Lecture Notes in Computer Science 10667

Commenced Publication in 1973
Founding and Former Series Editors:
Gerhard Goos, Juris Hartmanis, and Jan van Leeuwen

More information about this series at http://www.springer.com/series/7412

Yao Zhao · Xiangwei Kong
David Taubman (Eds.)

Image and Graphics

9th International Conference, ICIG 2017
Shanghai, China, September 13–15, 2017
Revised Selected Papers, Part II

 Springer

Editors
Yao Zhao
Beijing Jiaotong University
Beijing
China

David Taubman
UNSW
Sydney, NSW
Australia

Xiangwei Kong
Dalian University of Technology
Dalian
China

ISSN 0302-9743   ISSN 1611-3349 (electronic)
Lecture Notes in Computer Science
ISBN 978-3-319-71588-9   ISBN 978-3-319-71589-6 (eBook)
https://doi.org/10.1007/978-3-319-71589-6

Library of Congress Control Number: 2017960877

LNCS Sublibrary: SL6 – Image Processing, Computer Vision, Pattern Recognition, and Graphics

Printed on acid-free paper

This Springer imprint is published by Springer Nature
The registered company is Springer International Publishing AG
The registered company address is: Gewerbestrasse 11, 6330 Cham, Switzerland

Preface

These are the proceedings of the 8th International Conference on Image and Graphics (ICIG 2017), held in Shanghai, China, during September 13–15, 2017.

The China Society of Image and Graphics (CSIG) has hosted this series of ICIG conferences since 2000. ICIG is the biennial conference organized by the China Society of Image and Graphics (CSIG), focusing on innovative technologies of image, video, and graphics processing and fostering innovation, entrepreneurship, and networking. This time, Shanghai Jiaotong University was the organizer, and the Nanjing Technology University and Zong Mu Technology Ltd. Company were the co-organizers. Details about the past eight conferences, as well as the current one, are as follows:

Conference	Place	Date	Submitted	Proceeding
First (ICIG 2000)	Tianjin, China	August 16–18	220	156
Second (ICIG 2002)	Hefei, China	August 15–18	280	166
Third (ICIG 2004)	Hong Kong, China	December 17–19	460	140
4th (ICIG 2007)	Chengdu, China	August 22–24	525	184
5th (ICIG 2009)	Xi'an, China	September 20–23	362	179
6th (ICIG 2011)	Hefei, China	August 12–15	329	183
7th (ICIG 2013)	Qingdao, China	July 26–28	346	181
8th (ICIG 2015)	Tianjin, China	August 13–16	345	170
9th (ICIG 2017)	Shanghai, China	September 13–15	370	172

This time, the proceedings are published by Springer in the LNCS series. The titles, abstracts, and biographies of the three invited speakers of plenary talks are presented first. At ICIG 2017, 370 submissions were received, and 160 papers were accepted. To ease in the search of a required paper in these proceedings, the 160 regular papers have been arranged in alphabetical order according to their titles. Another 12 papers forming a special topic are included at the end.

Our sincere thanks go to all the contributors (around 200), who came from around the world to present their advanced works at this event. Special thanks go to the members of Technical Program Committee, who carefully reviewed every single submission and made their valuable comments for improving the accepted papers.

The proceedings could not have been produced without the invaluable efforts of the publication chairs, the web chairs, and a number of active members of CSIG.

September 2017

Yao Zhao
Xiangwei Kong
David Taubman

Organization

Honorary Chairs

Guanhua Xu   MOST, China
Yuan F. Zheng   Ohio State University, USA

General Chairs

Tieniu Tan   Chinese Academy of Sciences, China
Hongkai Xiong   Shanghai Jiaotong University, China
Zixiang Xiong   Texas A&M University, USA

Organizing Committee Chairs

Weiyao Lin   Shanghai Jiaotong University, China
Huimin Ma   Tsinghua University, China
Bo Yan   Fudan University, China

Technical Program Chairs

David Taubman   UNSW, Australia
Yao Zhao   Beijing Jiaotong University, China

Finance Chairs

Zhihua Chen   ECUST, China
Zhenwei Shi   Beihang University, China

Special Session Chairs

Jian Cheng   Chinese Academy of Sciences, China
Zhihai He   University of Missouri, USA
Z. Jane Wang   University of British Columbia, Canada

Award Chairs

Xin Li   West Virginia University, USA
Shiqiang Yang   Tsinghua University, China

Publicity Chairs

Mingming Cheng   Nankai University, China
Moncef Gabbouj   TUT, Finland

Exhibits Chairs

Zhijun Fang   Shanghai University of Engineering Science, China
Yan Lv   Microsoft Research, China

Publication Chairs

Xiangwei Kong   Dalian University of Technology, China
Jun Yan   Journal of Image and Graphics, China

International Liaisons

Xiaoqian Jiang   UCSD, USA
Huifang Sun   MERL, USA

Local Chairs

Wenrui Dai   UCSD, USA
Junni Zou   Shanghai Jiaotong University, China

Registration Chair

Chen Ye   Shanghai Jiaotong University, China

Webmasters

Chenglin Li   EPFL, Switzerland
Yangmei Shen   Shanghai Jiaotong University, China

Technical Program Committee

Ping An   Shanghai University, China
Ru An   Hohai University, China
Xiao Bai   Beijing University of Aeronautics and Astronautics, China
Lianfa Bai   Nanjing University of Science and Technology, China
Xiang Bai   Huazhong University of Science and Technology, China
Chongke Bi   Tianjin University, China
Hai Bian   Hangzhou Dica3d Technology Co., Ltd., China
Xiaochun Cao   Institute of Information Engineering,
                       Chinese Academy of Sciences, China

Yan-Pei Cao	Tsinghua University, China
Chong Cao	Tsinghua University, China
Qi Chen	Hainan University, China
Kang Chen	Tsinghua University, China
Mingkai Chen	Nanjing University of Posts and Telecommunications, China
Mingming Cheng	Nankai University, China
Yue Dong	MSRA, China
Zhijun Fang	Shanghai University of Engineering Science, China
Qianjin Feng	Southern Medical University, China
Xiaoyi Feng	Northwestern Polytechnical University, China
Dongmei Fu	University of Science and Technology Beijing, China
Junying Gan	Wuyi University, China
Lin Gao	ICT, CAS, China
Yue Gao	Tsinghua University, China
Xinbo Gao	Xidian University, China
Zexun Geng	Information Engineering University, China
Guanghua Gu	Yanshan University, China
Lin Gu	National Institute of Informatics, Japan
Yanwen Guo	Nanjing University, China
Hu Han	Nanyang Technological University, Singapore
Xiaowei He	Northwest University, China
Qiming Hou	Zhejiang University, China
Dong Hu	Nanjing University of Posts and Telecommunications, China
Hua Huang	Beijing Institute of Technology, China
Haozhi Huang	Tsinghua University, China
Yongfeng Huang	Tsinghua University, China
Rongrong Ji	Xiamen University, China
Yunde Jia	Beijing Institute of Technology, China
Sen Jia	Shenzhen University, China
Xiuping Jia	University of New South Wales, USA
Zhiguo Jiang	Beijing University of Aeronautics and Astronautics, China
Zhaohui Jiang	Central South University, China
Xiaoqian Jiang	University of California, San Diego, USA
Lianwen Jin	South China University of Technology, China
Bin Kong	Institute of Intelligent Machines, Chinese Academy of Sciences, China
Xiangwei Kong	Dalian University of Technology, China
Dengfeng Kuang	Nankai University, China
Jianhuang Lai	Sun Yat-Sen University, China
Congyan Lang	Beijing Jiaotong University, China
Changhua Li	Xi'an University of Architecture and Technology, China
Chenglin Li	Swiss Federal Institute of Technology in Lausanne, Switzerland
Hua Li	Institute of Computing Technology, Chinese Academy of Sciences, China
Jiming Li	Zhejiang Police College, China

Qi Li	Peking University, China
Shutao Li	Hunan University, China
Xi Li	Zhejiang University, China
Jie Liang	China Aerodynamics Research and Development Center, China
Pin Liao	Nanchang University, China
Chunyu Lin	Beijing Jiaotong University, China
Xiaojing Liu	Qinghai University, China
Changhong Liu	Jiangxi Normal University, China
Bin Liu	University of Science and Technology of China, China
Bin Liu	Tsinghua University, China
Chenglin Liu	Institute of Automation, Chinese Academy of Sciences, China
Wenyu Liu	Huazhong University of Science and Technology, China
Yue Liu	Beijing Institute of Technology, China
Qingshan Liu	Nanjing University of Information Science and Technology, China
Hongbing Lu	Fourth Military Medical University, China
Hanqing Lu	Institute of Automation, Chinese Academy of Sciences, China
Jiwen Lu	Tsinghua University, China
Jianhua Ma	Southern Medical University, China
Huimin Ma	Tsinghua University, China
Weidong Min	Nanchang University, China
Xuanqin Mou	Xi'an Jiaotong University, China
Taijiang Mu	Tsinghua University, China
Feiping Nie	Northwestern Polytechnical University, China
Yongwei Nie	South China University of Technology, China
Zhigeng Pan	Hangzhou Normal University, China
Yanwei Pang	Tianjin University, China
Yuxin Peng	Peking University, China
Yuntao Qian	Zhejiang University, China
Bo Ren	Nankai University, China
Jun Sang	Chongqing University, China
Nong Sang	Huazhong University of Science and Technology, China
Yangmei Shen	Shanghai Jiaotong University, China
Yuying Shi	North China Electric Power University, China
Huifang Sun	Mitsubishi Electric Research Laboratories, USA
Jiande Sun	Shandong University, China
Linmi Tao	Tsinghua University, China
Lei Tong	Beijing University of Technology, China
Yunhai Wang	Shandong University, China
Qi Wang	Northwestern Polytechnical University, China
Cheng Wang	Xiamen University, China
Meng Wang	Hefei University of Technology, China
Hanzi Wang	Xiamen University, China
Peizhen Wang	Anhui University of Technology, China
Tianjiang Wang	Huazhong University of Science and Technology, China

Bin Wang	Tsinghua University, China
Lili Wang	Beihang University, China
Shigang Wang	Jilin University, China
Miao Wang	Tsinghua University, China
Yunhong Wang	Beijing University of Aeronautics and Astronautics, China
Chunhong Wu	University of Science and Technology Beijing, China
Hongzhi Wu	Zhejiang University, China
Xiaojun Wu	Jiangnan University, China
Fei Wu	Zhejiang University, China
Zhongke Wu	Beijing Normal University, China
Dingyuan Xia	Wuhan University of Technology, China
Hongkai Xiong	Shanghai Jiaotong University, China
Mingliang Xu	Zhengzhou University, China
Chunxu Xu	Tsinghua University, China
Kun Xu	Tsinghua University, China
Zengpu Xu	Tianjin University of Science and Technology, China
Jianru Xue	Xi'an Jiaotong University, China
Xiangyang Xue	Fudan University, China
Bo Yan	Fudan University, China
Ling-Qi Yan	UC Berkeley, USA
Xiao Yan	Tsinghua University, China
Jingwen Yan	Shantou University, China
Jun Yan	Institute of Remote Sensing and Digital Earth, Chinese Academy of Sciences, China
Jinfeng Yang	Civil Aviation University of China, China
Sheng Yang	Tsinghua University, China
Yongliang Yang	Bath University, UK
Shiqiang Yang	Tsinghua University, China
Tao Yang	Tsinghua University, China
Hongxun Yao	Harbin Institute of Technology, China
Yong Yin	Dalian Maritime University, China
Shiqi Yu	Shenzhen University, China
Nenghai Yu	University of Science and Technology of China, China
Yinwei Zhan	Guangdong University of Technology, China
Aiqing Zhang	Anhui Normal University, China
Wei Zhang	Shandong University, China
Daoqiang Zhang	Nanjing University of Aeronautics and Astronautics, China
Jiawan Zhang	Tianjin University, China
Lei Zhang	Beijing Institute of Technology, China
Song-Hai Zhang	Tsinghua University, China
Shiliang Zhang	Peking University, China
Xinpeng Zhang	Shanghai University, China
Yanci Zhang	Sichuan University, China
Yongfei Zhang	Beijing University of Aeronautics and Astronautics, China
Fang-Lue Zhang	Victoria University of Wellington, New Zealand
Guofeng Zhang	Zhejiang University, China

Qiang Zhang	Dalian University, China
Yun Zhang	Zhejiang University of Media and Communications, China
Liangpei Zhang	Wuhan University, China
Shengchuan Zhang	Xiamen University, China
Xiaopeng Zhang	Shanghai Jiaotong University, China
Sicheng Zhao	Tsinghua University, China
Yao Zhao	Beijing Jiaotong University, China
Jieyu Zhao	Ningbo University, China
Chunhui Zhao	Harbin Engineering University, China
Ying Zhao	Central South University, China
Wei-Shi Zheng	Sun Yat-Sen University, China
Ping Zhong	National University of Defense Technology, China
Quan Zhou	China Academy of Space Technology, Xi'an, China
Jun Zhou	Griffith University, Australia
Liang Zhou	Nanjing University of Posts and Telecommunications, China
Linna Zhou	University of International Relations, China
Tao Zhou	Ningxia Medical University, China
Wengang Zhou	University of Science and Technology of China, China
Zhe Zhu	Duke University, USA
Wang-Jiang Zhu	Tsinghua University, China
Yonggui Zhu	Communication University of China, China

Contents – Part II

Compression, Transmission, Retrieval

5G Multimedia Communications

Artificial Intelligence

Computer Vision and Pattern Recognition

Boosting CNN-Based Pedestrian Detection via 3D LiDAR Fusion in Autonomous Driving

Jian Dou[1], Jianwu Fang[1,2], Tao Li[1], and Jianru Xue[1(✉)]

[1] Laboratory of Visual Cognitive Computing and Intelligent Vehicle,
Xi'an Jiaotong University, Xi'an, People's Republic of China
jrxue@mail.xjtu.edu.cn
[2] School of Electronic and Control Engineering,
Chang'an University, Xi'an, People's Republic of China

Abstract. Robust pedestrian detection has been treated as one of the main pursuits for excellent autonomous driving. Recently, some convolutional neural networks (CNN) based detectors have made large progress for this goal, such as Faster R-CNN. However, the performance of them still needs a large space to be boosted, even owning the complex learning architectures. In this paper, we novelly introduce the 3D LiDAR sensor to boost the CNN-based pedestrian detection. Facing the heterogeneous and asynchronous properties of two different sensors, we firstly introduce an accurate calibration method for visual and LiDAR sensors. Then, some physically geometrical clues acquired by 3D LiDAR are explored to eliminate the erroneous pedestrian proposals generated by the state-of-the-art CNN-based detectors. Exhaustive experiments verified the superiority of the proposed method.

1 Introduction

Pedestrian detection is the main task in autonomous driving, where the accurate and robust detection has the direct impact on the planning and decision of autonomous vehicles [14]. In addition, pedestrian detection forms as the basis for many promising vision tasks, such as pedestrian tracking [11], crowd sensing [25], activity reasoning [24], etc. Besides, pedestrian, as the main traffic element, plays an influential role for traffic scene understanding and mapping [6]. Hence, many efforts have been devoted for its progress. However, it still needs a large space to boost the detection performance, mainly because that there are many challenging factors: covering of all the pedestrians with different scales, distinct illumination, partial-occlusion, motion blur, similar appearance to other non-human objects, and so forth.

Facing these problems, many works have been proposed. Among them, convolutional neural network (CNN) module have established the most excellent performance. For example, faster region-based convolutional neural networks (Faster R-CNN) [20] is proposed with 9 anchor scales for bounding box regression, where a region proposal network (RPN) is embedded to speed up the

Y. Zhao et al. (Eds.): ICIG 2017, Part II, LNCS 10667, pp. 3–13, 2017.
https://doi.org/10.1007/978-3-319-71589-6_1

Fig. 1. The detection result of one image. Left is the one by Faster R-CNN [20] and right is generated by R-FCN [3].

proposal generation procedure. Redmon *et al.* [18] proposed a YOLO detection module which predicts the coordinates of bounding boxes directly using fully connected layers on top of the convolutional feature extractor. Subsequently, some variants of YOLO are put forward, such as YOLOv2 and YOLO 9000 [19]. Single shot multiBox detector (SSD) [12] initialized a set of default boxes over different aspect ratios and scales within a feature map, and discretized the output space of bounding boxes into these boxes. Although these works have complex architectures and delved into the instinct pedestrian representation, all of them cannot obtain a satisfactory performance, seeing Fig. 1 for a demonstration. One reason may be the dynamic challenging factors mentioned before, but one another more important reason is that it is difficult to learn an invariable representation of pedestrians in diverse environment. Supplemented by the 3D LiDAR sensor, we can gather the physically geometrical information of pedestrians, such as height from the ground, area of occupancy, etc. These information also can be treated as the spatial context clue for inferring. Actually, there is one former work [21] which addressed the pedestrian detection by fusing LiDAR and visual clues. However, this method cannot obtain a good calibration of visual and LiDAR clue, as well as an accurate detection by naive neural networks. Though there are some works for detection using LADAR or Laser sensors [13,23], they are based on the hypothesis that front dynamic objects are all pedestrians, where non object class knowledge is exploited. In other words, LiDAR cannot distinguish the class of different object, but cameras can. Hence, it is inevitable to fuse the camera and LiDAR sensors together, whereas needs a calibration for tackling their heterogeneous and asynchronous properties. Actually, vision+x module is becoming the main trend for scene understanding.

To this end, this work firstly dedicates to an accurate calibration for visual and LiDAR sensors, and update the calibration parameters with an online way. Second, we take Faster R-CNN as the basis for generating pedestrian proposals, and eliminate the wrong detections by considering constraints of physical geometrical clues, including the dominant distance of pedestrian within the proposals, height from the ground and dynamic area occupancy variation of pedestrians. By that, the pedestrian proposals generated by Faster R-CNN are significantly cleaned. The detailed flowchart is demonstrated in Fig. 2.

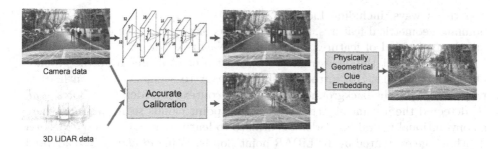

Fig. 2. The flowchart of the proposed method.

2 Related Works

This work mainly aims to boost the CNN based pedestrian detection performance with a 3D LiDAR sensor auxiliary. We will review the related works from CNN-based pedestrian detectors and other detection modules by non-vision approaches, such as LiDAR, Laser, etc.

CNN-based pedestrian detection: Recently, there have been a lot of detection works of interest deriving a convolutional deep neural networks (CNNs) [4,12]. Within this framework, great progress of pedestrian detection has been made compared with previous works with hand-craft feature, such as deformable part-based model (DPM) [5]. The core purpose of these CNN based detectors is to search the instinct or structural information implied by large-scale pedestrian samples with respect to the scale space [12,20,27] or geometry constraint, such as the part-geometry [16]. For example, Faster R-CNN [20], inspired by R-CNN [7], sampled the object proposal with multiple anchor scales, and speeded up the proposal generation by a region proposal networks (RPN). Cai *et al.* [2] proposed a unified multi-scale deep neural networks (denoted as MS-CNN) to address the scale issue. The similar issue was also concerned by the work of scale-adaptive deconvolutional regression (SADR) [27] and scale-aware Fast R-CNN [10]. Single shot multiBox detector (SSD) [12] predicted the category scores and box offsets for a set of default bounding boxes on feature maps, which is faster than single box module of YOLO [18]. Beside of the scale issue consideration, some studies concentrate on the structural information implied by different part of pedestrians. Within this category, Ouyang *et al.* [16] jointly estimated the visibility relationship of different parts of the same pedestrian to solve the partial-occlusion problem. They also proposed a deformable deep convolutional neural networks for generic object detection [17], where they introduced a new deformation constrained pooling layer modeling the deformation of object parts with geometric constraint and penalty. Although these CNN based detectors search for an instinct and structural representation of pedestrians, robust detection still remains very difficult because of the diverse environment.

Non-vision pedestrian detection: Except for the universal vision based module for pedestrian detection, some researchers exploited this problem using many non-vision ways, including Lidar [8,23], LADAR [13], and so on. Within this domain, geometrical features, such as the edge, skeleton, width of the scan line are the main kind of features. For example, Navarroserment *et al.* [13] utilized LADAR to detect the pedestrian by the constraint of height from the ground. Oliveira and Nunes [15] introduced Lidar sensor to segment the scan lines of pedestrian from the background with a spatial context consideration. Börcs *et al.* [1] detected the instant object by 3D LiDAR point clouds segmentation, where a convolutional neural networks was utilized to learn information of objects of a depth image estimated by 3D LiDAR point clouds. Wang *et al.* [23] also adopted the 3D LiDAR sensor to detect and track pedestrians. In their work, they first clustered the point cloud into several blobs, and labeled many samples manually. Then a support vector machine (SVM) was used to learn the geometrical clue of pedestrians.

In summary, the information acquired by non-vision sensors are all the geometrical clues without the explicit class information. Hence, in some circumstance, the frequent false detection is generated while the vision based methods can distinguish the different classes. Nevertheless, non-vision modules have the superior ability to the vision based ones for adapting different environment. It is inevitable to fuse the camera and non-vision modules together to obtain a boosted detection performance. Hence, this work utilizes 3D LiDAR sensor for an attempt.

3   Accurate Calibration of 3D LiDAR and Camera

For boosting the pedestrian detection performance, primary task is to calibrate camera to 3D LiDAR because of the demand for targeting the same objects. The work of calibration can be explained as to compute the intrinsic parameter of camera and extrinsic parameters correlation of two sensors, i.e., the translational vector $\mathbf{t}$ and rotate matrix $\mathbf{R} \in \mathbb{R}^{3\times3}$. In this work, the intrinsic camera parameter is computed by *Zhang Zhengyou* calibration [26]. For the extrinsic parameter, this work introduces an online automatic calibration method [9] to carry out the accurate calibration for our camera and 3D LiDAR sensors. It aims to pursue a maximization of overlapping geometry structure. Different from other off-line calibrations [22,26], it optimizes the the extrinsic parameter by latest observed several frames. Specifically, six values are calculated when optimization. They are $\{\Delta x,\ \Delta y,\ \Delta z\}$ translations, and the $\{roll,\ pitch,\ Eular\text{-}angle\}$ rotations between the camera and 3D LiDAR sensors. Given a calibration of $\mathbf{t}$ and $\mathbf{R}$, we first project the 3D LiDAR sensor onto the image plane captured by visual camera. Then, the objective function for optimization is specified as:

$$max: \sum_{f=n-w}^{n} \sum_{p=1}^{|V^f|} V_p^f S_{i,j}^f, \tag{1}$$

where w is the frame number for optimization (set as 9 frames in this work), n is the newest observed video frame, p is the index for 3D point set $\{V_p^f\}_{p=1}^{|V^f|}$

obtained by 3D LiDAR sensor, $S_{i,j}^f$ is the point (x,j) in the fth frame S. Note that, the point set in 3D LiDAR and camera is not the whole plane. Actually, the points in both sensors are all the edge points. For image, the point $S_{i,j}^f$ is extracted by edge detection appending an inverse distance transformation, and $\{V_p^f\}$ is obtained by calculating the distance difference of the scene from the 3D LiDAR (denoted as the origin of coordinates). Some typical calibration results are shown in Fig. 3. From Fig. 3, we obtain a high-accurate calibration results. As thus, we accomplish the calibration of camera and 3D LiDAR sensors.

Fig. 3. Typical calibration results of camera and 3D LiDAR.

4 Boosting CNN-Based Detectors by Fusing Physically Geometrical Clue of Pedestrian

4.1 Pedestrian Proposal Generation by CNN-Based Detectors

After the calibration, we obtain a fundamental precondition for tackling the pedestrian detection problem by fusing visual color and real distance of the target. However, despite the calibration is conducted, there remains some issues for detection. The main difficulty is the heterogeneous property, i.e., the sparsity and the physical meaning of the points in two sensors are rather different. In addition, the 3D point captured by LiDAR does not have the class information. Therefore, in this work, we treat the CNN-based detector as the basis, and take some physically geometrical clue of 3D point to rectify the generated pedestrian proposals. Recently, there are many works with a deep network architecture addressing the pedestrian detection. However, each of them does not perform a satisfactory performance. Therefore, his work takes Faster R-CNN [20] as an attempt, the erroneous pedestrian proposals are eliminated by fusing the following physically geometrical clues.

4.2 Physically Geometrical Clue Fusion for Pedestrian Detection

In this subsection, we will describe the method for how to fuse the physically geometrical clue extracted by 3D LiDAR in detail. As we all know that, the height of most of the walking person in the world belongs to the range of $[1,2]$

meters, and occupies a region with the maximum size of $0.5 \times 2 \, \text{m}^2$. In addition, the occupancy region of a human maintains relatively static. Therefore, this work extracts the static and dynamic physically geometrical clues of the pedestrian, including the height from the ground, occupancy dominance within a pedestrian proposals, and a dynamic occupancy variation in accordance with the scale variation of proposals.

(1) Static Geometrical Clues

Occupancy dominance (OD): The pedestrian proposals are generally represented by bounding boxes. By the observation, the 3D points locate in the bounding boxes sparsely and uniformly. The distance of the 3D points in each bounding box is computed by $r = \sqrt[2]{x^2 + y^2 + z^2}$, where r represents the distance of a 3D point (x, y, z). Specially, because the sparsity of 3D points, some pixels in color image have no distance information, usually denoted as (∞, ∞, ∞). Besides, the bounding box inevitably contain a few of background region whose distance is much larger than the ones of pedestrians. In addition, the distances of the 3D points within pedestrians always are similar, and the pedestrian occupies the dominant part of the bounding box. Inspired by this insight, this work puts forward an *occupancy dominance* to eliminate the bounding boxes whose scale is rather different from the pedestrian. Specifically, we sort the distance of the 3D points in a bounding box with ascending order, and observe that the truly pedestrian always have a largest width range of zone with constant distance, seeing Fig. 4 for an example. As thus, the main step of *occupancy dominance* is to extract the largest smooth part of the sorted distance curve. For this purpose, we compute the difference of two adjacent point in this distance curve, and set the difference as 0 when the distance difference is lower than 0.3 m. Then, we segment the curve into several fragments, and the length of each fragment is denoted as the *occupancy* in a bounding box. By this clue, we can get rid of the proposals without dominant object region.

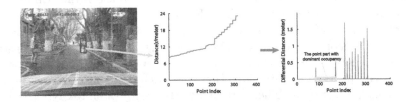

Fig. 4. The illustration of *occupancy dominance*.

Height-width constraint (HC): In the driving circumstances, the height of a walking pedestrian usually drops into a finite range, e.g., from 1.2 m to 2 m. Therefore, given a pedestrian proposal, its height cannot exceed 2.5 m. In this paper, for a bounding box, we specify the height constraint as $0.8 < (h_{max} - h_{min}) < 1.5$ m. With this constraint, the proposals with too little or large size are removed.

(2) Dynamic Geometrical Clues

Dynamic occupancy (DO): In addition to the static clues, we also exploit the dynamic clues for removing the proposals wrongly detected. That is because that the occupancy (defined before) of the human body in the bounding box maintains constant, i.e., the fragment length in Fig. 4 remains almost unchanged when varying the scale of the bounding box. On the contrary, the objects, such as the trees which are always detected as pedestrian, may have a rather different scale size, and have a *dynamic occupancy* (denoted as DO) when varying the scale of bounding boxes. Hence, we further determine the quality of the pedestrian proposal by varying the height of the bounding box, and examine whether the dominant occupancy of the bounding box variation has a direct proportion to height or not. If not, the proposal is a pedestrian proposal. Specifically, dynamic occupancy (DO) in this paper is fulfilled by enlarging the height of the bounding box with the size of 1.3 times.

Although the above clues are all quite simple, they are intuitive and can significantly boost the performance of the CNN based detector verified by the following experiments.

5 Experiments and Discussions

5.1 Dataset Acquisition

We collect the experimental data by an autonomous vehicle named as "Kuafu", which is developed by the Laboratory of Visual Cognitive Computing and Intelligent Vehicle of Xian Jiaotong University. In this work, a Velodyne HDL-64E S2 LIDAR sensor with 64 beams, and a high-resolution camera system with differential GPS/inertial information are equipped in the acquisition system. The visual camera is with the resolution of 1920×1200 and a frame rate of 25. In addition, the scanning frequency of the 3D-LiDAR is 10 Hz. In the dataset, there are 5000 frames containing 5771 pedestrians proposals in the ground-truth manually labeled by ourselves. It is worth noting that this work treats the detected proposals with a detection score larger than 0.8 as the truly detected pedestrian. Hence the performance of the proposed method cannot be represented by a precision-recall curve.

5.2 Metrics for Evaluation

To evaluate the performance, this paper introduces the precision and recall values. The precision value represents the ratio of proposals correctly detected as pedestrian to all the detected proposals, while the recall value specifies the percentage of detected pedestrian proposal in relation to the ground-truth number. For the performance evaluation, this work adds the constraints, i.e., OD, HC and DO gradually, by which the performance of different clues can be presented. In addition, occupancy dominance (OD) clue is essential for HC and DO. Therefore, we deploy it in all the configurations.

5.3   Performance Evaluation

The detection efficiency of the proposed method is 5 fps. Table 1 demonstrates the precision and recall values after embedding different physically geometrical clues. From this table, we can observe that the more the clues are added, the better precision the method generates and the worse recall is. It seems that the more clues make the detector cannot robustly detect all the pedestrians, seeing the 1606th and 1651th frames. Actually, through a checking in the visual results, more clues are necessary, which can remove the wrongly detected proposals to a larger extent. In the meantime, the margin of the recall value by embedding all

Table 1. The precision and recall values for different physically geometrical clue embedding. For a clearer comparison, we demonstrate the numbers of detected proposals (DPs) and the wrongly detected proposals (WDPs). Besides, the best precision and recall value are marked by **bold** font.

Sensor module	OD (N/Y)	HC (N/Y)	DO (N/Y)	DPs	WDPs	Recall (%)	Precision (%)
RGB only [20]	-	-	-	5177	633	**78.7**	87.7
RGB+3D-LiDAR	Y	N	Y	4537	268	73.9	94.1
RGB+3D-LiDAR	Y	Y	N	4650	316	75.1	93.2
RGB+3D-LiDAR	Y	Y	Y	4145	169	68.9	**95.9**

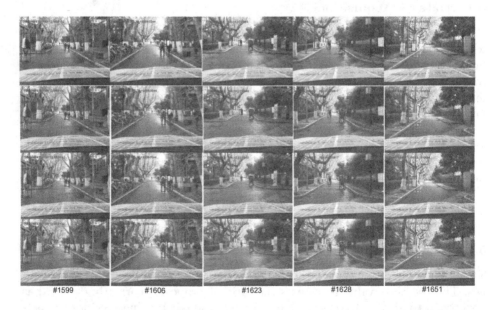

#1599   #1606   #1623   #1628   #1651

Fig. 5. Some typical snapshots of the results generated by embedding different clues. The first row is the results by Faster R-CNN [20]. The second row is the results by RGB+3D-LiDAR with the clue embedding of OD and DO. The third row is the results after embedding OD and HC, and the results with all of the physically geometrical clues are presented in the last row.

the clues is commonly caused by that we removed the pedestrian proposals whose distances are larger than about 50 m from our vehicle, which is totally acceptable in practical situations, taking the 1623th frame as an example (Fig. 5).

5.4 Discussions

In this work, we only take the Faster R-CNN [20] as an attempt. Actually, it is not the focus and similar for other CNN-based detectors. In addition, the utilization procedure of 3D-LiDAR is not restricted to this kind of module in this work. The purpose of this work aims to present that the performance of CNN-based detectors can be boosted by fusing some simple and intuitive geometrical clues extracted from 3D-LiDAR sensor, and the convincing results can be generated.

6 Conclusion

This paper novelly introduced the 3D-LiDAR sensor to boost the performance of CNN-based detectors. Faster R-CNN was utilized as an attempt. Facing the heterogeneous and asynchronous properties of two different sensors, this work firstly calibrated the RGB and LiDAR data with an online module which can adapt to the dynamic scene more effectively. Then, some physically geometrical clues acquired by 3D LiDAR were exploited to eliminate the erroneous pedestrian proposals. Exhaustive experiments verified the superiority of the proposed method. In the future, the more fusing module for camera and 3D-LiDAR is our focus.

Acknowledgement. This work is supported by the National Key R&D Program Project under Grant 2016YFB1001004, and also supported by the Natural Science Foundation of China under Grant 61603057, China Postdoctoral Science Foundation under Grant 2017M613152, and is also partially supported by Collaborative Research with MSRA.

References

1. Börcs, A., Nagy, B., Benedek, C.: Instant object detection in LiDAR point clouds. IEEE Geosci. Remote Sens. Lett. (2017, accepted)
2. Cai, Z., Fan, Q., Feris, R.S., Vasconcelos, N.: A unified multi-scale deep convolutional neural network for fast object detection. In: Leibe, B., Matas, J., Sebe, N., Welling, M. (eds.) ECCV 2016. LNCS, vol. 9908, pp. 354–370. Springer, Cham (2016). https://doi.org/10.1007/978-3-319-46493-0_22
3. Dai, J., Li, Y., He, K., Sun, J.: R-FCN: object detection via region-based fully convolutional networks. In: Advances in Neural Information Processing Systems, pp. 379–387 (2016)
4. Dai, J., Li, Y., He, K., Sun, J.: R-FCN: object detection via region-based fully convolutional networks. CoRR abs/1605.06409 (2016)
5. Felzenszwalb, P.F., Girshick, R.B., Mcallester, D., Ramanan, D.: Object detection with discriminatively trained part-based models. IEEE Trans. Pattern Anal. Mach. Intell. **32**(9), 1627–1645 (2010)

6. Geiger, A., Lauer, M., Wojek, C., Stiller, C., Urtasun, R.: 3D traffic scene understanding from movable platforms. IEEE Trans. Pattern Anal. Mach. Intell. **36**(5), 1012–1025 (2014)
7. Girshick, R., Donahue, J., Darrell, T., Malik, J.: Rich feature hierarchies for accurate object detection and semantic segmentation. In: Proceedings of the IEEE Conference on Computer Vision and Pattern Recognition, pp. 580–587 (2014)
8. Kidono, K., Miyasaka, T., Watanabe, A., Naito, T.: Pedestrian recognition using high-definition LiDAR. In: Proceedings of the Intelligent Vehicles Symposium, pp. 405–410 (2011)
9. Levinson, J., Thrun, S.: Automatic online calibration of cameras and lasers. In: Proceedings of the Robotics: Science and Systems (2013)
10. Li, J., Liang, X., Shen, S., Xu, T., Yan, S.: Scale-aware fast R-CNN for pedestrian detection. CoRR abs/1510.08160 (2015)
11. Li, J., Deng, C., Xu, R.Y.D., Tao, D., Zhao, B.: Robust object tracking with discrete graph-based multiple experts. IEEE Trans. Image Process. **26**(6), 2736–2750 (2017)
12. Liu, W., Anguelov, D., Erhan, D., Szegedy, C., Reed, S., Fu, C.-Y., Berg, A.C.: SSD: single shot multibox detector. In: Leibe, B., Matas, J., Sebe, N., Welling, M. (eds.) ECCV 2016. LNCS, vol. 9905, pp. 21–37. Springer, Cham (2016). https://doi.org/10.1007/978-3-319-46448-0_2
13. Navarroserment, L.E., Mertz, C., Hebert, M.: Pedestrian detection and tracking using three-dimensional LADAR data. Int. J. Robot. Res. **29**(12), 1516–1528 (2010)
14. Ohn-Bar, E., Trivedi, M.M.: Looking at humans in the age of self-driving and highly automated vehicles. IEEE Trans. Intell. Veh. **1**(1), 90–104 (2016)
15. Oliveira, L., Nunes, U.: Context-aware pedestrian detection using LiDAR. In: Intelligent Vehicles Symposium, pp. 773–778 (2010)
16. Ouyang, W., Zeng, X., Wang, X.: Modeling mutual visibility relationship in pedestrian detection. In: Proceedings of the IEEE Conference on Computer Vision and Pattern Recognition (2013)
17. Ouyang, W., Zeng, X., Wang, X., Qiu, S., Luo, P., Tian, Y., Li, H., Yang, S., Wang, Z., Li, H., Wang, K., Yan, J., Loy, C.C., Tang, X.: DeepID-Net: deformable deep convolutional neural networks for object detection. Int. J. Comput. Vis. 1–14 (2016)
18. Redmon, J., Divvala, S., Girshick, R., Farhadi, A.: You only look once: unified, real-time object detection. In: Proceedings of the IEEE Conference on Computer Vision and Pattern Recognition, pp. 779–788 (2016)
19. Redmon, J., Farhadi, A.: Yolo9000: better, faster, stronger. arXiv preprint arXiv:1612.08242 (2016)
20. Ren, S., He, K., Girshick, R., Sun, J.: Faster R-CNN: towards real-time object detection with region proposal networks. IEEE Trans. Pattern Anal. Mach. Intell. **PP**(99), 1 (2015)
21. Szarvas, M., Sakai, U., Ogata, J.: Real-time pedestrian detection using LiDAR and convolutional neural networks. In: Proceedings of the Intelligent Vehicles Symposium, pp. 213–218 (2006)
22. Unnikrishnan, R., Hebert, M.: Fast extrinsic calibration of a laser rangefinder to a camera. Carnegie Mellon University (2005)
23. Wang, H., Wang, B., Liu, B., Meng, X., Yang, G.: Pedestrian recognition and tracking using 3D LiDAR for autonomous vehicle. Robot. Auton. Syst. **88**, 71–78 (2017)

24. Yi, S., Li, H., Wang, X.: Pedestrian behavior modeling from stationary crowds with applications to intelligent surveillance. IEEE Trans. Image Process. **25**(9), 4354–4368 (2016)
25. Yuan, Y., Fang, J., Wang, Q.: Online anomaly detection in crowd scenes via structure analysis. IEEE Trans. Cybern. **45**(3), 562–575 (2015)
26. Zhang, Z.: A flexible new technique for camera calibration. IEEE Trans. Pattern Anal. Mach. Intell. **22**(11), 1330–1334 (2000)
27. Zhu, Y., Wang, J., Zhao, C., Guo, H., Lu, H.: Scale-adaptive deconvolutional regression network for pedestrian detection. In: Lai, S.-H., Lepetit, V., Nishino, K., Sato, Y. (eds.) ACCV 2016. LNCS, vol. 10112, pp. 416–430. Springer, Cham (2017). https://doi.org/10.1007/978-3-319-54184-6_26

Actual License Plate Images Clarity Classification via Sparse Representation

Yudong Cheng, Feng Liu[✉], Zongliang Gan, and Ziguan Cui

Jiangsu Key Laboratory of Image Processing and Image Communication,
Nanjing University of Posts and Telecommunications,
Nanjing, China
liuf@njupt.edu.cn

Abstract. The quality of the license plate image has a great influence on the license plate recognition algorithm. Predicting the clarity of license plate image in advance will help the license plate recognition algorithm set appropriate parameters to improve the accuracy of the recognition. In this paper, we propose a classification algorithm based on sparse representation and reconstruction error to divide license plate images into two categories: high-clarity and low-clarity. We produced over complete dictionaries of both two categories, and extract the reconstruction error of the license plate image that to be classified through the two dictionaries as the feature vector. Finally we send the feature vector to SVM classifier. Our Algorithm is tested by the license plate image database, reaching over 90% accuracy.

Keywords: Blind image quality assessment · Licenses plate
Dictionary learning · Sparse representation · Feature extraction

1 Introduction

In recent years, many problems in the industry, if supplemented by high-performance quality evaluation to do the pretreatment, the system will be stable and efficient. License plate image recognition system is the case. License plate recognition system (LPRS) which currently developing gradually, is one of the most popular research direction. LPRS is generally divided into the following sections [1]: license plate location, license plate segmentation, and license plate recognition (LPR) which is the main part of LPRS. At present, there are many LPR algorithms with the combination of the neural network, and the training samples of the algorithm has a very high demand [2–4]. If the license plate image training samples can be classified according to the clarity, thus making different network models, the final accuracy of LPR algorithm could be improved. Based on this, we propose a classification algorithm, dividing the license plate image into high-clarity and low-clarity two categories, to assist the LPRS.

© Springer International Publishing AG 2017
Y. Zhao et al. (Eds.): ICIG 2017, Part II, LNCS 10667, pp. 14–23, 2017.
https://doi.org/10.1007/978-3-319-71589-6_2

2 Relate Work

The clarity classification of license plate image is a brand new problem in the study of non-reference image quality assessment (NRIQA), and there are no research papers before. Compared with the general NRIQA algorithms, the clarity classification algorithm of the license plate images does not evaluate the quality score, but the image is classified by clarity according to the industrial demand. However, both are essentially the features that can accurately describe the image quality. Therefore, the recent study of NRIQA algorithm can give us a lot of help.

Early NRIQA algorithms generally assume the types of distortion model that affect the image quality are known [5–12]. Based on the presumed distortion types, these approaches extract distortion specific features to predict the quality. However, there are more types of image distortions in reality, and distortions may affect each other. The assumption limits the application of these methods.

Recent numbers of studies on NRIQA take similar architecture. First in the training stage, the data containing the distorted image and the associated subjective evaluation are trained [13] to extract feature vectors. Then a regression model is learned to map these feature vectors to subjective human scores. In the test stage, feature vectors are extracted from test images, and then send into the regression model to predict its quality model [14–18]. The strategy to classify the quality of license plate images is almost the same, but a classification model will replace the regression model.

Moorthy and Bovik proposed a two-step framework of BIQA, called BIQI [14]. Scene statistics that extracted form given distorted image firstly, are used to decide the distortion type this image belongs to. The statistics are also used to evaluate the quality of the distortion type. By the same strategy, Moorthy and Bovik proposed DIIVINE, which use a richer natural scene feature [15]. However, completely different to the actual application, both BIQI and DIIVINE assume that the distortion type in the test image is represented in the training data set.

Saad et al. assumed that the statistics of the DCT characteristics can be varied in a predictable manner as the image quality changes [16]. According to it, a probability model called BLIINDS is trained by the contrast and structural features extracted in the DCT domain. BLIINDS is extended to BLIINDS-II by using more complex NSS-based DCT functionality [17]. Another approach not only extract the DCT feature, but also the wavelet and curvelet [18]. Although this model achieve certain effects in different distortion types, it still cannot work on every type.

As there is a big difference between general natural images and license plate (LP) images, the general NRIQA pursuing universal can not be used on LP images directly. Statistical information of LP image, such as DCT domain, wavelet domain and gradient statistics, not only affected by the distortion, also affected by the LP characters. This makes it difficult for the general NRIQA algorithm to work on the LP image. However, the advantage of the LP image is that the image does not appear in addition to the license plate characters other than the image. This very useful priori information can help us solve the problem of clarity classification of LP images. Base on this, we can produce different large enough over complete dictionaries to represent all types of LP images and to classify them by extracting the LP images from different dictionary reconstruction errors as valid features.

3 Framework of License Plate Image Classification

Here are the six uniform size gray-scale LP images in Fig. 1. We can see that for the distinction between the obvious high-clarity images and low-clarity, their DCT transformation are no rules to follow, gradient statistics also mixed together indistinguishable, which makes the vast majority of known NRIQA algorithms cannot effectively extract the feature of the LP image quality can be described.

Here, we propose a method based on sparse representation algorithm to extract the appropriate feature vector, and then put the feature vector into the appropriate classification model.

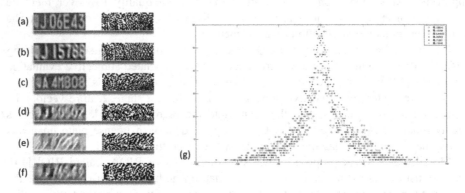

Fig. 1. Different clarity LP images and their DCT transform (a) (b) (c) are high-clarity images (d) (e) (f) are low-clarity images (g) is their gradient histogram

3.1 Classification Principle

Familiar with human subjective scoring that often used in general NRIQA algorithms as the final output, the clarity classification principle for LP images also needs to be artificially developed. In this algorithm, LP images are divided into two categories:

1. High-clarity LP image: the LP image that can be recognized all the last five characters by human.
2. Low-clarity LP image: the LP image that cannot be recognized all the last five characters by human.

Successful recognition of all the last five characters or not is one of the most intuitive manifestations of human eye's assessment. It is worth noting that we believe that the high/low clarity binary classification of images is a prerequisite for faithfully reflecting the subjective evaluation of image quality. Likewise, if the feature we extract can accurately distinguish between high and low clarity images, this feature can also be used to describe the image's quality score. Therefore, the classification principle that we propose is not unique. LP images could be classified into different categories by different principles.

3.2   The Algorithm of Feature Extraction

Sparse representation-based algorithms have been widely applied to computer vision and image processing like image denoising [19] and face recognition [20], especially the famous sparse representation-based classifier [21]. We follow this idea and describe in detail below.

Given sufficient samples of both high-clarity LP images and low, $A_1 = [v_{1,1}, v_{1,2}, \ldots, v_{1,n_1}] \in R^{m*n_1}$, $A_2 = [v_{2,1}, v_{2,2}, \ldots, v_{2,n_2}] \in R^{m*n_2}$, and test sample $y \in R^m$ from the same class would approximately lie in the subspace spanned by the training samples associated with either class:

$$y = a_{1,1} * v_{1,1} + a_{1,2} * v_{1,2} + \ldots + a_{1,n_1} * v_{1,n_1} \tag{1}$$

$$y = a_{2,1} * v_{2,1} + a_{2,2} * v_{2,2} + \ldots + a_{2,n_2} * v_{2,n_2} \tag{2}$$

and $a_{i,j} \in \mathbb{R}$, $j = 1, 2, \ldots n_i$ is a scalar.

Then we form a dictionary $\mathcal{D}$ by grouping all the samples from both classes.

$$\mathcal{D} = [A_1, A_2] = [v_{1,1}, v_{1,2}, \ldots v_{1,n_1}, v_{2,1}, \ldots, v_{2,n_2}] \tag{3}$$

and the linear representation of y can be written as:

$$y = \mathcal{D} * x_0 = a_{1,1} * v_{1,1} + a_{1,2} * v_{1,2} + \ldots + a_{2,n_2} * v_{2,n_2} \tag{4}$$

here x_0 is a coefficient vector whose entries are zero except those associated with the first class or second.

So to determine the class of clarity a test LP image is, it would be reconstructed and extracted the reconstruct error:

$$y_1 = D * \alpha_0(1) \tag{5}$$

$$y_2 = D * \alpha_0(2) \tag{6}$$

$$e(1) = \|y_{test} - y_1\|_2 \tag{7}$$

$$e(2) = \|y_{test} - y_2\|_2 \tag{8}$$

By compare these two error, the small one would be the clarity class the test image belongs to.

To learn the over-complete dictionary, K-SVD algorithm [22] would be used to solve the next optimization problem:

$$\langle D, \alpha \rangle = \operatorname{argmin}_{D,\alpha} \|Y - D * \alpha\|_2 \; s.t. \|\alpha\|_0 \leq L \tag{9}$$

However, the hypothesis of SRC algorithm is too strong to classify clarity of LP image directly. One of the prerequisites for the SRC algorithm is that the subspace of different classes are the same. To verify this, we create over complete dictionaries of the same parameters for the high/low clarity LP image training samples $D_1 D_2$.

$$\langle D_1, \alpha_1 \rangle = \text{argmin}_{D_1, \alpha_1} \|Y_1 - D_1 * \alpha_1\|_2 \ s.t. \|\alpha_1\|_0 \le L \tag{10}$$

$$\langle D_2, \alpha_2 \rangle = \text{argmin}_{D_2, \alpha_2} \|Y_2 - D_2 * \alpha_2\|_2 \ s.t. \|\alpha_2\|_0 \le L \tag{11}$$

In the process of making the dictionary, we found that for different image segmentation size, training error of dictionary produced by high-clarity image samples $E_1 = \|Y_1 - D_1 * \alpha_{1,training}\|_2$ is always larger than the error of low-clarity dictionary E_2 as shown in Fig. 2.

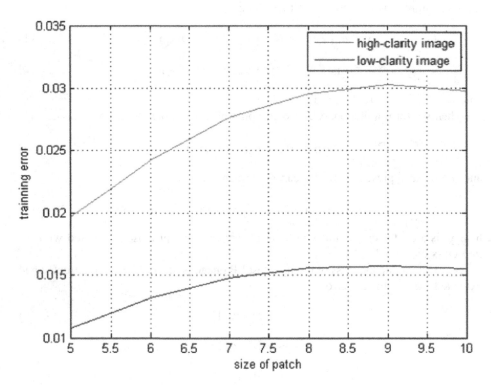

Fig. 2. Training error of different clarity LP images.

This means that high-clarity LP images can provide more information and are not more completely represented than low-clarity LP images that provide lower information. Although the frequency domain features that reflect the amount of LP image information cannot be effectively extracted, the same indirect reconstruction error can also represent the amount of information of the LP image.

The experimental results show that high-clarity LP images require more dictionary atoms to represent, and the dictionary's reconstruction error is related to the amount of information contained in the image. Although the SRC algorithm directly to the reconstruction error comparison method is not effective, the reconstruction error can still be extracted as LP image quality statistical feature.

So here we form two over complete dictionaries by high/low-clarity LP images with the same parameters. Then we get the reconstruction error $e(1)$ and $e(2)$ by Eqs. 5–8 as a two-dimensional feature vector of LP image.

In this algorithm, we utilize a support vector machine (SVM) for classification. While the feature vector was extracted, any classifier can be chosen to map it onto classes. The choice of SVM was motivated by the well performance [23] (Fig. 3).

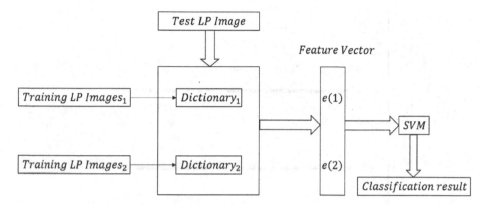

Fig. 3. Algorithm flowchart

4   Experiments and Analysis

4.1   Database Establishment

First of all, there is no public database of clarity classified LP images, so we have to build one. The size of LP images form the surveillance video should be uniformed to 20 * 60 pixels. Then, all the LP images will be evaluated artificially through the principle above. Based on this principle, we establishment a LP image database containing 500 high-clarity images and 500 low-clarity images. Low clarity LP images include a variety of common distortion types like motion blur, Gaussian blur, defocus blur, compression and noise.

4.2   Algorithm Performance and Analysis

There are a few parameters in the algorithm. We set L (the sparse prior in Eq. 9) to 2, so that we can get obvious reconstruction error with a small sparse prior. The kernel used in the SVM part is the radial basis function (RBF) kernel, whose parameters estimated by using cross-validation. In order to prevent over-fitting, we take random 30% of both clarity LP images, divide them into pieces with the size of n * n by sliding, and use the largest variance of 60% of each LP image to learn the dictionary. The other 70% images used as test samples. The figure reported here are the correct rate of classification by different algorithms.

We test our algorithm on the database we made above. Since we were the first to study this problem, there was no comparison of clarity classification algorithms for LP images. Here we test the performance of No-reference PSNR [24], BIQI [15], NIQE [14] and SSEQ [25]. We record the assessment score of No-reference PSNR, NIQE, SSEQ for the random selection of 150 high-clarity LP images and 150 low-clarity LP images in the database (Figs. 4, 5 and 6).

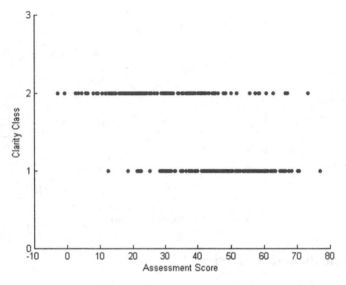

Fig. 4. Assessment score of no-reference PSNR

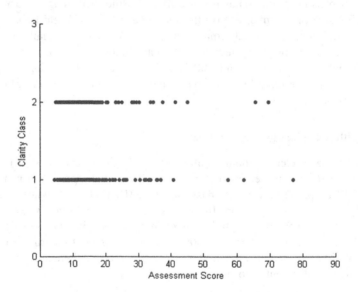

Fig. 5. Assessment score of NIQE

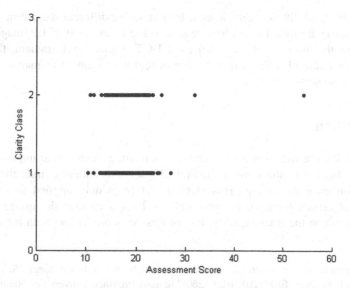

Fig. 6. Assessment score of SSEQ

It can be seen that these assessment scores are very close to the different LP image clarity, and cannot effectively distinguish between high-clarity images and low. Of course, these algorithms cannot evaluate the LP image quality.

For the BIQI algorithm, we tested the algorithm in another way. We did not directly calculate the assessment score of LP images, but sent the feature vector extracted from 9 wavelet transform into the SVM classifier. We compared this feature with ours (Table 1):

Table 1. Classification performance of algorithms on two clarity LP image database

		Class 1: high-clarity	Class 2: low-clarity
BIQI		38.00%	63.00%
Our algorithm	Patch size: 5	68.80%	95.80%
	Patch size: 6	81.80%	97.20%
	Patch size: 7	86.40%	**99.20%**
	Patch size: 8	88.20%	97.20%
	Patch size: 9	88.80%	97.80%
	Patch size: 10	**94.40%**	98.00%

It can be seen that the features extracted by BIQI also do not apply to the quality of LP image.

The result shows that our algorithm performs well especially with the large size of patch the LP image divided. Due to the lack of relevant databases and algorithms, we did not have more experiments. Based on SRC, our algorithm considered the expression ability of different dictionaries. By extracting different reconstruction error, this classification algorithm could be extended to the assessment of LP image quality. Familiar with the information extracted form DCT domain and gradient, the reconstruction error could also be used as feature in regression model to map to the associated human subjective scores.

5 Conclusion

We have proposed a well-performed clarity classification method that improves on the database we built. Not the same as traditional ones, this model extract the different reconstruction error as feature. This method can be widely applied to the quality assessment algorithm for fixed category objects. First determine the image category, and then determine the image quality, this process in more in line with human visual perception.

Acknowledgment. This research was supported in part by the National Nature Science Foundation, P.R. China (Nos. 61471201, 61501260), Jiangsu Province Universities Natural Science Research Key Grant Project (No. 13KJA510004), the Six Kinds Peak Talents Plan Project of Jiangsu Province (2014-DZXX-008), and the 1311 Talent Plan of NUPT.

References

1. Sharma, J., Mishra, A., Saxena, K., et al.: A hybrid technique for license plate recognition based on feature selection of wavelet transform and artificial neural network. In: 2014 International Conference on Optimization, Reliability, and Information Technology (ICROIT), pp. 347–352. IEEE (2014)
2. Nagare, A.P.: License plate character recognition system using neural network. Int. J. Comput. Appl. **25**(10), 36–39 (2011). ISSN 0975-8887
3. Akoum, A., Daya, B., Chauvet, P.: Two neural networks for license number plate recognition. J. Theoret. Appl. Inf. Technol. (2005–2009)
4. Masood, S.Z., Shu, G., Dehghan, A., et al.: License plate detection and recognition using deeply learned convolutional neural networks. arXiv preprint arXiv:1703.07330 (2017)
5. Ferzli, R., Karam, L.J.: A no-reference objective image sharpness metric based on the notion of just noticeable blur (JNB). IEEE Trans. Image Process. **18**(4), 717–728 (2009)
6. Narvekar, N.D., Karam, L.J.: A no-reference perceptual image sharpness metric based on a cumulative probability of blur detection. In: Proceedings of the IEEE International Workshop on Quality Multimedia Experience, July 2009, pp. 87–91 (2009)
7. Varadarajan, S., Karam, L.J.: An improved perception-based no-reference objective image sharpness metric using iterative edge refinement. In: Proceedings of the IEEE International Conference on Image Processing, October 2008, pp. 401–404 (2008)
8. Sadaka, N.G., Karam, L.J., Ferzli, R., Abousleman, G.P.: A no-reference perceptual image sharpness metric based on saliency-weighted foveal pooling. In: Proceedings of the IEEE International Conference on Image Processing, October 2008, pp. 369–372 (2008)
9. Sheikh, H.R., Bovik, A.C., Cormack, L.K.: No-reference quality assessment using natural scene statistics: JPEG2000. IEEE Trans. Image Process. **14**(11), 1918–1927 (2005)

10. Chen, J., Zhang, Y., Liang, L., Ma, S., Wang, R., Gao, W.: A no-reference blocking artifacts metric using selective gradient and plainness measures. In: Huang, Y.-M.R., Xu, C., Cheng, K.-S., Yang, J.-F.K., Swamy, M.N.S., Li, S., Ding, J.-W. (eds.) PCM 2008. LNCS, vol. 5353, pp. 894–897. Springer, Heidelberg (2008). https://doi.org/10.1007/978-3-540-89796-5_108

11. Suthaharan, S.: No-reference visually significant blocking artifact metric for natural scene images. J. Signal Process. **89**(8), 1647–1652 (2009)

12. Barland, R., Saadane, A.: Reference free quality metric using a region-based attention model for JPEG-2000 compressed images. In: Proceedings of SPIE, vol. 6059, pp. 605905-1–605905-10, January 2006

13. Mittal, A., Soundararajan, R., Bovik, A.C.: Making a 'completely blind' image quality analyzer. IEEE Signal Process. Lett. **20**(3), 209–212 (2013)

14. Moorthy, A.K., Bovik, A.C.: A two-step framework for constructing blind image quality indices. IEEE Signal Process. Lett. **17**(5), 513–516 (2010)

15. Moorthy, A.K., Bovik, A.C.: Blind image quality assessment: from natural scene statistics to perceptual quality. IEEE Trans. Image Process. **20**(12), 3350–3364 (2011)

16. Saad, M.A., Bovik, A.C., Charrier, C.: A DCT statistics-based blind image quality index. IEEE Signal Process. Lett. **17**(6), 583–586 (2010)

17. Saad, M.A., Bovik, A.C., Charrier, C.: Blind image quality assessment: a natural scene statistics approach in the DCT domain. IEEE Trans. Image Process. **21**(8), 3339–3352 (2012)

18. Shen, J., Li, Q., Erlebacher, G.: Hybrid no-reference natural image quality assessment of noisy, blurry, JPEG2000, and JPEG images. IEEE Trans. Image Process. **20**(8), 2089–2098 (2011)

19. Elad, M., Aharon, M.: Image denoising via sparse and redundant representations over learned dictionaries. IEEE Trans. Image Process. **15**(12), 3736–3745 (2006)

20. Zhang, Q., Li, B.: Discriminative K-SVD for dictionary learning in face recognition. In: 2010 IEEE Conference on Computer Vision and Pattern Recognition (CVPR). IEEE (2010)

21. Wright, J., et al.: Robust face recognition via sparse representation. IEEE Trans. Pattern Anal. Mach. Intell. **31**(2), 210–227 (2009)

22. Aharon, M., Elad, M., Bruckstein, A.: K-SVD: an algorithm for designing overcomplete dictionaries for sparse representation. IEEE Trans. Signal Process. **54**(11), 4311–4322 (2006)

23. Burges, C.: A tutorial on support vector machines for pattern recognition. Data Min. Knowl. Discov. **2**(2), 121–167 (1998)

24. Wang, Z., Sheikh, H.R., Bovik, A.C.: No-reference perceptual quality assessment of JPEG compressed images. In: Proceedings of the 2002 International Conference on Image Processing, vol. 1, p. I. IEEE (2002)

25. Liu, L., Liu, B., Huang, H., et al.: No-reference image quality assessment based on spatial and spectral entropies. Signal Process. Image Commun. **29**(8), 856–863 (2014)

Non-rigid 3D Object Retrieval with a Learned Shape Descriptor

Xiangfu Shi, Jieyu Zhao$^{(\boxtimes)}$, Long Zhang, and Xulun Ye

Department of Computer Science, Ningbo University, 818 Fenghua Road,
Ningbo 315211, China
xfu_shi@163.com, {zhao_jieyu,1401082013}@nbu.edu.cn,
1132548710@qq.com

Abstract. Non-rigid 3D objects are difficult to distinguish due to the structural transformation and noises. In this paper we develop a novel method to learn a discriminative shape descriptor for non-rigid 3D object retrieval. Compact low-level shape descriptors are designed from spectral descriptor, and the non-linear mapping of low level shape descriptors is carried out by a Siamese network. The Siamese network is trained to maximize the inter-class margin and minimize the intra-class distance. With an appropriate network hierarchy, we extract the last layer of the successfully trained network as the high-level shape descriptor. Furthermore, we successfully combine two low-level shape descriptors, based on the Heat Kernel Signature and the Wave Kernel Signature, and test the method on the benchmark dataset SHREC'14 Non-Rigid 3D Human Models. Experimental results show our method outperforms most of the existing algorithms for 3D shape retrieval.

Keywords: 3D object retrieval · Non-rigid · Siamese network
Laplace-Beltrami operator

1 Introduction

With the 3D objects widely used in a variety of fields, such as 3D games, movies entertainment, multimedia and so on, efficient and concise 3D shape analysis is be-coming more and more important. Retrieving non-rigid 3D objects has always been a hot and difficult topic. A large number of 3D retrieval methods have been proposed [1]. In [1] the authors present a review of the existing methods. Most of the methods represent a 3D shape as a shape descriptor. Shape descriptors are crucial for the 3D object representation. They not only need to describe the intrinsic attributes of shapes, but also need a good distinction for different models.

In the past decade, a large number of shape descriptors have been proposed, such as D2 shape distribution [2], statistical moments [3, 4], Fourier descriptor [5], Eigen-value Descriptor [6], etc. Those shape descriptors can effectively express 3D shapes, however they are relatively sensitive to non-rigid deformation and topological changes, and they are not suitable for non-rigid 3D shape retrieval.

Intrinsic descriptors with isometric invariance are proposed for non-rigid 3D models, the Laplace-Beltrami operator-based methods are the most common, includes the Global

© Springer International Publishing AG 2017
Y. Zhao et al. (Eds.): ICIG 2017, Part II, LNCS 10667, pp. 24–37, 2017.
https://doi.org/10.1007/978-3-319-71589-6_3

Point Signature (GPS) [7], the Heat Kernel Signature (HKS) [8], the Wave Kernel Signature (WKS) [9], the scale-invariant Heat Kernel Signature (SIHKS) [10], etc.

In the aforementioned methods, the shape descriptors are hand-crafted, rather than self-learning by data-driven. They are often not robust enough to deal with the deformation of the 3D models and geometric noises. In [11], the authors applied standard Bag-of-feature (BoF) to construct global shape descriptor. A set of HKSs of shapes are clustered using k-means to form the dictionary of words. Then they combine spatially-close words into histogram as shape descriptors. In [12], it combines the standard and spatial BoF descriptors for shape retrieval. Unlike the conventional BoF methods, the authors of [13] propose a supervised BoF approach with mean pooling to form discriminative shape descriptor. The authors of [14] adopt three levels for extracting high-level feature. They combine the SIHKS, the shape diameter function (SDF) and the averaged geodesic distance (AGD) three representative intrinsic features, then a position-independent BoF is extracted in mid-level. Finally a stack of restricted Boltzmann machines are used for high-level feature learning. [15–17] on the basis of histogram to optimize HKS by auto-encoder. In [14] they extract low level feature first, then neural networks are used to maximize the inter-class margin, minimize intra-class distance. [18] combines with SIHKS and WKS, the shape descriptor is obtained by the weight pooling, and linearly mapped into subspace using large margin nearest neighbor.

However, they almost have some common problems. Most high-level features are based on linear mapping. Although some methods extract high-level feature by deep learning, they have too few training samples. And the train set and test set always contain the same categories in their experiments.

2   Overview of Our Method

In this paper, we propose a novel non-rigid 3D object retrieval method. Our method improves both retrieval performance and time consumption. Inspired by mean pooling proposed in [13] and weighted pooling proposed in [18], we propose a simple and efficient method to simplify the multi-scale descriptor into a compact descriptor. We named it sum pooling descriptor. We use sum pooling instead of the weighted pooling, because the difference between the two is very small, with the increase in the number of points. This difference can be ignored when using the network optimization. So we use the simplest way to resolve this problem. This operation can be considered as the sum of the energy at each scale of each vertex on the meshes. it can describe the transformation of total energy. And we test this approach on HKS and WKS respectively.

Then we train a discriminative deformation-invariant shape descriptor via a two-stream network. It is called Siamese network in the field of computer vision and image processing. Figure 1 shows the pipeline of our proposed method, where the red arrows indicate the process of network training, and the blue arrows indicate test process. It included three steps:

- Multi-scale feature extraction. We extract two kinds of multi-scale features respectively, HKS and WKS, from 3D models to describe each non-rigid shape.

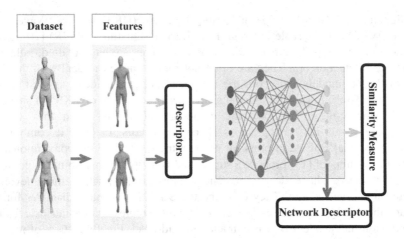

Fig. 1. The detailed framework of our method. We preprocess the 3D shapes from dataset and extract the point descriptors for each shape. The sum pooling step transforms the point descriptor into the compact descriptors, which can be represented by a vector. Finally, the high level descriptor is trained by the Siamese network. (Color figure online)

- Low level feature extraction. We employ the sum pooling operation on multi-scale features and get a succinct and compact representation of 3D shape. Each model can be represented as a vector.
- High level feature extraction. The low level features are mapped into subspace by a two-stream network which we design for 3D shape descriptor.

The reasons for choosing the two-stream network architecture for high-level feature extraction are as follows:

- The number of 3D models in one dataset is usually only a few tens or hundreds. The two-stream network architecture employ multiple inputs to increase the number of input samples of the network, it's a large extent and improve the ability of the network to fit.
- The low-level descriptors could be mapped into a better projection subspace in the Euclidean distance by the nonlinear mapping of the neural network.
- By comparing the differences between the different categories of samples in the loss function, the inter-class margin could be maximized and intra-class distance could be minimized.

3 Method

In this section, we describe the details of our method. In the first part, we describe the extraction of multi-scale features, includes HKS and WKS. The sum pooling operation and the design of the Siamese network are introduced in the second and third part.

3.1 Multi-scale Features Extraction

Heat Kernel Signature. The Heat Kernel Signature (HKS) [8] has been widely used in 3D shape analysis due to its capability of capturing significant intrinsic geometric properties, such as isometric invariance and robustness of geometric transformation. In HKS, a 3D model is represented as a Riemannian manifold M. The heat diffusion process on M is governed by the heat equation

$$\Delta_M u(x, t) = -\frac{\partial u(x, t)}{\partial t} \tag{1}$$

ΔM is the Laplace-Beltrami operator (LBO) on the Riemannian manifold M. And $k_t(x, y) : \Re^+ \times M \times M \to \Re$ is a function on M, which is heat kernel function used to describe the heat values between point x and point y on a given time t. The eigen-decomposition of the heat kernel is

$$k_t(x, y) = \sum_{k=0}^{\infty} e^{-\lambda k^t} \phi_k(x) \phi_k(y) \tag{2}$$

where λ_i and ϕ_i are the i-th eigenvalue and the i-th eigenfunction of the LBO respectively. The equation $k_t(x, x)$ can represent the heat values at point x from time t_0 to time t, where the unit heat sources u_0 aggregates on the 3D model surface S. Thus the HKS can be represented as

$$k_t(x, x) = \sum_{k=0}^{K-1} e^{-\lambda_k t} \phi_k(x)^2 \tag{3}$$

Note that we no longer choose all the eigenfunctions, just intercept the top k eigenfunctions of LBO. And the different diffusion time of HKS concatenated to obtain a descriptor of point x

$$HKS(x) = (k_{t_1}(x, x), k_{t_2}(x, x), \ldots, k_{t_\tau}(x, x)) \tag{4}$$

where the HKS(x) describes the local descriptor of point x on one model. It is showed as a T-dimensional vector. For a 3D model with n point $X = \{x_1, x_2, \ldots, x_n\}$, we finally get a global descriptor of size of $n * T$.

$$HKS = (HKS(x_1), HKS(x_2), \ldots, HKS(x_n)) \tag{5}$$

Wave Kernel Signature. The Wave Kernel Signature (WKS) [9] reflects the fact that the probability distribution of different energy of quantum particles. The energy of a quantum particle on a model surface is governed by the wave function $\psi(x, t)$ which is a solution of the Schrödinger equation

$$\frac{\partial \psi(x,t)}{\partial t} = i\Delta\psi(x,t) \tag{6}$$

Similar to HKS, WKS also depends on the LBO eigen-decomposition. We get an energy probability distribution with expectation value E. Therefore the wave equation can be written as

$$\psi_E(x,t) = \sum_{k=0}^{\infty} e^{i\lambda_k t}\phi_k(x)f_E(\lambda_k) \tag{7}$$

The probability to measure the particle at point x is $|\psi_E(x,t)|^2$. Considering that the time parameters do not have an intuitive explanatory of shape. The WKS define as the average probability over time is

$$p(x) = \lim_{x\to\infty}\frac{1}{T}\int_0^T |\psi_E(x,t)|^2 = \sum_{k=1}^{\infty}\phi_k(x)^2 f_E(\lambda_k)^2 \tag{8}$$

Therefor descriptor of different scales can be described by choose different distributions f_E. The multi-scales descriptor WKS with a set of energy distributions $E = \{e_1,\ldots,e_q\}$ is shown below

$$WKS(E,x) = (p_{e_1}(x),\ldots,p_{e_q}(x))^T \tag{9}$$

3.2 Sum Pooling Descriptor

For retrieval, a concise and compact descriptor to describe a shape is necessary, and there is a need for a good distinction between different no-rigid 3D shapes. Both HKS and WKS are multi-scale descriptors. They are not suitable for retrieval. In order to form a compact descriptor, we sum energy values at all points on each scale. It describes the process of the heat values changes on the shape surface over time. For a given shape S with V points, the scale size of multi-scale descriptor is N. We compute a sum pooling HKS or WKS over all point descriptors $d(x)$ computed from the points x of S. Thus, our shape descriptor is defined as

$$y(S) = \sum_{x\in S} d(x)/V \tag{10}$$

where $x \in S$ is a point from shape S. N is the number of all points. The descriptor of point x is represented by $d(x)$.

3.3 Siamese Network Architecture

As shown in Fig. 2, in order to make the descriptor map to the optimal Euclidean distance projection subspace while maximize the inter-class margin and minimize intra-class distance, we apply the two-stream network architecture to handle this part of work. Figure 3 shows that the Siamese network achieves the two-stream architecture by sharing network weights. It is proposed to be used for signature verification [19]. Later, various improvements to Siamese networks are applied in many missions, including face verification [20, 21], ground-to-aerial image matching [22], local path descriptor learning [23, 24] and stereo matching [25]. In this work, we design a novel Siamese network to learn a concise and compact descriptor for 3D shape retrieval.

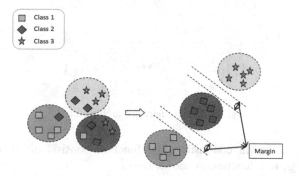

Fig. 2. The Siamese Network maps features to high-dimensional subspace, which narrowing the differences between the samples from same class and expanding the distance between the samples from different classes.

Note that Siamese network is a metric learning algorithm. Our aim is to get a compact descriptor. Considering that the hierarchical structure of the neural network and the distance of two samples are measured at the last layer in the European space. Thus we extract the last layer of the network as a descriptor after the training is finished.

Network Architecture. Figure 3 shows the architecture of our network. Here X_1 and X_2 are a pair of input samples of network. If they come from the same category then $Y = 1$, and we calls "positive pair" and otherwise $Y = 0$ ("negative pair"). The W is the sharing weights of network, and the function E_W that measures the Euclidean distance between the network outputs of X_1 and X_2. It is defined as

$$E_W(X_1, X_2) = ||G_W(X_1) - G_W(X_2)||_2 \tag{11}$$

where $G_W(X_1)$ and $G_W(X_2)$ are the high-level space vector after network mapping and $||G_W(X_1) - G_W(X_2)||_2$ is the Euclidean distance of two network's latent representations.

Considering that the input dimension is small, we do not incorporate the regularization term into the loss function, instead apply the RELU activation function directly in the first layer of the network, not only played a role of the regularization term, but also we find it increases the speed of convergence nearly ten times.

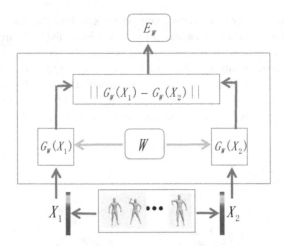

Fig. 3. Siamese network architecture.

Loss. We apply a margin contrastive loss function consists of squared error loss function and hinge loss function as shown below

$$loss(W) = YE_W^2 + (1 - Y) \max(0, \varepsilon - E_W) \tag{12}$$

where Y is a binary label of the pair indicates whether they are the same category or not and ε is a distance margin.

4 Experiments

4.1 Dataset and Evaluation Metric

Dataset. We evaluated our approaches on the dataset of the SHREC'14-Shape Retrieval of Non-Rigid 3D Human Model [26]. "Real" dataset contains real scans objects of 20 males and 20 females different persons altogether 40 subjects, each subject includes ten different poses a total of 400 models. "Synthetic" dataset includes 300 models with 15 groups (5 males, 5 females and 5 children). Each class has a unique shape with 20 different poses. Compared with other 3D datasets, the datasets we adopted are composed of human body models, rather than the different kinds of objects. It made these datasets particularly challenging.

Evaluation Metrics. We chose several evaluation metrics commonly used in 3D retrieval for evaluating the performance of our proposed descriptors.

- Nearest Neighbor (NN): The percentage of the closest matching objects and query are from the same class.
- First Tier (FT): The percentage of shapes is from the same class of the query are in the top K.

- Second Tier (ST): The percentage of shapes is from the same class of the query are in the top 2K.
- E-measure (EM): The EM is obtained by the precision and recall for top 32 of retrieved results.
- Discounted Cumulative Gain (DCG): a logarithmic statistic used to weighs correct results near the front of the ranked list and toward the end of the list.
- The Mean Average Precision (mAP): from the PR curves the average of all precision values computed in each relevant object in the retrieved list.

4.2 Implementation Details

In this subsection, we introduce our experimental settings. The LBO is limited to the first 100 eigenfunctions. For HKS, we choose 100 time scale. For WKS, the variance of the WKS Gaussian is set to 6. The dimension of WKS was 100. We down-sample all shapes to 10K vertexes and 20K faces with Meshlab [27].

We train a Siamese network which is made up of 3 layers fully connected network with size 150-516-256-150. We over sampling the number of "positive pair" ensure the number of two input samples of network is the same. The margin of safety ε in the loss function is set to 1.0.

4.3 Experiment 1

In this experiment, we divide the dataset into the training set and the test set according to [13]. We select 4 samples of each class as the training set, and the other as the test set.

We test the sum pooling HKS (SPHKS), the sum pooling WKS (SPWKS) and the stacked sum pooling HKS and WKS (SPHWKS) three low level descriptors and their corresponding trained descriptors by network. We run each test in this paper 20 times with different training set and test set splits, and take the average as the final results.

We test the performance of those features. After combining the Siamese network, our descriptor obtained significant results (Tables 1 and 2). And in this more challenging Real dataset, our approach is getting better results. It shows our method has a better effect on a dataset with noise and topology changes. The performance of stacked descriptors was worse than HKS. However, after network mapping, the performance of the descriptors is significantly improved.

Table 1. Shape descriptors evaluation on the SHREC'14 "Synthetic" dataset in experiment 1. We test the sum pooling descriptor (SPHKS, SPWKS, SPHWKS) with its corresponding descriptor trained by network.

Method	NN	FT	ST	EM	DCG
SPHKS	0.808	0.664	0.947	0.616	0.869
SPHKS+NN	0.841	0.722	0.939	0.607	0.890
SPWKS	0.747	0.603	0.871	0.569	0.840
SPWKS+NN	0.788	0.676	0.917	0.594	0.871
SPHWKS	0.844	0.697	0.970	0.628	0.904
SPHWKS+NN	0.928	0.861	0.984	0.632	0.957

Table 2. Shape descriptors evaluation on the SHREC'14 "Real" dataset in experiment 1.

Method	NN	FT	ST	EM	DCG
SPHKS	0.665	0.554	0.718	0.280	0.753
SPHKS+NN	0.804	0.726	0.901	0.270	0.866
SPWKS	0.181	0.169	0.274	0.157	0.425
SPWKS+NN	0.316	0.288	0.504	0.245	0.561
SPHWKS	0.513	0.438	0.643	0.245	0.672
SPHWKS+NN	0.898	0.851	0.966	0.270	0.933

We also compare the P-R curves Fig. 4 and the mean average accuracy (mAP) shows in Table 3.

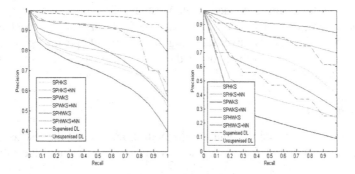

Fig. 4. Comparison of performance of three descriptors before and after network mapping on the SHREC'14 Synthetic dataset (left) and Real dataset (right) in experiment 1.

Our method compares with some state-of-the-art methods which are introduced in [30], including ISPM, DBN, HAPT, R-BIHDM, Shape Google, Unsupervised DL and supervised DL. We also compare our method with some methods that use deep learning or the recent learning methods, including CSD+LMNN [18], DLSD [28], RMVM [29]. Although our approach is not the best, but such as CSD+LMNN method, its training set and test set must have the same class which is not reasonable in the practical application.

By comparing the P-R curves and the results of the mAP, it's clear that our algorithm decreases slowly with the increase of Recall rate, which is more stable than other approaches. And the mAP of our proposed method is superior to most existing methods.

4.4   Experiment 2

We make two more interesting tests and choose some classes as training set, the rest as test set. One of the reasons we chose a two-stream architecture network is to weaken the label, so that the network have the power to find the difference between the different

Table 3. Comparison of different retrieval methods. The last six records are the results of our method. And the top three scores of each column are highlighted.

Method	Real	Synthetic
ISPM	25.8	90.2
DBN	30.4	84.2
R-BiHDM	64.0	64.2
HAPT	63.7	81.7
Shape Google(VQ)	51.4	81.3
Unsupervised DL	52.3	84.2
Supervised DL	79.1	95.4
CSD+LMNN	**97.92**	**99.67**
DLSD	75.4	**99.0**
RMVM	**79.5**	**96.3**
SPHKS(proposed)	61.9	73.2
SPHKS+NN	79.0	78.1
SPWKS	20.4	66.3
SPWKS+NN	36.2	73.8
SPHWKS	50.0	77.7
SPHWKS+NN	**89.5**	90.8

classes, rather only distinguishing between known classes. It is not difficult to find that out method is more suitable for this experiment than experiment 1. In both experiments, the number of negative sample pairs has been sufficient. However, in experiment 1, the Synthetic dataset and real dataset can only get 240 and 640 positive sample pairs. In this experiment, the number of positive sample pairs is significantly more than experiment 1, for the Synthetic dataset and the Real dataset we can obtain 2800 and 2000 sample pairs.

We choose half classes (20 calsses, 200 models in "Real" dataset and 7 classes, 2800 models in "Synthetic" dataset) as training set, and the rest as test set. The experiment results in (Tables 4 and 5) show that our method is more effective in improving the dataset with noise, which just shows the advantages of the neural network.

Obviously, as shown in Tables 4 and 5, even if the test classes are not in the training set, the results of our experiments are also significant. Our method is still more

Table 4. Shape descriptors devaluation on the SHREC'14 "Real" dataset in experiment 2.

Method	NN	FT	ST	EM	DCG
SPHKS	0.796	0.682	0.855	0.417	0.860
SPHKS+NN	0.899	0.803	0.950	0.436	0.923
SPWKS	0.311	0.278	0.449	0.278	0.562
SPWKS+NN	0.565	0.478	0.739	0.400	0.726
SPHWKS	0.687	0.587	0.790	0.400	0.800
SPHWKS+NN	0.944	0.915	0.989	0.439	0.966

Table 5. Shape descriptors evaluation on the SHREC'14 "Synthetic" dataset in experiment 2.

Method	NN	FT	ST	EM	DCG
SPHKS	0.896	0.794	0.981	0.695	0.927
SPHKS+NN	0.910	0.811	0.958	0.686	0.935
SPWKS	0.806	0.699	0.928	0.651	0.888
SPWKS+NN	0.812	0.675	0.875	0.617	0.873
SPHWKS	0.900	0.805	0.986	0.698	0.945
SPHWKS+NN	0.950	0.819	0.949	0.685	0.944

effective in SHREC'14 Real dataset. The SHREC'14 Synthetic dataset has little noise. The sum pooling descriptors have enough power to distinguish shapes from different classes.

The Precision-Recall plots Fig. 5 and the mAP Table 6 show the results of different descriptor. The network-optimized descriptors are more stable. Despite the stacked descriptor with HKS and WKS did not show good performance, it get a remarkable result trained by the Siamese network.

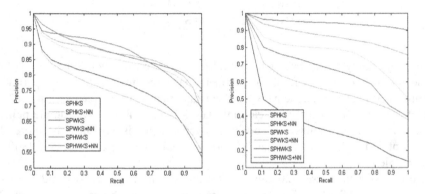

Fig. 5. Comparison of performance of three descriptors before and after network mapping on the SHREC'14 Synthetic dataset (left) and "Real" dataset (right) in experiment 2.

Table 6. The mean average precision of experiments evaluation on the SHREC'14 dataset in experiment 2.

Method	Real	Synthetic
SPHKS	74.3	84.1
SPHKS+NN	85.5	85.6
SPWKS	30.5	75.3
SPWKS+NN	54.0	73.0
SPHWKS	63.7	88.0
SPHWKS+NN	93.8	90.3

We visualized the trained SPHWKS descriptor, from Fig. 6 we find that no trained descriptors are difficult to distinguish visually. After training, there is a significant difference between classes.

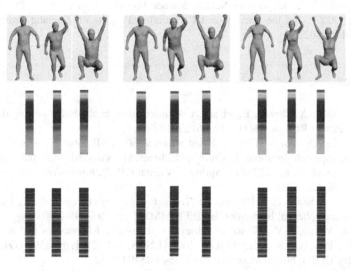

Fig. 6. Shape descriptors visualization. We choose three classes (left, middle, right) and the models between the different classes are chosen to have the same posture. From top to bottom are the models of human, the sum pooling descriptors and trained sum pooling descriptors.

4.5 The Time Consumption

We test our method on the PC with Inter(R) Core(TM) i5-4690 CPU and 8.0 GB RAM. It takes approximate 2.7 s for each shape to compute LBO eigenvalues and eigenvectors. It takes a total of 2.3 s to finish compute the low level descriptor for one shape, where the sum pooling process only needs 0.4 s. The time consumption in the high level descriptor extraction is mainly in the training stage. It take about 15 m to finish training a network.

5   Conclusion

We proposed a novel 3D shape descriptor via Siamese network. We first extracted a compact low level descriptor. We obtained it by sum pooling the point descriptor HKS and WKS. The HKS is more sensitive to the global information, the WKS is more effective for detail information. We stacked HKS and WKS, and further optimize it through the Siamese network. The network descriptor is obtained by extracting the last layer of Siamese network. We tested our proposed method on two challenging datasets, including Real and Synthetic dataset of SHREC'14 Human dataset. The results of our experiments showed that our proposed method is very effective for containing noises and indistinguishable data. The performance of our method is more than the existing method in many aspects.

Acknowledgements. This work is supported by National Natural Science Foundation of China under Grant 61571247, the National Natural Science Foundation of Zhejiang Province under Grant LZ16F030001, and the International Cooperation Projects of Zhejiang Province under Grant No. 2013C24027.

References

1. Lian, Z., Godil, A., Bustos, B., et al.: A comparison of methods for non-rigid 3D shape retrieval. Pattern Recogn. **46**(1), 449–461 (2013)
2. Elad, M., Tal, A., Ar, S.: Content based retrieval of VRML objects — an iterative and interactive approach. In: Jorge, J., Correia, N., Jones, H., Kamegai, M.B. (eds.) Multimedia 2001. Eurographics, pp. 107–118. Springer, Vienna (2002). https://doi.org/10.1007/978-3-7091-6103-6_12
3. Vranic, D.V., Saupe, D., Richter, J.: Tools for 3D-object retrieval: Karhunen-Loeve transform and spherical harmonics. In: IEEE MMSP, pp. 293–298 (2001)
4. Saupe, D., Vranić, D.V.: 3D model retrieval with spherical harmonics and moments. In: Radig, B., Florczyk, S. (eds.) DAGM 2001. LNCS, vol. 2191, pp. 392–397. Springer, Heidelberg (2001). https://doi.org/10.1007/3-540-45404-7_52
5. Chen, D., Tian, X., Shen, Y., et al.: On visual similarity based 3D model retrieval. Comput. Graph. Forum **22**(3), 223–232 (2010)
6. Jain, V., Zhang, H.: A spectral approach to shape-based retrieval of articulated 3D models. Comput.-Aided Des. **39**(5), 398–407 (2007)
7. Rustamov, R.M.: Laplace-Beltrami eigenfunctions for deformation invariant shape representation. In: Eurographics Symposium on Geometry Processing, pp. 225–233 (2007)
8. Sun, J., Ovsjanikov, M., Guibas, L.: A concise and provably informative multi-scale signature based on heat diffusion. In: Computer Graphics Forum, vol. 28, pp. 1383–1392. Wiley Online Library (2009)
9. Aubry, M., Schlickewei, U., Cremers, D.: The wave kernel signature: a quantum mechanical approach to shape analysis. In: 2011 IEEE International Conference on Computer Vision Workshops (ICCV Workshops), pp. 1626–1633. IEEE (2011)
10. Bronstein, M.M., Kokkinos, I.: Scale-invariant heat kernel signatures for non-rigid shape recognition. In: 2010 IEEE Conference on Computer Vision and Pattern Recognition (CVPR), pp. 1704–1711. IEEE (2010)
11. Bronstein, A.M., Bronstein, M.M., Guibas, L.J., et al.: Shape Google: geometric words and expressions for invariant shape retrieval. ACM Trans. Graph. **30**(1), 1 (2011)
12. Lavoué, G.: Combination of bag-of-words descriptors for robust partial shape retrieval. Vis. Comput. **28**(9), 931–942 (2012)
13. Litman, R., Bronstein, A.M., Bronstein, M.M., Castellani, U.: Supervised learning of bag-of-features shape descriptors using sparse coding. Comput. Graph. Forum **33**(5), 127–136 (2014)
14. Bu, S., Liu, Z., Han, J., Wu, J., Ji, R.: Learning high-level feature by deep belief networks for 3D model retrieval and recognition. IEEE Trans. Multimedia **16**(8), 2154–2167 (2013). CAESAR

15. Xie, J., Fang, Y., Zhu, F., et al.: Deepshape: deep learned shape descriptor for 3D shape matching and retrieval. In: Computer Vision and Pattern Recognition, pp. 1275–1283. IEEE (2015)
16. Fang, Y., Xie, J., Dai, G., et al.: 3D deep shape descriptor. In: Computer Vision and Pattern Recognition, pp. 2319–2328. IEEE (2015)
17. Zhu, Z., Wang, X., Bai, S., Yao, C., Bai, X.: Deep learning representation using autoencoder for 3D shape retrieval. In: Proceedings of 2014 International Conference on Security, Pattern Analysis, and Cybernetics (SPAC), pp. 279–284. IEEE (2014)
18. Chiotellis, I., Triebel, R., Windheuser, T., Cremers, D.: Non-rigid 3D shape retrieval via large margin nearest neighbor embedding. In: Leibe, B., Matas, J., Sebe, N., Welling, M. (eds.) ECCV 2016. LNCS, vol. 9906, pp. 327–342. Springer, Cham (2016). https://doi.org/10.1007/978-3-319-46475-6_21
19. Bromley, J., Guyon, I., Lecun, Y., et al.: Signature verification using a siamese time delay neural network. In: Advances in Neural Information Processing Systems, DBLP, pp. 737–744 (1993)
20. Chopra, S., Hadsell, R., LeCun, Y.: Learning a similarity metric discriminatively, with application to face verification. In: CVPR (2005)
21. Taigman, Y., Yang, M., Ranzato, M., Wolf, L.: Deepface: closing the gap to human-level performance in face verification. In: CVPR (2014)
22. Lin, T.Y., Cui, Y., Belongie, S., Hays, J.: Learning deep representations for ground-to-aerial geolocalization. In: CVPR (2015)
23. Han, X., Leung, T., Jia, Y., Sukthankar, R., Berg, A.C.: Matchnet: unifying feature and metric learning for patch based matching. In: CVPR (2015)
24. Zagoruyko, S., Komodakis, N.: Learning to compare image patches via convolutional neural networks. In: CVPR (2015)
25. Zbontar, J., LeCun, Y.: Computing the stereo matching 藝 cost with a convolutional neural network. In: CVPR (2015)
26. Pickup, D., Sun, X., Rosin, P.L., et al.: Shape retrieval of non-rigid 3D human models. In: Eurographics Workshop on 3D Object Retrieval, pp. 101–110. Eurographics Association (2014)
27. Visual Computing Lab, ISTI-CNR: Meshlab. http://meshlab.sourceforge.net/
28. Dai, G., Xie, J., Zhu, F., et al.: Learning a discriminative deformation-invariant 3D shape descriptor via many-to-one encoder. Pattern Recogn. Lett. 83, 330–338 (2016)
29. Gasparetto, A., Torsello, A.: A statistical model of Riemannian metric variation for deformable shape analysis. In: IEEE Conference on Computer Vision and Pattern Recognition (CVPR), June 2015
30. Pickup, D., Sun, X., Rosin, P.L., Martin, R.R., Cheng, Z., Lian, Z., Aono, M., Ben Hamza, A., Bronstein, A., Bronstein, M., Bu, S., Castellani, U., Cheng, S., Garro, V., Giachetti, A., Godil, A., Han, J., Johan, H., Lai, L., Li, B., Li, C., Li, H., Litman, R., Liu, X., Liu, Z., Lu, Y., Tatsuma, A., Ye, J.: SHREC'14 track: shape retrieval of non-rigid 3D human models. In: Proceedings of the 7th Eurographics Workshop on 3D Object Retrieval, EG 3DOR 2014. Eurographics Association (2014)

Adaptive Patch Quantization for Histogram-Based Visual Tracking

Lvran Chen[1,2,3], Huicheng Zheng[1,2,3]([✉]), Zijian Lin[1,2,3], Dajun Lin[1,2,3], and Bo Ke[1,2,3]

[1] School of Data and Computer Science, Sun Yat-sen University,
135 West Xingang Road, Guangzhou 510275, China
zhenghch@mail.sysu.edu.cn
[2] Key Laboratory of Machine Intelligence and Advanced Computing,
Ministry of Education, Sun Yat-sen University,
135 West Xingang Road, Guangzhou 510275, China
[3] Guangdong Key Laboratory of Information Security Technology,
Sun Yat-sen University, 135 West Xingang Road, Guangzhou 510275, China

Abstract. Color histogram-based trackers have shown favorable performance recently. However, most color histogram-based trackers employ pixel-wise information, incapable of distinguishing objects from backgrounds robustly. In this paper, we propose an adaptive patch quantization approach for histogram-based visual tracking. We first exploit neighboring pixels in the form of local patches to improve the discrimination between objects and backgrounds. Then we propose an adaptive quantization strategy for quantization space update and histogram adjustment to avoid model drifting. We further exploit a novel localization technique based on adaptive segmentation to improve the localization accuracy. The experimental results demonstrate that the proposed method performs superiorly against several state-of-the-art algorithms.

Keywords: Visual tracking · Histogram-based
Adaptive patch quantization

1 Introduction

Visual object tracking is one of the fundamental tasks in computer vision and has been applied to many applications [1,2] like surveillance, robotics, motion analysis, human-computer interface, and so on. In this paper, we focus on the problem of short-term, single-object tracking. Despite the significant progress in recent years, developing a robust tracking algorithm is still a challenging problem due to the real-world scenarios [3,4] such as illumination change, motion blur, deformation, heavy occlusion, and so on.

Recently, correlation filter (CF) based trackers enjoy a wide popularity due to their significant computational efficiency. However, CF-based tracker inherently learns a rigid template of the object, and thus it is vulnerable to deformation.

© Springer International Publishing AG 2017
Y. Zhao et al. (Eds.): ICIG 2017, Part II, LNCS 10667, pp. 38–50, 2017.
https://doi.org/10.1007/978-3-319-71589-6_4

On the contrary, histogram-based trackers like [5,6] cope well with this problem. However, most of them employ pixel-wise information for representation, which is incapable of distinguishing objects from backgrounds robustly. Moreover, the widely used fixed quantization is unable to adapt to the change of data, and it would degrade the model discrimination when objects and backgrounds share similar colors. Finally, smoothing-based localization strategy reduces the distinction between objects and backgrounds, and leads to erroneously located bounding boxes frequently. To resolve these issues, it is beneficial to exploit neighboring pixels for better representation.

To address the above issues, in this paper, we propose an adaptive patch quantization (APQ) approach for histogram-based visual tracking. We employ adaptively quantized patch information to distinguish objects from backgrounds robustly, address the model drifting issue, and further locate the objects with well-selected patches. The main contributions of our work can be summarized as follows.

1. We exploit neighboring pixels by using local patches in a discriminative histogram-based model to improve the discrimination between objects and backgrounds.
2. An adaptive quantization strategy is proposed to update quantization space and corresponding histograms to avoid the model drifting problem.
3. We exploit a novel localization technique based on adaptive segmentation to improve the localization accuracy.
4. Our extensive experiments demonstrate outstanding performance of the proposed algorithm compared to several state-of-the-art methods in three public benchmarks: VOT2016 [4], OTB-13 [1] and OTB-15 [2].

The rest of this paper is organized as follows. The related work is reviewed in Sect. 2. The adaptive patch quantization (APQ) approach for histogram-based visual tracking is discussed in Sect. 3. The experimental results of three popular benchmarks are presented in Sect. 4. Finally, Sect. 5 concludes this paper.

2   Related Work

Visual tracking is one of the fundamental problems in computer vision and gets a wide popularity recently. Most tracking algorithms can be either generative or discriminative. Generative algorithms learn the model of the object and search for the best matching region, such as incremental subspace learning [7], sparse representation [8], and so on. In contrast, discriminative models formulate the task as a binary classification problem, including multiple instance learning [9], P-N learning [10], support vector machines (SVM) [11,12], and so on.

The correlation filter (CF) based trackers enable dense samplings and high-dimensional features in training and detection while preserving real-time capacity. CF is first introduced to tracking field by Bolme et al. [13], and further extended by kernelized CF with multi-channel features [14]. Danelljan et al. [15]

propose a fast scale estimation with a pyramid representation. However, the periodic assumption introduces the unsatisfactory boundary effects. To solve this problem, the spatial regularization [16] is proposed to penalize CF coefficients based on their spatial locations. CF-based trackers are robust to illumination changes, but sensitive to dynamic situations like deformation.

Convolutional Neural Networks (CNNs) have become popular in visual tracking with the great power in feature representation. Trackers like [17] improve the representation effectiveness by large scale visual tracking data based on a pretrained CNN. Ma et al. [18] propose adaptive correlation filters to improve the tracking performance. Moreover, a formulation for learning continuous convolution filters is proposed in [19], which enables fusion of multi-resolution deep features. However, CNN-based trackers require heavy computations, and are therefore hard to achieve real-time performance without GPUs [17,19].

Recently, color-based trackers have attracted great attention [5,6,20,21]. The adaptive color tracker [21] proposes a temporally consistent strategy for model update, and adaptively selects the most important combinations of colors for tracking. To solve the drifting problem in color-based model, the distractor-aware tracker [5] suppresses distracting regions in similar colors with objects. Staple [6] improves the performance of discriminative color histogram-based model cooperated with CF, but the model is still unreliable in complicated backgrounds due to the limitation of pixel-wise information.

3   The Proposed Method

3.1   Discriminative Patch-Based Model

To distinguish objects from backgrounds robustly, patch information is employed in our model, and histograms are utilized for probability approximation. The first issue we face is the quantization of patch-based vectors. Fixed and homogeneous quantization is efficient and reliable when constructing histograms for low-dimensional vectors. However, for high-dimensional vectors, there are usually no sufficient data for such a quantization. As a result, a suitable method for space division is required. In this paper, K-Means clustering is introduced to quantize patch-based vectors due to its adaptivity to the data distribution.

We denote the search region, object region and background region by $\mathcal{S}$, $\mathcal{O}$ and $\mathcal{B}$, respectively. The three regions satisfy $\mathcal{O}, \mathcal{B} \subseteq \mathcal{S}$ and $\mathcal{O} \cap \mathcal{B} = \varnothing$. Patches are densely sampled from region $\mathcal{S}$ and arranged into vectors. We denote the set of these patch vectors by $E(\mathcal{S})$. For patch vector quantization, we obtain K centroids $\{\mathbf{c}_i\}_{i=1}^K$ by K-Means clustering on $E(\mathcal{S})$.

For each $\mathbf{u} \in E(\mathcal{S})$, let $\mathbf{b}(\mathbf{u})$ be the corresponding bin vector, which contains a unique non-zero element. Its i-th component, $b_i(\mathbf{u})$, is defined as

$$b_i(\mathbf{u}) = \begin{cases} 1, \forall j \neq i, d(\mathbf{u}, \mathbf{c}_i) \leq d(\mathbf{u}, \mathbf{c}_j) \\ 0, \text{otherwise} \end{cases}, i, j = 1, 2, \ldots, K \qquad (1)$$

where $d(\cdot, \cdot)$ calculates the Euclidean distance between two vectors. To distinguish patches from object region $\mathcal{O}$ and those from background region $\mathcal{B}$, the patch probability $p(\mathbf{u})$ is ideally set to be 1 for $\mathbf{u} \in E(\mathcal{O})$, and 0 for $\mathbf{u} \in E(\mathcal{B})$. We assume $p(\mathbf{u})$ to be a linear function, formulated as $p(\mathbf{u}) = \beta^T \mathbf{b}(\mathbf{u})$, where β is the model parameter.

Similar to [5,6], we obtain a discriminative patch-based model by linear Bayesian classifier,

$$\beta_i = \frac{H_i(\mathcal{O})}{H_i(\mathcal{O}) + H_i(\mathcal{S})}, i = 1, 2, \ldots, K, \qquad (2)$$

where β_i is the i-th component of β. $H(\mathcal{Q}) = \sum_{\mathbf{u} \in E(\mathcal{Q})} \mathbf{b}(\mathbf{u})$, $\mathcal{Q} \in \{\mathcal{O}, \mathcal{B}\}$ is the histogram on $\mathcal{Q}$, where $H_i(\mathcal{Q})$ is the i-th component of $H(\mathcal{Q})$.

The superiority of the proposed patch-based model is shown in Fig. 1, with more discriminative and smoother probability map (Fig. 1c) compared with pixel-wise model (Fig. 1b), where the probability map is obtained by evaluating $p(\mathbf{u})$ at pixels or centers of patches, located within the search region (Fig. 1a).

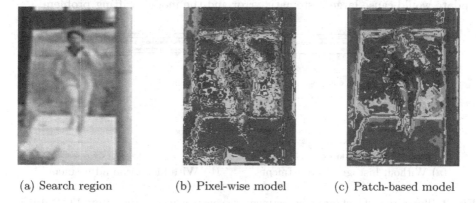

(a) Search region   (b) Pixel-wise model   (c) Patch-based model

Fig. 1. Example of object probability maps in sequence *graduate* in VOT2016 [4] at frame 67. The probability map of (b) pixel-wise model and (c) our patch-based model are calculated on (a) the search region. Hot colors correspond to high object probability scores. Best viewed in color.

3.2 Adaptive Quantization Strategy

In the proposed discriminative patch-based model, centroids $\{\mathbf{c}_i\}_{i=1}^{K}$ and histograms $H(\cdot)$ can be viewed as quantization space and results respectively. Both of them need to be updated over time to adapt to the change of object appearance.

Quantization Space. Similar to [22], we update the quantization space as:

$$n_i^{1:t+1} \cdot \mathbf{c}_i^{t+1} = n_i^{1:t} \cdot \mathbf{c}_i^t + \sum_{\mathbf{u} \in S_i^t} \mathbf{u} \qquad (3)$$

where $S_i^t = \{\mathbf{u}|\mathbf{u} \in E(\mathcal{S}^t), d(\mathbf{u}, \mathbf{c}_i^t) \leq d(\mathbf{u}, \mathbf{c}_j^t), \forall j \neq i, \text{where } j = 1, 2, \ldots, K\}$, $i = 1, 2, \ldots, K$ denotes the set of patches closest to $\mathbf{c}_i^t$, and $n_i^{1:t+1} = n_i^{1:t} + |S_i^t|$ is the number of patches closest to i-th cluster accumulated over time.

Histogram Adjustment. The linear interpolation $H^{1:t+1}(\cdot) = (1 - \eta_{\text{hist}})H^{1:t}(\cdot) + \eta_{\text{hist}}H^{t+1}(\cdot)$ is widely used for histogram update [5,6], which implicitly assumes that all histograms share the same quantization space over time. Due to the change of quantization space in our tracker, the assumption is invalid here. The histogram of previous patch vectors quantized by $\{\mathbf{c}_i^{t-\tau}\}_{i=1}^K$ may differ from that quantized by $\{\mathbf{c}_i^t\}_{i=1}^K$, where $\tau = 1, 2, \ldots, t-1$.

An intuitive illustration is shown in Fig. 2, where all curves denote histograms of $\mathbf{u} \in E(\mathcal{S}^1)$, but differ in quantization space. The red and blue curves in Fig. 2a denote histograms without adjustment strategy, quantized by $\{\mathbf{c}_i^{113}\}_{i=1}^K$ and $\{\mathbf{c}_i^1\}_{i=1}^K$ respectively, and sorted in an ascending order of the histogram in red in Fig. 2a. As shown in Fig. 2a, simply adopting the linear interpolation for histogram update would cause large systematic error and the model drifting problem.

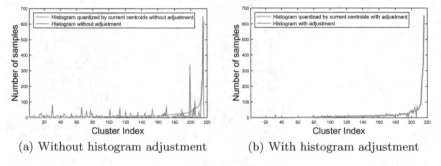

(a) Without histogram adjustment   (b) With histogram adjustment

Fig. 2. Illustration of histogram adjustment in sequence *gymnastics1* from VOT2016 [4] at frame 113. The red curves indicate histograms of patch vectors $\mathbf{u} \in E(\mathcal{S}^1)$ quantized by current centroids with or without the proposed histogram adjustment strategy, while the blue curves indicate histograms of the same patch vectors quantized by first-frame centroids updated with or without the proposed histogram adjustment strategy. (Color figure online)

To keep the consistency of quantization space in successive frames, we exploit a histogram adjustment strategy,

$$\tilde{H}_i^{1:t}(\mathcal{Q}) = \sum_{j \in F_i^t} H_j^{1:t}(\mathcal{Q}), \quad \mathcal{Q} \in \{\mathcal{O}, \mathcal{B}\} \tag{4}$$

where $\tilde{H}_i^{1:t}(\mathcal{Q})$ is the i-th component of adjusted histogram over time. The set $F_i^t = \{k|\forall j \neq i, d(\mathbf{c}_k^t, \mathbf{c}_i^{t+1}) \leq d(\mathbf{c}_k^t, \mathbf{c}_j^{t+1}), j, k = 1, 2, \ldots, K\}$, $i = 1, 2, \ldots, K$ indicates the index of clusters $\{\mathbf{c}_k^t\}_{k=1}^K$ closest to $\mathbf{c}_i^{t+1}$. We finally update the histogram as:

$$H_i^{1:t+1}(\mathcal{Q}) = (1 - \eta_{\text{hist}})\tilde{H}_i^{1:t}(\mathcal{Q}) + \eta_{\text{hist}}H_i^{t+1}(\mathcal{Q}), \quad \mathcal{Q} \in \{\mathcal{O}, \mathcal{B}\} \tag{5}$$

where η_{hist} is the learning rate. An illustration of histogram adjustment strategy is shown in Fig. 2b, where the red curve is the histogram of $\mathbf{u} \in E(\mathcal{S}^1)$ quantized by centroids $\{\mathbf{c}_i^{113}\}_{i=1}^K$ in a tracker with histogram adjustment strategy, while the blue curve is the adjusted histogram derived from that in the blue curve in Fig. 2a with the proposed adjustment strategy. The almost coincident curves in Fig. 2b indicate the validity of the proposed histogram adjustment strategy.

3.3 Adaptive Segmentation Based Localization

Different from the smoothing based localization strategy in [5,6], we exploit a novel localization technique based on adaptive segmentation to suppress the background and improve the localization accuracy.

For illustration, we denote by $r = [x, y, w, h]$ the object bounding box, with object location x, y, and object scale w, h, where w and h denote object width and height, respectively. Let $T(I, r)$ denotes an image transformation function, which extracts the rectangular region r in image I. Moreover, let $C(x; \theta)$ denotes a comparison function, which returns 1 for $x \geq \theta$ and 0 for otherwise.

To suppress the background, the threshold at frame t is obtained as:

$$\theta^t = \arg\max_{\theta} \frac{\sum_{\mathbf{u} \in E(\mathcal{R}^{t-1})} C(\boldsymbol{\beta}^T \mathbf{b}(\mathbf{u}); \theta)}{\sum_{\mathbf{u} \in E(\mathcal{S}^{t-1})} C(\boldsymbol{\beta}^T \mathbf{b}(\mathbf{u}); \theta)} \tag{6}$$

where $\mathcal{R}^{t-1} = T(I^{t-1}, r^{t-1}(\lambda))$ denotes the image region extracted by $r^{t-1}(\lambda)$ in I^{t-1}, and $r^{t-1}(\lambda) = [x^{t-1}, y^{t-1}, \lambda w^{t-1}, \lambda h^{t-1}]$ is the result of previous bounding box r^{t-1} scaled by parameter λ. The formulation searches for the threshold which leads to the segmentation result that best matches the scaled bounding box.

The bounding box r^t in image I^t is chosen from a set G^t by maximizing a score:

$$r^t = \arg\max_{r \in G^t} \left\{ \gamma f_{\text{APQ}}(\mathcal{X}_r^t) + (1 - \gamma) f_{\text{CF}}(\mathcal{X}_r^t) \right\} \tag{7}$$

where $\mathcal{X}_r^t = T(I^t, r)$, γ is the weighting between the two model, and $f_{\text{CF}}(\mathcal{X}_r^t)$ is the score obtained by correlation filter for localization, detailed in [15]. The score of discriminative patch-based model is formulated as:

$$f_{\text{APQ}}(\mathcal{X}_r^t) = \sum_{\mathbf{u} \in E(\mathcal{X}_r^t)} C(\boldsymbol{\beta}^T \mathbf{b}(\mathbf{u}); \theta^t) \cdot \boldsymbol{\beta}^T \mathbf{b}(\mathbf{u}) \cdot \omega(\mathbf{u}) \tag{8}$$

where $\omega(\mathbf{u})$ denotes a weighting function that penalizes patches according to their distances from the center of the region, with small values for patches at the border of the region, and large values for patches at the central region.

The superiority of our adaptive segmentation based localization is illustrated in Fig. 3. The localization by smoothing the original probability map (Fig. 3b) obtains a low-confident response map (Fig. 3c), leading to the unsatisfactory localization (Fig. 3a). In contrast, our adaptive segmentation based localization technique obtains a high-confident response map (Fig. 3f) with segmented probability map (Fig. 3e), leading to the improved localization (Fig. 3d).

An overview of the proposed APQ algorithm is summarized in Algorithm 1.

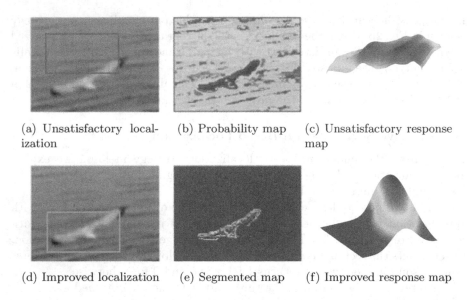

(a) Unsatisfactory local-   (b) Probability map   (c) Unsatisfactory response
ization   map

(d) Improved localization   (e) Segmented map   (f) Improved response map

Fig. 3. Exemplary adaptive segmentation based localization in sequence *birds1* from VOT2016 [4] at frame 219. First row illustrates the localization via simple smoothing, presented with (a) unsatisfactory localization, (b) probability map and (c) unsatisfactory response map. Second row illustrates our adaptive segmentation based localization, with (d) improved localization, (e) segmented probability map and (f) improved response map. Rectangles in the first column are estimated by the peak of the response maps shown in the third column. Hot colors correspond to high values. (Color figure online)

Algorithm 1. APQ tracking algorithm

Input: Frames $\{I^t\}_{t=1}^T$; initial object bounding box r^1.
Output: Object bounding box $\{r^t\}_{t=2}^T$.

1: **repeat**
2:      Crop search region $\mathcal{S}^t$ from image I^t centered at x^{t-1}, y^{t-1}.
3:      Extract patch vectors $\mathbf{u} \in E(\mathcal{S}^t)$ and get them quantized via Eq. (1).
4:      Detect the object location x^t, y^t via Eqs. (7) and (8).
5:      Estimate the object scale w^t, h^t as [15] and obtain r^t.
6:      Update quantization space $\{\mathbf{c}_i^{t+1}\}_{i=1}^K$ via Eq. (3).
7:      Adjust and update histograms via Eqs. (4) and (5).
8:      Update the discriminative patch-based model via Eq. (2).
9:      Obtain segmentation threshold for next frame via Eq. (6).
10:      Update correlation filters for localization and scale estimation as [15].
11: **until** end of video sequence

---

4   Experiment

We perform comprehensive experiments on benchmark datasets VOT2016 [4], OTB-13 [1] and OTB-15 [2], which demonstrate the competitive performance of our tracker APQ.

We first analyze various components in APQ, then compare our work with several state-of-the-art algorithms. All tracking results demonstrate the promising performance of APQ.

4.1   Implementation Details

The features used in APQ are composed of HOG features and patch-based color features, where the patch size is 3×3 pixel and a 27-dimensional vector is obtained in RGB image. 216 clusters are employed for feature quantization.

For stable cluster initialization, we start the iterative optimization at data distributed uniformly on the three dominant orientations according to principle component analysis (PCA), and take 3 iterations for quantization space update. We then update histogram with learning rate $\eta_{hist} = 0.013$. The weight γ is set to be 0.3 for combining patch-based histogram model and correlation filter. λ is set to be 0.6 for adaptive segmentation. The scaling factor of the observed search region $\mathcal{S}$ and object region $\mathcal{O}$ are set to be 1.5 and 0.8 relative to the target bounding box, respectively. The background region $\mathcal{B}$ is the complement set of a region with a scaling factor of 1.2 to the target bounding box on $\mathcal{S}$. The part of correlation filter is implemented as in [15], and so do the related parameter settings.

Our tracker is implemented in MATLAB with Intel Core i7-4790@3.4 GHz CPU and runs at 15.427 fps.

4.2   Analysis of Various Components in APQ

To demonstrate the effectness of various components proposed in APQ, including patch-based model, histogram adjustment, and segmentation based localization, we first test with different reduced versions of APQ on VOT2016 [4] with 60 challenge sequences. In our experiment, we denote APQ without histogram adjustment as APQ-Nh, APQ without segmentation based localization as APQ-Nseg, and APQ without either of them as APQ-N2.

To fully analyze the various components in APQ, similar to [4], we use the metrics accuracy and robustness for evaluation. The accuracy is computed by averaging per-sequence accuracy scores, where the per-sequence accuracy score is the average overlap between the predicted bounding box with the ground truth over valid frames. On the other hand, the robustness measures failure rate, where a failure is detected when a tracker predicts a bounding box with zero overlap with the ground-truth. To reduce the bias in the metrics, the tracker is re-initialized five frames after the failure, and ten frames after re-initialization are labeled as invalid for accuracy computation [23].

Table 1. Performance of different versions of APQ on VOT2016 [4]. Red and blue entries indicate the first and second best. The symbol $^\top$ denotes higher is better, while the symbol $^\perp$ denotes lower is better.

Tracker	Patch-based Model	Histogram Adjustment	Segmentation based Localization	Accuracy$^\top$	Failure$^\perp$
Staple [6]	No	No	No	0.529	81
APQ-N2	Yes	No	No	0.516	79
APQ-Nh	Yes	No	Yes	0.521	76
APQ-Nseg	Yes	Yes	No	0.527	74
APQ	Yes	Yes	Yes	0.520	72

As shown in Table 1, APQ shows the best performance in terms of failure without much decrease in the accuracy compared to Staple [6]. APQ-Nseg without the suppression of backgrounds causes inaccurate localization, and further leads to the drifting problem. APQ-Nh without the histogram adjustment strategy, updates histogram erroneously and further corrupts the model, and as a result, it gets a higher value in the metric of failure. Without both, APQ-N2 produces worse performance in terms of failure, but still performs a little better than Staple [6] due to the use of neighboring information. The results show that the proposed strategies improve the performance, especially in terms of failure.

4.3   Comparison with State-of-the-Art Results

We compare the results of our tracker APQ with those of state-of-the-art trackers including DAT [5], Staple [6], Struck [11], MEEM [12], KCF [14], DSST [15], ACT [21], DLSSVM [24], and LCT [25]. The compared methods cover color-based algorithms like DAT, ACT and Staple, correlation filter based trackers like DSST, KCF and LCT, methods based on structured SVM like DLSSVM and Struck, and ensemble based tracker like MEEM.

Table 2. Performance of our tracker APQ compared with several state-of-the-art trackers on VOT2016 [4]. Red, blue and green entries indicate the first, second and third best. The symbol $^\top$ denotes higher is better, while the symbol $^\perp$ denotes lower is better.

Tracker	Year	Where	Accuracy$^\top$	Robustness$^\perp$
APQ	-	-	0.520	0.336
DAT	2015	CVPR	0.476	0.480
Staple	2016	CVPR	0.529	0.378
Struck	2011	ICCV	0.417	0.942
KCF	2015	PAMI	0.467	0.569
DSST	2014	BMVC	0.471	0.704
ACT	2014	CVPR	0.421	0.662

VOT2016 Dataset. To ensure a fair and unbiased comparison, we use the raw results from the authors in comparison. Therefore, only algorithms provided with the related benchmark results are included in this comparison. As shown in Table 2, APQ shows the best performance in terms of robustness and second in terms of accuracy. Compared to Staple, APQ improved the robustness by 11.1% due to the patch-based information and segmentation-based localization. Compared to DSST, APQ takes color information into consideration, and therefore copes well with dynamic situations like deformation, which leads to improvement of the accuracy by 10.4% and that of the robustness by 52.3%, respectively. Moreover, APQ is superior to other state-of-the-art trackers like DAT, ACT, KCF and Struck.

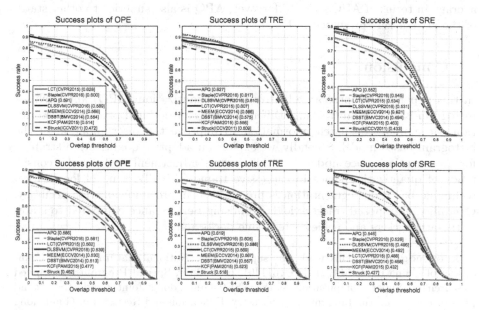

Fig. 4. The success plots of OPE, TRE, SRE on OTB-13 (first row) and OTB-15 (second row). The values in square brackets in legends denote the area under curve (AUC) scores of success plots. The original years and sources of these trackers are presented in legends as well. Higher ranking in legends indicates the better performance. Results are best viewed on high-resolution displays.

OTB-13 and OTB-15 Datasets. We further carry out experiments on the OTB-13 [1] and OTB-15 [2] benchmark datasets, which contain 50 and 100 sequences, respectively. Success plots are considered for evaluation of various methods in comparison, which present the success rates corresponding to different overlap thresholds. We also summarize the success scores based on the success plots, which correspond to areas under curve (AUC) of the success plots.

Moreover, one-pass evaluation (OPE), temporal robustness evaluation (TRE), and spatial robustness evaluation (SRE) are employed for robustness evaluation.

Figure 4 illustrates the success plots of OPE, TRE, and SRE on both OTB-13 and OTB-15, with success scores shown in brackets after the names of methods. In OPE evaluation metric, APQ performs the best in OTB-15 and ranks third in OTB-13 with a 0.037 decline rate compared with LCT. In TRE and SRE evaluation metrics, APQ performs best in both datasets due to the discriminative patch-based model, distinguishes objects from backgrounds robustly despite of the noise in first frame initialization. Moreover, the accurate localization strategy via segmentation reduces the error in tracking, and relieves the problem of model drifting. Since Struck performs best when it comes out, it can be viewed as the representation of previous trackers. Tracker APQ improves Struck by 24.8% on average in terms of AUC scores. Moreover, APQ is also superior to other state-of-the-art trackers presented in Fig. 4.

5   Conclusion

In this paper, we propose an adaptive patch quantization (APQ) approach for histogram-based visual tracking. Different from conventional pixel-wise description, we employ the patch information to improve the discrimination of the histogram-based model. Secondly, we exploit an adaptive quantization strategy for quantization space update and histograms adjustment to keep the consistency of quantization space in successive frames. Finally, a novel localization technique based on segmentation is proposed to improve localization accuracy. Overall, the proposed tracker yields promising performance compared to state-of-the-art trackers and achieves real-time performance.

Acknowledgments. This work was supported by National Natural Science Foundation of China (Nos. 61172141, U1611461, 61573387), Special Program for Applied Research on Super Computation of the NSFC-Guangdong Joint Fund (the second phase), Project on the Integration of Industry, Education and Research of Guangdong Province (No. 2013B090500013), Major Projects for the Innovation of Industry and Research of Guangzhou (No. 2014Y2-00213), and Science and Technology Program of Guangzhou (No. 2014J4100092).

References

1. Wu, Y., Lim, J., Yang, M.-H.: Online object tracking: a benchmark. In: IEEE Conference on Computer Vision and Pattern Recognition, pp. 2411–2418. IEEE Press, Portland (2013)
2. Wu, Y., Lim, J., Yang, M.-H.: Object tracking benchmark. IEEE Trans. Pattern Anal. Mach. Intell. **37**, 1834–1848 (2015)
3. Kristan, M., et al.: The visual object tracking VOT2014 challenge results. In: Agapito, L., Bronstein, M.M., Rother, C. (eds.) ECCV 2014. LNCS, vol. 8926, pp. 191–217. Springer, Cham (2015). https://doi.org/10.1007/978-3-319-16181-5_14

4. Kristan, M., et al.: The visual object tracking VOT2016 challenge results. In: Hua, G., Jégou, H. (eds.) ECCV 2016. LNCS, vol. 9914, pp. 777–823. Springer, Cham (2016). https://doi.org/10.1007/978-3-319-48881-3_54
5. Possegger, H., Mauthner, T., Bischof, H.: In defense of color-based model-free trackimg. In: IEEE Conference on Computer Vision and Pattern Recognition, pp. 2113–2120. IEEE Press, Boston (2015)
6. Bertinetto, L., Valmedre, J., Golodetz, S., Miksik, O., Torr, P.H.S.: Staple: complementary learners for real-time tracking. In: IEEE Conference on Computer Vision and Pattern Recognition, pp. 1401–1409. IEEE Press, Las Vegas (2016)
7. Ross, D.A., Lim, J., Lin, R.-S., Yang, M.-H.: Incremental learning for robust visual tracking. Int. J. Comput. Vis. **77**, 125–141 (2008)
8. Jia, X., Lu, H., Yang, M.-H.: Visual tracking via adaptive structural local sparse appearance model. In: IEEE Conference on Computer Vision and Pattern Recognition, pp. 1822–1829. IEEE Press, Providence (2012)
9. Babenko, B., Yang, M.-H., Belongie, S.: Robust object tracking with online multiple instance learning. IEEE Trans. Pattern Anal. Mach. Intell. **33**, 1619–1632 (2011)
10. Kalal, Z., Mikolajczyk, K., Matas, J.: Tracking-learning-detection. IEEE Trans. Pattern Anal. Mach. Intell. **34**, 1409–1422 (2012)
11. Hare, S., Saffari, A., Torr, P.H.: Struck: structured output tracking with kernels. In: IEEE International Conference on Computer Vision, pp. 263–270. IEEE Press, Barcelona (2011)
12. Zhang, J., Ma, S., Sclaroff, S.: MEEM: robust tracking via multiple experts using entropy minimization. In: Fleet, D., Pajdla, T., Schiele, B., Tuytelaars, T. (eds.) ECCV 2014. LNCS, vol. 8694, pp. 188–203. Springer, Cham (2014). https://doi.org/10.1007/978-3-319-10599-4_13
13. Bolme, D.S., Beveridge, J.R., Draper, B.A., Lui, Y.M.: Visual object tracking using adaptive correlation filters. In: IEEE Conference on Computer Vision and Pattern Recognition, pp. 2544–2550. IEEE Press, San Francisco (2010)
14. Henriques, J.F., Caseiro, R., Martins, P., Batista, J.: High-speed tracking with kernelized correlation filters. IEEE Trans. Pattern Anal. Mach. Intell. **37**, 583–596 (2015)
15. Danelljan, M., Hager, G., Khan, F.S., Felsberg, M.: Accurate scale estimation for robust visual tracking. In: British Machine Vision Conference, pp. 1–11. BMVA Press, Zurich (2014)
16. Danelljan, M., Hager, G., Shahbaz Khan, F., Felsberg, M.: Learning spatially regularized correltion filters for visual tracking. In: IEEE International Conference on Computer Vision, pp. 4310–4318. IEEE Press, Santiago (2015)
17. Nam, H., Han, B.: Learning multi-domain convolutional neural networks for visual tracking. In: IEEE Conference on Computer Vision and Pattern Recognition, pp. 4293–4302. IEEE Press, Las Vegas (2016)
18. Ma, C., Huang, J.-B., Yang, X., Yang, M.-H.: Hierarchical convolutional features for visual tracking. In: IEEE International Conference on Computer Vision, pp. 3074–3082. IEEE Press, Santiago (2015)
19. Danelljan, M., Robinson, A., Shahbaz Khan, F., Felsberg, M.: Beyond correlation filters: learning continuous convolution operators for visual tracking. In: Leibe, B., Matas, J., Sebe, N., Welling, M. (eds.) ECCV 2016. LNCS, vol. 9909, pp. 472–488. Springer, Cham (2016). https://doi.org/10.1007/978-3-319-46454-1_29
20. Oron, S., Bar-Hillel, A., Levi, D., Avidan, S.: Locally orderless tracking. In: IEEE Conference on Computer Vision and Pattern Recognition, pp. 1940–1947. IEEE Press, Providence (2012)

21. Danelljan, M., Shahbaz Khan, F., Felsberg, M., Van de Veijer, J.: Adaptive color attributes for real-time visual tracking. In: IEEE Conference on Computer Vision and Pattern Recognition, pp. 1090–1097. IEEE Press (2014)
22. Altun, O., Dursunoglu, N., Amasyali, M.F.: Clustering application benchmark. In: IEEE International Symposium on Workload Characterization, pp. 178–181. IEEE Press, San Jose (2007)
23. Kristan, M., et al.: The visual object tracking VOT2013 challenge results. In: IEEE International Conference on Computer Vision Workshops, pp. 98–111. IEEE Press, Sydney (2013)
24. Ning, J., Yang, J., Jiang, S., Zhang, L., Yang M.-H.: Object tracking via dual linear structured SVM and explicit feature map. In: IEEE Conference on Computer Vision and Pattern Recognition, pp. 4266–4274. IEEE Press, Las Vegas (2016)
25. Ma, C., Yang, X., Zhang C., Yang, M.-H.: Long-term correlation tracking. In: IEEE Conference on Computer Vision and Pattern Recognition, pp. 5388–5396. IEEE Press, Boston (2015)

Neural Image Caption Generation with Global Feature Based Attention Scheme

Yongzhuang Wang[✉] and Hongkai Xiong

Shanghai Jiao Tong University, Shanghai 200240, China
{wyz1036880293,xionghongkai}@sjtu.edu.cn

Abstract. The attention scheme is believed to align the words with objects in the task of image caption. Considering the location of objects vary in the image, most attention scheme use the set of region features. Compared with global feature, the region features are lower level features. But we prefer high-level features in image caption generation because words are high-level concepts. So we explore a new attention scheme based on the global feature and it can be appended to the original image caption generation model directly. We show that our global feature based attention scheme (GFA) can achieve the same improvement as the traditional region feature based attention scheme. And our model can achieve aligning the words with different regions as the traditional attention scheme. We test our model in Flickr8k dataset and Flickr30k dataset.

1 Introduction

Describing the visual scene or some details after a glance of an image is simple for people but quite difficult for visual recognition models. The task has great impact in some areas such as helping the blind people perceive the environment. So it becomes a focus in the computer vision community.

The task involves some subproblems such as object detection, behavior recognition etc. Therefore, most previous works are based on these tasks, they rely on hardcoded visual concepts and sentence templates [5,12]. However, the sentences templates limit the variety of generated sentences. But with the success of recurrent neural networks in processing the sequence problems like machine translation [25], some neural encoder-decoder models have been explored [23]. The neural encoder-decoder models take the task as a translation problem, which translate the image information to text information. In these models, the encoder is convolutional neural networks, which get a great success in some computer vision problems such as image classification, object detection, and the decoder is recurrent neural networks, which show a great potential in handling the sequence. And without the sentence templates, the generated sentences are more flexible and more similar to natural language.

Recently, with the attention scheme, which usually align each word of the sentence with some regions in the image, the neural encoder-decoder models make a great progress. However, these attention schemes need to get the region

© Springer International Publishing AG 2017
Y. Zhao et al. (Eds.): ICIG 2017, Part II, LNCS 10667, pp. 51–61, 2017.
https://doi.org/10.1007/978-3-319-71589-6_5

features and change the initial model structure. But our attention scheme is based on the global feature of the image, which is the input of the initial model. Thus we do not need extra procedure to get the feature of image regions. In summary, our main contribution is we propose a new attention scheme without any region features of the image, which can be directly appended to the initial model.

2   Related Work

2.1   Convolutional Neural Networks for Feature Extraction

Recently, convolutional neural networks achieve great success in the field of computer vision like image classification [8,19,20,22], object detection [6,7], image annotation. The success of CNNs is believed to be the result of its powerful ability to extract features. The feature extracted by CNNs works better than most of outstanding handcrafted features like HOG [3] and SIFT [16]. Thanks to the remarkable performance of the CNNs in the object detection and image annotation, which are the subproblems of image caption, we can represent nearly all the image information in a simple way. And it's comprehensive representation of objects and attribute, which build an essential foundation for the image caption task.

2.2   Image Caption with Templates

Based on the previous work of the image processing and sentence processing, a number of approaches take the task as a retrieval problem. They break up all the samples in the training set and the predict result is the combination of the result, which is stitched from the training annotations [13–15]. Other approaches generate caption with fixed templates whose place are filled with the results of object detection, attribute classification and scene recognition. But these approaches limit the variety of possible outputs.

2.3   Image Caption with Neural Networks

Inspired by the success of sequence-to-sequence encoder-decoder frameworks in the field of machine translation [1,2,19,21], the image caption task is regard as translating from image to text. [17] first develop a multimodal recurrent neural networks to translate the image into the text. [11] propose a feed forward neural network with a multimodal log-bilinear model to predict the next word given the previous output and image. [9] simplify the model and replace the feed forward network with a LSTM as the decoder, it also shows that the image only need to be input into the LSTM at the beginning of the model. [21] developes a new method to align the text with image, especially the word with region, by the output of bidirectional RNN [18] and the object detection results of the image from R-CNN [13]. The result of alignment in the joint embedding helps the caption generation. [4] replaces the vanilla recurrent neural networks with a multilayer LSTM as the decoder to generate caption. In their models, the first and second LSTM produce a joint representation of the visual and language inputs, the third and fourth LSTM transform the outputs of the previous LSTMs to produce the output.

2.4   Attention Scheme for Image Caption

Recently, attention scheme has been integrated into the encoder-decoder frameworks. [26] learns a latent alignment from scratch by incorporating the attention mechanisms when generating the word. [24] introduces a method to incorporate the high-level semantic concepts into the encoder-decoder approach. [27] reveals several architectures for augmenting high-level attributes from image to image representation for description generation. In all above attention schemes, some of them use the region features, which usually are mid-level features. Though [10] uses high-level semantic concepts, the high-level feature is extracted by manual selection which is unpractical for large data.

3   Our Model

In this section, we introduce our end-to-end neural network model. Our model is based on the encoder-decoder network in natural language translation. So it's a probabilistic framework, which directly maximize the probability of the correct sentence given the image. But the difference between the natural language translation model and our model is we use the CNNs as the encoder for the image, not the recurrent neural network for sequence input. Both of the models use recurrent neural networks as the decoder to generate the target sequence output. Therefore the problem can be solved by the following formulation

$$\theta^* = \underset{\theta}{\arg\max} \sum_{(I,S)} \log p(S|I;\theta) \tag{1}$$

where θ is the parameters of our model, I is the image, and S is the correct description. Because S is a sequence data, its length varies in different sentences. Therefore, we apply the chain rule to model the joint probability over $S_0, \ldots, S_N$ where N is the length of this particular sentence as

$$\log p(S|I;\theta) = \sum_{t=0}^{N} \log p(s_t|I, s_0, \ldots, s_{t-1}; \theta) \tag{2}$$

And given the image information and the information extracted from syntax structure, the attention scheme we used can control the model to focus on specific part of images information and decide the output content. Therefore the complete version of our model can be written as

$$\log p(S|I;\theta) = \sum_{t=0}^{N} \log p(s_t|I_t, s_0, \ldots, s_{t-1}; \theta) \tag{3}$$

$$I_t = f_a(I, s_0, \ldots, s_{t-1}) \bigodot I, t \in [0, N] \tag{4}$$

$$\theta^*, \theta_a^* = \underset{\theta, \theta_a}{\operatorname{argmax}} \sum_{(I,S)} \log p(S|I; \theta, \theta_a) \tag{5}$$

where θ is the parameter of basic model, θ_a is the parameter of attention scheme, $f_a(\cdot)$ means the attention scheme.

3.1   Encode Images

Following prior works [10,12], we regard the generated description as the combination of objects and their attributes which can be represented as some high-level features. Then we follow the work of NIC [23] to encode the image with CNNs, and we use the VGGNet as the image feature extractor. The VGGNet is pretrained on ImageNet, it can classify 1000 classes. So we believe it has powerful ability to extract features from image, which can obtain near all information we need such as object classes, attributes etc. Concretely, in our model, we use the 16-layers version of VGG-Net. Following NIC, we only use the second full connected layer in the CNNs, it's a 4096-dimensional vector. Since our model need to process both image information and text information, so we need convert all information we needed into the multimodal space. The encoder can be represented as

$$a = f(CNN_{\theta_c}(I)) \tag{6}$$

$$v = W_I a + b_I \tag{7}$$

where I represents the image, $CNN_{\theta_c}(I)$ translates the image pixel information into 4096-dimensinal feature vector, $W_I \in R^{m \times d}$ is weight to be learned, which translate the image information into the multimodal space, b_I is the bias. We set the activation function $f(\cdot)$ to the rectified linear unit (ReLU), which computes $f : x \mapsto \max(x, 0)$.

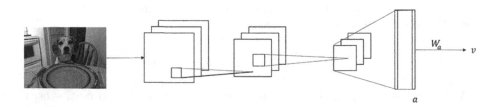

Fig. 1. The image encoding procedure.

Specifically, there are two reasons why we use the second full connected layer of the CNNs. On the one hand, the features extracted from the convolutional layer are distributed, and the data has stronger sparsity with the convolutional layer going deeper, while the bottom layer extract the underlying features we do not need. On the other hand, for the three full connected layers, we'd like to choose the top layers because we think it contains more higher-level features. But the last full connected layer has 1000 dimensions, which corresponds to the 1000 classes in the ImageNet Large Scale Visual Recognition Challenge, not all the 1000 classes are included in our image. Therefore, we choose the features extracted from the second full connected layer in VGGNet to represent the image. And before encoding the image features, we use ReLU function to remove the negative output (Fig. 1).

3.2 Decoding Sentences

Since our target is a sentence, which is in the form of a sequence of words, our decoder need to be able to handle sequence problem. So we choose the recurrent neural networks, it achieved a great success in sequence problem, especially in machine translation [25], which is the base of our model. In our model, we build a recurrent neural network which has 2 inputs, image and previous output. Both of them need be encoded into the multimodal space, the process for image has been declared in Sect. 3.1. When encoding the previous output, which is a word, we traverse all the sentences in the training data to formulate a vocabulary. And following [10], we cut out the words whose frequency is lower than the threshold, which is 5 in our model. And for convenience, we add the start and end symbol to each sentence. Then every word has a unique code by the method of one-hot encoding. The encoding result is sparse and high dimensional, thus we need to convert it into the dense multimodal space in the following from

$$x_t = W_s s_{t-1} + b_s \tag{8}$$

where s_{t-1} is the output of RNNs at time step $t-1$, which is the encoding result by the method of one-hot encoding, x_t is the encoding result in the multimodal space, W_s is the weight to be learned, which convert the word into the multimodal space, b_s is the bias.

Then with the multimodal data as inputs and the sequence of words as the labels, we can train our model by minimizing the cross-entropy loss. The full recurrent neural networks can be represented by the following formulations

$$h_t = f(v + x_t + W_h h_{t-1}) \tag{9}$$

$$s_t = softmax(W_o h_t + b_o) \tag{10}$$

where x_t is the input to the recurrent neural networks at time step t, v is the image encoding result in the multimodal result, h_t and h_{t-1} are the hidden layers state at time step t and $t-1$, s_t is the output of RNNs at time step t, $softmax(\cdot)$ is the softmax function. We use the Stochastic Gradient Descent algorithm to train our model (Fig. 2).

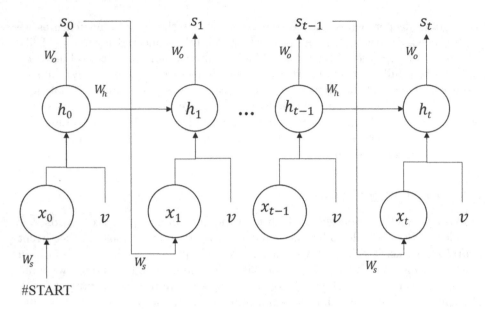

Fig. 2. The word decoding procedure.

3.3   Global Feature Based Attention Scheme

Attention scheme is the key of a good model when generating the description. Because the image is in a static state, but the description is dynamitic (i.e. the description is a list of words which are generated over time). So when generating different words, we need focus on different regions in the image, sometimes maybe the center of the image, sometimes just the background of the full image. It means the input should be dynamic not static. So when we generating the word, we need to decide which part of image information to be focused based on the content we previous generated, it's the core insight of attention scheme. The most similar model to our global feature based attention scheme (GFA) is [26], but the difference is we do not use features extracted from regions but from the full image and we use a different activation function.

In our model, we use a simple feed forward network with only one hidden layer to serve as attention scheme to decide the weights of different part of image information. The scheme can be represented as the following formulation

$$h_t^a = \sigma(W_g h_{t-1} + W_y s_{t-1} + a) \tag{11}$$

$$o_t^a = \sigma(W_m h_t^a) \tag{12}$$

$$a_t = o_t^a \bigodot a \tag{13}$$

where v is the image feature in the multimodal space, s_{t-1} is the previous output, h_t^a is the hidden layer state of our feed forward network at time step t, $\sigma(\cdot)$ means we use sigmoid function as the active function, o_t^a is the weight, $\odot$ means we use element-wise product, W_g, W_y, W_m are weights to be learned (Fig. 3).

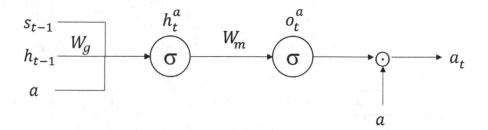

Fig. 3. Our global feature based attention scheme. And $\odot$ means the element-wise product.

The reason why we use sigmoid function is it can normalize the weight into the range of $(0, 1)$ and add nonlinearity as an activation function, and more importantly, the global feature based attention scheme do not need the competition between different parts of image information but other nonlinearity function like $softmax(\cdot)$ will compete between each other. Therefore, the input of our model can be written as

$$h_t = f(v_t + x_t + W_h h_{t-1}) \tag{14}$$

$$v_t = W_a a_t + b_a \tag{15}$$

where v_t is the result of global feature based attention scheme worked in multimodal space.

3.4 Our Full Model

Because our attention scheme is based on the image feature, we do not need other information. We can append our attention scheme to the initial model directly. And we can train the attention scheme with our original model as an end to end system.

Therefore, at each time step, the image feature will be input into the attention scheme first, then the output will instead the original image feature. So we do not need change the structure of the initial model.

4 Results

4.1 Implementation Details

Encoder-CNN. We use the 16-layer version of VGG-Net as the encoder-CNN, specifically, the second fully connected layer outputs are used as the representation of images, which is a 4096-dimension vector. Besides, we add a ReLU function to remove the negative outputs. In our training stage, we fix the convolutional layers and fine-tune the full connected layers on the ISLVRC16 dataset for 10 epochs (Fig. 4).

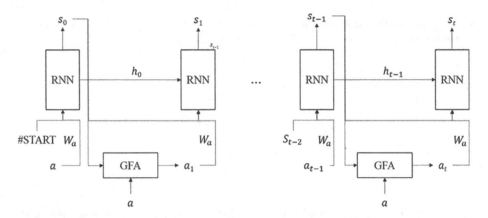

Fig. 4. Our neural image caption model with global feature based attention scheme.

Decoder-RNN. We concatenate the word embedding vector and image feature to get the input in multimodal space. Our decoder-RNN only has one hidden layer with the size of 256. And in order to make our model be a nonlinear system, we add ReLU function after the hidden layer, which can also avoid the vanishing gradient problem. Besides, we use dropout to avoid over-fitting problem, the dropout ratio is set to 0.4 in our model.

Training. We set the learning rate to 0.001 and decayed by 0.1 after every 50 epochs. Because every image has several descriptions in the dataset, we extract the image with only one description for each sample. We use the Stochastic Gradient Descent algorithm to train our model and the batch size is 128.

Evaluation. Because the target output of our image caption model is the same as the machine translation problem. We use the same evaluation criteria to evaluate our model and we choose the BLEU algorithm and METEOR.

4.2 Quantitative Analysis

We test our model on Flickr8k dataset and Flickr30k dataset, and we contrast our model with some classic models. Our original model is based on RNNs, which is proved to have poor performance than LSTM used in NIC. But our GFA shows the same improvement performance compared with classic models. Our GFA improves the BLEU-n score and METEOR score by 5.0/4.8/4.8/3.9/0.017 in Flickr8k and 1.6/0.9/0.8/0.5/0.012 in Flickr30k, compared with hard-attention, which improves the score by 4/4.7/4.4/-/0.015 in Flickr8k and 0.6/1.6/1.9/1.6/0.003 in Flickr30k, and soft-attention, which improves the score by 4/3.8/2.9/-/0.001 in Flickr8k and 0.4/1.1/1.1/0.8/0.002 in Flickr30k.

Since our GFA is based on the global feature and we know the weights and biases of full connected layers in CNNs. Then we can derive the equation to get the weights of the different parts of the last convolutional neural networks. In the derivation procedure, we use least-square method to solve the over-determined system of equations, and we ignore the influence of ReLU function attached to the second full connected layer. Finally, we use Polynomial Interpolation Algorithm to recover the weighs of different parts of original image. Because in the procedure of derivation, we ignore the affection of the nonlinearity function, the derivation result is just the inference of the alignment between the word and the image. Even so, the result shows our global feature based attention scheme can achieve aligning the word with relevant regions (Tables 1 and 2) (Fig. 5).

Table 1. Results compared with other models.

Dataset	Approach	B-1	B-2	B-3	B-4	METEOR
Flickr8k	Google NIC	63	41	27	-	0.172
	Hard-attention	**67**	**45.7**	**31.4**	**21.3**	**0.187**
	Soft-attention	**67**	44.8	29.9	19.5	0.173
	Initial model	56.9	38.3	23.7	14.6	0.154
	GFA	61.9	43.1	28.5	18.5	0.171
Flickr30k	Google NIC	66.3	42.3	27.7	18.3	0.182
	Hard-attention	**66.9**	**43.9**	**29.6**	**19.9**	**0.185**
	Soft-attention	66.7	43.4	28.8	19.1	0.184
	Initial model	56.3	37.3	24.5	15.3	0.151
	GFA	57.9	38.2	25.3	15.8	0.163

Table 2. The improvement of different attention models.

Dataset	Approach	B-1	B-2	B-3	B-4	METEOR
Flickr8k	Hard-attention	4	4.7	4.4	-	0.015
	Soft-attention	4	3.8	2.8	-	0.001
	GFA	**5.0**	**4.8**	**4.8**	**3.9**	**0.017**
Flickr30k	Hard-Attention	0.6	**1.6**	**1.9**	**1.6**	0.003
	Soft-attention	0.4	1.1	1.1	0.8	0.002
	GFA	**1.6**	0.9	0.8	0.5	**0.012**

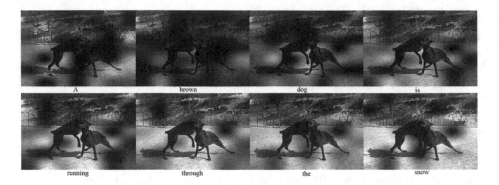

Fig. 5. The alignment result between regions and words.

5   Conclusion

We propose a neural image caption extractor with a new attention scheme. Our global feature based attention scheme is based on the features of the full image rather than regions and we use a simpler structure. And we achieve the same improvement result compared with other attention scheme.

References

1. Bahdanau, D., Cho, K., Bengio, Y.: Neural machine translation by jointly learning to align and translate. In: Computer Science (2014)
2. Cho, K., Van Merriënboer, B., Gulcehre, C., Bahdanau, D., Bougares, F., Schwenk, H., Bengio, Y.: Learning phrase representations using RNN encoder-decoder for statistical machine translation. In: Computer Science (2014)
3. Dalal, N., Triggs, B.: Histograms of oriented gradients for human detection. In: IEEE Computer Society Conference on Computer Vision and Pattern Recognition, CVPR 2005, pp. 886–893 (2005)
4. Donahue, J., Hendricks, L.A., Rohrbach, M., Venugopalan, S., Guadarrama, S., Saenko, K., Darrell, T.: Long-term recurrent convolutional networks for visual recognition and description. Elsevier (2015)
5. Farhadi, A., Hejrati, M., Sadeghi, M.A., Young, P., Rashtchian, C., Hockenmaier, J., Forsyth, D.: Every picture tells a story: generating sentences from images. In: Daniilidis, K., Maragos, P., Paragios, N. (eds.) ECCV 2010. LNCS, vol. 6314, pp. 15–29. Springer, Heidelberg (2010). https://doi.org/10.1007/978-3-642-15561-1_2
6. Girshick, R.: Fast R-CNN. In: Computer Science (2015)
7. Girshick, R., Donahue, J., Darrell, T., Malik, J.: Rich feature hierarchies for accurate object detection and semantic segmentation. In: 2014 IEEE Conference on Computer Vision and Pattern Recognition (CVPR), pp. 580–587 (2014)
8. He, K., Zhang, X., Ren, S., Sun, J.: Deep residual learning for image recognition. In: Computer Vision and Pattern Recognition, pp. 770–778 (2016)
9. Karpathy, A., Feifei, L.: Deep visual-semantic alignments for generating image descriptions. IEEE Trans. Pattern Anal. Mach. Intell. **39**(4), 664–676 (2017)

10. Karpathy, A., Joulin, A., Li, F.-F.: Deep fragment embeddings for bidirectional image sentence mapping, vol. 3, pp. 1889–1897 (2014)
11. Kiros, R., Salakhutdinov, R., Zemel, R.: Multimodal neural language models. In: International Conference on International Conference on Machine Learning, pp. II-595 (2014)
12. Kulkarni, G., Premraj, V., Dhar, S., Li, S.: Baby talk: understanding and generating simple image descriptions. In: IEEE Conference on Computer Vision and Pattern Recognition, pp. 1601–1608 (2011)
13. Kuznetsova, P., Ordonez, V., Berg, A.C., Berg, T.L., Choi, Y.: Collective generation of natural image descriptions. In: Meeting of the Association for Computational Linguistics: Long Papers, pp. 359–368 (2012)
14. Kuznetsova, P., Ordonez, V., Berg, T.L., Choi, Y.: TREETALK Composition and compression of trees for image descriptions. TACL **2**, 351–362 (2014)
15. Li, S., Kulkarni, G., Berg, T.L., Berg, A.C., Choi, Y.: Composing simple image descriptions using web-scale n-grams. In: Fifteenth Conference on Computational Natural Language Learning, pp. 220–228 (2011)
16. Lowe, D.G.: Object recognition from local scale-invariant features. In: The Proceedings of the Seventh IEEE International Conference on Computer Vision, p. 1150 (2002)
17. Mao, J., Xu, W., Yang, Y., Wang, J., Huang, Z., Yuille, A.: Deep captioning with multimodal recurrent neural networks (m-rnn), Eprint Arxiv (2014)
18. Mikolov, T., Karafiát, M., Burget, L., Cernocký, J., Khudanpur, S.: Recurrent neural network based language model. In: INTERSPEECH 2010, Conference of the International Speech Communication Association, Makuhari, Chiba, Japan, September, pp. 1045–1048 (2010)
19. Simonyan, K., Zisserman, A.: Very deep convolutional networks for large-scale image recognition. In: Computer Science (2014)
20. Smirnov, E.A., Timoshenko, D.M., Andrianov, S.N.: Comparison of regularization methods for imagenet classification with deep convolutional neural networks. Aasri Proc. **6**(1), 89–94 (2014)
21. Sutskever, I., Vinyals, O., Le, Q.V.: Sequence to sequence learning with neural networks. **4**, 3104–3112 (2014)
22. Szegedy, C., Liu, W., Jia, Y., Sermanet, P., Reed, S., Anguelov, D., Erhan, D., Vanhoucke, V., Rabinovich, A.: Going deeper with convolutions. In: Computer Vision and Pattern Recognition, pp. 1–9 (2015)
23. Vinyals, O., Toshev, A., Bengio, S., Erhan, D.: Show and tell: a neural image caption generator. In: Computer Vision and Pattern Recognition, pp. 3156–3164 (2015)
24. Wu, Q., Shen, C., Liu, L., Dick, A., Van Den Hengel, A.: What value do explicit high level concepts have in vision to language problems? In: Computer Vision and Pattern Recognition, pp. 203–212 (2016)
25. Yonghui, W., Schuster, M., Chen, Z., Le, Q.V., Norouzi, M., Macherey, W., Krikun, M., Cao, Y., Gao, Q., Macherey, K.: Bridging the gap between human and machine translation. In: Google's Neural Machine Translation System (2016)
26. Kelvin, X., Ba, J., Kiros, R., Cho, K., Courville, A., Salakhutdinov, R., Zemel, R., Bengio, Y.: Show, attend and tell: neural image caption generation with visual attention. In: Computer Science, pp. 2048–2057 (2015)
27. Yang, Z., Yuan, Y., Wu, Y., Salakhutdinov, R., Cohen, W.W.: Encode, review, and decode: reviewer module for caption generation (2016)

Activation-Based Weight Significance Criterion for Pruning Deep Neural Networks

Jiayu Dong[1,2,3], Huicheng Zheng[1,2,3]($\boxtimes$), and Lina Lian[1,2,3]

[1] School of Data and Computer Science, Sun Yat-sen University,
135 West Xingang Road, Guangzhou 510275, China
`zhenghch@mail.sysu.edu.cn`
[2] Key Laboratory of Machine Intelligence and Advanced Computing,
Ministry of Education, Sun Yat-sen University, 135 West Xingang Road,
Guangzhou 510275, China
[3] Guangdong Key Laboratory of Information Security Technology,
Sun Yat-sen University, 135 West Xingang Road, Guangzhou 510275, China

Abstract. Due to the massive amount of network parameters and great demand for computational resources, large-scale neural networks, especially deep convolutional neural networks (CNNs), can be inconvenient to implement for many real world applications. Therefore, sparsifying deep and densely connected neural networks is becoming a more and more important topic in the computer vision field for addressing these limitations. This paper starts from a very deep CNN trained for face recognition, then explores sparsifying neuron connections for network compression. We propose an activation-based weight significance criterion which estimates the contribution that each weight makes in the activations of the neurons in the next layer, then removes those weights that make least contribution first. A concise but effective procedure is devised for pruning parameters of densely connected neural networks. In this procedure, one neuron is sparsified at a time, and a requested amount of parameters related to this neuron is removed. Applying the proposed method, we greatly compressed the size of a large-scale neural network without causing any loss in recognition accuracy. Furthermore, our experiments show that this procedure can work with different weight significance criterions for different expectations.

Keywords: Pruning · Network compression · Weight significance

1 Introduction

Since the breakthrough in [1], deep convolutional neural networks have become the state-of-the-art techniques for various computer vision tasks, especially for image classification and recognition problems. Different architectures [1–5] have been proposed over the years and achieved better and better classification or recognition accuracy. One of the main trends of improving the network architectures is by increasing their depth, adding more layers to the network structures.

© Springer International Publishing AG 2017
Y. Zhao et al. (Eds.): ICIG 2017, Part II, LNCS 10667, pp. 62–73, 2017.
https://doi.org/10.1007/978-3-319-71589-6_6

While improving the classification or recognition results, a deeper network always requires higher computational complexity and larger disk memory, which in a way hinders its utilization in certain scenarios, such as embedded systems or real-time applications.

Face recognition is one of the most challenging problems in image processing and computer vision. Many excellent works [13,17,19] have successfully applied deep CNNs to tackle face recognition tasks. Massive parameters ensure the ability of deep CNNs to express and discriminate complex face images. And deeper architectures are often useful in learning better and more abstract features. Another critical factor to the success of deep CNNs in face recognition is their capability to exploit large training datasets, which sometimes may be difficult to obtain, though. Meanwhile, these factors also contribute to their rapidly growing demand for model storage and computational resources.

To balance recognition performance against the size of network models, we can first train a densely connected baseline model to learn good face features, and then prune redundant connections to perform compression while preserving good recognition accuracy as much as possible.

Sparsifying connections is often performed in fully-connected layers, in which weights are sorted according to some significance criterions, and those weights with less significance are pruned. Such criterions are sometimes defined in terms of saliency. In this paper, we propose an activation-based criterion to sort the connections by their contributions in the activations of the next layer. Our pruning procedure sparsifies one neuron at a time, pruning a certain amount of connections of a neuron and then continues pruning the next one until the expected compression rate is reached. It also includes a surgeon step, in which whenever weights are removed in a pruning step, the remaining weights would be adjusted to maintain the whole network status. Therefore, after a model is pruned, the retraining or fine-tuning process is not requested. However, many observations including ours show that fine-tuning the pruned models can further improve their recognition performance, which would be verified by experimental results in this paper.

The main contributions that we made in this paper are as follows: (1) we propose a simple and yet effective weight pruning procedure, which performs well in compressing deep convolutional neural networks with large parameter sets; (2) we propose an activation-based weight significance criterion, which indicates that weights with less contribution to the activations of neurons in the next layer should be removed first; (3) The pruning procedure that we devise can be combined with different weight significance criterions for different performance improvements, such as higher compression rate or better recognition results.

The rest of this paper is organized as follows. Section 2 introduces some related works in sparsifying deep neural networks. The proposed method is described in detail in Sect. 3. The experimental results are displayed and analyzed in Sect. 4. Finally, we conclude this paper by Sect. 5.

2 Related Work

The motivation of pruning densely connected networks is that it helps to reduce the model size and therefore make it easier to implement deep neural networks in certain scenarios like embedded platforms with limited disk memory and computational resources. And also in many studies like [7,9], it is believed that smaller and sparser models can address the over-fitting problem and lead to better generalization.

One of the most classical works of dropping weights in deep neural networks is done by LeCun *et al.* [6] and known as Optimal Brain Damage (OBD). The authors used second derivative information to evaluate the saliencies of weights and perform pruning. Optimal Brain Surgeon (OBS) [11] further calculates the second derivative by dropping some approximations made by OBD.

Instead of trying to minimize the growth of the objective function during pruning parameters like the above two methods, Srinivas and Babu [12] suggested removing those neurons in a layer whose absence cause the minimum change of the activations of the neurons in the next layer. They proposed a data-free pruning procedure, which prunes an entire neuron at a time whenever two neurons have similar weight sets. The saliency is then defined as:

$$S_{i,j} = \langle a_j^2 \rangle \| \varepsilon_{i,j} \|_2^2 \tag{1}$$

$S_{i,j}$ represents the saliency that is evaluated between two neurons i and j. And a_j is the parameter that connects neuron j to a neuron in the next layer, and $\langle a_j^2 \rangle$ denotes the average of the square of the scalar a_j over all neurons in the next layer, and $\| \varepsilon_{i,j} \|_2$ is the Euclidean distance between two weight sets corresponding to the two neurons.

In [13], the authors proposed a correlation-based criterion for weight pruning, which removes those weights that have small neural correlations first. Their method performs pruning in one layer at a time, and after a layer is sparsified, the pruned model needs to be retrained. Due to the lack of the surgeon operation, OBD also requires retraining after each pruning operation. In the cases of OBS and [12], they would adjust the rest of the parameters after each pruning step to maintain the objective function or activations in the next layer, so they do not need retraining or fine-tuning.

All of the above methods only consider the significance of weights when pruning and do not care about the structure of pruned networks. To avoid irregular network structures after pruning, [8] introduces a structure pruning method which fits the pruned network on parallel computation.

As another line of reducing the size of neural network models, [14–16] applied singular value decomposition, low rank matrices approximation or vector quantization of weight matrices of the network to perform compression. Only small amount of parameters are needed to represent or predict all the parameters of the deep architecture. These methods do not prune weights in the same way as the above methods. Rather than pruning them, they use the approximations of weight matrices by which they can store much fewer weights than the original networks.

In [10], they used pruning, trained quantization and Huffman coding together to deeply compress the neural network and achieved good results, which shows that pruning methods and numerical computation methods can be well implemented together to further reduce the model size. In this paper we focus on finding a good pruning strategy, including the weight significance criterion and pruning procedure. And our proposed method is demonstrated to be superior in the experiments.

3 Pruning Connections of Deep Neural Networks

We choose the classical VGG-16 architecture proposed in [17] as our baseline model, which starts from a series of convolutional layers and ends with three fully-connected layers. The fc6 layer and fc7 layer are two fully-connected layers following the last convolutional layer. The fc8 layer is a n-ways classifier whose dimension depends on training datasets.

The fully-connected layer fc6 and fc7 contain most of the parameters of the whole architecture, and many researches [12,13] also point out that most of the redundancy exists in fully-connected layers. Therefore, our pruning operation is performed in the fc6 and fc7 layers.

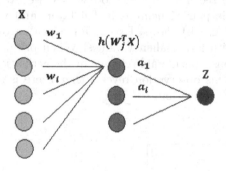

Fig. 1. Illustration of the forward propagation in a neural network.

3.1 Maintaining the Activations of the Next Layer

In [12], the authors proposed to remove neurons that cause the least change in the activations of the next layer. The weight matrix W connects the neurons in the previous layer to the neurons in the current layer. A neuron in the current layer is connected to the previous layer through a weight set W_i (i indicates the index of a neuron), and is connected to the next layer by a parameter a_i. The forward propagation process is demonstrated in Fig. 1. In order to make it easy to illustrate the process, let us assume there is only one neuron in the next layer, when there are two or more neurons, we average the values of a_i over all of the neurons. And the activation of the next layer can be written as:

$$z = a_1 h(W_1^T X) + \cdots + a_i h(W_i^T X) + \cdots + a_j h(W_j^T X) + \cdots + a_n h(W_n^T X). \quad (2)$$

When $W_i = W_j$, the activation z can be written as:

$$z' = a_1 h(W_1^T X) + \cdots + (a_i + a_j) h(W_i^T X) + \cdots + a_n h(W_n^T X) \qquad (3)$$

Equation(3) shows whenever two weight sets are equal, one of them can be effectively remove without causing any change in the activations of neurons in the next layer. $h(x)$ is the non-linear activation function. In this paper we use the ReLU function, so that $h(x) = max(0, x)$.

If we keep pruning weights without causing any change in the next layer, then the output of the network will remain the same, so that the recognition accuracy will be well retained as the size of model shrinks.

However, in large scale neural networks, a weight set in fully-connected layers contains a large amount of parameters, and there may not be two weight sets which are exactly the same. When $W_i \neq W_j$, the change of the activation is:

$$(z - z')^2 = a_j^2 \left(h(W_j^T X) - h(W_i^T X) \right)^2. \qquad (4)$$

As the above equation shows, the change of the activation is no longer zero. In order to minimize it, we can find two most similar weight sets which minimize (4), and remove one of the neuron accordingly. Then we come to the definition of saliency as (1). To see how this method works, we evaluate the saliencies between every possible pair of neurons in fc6 layer, and we get the distribution of saliencies as Fig. 2(b) shows. Except for a peak around zero, there are many neuron pairs with large saliency values. When pruning process proceeds to remove those neurons, considerable change in the activations of the next layer becomes inevitable. This observation reveals that there is still much room for better maintaining the activation.

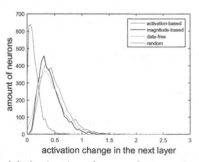   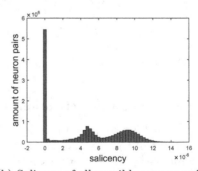

(a) Activation change after pruning   (b) Saliency of all possible neuron pairs

Fig. 2. Activation change after pruning

3.2 Activation-Based Criterion for Further Maintaining the Activations

In this part, instead of pruning the whole neuron, we propose an activation-based criterion to prune weights within a neuron, keeping a small amount of weights to compensate for the change in the activation. By keeping a small amount of parameters, for example 1%, we can remove 99% parameters in W_j and obtain the sparsified weight set W_j'. The change in activation becomes:

$$a_j^2 \left(h(W_j^T X) - h(W_j'^T X) \right)^2 \tag{5}$$

When $h(W_j^T X) = h(W_j'^T X)$, the change of activation is minimized. It is known that $h(W_j^T X) \geq 0$. When $h(W_j^T X) = 0$, we can simply set $a_j = 0$. When $h(W_j^T X) > 0$, we have:

$$h(W_j^T X) = \sum_{i=1}^{n} w_i x_i. \tag{6}$$

In the above equation, $w_1, \ldots, w_n$ and $x_1, \ldots, x_n$ represent the elements in the weight sets and input vectors, respectively. We can use a relatively small dataset to evaluate

$$E\left(h(W_j^T X)\right) = \sum_{i=1}^{n} E(w_i x_i) \tag{7}$$

Parameter w_i of bigger $abs\left(E(w_i x_i)\right)$ contributes more to the activations of neurons in the next layer. Therefore, we can sort w_i by their $abs\left(E(w_i x_i)\right)$ value in the descending order, reserve the first 1%, and remove the rest of parameters in W_j. Then we get the sparsified weight vector W_j''. We use the dataset to calculate $E\left(h(W_j''^T X)\right)$. Let

$$W_j' = \frac{E\left(h(W_j^T X)\right)}{E\left(h(W_j''^T X)\right)} W_j'' \tag{8}$$

Finally we obtain

$$E\left(h(W_j^T X)\right) = E\left(h(W_j'^T X)\right) \tag{9}$$

This method can better maintain the activations of the next layer than simply removing the whole neuron at a time. To verify this point, we estimate and compare the activation changes in fc7 layer, after 99% of the parameters in the fc6 layer are pruned using different pruning methods. Figure 2(a) shows the distribution of the activation changes of all neurons in fc7 layer after pruning. The method that removes one neuron at a time is referred to as data-free on account of requiring no training data to perform pruning, and is described in detail in [12]. Our method is referred to as activation-based. The other two methods are naive pruning techniques by removing weights randomly or removing those weights with small magnitudes. We can see from Fig. 2(a) that our method is significantly better than the other methods in maintaining the activations of the next layer. The pruning procedure that we propose is summarized in Algorithm 1. The order of the list of neurons to be pruned is the same as the data-free method.

Algorithm 1. The proposed algorithm for weight pruning

Input: A list of weight sets W_i that connect the neurons to be pruned to the previous layer.

Start from the first neuron in the input neuron list.

1: **while** the requested compression rate is not reached **do**
2:      Sort all the weights in W_i by the weight significance criterion described in Sect. 3.2 in the descending order.
3:      Keep the first 1% weights and drop the rest of the weights in W_i, and get the sparsified weight set $W_i^{''}$.
4:      Evaluate $E\left(h(W_i^T X)\right)$ and $E\left(h(W_i^{''T} X)\right)$, and let

$$W_i^{'} = \frac{E\left(h(W_i^T X)\right)}{E\left(h(W_i^{''T} X)\right)} W_i^{''}$$

5:      Move on to the next neuron to be pruned.
6: **end while**
7: Retrain or fine-tune the pruned model if requested.

Output:The sparsified weight matrices $W_i^{'}$.

As illustrated above, we propose an activation-based weight significance criterion as well as a pruning procedure (see Algorithm 1). We believe that this algorithm can also be combined with other existing criterions to pursue other expectations. Here we present this point by introducing the correlation criterion into this procedure.

In [13], the authors found that connections that are strongly correlated have stronger predictive power for the activities of the latter layers in a deep architecture. A parameter or weight in neural networks represents a connection of two neurons in two adjacent layers. We compute correlations in the connections and sort them in a descending order, and remove those connections with small correlation values. In fact, we just simply replace activation-based criterion with correlation-based criterion in step 2 of Algorithm 1. By doing so, we can see if this algorithm can work well with other criterions and also compare our activation-based criterion with the correlation-based criterion.

3.3   Testing and Fine-Tuning

We use a pre-trained model and the pruned models to deal with the face verification task on the LFW face dataset [18], and compare the results by following the standard evaluation protocol. 6000 face pairs are evaluated to decide whether the two faces in a pair belong to the same person. The last fully-connected layer fc8 is removed during testing, and the output 4096-dimensional vectors of the fc7 layer are extracted as features of the corresponding faces. Every face image is first rescaled to three different sizes: 256×256, 384×384, and 512×512. For each size, five patches of 224×224 pixel are cropped from the four corners and the center of the image with horizontal flip. As in [2], these 30 cropped image patches are input to the network, and 30 feature vectors of the face are extracted and averaged. The final averaged feature vectors will be compared by using the Euclidean distance.

A pre-trained baseline model would be used in our pruning experiments. Certain amount of parameters of certain layers will be pruned, and then the pruned model would be fine-tuned when requested. A deep neural network would converge to a minimum point during training. Any vibration on the parameters of the trained network would deviate the network from the minimum point. The motivation of minimizing the change in activations of the next layer is that it helps to keep the trained model remaining close to the minimum point. However, the optimal status of the trained network would be sabotaged inevitably by pruning operations. Fine-tuning the pruned network tries to make it converge to a minimum point again.

The collection of the training dataset is described in detail in [17]. Although the training dataset contains a massive amount of face images, the image quality of this dataset is not of satisfaction. So we used an augmented subset of the training dataset to fine-tune the pruned model. This dataset contains face

Table 1. Verification accuracy on LFW after pruning (the data-free method performs pruning in both of the fc6 and fc7 layers since it removes the whole neurons)

fc6 pruned	Random	Magnitude-based	Activation-based	Data-free [12]
0.25	0.9606	0.9613	0.9613	0.9613
0.50	0.9583	0.9611	0.9573	0.9531
0.75	0.9555	0.9573	0.9572	0.9420
0.99	0.6716	0.9303	0.9483	0.9202

Table 2. Verification accuracy on LFW after pruning and fine-tuning (pruning operation is performed on the fc6 layer except for the data-free method, which removes the whole neurons)

Weights pruned	Random	Magnitude-based	Activation-based	Correlation-based	Data-free [12]
97 MB	0.9743	0.9694	0.9737	0.9723	0.9730
194 MB	0.9707	0.9743	0.9720	0.9758	0.9712
291 MB	0.9680	0.9716	0.9703	0.9700	0.9697
384 MB	0.9510	0.9649	0.9657	0.9547	0.9644

images of 300 identities. These images were detected for face regions using the Viola&Jones face detector [20]. The faces were cropped out along with part of the background and then resized to the same scale. Erroneous faces were further filtered manually. We used this augmented dataset to retrain the pruned model for 5 epochs, and the learning rate is set to decrease from 10^{-4} to 10^{-6}.

4   Experimental Results

The pre-trained baseline model that we use in our pruning experiments is trained and released by the group of [17]. When it is tested on the LFW verification task, it reports an accuracy of 96.13%. Experimental results of various pruning methods performed on the pre-trained model are shown in Table 1. The pruning procedures are carried out on the fully-connected layer fc6. As it is shown in Table 1, when 25% of the parameters in the fc6 layer are pruned using the magnitude-based or the activation-based method, the verification accuracies of the network do not degrade at all. When 50% or 75% of the parameters are pruned, the activation-based method does not show its edge over the other two methods. However, after pruning 99% parameters which means compressing the fc6 layer by 100 times, the model pruned with the activation-based method achieves a significantly better accuracy than those of the other methods. We also conduct experiments using the method in [12], which prunes a whole neuron (two layers related) at a time. When it removes the same amount of parameters in the two layers as the other methods do in one layer, it achieves accuracies of 0.9613, 0.9530, 0.9420, and 0.9202, which cannot compare to the proposed activation-based method.

Table 3. Experimental results after pruning two fc layers and fine-tuning

fc6 pruned	fc7 pruned	Activation-based	Correlation-based	Data-free [12]
194 MB	32 MB	0.9605	0.9694	0.9611
291 MB	48 MB	0.9704	0.9610	0.9590
384 MB	32 MB	0.9549	0.9406	–
384 MB	63 MB	0.9547	0.9268	0.9430

Experimental results after fine-tuning the pruned models are shown in Table 2. As we can see, after fine-tuning, the results of all pruned models are improved. The best accuracy achieved by the correlation-based method after fine-tuning is up to 97.58%, while the best results of other methods are around 97.4%, which suggests that the correlation criterion provides a better initialization for fine-tuning when certain amount of weights are removed. Also, these results in a way resonate the idea that sparse networks lead to better generalization. However, when it comes to removing 99% of the parameters in fc6 (384 MB), the activation-based method still gets the best result, which means

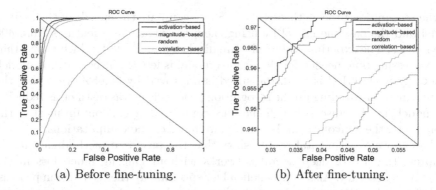

(a) Before fine-tuning.   (b) After fine-tuning.

Fig. 3. ROC curves of pruned models, where 99% of parameters of the fc6 layer are removed.

that this method is a better choice for performing deeper pruning. The ROC curves of the models pruned by different methods are shown in Fig. 3. From these ROC curves we can know the advantage of the activation-based method when pruning a large amount of parameters of the network. Removing 99% of parameters in fc6 using the proposed method, we can reduce the model size from 553 MB to 128 MB, and the pruned model achieves an accuracy of 96.57%, which is even higher than the baseline model.

We have also conducted experiments on pruning both of the fc6 layer and the fc7 layer at the same time. And the results are shown in Table 3. We can see that the activation-based method performs significantly better than the correlation-based method and the data-free method, when it comes to pruning two fc layers at the same time. Even when both of fc6 and fc7 layers are deeply pruned using the activation-based technique, which amounts to compressing the network size from 553 MB to 65 MB, there is still only a slight drop in accuracy.

Compared to the study in [17], which improves the verification accuracy to 97.27% by increasing the depth of the network architecture, in this paper, we improve the accuracy to around 97.4% by sparsifying the network structure, and reduce the model size at the same time.

Table 4. The computational speeds

Model size	Total time	Time per face	Total time (GPU-accelerated)	Time per face (GPU-accelerated)
553 MB	193.81 s	0.48453 s	18.65 s	0.04662 s
65 MB	185.78 s	0.46445 s	12.18 s	0.03045 s

After the baseline model is pruned, the size of the model shrinks greatly. In the meantime, the decrease in the amount of parameters reduces the total times of addition and multiplication needed in forward propagation, which can speed up the recognition process theoretically. So we compare the speeds of the pruned model and the baseline model by using them to extract face features from 400 face images. The experimental results are displayed in Table 4, which shows that the processing time needed for the pruned model is less than the baseline model. Especially when GPU is used, the speed is improved by 34.68%. However, the improvement in speeding up the recognition process is not as distinct as reducing the model size, because although the fully-connected layers contain most of the parameters, the convolutional layers require most of the computations.

The above experimental results show that the proposed method can deeply compress the size of deep neural networks without causing much loss in the recognition accuracy. Also, it is beneficial for speeding up the recognition process. Therefore, it has the potential to make deep neural networks easier to implement in many real applications.

5   Conclusion

In this paper, we propose an activation-based criterion to evaluate the importance of weights in deep convolutional neural networks. The proposed criterion is applied to a deep CNN trained for face recognition. We have carried out a series of experiments to verify the effectiveness of the proposed method. It is demonstrated that when the pre-trained baseline model is deeply compressed, the proposed method achieves the best performance, indicating that the activation information can be a useful indicator for estimation of weight significance. The study reported in this paper provides insights for reducing deep CNNs for face recognition. We believe that the proposed method is applicable in many deep learning scenarios independently or when combined with other methods.

Acknowledgements. This work was supported by National Natural Science Foundation of China (Nos. 61172141, U1611461, 61573387), Special Program for Applied Research on Super Computation of the NSFC-Guangdong Joint Fund (the second phase), Project on the Integration of Industry, Education and Research of Guangdong Province (No. 2013B090500013), Major Projects for the Innovation of Industry and Research of Guangzhou (No. 2014Y2-00213), and Science and Technology Program of Guangzhou (No. 2014J4100092).

References

1. Krizhevsky, A., Sutskever, I., Hinton, G.E.: Imagenet classification with deep convolutional neural networks. In: International Conference on Neural Information Processing Systems, pp. 1097–1105 (2012)
2. Simonyan, K., Zisserman, A.: Very deep convolutional networks for large-scale image recognition. In: International Conference on Learning Representations, pp. 1–14 (2015)
3. LeCun, Y., Bottou, L., Bengio, Y., Haffner, P.: Gradient-based learning applied to document recognition. Proc. IEEE **86**(11), 2278–2324 (1998)

4. Szegedy, C., Liu, W., Jia, Y., et al.: Going deeper with convolutions. In: IEEE Conference on Computer Vision and Pattern Recognition, pp. 1–9 (2015)
5. He, K., Zhang, X., Ren, S., Sun, J.: Deep residual learning for image recognition. In: IEEE Conference on Computer Vision and Pattern Recognition, pp. 770–778 (2016)
6. LeCun, Y., Denker, J.S., Solla, S.A.: Optimal brain damage. In: Advances in Neural Information Processing Systems, pp. 598–605 (1989)
7. Liu, C., Zhang, Z., Wang, D.: Pruning deep neural networks by optimal brain damage. In: Interspeech, pp. 1092–1095 (2014)
8. Anwar, S., Hwang, K., Sung, W.: Structured pruning of deep convolutional neural networks. ACM J. Emerg. Technol. Comput. Syst. **13**(3), 32.1–32.18 (2017)
9. Wolfe, N., Sharma, A., Drude, L., Raj, B.: The incredible shrinking neural network: New perspectives on learning representations through the lens of pruning (2017). arXiv preprint arXiv:1701.04465
10. Han, S., Mao, H., Dally, W.J.: Deep compression: compressing deep neural networks with pruning, trained quantization and huffman coding. In: International Conference on Learning Representations, pp. 1–14 (2016)
11. Hassibi, B., Stork, D.G.: Second order derivatives for network pruning: optimal brain surgeon. In: Advances in Neural Information Processing Systems, pp. 164–171 (1992)
12. Srinivas, S., Babu, R.V.: Data-free parameter pruning for deep neural networks. In: British Machine Vision Conference, pp. 31.1–31.12 (2015)
13. Sun, Y., Wang, X., Tang, X.: Sparsifying neural network connections for face recognition. In: IEEE Conference on Computer Vision and Pattern Recognition, pp. 4856–4864 (2016)
14. Denil, M., Shakibi, B., Dinh, L., et al.: Predicting parameters in deep learning. In: Advances in Neural Information Processing Systems, pp. 2148–2156 (2013)
15. Jaderberg, M., Vedaldi, A., Zisserman, A.: Speeding up convolutional neural networks with low rank expansions. In: British Machine Vision Conference, pp. 1–12 (2014)
16. Gong, Y., Liu, L., Yang, M., Bourdev, L.D.: Compressing deep convolutional networks using vector quantization (2014). arXiv preprint arXiv:1412.6115
17. Parkhi, O.M., Vedaldi, A., Zisserman, A.: Deep face recognition. In: British Machine Vision Conference, pp. 41.1–41.12 (2015)
18. Huang, G.B., Mattar, M., Berg, T., Learned-Miller, E.: Labeled faces in the wild: a database for studying face recognition in unconstrained environments, Technical report 07–49. University of Massachusetts, Amherst (2007)
19. Schroff, F., Kalenichenko, D., Philbin, J.: FaceNet: a unified embedding for face recognition and clustering. In: The IEEE Conference on Computer Vision and Pattern Recognition, pp. 815–823 (2015)
20. Viola, P., Jones, M.: Robust real-time face detection. Int. J. Comput. Vision **57**(2), 137–154 (2004)

Local and Global Sparsity
for Deep Learning Networks

Long Zhang, Jieyu Zhao[(✉)], Xiangfu Shi, and Xulun Ye

Department of Computer Science, Ningbo University,
818 Fenghua Road, Ningbo 315211, China
{1401082013, zhao_jieyu}@nbu.edu.cn, xfu_shi@163.com,
1132548710@qq.com

Abstract. It has been proved that applying sparsity regularization in deep learning networks is an efficient approach. Researchers have developed several algorithms to control the sparseness of activation probability of hidden units. However, each of them has inherent limitations. In this paper, we firstly analyze weaknesses and strengths for popular sparsity algorithms, and categorize them into two groups: local and global sparsity. $L_{1/2}$ regularization is first time introduced as a global sparsity method for deep learning networks. Secondly, a combined solution is proposed to integrate local and global sparsity methods. Thirdly we customize proposed solution to fit in two deep learning networks: deep belief network (DBN) and generative adversarial network (GAN), and then test on benchmark datasets MNIST and CelebA. Experimental results show that our method outperforms existing sparsity algorithm on digits recognition, and achieves a better performance on human face generation. Additionally, proposed method could also stabilize GAN loss changes and eliminate noises.

Keywords: Sparsity · Regularization · Deep learning · GAN

1 Introduction

In the last decade, deep learning networks have an ambitious development. Its success has influenced not only many research fields but also our lives (self-piloting, language translation, etc.). From many experimental results, deep learning algorithms overcome most of traditional machine learning methods. Similar with human brain, deep learning networks contain multiple layers of neuron. Connections are built to link neurons between adjoining layers. Given an input, a deep learning network could abstract features through its deep architecture. It has been successfully applied to different fields like object recognition [1], human motion capture data [2, 3], information retrieval [4], speech recognition [5, 6], visual data analysis [7], and archives a wonderful performance.

There are several famous deep learning network structures. Deep belief network was firstly introduced by Hinton [4] in 2006, which started the age of deep learning. DBN brings researchers a new vision that a stack of generative models (like RBMs) is trainable by maximizing the likelihood of its training data. Unsupervised learning and generative models play key roles in this kind of network structure, and become more

© Springer International Publishing AG 2017
Y. Zhao et al. (Eds.): ICIG 2017, Part II, LNCS 10667, pp. 74–85, 2017.
https://doi.org/10.1007/978-3-319-71589-6_7

and more important in the later deep learning network development. In 2012, Krizhevsky [8] applied a deep CNN on ImageNet dataset, and won the contest of ILSVRC-2012. GPU was implemented to accelerate training process, while "dropout" theory [9] was also implemented to solve "overfitting" problems. GAN (Generative Adversarial Nets) has drawn a lot of attentions from deep learning researchers. It was firstly introduced by Goodfellow [10] in 2014 and became a hot topic in recent two years [11]. Even Prof. LeCun said "Adversarial training is the coolest thing since sliced bread".

Although deep learning networks have achieved a great success, without constraints on the hidden layers and units, it may produce redundant, continuous-valued codes and unstructured weight patterns [12]. Researchers have developed several useful constraints which improved networks performance greatly. Among them, adding sparsity regularization to networks has been proved as an efficient and effective approach.

This paper focus on the usage of sparsity regularization in deep learning networks. Section 2 presents related works. Section 3 categories different sparsity methods, lists their pros and cons. A novel sparsity regularization framework is introduced which could be customized to fit different networks structure. L1/2 regularization is first time applied with deep learning network. Section 4 presents two applications with our proposed method – Sparse DBN and Sparse GAN. Section 5 demonstrates experiments on two benchmarks, results support our proposal. Finally, this paper is conclude with a summary in Sect. 6.

2   Related Works

Bengio [13] said that if one is going to have fixed size representations, then sparse representations are more efficient in an information-theoretic sense, allowing for varying the effective number of bits per example. Traditional sparse coding learns low-level features for unlabeled data. However, deep learning networks provide a deep architecture with multiple layers. Network abstracts high-level features from lower ones. Applying sparse coding algorithm straightforwardly to build multiple levels of hierarchy is difficult. Firstly, building sparse coding on top of another sparse coding output may not satisfy the modeling assumption. Secondly, optimization is expensive [11, 14].

Luckily, there are several methods proposed to solve this problem. In 2008, Lee [15] developed a sparsity variant based on deep belief networks. A regularization term was added to loss function which penalized as the deviation of the expected activation of hidden units. Keyvanrad [14] applies a normal distribution on the deviation of the expected activation to control the degree of sparseness. The activation probability of hidden units get little penalty when they are close to zero or one. Similarly, Ji [12] implements L_1-norm on the activation probability of hidden units together with rate distortion theory. According to Xu [16], the L_q regularization plays special important role on sparse modeling. However, it is a non-convex, non-smooth, and non-Lipschitz optimization problem which is difficult in general to have a thorough theoretical understanding and efficient algorithms for solutions. Somehow, studies in [16–18] have resolved partially these problems. Krishnan and Fergus [17] demonstrated that $L_{1/2}$ and $L_{2/3}$ regularization are very efficient when applied to image deconvolution. Xu [18] ensured that $L_{1/2}$ plays a representative role among all L_q regularization with q in (0, 1). Xu [16] also proved the superiority of $L_{1/2}$ over L_1 regularization.

Another approach for sparsity in deep learning networks is the choice of activation function. For a certain period, sigmoid and hyperbolic tangent functions were widely used in the literature. However in practice, training process has a slow convergence speed. Network may stuck at a poor local solution. Then, Nair [19] achieved a promising result by using rectifier linear unit (ReLU) in network. Compared with sigmoid or hyperbolic tangent functions, about 50% to 75% of hidden units are inactivate, and also with Leaky ReLU [20, 21] for higher resolution modeling.

3 Local and Global Sparsity

According to previous research results [12, 14, 15], applying sparsity terms to the activation probability of hidden units in deep learning networks could gain a much better performance. Some papers focus on individual hidden unit's probability, and others focus on the aggregation of them. We name the local sparsity for the prior ones, and the global sparsity for the after ones. However, deficiencies exist for each of them, it is inherent and difficult to solve. After a study of those methods, we found out that the weakness of local sparsity is just the strength of global sparsity, and vice versa. Therefore we propose a combined sparsity regularization, which could outcome each single ones.

3.1 Local Sparsity

The optimization problem of a sparse deep learning network is generally done by

$$\min f(x) + \lambda_1 L_{sparse} \tag{1}$$

where $f(x)$ is deep learning network's original loss function, λ_1 is a regularization constant, a tradeoff between "likelihood" and "sparsity" [14]. L_{sparse} is the sparsity regularization term.

Local sparsity methods in the deep belief network use a sparse variant or function to control average activation probability of hidden units. Different methods implement L_{sparse} in different way. In paper [15], the regularization term penalizes a deviation of the expected activation of hidden units from a fixed level p. Authors in [15] believe it could keep the "firing rate" of network neurons at a low value, so that network neurons are sparse. Given a training set $\{v^1, \ldots, v^m\}$, regularization term is defined as

$$L_{sparse} = \sum_{j=1}^{n} |p - \frac{1}{m} \sum_{l=1}^{m} E[h_j^{(l)} | v^{(l)}]|^2 \tag{2}$$

where p is a constant which control the sparseness of hidden units, n is the number of hidden units, $E[\cdot]$ is the conditional expectation on hidden unit h_j. Since it is implemented on RBM, therefore we can call it sparseRBM. This method achieved a great performance in 2008.

However, p is a fixed value. All hidden units share the same deviation level is logically inappropriate and crude. In paper [14], situation is improved by replacing with a normal function and a variance parameter to control the force degree of sparseness, so called normal sparse RBM (nsRBM). According to its authors, network parameters get little updates only when activation probability of hidden units are near to zero or one. That indicates hidden units with activation probability near one are important factors, therefor gradient penalizations are little. Given a training set $\{v^1, \ldots, v^m\}$, regularization term is constructed as

$$L_{sparse} = -\sum_{j=1}^{n} f(k_j, p, \sigma^2) = -\sum_{j=1}^{n} \frac{1}{\sigma\sqrt{2\pi}} e^{-\frac{1}{2}\left(\frac{k_j-p}{\sigma}\right)^2} \tag{3}$$

$$k_j = \frac{1}{m} \sum_{l=1}^{m} E[h_j^{(l)} | v^{(l)}] \tag{4}$$

where $f(\cdot)$ is a normal probability density function, k_j is the average of conditional expectation on hidden unit h_j, p is a constant, σ is the standard deviation. Same with sparseRBM, p controls the sparseness level, but changing σ can control the force degree of sparseness.

nsRBM can be seen as a "soft" version of sparseRBM. It softens the "hard" influence of the fixed p level, and achieves a better performance. However, fixed p level is still in use. Currently there is no good way to get the right level except try-and-error. Secondly, there is too many parameters. Finding a good combination is time-consuming. Thirdly, interactions cross hidden units are not considered.

3.2 Global Sparsity

Global sparsity in deep learning networks focus on the aggregation of activation probability of hidden units. It provides an overview on network's sparseness. L_q-norm is generally applied as the regularization term. In deep learning networks, given a training set $\{v^{(1)}, \ldots, v^{(m)}\}$, L_q regularization can be described as

$$L_{sparse} = L_q = \left(\sum_{j=1}^{n} |k_j|^q\right)^{\frac{1}{q}} \tag{5}$$

where q is a constant $(0 < q \le 1)$, k_j is the average of conditional expectation on hidden unit h_j, see Eq. (4). In [12], Ji has implemented L_1 regularization in deep belief networks, with its help the activation probability of hidden units has been greatly reduced near to zero. L_1 regularization is just an instance of L_q regularization. Recent studies [16, 18] shows $L_{1/2}$ regularization could generate more sparse solutions than it. Our experiments also prove that applying $L_{1/2}$ regularization in deep learning networks could achieve a better performance that L_1.

Compare with local sparsity methods, global sparsity aggregates activation possibility of hidden units. It has no fixed p level ($p = 0$), and no additional parameters to adjust. Sparsity logic is easy to understand and simple to use. However, it has no control on the sparseness of each hidden unit. All hidden units have the same penalty mechanism. If a hidden unit with activation possibility near one indicates an "important" factor, global sparsity forces "less important" hidden units (between zero and one) become to zero. This is not a good behavior if we want to see more details from network results.

3.3   A Combined Solution

Problems of local and global sparsity are inherent, and difficult to resolve. Therefore we propose a combined solution, ideally local and global sparsity can complement with each other. The new sparsity regularization is constructed as

$$L_{sparse} = L_{local} + \lambda_2 L_{global} \tag{6}$$

where L_{local} indicates one of local sparsity methods, L_{global} indicates an instance of L_q regularization, λ_2 is a constant, a tradeoff between local and global sparsity. Experiments in Sect. 5 demonstrate this combined solution outperforms each single sparsity method mentioned above.

4   Sparse DBN and Sparse GAN

In this section, we implement proposed method in a deep belief network (DBN) and a generative adversarial network (GAN). The purpose for the sparse DBN is to compare with previous single sparsity methods [12, 14, 15]. Sparse GAN shows our proposed method could benefit data generations, stabilize loss changes and eliminate noises.

4.1   Sparse DBN

Deep belief network is consist of several RBMs. Therefore, sparse DBN means sparse RBM. RBM is a two layer, bipartite, undirected graphical model (see Fig. 1) with a set of visible units v, and a set of hidden units h. Visible units represent observable data, hidden units represent features captured from observable data. Visible layer and hidden layer are connected by a symmetrical weight matrix. There is no connection within the same layer.

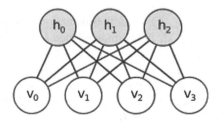

Fig. 1. Undirected graphical model of an RBM

If units are binary-valued, the energy function of RBM can be defined as

$$E(v,h) = -\sum_{i=1}^{n}\sum_{j=1}^{m} v_i w_{ij} h_j - \sum_{i=1}^{n} a_i v_i - \sum_{j=1}^{m} b_j h_j \tag{7}$$

where n and m are the total number of visible units and hidden units. v_i and h_j represent the value of visible neuron i and hidden neuron j. a_i and b_j are bias terms. w_{ij} represents the connection weight between i and j. The joint probability distribution for visible and hidden units can be defined as

$$P(v,h) = \frac{1}{Z} e^{-E(v,h)} \tag{8}$$

$$Z = \sum_{v}\sum_{h} e^{-E(v,h)} \tag{9}$$

where Z is the normalization factor. And the probability assigned to a visible vector v by the network, is obtained by marginalizing out hidden vector h

$$P(v) = \sum_{h} P(v,h) = \frac{1}{Z}\sum_{h} e^{-E(v,h)} \tag{10}$$

Parameters can be optimized by performing stochastic gradient descent on the log-likelihood of training data. Given a training set $\{v^1, \ldots, v^m\}$, loss function of RBM can be defined as

$$\min \frac{1}{m}\sum_{l=1}^{m} \log(P(v^{(l)})) \tag{11}$$

Finally, by integrating Eqs. (1) and (11), we can get the loss function for proposed sparse RBM method as

$$\min \frac{1}{m}\sum_{l=1}^{m} \log(P(v^{(l)})) + \lambda_1 L_{local} + \lambda_2 L_{global} \tag{12}$$

Results in Sect. 5.1 shows our proposed method is efficient, and achieved the best recognition accuracy in MNIST dataset for all different number of training and testing samples. The performance overcomes each single local and global sparsity algorithms mentioned above.

4.2 Sparse GAN

GAN contains two models: generative and discriminative model. The objective of generative model is to synthesize data resembling real data, while the objective of discriminative model is to distinguish real data from synthesized ones [22]. They both are multilayer perceptrons.

Given the training data set $\{x^1, \ldots, x^n\}$, p_x is the data's distribution. Let z be a random vector sampled from p_z, generative model takes z as input and output synthesize data as $G(z)$. Input of discriminative model is a mix of training data and synthesize data, output is a single scalar as $D(x)$ or $D(G(z))$ depending on input's source, which demonstrates the probability of input data come from real training dataset. Ideally $D(x) = 1$ and $D(G(z)) = 0$. Network plays a two-player minimax game, and they can be trained by solving

$$\min_G \max_D E_{x \sim p_x}[\log D(x)] + E_{z \sim p_z}[\log(1 - D(G(z)))] \tag{13}$$

If we denote the distribution of $G(z)$ as p_G, this minimax game has a global optimum for $p_G = p_x$ [1]. The training processes of generative and discriminative model are proceeded alternately. Parameters of generative model are fixed when updating discriminative model, vice versa. Be aware that discriminative model might learn faster than generative model. To keep in sync, we could train discriminative model k times, and then train generative model one time.

Due to the special mechanism of GAN, sparsity terms are added separately into the loss function of generative and discriminative models. The loss function for discriminative model is

$$\max E_{x \sim p_x}[\log D(x)] + E_{z \sim p_z}[\log 1 - D(G(z))] + \lambda_{d1} L_{local} + \lambda_{d2} L_{global} \tag{14}$$

Meanwhile the loss function for generative model is

$$\min E_{z \sim p_z}[\log 1 - D(G(z))] + \lambda_{g1} L_{local} + \lambda_{g2} L_{global} \tag{15}$$

Result in Sect. 5.2 shows, with the help of sparsity terms, quality of generated images are significantly improved. Moreover, the loss changes of generative and discriminative models are stabilized and noises in later iterations can be eliminated by our proposed method.

5   Experiments

5.1   MNIST

The MNIST digit dataset contains 60,000 training and 10,000 test images of 10 handwritten digits (0–9), each image with size 28×28 pixels [23]. The image pixel values are normalized between 0 and 1. In our experiment, we implement proposed sparsity method in a RBM network with 500 hidden units. Contrastive divergence and stochastic gradient descent are applied for sampling and parameter updating. Mini-batch size is set to 100. Sparsity term in nsRBM is selected as L_{local} regularization term, while $L_{1/2}$ is selected as L_{global} regularization term. Original nsRBM contains two parameters: p level and standard deviation σ, in our experiment we use standard normal distribution ($p = 0, \sigma = 1$). We get the best performance when "tradeoff" constants are set to $\lambda_1 = 3, \lambda_2 = 0.005$.

Similar with [12, 14], we firstly train proposed method and several other sparsity regularization algorithms (RBM, sparseRBM [15], nsRBM [14], L_1 [12], $L_{1/2}$, and proposed method) on 20,000 images (2000 images per class), and then the learnt features are used as input for the same linear classifier. For the classification, we use 500, 1000 and 5000 images per class for training, 10,000 images for testing. We train 1000 epochs for all different methods. From Table 1, we can see our proposed method achieves the best recognition accuracy for all different number of training and testing samples. We demonstrate error rate changes for every 100 epochs in Fig. 2, and our method also achieves the best.

Table 1. Recognition error rate for training 100, 500, 1000 samples per class on MNIST dataset

Algorithms	100 Samples		500 Samples		1000 Samples	
	Training	Testing	Training	Testing	Training	Testing
RBM	10.80	11.47	5.84	6.38	4.54	5.06
sparseRBM	11.78	12.77	6.44	6.99	4.18	4.74
nsRBM	10.99	11.82	5.92	6.15	3.59	4.06
L1	11.21	12.34	6.31	6.78	3.63	4.07
L1/2	**10.77**	12.09	5.89	6.14	3.44	3.95
Ours	**10.77**	**11.33**	**5.32**	**5.75**	**3.14**	**3.63**

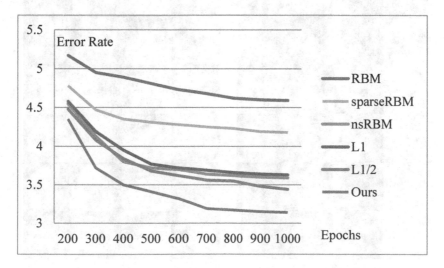

Fig. 2. Recognition error rate for every 100 epochs on MNIST dataset

5.2   CelebA

CelebA is a large-scale dataset with 202,599 number of face images [24]. Images cover large pose variations and background clutter. We implement our proposed sparsity algorithm in a deep convolutional generative adversarial network [11] with 5 convolutional layers. For the generative model, input is a 64-dimension vector which is randomly sampled from a uniform distribution. Filter numbers for each layers are 1024, 512, 256, 128, and 3, kernel size is 4×4 and stride is 2, output is a 64×64 synthesized human face. Structure of discriminative model is reverse expect output is a scalar. For training, mini-batch size is set to 64, and totally 3166 batches for one epoch.

Figure 3 shows some synthetic images generated by GAN (left side) and sparse GAN (right side). First row of images are sampled after epoch 1 iteration 500 of 3166, images generated by sparse GAN could describe face contours roughly. In the third row (sampled after epoch 1 complete), a human face could be easily recognized. Images generated at same steps by GAN could not achieve that. Last row of images are sampled after epoch 6, images on right side are obviously better.

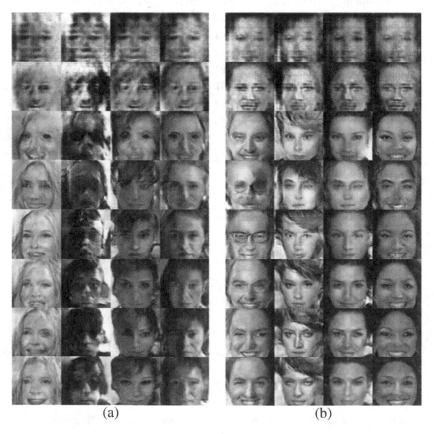

(a)   (b)

Fig. 3. Synthetic images generated after different epochs by (a) GAN (b) sparse GAN.

Figures 4 and 5 demonstrate that sparsity terms could also stabilize loss changes while GAN playing minimax game. Moreover, noises in later iterations are surprisingly eliminated by sparse GAN. This is beyond our expectation.

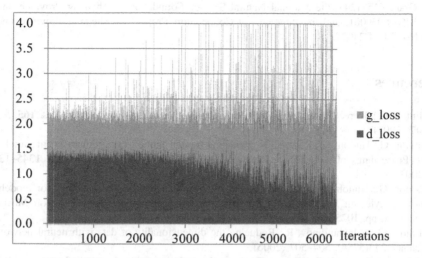

Fig. 4. Loss values of discriminator and generator models in GAN

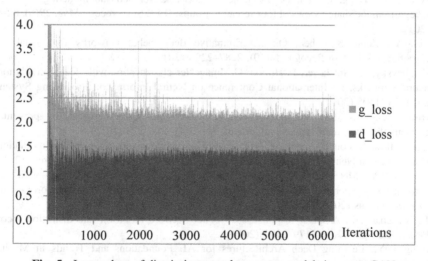

Fig. 5. Loss values of discriminator and generator models in sparse GAN

6 Conclusion

We studied popular sparsity algorithms and categorized according to their mechanism. After analyze their weaknesses and strengths, we presented a combined solution for local and global sparsity regularization. Two deep learning networks (DBN and GAN)

were implemented to verify proposed solution. Additionally, experiments on two benchmarks showed promising results of our method.

Acknowledgments. This work was supported by National Natural Science Foundation of China under Grant 61571247, the National Natural Science Foundation of Zhejiang Province under Grant LZ16F030001, and the International Cooperation Projects of Zhejiang Province under Grant No. 2013C24027.

References

1. Hinton, G.: To recognize shapes, first learn to generate images. Prog. Brain Res. **165**, 535–547 (2007)
2. Taylor, G., Hinton, G., Roweis, S.: Modeling human motion using binary latent variables. In: Proceedings of Advances in Neural Information Processing Systems, pp. 1345–1352 (2007)
3. Taylor, G., Hinton, G.: Factored conditional restricted Boltzmann machines for modeling motion style. In: Proceedings of the 26th Annual International Conference on Machine Learning, pp. 1025–1032 (2009)
4. Hinton, G., Salakhutdinov, R.: Reducing the dimensionality of data with neural networks. Science **313**(5786), 504–507 (2006)
5. Mohamed, A., Dahl, G., Hinton, G.: Acoustic modeling using deep belief networks. IEEE Trans. Audio Speech Lang. Process. **20**(1), 14–22 (2012)
6. Hinton, G., Deng, L., Yu, D.: Deep neural networks for acoustic modeling in speech recognition: the shared views of four research groups. IEEE Sig. Process. Mag. **29**(6), 82–97 (2012)
7. Liu, Y., Zhou, S., Chen, Q.: Discriminative deep belief networks for visual data classification. Pattern Recogn. **44**(10), 2287–2296 (2011)
8. Krizhevsky, A., Sutskever, I., Hinton, G.: ImageNet classification with deep convolutional neural networks. In: International Conference on Neural Information Processing Systems, pp. 1097–1105 (2012)
9. Hinton, G., Srivastava, N., Krizhevsky, A.: Improving neural networks by preventing co-adaptation of feature detectors. Comput. Sci. **3**(4), 212–223 (2012)
10. Goodfellow, I., Pouget-Abadie, J., Mirza, M.: Generative adversarial nets. In: International Conference on Neural Information Processing Systems, pp. 2672–2680 MIT Press (2014)
11. Radford, A., Metz, L., Chintala, S.: Unsupervised representation learning with deep convolutional generative adversarial networks. In: 4th International Conference on Learning Representations (2016)
12. Ji, N., Zhang, J.: A sparse-response deep belief network based on rate distortion theory. Pattern Recogn. **47**(9), 3179–3191 (2014)
13. Bengio, Y.: Learning Deep Architectures for AI. Foundations and Trends in Machine Learning (2009)
14. Keyvanrad, M., Homayounpour, M.: Normal sparse deep belief network. In: International Joint Conference on Neural Networks, pp. 1–7 (2015)
15. Lee, H., Ekanadham, C., Ng, A.: Sparse deep belief net model for visual area V2. In: Advances in Neural Information Processing Systems, pp. 873–880 (2008)
16. Xu, Z., Chang, X., Xu, F., Zhang, H.: L1/2 regularization: a thresholding representation theory and a fast solver. IEEE Trans. Neural Networks Learn. Syst. **23**(7), 1013–1027 (2012)

17. Krishnan, D., Fergus, R.: Fast image deconvolution using hyper-Laplacian priors. In: Advances in Neural Information Processing Systems, pp. 1033–1041. MIT Press, Cambridge (2009)
18. Xu, Z., Guo, H., Wang, Y., Zhang, H.: Representative of L1/2 regularization among Lq $(0 < q \leq 1)$ regularizations: an experimental study based on phase diagram. Acta Automatica Sinica **38**(7), 1225–1228 (2012)
19. Nair, V., Hinton, G.: Rectified linear units improve restricted boltzmann machines. In: Proceedings of the 27th International Conference on Machine Learning, pp. 807–814 (2010)
20. Maas, A., Hannun, A., Ng, A.: Rectifier nonlinearities improve neural network acoustic models. In: Proceedings of the 30th International Conference on Machine Learning, vol. 30, no. 1 (2013)
21. Xu, B., Wang, N., Chen, T., Li, M.: Empirical evaluation of rectified activations in convolutional network. arXiv preprint arXiv:1505.00853 (2015)
22. Liu, M., Tuzel, O.: Coupled generative adversarial networks. In: Advances in Neural Information Processing Systems (2016)
23. The MNIST database of handwritten digits. http://yann.lecun.com/exdb/mnist. Accessed 29 May 2017
24. Large-scale CelebA Dataset. http://mmlab.ie.cuhk.edu.hk/projects/CelebA.html. Accessed 29 May 2017

Object Detection by Learning Oriented Gradients

Jiajie Chen[1,2,3], Huicheng Zheng[1,2,3(✉)], Na He[1,2,3],
Ziquan Luo[1,2,3], and Rui Zhu[1,2,3]

[1] School of Data and Computer Science, Sun Yat-sen University,
135 West Xingang Road, Guangzhou 510275, China
`zhenghch@mail.sysu.edu.cn`
[2] Key Laboratory of Machine Intelligence and Advanced Computing,
Ministry of Education, Sun Yat-sen University, 135 West Xingang Road,
Guangzhou 510275, China
[3] Guangdong Key Laboratory of Information Security Technology,
Sun Yat-sen University, 135 West Xingang Road, Guangzhou 510275, China

Abstract. This paper proposes a method of learning features corresponding to oriented gradients for efficient object detection. Instead of dividing a local patch into cells with fixed sizes and locations such as in the traditional HOG, we employ a data-driven method to learn the sizes and locations of cells. Firstly, oriented gradient patch-maps of a local patch are constructed according to the orientations. Secondly, rectangular cells of various sizes and locations are constructed in each patch-map to sum up the magnitudes of oriented gradients and produce candidate local features. The local features are then selected by using a boosting procedure. Finally, a local patch is represented by a feature vector in which each component corresponds to the sum of oriented gradients in a rectangular cell. An object detector is then trained over the local patches by using a higher-level boosted cascade structure. Extensive experimental results on public datasets verified the superiority of the proposed method to existing related methods in terms of both the training speed and the detection accuracy.

Keywords: Oriented gradients · Boosting · Object detection

1 Introduction

With its wide applications in computer vision, object detection has become one of the most studied problems for several decades. Developing a reliable object detector enables a vast range of applications such as video surveillance [3] and the practical deployments of autonomous and semiautonomous vehicles [2] and robotics [1]. It is also a key component of many other computer vision tasks, such as object tracking [11], object recognition [7], scene understanding [5], and augmented reality [6]. The fundamental goal of object detection is to detect the locations and categories of multiple object instances in the images efficiently.

© Springer International Publishing AG 2017
Y. Zhao et al. (Eds.): ICIG 2017, Part II, LNCS 10667, pp. 86–96, 2017.
https://doi.org/10.1007/978-3-319-71589-6_8

Generally, object detection consists of two steps: (1) feature extraction and (2) classification. Object detection based on deep learning attracted wide interests and showed promising performance recently [20,21]. However, the training process of deep learning models is generally very time-consuming even with the support of GPUs and requires large training datasets. In the milestone work of Viola and Jones [8], a boosted cascade of simple features is proposed for efficient object detection. Since then, many researchers have made efforts to extend the approach. The impressive improvement has been made mainly via: (1) improving the boosted cascade structure [4,23,25], and (2) learning low-level features based on appearance models [12–14]. There are three representative low-level features constructed based on gradient information, i.e., Histogram of Oriented Gradients (HOG) [15], SIFT [9], and SURF [24]. All the descriptors adopt position-fixed histograms computed in local cells for representation of local patches.

The cascade-HOG framework [10] is a representative method for constructing weak classifiers based on HOG features in local patches. To construct the HOG features, it is necessary to compute magnitudes and orientations of image gradients. The histograms are generated by adding up the gradient information in small spatial regions (cells). In this way, local object appearance and shape can be generally characterized by the distribution of local intensity gradients or edge directions. Such descriptions are invariant to local geometric and photometric transformations. Nevertheless, the handcrafted features are not adaptive to complicated distributions in real-world applications. In the HOG, a local patch is evenly divided into 4 cells to construct the histograms separately [10,15,19]. Such a fixed construction of cells, however, may not cope well with variations in various object classes, which could limit the capability of object detectors trained over local patches. To address this issue, in this paper, instead of dividing a local patch into cells with fixed sizes and locations such as HOG, we propose a data-driven method to learn local features corresponding to oriented gradients, intending to better capture the appearance and shape of various objects.

The proposed feature learning chain is summarized in Fig. 1. Firstly, by computing the orientation of the gradients for each local patch, we create k oriented gradient maps for each local patch. These maps, namely patch-maps in this paper, have the same size as the local patch. We then construct rectangular cells of various sizes and locations in each patch-map. Within each cell, the magnitudes of oriented gradient are accumulated over the pixels of cell as one candidate feature. Secondly, we use a boosting procedure to learn the local features, which selects a few features corresponding to dominant oriented gradients for each patch-map. The selected features of each patch-map are concatenated to form the descriptor of local patches. Finally, we train object detector over these local patches with a higher-level boosted cascade, which replaces the two conflicted criteria (false-positive rate and hit rate) with a single criterion AUC (area under the curve) for convergence test. Experiments on various public datasets verified that the proposed method obtained better performance than existing related methods both in terms of the training speed and the detection accuracy.

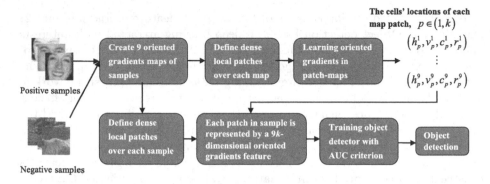

Fig. 1. An overview of the proposed method for oriented gradient learning and object detection.

The rest of this paper is organized as follows. Section 2 describes the process of learning local features corresponding to oriented gradients in detail, and constructs the corresponding object detector. Experimental analysis is presented in Sect. 3. This paper is finally concluded by Sect. 4.

2   The Proposed Method

2.1   Learning Oriented Gradients

We collect positive and negative samples from the training set, and compute gradients of the sample images in advance.

In general, we define $G_x(x, y)$ as the horizontal gradient of a pixel at (x, y) by using the filter kernel $[-1, 0, 1]$, and $G_y(x, y)$ as the vertical gradient by the filter kernel $[-1, 0, 1]^T$. The magnitude $G(x, y)$ and orientation $\alpha(x, y)$ of the gradient are computed as follows.

$$G(x, y) = \sqrt{G_x(x, y)^2 + G_y(x, y)^2}, \tag{1}$$

$$\alpha(x, y) = \tan^{-1}\left(\frac{G_y(x, y)}{G_x(x, y)}\right), \tag{2}$$

The orientations of gradients ranging from $0°$ to $360°$ are evenly divided into k bins, k is set as 9 here. We generate an oriented gradient map with the same size as the input sample for each bin. If the gradient orientation of a pixel at (x, y) belongs to the i-th bin, we set the value at the same location in the i-th map to be the gradient magnitude of the pixel. The same locations in the other maps are then filled with 0.

We define patches of various sizes for reliable detection. For instance, given a template with 40×40 pixels, the patch sizes are set as 16×16 pixels, 16×32 pixels, 32×16 pixels, and 32×32 pixels. A window with a stride of 4 pixels slides over the oriented gradient maps to extract the local patches. We obtain a patch-map set for each oriented gradient map. The patch-map set is utilized for learning local features corresponding to oriented gradients, in which positive patch-maps are generated from the oriented gradient maps of positive samples and negative patch-maps are from negative samples. We take rectangular cells of various locations and sizes in a patch-map, and accumulate all gradients in a rectangular cell as one candidate feature. One weak classifier is built over each rectangular cell in parallel from the patch-map set. The decision tree is chosen as the model for weak classifiers for convenience.

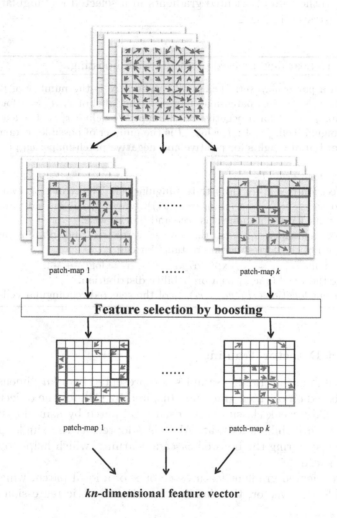

Fig. 2. The extraction process of oriented gradient features for a local patch. The arrow direction defines the orientation of gradients of a pixel, whereas the arrow length denotes the magnitude. There are k patch-maps corresponding to k orientation bins, where each one yields n features by summarizing gradients in n rectangular cells (the small rectangular regions in patch-maps). Totally kn oriented gradient features are generated for each local patch.

The AdaBoost learning algorithm is used to select a small number of weak classifiers, which can also be regarded as a process of rectangular cell selection. The boosting procedure is illustrated in Algorithm 1. We preserve the first n rectangular cells selected by boosting, where $n = 10$ according to our experiments. $(h_p^q, v_p^q, c_p^q, r_p^q)$ is recorded as the location of the rectangular cell, where (h_p^q, v_p^q) represents the coordinates of the upper left corner of the cell, c_p^q and r_p^q represent its width and height, $p = 1 : n$, $q = 1 : k$. Each local patch in the training sample is represented by a kn-dimensional feature vector where each component corresponds to the sum of oriented gradients in a selected rectangular cell. The process is illustrated in Fig. 2.

Algorithm 1. Learning oriented gradients with boosting.

Input: Given a patch-map set: $\{(x_i, y_i)\}_{i=1}^N$, where N is the number of patch-maps in the set, x_i is the i-th patch-map and y_i is the label of x_i, $y_i = 1$ for a positive patch-map, $y_i = -1$ for a negative patch-map. We define x_i^j as the feature of the j-th rectangular cell, $j = 1 : J$, where J is the number of possible rectangular cells.

1: **Initialize:** Initial weights for positive and negative patch-maps: $w_{1,i} = \frac{1}{N}$, $i = 1 : N$.

2: **Boosting:** for $t = 1 : T$

3: Train a decision tree s_j for the j-th rectangular cell. The error ε_j is evaluated with respect to w_t: $\varepsilon_j = \sum_{i=1}^N w_{t,i} \delta(y_i \neq s_j(x_i))$, where $\delta(\cdot)$ is an indicator function, which outputs 1 if the argument is true and 0 otherwise.

4: Choose the classifier $\hat{s}_t$ with the lowest error $\hat{\varepsilon}_t$, and obtain the location (h_t, v_t, c_t, r_t) of the corresponding rectangular cell.

5: Update weight $w_{t+1,i} = w_{t,i} \exp(-\alpha_t y_i \hat{s}_t(x_i))$, $\alpha_t = \log(\frac{(1-\hat{\varepsilon}_t)}{\hat{\varepsilon}_t})$.

6: Normalize the weights w_{t+1} as a probability distribution.

Output: Output locations $(h_t, v_t, c_t, r_t)_{t=1}^T$ of the selected rectangular cells.

2.2   Object Detector Training

Each local patch in the training samples is represented by a kn-dimensional feature vector based on oriented gradients. Inspired by [24], for the object detector, we further build a weak classifier over each local patch by using logistic regression as it has probabilistic output. AUC is adopted as the single criteria for convergence test during the boosted cascade learning, which helps to accelerate the training speed.

Given an oriented gradient feature vector $\mathbf{x}$ of a local patch, which is a kn-dimensional feature vector, the classifier based on logistic regression is defined as follows:

$$g(\mathbf{x}) = \frac{1}{1 + \exp(-y(\mathbf{w}^T \mathbf{x} + b))}, \tag{3}$$

where $y \in \{-1, 1\}$ is the label of the local patch, $\mathbf{w}$ is a kn-dimensional weight vector and b is a bias term. We solve the following unconstrained optimization problem to obtain the parameters by using Liblinear [22],

$$\min_{\mathbf{w},b} C \sum_{i=1}^{L} \log \left(1 + \exp(-y_i(\mathbf{w}^T \mathbf{x}_i + b))\right) + \|\mathbf{w}\|_1, \tag{4}$$

where $C > 0$ is a penalty parameter, $\| \cdot \|_1$ denotes the l_1-norm, L is the number of training samples, $\mathbf{x}_i$ is a kn-dimensional feature vector of a local patch on the i-th training sample, y_i is the corresponding label of the local patch.

We implement the boosted cascade framework to train the object detector. Each stage of the cascade is a boosted learning procedure. In the r-th boosting round, we build a logistic regression model $g(\mathbf{x})$ for each local patch in parallel from the training set. Assume that there are M local patches in a sample. Then M logistic regression classifiers $\{g_m(\mathbf{x})\}_{m=1}^M$ would be created. $G^{r-1}(\mathbf{x}) + g_m(\mathbf{x})$ is tested on all training samples to get an AUC score , where $G^{r-1}(\mathbf{x})$ is a combined classifier of previous $r-1$ rounds. We seek the classifier $g_r(\mathbf{x})$ which produces the highest AUC score. Gentle AdaBoost is adopted to combine the weak classifiers at the end of each boosting round.

The decision threshold θ of the strong classifier per stage is determined by searching on the ROC curve to find the point (d, f) such that the hit rate $d = d_{min}$, where d_{min} is the minimal hit rate for each stage. The value f is then the false positive rate (FPR) at the current stage. Therefore, FPR is adaptive across different stages, usually with values much smaller than 0.5. It means that the overall FPR can reach the overall goal of the cascade quickly. As a result, the cascade of stages tends to be short.

2.3 Object Detection

The trained object detector works on a fixed template size, but objects in images may have various sizes in practice. To guarantee effective detection of these objects, we build an image pyramid by scaling the input image.

The object detector scans across all scales in the pyramid to find objects. Considering that the detector may not be sensitive to small changes of scales, multiple detections may appear around a candidate object. We merge these duplicated detections with a simple strategy. All detections in an image are partitioned into disjoint subsets at first. Specifically, detections are in the same subset if their bounding boxes overlap. Each subset generates a final bounding box as detection, whose corners are the averages of the corresponding corners of all detections in the subset.

3 Experimental Results

The proposed approach is evaluated experimentally on three public datasets: UMass FDDB, PASCAL VOC 2007, and PASCAL VOC 2005. The experiments were all carried out with an Intel Xeon E5-2609 v4@1.70 GHz CPU.

3.1   Experiments on the FDDB Dataset

The FDDB dataset contains 2845 images with a total of 5771 faces that may be subject to substantial occlusion, blur, or pose variations. Five face detectors are separately trained for various views: the frontal view, the left/right half-profile views, and the left/right full-profile views.

For positive training samples, we collected 14000 faces from the frontal view, 8000 faces from the half-profile views, and 5000 faces from the full-profile views, which were all resized to 40×40 pixels. We also collected about 8000 images without faces, which were scanned by using sliding windows to construct negative training samples. The training procedure only took about 2 h to converge at the 6th stage, while the Haar training module provided by OpenCV took more than 2 days to finish training with the same dataset and CPU.

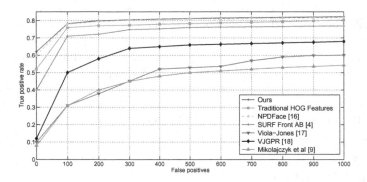

Fig. 3. ROC curves of various methods obtained on the FDDB dataset.

To demonstrate the advantage of the proposed features based on learning oriented gradients in local patches, we replaced the proposed feature vector with the traditional HOG in the boosted cascade detector. Figure 3 shows the ROC curves of various methods including ours on the FDDB dataset [4,9,16–18]. The proposed approach outperforms most of existing methods significantly. Specifically, the proposed features show clear improvement over the common HOG features. The proposed detector also slightly surpasses NPDFace specifically designed for face detection [16].

Figure 4 shows some examples of the detected faces by using the proposed features learned from oriented gradients in local patches in comparison to those by using traditional HOG features. The proposed method can successfully detect faces subject to various poses, occlusion, and illumination conditions, while the method based on the traditional HOG features failed to detect some partly occluded or blurred faces, and produced a number of false detections. Traditional HOG method with fixed cells in local patch can not capture the appearance and shape precisely. When applied to detect some partly occluded or blurred faces, HOG performs not so well. The results verified the superiority of the proposed features to the traditional HOG features in terms of face detection.

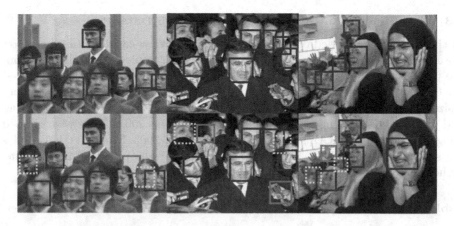

Fig. 4. Examples of face detection on the FDDB dataset. First row: detections obtained by the proposed method. Second row: detections obtained by using traditional HOG features. Correct detections are indicated by green boxes, while missing ones by dashed yellow boxes and false ones by red boxes. (Color figure online)

3.2   Experiments on the PASCAL VOC 2007 Dataset

The PASCAL VOC 2007 dataset contains a number of visual object classes in realistic scenes. We carried out experiments on four object classes from this dataset, including person, car, bicycle, and dog, since they contain more positive training samples than the others to allow learning without external datasets. We simply trained a general detector for each object class. The trained detectors were evaluated on the test set of PASCAL VOC 2007. Table 1 shows the results of detection by the proposed method in comparison to the results of state-of-the-art algorithms [8,14,25–27]. The proposed method obtained the highest detection rates on 2 out of 4 classes. On the bicycle class, the proposed method performs better than other methods except for [14]. On the dog class, our method does not work so well. The reason is that oriented gradient features of furry animals are not so evident and it is easy to mistaken dogs as other furry animals. But our method still has a higher detection rate than the traditional HOG features, which indicates that the learned oriented gradient features can better capture the appearance and shape of furry animals. As for RCNN [26], it applies high-capacity convolutional neural networks to bottom-up region proposals and thus can learn more powerful features to describe objects. However, the detection of RCNN is slow. At test time, features are extracted from each object proposal in each test image. Detection with VGG16 takes 47 s/image on a GPU. Our method only takes 0.4 s/image on a CPU. On the whole, the improvement of our method over HOG features indicates that the learned oriented gradients are better adapted to challenging objects.

3.3   Experiments on the PASCAL VOC 2005 Dataset

In this section, we carried out experiments on side-view car detection based on the PASCAL VOC 2005 dataset. 600 side-view car samples were collected from the UIUC subset and ETHZ subset in PASCAL VOC 2005. We further mirrored the 600 samples to generate 1200 positive training samples. All car samples were resized to 80 × 30 pixels. The proposed method took 39 min to finish training and produced 6 stages in cascade. The test set contains 200 side-view cars in 170 images from the TUGRAZ subset in PASCAL VOC 2005. The detection results are summarized in Table 2, which demonstrate that the proposed method has higher detection rate compared to HOG, SURF, and Haar features.

Table 1. Detection rates on four object classes from the PASCAL VOC 2007 dataset.

Method	Person	Car	Bicycle	Dog
Ours	**48.4**	**60.3**	59.2	11.8
Traditional HOG features	43.2	54.1	55.7	10.9
Viola and Jones [8]	40.4	52.3	52.7	8.1
RCNN fc_7 [26]	43.3	58.9	57.9	**46.0**
iCCCP [25]	36.6	51.3	55.8	12.5
HOG-LBP [14]	44.6	58.2	**59.8**	15.1
MILinear [27]	21.9	45.0	39.7	21.3

Table 2. Detection results on side-view cars from the PASCAL VOC 2005 dataset.

	Detection rate	False positives
Ours	**80.5**	21
SURF cascade [24]	70	18
Traditional HOG features	74	29
Viola and Jones [8]	68	34

4   Conclusion

This paper presents a method of learning features from oriented gradients in local patches for robust object detection. Gradients in a local patch are grouped according to their orientations, which leads to 9 patch-maps. Rectangular cells are constructed in each patch-map, which are used to generate candidate local features by summing up magnitudes of oriented gradients therein. The local features are then selected by boosting. Eventually, each local patch is represented by a 90-dimensional feature vector. A higher-level boosting is then carried out over local patches in the detection window. Experimental results on three public datasets demonstrated the superiority of the proposed approach in comparison to existing methods in terms of both training efficiency and detection accuracy.

Acknowledgements. This work was supported by National Natural Science Foundation of China (Nos. 61172141, U1611461, 61573387), Special Program for Applied Research on Super Computation of the NSFC-Guangdong Joint Fund (the second phase), Project on the Integration of Industry, Education and Research of Guangdong Province (No. 2013B090500013), Major Projects for the Innovation of Industry and Research of Guangzhou (No. 2014Y2-00213), and Science and Technology Program of Guangzhou (No. 2014J4100092).

References

1. Coates, A., Ng. A.Y.: Multi-camera object detection for robotics. In: ICRA, pp. 412–419 (2010)
2. Satzoda, R.K., Trivedi, M.M.: Overtaking and receding vehicle detection for driver assistance and naturalistic driving studies. In: ITSC, pp. 697–702 (2014)
3. Fang, S., Tong, S., Xu, X., Xie, Z.: A method of target detection and tracking in video surveillance. In: ICIG, pp. 84–87 (2004)
4. Li, J., Wang, T., Zhang, Y.: Face detection using SURF cascade. In: ICCV, pp. 2183–2190 (2011)
5. Li, L.J., Li, R., Fei-Fei, L.: Towards total scene understanding: classification, annotation and segmentation in an automatic framework. In: CVPR, pp. 2036–2043 (2009)
6. Hayashi, T., Uchiyama, H., Pilet, J., Saito, H.: An augmented reality setup with an omnidirectional camera based on multiple object detection. In: ICPR, pp. 3171–3174 (2010)
7. He, Z., Sun, Z., Tan, T., Qiu, X., Qiu, C., Dong, W.: Boosting ordinal features for accurate and fast iris recognition. In: CVPR, pp. 1–8 (2008)
8. Viola, P.A., Jones, M.J.: Rapid object detection using a boosted cascade of simple features. In: CVPR, pp. 511–518 (2001)
9. Mikolajczyk, K., Schmid, C., Zisserman, A.: Human detection based on a probabilistic assembly of robust part detectors. In: Pajdla, T., Matas, J. (eds.) ECCV 2004. LNCS, vol. 3021, pp. 69–82. Springer, Heidelberg (2004). https://doi.org/10.1007/978-3-540-24670-1_6
10. Zhu, Q., Yeh, M., Cheng, K., Cheng, S.: Fast human detection using a cascade of histograms of oriented gradients. In: CVPR, pp. 1491–1498 (2006)
11. Breitenstein, M.D., Reichlin, F., Leibe, B., Koller-Meier, E., Gool, L.V.: Robust tracking-by-detection using a detector confidence particle filter. In: ICCV, pp. 1515–1522 (2015)
12. Vedaldi, A., Gulshan, V., Gulshan, M., Zisserman, A.: Multiple kernels for object detection. In: ICCV, pp. 606–613 (2009)
13. Deselaers, T., Ferrari, V.: Global and efficient self-similarity for object classification and detection. In: CVPR, pp. 1633–1640 (2010)
14. Zhang, J., Zhang, K., Yu, Y., Tan, T.: Boosted local structured HOG-LBP for object localization. In: CVPR, pp. 1393–1400 (2011)
15. Dalal, N., Triggs, B.: Histograms of oriented gradients for human detection. In: CVPR, pp. 886–893 (2005)
16. Liao, S., Jain, A.K., Li, S.Z.: A fast and accurate unconstrained face detector. IEEE Trans. PAMI **38**(2), 211–223 (2015)
17. Viola, P.A., Jones, M.J.: Robust real-time face detection. Int. J. Comput. Vis. **57**(2), 137–154 (2004)

18. Jones, V., Miller, E.L.: Online domain adaptation of a pre-trained cascade of classifiers. In: CVPR, pp. 577–584 (2011)
19. Girshick, R., Iandola, F., Iandola, T., Malik, J.: Deformable part models are convolutional neural networks. In: CVPR, pp. 437–446 (2015)
20. Girshick, R.: Fast R-CNN. In: ICCV, pp. 1440–1448 (2015)
21. Yang, F., Choi, W., Lin, Y.: Exploit all the layers: fast and accurate CNN object detector with scale dependent pooling and cascaded rejection classifiers. In: CVPR, pp. 2129–2137 (2016)
22. Fan, R., Chang, K., Hsieh, C.J., Wang, X., Lin, C.: Liblinear: a library for large linear classification. J. Mach. Learn. Res. 9, 1871–1874 (2008)
23. Schnitzspan, P., Fritz, M., Roth, S., Schiele, B.: Discriminative structure learning of hierarchical representations for object detection. In: CVPR, pp. 2238–2245 (2009)
24. Li, J., Zhang, Y.: Learning SURF cascade for fast and accurate object detection. In: CVPR, pp. 3468–3475 (2013)
25. Zhu, L., Chen, Y., Yuille, A., Freeman, W.: Latent hierarchical structural learning for object detection. In: CVPR, pp. 1062–1069 (2010)
26. Girshick, R., Donahue, J., Darrell, T., Malik, J.: Rich feature hierarchies for accurate object detection and semantic segmentation. In: CVPR, pp. 580–587 (2014)
27. Ren, W., Huang, K., Tao, D., Tan, T.: Weakly supervised large scale object localization with multiple instance learning and bag splitting. IEEE Trans. PAMI 38(2), 405–416 (2016)

Unsupervised Representation Learning with Deep Convolutional Neural Network for Remote Sensing Images

Yang Yu, Zhiqiang Gong, Ping Zhong[✉], and Jiaxin Shan

ATR Laboratory, School of Electronic Science and Engineering,
The National University of Defense Technology,
Changsha 410073, Hunan, China
zhongping@nudt.edu.cn

Abstract. With the rapid growth in quantity and quality of remote sensing images, extracting the useful information in them effectively and efficiently becomes feasible but also challenging. Convolutional neural network (CNN) is a suitable method to deal with such challenge since it can effectively represent and extract the information. However, the CNN can release their potentials only when enough labelled data provided for the learning procedure. This is a very time-consuming task and even infeasible for the applications with non-cooperative objects or scenes. Unsupervised CNN learning methods, which relieve the need for the labels in the training data, is a feasible solution for the problem. In this work, we investigate a real-world motivated sparsity based unsupervised deep CNN learning method. At first, the method formulates a balanced data driven population and lifetime sparsity prior and thus construct the unsupervised learning method through a layerwise mean. Then we further perform the method on the deep model with multiple CNN layers. Finally, the method is used for the remote sensing image representation and scenes classification. The experimental results over the public UC-Merced Land-use dataset demonstrate that the developed algorithm obtained satisfactory results compared with the recent methods.

Keywords: Unsupervised representation learning
Convolutional neural network · Scene classification
Remote sensing images · Sparsity

1 Introduction

In the last decades, remote sensing imaging has become increasingly important in environmental monitoring, military reconnaissance, precision farming and other domains. Both the quantity and quality of remote sensing images are growing rapidly. How to mine the useful information in such huge image repositories has been a challenging task. Traditional machine learning methods including the feature representation and classification algorithms cannot tackle this challenge well for their limited representation ability.

© Springer International Publishing AG 2017
Y. Zhao et al. (Eds.): ICIG 2017, Part II, LNCS 10667, pp. 97–108, 2017.
https://doi.org/10.1007/978-3-319-71589-6_9

Recently, the emergence of deep learning combined with hierarchical feature representation has brought changes for the analysis of huge remote sensing images. Convolutional neural networks (CNN) [1], as one of the famous deep learning architectures, demonstrated impressive performances in the literature of computer vision. CNN can not only capture and represent more complicated and abstract images by powerful fitting capacity coming from deep structures but also make full use of a great number of training samples to achieve better results. The representation ability of CNN derives main from its deep model structure, and also a large number of model parameters. Estimating the model parameters usually need huge labelled data in the supervised learning framework. Preparing the numerous labelled data is a very time-consuming task. Moreover, in the applications for non-cooperative objects and scenes, it is impossible to get the labels for the observed data. Semi-supervised and unsupervised learning methods could deal with this problem. In this work, we mainly investigate the unsupervised learning method for the CNN model and aim to relieve the heavy consumption of the numerous labelled training data and meanwhile to maintain its performance on representation ability.

The goal of unsupervised deep learning is utilizing the observed data only (no need for the corresponding semantic labels) to learn a rich representation that exposes relevant semantic features as easily decodable factors [2]. The deep learning community has completed primary researches on this topic. There are three kinds of methods to implement the unsupervised deep learning. The first is to design specific models which naturally allow the unsupervised learning. The conventional models are autoencoders [3] and recently their variants, such as denoising autoencoders (DAE [3]) and ladder network [4]. The restricted Boltzman machines (RBMs) can also be trained in an unsupervised way [5]. Besides, stacking multiple autoencoders layers or RBMs produce the well-known deep belief network (DBN) [6], which naturally has the ability from autoencoders and RBMs on allowing unsupervised learning.

The second kind of unsupervised deep learning methods is implemented through a particular model structure and learning strategy. The generative adversarial networks (GANs) is the recent popular method for unsupervised learning [7]. The GAN method trains a generator and a discriminator by the learning strategy as rule of minimax game. Following the research direction of GANs, deep convolutional generative adversarial networks (DCGAN [8]) also obtained a good performance on the generation and feature learning of images, and Wasserstein GAN [9] improved the defects of GAN and achieved a more robust framework. From the application view, the structure of DCGAN has been successfully introduced into the remote sensing literature and obtained impressive remote sensing image representation and scene classification results [2]. But the difficulty in training procedure is the GAN' defect that cannot be ignored.

The third kind of unsupervised deep learning method is substantially embedded into the learning process through formulating specific loss objectives, which usually follow the real-world rules and can be computed with no needs of semantic labels in the training samples. The principles of sparsity and diversity can be used to construct loss function for deep unsupervised learning. Enforcing population and lifetime sparsity

(EPLS) [10] is such a method with simple ideas but remarkable performance. The EPLS enforces the output of each layer conform to population sparsity and lifetime sparsity. It is an entirely unsupervised method that can be trained with unlabeled image patches layer by layer and does not need a fine-tuning process. In contrast to other deep learning methods, especially GAN, EPLS is very easy to train and also very robust to convergence.

Considering the easy implementation and also the superior representation ability obtained through only the unsupervised learning, this work investigates the EPLS based unsupervised representation learning with Deep CNN for remote sensing images. Especially this work investigates a balanced data driven sparsity (BDDS) [11] EPLS algorithm in the deep CNN. In this method, the CNN is trained through the extended EPLS with a balanced data driven sparsity, and the multiple convolutional layers are stacked to form the deep network obtained through entirely unsupervised learning method.

2   EPLS

EPLS builds a sparse objective through enforcing lifetime sparsity and population sparsity to filters output and optimizes the parameters by minimizing the error between the filters output and the sparse target. The reasons why enforcing lifetime and population sparsity will be explained in Subsect. 2.1. Subsection 2.2 will present the algorithm details.

2.1   Population and Lifetime Sparsity

Sparsity is one of the desirable properties of a good network's output representation. Its primary purpose is to reduce network's redundancy and improve its efficiency and diversity. Sparsity can be described in terms of population sparsity and lifetime sparsity [12]. Population sparsity means that the fraction of neurons activated by a particular stimulus should be relatively small. The sparsity assumption can reduce the number of redundant neurons and enhance the networks' ability of description and efficiency. Lifetime sparsity expresses that a neuron is constrained to respond to a small number of stimuli and each neuron must have a response to some stimuli. So lifetime sparsity plays a significant role in preventing bad solutions such as dead outputs.

The degree of population and lifetime sparsity can be adjusted for specific task and requirement for better performances. In our task at hand, the sparsity degrees are set as follows. On the one hand, strong population sparsity is demanded that for each training sample (stimulus) in a mini-batch only one neuron must be activated as active or inactive (no intermediate values are allowed between 1 and 0). On the other hand, we enforce a strict lifetime sparsity since each neuron must be activated only one time by a certain training simple in one mini-batch. So the ideal outputs of a mini-batch in training EPLS are one-hot matrices, as shown in Fig. 1(d). Besides, Fig. 1 also shows other three situations of output according to different kinds of sparsity for comparisons.

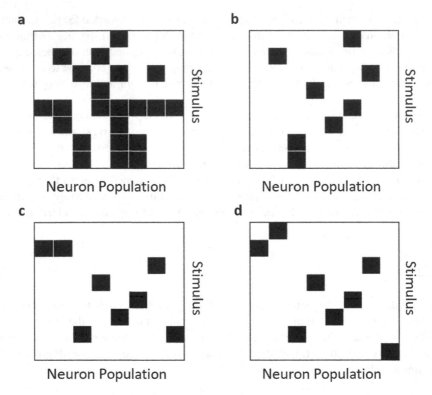

Fig. 1. Understanding strong population and lifetime sparsity. (a) Outputs that disobey the rule of sparsity. (b) Strong population sparsity. (c) Strong lifetime sparsity. (d) Outputs that conform both population and lifetime sparsity.

2.2 EPLS Algorithm

EPLS is usually used for the unsupervised learning in a layer-wise way. For the layer l in CNN, EPLS builds a one-hot target matrix T^l (as shown in Fig. 1(d)) to enforce both lifetime and population sparsity of the output H^l from a mini-batch. The parameters of this layer will be optimized by minimizing the L_2 norm of the difference between H^l and T^l,

$$H^l = \sigma\left(D^l W^l + b^l\right) \tag{1}$$

$$\{W^l, b^l\} = argmin_{\{W^l, b^l\}} \left\|H^l - T^l\right\|_2^2 \tag{2}$$

where D^l is the mini-batch matrix of layer l, W^l and b^l are weights and bias of the layer, $\sigma(*)$ is the pointwise nonlinearity, $H^l, T^l \in \Re^{m \times r}$, m is the number of patches in a mini-batch, r is the number of neurons of layer, l, N is the total number of training patches. For the optimization of parameters in layer l, the mini-batch stochastic gradient descent algorithm will be performed.

Algorithm 1 presents the steps to implement EPLS. The primary objective of EPLS is to build the target matrix T^l, which will be assigned to be a one-hot matrix depending on the maximum values in H^l. EPLS will process rows of H^l one by one iteratively. In each row, the algorithm selects the neuron k of the nth row that has the maximal activation value (h_j minus an inhibitor a_j) to be set as the only one "hot code", and thus ensure population sparsity [10]. Once the neuron k has been selected, the corresponding inhibitor a_k will be increased by r/N. The inhibitor which can measure the number of each neuron has been selected, and the phenomenon of dead outputs or one neuron form being selected too many times is prevented, and thus ensure lifetime sparsity. More details on the EPLS algorithm can be found in [10].

Algorithm 1 EPLS [11]

Input: H^l, a, N

Output: T^l, a

1: $T^l = 0$

2: $H^l = (H^l - min(H^l))/(max(H^l) - min(H^l))$

3: **for** $n = 1 \rightarrow m$ **do**

4: $\quad h_j = H_{n,j}^l \ \forall j \in \{1,2,...,r\}$

5: $\quad k = argmax_j(h_j - a_j)$

6: $\quad T_{n,k}^l = 1$

7: $\quad a_k = a_k + (r/N)$

8: **end for**

9: Remap T^l to active/inactive values

Though EPLS tactfully enforce lifetime sparsity through the inhibitors, a defect will exist when the inhibitor of a certain neuron k is too big, wrong neurons will be activated by patches corresponding to the neuron k. It will influence the performance of EPLS, and we call it "neuron saturation" that will be discussed in the next section.

3 Unsupervised Learning of Deep CNN with BDDS Based EPLS

3.1 Flowchart of the Method

The method contains both training and testing processes, as shown in Fig. 2. The testing process is similar with the one in other deep learning algorithms, which applies the deep networks on testing samples to get discriminative features. Because of the feature of EPLS' loss function (2) training process is different, parameters are independent of each layer. It is impossible to train all the parameters at one time, an algorithm to update the parameters layer by layer is needed and it will be discussed in Subsect. 3.3. It is also noteworthy that we perform a BDDS operation before training the network, which makes up the shortcomings of EPLS and will be discussed in Subsect. 3.2.

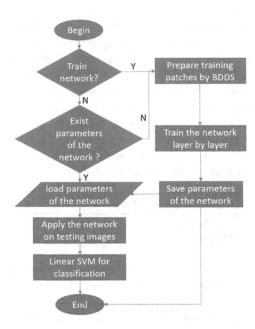

Fig. 2. Flow chart of the method.

3.2   Balanced Data Driven Sparsity (BDDS) Based EPLS

"Neuron Saturation" Phenomenon. EPLS achieves lifetime sparsity by enforcing a neuron being selected only once in a mini-batch through inhibitors. Such operation must face two drawbacks. On the one hand, training image patches randomly abstracted from remote sensing images are unbalanced, i.e., the numbers of patches from different potential classes could be very different, some are huge while some are small. Just part of such kinds of patches with a huge number will greatly improve value of the inhibitor corresponding to a neuron, thus the neuron will be saturated. Other neurons that respond to the different patches will be enforced to respond to the remaining part of that kind of training patches. We call such phenomenon "neuron saturation" which will reduce the diversity of filters. Figure 3 shows how the unbalanced data influences the target matrix. Training patch set 1 is a balanced training set corresponding to a "healthy" target matrix T_1^l. If there are too many red patches and too little yellow patches just like training patch set 2, a "sick" target matrix T_2^l will appear. It is because additional red patches may enforce the yellow neuron make the weights that were learned for yellow patches turn to respond to the red patches.

On the other hand, even though the whole training patches is balanced, inputting too many similar patches to the network at the same time will also lead to a local "neuron saturation". Patches enforced to activate the wrong neuron will be wasted, and unrelated neuron will be "contaminated". It will reduce the efficiency of the training process and decrease the network's performance. A balanced data driven sparsity (BDDS) based EPLS will be introduced to solve the problem from local and global "neuron saturation" phenomenon in next subsection.

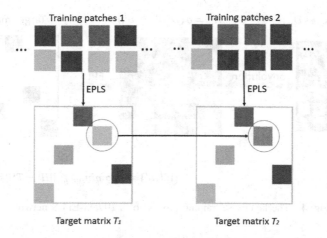

Fig. 3. The effect of the unbalanced training data [11]. (Color figure online)

BDDS Based EPLS. To address the issue of local and global "neuron saturation" phenomenon and achieve a more natural sparsity, we construct the balanced training samples for EPLS. There are four steps to implement the proposed method. (1) **Patches Extraction.** The patches are randomly extracted from remote sensing image datasets. (2) **Clustering.** All patches are clustered into n classes (Sect. 4 will set an experiment to explore the suitable value of n). In this work, we perform the clustering over the color LBP features of training patches. We perform LBP [13] to all three channels of training patches and concatenate all these features to LBP texture features, thus color LBP features is obtained. The classes without enough patches will be supplemented at random. (3) **Arrangement.** This step extracts one sample per category to constitute a balanced mini-batch. As a result, every mini-batch contains samples covering all classes, and the numbers of samples from different classes are same. (4) **EPLS.** This step uses the balanced mini-batches to train EPLS and the problems from local and global "neuron saturation" phenomenon could be solved.

3.3 Applying BDDS Based EPLS on Multiple Layers

BDDS-EPLS is usually performed layerwise. Moreover, a single layer trained by BDDS-EPLS could obtain impressive results. In this work, we further investigate to apply the BDDS-EPLS method to multiple layers for more powerful representation ability. Because global backpropagation cannot be used on EPLS' layerwise loss function, perform EPLS training on deep CNN model is different from the training of other deep networks. Since EPLS needs to be trained layer by layer, a greedy layerwise unsupervised pretraining [14] will be performed to implement the EPLS training over the deep model. It is based on the idea that a layerwise unsupervised criterion can be applied to pretrain the network's parameters, allowing the use of large amounts of unlabeled data. Figure 4 shows the layerwise training process of a BDDS-EPLS network. All parameters in every layer need to be optimized by greedy layerwise unsupervised training.

Training patches D^l　　　　$H^l = \sigma(D^l W^l + b^l)$　　　　Target matrix T^l

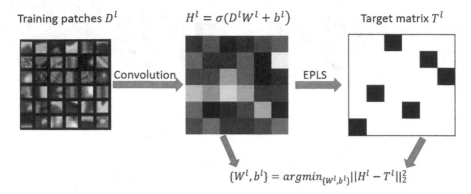

Convolution　　　　　　　　EPLS

$$\{W^l, b^l\} = argmin_{\{W^l, b^l\}} ||H^l - T^l||_2^2$$

Fig. 4. The layerwise training process of a BDDS-EPLS network

Algorithm 2 shows the detail steps to train BDDS-EPLS. For each layer, parameters are updated independently. The updating process as follows: firstly, the method performs BDDS algorithm for balanced training patches. Secondly, the feature matrix H^l is obtained through (1) and the target matrix through EPLS algorithm. Finally, mini-batch stochastic gradient descent algorithm is performed on minimizing (2) to optimize parameters in layer l. Repeat the training process until the stop condition is reached.

Algorithm 2 Greedy layerwise unsupervised training of BDDS-EPLS

1: **for** $l = 1 \to L$ **do**

2:　　$D^l \leftarrow$ BDDS(l)

3:　　**do**

4:　　　$H^l \leftarrow$ EPLS(D^l)

5:　　　$\{W^l, b^l\} \leftarrow$ updated by minimising $||H^l - T^l||_2^2$

6:　　**while** achieving stop condition

7: **end for**

4　Experiments

4.1　Experimental Setup

In this section, experiments are set to show the effects of the single layer and multiple layers BDDS-EPLS in different scenarios of image classification on Ucmerced dataset [15]. We randomly select 80 images per class for training and leave the remaining 20 ones for testing. Both the number of neurons and the size of mini-batch are set to 500 to all experiments and the number of training samples will be set to 105000 in every layer. The receptive field is set to 7×7 with stride 1 pixel. And we applied a non-overlapping max-pooling of 2×2 pixels at each representation layer, except for the last layer, which divides the output feature map into 2×2 pixels and feeds into a linear SVM.

4.2   General Performance

Representation and Classification Performance. The two-layer BDDS-EPLS network obtains a classification accuracy on 85.95% that significantly improves the performance of two-layer EPLS network reported in [10]. Figure 5 shows the confusion matrices of the representation features of the two-layer BDDS-EPLS learned. Errors concentrate on close classes such as dense-residential, building and mobile-home-park, and the other classes are classified well even 100% accuracy appears in some classes. It shows that BDDS-EPLS has the powerful capacity of unsupervised feature representation only with unlabeled image patches as training samples.

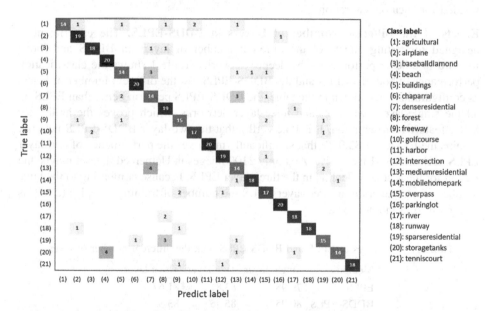

Fig. 5. Confusion matrices of the two-layer BDDS-EPLS

Effects of the Different Number of Clustering Centers. The experiment is designed for testing effects of the different number of clustering centers m in BDDS. We follow the experimental pipeline setup of [10]. The only difference is the way selecting training patches in which we use color LBP features of training patches for BDDS. m is set to 100, 200, 500, 1000 respectively and Fig. 6 shows that the highest classification 80.95% appears on m equal to 500. It maybe means that when the number of clustering

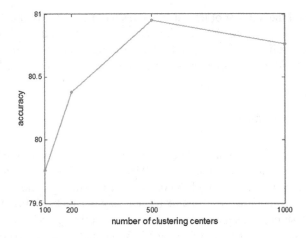

Fig. 6. Effects of the different number of clustering centers

centers equals to the number of neurons in the network, the best suppression was yielded for "neuron saturation".

Effects of the Different Number of Layers in BDDS-EPLS. The experiment is designed for testing effects of the different number of layers in BDDS and looks forward to a better performance by deeper networks. Table 1 shows the classification performance of both the EPLS and the BDDS-EPLS, for the different number of layers as configurations. As shown in the table, the BDDS-EPLS perform better than EPLS on all the single-layer, two-layer and three-layer networks, which proves the ability for better feature representation. It is noteworthy that the two-layer BDDS-EPLS network obtains the best result 85.95% that significantly improves the performance of two-layer EPLS network 83.81 by 2.14%. And only 2100 images in Ucmerced dataset maybe the reason for the accuracy decline in the three-layer EPLS, because comparing to the huge number of parameters in a three-layer EPLS the number of training samples (2100) is too small to fit the network.

Table 1. Accuracies of EPLS and BDDS-EPLS with the different number of layers.

Methods	Single-layer	Two-layer	Three-layer
EPLS	79.98	83.81	81.67
BDDS-EPLS	80.95	**85.95**	83.33

4.3   Comparing with Other State of the Art Unsupervised Algorithms

Table 2 shows the classification accuracies of several state of the art algorithms on Ucmerced dataset. Our two-layer based BDDS-EPLS gets the best performance 85.95% even higher than the six-layer DCGANs and MARTA GANs (without data augmentation). EPLS that combines CNN with strong population sparsity and lifetime sparsity has the great ability of unsupervised representation learning. The BDDS

Table 2. Classification accuracies of some state of the art algorithms. Best result in bold.

Method	Accuracy
OMP-k [16]	81.67
SPCK++ [17]	76.05
DCGANs [2]	80.36
MARTA GANs [2]	85.37
EPLS [10]	84.53
BDDS-EPLS (ours)	**85.95**

method addresses the "neuron saturation" phenomenon in EPLS and release EPLS's ability, thus achieve the best performance. It is also noteworthy that EPLS' classification accuracy in [10] achieves 84.53% with 1000 neurons per layer, while our method's classification accuracy reaches 85.95% with only 500 neurons per layer. It shows the power of our BDDS-EPLS method.

5 Conclusions and Future Work

In this work, we apply a deep BDDS-EPLS network on Ucmerced dataset, and significantly improve the classification accuracy. In the future, we will try to increase the depth of the network and generalize BDDS-EPLS for hyperspectral imagery.

Acknowledgement. This research was conducted with the support of the Natural Science Foundation of China under Grant 61671456 and 61271439, A Foundation for the Author of National Excellent Doctoral Dissertation of P. R. China (FANEDD) under Grant 201243, Program for New Century Excellent Talents in University under Grant NECT-13-0164.

References

1. Chen, K., Ding, G., Han, J.: Attribute-based supervised deep learning model for action recognition. Front. Comput. Sci. **11**, 219–229 (2017)
2. Bengio, Y.: Learning Deep Architectures for AI. Foundations and Trends in Machine Learning. Now Publishers Inc, Breda (2009)
3. Vincent, P., Larochelle, H., Bengio, Y., Manzagol, P.A.: Extracting and composing robust features with denoising autoencoders. In: International Conference on Machine Learning, pp. 1096–1103 (2008)
4. Valpola, H.: From neural PCA to deep unsupervised learning. arXiv preprint (2014)
5. Smolensky, P.: Information processing in dynamical systems: foundations of harmony theory. In: David, E.R., James, L.M. (eds.) Parallel Distributed Processing: Explorations in the Microstructure of Cognition, vol. 1, pp. 194–281 (1986). Chapter 6
6. Hinton, G.E., Osindero, S., Teh, Y.W.: A fast learning algorithm for deep belief nets. Neural Comput. **18**, 1527–1554 (2006)
7. Goodfellow, I.J., Pouget-Abadie, J., Mirza, M., Xu, B., Warde-Farley, D., Ozair, S.: Generative adversarial nets. In: Conference on Neural Information Processing Systems, vol. 3, pp. 2672–2680 (2014)

8. Radford, A., Metz, L., Chintala, S.: Unsupervised representation learning with deep convolutional generative adversarial networks. In: Computer Science (2015)
9. Martin, A., Soumith, C., Léon, B.: Wasserstein GAN. arXiv preprint (2017)
10. Romero, A., Gatta, C., Camps-Valls, G.: Unsupervised deep feature extraction for remote sensing image classification. IEEE Trans. Geosci. Remote Sens. 54(3), 1–14 (2015)
11. Yang, Y., Zhiqiang, G., Ping, Z.: Balanced data driven sparsity for unsupervised deep feature learning in remote sensing images classification. In: IEEE International Geoscience and Remote Sensing Symposium (2017)
12. Willmore, B., Tolhurst, D.J.: Characterizing the sparseness of neural codes. Network 12(12), 255–270 (2001)
13. Ojala, T., Pietikäinen, M., Mäenpää, T.: Gray scale and rotation invariant texture classification with local binary patterns. In: European Conference on Computer Vision, pp. 404–420 (2000)
14. Bengio, Y., Lamblin, P., Popovici, D., Larochelle, H.: Greedy layerwise training of deep networks. In: Conference on Neural Information Processing Systems, pp. 153–160 (2006)
15. Yang, Y., Newsam, S.: Bag-of-visual-words and spatial extensions for land-use classification. In: ACM SIGSPATIAL GIS, pp. 270–279 (2010)
16. Cheriyadat, A.: Unsupervised feature learning for aerial scene classification. IEEE Trans. Geosci. Remote Sens. 52(1), 439–451 (2014)
17. Yang, Y., Newsam, S.: Spatial pyramid co-occurrence for image classification. In: Proceeding of IEEE International Conference on Computer Vision, pp. 1465–1472, November 2011

Image Captioning with Object Detection and Localization

Zhongliang Yang[✉], Yu-Jin Zhang, Sadaqat ur Rehman,
and Yongfeng Huang

Tsinghua University, Beijing 100084, China
yangzll5@mails.tsinghua.edu.cn

Abstract. Automatically generating a natural language description of an image is a task close to the heart of image understanding. In this paper, we present a multi-model neural network method closely related to the human visual system that automatically learns to describe the content of images. Our model consists of two sub-models: an object detection and localization model, which extracts the information of objects and their spatial relationship in images respectively; besides, a deep recurrent neural network (RNN) based on long short-term memory (LSTM) units with attention mechanism for sentences generation. Each word of the description will be automatically aligned to different objects of the input image when it is generated. This is similar to the attention mechanism of the human visual system. Experimental results on the COCO dataset show the merit of the proposed method, which outperforms previous benchmark models.

Keywords: Neural networks · Image caption · Object detection
Deep learning

1 Introduction

In the past few years, deep neural network has made significant progress in image processing area, like image classification [1–3], object detection [4–6]. However, tasks like image classification and object detection are far from the end of image understanding. One ultimate goal of image understanding is to understand the whole image scenario but not individual objects. Image captioning follows the same path by extracting the complete detail of individual object and their associated relationship from image. Finally, the system can automatically generate a sentence to describe the image. This problem is extremely important, as well as difficult because it connects two major artificial intelligence fields: computer vision and natural language processing.

Previous studies are mostly inspired by the works of machine translation, where the task is to translate a source sentence written in one language (like French) into a target sentence written in a different language (like English), keeping logic and syntax precise. Associating image captioning and machine translation together makes sense because they can be placed in the same framework, called Encoder-Decoder framework. In the Encoding step, we encode the source information, which is an image in image captioning task and source sentence in translation task, into a target vector. Followed by the decoding step, in which sentences are generated by decoding the target

© Springer International Publishing AG 2017
Y. Zhao et al. (Eds.): ICIG 2017, Part II, LNCS 10667, pp. 109–118, 2017.
https://doi.org/10.1007/978-3-319-71589-6_10

vector. The core part of this framework is how to encode the source information (image or sentence) and how to decode the target vectors.

Previous works are align in the decoding step, they usually use recurrent neural networks (RNN) based on long short-term memory (LSTM) [7] units as a decoder. As for the encoding step is concerned, the work is divided into two major classes: CNN-RNN models [8–10] and attention based models [11, 12]. CNN-RNN models represent an image as a single feature vector from the top layer of a pre-trained convolutional network, whereas attention based models use the vector made up by the representations of image's subregions as the source vector. The biggest drawback of CNN-RNN models is that they hardly align different visual parts of the input image to words in captions. Attention based model like [11] allowed their model to attend any visual parts of the input image but most of the subregions it attends are meaningless.

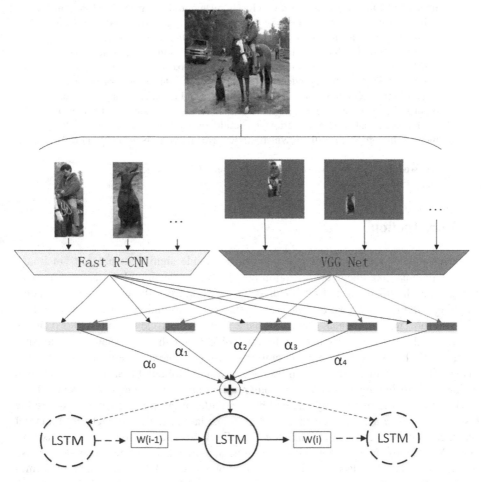

Fig. 1. An overview of the proposed framework. The encoding part first extract the information of objects (left) and their spatial relationships (right) in the image, then the decoding part generate words based on these features.

Our model also follows the Encoder-Decoder framework, however, it is totally different from the previous models as shown in Fig. 1. Our motivation in describing an image is to find out its contents, rather than focusing on some meaningless regions associated with it. The locations of different objects in an image is also a positive information for describing an image, since they reflect the spatial position relationships of objects in an image. Due to the aforementioned reason, we combine object detection with image captioning to focus on the real meaningful information domain in the images to generate the resulting sentences much better and efficient. The encoding part of our model consists of two steps. Initially, we use an object detection model to detect objects in the image followed by a deep Convolutional Neural Network to extract their spatial relationships. All these information will be represented as a set of feature vectors, which is then fed into the decoding part where the description sentence will be generated.

In order to measure the performance, we evaluate our model on COCO dataset using seven standard metrics: BLEU-1, 2, 3, 4, METEOR, CIDEr and ROUGH-L. Experimental results shows that our proposed model perform better than the baseline soft attention model [11] and is similar to the benchmark ATT model [12] in performance evaluation.

2   Our Model

This section describes the detail of the proposed model, which consists of two main parts: encoding and decoding. The input to our model is a single image I, while the output is a descriptive sentence S consists of K encoded words: $S = \{w_1, w_2, \ldots, w_K\}$.

In the encoding part, firstly, we present a model that recognizes objects in the input image followed by a deep CNN to extract their locations, which reflect the spatial relationship associated. All the information will be represented as a set of feature vectors referred as annotation vectors. The encoding part produces L annotation vectors, each of which is a D-dimensional representation corresponding to an object and also its spatial location in the input image: $A = \{A_1, A_2, \ldots, A_L\}, A_i \in R^D$.

In the decoding part, all these annotation vectors are fed into a deep Recurrent Neural Network model to generate a description sentence.

2.1   Encoding Part

Our core insight is that when human beings try to describe an image using sentence (combination of words), it's natural to first find out objects and their relation-ships in the desired image. To imitate human beings, our encoding part has two steps, first we use an object detection model to detect objects in the image followed by a deep Convolutional Neural Network to get their spatial locations.

Object Detection. In the past few years, significant progress have been done in object detection. These advances are driven by the success of region proposal methods (e.g. [13]) and region-based convolutional neural networks (R-CNN) [5]. In our model, we choose Faster R-CNN [6] as object detection model due to its efficiency and effectiveness in object detection task. Faster R-CNN is composed of two modules. The first module is a deep fully convolutional network that propose regions, the second module is the Fast R-CNN detector [5] which uses the proposed regions. To generate region proposals, the authors of [6] slides a small network over the convolutional feature map output by the last shared convolutional layer. For each sliding window of the input convolutional feature map, this small network maps it to a lower-dimensional feature. Then this feature fed into two sibling fully-connected layers: a box-regression layer (*reg*) and a box-classification layer (*cls*). After training, the Faster R-CNN takes an image (of any size) as an input and produce a set of rectangular object proposals, each with an objectness score. Then we sort these boxes according to their scores in descending order and choose the top-n boxes as the regions of objects in the input image. Each rectangular object region is mapped to a feature vector by fully connected layers (in our implementation it's 'fc7' layer) of the Faster R-CNN model. More explicitly, for every input image we detect n objects in an image and each object is represented as a d-dimension vector: $\{obj_1, obj_2, \ldots, obj_n\}, obj_i \in d^d$. Images in Fig. 2 are some results of object detection part, each object detected has an objectness score on it, captions below each image are generated by the proposed model and the words in red align to the objects detected in each image.

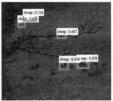

Caption: A vase of flowers on a table.   Caption: A man is riding a horse on the street.   Caption: A herd of sheep grazing in a field.   Caption: A man is sitting on a bench in the park.

Fig. 2. Some results of object detection part. The captions are generated by the proposed model.

Object Localization. This part is designed to extract the information of objects spatial locations which in turn reflect their spatial relationships. Junqi et al. [14] also considered the locations of different localized regions. However, they just added the boxes central's with x location, y location, width, height and area ratio with respect to the entire image's geometry to the end of the vector of each localized regions. In this paper, the implementation of extracting information of each object location is completely different from [14]. In object detection part, we know that for each input image, the output is n rectangular object regions, each with an objectness score. For each object in this image, we keep the region of its bounding box unchanged and set remaining regions to mean value of the training set. So we get a new image, which has the same size as the original image but just consists the bounding box region of one object as shown in Fig. 1. As we detected n objects for each image therefore, we get n new images for individual image. Each new image will then be fed into the VGG net [2] and the feature vector of its 'fc7' layer will be extracted, which yields to the vectorized representation of object location. Furthermore, we get another n vectors of t-dimension in which each vector represents the information of spatial location of each object: $\{loc_1, loc_2, \ldots, loc_n\}, loc_i \in d^t$.

Each annotation vector A_i consists of two parts: First, vector obj_i represents the feature of object which particularly describes the contents of image. Second, vector loc_i represents the feature of object location which tell us about the location of individual object.

$$A_i = [\mathbf{obj}_i; \mathbf{loc}_i], A_i \in d^D, D = d + t \tag{1}$$

2.2 Decoding Part

In this paper, we describe a decoding part based on an LSTM network with attention mechanism. Attention mechanism was first used in neural machine translation area by [15]. Following the same mechanism, the authors of [11, 16, 17] introduced it into image processing domain whereas, [11] was the first to apply it in image captioning task. The key idea of attention mechanism is that when a sentence is used to describe an image, not every word in the sentence is "translated" from the whole image but actually it just has relation to a few subregions of an image. It can be viewed as a form of alignment from words of the sentence to subregions of the image. The feature vectors of these subregions are referred to as annotation vectors. Here in our implementation, subregions are referred to as the bounding box of objects and annotation vectors are referred to as $\{A_i\}$, which is already discussed in the encoding part.

In the decoding part we follow [11] to use a long short-term memory (LSTM) network [7] as a decoder. LSTM network products one word at every step j conditioned on a context vector z_j, the previous hidden state h_{j-1} and the previously generated words w_{j-1} using the following formulations:

$$In_j = \sigma\left(W_i E w_{j-1} + U_i h_{j-1} + Z_i z_j + b_i\right) \tag{2}$$

$$f_j = \sigma\left(W_f E w_{j-1} + U_f h_{j-1} + Z_f z_j + b_f\right) \tag{3}$$

$$c_j = f_j c_{j-1} + tanh\left(W_c E w_{j-1} + U_c h_{j-1} + Z_c z_j + b_c\right) \tag{4}$$

$$o_j = \sigma\left(W_o E w_{j-1} + U_o h_{j-1} + Z_o z_j + b_o\right) \tag{5}$$

$$h_j = o_j tanh\left(c_j\right) \tag{6}$$

Here In_j, f_j, c_j, o_j, h_j represent the state of input gate, forget gate, cell, output gate and hidden layer respectively. W, U, Z and b are learned weight matrices and biases. E is an embedding matrix and σ is the logistic sigmoid activation. The context vector z_j is generated from the annotation vectors A_j, $i = 1, \ldots, n$, corresponding to the feature vectors of different objects.

There are two different versions in [11] to compute the context vector z_j and we use the "soft" version, that is

$$\mathbf{z}_j = \sum_{i=1}^{n} \alpha_{ji} \mathbf{A}_i \tag{7}$$

where α_{ji} is a scalar weighting of annotation vector $\mathbf{A}_i$ at time step j, defined as follows:

$$\mathbf{e}_{ji} = f_{att}(\mathbf{A}_i, h_{j-1}) \tag{8}$$

$$\alpha_{ji} = \frac{\exp(\mathbf{e}_{ji})}{\sum_{k=1}^{n} \exp(\mathbf{e}_{jk})} \tag{9}$$

$$\sum_{i=1}^{n} \alpha_{ji} = 1 \tag{10}$$

where f_{att} is a multilayer perceptron conditioned on the previous hidden state h_{j-1}.

We predict the next word W_j with a softmax layer, the input of it are the context vector, the previously generated word and the decoder state h_j:

$$p(w_j) \propto \exp(L_o(Ew_{j-1} + L_h h_j + L_z z_j)) \tag{11}$$

where L_o, E, L_h, L_z are learned parameters. The positive weight α_{ji} can be viewed as the probability that the word generated at time step j "translated" from annotation vector $\mathbf{A}_i$. Since $\mathbf{A}_i$ contains both the content information and the spatial location information of object i, α_{ji} will learns both the content relationships and spatial relationships of the objects in the input image when predict the next word w_j. Examples in Fig. 3 shows how the spatial relationships of objects can be reflected in the generated sentences.

Baseline: A kitchen with a refrigerator and a microwave.

Ours: A black and white cat sitting on top of a refrigerator

Baseline: A desk with a laptop and a monitor.

Ours: A man sitting in front of a laptop computer

Baseline: A couple of giraffe standing next to each other.

Ours: A couple of giraffe standing in the grass near trees

Baseline: A baseball player holding a bat on a field.

Ours: A baseball player swinging a bat at a ball

Fig. 3. Illustration of how the proposed model use the information of objects and their spatial relationships in the image to generate sentences. The baseline results are generated by Neural-Talk2 (version2.0 of Deep VS [10]). "Ours" are generated by the proposed model. Words in red align to the objects which are not recognized by the baseline model and the blue words show objects spatial relationships.

2.3   Training

This section describe the training of proposed model. The training data for each image consists of input image features $\{A_i\}$ and output caption words sequence $\{w_k\}$. Parameters of the proposed encoding part is fixed, so we only need to learn the parameters of the proposed decoding part, which are all the attention model parameters $\Theta_{Att} = \{W, U, Z, b\}$ jointly with RNN parameters Θ_{RNN}.

We train our model using maximum likelihood with a regularization term on the attention weights by minimizing a loss function over training set. The loss function is a negative log probability of the ground truth words $w = \{w_1, w_2, \ldots, w_K\}$:

$$LOSS = - \sum_t \log(p(w_j)) + \lambda \sum_i \left(1 - \sum_t \alpha_{i,j}\right)^2 \qquad (12)$$

where w_j is the ground truth word and $\lambda > 0$ is a balancing factor between the cross entropy loss and a penalty on the attention weights. We use stochastic gradient descent with momentum 0.9 to train the parameters of our network.

3 Experiments

In this section, we first describe the dataset used in our experiments as well as the experimental methodology followed by the detail results discussion. We report all the results using Microsoft COCO caption evaluation tool [18], including BLEU-1, 2, 3, 4, METEOR, CIDEr and ROUGH-L.

3.1 Dataset

We use COCO dataset [21] for experimental purpose to show the efficiency of proposed method, which includes 123287 color images. For each image, there are at least five captions given by different AMT workers. To make the results comparable to other methodologies, we use the commonly adopted [18] splits of the dataset, which assigns 5000 for validation, 5000 for testing and keep the rest for training. For each sentence, we limit the length size to 50 words and truncate the rest. Each sentence ends with a character "<end>". Words that appear less than five times are marked as a character "<unk>". When dictionary is build, resulting in the final vocabulary with 10020 unique words in COCO dataset.

3.2 Experimental Setting

In the encoding part of the proposed model, we use faster R-CNN [5] pre-trained on COCO dataset for object detection and VGG net [2] pre-trained on ImageNet dataset for feature extraction. For each input image, Faster R-CNN output a set of rectangular object proposals with an objectness score. We sort these scores and select the top-5 areas as the objects detected in this image. Each object then is represented as a vector of 4096 dimensions by the 'fc7' layer of faster R-CNN. Also, the spatial location of each object is represented as a vector of 4096 dimensions by the 'fc7' layer of VGG net. We concatenate these two vectors to form annotation vectors $\{A_i\}$, which yields the dimension of annotation vectors as 8192. We also use the 'fc7' layer of VGG Net to extract features of the whole image and repeat this vector twice. So for each individual input image, the output of the proposed encoding part is a matrix of 6 * 8192 dimensions.

The proposed decoding part is the LSTM network [7] with attention mechanism. We map each word to a vector of 1000 dimensions and set the hidden layers of LSTM to be 1000 dimensions. We use *tanh* as nonlinear activation function σ. For training, we use stochastic gradient descent with momentum = 0.9 to do model updating with a mini-batch size of 100, we set initial learning rate to 0.01 and decrease it by half after every 20,000 iterations. During testing, we use beam search method which selects the top-k best sentences and keep them to be expanded with new words in future until the end of sentence symbol is reached. During testing, we use beam search method which selects the top-k best sentences and keep them to be expanded with new words in future until the end of sentence symbol is reached. By comparing the results of different value of k, we find we can get the best results when k is set to 4.

3.3   Evaluation Results

Following previous works, we evaluate the proposed model using standard metrics: BLEU-1,2,3,4, METEOR, CIDEr and ROUGH-L (the higher the better), all the metrics are computed by using the codes released by COCO Evaluation Server [18]. The results are shown in Table 1, where "Ours" indicates the performance of the proposed model. Comparing the results of [8–10, 19], which are CNN-RNN models, with results of [11, 14, 20], which are attention based models, we can find that to encode each image into a set of annotation vectors which represent different subregions of the input image is better and more optimized then to encode the whole image into a single feature vector. Since the proposed model is directly developed from the soft-attention approach [11], therefore, its comparison is highly demanding. The major difference between the proposed model and the soft-attention approach [11] is that we use the information of objects and their spatial information in images for sentence generation. From Table 1, it's clear that the proposed model has achieve better performance than the soft-attention approach [11], which proves that the additional information really help machines to achieve better image understanding. Comparing with the best model which is ATT

Table 1. Results on the MSCOCO dataset.

Method	BLEU-1	BLEU-2	BLEU-3	BLEU-4	METEOR	CIDEr	ROUGH-L
NIC [8]	66.6	46.1	32.9	24.6	–	–	–
LRCN [19]	62.79	44.19	30.41	21	–	–	–
DeepVS [10]	62.5	45	32.1	23	19.5	66	–
m-RNN [9]	67	49	35	25	–	–	–
soft-att [11]	70.7	49.2	34.4	24.3	23.9	–	–
hard-att [11]	71.8	50.4	35.7	25	23.04	–	–
g-LSTM [20]	67	49.1	35.8	26.4	22.74	81.25	–
ATT [12]	70.9	53.7	40.2	30.4	24.3	–	–
RA + SF [14]	69.1	50.4	35.7	24.6	22.1	78.3	50.1
(RA + SF)-BEAM10 [14]	69.7	51.9	38.1	28.2	23.5	83.8	50.9
Ours	70.4	53.1	39.2	29	23.8	85	52.1

model [12] up to date, our results are still comparable even though they used a stronger CNN construction which is GoogLeNet instead of VGG16 in our case. Also, we claim that the proposed model takes less computation and more optimized than ATT model since GoogLeNet is more deeper model than VGG16.

4 Conclusion

In this paper, we present a multi-model Neural Network that automatically learns to describe the content of images. Our model first extracts the information of objects and their spatial locations in an image, and then a deep recurrent neural network (RNN) based on LSTM units with attention mechanism generates a description sentence. Each word of the description is automatically aligned to different objects in the input image when it is generated. The proposed model is more optimized compared to other benchmark algorithms on the ground that its implementation is totally made on human visual system. We hope that this paper will serve as a reference guide for researchers to facilitate the design and implementation image captioning.

Acknowledgment. This work has been supported by the National Natural Science Foundation of China under Grants NNSF-61171118, NNSF-61673234 and U-1636124.

References

1. Krizhevsky, A., Sutskever, I., Hinton, G.E.: Imagenet classification with deep convolutional neural networks. In: Advances in Neural Information Processing Systems, pp. 1097–1105 (2012)
2. Simonyan, K., Zisserman, A.: Very deep convolutional networks for large-scale image recognition. arXiv preprint arXiv:1409.1556 (2014)
3. Szegedy, C., et al.: Going deeper with convolutions. In: Proceedings of the IEEE Conference on Computer Vision and Pattern Recognition, pp. 1–9 (2015)
4. Girshick, R., Donahue, J., Darrell, T., Malik, J.: Region-based convolutional networks for accurate object detection and segmentation. IEEE Trans. Pattern Anal. Mach. Intell. **38**(1), 142–158 (2016)
5. Girshick, R.: Fast R-CNN. In: Proceedings of the IEEE International Conference On Computer Vision, pp. 1440–1448 (2015)
6. Ren, S., He, K., Girshick, R., Sun, J.: Faster R-CNN: towards real-time object detection with region proposal networks. In: Advances in Neural Information Processing Systems, pp. 91–99 (2015)
7. Hochreiter, S., Schmidhuber, J.: Long short-term memory. Neural Comput. **9**(8), 1735–1780 (1997)
8. Vinyals, O., Toshev, A., Bengio, S., Erhan, D.: Show and tell: a neural image caption generator. In: Proceedings of the IEEE Conference on Computer Vision and Pattern Recognition, pp. 3156–3164 (2015)
9. Mao, J., Xu, W., Yang, Y., Wang, J., Huang, Z., Yuille, A.: Deep captioning with multimodal recurrent neural networks (m-RNN). arXiv preprint arXiv:1412.6632 (2014)

10. Karpathy, A., Fei-Fei, L.: Deep visual-semantic alignments for generating image descriptions. In: Proceedings of the IEEE Conference on Computer Vision and Pattern Recognition, pp. 3128–3137 (2015)
11. Xu, K., et al.: Show, attend and tell: neural image caption generation with visual attention. In: Proceedings of the International Conference on Machine Learning, pp. 2048–2057 (2015)
12. You, Q., Jin, H., Wang, Z., Fang, C., Luo, J.: Image captioning with semantic attention. In: Proceedings of the IEEE Conference on Computer Vision and Pattern Recognition, pp. 4651–4659 (2016)
13. Uijlings, J.R., Van De Sande, K.E., Gevers, T., Smeulders, A.W.: Selective search for object recognition. Int. J. Comput. Vis. **104**(2), 154–171 (2013)
14. Jin, J., Fu, K., Cui, R., Sha, F., Zhang, C.: Aligning where to see and what to tell: image caption with region-based attention and scene factorization. arXiv preprint arXiv:1506.06272 (2015)
15. Bahdanau, D., Cho, K., Bengio, Y.: Neural machine translation by jointly learning to align and translate. arXiv preprint arXiv:1409.0473 (2014)
16. Mnih, V., Heess, N., Graves, A.: Recurrent models of visual attention. In: Advances in Neural Information Processing Systems, pp. 2204–2212 (2014)
17. Ba, J., Mnih, V., Kavukcuoglu, K.: Multiple object recognition with visual attention. arXiv preprint arXiv:1412.7755 (2014)
18. Karpathy, A.: neuraltalk2. https://github.com/karpathy/neuraltalk2
19. Donahue, J., et al.: Long-term recurrent convolutional networks for visual recognition and description. In: Proceedings of the IEEE Conference on Computer Vision and Pattern Recognition, pp. 2625–2634 (2015)
20. Jia, X., Gavves, E., Fernando, B., Tuytelaars, T.: Guiding the long-short term memory model for image caption generation. In: Proceedings of the IEEE International Conference on Computer Vision, pp. 2407–2415 (2015)
21. Lin, T.-Y., Maire, M., Belongie, S., Hays, J., Perona, P., Ramanan, D., Dollár, P., Zitnick, C. L.: Microsoft COCO: common objects in context. In: Fleet, D., Pajdla, T., Schiele, B., Tuytelaars, T. (eds.) ECCV 2014. LNCS, vol. 8693, pp. 740–755. Springer, Cham (2014). https://doi.org/10.1007/978-3-319-10602-1_48

Image Set Representation with L_1-Norm Optimal Mean Robust Principal Component Analysis

Youxia Cao, Bo Jiang$^{(\boxtimes)}$, Jin Tang, and Bin Luo

School of Computer Science and Technology, Anhui University,
No. 111 Jiulong Road, Hefei, China
ahu_youxia@foxmail.com, {jiangbo,tj,luobin}@ahu.edu.cn

Abstract. Many problems in computer vision area can be formulated as image set representation and classification. One main challenge is that image set data usually contains various kinds of noises and outliers which usually make the recognition/learning tasks of image set more challengeable. In this paper, we propose a new L_1 norm optimal Mean Principal Component Analysis (L1-MPCA) to learn an optimal low-rank representation for image set. Comparing with original observed image set, L1-MPCA based low-rank representation is generally noiseless and thus can encourage more robust learning process. An effective update algorithm has been proposed to solve the proposed L1-MPCA model. Experimental results on several datasets demonstrate the effectiveness and robustness of the proposed L1-MPCA method.

1 Introduction

Object recognition/learning based on visual content information is a fundamental problem in computer vision area. Recently, image set based object recognition approaches have been widely studied and attracted more and more interest. For image set based object recognition, it aims to achieve object recognition/learning problem by using multiple images (or video) that belong to one object.

One problem for image set based object recognition process is how to effectively represent an image set [5,9,11,22,26]. In recent years, many methods have been proposed for this problem. One kind of popular methods is to use statistical models. These methods usually aim to represent an image set by using some distributions, such as Gaussian, GMM, etc. [24]. Based on these representation, the similarity measurement between two image sets can be computed by metric measurement between distributions [1,18,20,22]. Another kind of methods is to use linear subspace models which aims to represent an image set by using a linear or affine subspace. Based on these representation, one can compute the distance between two image sets by measuring the distance between two subspaces [9,10,15,25]. Recent studies also aim to represent an image set using a nonlinear manifold or several sub-manifolds. Then, they generally use the metric learning method of manifolds to achieve image set recognition/learning tasks [3,4,7,11,21,23,26]. Some other methods have also been proposed [6].

© Springer International Publishing AG 2017
Y. Zhao et al. (Eds.): ICIG 2017, Part II, LNCS 10667, pp. 119–128, 2017.
https://doi.org/10.1007/978-3-319-71589-6_11

Previous works generally focus on developing a method for image set feature extraction and classification problems. In this paper, we focus on image set itself and propose a robust low-rank representation for image set. Our method is motivated by the following observation. Motivated by recent work on low-rank representation [12, 19], we propose a new low-rank representation, called L_1 norm based robust optimal Mean Principal Component Analysis (L1-MPCA), for image set recovery and representation. The aim of L1-MPCA is to integrate the mean calculation into L1-norm PCA low-rank approximation objective and thus the optimal mean can be obtained to enhance the low-rank approximation and representation. An effective optimization algorithm has been derived to solve the proposed L1-MPCA. Comparing with original observed image sets, L1-MPCA of image sets are generally noiseless and more regular, which significantly encourages the robust learning and recognition process. Experimental results on four datasets demonstrate the effectiveness and robustness of the proposed L1-MPCA methods.

2 Brief Review of Optimal Mean PCA

In this section, we give a brief introduction of Optimal Mean Principal Component Analysis (OMPCA) model [19]. Let $\mathbf{X} = (\mathbf{x}_1, \mathbf{x}_2, \cdots \mathbf{x}_n) \in \mathbb{R}^{p \times n}$ be the input data matrix containing the collection of n data column vectors in p dimension space. In image set representation, each column $\mathbf{x}_i$ denotes one linearized array of pixels gray levels. The aim of Optimal Mean Principal Component Analysis (OMPCA) [19] is to find the optimal low-dimensional matrices $\mathbf{U} = (\mathbf{u}_1, \mathbf{u}_2, \cdots \mathbf{u}_k) \in \mathbb{R}^{p \times k}$, $\mathbf{V} = (\mathbf{v}_1, \mathbf{v}_2, \cdots \mathbf{v}_k) \in \mathbb{R}^{n \times k}$ and mean vector $\mathbf{b} \in \mathbb{R}^p$ by minimizing,

$$\min_{\mathbf{U}, \mathbf{V}, \mathbf{b}} \sum_{i=1}^{n} \|\mathbf{x}_i - \mathbf{U}\mathbf{v}_i - \mathbf{b}\|_2^2 = \|\mathbf{X} - \mathbf{U}\mathbf{V}^{\mathrm{T}} - \mathbf{b}\mathbf{1}^{\mathrm{T}}\|_F^2 \qquad s.t. \quad \mathbf{U}\mathbf{U}^{\mathrm{T}} = \mathbf{I} \qquad (1)$$

where $\mathbf{1} = (1, 1, \cdots, 1) \in \mathbb{R}^n$. Let $\mathbf{Z} = \mathbf{U}\mathbf{V}^{\mathrm{T}} + \mathbf{b}\mathbf{1}^{\mathrm{T}}$, then $\mathbf{Z}$ provides a kind of low-rank representation for original input data $\mathbf{X}$. It is known that the squared loss function used in the above MPCA is very sensitive to outliers. In order to overcome this problem, Nie et al. [19] also propose a kind of Robust MPCA by using $L_{2,1}$ norm and solve the optimization problem as

$$\min_{\mathbf{U}, \mathbf{V}, \mathbf{b}} \sum_{i=1}^{n} \|\mathbf{x}_i - \mathbf{U}\mathbf{v}_i - \mathbf{b}\|_2 = \|\mathbf{X} - \mathbf{U}\mathbf{V}^{\mathrm{T}} - \mathbf{b}\mathbf{1}^{\mathrm{T}}\|_{2,1} \qquad s.t. \quad \mathbf{U}\mathbf{U}^{\mathrm{T}} = \mathbf{I} \qquad (2)$$

Comparing with Frobenious norm loss function, $L_{2,1}$-norm loss function performs robustly w.r.t outliers because it uses a non-squared loss function.

3 L_1-Norm Based Robust MPCA

The above $L_{2,1}$-norm OMPCA is robustness to outliers. However, it is sensitive to the corruptions or large errors existing in each image $\mathbf{x}_i$ because of L2 norm loss function for each image data. Our aim in this section is to propose a new kind of robust OMPCA by using L_1 norm loss function instead of $L_{2,1}$ norm loss function.

Model formulation. Formally, let $\mathbf{X} = (\mathbf{x}_1, \mathbf{x}_2, ..., \mathbf{x}_n) \in \mathbb{R}^{p \times n}$ be the image set data, our L_1 norm based MPCA (L1-MPCA) is formulated as,

$$\min_{\mathbf{U}, \mathbf{V}, \mathbf{b}} \sum_{i=1}^{n} \|\mathbf{x}_i - \mathbf{U}\mathbf{v}_i - \mathbf{b}\|_1 = \|\mathbf{X} - \mathbf{U}\mathbf{V}^T - \mathbf{b}\mathbf{1}^T\|_1 \quad s.t. \quad \mathbf{U}\mathbf{U}^T = \mathbf{I} \quad (3)$$

where L_1 norm loss function is defined as $\|\mathbf{A}\|_1 = \sum_i \sum_j |\mathbf{A}_{ij}|$. It is known that the L_1 norm loss function will make the the proposed L1-MPCA robust to both corruptions noise/large errors and outliers. Note that the above L1-MPCA can be regarded as a natural extension of the tractional L1-PCA model [2,13] by further removing optimal mean automatically from the input data set $\mathbf{X}$.

Optimization. We present an effective updating algorithm to solve L1-MPCA model. Firstly, Eq. (3) can be rewritten equivalently as

$$\min_{\mathbf{U}, \mathbf{V}, \mathbf{E}, \mathbf{b}} \|\mathbf{E}\|_1 \quad s.t. \quad \mathbf{E} = \mathbf{X} - \mathbf{U}\mathbf{V}^T - \mathbf{b}\mathbf{1}^T, \mathbf{U}\mathbf{U}^T = \mathbf{I} \quad (4)$$

We use the Augmented Lagrange Multiplier (ALM) method to solve this problem. ALM solves a sequences of subproblems

$$\min_{\mathbf{U}, \mathbf{V}, \mathbf{E}, \mathbf{b}} \|\mathbf{E}\|_1 + \mathrm{Tr} \quad \Omega^T(\mathbf{E} - \mathbf{X} + \mathbf{U}\mathbf{V}^T + \mathbf{b}\mathbf{1}^T) + \frac{2}{\mu}\|\mathbf{E} - \mathbf{X} + \mathbf{U}\mathbf{V}^T + \mathbf{b}\mathbf{1}^T\|_F^2$$
$$s.t. \quad \mathbf{U}\mathbf{U}^T = \mathbf{I} \quad (5)$$

where Ω is Lagrange multipliers and μ is the penalty parameter. There are two major parts of this algorithm, i.e., solving the sub-problem and updating parameters (Ω, μ).

First, we rewrite the objective function of Eq. (5) as

$$\min_{\mathbf{U}, \mathbf{V}, \mathbf{E}, \mathbf{b}} \|\mathbf{E}\|_1 + \frac{2}{\mu}\|\mathbf{E} - (\mathbf{X} - \mathbf{U}\mathbf{V}^T - \mathbf{b}\mathbf{1}^T + \frac{\Omega}{\mu})\|_F^2 \quad s.t. \quad \mathbf{U}\mathbf{U}^T = \mathbf{I} \quad (6)$$

Then, we iteratively solve the following sub-problems until convergence.

(1) Solve $\mathbf{U}, \mathbf{V}, \mathbf{b}$ while fixing $\mathbf{E}$. The problem becomes

$$\min_{\mathbf{U}, \mathbf{V}, \mathbf{b}} \|(\mathbf{X} - \mathbf{E} - \frac{\Omega}{\mu}) - \mathbf{b}\mathbf{1}^T - \mathbf{U}\mathbf{V}^T\|_F^2 \quad s.t. \quad \mathbf{U}\mathbf{U}^T = \mathbf{I} \quad (7)$$

This is standard MPCA [19] and can be solved effectively using a closed-form solution.

(2) Solve $\mathbf{E}$ while fixing $\mathbf{U}, \mathbf{V}, \mathbf{b}$. The problem becomes

$$\min_{\mathbf{E}} \|\mathbf{E}\|_1 + \frac{2}{\mu}\|\mathbf{E} - (\mathbf{X} - \mathbf{U}\mathbf{V}^T - \mathbf{b}\mathbf{1}^T + \frac{\Omega}{\mu})\|_F^2 \quad (8)$$

It is well known that, this problem has closed-form solution,

$$\mathbf{E}_{ij} = \text{sign}(\mathbf{K}_{ij})(|\mathbf{K}_{ij}| - \frac{1}{\mu})_+, \quad \mathbf{K} = \mathbf{X} - \mathbf{U}\mathbf{V}^{\mathrm{T}} - \mathbf{b}\mathbf{1}^{\mathrm{T}} + \frac{\Omega}{\mu} \qquad (9)$$

(3) At the end of each ALM iteration, Ω, μ are updated as

$$\Omega = \Omega + \mu(\mathbf{X} - \mathbf{U}\mathbf{V}^{\mathrm{T}} - \mathbf{E})$$
$$\mu = \rho\mu \qquad (10)$$

where $\rho > 1$.

4   Application: Image Set Representation and Classification

In this section, we apply the proposed L1-MPCA in image set representation and classification tasks. Our image set representation and classification method contains two main steps.

First, given an image set $\mathbf{X} = (\mathbf{x}_1, \mathbf{x}_2, \cdots \mathbf{x}_n)$, we first use the proposed L1-MPCA to compute the optimal $\mathbf{U}^*, \mathbf{V}^*$ and mean vector $\mathbf{b}^*$. We then obtain the optimal low-rank representation $\mathbf{Z}$ as

$$\mathbf{Z} = \mathbf{X} - \mathbf{U}^*\mathbf{V}^{*\mathrm{T}} - \mathbf{b}^*\mathbf{1}^{\mathrm{T}}$$

Comparing with the original image set data $\mathbf{X}$, the noises of images and outliers in image set $\mathbf{X}$ can be well suppressed in its low-rank representation $\mathbf{Z}$.

Second, based on low-rank representation $\mathbf{Z}$, we can use some image set feature extraction and learning methods such as Covariance Discriminative Learning (CDL) [22], Covariate-relation graph (CRG) [6] and Manifold-Manifold Distance (MMD) [23] to conduct image set classification tasks.

5   Experiments

To evaluate the effectiveness of the proposed L1-MPCA method, we apply it in image set representation and classification tasks. For image set learning methods, we use some recent methods: Covariance Discriminative Learning (CDL) [22], Covariate-relation graph (CRG) [6], Manifold-Manifold Distance (MMD) [23], Set to Set Distance Metric Learning (SSDML) [27] and Canonical Correlations (DCC) [15]. According to [23], MMD method does the subspaces learning with 95% data energy based on PCA. For the discriminative learning method of CDL, we choose PLS to do the learning task. For SSDML method, we set $\nu = 1, \lambda_1 = 0.001$ and $\lambda_2 = 0.1$.

5.1 Datasets and Settings

In our experiments, we test our L1-MPCA on four datasets including YouTube Celebrities (YTC) [14], ETH-80 [17], Honda/UCSD [16] and CMU MoBo [8]. In each image set data, we resize all the images into 20×20 intensity images. The datasets are described as following.

- ETH-80 [17] dataset has image sets of 8 categories and each category contains 10 objects with 41 views per object, spaced equally over the viewing hemisphere, for a total of 3280 images. For each subject of this dataset, we randomly choose 5 sets for training and the rest 5 object for testing.
- YouTube-Celebrities (YTC) [14] dataset contains 1910 video clips of 47 celebrities (actors and politicians), most of the videos are low resolution and highly compression, which leads to noisy, low-quality image frames. Each clip contains hundreds of frames. For this dataset, we randomly chose 3 sets for training and 6 sets for testing.
- Honda/UCSD [16] dataset consists of 59 video sequences belonging to 20 different persons. Each sequence contains about 400 frames covering large variations. Each individual in our database has at least two videos. For this dataset, we randomly select one sequence for training set and the rest for testing.
- CMU MoBo [8] dataset has 96 sequences of 24 persons and the sequences are captured from different walking situations inclined walk, and slow walk holding a ball (to inhibit arm swing). Each video further divided into four illumination sets, the first set for training and the rest sets for testing.

5.2 Results Analysis

To evaluate the benefit of the proposed L1-MPCA low-rank representation method, we compare our method with original data and L1-PCA method [2,13]. Figure 1 summarizes the average classification results on four datasets, respectively. (1) Comparing with original image set $\mathbf{X}$, the proposed L1-MPCA method can significantly improve the image set classification results, which clearly demonstrates the desired benefit and effectiveness of the proposed L1-MPCA method on conducting image set representation problem and thus leads to better classification result. (2) The proposed L1-MPCA methods generally performs better than L1-PCA method [2]. This clearly demonstrates the benefit of the proposed L1-MPCA by further considering the optimal mean vector value in low-rank representation.

5.3 Robust to Noise

To evaluate the robustness of L1-MPCA method to the noise possibly appearing in the testing image set data, we randomly add some noise to the image set datasets. Here, we add two kinds of noises including salt & pepper and block

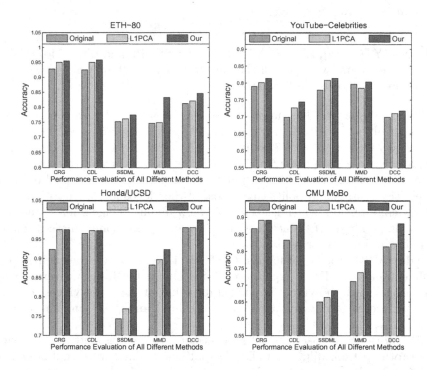

Fig. 1. Average accuracies of different methods on four datasets.

Table 1. Classification accuracies on ETH80 dataset with different noises.

Methods	Noisead	Salt & Pepper					Block noise				
		0.1	0.2	0.3	0.4	0.5	5	15	25	35	45
CDL	Original	0.800	0.700	0.625	0.583	0.425	0.833	0.750	0.708	0.637	0.405
	L1-PCA	0.875	0.739	0.667	0.617	0.458	0.901	0.843	0.763	0.665	0.567
	L1-MPCA	**0.917**	**0.845**	**0.738**	**0.708**	**0.667**	**0.922**	**0.861**	**0.783**	**0.696**	**0.607**
CRG	Original	0.875	0.800	0.775	0.653	0.550	0.875	0.833	0.747	0.675	0.475
	L1-PCA	0.901	0.833	0.797	0.732	0.625	0.911	0.866	0.774	0.697	0.583
	L1-MPCA	**0.916**	**0.875**	**0.811**	**0.767**	**0.673**	**0.937**	**0.875**	**0.801**	**0.721**	**0.595**
MMD	Original	0.712	0.625	0.550	0.525	0.475	0.666	0.583	0.500	0.466	0.431
	L1-PCA	0.750	0.667	0.625	0.542	0.491	0.776	0.673	0.575	0.533	0.461
	L1-MPCA	**0.811**	**0.708**	**0.650**	**0.593**	**0.500**	**0.807**	**0.767**	**0.702**	**0.647**	**0.573**
SSDML	Original	0.700	0.650	0.575	0.473	0.438	0.708	0.671	0.583	0.501	0.467
	L1-PCA	0.733	0.666	0.583	0.483	0.443	0.750	0.683	0.596	0.511	0.475
	L1-MPCA	**0.767**	**0.708**	**0.611**	**0.573**	**0.542**	**0.783**	**0.713**	**0.633**	**0.575**	**0.511**
DCC	Original	0.733	0.613	0.553	0.437	0.339	0.700	0.627	0.566	0.483	0.408
	L1-PCA	0.803	0.722	0.637	0.583	0.524	0.788	0.718	0.643	0.522	0.466
	L1-MPCA	**0.833**	**0.797**	**0.703**	**0.627**	**0.573**	**0.800**	**0.758**	**0.650**	**0.567**	**0.511**

Table 2. Classification accuracies on YTC dataset with different noises.

Methods	Noisead	Salt & Pepper					Block noise				
		0.1	0.2	0.3	0.4	0.5	5	15	25	35	45
CDL	Original	0.651	0.573	0.432	0.358	0.238	0.650	0.510	0.413	0.366	0.227
	L1-PCA	0.703	0.654	0.587	0.422	0.317	0.713	0.654	**0.583**	**0.471**	0.328
	L1-MPCA	**0.709**	**0.666**	**0.595**	**0.433**	**0.344**	**0.733**	**0.682**	0.573	0.453	**0.393**
CRG	Original	0.742	0.666	0.521	0.453	0.373	0.707	0.611	0.532	0.444	0.309
	L1-PCA	0.771	0.683	0.511	**0.475**	**0.383**	0.783	0.627	0.575	0.467	0.350
	L1-MPCA	**0.783**	**0.683**	**0.537**	0.465	0.377	**0.802**	**0.741**	**0.666**	**0.583**	**0.405**
MMD	Original	0.701	0.621	0.575	0.466	0.393	0.696	0.605	0.528	0.499	0.336
	L1-PCA	0.766	0.666	**0.611**	0.505	0.423	0.750	0.653	**0.583**	0.511	0.471
	L1-MPCA	**0.783**	**0.683**	0.601	**0.542**	**0.447**	**0.778**	**0.683**	0.566	**0.533**	**0.505**
SSDML	Original	0.701	0.621	0.531	0.401	0.389	0.711	0.627	0.550	0.448	0.342
	L1-PCA	0.773	0.646	0.562	0.473	0.382	0.766	0.631	0.575	**0.499**	0.377
	L1-MPCA	**0.792**	**0.696**	**0.583**	**0.481**	**0.393**	**0.773**	**0.674**	**0.586**	0.473	**0.383**
DCC	Original	0.656	0.567	0.441	0.397	0.217	0.683	0.578	0.450	0.349	0.207
	L1-PCA	0.697	0.577	0.465	**0.453**	0.311	0.721	0.649	0.557	0.467	0.350
	L1-MPCA	**0.703**	**0.650**	**0.583**	0.437	**0.343**	**0.727**	**0.673**	**0.579**	**0.483**	**0.366**

Table 3. Classification accuracies on Honda dataset with different noises.

Methods	Noisead	Salt & Pepper					Block noise				
		0.1	0.2	0.3	0.4	0.5	5	15	25	35	45
CDL	Original	0.871	0.799	0.730	0.666	0.432	0.883	0.777	0.653	0.577	0.450
	L1-PCA	0.875	0.783	**0.741**	0.696	0.601	0.911	0.833	0.713	0.641	0.522
	L1-MPCA	**0.916**	**0.833**	0.731	**0.700**	**0.626**	**0.921**	**0.850**	**0.743**	**0.650**	**0.583**
CRG	Original	0.910	0.811	0.696	0.633	0.473	0.899	0.751	0.583	0.434	0.405
	L1-PCA	0.948	0.833	0.701	0.650	0.515	0.911	0.811	0.637	0.557	0.466
	L1-MPCA	**0.950**	**0.844**	**0.733**	**0.666**	**0.533**	**0.937**	**0.823**	**0.710**	**0.595**	**0.511**
MMD	Original	0.871	0.734	0.590	0.550	0.433	0.846	0.711	0.573	0.466	0.437
	L1-PCA	0.866	0.750	0.611	0.576	0.433	0.897	0.801	0.695	0.505	0.444
	L1-MPCA	**0.883**	**0.786**	**0.650**	**0.592**	**0.498**	**0.901**	**0.811**	**0.722**	**0.583**	**0.466**
SSDML	Original	0.743	0.666	0.511	0.433	0.399	0.718	0.635	0.544	0.473	0.366
	L1-PCA	0.769	0.683	0.573	0.450	0.409	0.766	0.677	0.595	0.500	0.415
	L1-MPCA	**0.794**	**0.693**	**0.610**	**0.493**	**0.433**	**0.808**	**0.731**	**0.606**	**0.593**	**0.511**
DCC	Original	0.950	0.883	0.766	0.613	0.526	0.943	0.837	0.727	0.579	0.433
	L1-PCA	0.967	**0.922**	0.776	0.696	0.633	0.950	0.871	0.733	0.652	0.566
	L1-MPCA	**0.983**	0.911	**0.797**	**0.701**	**0.650**	**0.974**	**0.883**	**0.766**	**0.666**	**0.583**

noise. For each kind of noise, we add various levels of the noises and test our method on these noise image set data. Tables 1, 2, 3 and 4 show the accuracies of all the traditional methods across different noise level. From the results, we can note that: (1) As the level of noise increasing. Our L1-MPCA method still maintains better performance comparing with the original image set data. This obviously indicates the noise removing ability of the proposed L1-MPCA method. (2) L1-MPCA performs better than L1-PCA method [2], indicating the more robustness of the L1-MPCA method on noise data reconstruction.

Table 4. Classification accuracies on CMU dataset with different noises.

Methods	Noisead	Salt & Pepper					Block noise				
		0.1	0.2	0.3	0.4	0.5	5	15	25	35	45
CDL	Original	0.797	0.691	0.618	0.543	0.344	0.808	0.750	0.666	0.487	0.301
	L1-PCA	0.833	0.766	0.650	0.575	0.483	0.827	0.775	0.683	0.506	0.466
	L1-MPCA	**0.850**	**0.799**	**0.723**	**0.644**	**0.490**	**0.866**	**0.818**	**0.750**	**0.566**	**0.482**
CRG	Original	0.825	0.766	0.671	0.543	0.321	0.803	0.733	0.683	0.450	0.320
	L1-PCA	0.873	0.800	**0.743**	0.628	0.495	0.850	0.766	0.679	0.637	0.449
	L1-MPCA	**0.875**	**0.810**	0.723	**0.683**	**0.506**	**0.866**	**0.797**	**0.683**	**0.650**	**0.455**
MMD	Original	0.711	0.622	0.533	0.505	0.341	0.666	0.550	0.471	0.416	0.283
	L1-PCA	0.750	0.683	0.621	0.575	0.483	0.776	0.707	0.650	0.571	0.361
	L1-MPCA	**0.811**	**0.755**	**0.643**	**0.591**	**0.513**	**0.807**	**0.732**	**0.666**	**0.583**	**0.421**
SSDML	Original	0.696	0.611	0.550	0.466	0.377	0.700	0.650	0.541	0.483	0.322
	L1-PCA	0.703	0.647	0.595	0.517	0.466	0.717	**0.666**	0.606	0.533	0.450
	L1-MPCA	**0.731**	**0.650**	**0.601**	**0.543**	**0.483**	**0.733**	0.650	**0.622**	**0.571**	**0.500**
DCC	Original	0.783	0.711	0.637	0.550	0.366	0.803	0.733	0.677	0.543	0.391
	L1-PCA	0.791	0.710	**0.672**	0.606	0.450	0.845	0.750	0.683	0.577	0.411
	L1-MPCA	**0.810**	**0.737**	0.666	**0.611**	**0.473**	**0.850**	**0.758**	**0.683**	**0.601**	**0.483**

6   Conclusion

In this paper, we propose a new method, called L_1 norm Mean PCA (L1-MPCA) model for image set representation and learning problems. L1-MPCA is robust to both noises and outliers, which encourages robust image set learning tasks. An effective update algorithm has been proposed to solve the proposed L1-MPCA model. Experimental results on several datasets show the benefit and robustness of the proposed L1-MPCA method. In our future, we will further consider the manifold structure of data in our L1-MPCA model.

Acknowledgment. This work is supported by the National Natural Science Foundation of China (61602001, 61472002, 61671018); Natural Science Foundation of Anhui Province (1708085QF139); Natural Science Foundation of Anhui Higher Education Institutions of China (KJ2016A020); Co-Innovation Center for Information Supply & Assurance Technology, Anhui University The Open Projects Program of National Laboratory of Pattern Recognition.

References

1. Arandjelovic, O., Shakhnarovich, G., Fisher, J., Cipolla, R., Darrell, T.: Face recognition with image sets using manifold density divergence. In: 2005 IEEE Conference on Computer Vision and Pattern Recognition (CVPR), pp. 581–588. IEEE (2005)
2. Cao, Y., Jiang, B., Chen, Z., Tang, J., Luo, B.: Low-rank image set representation and classification. In: Liu, C.-L., Hussain, A., Luo, B., Tan, K.C., Zeng, Y., Zhang, Z. (eds.) BICS 2016. LNCS (LNAI), vol. 10023, pp. 321–330. Springer, Cham (2016). https://doi.org/10.1007/978-3-319-49685-6_29

3. Cevikalp, H., Triggs, B.: Face recognition based on image sets. In: 2010 IEEE Conference on Computer Vision and Pattern Recognition (CVPR), pp. 2567–2573. IEEE (2010)
4. Chen, S., Sanderson, C., Harandi, M.T., Lovell, B.C.: Improved image set classification via joint sparse approximated nearest subspaces. In: 2013 IEEE Conference on Computer Vision and Pattern Recognition (CVPR), pp. 452–459. IEEE (2013)
5. Chen, S., Wiliem, A., Sanderson, C., Lovell, B.C.: Matching image sets via adaptive multi convex hull. In: 2014 IEEE Winter Conference on Applications of Computer Vision (WACV), pp. 1074–1081. IEEE (2014)
6. Chen, Z., Jiang, B., Tang, J., Luo, B.: Image set representation and classification with covariate-relation graph. In: IEEE Conference on Asian Conference and Pattern Recognition (ACPR), pp. 750–754. IEEE (2015)
7. Cui, Z., Shan, S., Zhang, H., Lao, S., Chen, X.: Image sets alignment for video-based face recognition. In: 2012 IEEE Conference on Computer Vision and Pattern Recognition (CVPR), pp. 2626–2633. IEEE (2012)
8. Gross, R., Shi, J.: The CMU motion of body (MoBo) database. Technical report CMU-RI-TR-01-18, Robotics Institute, Carnegie Mellon University (2001)
9. Hamm, J., Lee, D.D.: Grassmann discriminant analysis: a unifying view on subspace-based learning. In: Proceedings of the 25th International Conference on Machine Learning, pp. 376–383. ACM (2008)
10. Harandi, M.T., Sanderson, C., Shirazi, S., Lovell, B.C.: Graph embedding discriminant analysis on grassmannian manifolds for improved image set matching. In: 2011 IEEE Conference on Computer Vision and Pattern Recognition (CVPR), pp. 2705–2712. IEEE (2011)
11. Hu, Y., Mian, A.S., Owens, R.: Sparse approximated nearest points for image set classification. In: 2011 IEEE Conference on Computer Vision and Pattern Recognition (CVPR), pp. 121–128. IEEE (2011)
12. Jiang, B., Ding, C., Luo, B., Tang, J.: Graph-laplacian PCA: closed-form solution and robustness. In: 2013 IEEE Conference on Computer Vision and Pattern Recognition (CVPR), pp. 3492–3498. IEEE (2013)
13. Ke, Q., Kanade, T.: Robust L1 norm factorization in the presence of outliers and missing data by alternative convex programming. In 2005 IEEE Conference on Computer Vision and Pattern Recognition (CVPR), pp. 739–746. IEEE (2005)
14. Kim, M., Kumar, S., Pavlovic, V., Rowley, H.: Face tracking and recognition with visual constraints in real-world videos. In: 2008 IEEE Conference on Computer Vision and Pattern Recognition (CVPR), pp. 1–8. IEEE (2008)
15. Kim, T.-K., Kittler, J., Cipolla, R.: Discriminative learning and recognition of image set classes using canonical correlations. IEEE Trans. Pattern Anal. Mach. Intell. **29**(6), 1005–1018 (2007)
16. Lee, K.-C., Ho, J., Yang, M.-H., Kriegman, D.: Video-based face recognition using probabilistic appearance manifolds. In: 2003 IEEE Conference on Computer Vision and Pattern Recognition (CVPR), pp. I–313. IEEE (2003)
17. Leibe, B., Schiele, B.: Analyzing appearance and contour based methods for object categorization. In: 2003 IEEE Conference on Computer Vision and Pattern Recognition (CVPR), pp. II–409. IEEE (2003)
18. Lu, J., Wang, G., Moulin, P.: Image set classification using holistic multiple order statistics features and localized multi-kernel metric learning. In: 2013 IEEE International Conference on Computer Vision (ICCV), pp. 329–336. IEEE (2013)
19. Nie, F., Yuan, J., Huang, H.: Optimal mean robust principal component analysis. In: Proceedings of the 31st International Conference on International Conference on Machine Learning, vol. 32, pp. 1062–1070 (2014)

20. Shakhnarovich, G., Fisher, J.W., Darrell, T.: Face recognition from long-term observations. In: Heyden, A., Sparr, G., Nielsen, M., Johansen, P. (eds.) ECCV 2002 Part III. LNCS, vol. 2352, pp. 851–865. Springer, Heidelberg (2002). https://doi.org/10.1007/3-540-47977-5_56

21. Wang, R., Chen, X.: Manifold discriminant analysis. In: 2009 IEEE Conference on Computer Vision and Pattern Recognition (CVPR), pp. 429–436. IEEE (2009)

22. Wang, R., Guo, H., Davis, L.S., Dai, Q.: Covariance discriminative learning: a natural and efficient approach to image set classification. In: 2012 IEEE Conference on Computer Vision and Pattern Recognition (CVPR), pp. 2496–2503. IEEE (2012)

23. Wang, R., Shan, S., Chen, X., Gao, W.: Manifold-manifold distance with application to face recognition based on image set. In: 2008 IEEE Conference on Computer Vision and Pattern Recognition (CVPR), pp. 1–8. IEEE (2008)

24. Wang, W., Wang, R., Huang, Z., Shan, S., Chen, X.: Discriminant analysis on Riemannian manifold of Gaussian distributions for face recognition with image sets. In: 2015 IEEE Conference on Computer Vision and Pattern Recognition (CVPR), pp. 2048–2057. IEEE (2015)

25. Yamaguchi, O., Fukui, K., Maeda, K.-I.: Face recognition using temporal image sequence. In: 1998 Proceedings of the Third IEEE International Conference on Automatic Face and Gesture Recognition, pp. 318–323. IEEE (1998)

26. Yang, M., Zhu, P., Van Gool, L., Zhang, L.: Face recognition based on regularized nearest points between image sets. In: 2013 10th IEEE International Conference and Workshops on Automatic Face and Gesture Recognition (FG), pp. 1–7. IEEE (2013)

27. Zhu, P., Zhang, L., Zuo, W., Zhang, D.: From point to set: extend the learning of distance metrics. In: 2013 IEEE International Conference on Computer Vision (ICCV), pp. 2664–2671. IEEE (2013)

Object Tracking Based on Multi-modality Dictionary Learning

Jing Wang, Hong Zhu$^{(\boxtimes)}$, Shan Xue, and Jing Shi

Faculty of Automation and Information Engineering,
Xi'an University of Technology, Xi'an 710048, China
jjing63@hotmail.com, zhuhong@xaut.edu.cn,
xueshanmath@163.com, shijing1003@163.com

Abstract. Sparse representation based methods have been increasingly applied to object tracking. However, complex optimization and a single dictionary limit their deployment during tracking. In this paper, we propose a tracking method based on multi-modality dictionary learning in particle filter framework. First, multi-modality dictionary is formed by background templates and object templates including short-term templates and long-term templates that are updated by K-means clustering. Second, coarse tracking results are achieved by computing the coefficients of object with respect to templates from multi-modality dictionary. Finally, the Local Maximal Occurrence (LOMO) features of coarse tracking results and multi-modality dictionary are compared through observation likelihood function, a candidate result with highest observation score is regarded as the final tracking result. The experimental results demonstrated the effectiveness of our method compared to some state-of-the-art methods.

Keywords: Object tracking · Multi-modality dictionary · Particle filter
K-means clustering

1 Introduction

Object tracking plays an important role in computer vision, which has been widely used in the field of surveillance, intelligent transportation control, medical image and military simulation [1] etc. Even though numerous tracking problems have been studied for decades, and reasonable good results have been achieved, it is still challenging to track general objects in a dynamic environment accurately due to various factors that include noise, occlusion, background cluttering, illumination changes, fast motions, and variations in pose and scale. At present, most of state-of-the-art object tracking methods can be categorized into two types: generative models and discriminative models [2].

The generative methods take the candidate having the best compatibility with the appearance model as the tracked object. For example, Ross et al. proposed an incremental subspace model to adapt object appearance variation [3]. Wang et al. put forward multi-features fusion object model under the guidance of color-feature, and tracking object accurately is realized by the principle of spatial consistency [4]. Wang et al. proposed a probability continuous outlier model to cope with partial occlusion via

© Springer International Publishing AG 2017
Y. Zhao et al. (Eds.): ICIG 2017, Part II, LNCS 10667, pp. 129–138, 2017.
https://doi.org/10.1007/978-3-319-71589-6_12

holistic object template [5]. The latter addresses object tracking as a binary classification to separate the object from background. For example, Kalal et al. first utilized structured unlabeled data and used an online semi-supervised learning method [6], then tracking-learning-detection (TLD) for object tracking in long sequences is proposed subsequently [7]. Babenkon et al. formulated object tracking as an online multiple instance learning [8]. Generally speaking, the former can get more accurate characteristic of object but with high computational complexity. The latter can obtain better tracking accuracy but has to process a large number of training samples. Object needs to be retrained if its appearance changed, and tracking failure can be easily caused by inadequate training samples. In addition, there are some combine both generative and discriminative models [9–11] to get more desirable results.

Recently, sparse representation based methods [9–13] have shown promising results in various tests. Object is represented as a linear combination of a few templates, which are helpful to remove the influences from partial occlusion, illumination and other factors on object based on sparse coding. However, this kind of method is based on solving ℓ_1 minimization that has large computational load, and sparse code is solved by complex optimization. Therefore, a multi-modality dictionary is built in this paper to simplify the sparse coding, and then follow the idea of combination of generative and discriminative to achieve object tracking.

The remainder of this paper is organized as follows. In Sect. 2, particle filter and object representation that are related to our work are reviewed. Section 3 introduces the details of the proposed tracking method. Experimental results and analysis are shown in Sect. 4, and we conclude this paper in Sect. 5.

2 Preliminary

2.1 Particle Filter

Particle filter as the tracking framework in this paper, the object of the next frame is estimated by the observation probability of particles at the current frame [14]. Suppose $Y_t = [y_1, \ldots, y_t]$ are observed images at frames 1 to t, x_t is the state variable that describing object motion parameters at frame t, and follows the following probability distribution:

$$p(x_t \mid Y_t) \propto p(y_t \mid x_t) \int p(x_t \mid x_{t-1}) p(x_{t-1} \mid Y_{t-1}) dx_{t-1} \qquad (1)$$

where $p(x_t \mid x_{t-1})$ is state transition distribution, $p(y_t \mid x_t)$ estimates the likelihood of observing y_t at state x_t. Particles are sampled as Gaussian distribution with the center position of previous tracking result. As the number of particles will affect the tracking efficiency, irrelevant particles need to be filtered to reduce the tracking redundancy.

2.2 Object Representation

Liao et al. proposed Local Maximal Occurrence (LOMO) feature [15] for the performance of the target in different cameras is inconsistent, which is an effective handmade feature that can be compared with the characteristics of deep learning network in recent years. The LOMO feature analyzes the horizontal occurrence of local features, and maximizes the occurrence to make a stable representation against viewpoint changes. Specifically, the Retinex algorithm is firstly applied to produce a color image that is consistent to human observation of the scene, then HSV color histogram is used to extract color features of Retinex images, finally, Scale Invariant Local Ternary Pattern (SILTP) descriptor [16] is applied to achieve invariance to intensity scale changes and robustness to image noises.

Since the challenging problems in object tracking and person re-identification are actually the same, in view of the validity of the LOMO feature has been verified, the LOMO feature as the object feature in this paper.

3   Proposed Method

In this paper, object tracking is regarded as the dictionary learning problem. By constructing multi-modality dictionary properly that can describe object precisely, thus the complex optimization can be simplified. The proposed tracking method is presented in Algorithm 1.

Algorithm 1: Proposed Tracking Method

Input: image at frame t
Output: tracking result $\hat{x}_t$ of image at frame t
Initialization: construct the multi-modality dictionary by using the first frame of a video
Tracking:
for t=2:end of the video
    1.   Sample particles based on the tracking result of previous frame, and candidates are filtered by the distance constraint;
    2.   Solve the coefficients of candidates with respect to multi-modality dictionary using the LARS method;
    3.   Get the candidate tracking results R according to the coefficients of each candidate (Eq. (6));
    4.   Compute the observation likelihood score of each candidate result from R by Eq. (8);
    5.   Candidate with the highest observation score is regarded as the final tracking result;
    6.   Update the multi-modality dictionary through K-means clustering (Sect. 3.1).
end for

3.1   Multi-modality Dictionary Building and Updating

In general, sparse representation based tracking method usually uses over-complete dictionary to encode the object. Sparse code learning involves two problems: sparse coding that is to solve the computation of the coefficients to represent the object with the learned dictionary, and dictionary learning that is to solve the problem of constructing the dictionary [17]. With the sparse assumption, a candidate object x_i can be represented as a linear combination of sparse code α_i from dictionary D. The sparse code $\alpha_i \in \mathbb{R}^{n+m}$ corresponding to x_i is calculated by

$$\min_{\alpha_i} \frac{1}{2} \|x_i - D\alpha_i\|_2^2 + \lambda \|\alpha_i\|_1 \tag{2}$$

where over-complete dictionary $D = [D_p, D_n] \in \mathbb{R}^{d \times (n+m)}$ that is formed by the foreground dictionary $D_p \in \mathbb{R}^{d \times n}$ and background dictionary $D_n \in \mathbb{R}^{d \times m}$. The above problem is also referred to as dictionary learning, which is actually the Lasso regression [18] that can be solved by LARS [19], and then get the sparse code α_i of x_i.

However, the method mentioned above not only requires a large number of templates for over-complete dictionary, but also makes the tracking process more complicated. Actually, for objects in the ideal state without severe external influences, a small number of dictionary templates can distinguish objects from background well; for objects with appearance changed, more dictionary templates will bring many errors. So if a suitable dictionary for the current object can be obtained in real time, there is no need to build over-complete dictionary and experience complex optimization process.

In this paper, object dictionary is formed by short-term templates D_s and long-term templates D_l, the templates of background dictionary D_n are selected randomly from non-object area of video image. Therefore, multi-modality dictionary D is built by the two parts, that is $D = [D^S, D^L]$, where $D^S = [D_s, D_n] \in \mathbb{R}^{d \times (m_s + n_s)}$, $D^L = [D_l, D_n] \in \mathbb{R}^{d \times (m_l + n_l)}$, and the dictionary template is represented by the observed pixel values. More specifically, D_s is initialized by the transformed object templates of the first frame, that is the current object moves 1–2 pixels along four directions (up, down, left and right). D_l is initialized by the clustering center of D_s, that is $D_l = \frac{1}{l_s} \sum_{i=1}^{l_s} D_s^{(i)}$, where l_s represents the number of templates in D_s, here let $l_s = 9$. It should be noted that the observation vector of each template usually constraints its columns to have ℓ_2-norm less than or equal to 1.

For multi-modality dictionary, when object appearance changes little, short-term dictionary can distinguish object from background effectively, and long-term dictionary can reduce errors accumulation; when object appearance changes greatly, short-term dictionary can track object continuously, and long-term dictionary can prevent loss of correct sampled object. Thus, the combination of two modality dictionaries can better balance the adaptability and robustness of ℓ_1 trackers, and it is crucial for updating multi-modality dictionary. D_s is trained and updated using the candidates sampled in the previous frame. D_l is trained and updated using accurate result in all previous frames, and then according to the theory of K-means clustering, the category that the current object belongs to is identified by calculating the Euclidean distance between the current object and the clustering centers of long-term dictionary, as shown in Eq. (3). The long-term dictionary is represented by the cluster center of each category, which reduces the amount of computation effectively.

$$\begin{cases} x^t \in D_l^{c^i}, & d\left(f(x^t), f\left(D_l^{c^i}\right)\right) \in [0, d\_max + \Delta] \\ x^t \in D_l^{c^{new}}, & d\left(f(x^t), f\left(D_l^{c^i}\right)\right) > d\_max + \Delta \end{cases} \tag{3}$$

where $D_l^{c^i}$ represents the existed category of long-term dictionary, $D_l^{c^{new}}$ represents the new category of long-term dictionary, $d(\cdot)$ denotes Euclidean distance, $f(\cdot)$ indicates the corresponding LOMO feature, d_max represents the maximum value of Euclidean distance between templates $d(D_s, D_s')$ in initialized short-term dictionary D_s, and Δ is variable.

3.2 Tracking Based on Multi-modality Dictionary

The proposed method is based on particle filter framework, and all the sampled particles are expressed as $Y = \{y_1, y_2, \ldots, y_N\} \in \mathbb{R}^{d \times N}$. Then irrelevant particles are filtered by the distance constraint that is the distance between the center coordinate of the sampled object $p(y_i^t)$ and the center coordinate of tracking result of previous frame $p(x_{t-1})$ should meet $\|p(y_i^t) - p(x_{t-1})\|_2 \leq \max(w, h)$, where w and h represent the width and height of bounding box of previous tracking result respectively. The candidate samples are expressed as $X = \{x^i \mid i \in [1, q]\} \in \mathbb{R}^{d \times q}(q \ll N)$.

Assuming that the multi-modality dictionary can be adapt to the object appearance changes well, the value of the cost function between the ideal tracking result and the templates of object dictionary should be minimal. The cost function of short-term dictionary and long-term dictionary are expressed as Eqs. (4) and (5) respectively. Then the best coefficients are solved using the LARS method [19].

$$l_S(x^i, D^S) = \min_{\alpha_s^i} \frac{1}{2} \|x^i - D^S \cdot \alpha_s^i\|_2^2 + \lambda \|\alpha_s^i\|_1 \tag{4}$$

$$l_L(x^i, D^L) = \min_{\alpha_l^i} \frac{1}{2} \|x^i - D^L \cdot \alpha_l^i\|_2^2 + \lambda \|\alpha_l^i\|_1 \tag{5}$$

Generally, an image observation of a "good" object candidate is effectively represented by the object templates and not the background templates, thereby, leading to a sparse representation. Likewise, an image observation of a "bad" object candidate can be more sparsely represented by a dictionary of background templates. Therefore, for ideal sampled object, the difference between the $\ell_1 - norm$ of coefficients of object templates and background templates should be larger. Then the candidate tracking results R are formed by the first p samples satisfying the condition, as shown in Eqs. (6) and (7).

$$R = [R_S, R_L] = \left[I_S^i\big|_p, I_L^i\big|_p\right] \quad (i \in [1, q]) \tag{6}$$

$$\begin{aligned} I_S^i &= \max\left(\|\alpha_{s+}^i\|_1 - \|\alpha_{s-}^i\|_1\right) \\ I_L^i &= \max\left(\|\alpha_{l+}^i\|_1 - \|\alpha_{l-}^i\|_1\right) \end{aligned} \tag{7}$$

where α^i_{s+} and α^i_{s-} represent the coefficients of object templates and background templates in short-term dictionary, α^i_{l+} and α^i_{l-} represent the coefficients of object templates and background templates in long-term dictionary.

Eventually, the observation likelihood function is built for each candidate tracking result, then the candidate tracking result with the highest similarity is regarded as the final tracking result $\hat{x}$, as shown in Eqs. (8–9).

$$\hat{x} = \arg\max(\omega_s \cdot s_s + \omega_l \cdot s_l) \quad s_l = sim\big(f(R^j_L), f(D_L)\big) \tag{8}$$

$$\begin{aligned} s_s &= sim\big(f(R^j_s), f(D_S)\big) \\ s_l &= sim\big(f(R^j_L), f(D_L)\big) \end{aligned} \quad j \in [1, p] \tag{9}$$

where $sim(\cdot)$ represent the similarity that is calculated by Bhattacharyya distance, $f(\cdot)$ is the LOMO feature of the corresponding image area. $\omega_s = s_s/(s_s + s_l)$ and $\omega_s = s_s/(s_s + s_l)$ are the weights.

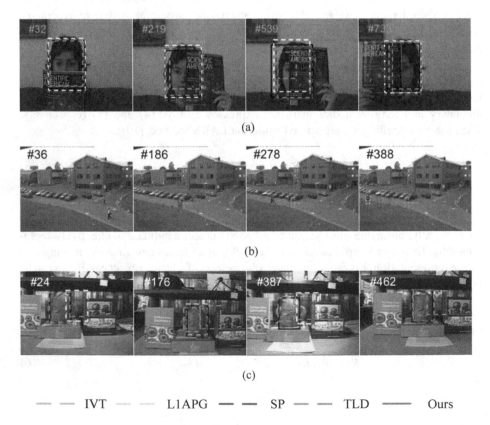

(a)

(b)

(c)

— — IVT — — L1APG — — SP — — TLD —— Ours

Fig. 1. Some representative results of test sequences. (a) *FaceOcc1*; (b) *Walking*; (c) *Fish*.

4 Experiments and Analysis

The test video sequences (*FaceOcc1*, *Walking* and *Fish*) are selected from object tracking benchmark [1]. We test four state-of-the-art methods on the same video sequences for comparison. They are IVT [3], L1APG [13], TLD [7] and SP [5]. The code of all those trackers are public available, and we keep the parameter settings provided by authors for all the test sequences. In this paper, we use the error rate (*error*) and overlap rate (*overlap*) to evaluate the tracking performance of each tracking method. *error* is the Euclidean distance between the center coordinate obtained from tracking method and tracking ground truth, which means the smaller the value, the more accurate position the method tracks. *overlap* is the overlap ratio between the tracking window of the method and the ideal tracking window, which means the larger the value, the more suitable window the method has. Figure 1 shows some representative results of test sequences.

Tracking error plots and tracking overlap plots for all the test sequences are shown in Figs. 2 and 3. The main tracking problem in *FaceOcc1* is that the object is occluded in large area for a long time. TLD fails to track when object is occluded in large area,

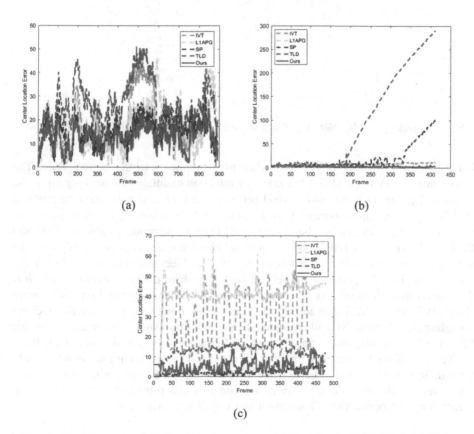

(a)

(b)

(c)

Fig. 2. Tracking error plots for all test sequences. (a) *FaceOcc1*; (b) *Walking*; (c) *Fish*.

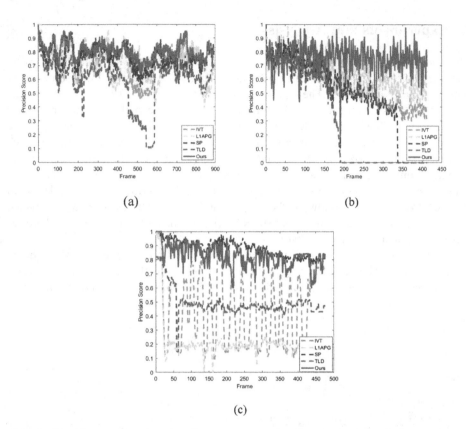

Fig. 3. Tracking overlap plots for all test sequences. (a) *FaceOcc1*; (b) *Walking*; (c) *Fish*.

but it can back to track object well when object remains in the normal state. The performance of IVT, L1APG, SP and our method can maintain low tracking error and high overlap rate, in which, our method performs the best. The main tracking problem in *Walking* is partially occlusion and object scales variation. When object scale becomes small, object cannot be distinguished from background clearly, so TLD and SP lose object. IVT, L1APG and our method can track object continuously, but the tracking bounding box of IVT is too large to fit the object size. Our method performs the best and L1APG performs the second best. The main tracking problem in *Fish* is the illumination changes. As the object is affected by the illumination and camera shake, IVT and L1APG start to drift. TLD can track object roughly, but the tracking bounding box is small. SP and our method show the promising performance, in which SP is the best tracker, and there is a slightly difference between SP and our method.

Table 1 shows the mean of tracking error and tracking overlap rate, in which bold fonts indicate the best performance while the Italic underlined fonts indicate the second best ones. From these data, we can conclude that the proposed method has good performance on occlusions, illumination and object scale variation, etc.

Table 1. The mean of tracking error and tracking overlap rate.

Method	FaceOcc1		Walking		Fish	
	error (pixel)	overlap (%)	error (pixel)	overlap (%)	error (pixel)	overlap (%)
IVT	17.92	74.92	7.62	56.57	24.42	47.38
L1APG	16.99	71.57	*2.92*	*65.34*	40.70	21.43
SP	*14.61*	*75.13*	19.32	48.88	**2.48**	**88.38**
TLD	27.38	59.69	95.89	29.06	13.22	49.54
Ours	**13.73**	**80.46**	**2.23**	**75.29**	*4.08*	*82.62*

5   Conclusions

In this paper, object tracking method based on multi-modality dictionary is proposed, which addresses object tracking as a problem of learning a dictionary that can represent object accurately. Under the particle filter framework, a multi-modality dictionary is built and updated by clustering, which makes the candidate tracking result can be obtained easily by comparing the coefficients difference with respect to multi-modality dictionary. And then the final tracking result is determined by calculating observation function precisely through employing LOMO feature. By applying some benchmark videos, the experimental results show that the proposed method is more robust against occlusions, illumination changes and background interference.

Acknowledgment. This work is supported in part by National Natural Science Foundation of China (No. 61673318), Natural Science Basic Research Plan in Shaanxi Province of China (No. 2016JM6045) and Scientist Research Program Funded by Shaanxi Provincial Education Department (No. 16JK1571).

References

1. Wu, Y., Lim, J., Yang, M.-H.: Online object tracking: a benchmark. In: Proceedings of IEEE Computer Society Conference on Computer Vision and Pattern Recognition, pp. 2411–2418 (2013)
2. Li, X., Hu, W., Shen, C., Zhang, Z., Dick, A., Hengel, A.V.D.: A survey of appearance models in visual object tracking. ACM Trans. Intell. Syst. Technol. 4(4), 478–488 (2013)
3. Ross, D., Lim, J., Lin, R.-S., Yang, M.-H.: Incremental learning for robust visual tracking. Int. J. Comput. Vis. 77, 125–141 (2008)
4. Wang, J., Zhu, H., Yu, S., Fan, C.: Object tracking using color-feature guided network generalization and tailored feature fusion. Neurocomputing 238, 387–398 (2017)
5. Wang, D., Lu, H., Yang, M.-H.: Online object tracking with sparse prototypes. IEEE Trans. Image Process. 22, 314–325 (2013)
6. Kalal, Z., Matas, J., Mikolajczyk, K.: P-N learning: bootstrapping binary classifiers by structural constraints. Comput. Vis. Pattern Recognit. 238(6), 49–56 (2010)
7. Kalal, Z., Mikolajczyk, K., Matas, J.: Tracking-learning-detection. IEEE Trans. Pattern Anal. Mach. Intell. 34, 1409–1422 (2012)

8. Babenko, B., Yang, M.-H., Belongie, S.: Robust object tracking with online multiple instance learning. IEEE Trans. Pattern Anal. Mach. Intell. **33**, 1619–1632 (2011)
9. Zhong, W., Lu, H., Yang, M.-H.: Robust object tracking via sparsity-based collaborative model. In: Proceedings of IEEE Computer Society Conference on Computer Vision and Pattern Recognition, pp. 1838–1845 (2012)
10. Wang, N., Wang, J., Yeung, D.Y.: Online robust non-negative dictionary learning for visual tracking. In: Proceedings of IEEE Computer Society Conference on Computer Vision, pp. 657–664 (2013)
11. Xing, J., Gao, J., Li, B., Hu, W., Yan, S.: Robust object tracking with online multi-lifespan dictionary learning. In: Proceedings of IEEE Computer Society Conference on Computer Vision, pp. 665–672 (2013)
12. Mei, X., Ling, H.: Robust visual tracking and vehicle classification via sparse representation. IEEE Trans. Pattern Anal. Mach. Intell. **33**, 2259–2272 (2011)
13. Bao, C., Wu, Y., Ling, H., Ji, H.: Real time robust L1 tracker using accelerated proximal gradient approach. In: Proceedings of IEEE Computer Society Conference on Computer Vision, pp. 1830–1837 (2012)
14. Chang, C., Ansari, R.: Kernel particle filter for visual tracking. IEEE Sig. Process. Lett. **12**, 242–245 (2005)
15. Liao, S., Hu, Y., Zhu, X., Li, S.Z.: Person re-identification by local maximal occurrence representation and metric learning. In: Proceedings of IEEE Computer Society Conference on Computer Vision and Pattern Recognition, pp. 2197–2206 (2015)
16. Liao, S., Zhao, G., Kellokumpu, V., Pietikäinen, M., Li, S.Z.: Modeling pixel process with scale invariant local patterns for background subtraction in complex scenes. In: Proceedings of IEEE Computer Society Conference on Computer Vision and Pattern Recognition, pp. 1301–1306 (2010)
17. Aharon, M., Elad, M., Bruckstein, A.: K-SVD: an algorithm for designing overcomplete dictionaries for sparse representation. IEEE Trans. Sig. Process. **54**, 4311–4322 (2006)
18. Tibshirani, R.: Regression shrinkage and selection via the lasso. J. Roy. Stat. Soc. **73**, 273–282 (2011)
19. Rosset, S., Zhu, J.: Least angle regression. Ann. Stat. **32**, 407–499 (2004)

Hardness Prediction for Object Detection Inspired by Human Vision

Yuwei Qiu, Huimin Ma[⊠], and Lei Gao

Department of Electronic Engineering, Tsinghua University, Beijing, China
{qyw14,gao-115}@mails.tsinghua.edu.cn, mhmpub@tsinghua.edu.cn

Abstract. We introduce eye tracking features including existing features like (1) scan path and (2) heat map, and novel features including (1) components of scan path and (2) peaks of heat to better define and understand human vision. In this paper, these features are used to describe the eye movements of a person when he/she is watching an image and looking for the target object in it. Based on these features, a new image complexity called *eye tracking complexity* is defined. Eye tracking complexity can be computed either by carrying out eye tracking experiments and extracting eye tracking features or through a convolutional neural network (CNN), which is introduced in this paper. This CNN computes eye tracking complexity directly from images. It has been validated that eye tracking complexity of an image corresponds to the detection algorithms average precision over an image. Thus, eye tracking complexity can be used to predict the hardness of object detection, which can yield guidelines for the hierarchical algorithms design.

1 Introduction

Prediction of bad results of object detection is quite useful, with which computing resources can be rearranged and algorithms can be designed as hierarchical to improve the efficiency. When a person is watching a image, he/she knows whether it will be a tough task to find a target in the image. However, it is challenging for computers to predict how difficult it will be to detect objects before carrying out automatic detection algorithms.

Generally, object detection in human vision is transparent and all human beings carry out such task without any difficulty but with high accuracy and efficiency. However, automatic algorithms like neural networks are designed on a basis of math without taking any human perception into consideration. There is rare study combining *human factor* with automatic algorithms in the task of object detection. Inspired by the process of object detection in human vision, this paper aims at abstracting or modeling the essential of human vision and defining an image complexity for hardness prediction of object detection algorithms.

As for modeling human vision reasonably, it is still a tough task given that eye movements of a person during observation is complex. According to some psychological studies [1–4], eye tracking is one of the most prevalent methods

© Springer International Publishing AG 2017
Y. Zhao et al. (Eds.): ICIG 2017, Part II, LNCS 10667, pp. 139–150, 2017.
https://doi.org/10.1007/978-3-319-71589-6_13

used for analyzing eye movements. However, the raw eye tracking data are enormous two or three dimensional coordinates of gazes. Such forms are too massive to indicate any meaningful pattern of human vision. Valid features are required to be extracted.

In this paper, equipped with eye trackers, eye movements are recorded when people are watching images and looking for target object. The characteristics in eye tracking data like (1) the number of gazes, (2) the distance between gazes, (3) the density of gazes or the (4) angle of two neighboring scan lines is the basis of the eye tracking feature definition. Existing eye tracking features including (1) scan path and (2) heat map [5] are introduced. Novel features like (1) components of scan path and (2) peaks of heat are newly defined. These features are used to describe the eye movements.

Based on these features, a metric of image complexity is further defined: *eye tracking complexity (ETC)*. Eye tracking complexity can be computed either by carrying out eye tracking experiments and extracting eye tracking features, or through a convolutional neural network (CNN). Replacing time-consuming eye tracking experiments, the CNN can directly compute eye tracking complexity from raw images. Note that our purpose is to build direct connection between images and eye tracking complexity, or in other words, to classify images into categories according to the eye tracking complexity. CNN is adopted due to its well-known performance in image classification [6].

The effectiveness of the proposed complexity definition has been validated through numerical experiments. According to the results, eye tracking complexity corresponds to the average precision of automatic detection algorithms over an image. Namely, eye tracking complexity can be used to predict how difficult it is for the object to be detected by automatic algorithms. Based on the hardness prediction results, adaptations (e.g., changing object detection algorithms used for the image or slightly increasing or decreasing the iterations of the detection networks) can be carried out to improve the efficiency (Fig. 1).

To sum up, the contribution of this paper includes: (1) Large numbers of eye tracking experiments based on ImageNet dataset are conducted. Eye tracking features including components of scan path, and peaks of heat are newly defined. (2) A new metric of image complexity is defined based on these eye tracking features. It also has been validated that the new complexity corresponds to the detection algorithms average precision. (3) We train a CNN to directly compute the new image complexity in place of the time-consuming eye tracking experiments. (4) Given the prediction result, a simple example of the hierarchical algorithm design shows the benefit of the proposed scheme.

The rest of this paper will be organized as follows. Section 2 is a review of related works including various definitions of image complexity, the application of CNN in computer vision and the studies using eye tracking. In Sect. 3, implementation details of eye tracking experiments are described. In Sect. 4, eye tracking features including existing ones (scan path and heat map) and novel ones (components of scan path and peaks of heat) are introduced. In Sect. 5, the ETC is defined based on eye tracking features introduced in Sect. 4. In Sect. 6,

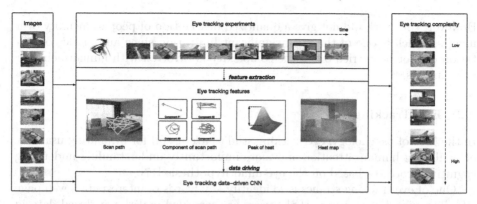

Fig. 1. Briefly summarize, we carried out eye tracking experiments and collected the eye tracking data. Next, eye tracking features are extracted from the data and eye tracking complexity is computed. Also, a CNN is trained to compute eye tracking complexity directly from the images. Eye tracking complexity can be either computed from this CNN or eye tracking experiments.

the typical process of hardness prediction is built up. We draw conclusions and discuss about the numerical results in Sect. 7.

2   Related Works

There have been a lot of studies about image complexity and we discuss pros and cons of some of the previous definitions of image complexity. Meanwhile, the using of eye tracking data or human visual system (like saliency) is also introduced in this part.

2.1   Image Complexity

Digital images can be analyzed at wide range of levels ranging from pixel arrangement to the level of human understanding [7] and there have been numerous studies.

In the level of image analysis by machines [8–13]. The method adopting neural network from three aspects including texture, edge information and significant area to describe the complexity of the image has been raised in [8]. Also in [9], the researcher used color similarity. However, the features like texture, edges, or significant areas can only represent the local complexity and lose some global information.

As for studies using human perception over the content to describe image complexity [14–16], a measurement method based on SIFT & K-means algorithm, namely the estimation of the mismatch between the target and the interesting points has been introduced by Huo [16]. He carried out memory experiments, which asked people to memorize the content like objects, style or context of the images then analyzed the difference to study the complexity of the images.

However, this work did not give a quantized description of peoples memory over images, which is one of the most significant limitation since automatic computation cannot be carried out if the complexity is involved with human behavior experiments.

2.2 Eye Tracking

In the field of psychology, eye tracking studies are useful for evaluating usability or analyzing human attention and more importantly understanding underlying cognitive processes based on the eye-mind hypothesis [17].

One of eye tracking studies is to identify key words of interests in a web page [18]. The visual experiences of the users are recorded and the analyzed data in the form of heat maps of the concern keywords explains the user eye behavior over the screen.

2.3 Convolutional Neural Network

A CNN contains one or more layers containing neurons with neighboring interactions, which has various implementations like face or object detection, text detection or recognition or image classification. The application of CNN in image classification is introduced in [6]. This architecture of CNN has been adapted to various forms for printed or handwritten character detection or recognition, face detection or recognition.

3   Eye Tracking Experiments

In this section, implementation details are shown for eye tracking experiments.

Participants: All of the 1280 times of eye tracking experiments are carried out by adults (aged above 18, with an educational level above college and without any mental diseases or ophthalmic diseases) and supervised by our group.

Eye tracker: Participants are equipped with *Tobii* eye trackers in the experiments and all of the eye movements are recorded. The average time for each time of experiment is around 6 min and the interval between two gazes recorded is 500 ms.

Task for participants: In the experiments, people are asked to watch a series of images switching over the computer screen. Participants are able to control the computer to switch from the first image toward the second one. Each of the participants has a different target object to seek out in one section of the experiment and this target appears somewhere in the images.

Images set: 1280 natural scene images used for participants to observe in the experiments are natural scenes from ImageNet database [19]. These images are chosen from 20 different classes in ImageNet. And for each class, 64 different images are selected randomly. Each experiment are divided into two sections of

Table 1. The images used in the eye tracking images are chosen from the classes in this form. And for each classes, 6 different images are selected randomly. Times of valid experiments are also listed here. We note that for each time of experiment, two sections are contained with 12 images of two different classes. Therefore, there will be approximately 2560 groups of eye tracking data and each group is recorded for 6 images of the same class.

Classes	Airplane	Bear	Chair	Furniture	Giraffe	Glasses	Helmet	Horse	Ladle	Monkey
Num.	140	128	118	124	152	124	128	162	128	130
Classes	Person	Purse	Piano	Rabbit	Sheep	Sofa	Table	Tiger	Whale	Zebra
Num.	136	134	124	156	138	136	128	126	132	132

12 images (6 images in one section). Each section contains 6 images from one class, therefore, eye tracking data for one image is collected 12 times repeatedly in case of unexpected errors.

Note that: (1) Participants are required to take off their glasses during the process of the experiments; (2) In one experiment, the participants are not allowed to take any rest and all of their eyes movements are recorded; (3) All of the data collected from eye tracking experiments will be firstly filtered in case of malfunction of eye trackers. The number of valid experiments are listed in Table 1.

4   Features Extraction from Eye Tracking Data

Generally, the eye tracking features including (1) scan path and (2) heat map are existing ideas for eye tracking data analysis [5]. Apart from these, novel features are newly defined to further illustrate characteristics including (1) the number of gazes, (2) the distance between gazes, (3) the density of gazes or the (4) angle of two neighboring scan lines.

The eye tracking data contains massive points which denote gazes of human eye balls. Furthermore, the gazes are cut up in groups for each image and each group contains all of the gazes of a person when he/she is observing one image. In the following, detailed definitions of eye tracking features are introduced:

(1) **Scan path**: A broken line connecting every two gazes which have neighboring time stamps. It illustrates the moving path of human eye balls and can be directly computed by raw eye tracking data.

(2) **Heat map**: A map presenting the density of gazes over an image when people are watching it. Note that heat maps have various forms. Specifically, in this paper a gray level form is chosen. Basically, the denser the gazes located in an area, the higher the grey level (the darker) of the pixels. Besides, values of pixels in the heat map are normalized, ranging from 0 to 1.

Both the above two features can be easily extracted by simple signal processing techniques. Two more novel features are introduced in this paper:

(3) **Components of scan path**: Massive gazes are connected in scan path, which is composed of basically four types of components: (1) one-way lines, (2) back-and-forth straight lines, (3) typical polygon and (4) dense polygon. These types of components can successfully form up any scan path (See Fig. 2). Moreover, judging from the (1) density of gazes and (2) the number of lines involved in each type of components, one-way lines, back-and-forth straight lines, typical polygon and dense polygon are scored $1, 2, 3$ and 4. This score will be used for complexity definition in the next section.

We note that the judgment is made by detailed analyzing (1) the distance between points, (2) the angle of two neighboring lines and (3) the density of points. The main process of this judgment goes as follows:

– Given that two gazes at time t and time $t + 1$ are adjacent, compute the distance between them. Carry out the same procedure to gazes at time $t + 1$ and time $t + 2$.
– Compute the distances between gaze t and $t + 1$, and gaze $t + 1$ and $t + 2$.
– Compute the angle between line(t, $t + 1$) and line($t + 1$, $t + 2$).
– By asking yes/no questions like "Is the distance between current gaze and last gaze larger than threshold?" or "Is the angle between current-next and current-last smaller than 90 degrees?", complex scan paths will be cut up into components (See Fig. 4 to see the whole procedure).

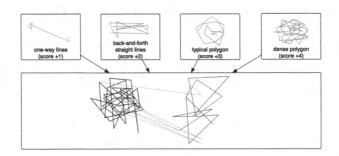

Fig. 2. Four types of scan path components. Any scan path can be formed up by these four components roughly.

(4) **Peaks of heat**: In the heat map, which illustrates the density of gazes locally, local maximum value of density is picked as local peak of heat. Note that since local maximum values are not unique in a heat map, there will be more than one peak of heat in a heat map as well. Peaks will be picked by *steepest ascent*.

We refer the reader to Fig. 3 to see an illustration.

Scan Path   Components of Scan Path   Heat Map   Peak of Heat

Fig. 3. Existing eye tracking features include scan path and heat map and novel features include scan path component and peak of heat.

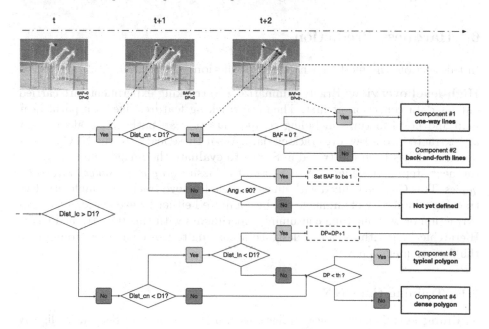

Fig. 4. Scan path segmentation can be accomplished by asking yes/no questions as it is shown in this figure. We note that Dist_lc (Dist_cn) is the distance between the last and current (current and next) gaze. Ang is the angle of the lines between current-last and current-next.

5 Eye Tracking Complexity

In this section, the newly introduced eye tracking complexity is defined based on novel eye tracking features (components of scan path and peaks of heat).

Generally, the components of scan path illustrate how a person distributes his/her attention, or the time of observation. More complex components means a higher complexity. The peak of heat describes the level of how much attention this person has paid to specific areas. A high value means the person may be confused or interested in that area. Human attention over a whole image should be measured as the sum of the distributions of attention in each part of the image.

Inspired by this, eye tracking complexity (ETC) of an image is defined as follows:

$$\text{ETC} = \left\lfloor \sum_{c_i \in \mathcal{C}} s_i \times p_i + \frac{1}{2} \right\rfloor \tag{1}$$

where $\mathcal{C} = \{c_1, c_2, \ldots, c_K\}$ is the set of scan path components extracted from the image, s_i and p_i is the corresponding score and the peak value of heat in local areas of the component c_i, respectively. Note that for each of the images, eye tracking complexity is an integer, which serves as labels in the classifier.

6 Hardness Prediction

In this section, the model for hardness prediction is presented.

High-level overview: Briefly summarize, eye tracking experiments are carried out for data collection at first. Then eye tracking features like scan path, heat map and novel features including components of scan path and peaks of heat are extracted from raw eye tracking data. With these features, the ETC is computed as it has been illustrated in Sect. 4 to evaluate the image complexity. For the next step, a classifier (CNN) is used to classify *gray level images into categories*. This CNN is trained with images labeled by eye tracking complexity. Eye tracking complexity of an image can be computed either by eye tracking features extraction or without time-consuming experiments with this fully trained CNN. Hierarchical algorithms can be designed according to this complexity to improve the detection efficiency.

6.1 Training the CNN

Training set: The eye tracking features, which is stated in Sect. 4, is slightly updated for network training in this part. The number of input images is multiplied by 5 times with adaptations including (1) mirroring, (2) vertical clockwise rotation, (3) vertical anti-clockwise rotation and (4) horizontal rotation to be 6400. 80% of these images (5120) are used as training set and the rest (1280) is for testing.

Architecture: We adjust the architecture of *LeNet* [20] to the CNN used for hardness prediction because this network functions well in gray level images classification. Briefly summarize, this CNN contains two convolutional layers, two pooling layers and two fully connected layers. The input gray level images are re-sized to 32×32.

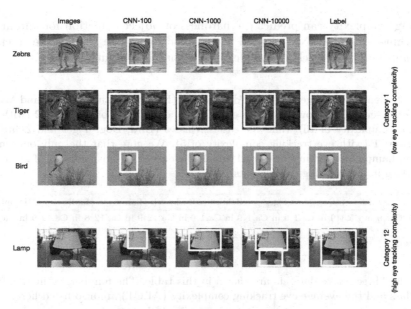

Fig. 5. All of the three CNNs performed equally on precision over images in **Category 1** (Bird, Tiger and Zebra) but quite different on **Category 12** (Lamp).

6.2 Hardness Prediction

Images for test: To validate the effectiveness of eye tracking complexity as hardness prediction for object detection, 72 images are chosen from ImageNet. These 72 images are from 8 categories (each category has 9 images, randomly selected). 4 of the 8 categories are the hardest (with the highest possibility for algorithms to fail) and the rest of them are the easiest (with the lowest possibility for algorithms to fail) classes for object detection according to the result of ILSVRC 2016.

Note that the so-called "hardest" and "easiest" classes are illustrated by ImageNet in the purpose of warning participants of ILSVRC worldwide. Generally, hardest classes attain the lowest mean Average Precision (mAP).

Eye tracking complexity can also be computed by experiments. However, in our experiment, the classifier CNN replaces eye tracking experiments for the computation of eye tracking complexity of these images and the output is shown in Table 2.

Results: Generally, images of the hardest classes (Backpack, Ladle, Lamp and Microphone) cluster in **Category 11** (with eye tracking complexity of 15) and **12** (with eye tracking complexity of 16) while the easiest classes (Bird, Dog, Tiger and Zebra) in **Category 1** (with eye tracking complexity of 5). We note that the only one image of Class Lamp clustered in Category 11 might be caused by unsteadiness of attention distraction in eye tracking experiments.

This result indicates that the output of this CNN, namely the eye tracking complexity, corresponds to the performance of automatic algorithms. Eye tracking complexity can predict the hardness of object detection for automatic algorithms. And the CNN adopted in our experiment can replace eye tracking experiments for eye tracking complexity automated computation.

Table 2. Generally, images of the hardest classes (Backpack, Ladle, Lamp and Microphone) cluster in **Category 11** (with eye tracking complexity of 15) and **12** (with eye tracking complexity of 16) while the easiest classes (Bird, Dog, Tiger and Zebra) in **Category 1** (with eye tracking complexity of 5). We note that the only one image of Class Lamp clustered in Category 11 might be caused by unsteadiness of attention distraction in eye tracking experiments.

Classes	Bird	Dog	Tiger	Zebra	Backpack	Lamp	Ladle	Microphone
Output Ca.	9 in Ca.1	9 in Ca.1	9 in Ca.1	9 in Ca.1	9 in Ca.12	9 in Ca.12	8 in Ca.12 1 in Ca.11	9 in Ca.12

Table 3. Three image datasets are shown in this table. The numbers of images from each class and the average eye tracking complexity (AECT) are also listed here.

Classes	Bird	Dog	Tiger	Zebra	Backpack	Lamp	Ladle	Microphone	AETC
Set 1	12	12	12	12	0	0	0	0	**4.8**
Set 2	6	6	6	6	6	6	6	6	**10.1**
Set 3	0	0	0	0	12	12	12	12	**14.8**

Table 4. Increasing iterations does improve the performance of automatic algorithms over the dataset that consists of images with lower ETC, while a larger number of iterations is useful for performance improvement over a dataset with high ETC.

mAP	Set 1	Set 2	Set 3
CNN-100	**0.632**	0.142	0.017
CNN-1000	**0.637**	0.254	0.086
CNN-10000	**0.637**	0.365	0.118

6.3   Hierarchical Algorithms Design

According to the eye tracking complexity of an image, hardness of detection can be predicted in advance, which means hierarchical algorithms can be designed accordingly.

One of possible design for hierarchical algorithms based on eye tracking complexity is presented here.

Networks: Three CNNs with different iterations (CNN-100, CNN-1000 and CNN-10000) are all trained with the same starting point and the same training sets including 50,000 images for training and 10,000 for validation. All of the images used for training are from ImageNet.

Test datasets: Three test datasets are built up and the contents are shown in Table 3. Average eye tracking complexity (AETC) of each dataset is also listed here. CNN-100, CNN-1000 and CNN-10000 are tested on all of these three datasets and the mean Average Precision (mAP) of each dataset is shown in Table 4.

Results: The results of hierarchical, non-hierarchical algorithms and bounding boxes are shown in Fig. 5.

What has been shown from the results is that: (1) All of the three CNNs performed equally on precision over images in **Category 1** (Bird, Tiger and Zebra) but quite different on **Category 12** (Lamp). (2) Increasing iterations does improve the performance of automatic algorithms over datasets that consist of images with higher average eye tracking complexity. However, for a dataset with lower eye tracking complexity, a large number of iterations is invalid for performance improvement.

Therefore, in computation of eye tracking complexity before training detection network or designing algorithms, efforts in vain can be avoided by choosing suitable iteration times.

Further studies about eye tracking complexity will be focused on performance of networks with different (1) depth, (2) architecture or (3) kernels, on images with different eye tracking complexity, which yields more guidelines for hierarchical detection algorithms design.

7   Conclusion and Discussion

To sum up, novel eye tracking features including (1) components of scan path and (2) the peak of heat are defined in this paper. Based on these features, a kind of image complexity, eye tracking complexity, and a CNN for its computation in place of eye tracking experiments are introduced. Generally, this complexity corresponds to the hardness of object detection. These results can yield useful guidelines for hierarchical algorithms design and the arrangement of computing resources.

References

1. Kiili, K., Ketamo, H., Kickmeier-Rust, M.D.: Evaluating the usefulness of eye tracking in game-based learning. Int. J. Serious Games 1(2) (2014)
2. Longman, C.S., Lavric, A., Monsell, S.: More attention to attention? An eye-tracking investigation of selection of perceptual attributes during a task switch. J. Exp. Psychol.: Learn. Mem. Cogn. **39**(4), 1142 (2013)
3. Kassner, M., Patera, W., Bulling, A.: Pupil: an open source platform for pervasive eye tracking and mobile gaze-based interaction. In: Proceedings of the 2014 ACM International Joint Conference on Pervasive and Ubiquitous Computing: Adjunct Publication, pp. 1151–1160. ACM (2014)

4. Duque, A., Vázquez, C.: Double attention bias for positive and negative emotional faces in clinical depression: evidence from an eye-tracking study. J. Behav. Ther. Exp. Psychiatry **46**, 107–114 (2015)
5. Blascheck, T., Kurzhals, K., Raschke, M., Burch, M., Weiskopf, D., Ertl, T.: State-of-the-art of visualization for eye tracking data. In: Proceedings of EuroVis, vol. 2014 (2014)
6. Krizhevsky, A., Sutskever, I., Hinton, G.E.: Imagenet classification with deep convolutional neural networks. In: Advances in Neural Information Processing Systems, pp. 1097–1105 (2012)
7. Cardaci, M., Di Gesù, V., Petrou, M., Tabacchi, M.E.: A fuzzy approach to the evaluation of image complexity. Fuzzy Sets Syst. **160**(10), 1474–1484 (2009)
8. Chen, Y.-Q., Duan, J., Zhu, Y., Qian, X.-F., Xiao, B.: Research on the image complexity based on neural network. In: 2015 International Conference on Machine Learning and Cybernetics, ICMLC, vol. 1, pp. 295–300. IEEE (2015)
9. Yang, S., Gao, P., Meng, F., Jiang, X., Liu, H.: Objective image quality assessment based on image complexity and color similarity. In: 2013 Fourth World Congress on Software Engineering, WCSE, vol. 1, pp. 5–9. IEEE (2013)
10. Rigau, J., Feixas, M., Sbert, M.: An information-theoretic framework for image complexity. In: Proceedings of the First Eurographics Conference on Computational Aesthetics in Graphics, Visualization and Imaging, pp. 177–184. Eurographics Association (2005)
11. Peters, R.A., Strickland, R.N.: Image complexity metrics for automatic target recognizers. In: Automatic Target Recognizer System and Technology Conference, pp. 1–17. Citeseer (1990)
12. Yu, H., Winkler, S.: Image complexity and spatial information. In: 2013 Fifth International Workshop on Quality of Multimedia Experience, QoMEX, pp. 12–17. IEEE (2013)
13. Yaghmaee, F., Jamzad, M.: Introducing a new method for estimation image complexity according to calculate watermark capacity. In: 2008 International Conference on Intelligent Information Hiding and Multimedia Signal Processing, IIHMSP 2008, pp. 981–984. IEEE (2008)
14. Da Silva, M.P., Courboulay, V., Estraillier, P.: Image complexity measure based on visual attention. In: 2011 18th IEEE International Conference on Image Processing, pp. 3281–3284. IEEE (2011)
15. Mario, I., Chacon, M., Alma, D., Corral, S.: Image complexity measure: a human criterion free approach. In: 2005 Annual Meeting of the North American Fuzzy Information Processing Society, NAFIPS 2005, pp. 241–246. IEEE (2005)
16. Huo, J.: An image complexity measurement algorithm with visual memory capacity and an EEG study. In: 2016 SAI Computing Conference (SAI), pp. 264–268. IEEE (2016)
17. Just, M.A., Carpenter, P.A.: Eye fixations and cognitive processes. Cogn. Psychol. **8**(4), 441–480 (1976)
18. Kumar, N., Maheshwari, V., Kumar, J.: A comparative study of user experience in online social media branding web pages using eye tracker. In: 2016 International Conference on Advances in Human Machine Interaction (HMI), pp. 1–8. IEEE (2016)
19. Deng, J., Dong, W., Socher, R., Li, L.-J., Li, K., Fei-Fei, L.: Imagenet: a large-scale hierarchical image database. In: 2009 IEEE Conference on Computer Vision and Pattern Recognition, CVPR 2009, pp. 248–255. IEEE (2009)
20. LeCun, Y., Cortes, C., Burges, C.J.: The MNIST database of handwritten digits (1998)

Orientation Estimation Network

Jie Sun, Wengang Zhou[✉], and Houqiang Li

Department of Electronic Engineering and Information Science,
University of Science and Technology of China, Hefei 230026, Anhui, China
`zhwg@ustc.edu.cn`

Abstract. We propose the Orientation Estimation Network (OEN) to
predict the dominant orientation of the outdoor images and rotate the
images to a canonical orientation which is visually comfortable. The OEN
outputs the sine and cosine of the angle which are continuous in contrast to the angle. We collect a new dataset called the Outdoor Images
dataset for this task. This dataset contains various kinds of outdoor
images, such as buildings, landscape, persons and boats, and the orientation information has been manually annotated. We choose AlexNet,
MobileNet and VGGNet to extract image features and regress to the
angle of images. In our task, MobileNet achieves high performance while
needing less resource, and can be applied to mobile and embedded vision
applications. We compare our method with the hand-crafted methods on
our dataset. In the evaluation, our learning based method significantly
outperforms the hand-crafted methods in the task of outdoor images
orientation estimation.

Keywords: Outdoor images · Orientation estimation · Deep learning

1 Introduction

In recent years, convolutional neural networks have been used in various tasks in
computer vision, such as classification [4–7,26], detection [8–10,25], segmentation
[11], image search [15,16], and have achieved state-of-the-art performance in
these tasks. CNN has got unprecedented success ever since AlexNet [4] won
the ImageNet Challenge in 2012 because of the power of hierarchical abstract
representation, but it also has the limit when dealing with rotation invariance
only by convolution and pooling.

To overcome such limit, the traditional solution is data augmentation. Training samples are rotated into multi-oriented versions. Although data augmentation improves the performance by extending the training data, the network
tends to be more fitted to the training data and would lose some generalization
capacity, and more training time is required. Another way is rotating the filters.
Usually, one filter in the network can detect one specific pattern in the image, so
we can rotate this filter to detect the same pattern with different orientations. It
can alleviate the network to learn all different orientations and achieve rotation
invariance. The motivation is straight-forward, but it has to change the way of

© Springer International Publishing AG 2017
Y. Zhao et al. (Eds.): ICIG 2017, Part II, LNCS 10667, pp. 151–162, 2017.
https://doi.org/10.1007/978-3-319-71589-6_14

forward and backward propagation which is not convenient and the angle of the filters is discontinuous.

In this paper, we directly predict the image orientation, instead of making a rotate invariant representation, and then align the images according to the angle predicted by the OEN to achieve upright configuration of the visual content. This approach is inspired by hand-crafted features, such as SIFT [1]. SIFT calculates the domain orientation of the keypoint and aligns the patch by the domain orientation. After that, SIFT gets the descriptor for this key-point. Unlike SIFT, we predict the global orientation of images instead of local orientation. Here we choose the outdoor scene images as our target images because they usually have a clearly defined principal orientation in human perception.

In this paper, we make orientation estimation by regressing to the human annotated ground truth. In contrast to our method, Spatial Transformer Network [12] uses the classification information as ground truth to learn the transform indirectly. Spatial Transformer Layer learns the way to transform a feature map or a region of images. And the transform is forwarded to the next layer. But STN can only handle a limited range of orientation variance. Here we give the outdoor images a canonical orientation and we learn this orientation directly by OEN. So we can learn the images with arbitrary orientation and finally rotate images to the appropriate orientation. Figure 1 shows the different orientations of the same scene. The contributions of this paper are summarized as follows:

- We propose a new task of predicting the canonical orientation of outdoor images and present a solution for this task.
- We collect a new dataset called Outdoor Images for our task. The dataset is composed of outdoor images and the orientation information has been manually annotated.
- We compare our method with hand-crafted methods and study AlexNet, MobileNet [19] and VGGNet [5] in our task.

Fig. 1. Different orientations of same scene

2   Related Work

The related works to achieve rotation invariance: (1) the hand-crafted orientation estimation, (2) data augmentation and (3) Spatial Transformer Network.

2.1   Hand-Crafted Orientation Estimation

Orientation information is important for hand-crafted feature to align local patches to achieve rotation invariance. SIFT detector calculates the dominant orientation of key-point by statistics of local gradient direction of image intensities. ORB detector [2] uses the moment of a patch to find the offset between the patch's intensity and its center and then this offset vector is used as the orientation of key-point. BRISK detector [3] and FREAK detector [13] sample the neighborhood of the key-point by using a pattern. The long distance point pairs are used to calculate the orientation of key-point.

In contrast to hand-crafted orientation estimation, our learning-based method automatically predicts the orientation without hand-crafted feature detectors. The power of CNN to extract feature is more effective than hand-crafted method. In recent years, traditional methods have been replaced gradually and usually are used as baselines.

2.2   Data Augmentation

Deep convolution neural network have the ability of dealing with transitions, scale changes, and limited rotations. And the capability comes from rich convolutional filters, and pooling. Data augmentation is used to achieve local or global transform invariance with rich convolutional filters [14]. Therefore, data augmentation can improve performance for many tasks. However, the network tends to be more fitted to the training data and would loss some generalization capacity, and more training time is required.

In contrast to data augmentation, our method based on network predict the canonical orientation directly. Then the learned orientation can been used to other tasks to achieve higher performance.

2.3   Spatial Transformer Network

The Spatial Transformer Layer is proposed by Jaderberg et al. [12], and learns the way to transform a feature map or a region of images. The transform is forwarded to the next layer. A general framework for spatial transform comes out by STN, but the problem about how the complex transform parameters use CNN to precisely estimate has not been well solved. Most recent work [17,18,20,21,23,24] have tried rotating conventional filters to achieve rotation invariance. But they have to change the way of forward and backward propagation.

In contract to STN, our method learns the orientation directly using the ground truth of the explicit orientation. And STN learns the orientation implicitly using the ground truth of the task, such as classification information. STN has the limit to significant change of orientation. So we solve this problem by learning orientation directly in our method.

3   Orientation Estimation Network

In this work we focus on predicting the canonical orientation for outdoor images and making images visually comfortable. The Orientation Estimation Network takes outdoor images as input, and outputs the angle of images which is consistent with human perception. Then we take the predicted angle outputs to rotate the images to a canonical orientation.

In the following, we introduce the detail of Orientation Estimation Network by three parts: (1) Learning stage, (2) Fine-tuning stage and (3) Predicting stage.

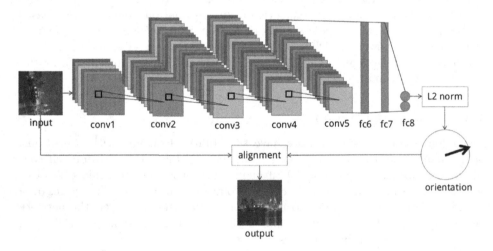

Fig. 2. The framework of our method based on AlexNet

3.1   Learning Stage

In this stage, we take the images as the input, through a classic network, such as AlexNet, the champion of ImageNet 2012. Then we get the CNN features extracted from images. We combine the features and output two values which are defined as sine and cosine of the angle. We choose sine and cosine of angle, because sine and cosine are continuous with respect to the angle. So it is easy to optimizes and train. Besides, we add a normalization layer which normalizes the output vector to unit-norm to ensure the validity of sine and cosine. We use L2 loss between the predicted values and the ground truth in training. We calculate the angle by the arctangent function. Figure 2 shows the framework of our method.

3.2 Fine-Tuning Stage

It is not enough robust only based on learning stage, where the network learns one image at one time. And the orientation can be transformed by rotating the image. So two images at same scene with different orientations can help network to learn the orientations of them by each other. In this stage, we learn the rotated angle between two images at same scene to help improve the performance of orientation estimation.

In the fine-tuning stage, we extend our framework to a Siamese architecture. The input images are the same scene with two different orientations. The ground truth is the difference between the orientations of input images. The predicted angle is the difference between the orientations which are outputted by the two sub-networks for input images. The loss is the difference between the ground truth angle and the predicted angle. After the single network learning stage, we have got a good performance for prediction. Based on that, we improve the performance by fine-tuning. We fine-tune the fully-connected layers for AlexNet and VGGNet, and last convlutional layer for MobileNet. Figure 3 shows the framework of the fine-tuning stage.

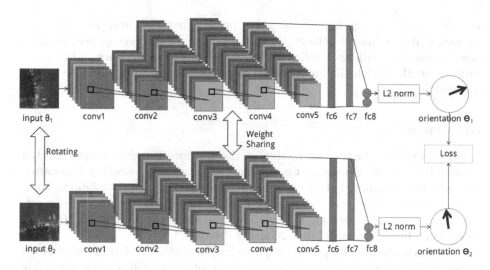

Fig. 3. The framework of the fine-tuning stage based on AlexNet. Two input images are same scene with different orientations, which are θ_1 and θ_2. Two output orientations are Θ_1 and Θ_2. And the loss is $||\theta_1 - \theta_2| - |\Theta_1 - \Theta_2||^2$.

3.3 Predicting Stage

In the predicting stage, we take the image as the input and output the orientation. We use a sub-network from the Siamese architecture to predict the angle. Then we rotate the image using the predicted orientation. Table 1 reports the detail of OEN architecture based on AlexNet.

Table 1. The architecture of the orientation estimation network based on AlexNet

Type	Size
Input	227 * 227 * 3
Conv1+Pool1	27 * 27 * 96
Conv2+Pool2	13 * 13 * 256
Conv3	13 * 13 * 384
Conv4	13 * 13 * 384
Conv5+Pool5	6 * 6 * 256
FC6	1 * 1 * 4096
FC7	1 * 1 * 4096
FC8	1 * 1 * 2
L2 normalization	1 * 1 * 2
Output	1 * 1 * 1

4 Experiment

We introduce the experiments by three parts. First, we introduce our new dataset, Outdoor Images dataset. Second, we compare the performance of three classic networks which are applied to Oriented Estimation Network and we compare our method with the hand-crafted methods. Third, we analyze the result of the experiments.

4.1 Dataset

In our experiment, we test our method in the Outdoor Images dataset collected by ourselves, where the orientations of images have been manually annotated. The dataset is composed of several kinds outdoor scene, such as buildings, landscape, persons, boats, and has been divided into the training set and test set. The images in our dataset are selected from the Flickr1M dataset [22]. Figure 4 shows some images in our Outdoor Images dataset.

The images have been preprocessed to keep the information in the circle of center while dropping outside. The pixels out of circle will go to the outside of images when we rotate the images, so these pixels are abandoned. They are colored as black in case of influencing the experiment result.

4.2 Experiment Setup

In our experiment, we first compare the performance of AlexNet, MobileNet and VGGNet for predicting the orientation of images. AlexNet contains five convolutional layers and three fully-connected layers. The fully-connected layers almost take up 90% parameters of AlexNet, and MobileNet drops the fully-connected layers to compress model. MobileNet takes many 3×3 depthwise convolutional

Fig. 4. Sample images in the outdoor images dataset

filters and 1×1 pointwise convolutional filters to reduce a large number of parameters. MobileNet only has 4.2 million parameters while 60 million for AlexNet. And VGGNet has 16 layers and 138 million parameters. So MobileNet has the advantage to be applied to mobile and embedded vision applications.

We also compare our CNN method with the hand-crafted methods. In our experiment, SIFT calculates the dominant orientation of the whole image by statistics of global gradient direction of image intensities, instead of local gradient information. ORB uses the moment of the whole image to find the offset between the image's intensity and its center and then this offset vector is used as the orientation of image. BRISK and FREAK sample the neighborhood of the whole image by using a pattern. The long distance point pairs are used to calculate the orientation of the image. We use the average error of orientation as the criteria for evaluation.

4.3 Results

In our experiment, we use L2 loss for training. And we set initial learning rate as 0.0001 and every epoch drops to 0.96 of the last learning rate. We set the batch size as 128 and the size of input image as 227×227.

Table 2 shows the average error of AlexNet, MobileNet and VGGNet in our task for predicting the orientation of images. We set the same learning rate and other experiment parameters for them. The results show that MobileNet has better performance than AlexNet and has comparable performance with VGGNet.

But MobileNet needs few resources. So it is suitable to choose MobileNet in our task to predict the orientation.

Table 2. Average error of AlexNet, MobileNet and VGGNet for predicting the orientation of images

Network	AlexNet	MobileNet	VGGNet
Average error (degree)	25.85	23.63	23.61

Table 3 shows the average error of the OEN and the hand-crafted methods for predicting the global orientation of images. The results show that our method significantly outperforms the hand-crafted methods. Because SIFT and ORB which use the information of intensities to decide the orientation have no relationship with the global orientation which is visually comfortable. BRISK and FREAK which use the long distance point pairs have the same reason with SIFT and they are easy to change orientation after moving a few pixels.

Table 3. Average error of our method and the hand-crafted methods for predicting the global orientation of images

Method	Our method	SIFT	ORB	BRISK	FREAK
Average error (degree)	25.85	40.08	52.76	70.98	68.47

Figure 5 shows the angle error histogram of our method. The error of the angle is mostly below 20°. Therefore, our method is stable to predict the orientation of images. It is reliable to rotate the images by the predicted orientation through our method.

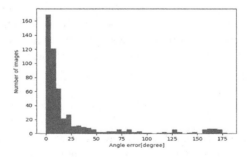

Fig. 5. The angle error histogram of our method

Figure 6 shows examples of predicting the orientation of images with little error. The left column is the ground truth images, the middle column is the

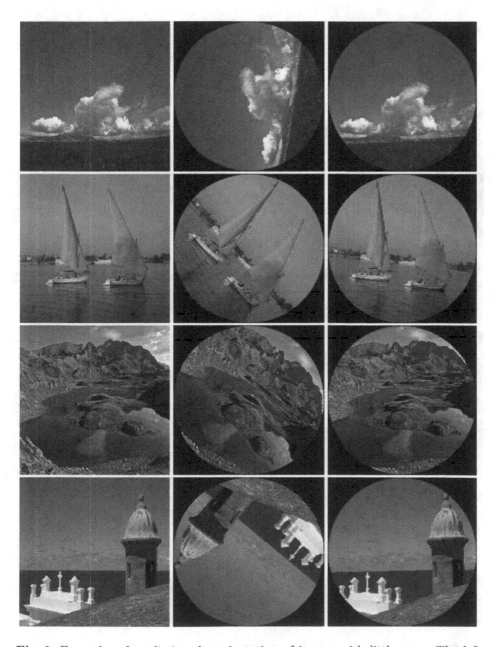

Fig. 6. Examples of predicting the orientation of images with little error. The left column is the ground truth images, the middle column is the input images for prediction and the right column is the results of the images rotated by the predicted orientation.

Fig. 7. Examples of predicting the orientation of images with large error. The left column is the ground truth images, the middle column is the input images for prediction and the right column is the results of the images rotated by the predicted orientation.

input images for predicting and the right column is the results of the images rotated according to the predicted orientation.

The results show the examples with little error and they catch the information of background for outdoor images. These images are typical ones mostly occupied by background. So it can be predicted well.

Figure 7 shows examples with larger error than examples in Fig. 6. In the images which contain buildings, the height of buildings are not same. So the line for top of buildings is not parallel with the ground. It is confusing for the network to predict the orientation of images and it causes error. In the images which contain persons, it has large error for predicting orientation. The reason we thought is that persons occupy too much space and have a little background while other kinds images have more background information. So the images contain persons are not predicted well. A solution to address this problem is to train for the images contain persons alone, if the task is predicting an orientation only for images with persons.

5 Conclusion

We have presented a new task of calculating the holistic dominant angle for outdoor images, and aligning the images to be visually comfortable. We compare CNN method with hand-crafted methods and show the advantage of convlutional neural network. Experiment on AlexNet, MobileNet and VGGNet demonstrates the performance for predicting the canonical orientation of outdoor images. And it turns out that MobileNet is more suitable for this work with less average error and less resource.

Acknowledgements. This work was supported by NSFC under contract No. 61472378 and No. 61632019, the Fundamental Research Funds for the Central Universities, and Young Elite Scientists Sponsorship Program By CAST (2016QNRC001).

References

1. Lowe, D.G.: Object recognition from local scale-invariant features. In: ICCV, pp. 1150–1157 (1999)
2. Rublee, E., Rabaud, V., Konolige, K., Bradski, G.: ORB: an efficient alternative to SIFT or SURF. In: ICCV, pp. 2564–2571 (2011)
3. Leutenegger, S., Chli, M., Siegwart, R.Y.: Brisk: binary robust invariant scalable keypoints. In: ICCV, pp. 2548–2555 (2011)
4. Krizhevsky, A., Sutskever, I., Hinton, G.E.: Imagenet classification with deep convolutional neural networks. In: NIPS, pp. 1097–1105 (2012)
5. Simonyan, K., Zisserman, A.: Very deep convolutional networks for large-scale image recognition. arXiv preprint arXiv:1409.1556 (2014)
6. He, K., Zhang, X., Ren, S., Sun, J.: Deep residual learning for image recognition. In: CVPR, pp. 770–778 (2016)
7. Szegedy, C., Liu, W., Jia, Y., Sermanet, P., Reed, S., Anguelov, D., Erhan, D., Vanhoucke, V., Rabinovich, A.: Going deeper with convolutions. In: CVPR, pp. 1–9 (2015)

8. Girshick, R., Donahue, J., Darrell, T., Malik, J.: Rich feature hierarchies for accurate object detection and semantic segmentation. In: CVPR, pp. 580–587 (2014)
9. Girshick, R.: Fast R-CNN. In: ICCV, pp. 1440–1448 (2015)
10. Ren, S., He, K., Girshick, R., Sun, J.: Faster R-CNN: towards real-time object detection with region proposal networks. In: NIPS, pp. 91–99 (2015)
11. He, K., Gkioxari, G., Dollár, P., Girshick, R.: Mask R-CNN. arXiv preprint arXiv:1703.06870 (2017)
12. Jaderberg, M., Simonyan, K., Zisserman, A.: Spatial transformer networks. In: NIPS, pp. 2017–2025 (2015)
13. Alahi, A., Ortiz, R., Vandergheynst, P.: Freak: fast retina keypoint. In: CVPR, pp. 510–517 (2012)
14. Van Dyk, D.A., Meng, X.L.: The art of data augmentation. J. Comput. Graph. Stat. 10(1), 1–50 (2001)
15. Liu, Z., Li, H., Zhou, W., Tian, Q.: Uniting keypoints: local visual information fusion for large scale image search. IEEE Trans. Multimed. 17(4), 538–548 (2015)
16. Zhou, W., Lu, Y., Li, H., Song, Y., Tian, Q.: Spatial coding for large scale partial-duplicate web image search. In: ACM MM, pp. 131–140 (2010)
17. Wu, F., Hu, P., Kong, D.: Flip-rotate-pooling convolution and split dropout on convolution neural networks for image classification. arXiv preprint arXiv:1507.08754 (2015)
18. Marcos, D., Volpi, M., Tuia, D.: Learning rotation invariant convolutional filters for texture classification. arXiv preprint arXiv:1604.06720 (2016)
19. Howard, A.G., Zhu, M., Chen, B., Kalenichenko, D., Wang, W., Weyand, T., Andreetto, M., Adam, H.: Mobilenets: efficient convolutional neural networks for mobile vision applications. arXiv preprint arXiv:1704.04861 (2017)
20. Zhou, Y., Ye, Q., Qiu, Q., Jiao, J.: Oriented response networks. arXiv preprint arXiv:1701.01833 (2017)
21. Marcos, D., Volpi, M., Komodakis, N., Tuia, D.: Rotation equivariant vector field networks. arXiv preprint arXiv:1612.09346 (2016)
22. http://press.liacs.nl/mirflickr/
23. Cohen, T.S., Welling, M.: Steerable CNNs. arXiv preprint arXiv:1612.08498 (2016)
24. Worrall, D.E., Garbin, S.J., Turmukhambetov, D., Brostow, G.J.: Harmonic networks: deep translation and rotation equivariance. arXiv preprint arXiv:1612.04642 (2016)
25. Mao, J., Li, H., Zhou, W., Yan, S., Tian, Q.: Scale-based region growing for scene text detection. In: ACM MM (2013)
26. Zhang, X., Xiong, H., Zhou, W., Lin, W., Tian, Q.: Picking deep filter responses for fine-grained image recognition. In: CVPR, pp. 1134–1142 (2016)

A Method for Detecting Surface Defects in Insulators Based on RPCA

Wei Hu[1(✉)], Hongyu Qi[2], Zhenbing Zhao[2(✉)], and Leilei Xu[2]

[1] Dispatching and Control Center, State Grid Information
and Telecommunication Branch, Beijing 100761, China
whu@sgcc.com.cn
[2] North China Electric Power University, Baoding 071003, China
zhaozhenbing@ncepu.edu.cn

Abstract. To solve such problems of existing methods for detecting surface defects in insulators as monotonous detectable category and long processing time, this paper presents a simple but effective detection approach based on Robust Principal Component Analysis (RPCA). Firstly, our method is based on insulator strings. We divide insulator string image into multiple insulators images, and then use these images as a test set. Secondly, due to the insulator has the characteristic of strong similarity, we decompose an insulator into a non-defective low-rank component and a defective sparse component by RPCA, and detect whether the insulator is defective. Through the Probabilistic Robust Matrix Factorization (PRMF) algorithm, the operation efficiency is improved. Furthermore, we verify the feasibility and effectiveness of the method by taking a great deal of experimental data.

Keywords: Detection · Insulator · Defect · RPCA · PRMF

1 Introduction

Insulators play an important role in transmission lines. However, it is vulnerable and can be thwarted by a fracture or other faults. These faults even cause power failure and serious economic losses or casualties. Therefore, monitoring the condition of insulators is of great significance.

As per literature [1, 2], the damage of insulators can be determined by the minimum law of the vertical gray statistic chart. Works [1, 2] realizes the damage detection of insulator without cover, but when the insulator is occluded partially, their method will destroy the minimum law of the insulator and lead to miscalculation. Work [3] divides an insulator into 10 parts, defines the standard of Contract-Mean-Variance (CMV) curve by three texture parameters of each part, and then detects whether the

This work was supported in part by the National Natural Science Foundation of China under grant number 61401154, by the Natural Science Foundation of Hebei Province of China under grant number F2016502101 and by the Fundamental Research Funds for the Central Universities under grant number 2015ZD20.

© Springer International Publishing AG 2017
Y. Zhao et al. (Eds.): ICIG 2017, Part II, LNCS 10667, pp. 163–173, 2017.
https://doi.org/10.1007/978-3-319-71589-6_15

insulator is broken. However, when the insulator is divided, the damage is distributed on two adjacent parts. Under this condition, the stability of the CMV curve will be increased, thus probably causing miscalculation. Work [4] uses the edge slope feature model of crack to detect crack and obtains satisfactory results from the smooth insulators. But when the insulator surface is unsmooth, the method may cause miscalculation. Work [5] extracts the crack of binary image vertical projection, horizontal projection and two-order moment invariant of geometric moment invariants as the feature value, and detects the category of crack by Adaptive Resonance Theory (ART) network. The features extracted by this method is only applicable to the classification of the crack and it is monotonous. In [1–5], the number of fault categories is so limited, and the criterion of insulator fault is monotonous. They cannot deal with a variety of defects [6].

This paper presents a simple but effective approach to detect surface defects of insulators based on RPCA. The approach decomposes the image matrix of insulator into a low-rank component and a sparse component effectively. The low-rank image and the sparse image correspond to the non-defective component and the defective component, respectively. The advantages of the method are that the defects can be identified by separating the sparse component image and their categories can be determined. Moreover, we have reduced the computational complexity relatively.

2 Low-Rank Matrix Restoration Based on RPCA

RPCA is also called sparse and low-rank matrix decomposition [7] and it is evolved from the Principal Component Analysis (PCA) algorithm. PCA is the method that makes high-dimensional data in a low-dimensional space. It reduces the data dimension. Meanwhile, it can preserve more details in source images. The formula is as follows:

$$\min \|\mathbf{E}\|_F$$
$$s.t. \quad rank(\mathbf{A}) \le r, \mathbf{A} + \mathbf{E} - \mathbf{D} \tag{1}$$

where $\mathbf{A}$ is a low-rank component, $\mathbf{E}$ is a sparse-error component, $\mathbf{D}$ is original input data and each column represents the data of an observed image. $\|\cdot\|_F$ is the Frobenius matrix norm. However, there is a difficult problem in most error matrices, which is to recover low-rank matrices from high-dimensional data of observation matrices. These error matrices do not belong to the independent distribution of Gaussian noise. Moreover, PCA needs to know the dimensionality of low-dimensional feature space. But these problems are difficult to solve generally.

Based on the above PCA problems, Wright et al. [8] proposed RPCA to solve the question that data in $\mathbf{A}$ have been seriously damaged. In other words, they transformed the PCA problem into the RPCA problem. We describe the RPCA problem abstractly as follows: when we know the observation matrix $\mathbf{D}$ and $\mathbf{A} + \mathbf{E} = \mathbf{D}$, although we do not know $\mathbf{A}$ and $\mathbf{E}$, but we know that $\mathbf{A}$ is a low-rank component and $\mathbf{E}$ is a sparse component in which nonzero elements can be arbitrarily large. And then we try to restore $\mathbf{A}$ in this condition. The formula can be described as follows:

$$\min_{\mathbf{A,E}} \quad rank(\mathbf{A}) + \lambda \|\mathbf{E}\|_0$$
$$s.t. \quad \mathbf{A} + \mathbf{E} = \mathbf{D} \tag{2}$$

where the rank of matrix $\mathbf{A}$ is represented by $rank(\mathbf{A})$, and $\|\cdot\|_0$ denotes the L_0 norm, λ denotes the weight of noise. If we can solve the RPCA problem by the correct λ, $(\mathbf{A}, \mathbf{E})$ can be accurately recovered as well. Nevertheless, Eq. (2) belongs to the NP-Hard and Strictly Non-convex Optimization problem, and there is no efficient solution [9, 10].

We can turn the RPCA problem into a convex optimization problem which can be solved easily by making the stress relaxation of Eq. (2). In other words, we use the L_1 norm instead of the l_0 norm and use the kernel norm $\|\mathbf{A}\|_* = \sum_i \sigma_i(\mathbf{A})$ of $\mathbf{A}$ instead of the rank $(\mathbf{A})$. Then we turn Eq. (2) into Eq. (3). And then we turn the problem into a convex optimization problem which is easy to solve relatively. The result as Eq. (3): under certain conditions, $(\mathbf{A}, \mathbf{E})$ can be solved uniquely and recovered ideally.

$$\min_{\mathbf{A,E}} \quad \|\mathbf{A}\|_* + \lambda \|\mathbf{E}\|_1$$
$$s.t. \quad \mathbf{A} + \mathbf{E} = \mathbf{D} \tag{3}$$

Where $\|\mathbf{A}\|_* = \sum_i \sigma_i(\mathbf{A})$, $\sigma_i(\mathbf{A})$ represents the ith singular value of matrix $\mathbf{A}$, $\|\mathbf{E}\|_1 = \sum_{ij} \sigma_{ij}(\mathbf{A})$ represents the sum of the absolute values of elements in matrix $\mathbf{E}$.

The relaxation method is mainly to replace the non-convex l_0 norm into the l_1 norm which can measure the sparsity function easily. Thus, we can solve the RPCA problem by using the Convex optimization or non-linear programming to approximate the original problem [11]. In practical applications, with an increasing in detection frames, the input matrix $\mathbf{D}$ increases rapidly. The difficulty of computer processing and the time of processing is increasing as well. Hence the processing method for real-time updating is essential.

3 PRMF Algorithm

With the increasing application of RPCA in computer vision and image processing, scholars have proposed a series of algorithms to solve the RPCA problem, such as Singular Value Decomposition (SVD) [12], Accelerated Proximal Gradient (APG) [13], Alternating Direction Method (ADM) [14] and Augmented Lagrange Multiplier (ALM) [15]. However, with an increase in the sequence of video frames, the number of the input matrix is increasing rapidly and it extends the calculation time and affects the efficiency. To solve this problem, this paper uses RPCA based on PRMF [16] to realize real-time processing of input sequence and our method can solve the above problems effectively.

3.1 Matrix Decomposition

$\mathbf{Y}$ is a matrix with outliers and $\mathbf{Y} = [y_{ij}] \in R^{m \times n}$. The matrix decomposition of $\mathbf{Y}$ is expressed as follows:

$$\min_{U \in R^{m \times r}, V \in R^{n \times r}} \left\| W \otimes \left(Y - UV' \right) \right\|_a^a \tag{4}$$

where $W = [w_{ij}]$ is a matrix of size $m \times n$ pixels and only contains 0, 1. When the element y_{ij} in matrix Y is not damaged, $w_{ij} = 1$; when y_{ij} is damaged, $w_{ij} = 0$.

a is the coefficient of the loss function: when $a = 1$, it corresponds to the L_1 norm; when $a = 2$, it corresponds to the L_2 norm.

For Eq. (4), we obtained the following formula by the regularization procedure.

$$\min_{U,V} \left\| W \otimes \left(Y - UV' \right) \right\|_a^a + \frac{\lambda_u}{2} \|U\|_2^2 + \frac{\lambda_v}{2} \|V\|_2^2 \tag{5}$$

In Eq. (5), λ_u and λ_v are the parameters of regularization, and they are greater than zero.

3.2   Matrix Decomposition Based on Likelihood Probability

From the perspective of Bayesian probability, the problem in Eq. (5) can be regarded as a Maximum A Posteriori problem. To improve robustness, we use the L_1 norm to decompose a matrix. The model of matrix decomposition based on probability is as follows:

$$Y = UV' + E \tag{6}$$

$$u_{ij}|\lambda_u \sim N\left(u_{ij}|0, \lambda_u^{-1}\right) \tag{7}$$

$$v_{ij}|\lambda_v \sim N\left(v_{ij}|0, \lambda_v^{-1}\right) \tag{8}$$

where $E = [e_{ij}]$ is the error matrix of size $m \times n$ pixels and each of its elements e_{ij} follows a separate Laplace distribution $L(e_{ij}|0,\lambda)$. We get the following expression:

$$p(E|\lambda) = \left(\frac{\lambda}{2}\right)^{mn} \exp\{-\lambda\|E\|_1\} \tag{9}$$

To calculate U and V, we set λ_u, λ_v and λ to fixed values and then use the MAP based on Bayes' Rule, and we can get:

$$p(U,V|Y, \lambda_u, \lambda_v) \propto p(Y|U,V, \lambda)p(U|Y, \lambda_u)p(V|Y, \lambda_v) \tag{10}$$

$$\log p(U,V|Y, \lambda_u, \lambda_v) = -\lambda\left\| Y - UV' \right\|_1 - \frac{\lambda_u}{2}\|U\|_2^2 - \frac{\lambda_v}{2}\|V\|_2^2 + C \tag{11}$$

where C is a constant independent of U, V. Thus, the problem of solving the maximum value of $\log_p (U, V|Y, \lambda_u, \lambda_v)$ is equivalent that of solving the minimum problem of the following equation:

$$\min_{\mathbf{U},\mathbf{V}} \left\| \mathbf{Y} - \mathbf{U}\mathbf{V}' \right\|_1 + \frac{\lambda_u'}{2} \|\mathbf{U}\|_2^2 + \frac{\lambda_v'}{2} \|\mathbf{V}\|_2^2 \qquad (12)$$

In Eq. (12), $\lambda_u' = \lambda_u'/\lambda$ and $\lambda_v' = \lambda_v'/\lambda$.

3.3 PRMF Algorithm Based on RPCA

The general equation for RPCA has been presented in the previous section:

$$\min_{\mathbf{A}} \quad \|\mathbf{A}\|_* + \lambda \|\mathbf{D} - \mathbf{A}\|_1 \qquad (13)$$

We have known that Eq. (12) is the matrix decomposition equation based on probability and Eq. (13) is the general equation of RPCA, and there are some similarities between them. Literature [17] proposes a theorem of matrix factorization. For any matrix $\mathbf{Z} \in R^{m \times n}$, we have the following expression:

$$\|\mathbf{Z}\|_* = \min_{\mathbf{U},\mathbf{V},\mathbf{Z}=\mathbf{U}\mathbf{V}'} \frac{1}{2} \left(\|\mathbf{U}\|_2^2 + \|\mathbf{V}\|_2^2 \right) \qquad (14)$$

When $\lambda_u' = \lambda_v' = \lambda_r$ and $r = k$, we can get the following results by substituting Eq. (12) for Eq. (14):

$$\min_{\mathbf{U},\mathbf{V}} \left\| \mathbf{Y} - \mathbf{U}\mathbf{V}' \right\|_1 + \frac{\lambda_u'}{2} \|\mathbf{U}\|_2^2 + \frac{\lambda_v'}{2} \|\mathbf{V}\|_2^2$$
$$= \min_{\mathbf{U},\mathbf{V}} \left\| \mathbf{Y} - \mathbf{U}\mathbf{V}' \right\|_1 + \lambda_r \|\mathbf{U}\mathbf{V}'\|_* \qquad (15)$$
$$= \min_{\mathbf{X},rank(\mathbf{X})=k} \|\mathbf{Y} - \mathbf{X}\|_1 + \lambda_r \|\mathbf{X}\|_*$$

Through the above analysis, we established the RPCA method based on the PRMF. Next, we will use our method to solve the problems of surface defects detection of insulators effectively.

4 Analysis of Insulators Surface Defects Detection

4.1 Experiment on Public Datasets

Background modeling is a common application in computer vision processing, with the purpose of separating the dynamic part from the static background. The dynamic part includes moving objects and illumination variations. The static part of surveillance video is generally unchangeable, which can be regarded as the low-rank component $\mathbf{A}$. Moving objects and illumination variations change over time and they can be regarded as sparse component $\mathbf{E}$. This paper selects 200 frames of size 144×176 pixels from public datasets as test samples. As shown in Fig. 1:

(a)   (b)   (c)

Fig. 1. Foreground extraction results based on PRMF-RPCA, (a) original image frame, (b) the low-rank component, (c) the sparse component

From the perspective of computation time, we compared the PRMF-RPCA algorithm with several common RPCA algorithms. From Table 1, we found that PRMF-RPCA algorithm improves the efficiency effectively.

Table 1. The running time of several common RPCA algorithms

	PRMF	APG	IALM	ALM
Time/s	40.45	632.43	119.54	135.93

4.2   Surface Defects Detection of Insulator Strings

Insulators are an indispensable element for transmission lines. The good state of insulators is a prerequisite for power transmission line operation. But insulators can still be damaged by the wind and the sun in a natural environment. Harsh environments will lead to weathered oxidation, breakage and cracks of insulator strings. [18]. This paper presents a method for detecting surface defects in insulators based on PRMF-RPCA. The experiment used 8 insulator images from aerial video as an example. The experimental results are shown in Fig. 2.

As is shown, Fig. 2(a) displays the images of an insulator string. We can find that the insulator string is oxidized into holes in the first image. In the third image, the insulator has a little breakage. Other images exhibit different defects. Figure 2(b) shows the non-defect low-rank component. Figure 2(c) a defective sparse component. From Fig. 2, we can find that except for the defective part, the sparse component is in white and the rest is in black. The rate of defect detection of insulator strings is close to 100%.

4.3   Insulator Surface Defects Detection

To further detect tiny defects of the insulator string, our method is based on insulators. Insulators share a strong similarity which is expressed as the linear low-rank component in the image matrix. The defects on the insulator surface are different generally, as expressed by non-zero elements in the sparse matrices. Therefore, based on the above analysis, we use RPCA to detect surface defects of insulators.

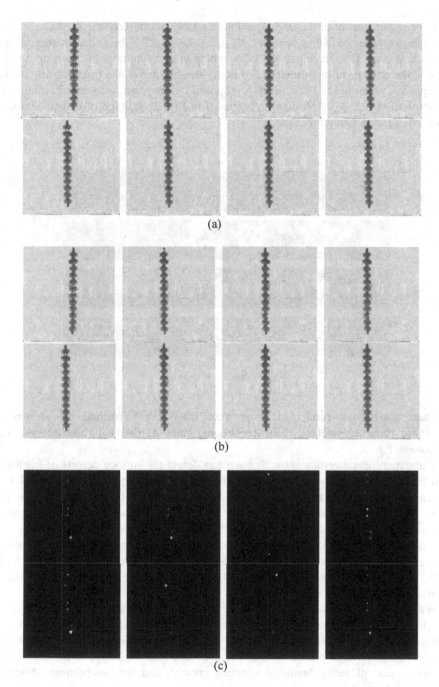

Fig. 2. Surface defects detection results of insulator, (a) the to-be-detected insulator string, (b) the low-rank component, (c) the sparse component

We convert a set of insulator images into a set of column vectors: $X_1, X_2,\ldots\ldots, X_N$. And then we generate matrix $\mathbf{D} = [X_1, X_2,\ldots\ldots, X_N] \in R^{m\times n}$ by concatenating all the vectors and using $\mathbf{D}$ as the input of RPCA, where m is the number of pixels per image and n is the number of input images. To verify the feasibility and practicability of the principle and algorithm of PRMF-RPCA proposed in this paper, we select 20 images of insulators of size 256×256 pixels. As shown in Fig. 3: the type of defects includes noise, cracks, and string breakage.

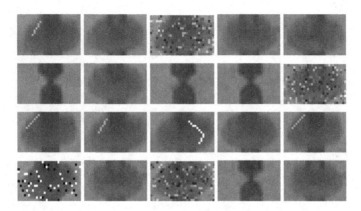

Fig. 3. Insulator images

The experimental results of using the PRMF-RPCA method are shown in Fig. 4: (a) is the non-defective low-rank component $\mathbf{A}$, (b) is the defective sparse component $\mathbf{E}$.

The experimental results show that we can detect the surface defects of insulator from 20 similar images by PRMF-RPCA algorithm successfully. From Figs. 3 and 4(b) we can see that the defects information which got by PRMF-RPCA is the same as the result of manual detection exactly and it is marked with white clearly. The non-defective information is displayed as a black picture in Fig. 4(b).

From Table 2 we can see that our method's running time of 20 images is 24.60 s; the average time is about 1.2 s, but the detection time of APG is 850.32 s, IALM is 122.52 s, and ALM is 168.5 s. From a real-time perspective, our approach has made significant progress over other methods.

We can distinguish the categories of insulator surface defects simply by the sparsity. But the different defects of insulators are expressed by sparse component, which is inadequate. As the experimental results shown in Fig. 4, we found that the gray value of sparse component of normal insulator is low, and then the image is smoother. But the gray value of string breakage changes greatly, and the smoothness of string breakage is poor.

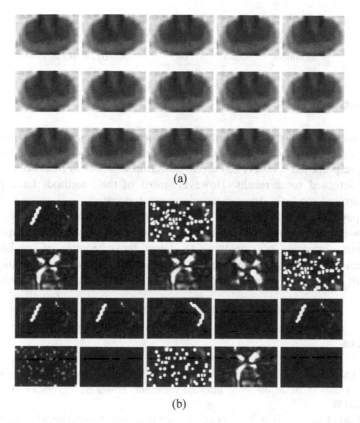

(a)

(b)

Fig. 4. Detection results of surface defects of insulator, (a) low-rank matrix image, (b) sparse matrix image

Table 2. Detection time of insulator surface defects in several common algorithms

	PRMF	APG	IALM	ALM
Time/s	24.60	850.32	122.52	168.46

$$S_p = \frac{1}{M} \sum_{i=0}^{M-1} (x_i - \bar{x})^2 \qquad (16)$$

In Eq. (16), x_i is the value of each pixel of image, $\bar{x}$ is the mean of the image. To distinguish the categories of surface defects of insulators better, we introduce a measure of smoothing to detect the categories of insulators. The smoothness of each category is shown in Table 3: we can conclude that the smoothness of normal insulators is smaller and its image is smoother, but the smoothness of the crack is relatively smaller. Because the noise is dispersed in insulators and it is heterogeneous, and the smoothness of the noise is larger than others'. Thus, we can detect the insulator surface defects better by the smoothness.

Table 3. Smoothness values of insulation surface defects

Defect category	Normal	String breakage	Crack	Noisy
Smoothness	0.0007	0.0667	0.0273	0.1195

5 Conclusion

To detect insulator surface defects from a mess of aerial images, the traditional artificial method is difficult to feed the actual requirements of the engineering. Subsequent scholars have proposed a variety of defects detection methods of insulator surface and they have achieved some results. However, most of their methods have plenty of shortcomings and can only detect categories monotonously.

In this paper, for the similarities of insulators, we decompose the defective insulator into the low-rank component and the sparse component by PRMF-RPCA. Specifically, we introduce a measure of smoothing to detect the categories of insulators. The experimental results show that the method improves the efficiency and ability of surface defects detection of insulators, and realizes the real-time updating detection of insulators.

References

1. Yang, H.M., Liu, Z.G., Han, Y., et al.: Foreign body detection between insulator pieces in electrified railway based on affine moment invariant. Power Syst. Technol. **37**(8), 2297–2302 (2013)
2. Yang, H.M., Liu, Z.G., Han, Z.W., et al.: Foreign body detection between insulator pieces in electrified railway based on affine moment invariant. J. China Railw. Soc. **35**(4), 30–36 (2013)
3. Zhang, X.Y., An, J.B., Chen, F.M.: A method of insulator fault detection from airborne images. In: 2010 Second WRI Global Congress on Intelligent Systems (GCIS), vol. 2, pp. 200–203 (2010)
4. Sun, J.: Research on crack detection of porcelain insulators based on image detection. North China Electric Power University, Baoding, China (2008)
5. Liu, G.H., Jiang, Z.J.: Recognition of porcelain bottle crack based on modified ART-2 network and invariant moment. Chin. J. Sci. Instrum. **30**(7), 1420–1425 (2009)
6. Yao, M.H., Li, J., Wang, X.B.: Solar cells surface defects detection using RPCA method. Chin. J. Comput. **36**(9), 1943–1952 (2013)
7. Jean, J.H., Chen, C.H., Lin, H.L.: Application of an image processing software tool to crack inspection of crystalline silicon solar cells. In: Machine Learning and Cybernetics (ICMLC), vol. 4, pp. 1666–1671, Singapore (2011)
8. Wright, J., Peng, Y.G., Ma, Y., et al.: Robust principal component analysis: exact recovery of corrupted low-rank matrices via convex optimization. Adv. Neural Inf. Process. Syst. **87**(4), 20:3–20:56 (2009)
9. Chen, M.M., Lin, Z.C., Shen, X.Y.: Algorithm and implementation of matrix reconstruction. University of Chinese Academy of Sciences, Beijing (2010)
10. Candès, E.J., Li, X., Ma, Y., et al.: Robust principal component analysis? J. ACM (JACM) **58**(3), 11 (2011)

11. Jin, J.Y.: Separation of image based on sparse representation. Xidian University, Xi'an, China (2011)
12. Cai, J.F., Candès, E.J., Shen, Z.: A singular value thresholding algorithm for matrix completion. SIAM J. Optim. **20**(4), 1956–1982 (2010)
13. Peng, Y., Ganesh, A., Wright, J., et al.: RASL: robust alignment by sparse and low-rank decomposition for linearly correlated images. IEEE Trans. Pattern Anal. Mach. Intell. **34** (11), 2233–2246 (2012)
14. Ke, Q., Kanade, T.: Robust L1 norm factorization in the presence of outliers and missing data by alternative convex programming. In: 2005 IEEE Conference on Computer Vision and Pattern Recognition, pp. 739–746. IEEE (2005)
15. Lin, Z., Chen, M., Ma, Y.: The augmented lagrange multiplier method for exact recovery of corrupted low-rank matrices. arXiv preprint arXiv:1009.5055 (2010)
16. Wang, N., Yao, T., Wang, J., Yeung, D.-Y.: A probabilistic approach to robust matrix factorization. In: Fitzgibbon, A., Lazebnik, S., Perona, P., Sato, Y., Schmid, C. (eds.) ECCV 2012. LNCS, vol. 7578, pp. 126–139. Springer, Heidelberg (2012). https://doi.org/10.1007/978-3-642-33786-4_10
17. Mazumder, R., Hastie, T., Tibshirani, R.: Spectral regularization algorithms for learning large incomplete matrices. J. Mach. Learn. Res. **11**(Aug), 2287–2322 (2010)
18. Cui, K.B.: Research on the key technologies in insulator defect detection based on image. North China Electric Power University, Beijing (2016)

A Dim Small Target Detection Method Based on Spatial-Frequency Domain Features Space

Jinqiu Sun[1], Danna Xue[1(✉)], Haisen Li[2], Yu Zhu[2], and Yanning Zhang[2]

[1] School of Astronautics, Northwestern Polytechnical University, Xi'an 710072, China
donna93826@gmail.com
[2] School of Computer Science and Technology, Northwestern Polytechnical University, Xi'an 710072, China

Abstract. The target detection, especially extracting low SNR potential targets and stars from the star images, plays as a key technology in the space debris surveillance. Due to the complexity of the imaging environment, the detection of dim small targets in star images faces many difficulties, including low SNR and rare unstable features. This paper proposes a dim small target detection method based on the high dimensional spatial-frequency domain features extracted by filter bank, and training the support vector machine (SVM) classifier. The experimental results demonstrate that the proposed method exceeds the state-of-the-art on the ability to detect low SNR targets.

Keywords: Dim and small target detection · Filter bank
Support vector machine (SVM)

1 Introduction

The space debris number increases greatly in the last decades due to the intense outer space exploration, making a deteriorating earth orbit. The space debris detecting, dodging and removing become a remarkable international issue. In this case, the surveillance of the space debris becomes a hot topic in the space exploration. Meanwhile, the improvement of the space debris surveillance and early warning system, especially the detection of dim small targets, plays as a key technology.

Due to the complexity of the imaging environment in space, the detection of dim small targets in star images is influenced by low noise-signal ratio and rare unstable features and the similarity between stars and targets. As the imaging distance is too far, and the size of the space debris itself is also small, the spot of the target in the star image target has only 3–100 pixels without obvious texture features. Many commonly used feature extraction operators, such as Canny, LBP, SIFT and etc., cannot effectively extract the features in the star image. The target is approximately Gaussian distribution on the image with the brightest pixel as the center, and the surroundings are scattered into a circular or elliptical spot. The gray value of the surrounding pixels is lower than the center pixel. In the image sequence, since the movement of the target

© Springer International Publishing AG 2017
Y. Zhao et al. (Eds.): ICIG 2017, Part II, LNCS 10667, pp. 174–183, 2017.
https://doi.org/10.1007/978-3-319-71589-6_16

and background noise, the gray level, area, SNR and other intuitive features of the target are constantly changing.

Due to the characteristic of the star image, most of the existing detectors handle the problem from two aspects. The first one is to choose better threshold for segmentation. Consider of the uneven illumination, adaptive local threshold segmentation method [1–3] was proposed. The segmentation threshold is calculated in each divided sub-image instead of setting a global threshold [4–6]. However, the relationship between the adjacent target pixels and the distribution of the gray level are not taken into account. The other make uses of other features of the image, such as the target geometry the detection method based on mathematical morphology [7], the target detection method based on the statistical model [8], the target detection based on wavelet analysis method [9], and the genetic algorithm [10] which is robust to complex background. Pixel based methods usually use multi-frame image to detect target. For example, the method based on inter-frame difference [11] and the self-adaptive optical flow method [12] need at least 2 images to determine the motion of the targets. Although these algorithms have improved accuracy, there are still limitation on detecting the low SNR target.

In this paper, we consider the problems mentioned above and propose dim small target detecting method with feature learning. The main contributions of our work can be summarized as follows:

- We design a filter bank based on the imaging characteristics of the small debris and noises, to makes full use of the correlation between the adjacent pixels of the target. The experimental results demonstrated that the features extracted by the designed filter banks achieve better than the traditional features such as gray level, etc.
- We take the detection problem as a classification problem. A SVM classifier trained by labeled star image is used to detect the stars and potential targets. The training process of the SVM classifier is simple but the effective.

2 The Spatial-Frequency Domain Features Based Dim Small Target Detection

2.1 Dim Small Target Imaging Model

The target imaging model in a single frame is shown in Eq. (1):

$$T^t + B^t = \alpha^t_{(x_i,y_j)} \delta^t(x_i, y_j) \otimes h_o \otimes h_T^t + n^t(x, y) \quad x, y \in N_T \tag{1}$$

where T^t is the ideal imaging model for the target at the moment, B^t is the background in the moment of the imaging model. The real target imaging model is the result of the superposition of the target itself and the noises. $\alpha^t_{(x_i,y_j)}$ is the brightness of target, $\delta^t_{(x_i,y_j)}$ is the impact function, h_o for the optical system blur kernel, which is generated by the design and manufacture of camera optical system. h_T^t is the target motion blur kernel, which is generated by the relative motion between the camera and targets, $n^t_{(x,y)}$ is the noise gray level at pixel on location of (x, y).

The only difference between stars and targets is the motion blur kernel. In this paper, we only focus on detection in single frame, so we treat star and debris target as the same class. The stars and targets will be distinguished by their motion features with multi-frame in subsequent steps.

2.2 Dim Small Target Detection

In this paper, we use a filter bank consisting of 29 filters to extract the features of each pixel in the star images. The features extracted from the labeled real star image are then used to train the SVM classifier. After obtaining the optimal parameters, target in new star image can be detected by the trained SVM classifier (Fig. 1).

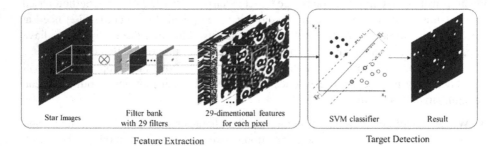

Fig. 1. The workflow of the proposed method

Feature Extraction with Filter Bank. Consider of the distribution of the gray level and the motion blur, we design a filter bank consisting of 29 filters to extract the features of the stars and potential targets in different scales (Fig. 2).

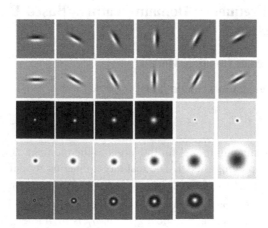

Fig. 2. The filter bank has a mix of edge, bar and spot filters at multiple scales and orientations. It has a total of 29 filters - 2 Gaussian derivative filters at 6 orientations, 8 Laplacian of Gaussian filters, 4 Gaussian filters and 5 S filters.

The labeled images are convolved with the 29 filters respectively. The feature vector of every pixel in the image is 29-dimentional.

$$Feature_i = I_{train} \otimes filter_i \quad i = 1, \ldots, 29 \tag{2}$$

The Gaussian filters. The Gaussian derivative filters consist of 4 rotationally invariant filters of the form.

$$G(x, y) = \frac{1}{2\pi\sigma^2} e^{-\frac{x^2+y^2}{2\sigma^2}} \tag{3}$$

where x, y are the two-dimensional coordinates, σ is $\sqrt{2}, 2, 2\sqrt{2}, 4$.

The Gaussian derivative filters. The Gaussian derivative filters consist of filters at 6 orientations.

$$\begin{bmatrix} x' \\ y' \end{bmatrix} = \begin{bmatrix} \cos\theta & -\sin\theta \\ \sin\theta & \cos\theta \end{bmatrix} \begin{bmatrix} x \\ y \end{bmatrix} \tag{4}$$

where x, y are the two-dimensional coordinates, x', y' are the coordinates after rotation, θ is the direction, respectively, taking 0°, 30°, 60°, 90°, 120° and 150°.

$$\frac{\partial G}{\partial x'} = \left(-\frac{1}{2\pi\sigma_x^4}\right) x e^{-\frac{x^2+y^2}{2\sigma_x^2}}, \frac{\partial G}{\partial y'} = \left(-\frac{1}{2\pi\sigma_y^4}\right) y e^{-\frac{x^2+y^2}{2\sigma_y^2}} \tag{5}$$

$$\frac{\partial^2 G}{\partial x'^2} = \left(-\frac{1}{2\pi\sigma_x^4}\right)\left(1 - \frac{x^2}{\sigma_x^2}\right) e^{-\frac{x^2+y^2}{2\sigma_x^2}}, \frac{\partial^2 G}{\partial y'^2} = \left(-\frac{1}{2\pi\sigma_y^4}\right)\left(1 - \frac{y^2}{\sigma_y^2}\right) e^{-\frac{x^2+y^2}{2\sigma_y^2}} \tag{6}$$

where σ_x is $6\sqrt{2}$, σ_y is $2\sqrt{2}$.

The Laplacian of Gaussian filters. The LOG filters consist of 8 rotationally invariant filters.

$$LoG(x, y) = -\frac{1}{\pi\sigma^4}\left[1 - \frac{x^2+y^2}{2\sigma^2}\right] e^{-\frac{x^2+y^2}{2\sigma^2}} \tag{7}$$

where σ takes $\sqrt{2}, 2, 2\sqrt{2}, 4, 3\sqrt{2}, 6, 6\sqrt{2}, 12$, respectively.

The Schmid (S) filters. The S filters [13] consist of 5 rotationally invariant filters.

$$S(r, \sigma, \tau) = \cos\left(\frac{\pi\tau r}{\sigma}\right) \exp\left(-\frac{r^2}{2\sigma^2}\right) \tag{8}$$

where $F0(\sigma, \tau)$ is added to obtain a zero DC component with the (σ, τ) pair taking values (2, 1), (4, 1), (6, 1), (8, 1), and (10, 1). The filters have rotational symmetry.

In this paper, we use the Eq. (9) to normalize the data range to $[-1,1]$, to get rid of influence of scale difference.

$$x^* = x_{\min} + 2 \times \frac{x - x_{\min}}{x_{\max} - x_{\min}}, x \in D, x^* \in D^* \tag{9}$$

where D is the dataset need to be normalized, D^* is the normalized dataset, x and x^* are the element of D and D^*, respectively. $x_{\max}$ and $x_{\min}$ are the largest and smallest elements in D.

Balance of the sample. In the star image, the number of background pixels far exceed the number of target pixels, which more than one order of magnitude. When the number of positive and negative samples are very disparity, the classifier only classifying the major class correctly can achieve high precision. Therefore, in order to ensure the balance amount of training samples, we select a part of the background pixels as the negative samples for training from the feature space corresponding to the star image.

Since the influence of the inconsistent background illumination may influence the performance, we divide the image into several regions, and the background pixels are taken randomly from every region of the image to ensure the pixel samples are distributed on the whole image. In this paper, every training image is divided into 16 regions, and the same number of background points are randomly sampled in each area as the training sample input.

SVM Classifier Training. In the feature space obtained by the above processing, the training data set T can be expressed as:

$$T = \{(\mathbf{x}_1, \mathbf{y}_1), (\mathbf{x}_2, \mathbf{y}_2), \ldots (\mathbf{x}_N, \mathbf{y}_N)\}, \mathbf{x}_i \in \chi = R^n, 1 \leq i \leq N \tag{10}$$

where $\mathbf{x}_i$ is the n dimensional feature vector of the ith training sample, $\mathbf{y}_i$ is the class label of the ith training sample, N is the number of samples in the training data set.

Each pixel has an n-dimensional feature vector. In this n-dimensional feature space, the features are linearly inseparable, so it is necessary to map the space to high-dimensional space and then classify it.

In the original linear space $\chi \subset \mathbf{R}^n, \mathbf{x} = \left(x^{(1)}, x^{(2)}, \cdots, x^{(n)}\right)^T \in \chi$, where χ is the input of low-dimensional space. The mapping high-dimensional space is $Z \subset \mathbf{R}^m, \mathbf{z} = \left(z^{(1)}, z^{(2)}, \cdots, z^{(m)}\right)^T \in Z, (m > n)$. Here, the radial basis function (RBF) is used to map the nonlinear samples to the high-dimensional space.

$$K(\mathbf{x}, \mathbf{z}) = \exp\left(-\gamma \|\mathbf{x} - \mathbf{x}_c\|^2\right) \quad \gamma > 0 \tag{11}$$

where $\mathbf{x}$ the original feature vector. $\mathbf{z}$ is the corresponding feature vector in the high dimensional space. $\mathbf{x}_c$ is the center of the kernel function.

And then use the idea of maximizing the interval to find a class of hyperplanes as shown in Eq. (12) in the training data set.

$$w^T \mathbf{z} + b = 0 \tag{12}$$

where w and b are the normal vector and the intercept of the classification hyperplane. The corresponding decision function is formula (13).

$$f(x) = sign(w^T \mathbf{z} + b) = \begin{cases} 1 & w^T \mathbf{z} + b > 0 \\ 0 & w^T \mathbf{z} + b < 0 \end{cases} \tag{13}$$

The training of the SVM classifier minimizes the objective function in Eq. (13). The aim is to maximize the support vector, at the same time, minimize the number of misclassified samples.

$$\min_{\omega, b, \xi} \frac{1}{2} \|w\|^2 + C \sum_{i=1}^{N} \xi_i$$
$$s.t \ y_i(w^T z_i + b) \geq 1 - \xi_i, \xi_i \geq 0, i = 1, 2, \ldots, N \tag{14}$$

where ξ_i is the relaxation variable, and $\xi_i \geq 0$, C is the penalty parameter, $C > 0$.

The optimal classification parameters C and γ corresponding to the SVM classifier are determined through twice grid search. The range of parameters are divided into different grids according to a certain separation method. Then the algorithm iterates through the points in each grid to determine the relative optimal parameters for the classifier.

The bigger grids are applied in the first search. After finding out the best interval, the smaller grids are creating within the interval for the second search. The specific search method is as follows (Table 1):

Table 1. The process of grid search

	Input: the search range and search grid size for C and γ
	Output: optimal parameter C and γ
1	Grid search
2	Cross validation to find the optimal classification prediction results
3	If the search condition is satisfied, the optimal search range is obtained, otherwise return Step 1
4	Determine the small search interval and the grid size
5	Grid search
6	Cross validation to find the optimal classification prediction results
7	If the search condition is satisfied, the optimal parameter C and γ is obtained, otherwise return Step 5
8	End

Here we use 5-fold cross validation to determine the classification performance of the classifier in a single training process. The original data is divided into five parts, four of which as a data training set, the rest one as the validation set. During the training process, the training set is used to train the classifier, and then the verification set is used to verify the classification performance of the classifier. The average of the five results is the classification performance of the classifier.

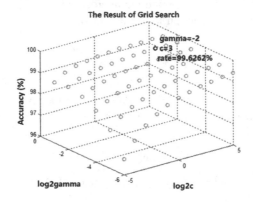

Fig. 3. The results of grid search (Color figure online)

As shown in Fig. 3, each blue circle represents a grid parameter optimization process. When the penalty function parameter C is 3, and the parameter γ is −2, the classifier classification performance is optimal, classification accuracy rate of 99.626%.

3 Experiments

In this section, more than 3000 labeled star images with hot-pixel, cosmic rays and other noises are experimented with the proposed method. The environment is Windows 7, Core i3 processor, memory 6 G, the program is coded in MATLAB R2013a.

3.1 Detection Rate

In this paper, the detection is on pixel level, so the detection rate is defined as the proportion of correctly classified target pixels in the ground truth target pixels (Fig. 4).

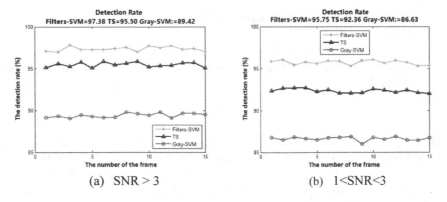

(a) SNR > 3   (b) 1<SNR<3

Fig. 4. The detection rate of target with different SNR

The Filters-SVM method tends to have a better detection rate when processing the same sequence of images. The detection rate of the Filters-SVM method is higher than 95% for different SNR targets. The average detection rate of adaptive local threshold segmentation is only 92.36% when the target SNR is lower.

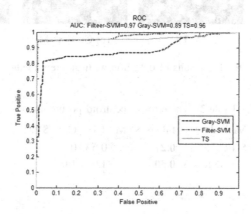

Fig. 5. The ROC line graph of different methods

The ROC curve of our method higher than the other methods, and the AUC value of Filters-SVM is 0.97, which is greater than the AUC value of adaptive local threshold segmentation (0.96) and Gray-SVM method (0.89).

3.2   Shape Retention Ability

Haralick [14] established four criteria to evaluate the performance of segmentation. (a) For some features, such as gray level and texture, the same region should be coincident and uniform. (b) The area should be simple and without a lot of holes. (c) There are significant differences between the adjacent regions. (d) The boundary of each region should be simple but not rough, and the space position is accurate.

The target shape is a key factor in the process of target centroid localization. The more complete the target shape, the more accurate the centroid positioning results. The retention of the target shape in the three methods is analyzed. The results are shown in Fig. 6.

The proposed method (Filters-SVM) is compared with adaptive local threshold segmentation (TS), and gray based SVM (Gray-SVM), which use only gray level as features to train the SVM classifier. The result demonstrates that the Filters-SVM method (in Fig. 5) has least incorrectly classification on the background noise. The edge of the target is smooth.

The centroid position of target in the image will be later used to determine the orbit. A very small error can lead to several kilometers of track position error. In this paper, we evaluate the performance of detection method also by the centroid positioning error. Here we use the energy accumulation centroid positioning method proposed in [15] (Table 2).

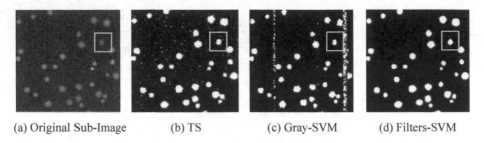

| (a) Original Sub-Image | (b) TS | (c) Gray-SVM | (d) Filters-SVM |

Fig. 6. The results of detection with different method

Table 2. The error of centroid positioning

Method	Filters-SVM	TS	Gray-SVM
SNR > 3	**0.27**	0.53	0.72
1 < SNR < 3	**0.50**	1.07	1.05

3.3 Speed

Due to the real-time requirement of dim small target detection in star image, the processing time of single-frame image is also an important criterion of small target detection method. In this experiment, the single frame image processing time is analyzed.

Table 3. The average processing time in single frame

Method	Filters-SVM	TS (with post-process)	Gray-SVM
Average processing time	0.27 s	0.14 s (0.34 s)	0.24 s

Table 3 shows the single frame processing time for three different target detection methods. The result of adaptive local threshold segmentation consist of many wrongly classified pixels, and generally cooperated with the post-process to deal with the wrong pixels. Therefore, this experiment also considered its impact on single-frame image processing time. The Filters-SVM method meets the requirements of real-time processing.

4   Conclusion

This paper proposes a low-signal-to-noise star point detection method for star images based on the high-dimensional features. In this paper, the target detection is solved as an image classification problem. Firstly, the designed filter banks is used to extract the high-dimensional features, and then the classifier is trained according to the characteristics. Finally, the detection of potential targets and stars is realized by the trained classifier. The experimental results show that our method can detect the dim and small targets and stars in the star image, and can effectively prevent the interference of the noise. The weak targets with small spots, low brightness and low signal-to-noise ratio are well extracted.

Acknowledgements. This work is supported by the Major Program of National Natural Science Foundation of China (No. 61231016); the National High Technology Research and Development Program of China (No. 2015AA016402); the Seed Foundation of Innovation and Creation for Graduate Students in Northwestern Polytechnical University (Z2017003).

References

1. Gueguen, L., Velasco-Forero, S., Soille, P.: Local mutual information for dissimilarity-based image segmentation. J. Math. Imaging Vis. **48**(3), 625–644 (2014)
2. Xia, Y., Ji, Z., Zhang, Y.: Brain MRI image segmentation based on learning local variational Gaussian mixture models. Neurocomputing **204**, 189–197 (2016)
3. Wang, X.F., Min, H., Zhang, Y.G.: Multi-scale local region based level set method for image segmentation in the presence of intensity inhomogeneity. Neurocomputing **151**, 1086–1098 (2015)
4. Wang, X., Tang, Y., Masnou, S., et al.: A global/local affinity graph for image segmentation. IEEE Trans. Image Process. **24**(4), 1399–1411 (2015). A Publication of the IEEE Signal Processing Society
5. Wang, H., Huang, T.Z., Xu, Z., et al.: A two-stage image segmentation via global and local region active contours. Neurocomputing **205**, 130–140 (2016)
6. Altarawneh, N.M., Luo, S., Regan, B., et al.: Global threshold and region-based active contour model for accurate image segmentation. Signal Image Process. **5**(3), 1–11 (2014)
7. Caponetti, L., Castellano, G., Basile, M.T., et al.: Fuzzy mathematical morphology for biological image segmentation. Appl. Intell. **41**(1), 117–127 (2014)
8. Chen, B., Zou, Q.H., Li, Y.: A new image segmentation model with local statistical characters based on variance minimization. Appl. Math. Model. **39**(12), 3227–3235 (2015)
9. Meng, X., He, Z., Feng, G., et al.: An improved wavelet denoising algorithm for wideband radar targets detection. Circuits Syst. Signal Process. **32**(4), 2003–2026 (2013)
10. Maity, S.P., Nandi, P.K., Kundu, M.K.: Genetic algorithm for improvement in detection of hidden data in digital images. In: The Sixth International Conference on Advances in Pattern Recognition, pp. 164–169 (2011)
11. Cheng, Y.H., Wang, J.: A motion image detection method based on the inter-frame difference method. Appl. Mech. Mater. **490–491**, 1283–1286 (2014)
12. Xin, Y., Hou, J., Dong, L., et al.: A self-adaptive optical flow method for the moving object detection in the video sequences. Opt. – Int. J. Light Electron Opt. **125**(19), 5690–5694 (2014)
13. Varma, M., Zisserman, A.: A statistical approach to texture classification from single images. Int. J. Comput. Vis. **62**(1), 61–81 (2005)
14. Haralick, R.M., Shapiro, L.G.: Image segmentation techniques. Comput. Vis. Graph. Image Process. **29**(1), 100–132 (1985)
15. Sun, J.Q., Zhou, J., Zhang, Z., et al.: Centroid location for space targets based on energy accumulation. Opt. Precis. Eng. **19**(12), 3043–3048 (2011)

Compression, Transmission, Retrieval

An Algorithm for Tight Frame Grouplet to Compute Association Fields

Jingwen Yan[1] ⓘ, Zhenguo Yuan[1](✉) ⓘ, Tingting Xie[1] ⓘ,
and Huimin Zhao[2,3] ⓘ

[1] Department of Electronic Engineering, Shantou University,
Shantou, Guangdong, China
16zgyuan@stu.edu.cn
[2] School of Electronic and Information,
Guangdong Polytechnic Normal University, Guangzhou, Guangdong, China
[3] Key Laboratory of Digital Content Processing and Security Technology
of Guangzhou City, Guangzhou, Guangdong, China

Abstract. Tight frame grouplet transform is a kind of weighted multiscale Haar transform with a causality imposed on the association field. Defined with a causality property, multiscale association fields become more flexible to construct grouplets which can adapt the different geometry structure in different scales. Grouplet transform uses the block matching algorithm to compute association field coefficients, which needs more operations than the computation of grouplet coefficients. An algorithm named LD-PO based on line detection and partial ordering is proposed to make grouplet transform become more efficient. It takes the place of block matching algorithm to compute association field coefficients. The LD-PO algorithm uses line detection masks and the feature of partial ordering to compute geometric flow in an image. Experimental results show that tight frame grouplet using LD-PO algorithm can also reconstruct an image with no loss. Compared with the block matching algorithm, it's complexity to compute association field coefficients is fewer and the loss of grouplet coefficients' sparsity can be ignored.

Keywords: Grouplet transform · Association field · Line detection
Partial ordering · Complexity

1 Introduction

Images often contain regions composed of locally oriented structures. These geometric structures provide fundamental features for many problems in computer vision and image processing [1]. It is required to improve state of image processing algorithms to efficiently represent these complex structures.

Wavelet bases are the optimal bases that represent point singularity. They can adapt the processing resolution to the local image regularity [2]. However, the discontinuity of natural images is usually represented by smooth curves because natural objects' edges and borders are smooth. Wavelet bases are suboptimal to represent images that contain complex geometrical structures because their square support is not adapted to

© Springer International Publishing AG 2017
Y. Zhao et al. (Eds.): ICIG 2017, Part II, LNCS 10667, pp. 187–196, 2017.
https://doi.org/10.1007/978-3-319-71589-6_17

represent linear singularity. To take advantage of geometrical image regularities in space or time, Mallat proposed grouplet orthogonal bases and tight frames [3]. In spirit of the "Gestalt" psychophysics school [4–6], the geometry is constructed with grouping processes which define multiscale association fields [7]. Many researchers have applied grouplet model to practice. A reduced reference perceptual image quality measure based on the grouplet transform is proposed in [8]. In order to get better fusion effect, grouplet transform is applied and coefficients are fused by PCNN [9]. An advanced grouplet transform is proposed that make use of the advantage of Greedy algorithm and Dynamic Programming algorithm in association fields pruning [10]. A grouplet framework is presented to be applied to inpainting and synthesis [11].

This paper introduces algorithm based on line detection and partial ordering to compute association fields which is along the orientation of geometric flow [12–14]. Section 2 describes the coefficient layer computation of tight frame grouplet. Section 3 introduces algorithm based on line detection and partial ordering in the association field layer computation. Experimental results are described in Sect. 4 to show advantages of the presented algorithm LD-PO.

2   Tight Frame Grouplet Coefficients Layer Computation

2.1   Forward Decomposition

Different from orthogonal grouplet, tight frame grouplet is redundant and can be constructed without an embedded subgrid structure. It ascribes to the use of partial ordering. To an image F including N samples, a grouplet frame transforms it into multiscale difference coefficients and coarse scale average coefficients. We can get these coefficients from successive grouping and computation according to multiscale association fields.

Initialize $a = F$. A new array $s[n]$ which ensures energy conservation is created to store the support size of the averaging coefficients of F. At the initialization, for $j = 0$, since $a = F$, it results that $s[m] = 1$ for any integer $1 \leq m \leq N$. For j going from 1 to J, the averaging size is update by

$$\hat{s} = s[m] + s[\tilde{m}], \tag{1}$$

difference coefficient is computed by

$$d_j[\tilde{m}] = (a[\tilde{m}] - a[m])\sqrt{\frac{s[m]s[\tilde{m}]}{\hat{s}}}, \tag{2}$$

average coefficient is computed by

$$\hat{a} = \frac{s[m]a[m] + s[\tilde{m}]a[\tilde{m}]}{\hat{s}}. \tag{3}$$

These values are stored "in place": $a[m] = \hat{a}$ and $s[m] = \hat{s}$. At the coarsest scale 2^J, for all m, the average coefficients are normalized:

$$a_J[m] = a[m]\sqrt{s[m]}.$$ (4)

A forward decomposition transforms an image F of size N into a family of $J+1$ grouplet coefficient arrays $\{d_j[m], a_J[m]\}_{1 \leq j \leq J}$. For a signal of N, Eqs. (1), (2) and (3) compute the $(J+1)N$ grouplet coefficients with $O(JN)$ operations.

2.2 Backward Decomposition

A backward decomposition can restore an image F from its grouplet coefficients $\{d_j[m], a_J[m]\}_{1 \leq j \leq J}$. Tight frame grouplet has an infinite number of left inverses because of the redundant representation. The best inverse for noise removal by thresholding is the pseudo-inverse [3].

The average coefficient normalization (4) is then inverted

$$\forall m, a[m] = \frac{a_J[m]}{\sqrt{s[m]}}.$$ (5)

Each grouping operator is then inverted in the reverse order it was calculated. For j decreasing from J to 1, the scale support is updates by

$$\tilde{s} = s[m] - s[\tilde{m}].$$ (6)

By inverting the grouplet transform (2) and (3), the finer scale average coefficients are computed:

$$\tilde{a}_- = a[m] + d_j[\tilde{m}] \frac{\sqrt{\tilde{s}}}{\sqrt{s[\tilde{m}]s[m]}}$$ (7)

and

$$\tilde{a}_+ = a[m] - d_j[\tilde{m}] \frac{\sqrt{s[\tilde{m}]}}{\sqrt{\tilde{s}s[m]}}.$$ (8)

[3] also proves that the pseudo-inverse is implemented with equal averaging weights on causal and anti-causal reconstructions:

$$\tilde{a} = \frac{\tilde{a}_- + a[\tilde{m}]}{2} \quad \text{and} \quad a[\tilde{m}] = \tilde{a}.$$ (9)

The averaging size is then updated $s[m] = \tilde{s}$.

At the end of the loop over all j and n, this left inverse reconstructs the image $F = a$. If F has N samples, this reconstruction is performed with $O(JN)$ operations.

3 Tight Frame Grouplet Association Field Layer Computation

3.1 The Complexity of Block Matching Algorithm

For a giving image $F \in \mathbb{R}^2$ that has $N = n \times n$ pixels, we need to estimate the local texture orientation and the association fields $\{A_j[m]\}$ store the difference of positions among different points. Block matching algorithm [15] is used to compute association fields in [3], it finds the $p = m$ which minimizes this distance:

$$\mathrm{m} = \underset{\substack{p \in N(\hat{m}) \\ p \; before \; \tilde{m}}}{\arg\min} \sum_{n \in B(p)} |a[n] - a[n+m-p]|^k with \;\; k = 1 \;\; or \;\; \mathrm{k} = 2. \qquad (10)$$

In Eq. (10), the size of the neighborhoods $N(\hat{m})$ is $K \cdot B(p)$ is a block of P points. The block matching computes the JN values of the J association fields A_j with $O(JNKP)$ operations. If we compute all association fields from the finest scale association field A_1, the computational complexity becomes $O(NKP + JN)$. It's important to point out that the value of J is usually far less than the value of KP when it comes to the practical application. It means that the complexity of a whole tight frame grouplet is up to the complexity of association field layer computation. Proposed algorithm in this paper is aimed to reduce the complexity and it just need $O(JN)$ operations, which will be proved in Sect. 3.2.

3.2 Proposed Algorithm Based on Line Detection and Partial Ordering

It is well known that discrete wavelet transform has an orientation selectivity. For example, for a scale 2^j that increases from 2^1 to 2^J, and for all $0 \leq n < 2^{-j}N$, the Haar transform groups consecutive average coefficients $a[2n]$ and $a[2n+1]$, and it computes a next scale average

$$a[n] = \frac{a[2n] + a[2n+1]}{2}, \qquad (11)$$

together with a normalized difference:

$$d_j[n] = (a[2n+1] - a[2n])\sqrt{2^{(j-1)}}. \qquad (12)$$

In scale 2^j, we first compute coefficients along the horizontal direction and then along the vertical direction according to Eqs. (11) and (12). The image is then divided into four parts: average coefficients LL, difference coefficients along the horizontal direction HL, difference coefficients along the vertical direction LH and difference coefficients along the diagonal direction HH.

It is obviously not enough to express images with complex shapes and textures in three orientations. In contrast to determining the direction from the coarse scale in discrete wavelet transform, a new geometric flow computation algorithm named

LD-PO based on line detection and partial ordering is proposed. For spatial geometric grouping, a grouplet partial ordering can be defined with respect to a preferential direction of angle θ. A point $x = (x_1, x_2) \in \mathbb{R}^2$ is said to be before $\tilde{x} = (\tilde{x}_1, \tilde{x}_2) \in \mathbb{R}^2$ with respect to a partial ordering of angle θ if

$$x_1 \cos \theta + x_2 \sin \theta < \tilde{x}_1 \cos \theta + \tilde{x}_2 \sin \theta. \tag{13}$$

Proposed algorithm LD-PO aims to compute geometric flow from pixel level. It is normally hard to complete the computation, but the use of partial ordering dramatically simplifies the computation. Figure 1(a) shows a binary image. The red line is discretized and represented by black pixels. If partial ordering of angle $\theta = 0$ in Eq. (13) is used, which means that coefficients are ordered by columns by columns, the red line then can be regard as a geometric flow of this binary image and the flow's orientation is from right to left. A point $\tilde{m}$ is grouped with m which is before $\tilde{m}$, if point $\tilde{m}$ and m are along the same geometric flow. The angle range from m to $\tilde{m}$ is $(-90°, +90°)$. The difference of positions is stored in an association field array: $A_j[\tilde{m}] = m - \tilde{m}$.

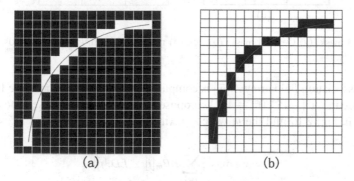

Fig. 1. Binary image. (Color figure online)

In this paper, geometric flow is regarded as the composition of numerous polygonal lines in pixel-level. Proposed algorithm LD-PO looks for polygonal lines by running a 3×3 mask through the image. The response of the mask at any point is acquired by computing the sum of products of the coefficients with the gray levels contained in the region encompassed by the mask:

$$R = \sum_{i=1}^{9} w_i z_i. \tag{14}$$

In Eq. (14), z_i is the gray level of the pixel associated with mask coefficient w_i Particularly, z_i takes value in set $\{0, 1\}$ in binary image. As usual, the response of the mask is defined with respect to its center location. Figure 2 (b), (c) and (d) are line detection masks which will respond strongly to lines oriented at $0°$, lines oriented at $+45°$ and lines oriented at $-45°$ respectively.

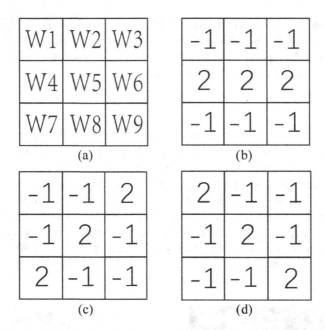

Fig. 2. 3×3 mask. (a) General mask; (b), (c), (d) mask of detecting direction of $0°$, $+45°$ and $-45°$ separately.

When association field array $A_j[\tilde{m}]$ is computed by 3×3 mask, the angle from m to $\tilde{m}$ takes value in set $\{-45°, 0°, +45°\}$. Proposed algorithm LD-PO uses line detection masks LD_i in Fig. 2 to find the m which maximizes:

$$m = \arg\max |\sum_{j=1}^{9} BP_{\tilde{m}}[j] \times LD_i[j]|. \tag{15}$$

$BP_{\tilde{m}}$ is a 3×3 image matrix, in which center location point $\tilde{m}$ is. It's then transformed into a binary matrix by:

$$BP_{\tilde{m}}[i] = \begin{cases} 0 & if \ BP_{\tilde{m}}[i] < Av \\ 1 & others \end{cases}, \text{for integer } i \in [1, 9]. \tag{16}$$

Thresholding criteria Av is the average gray value of image matrix $BP_{\tilde{m}}$ in Eq. (16). Notation i in Eq. (15) represents the direction that mask LD detects. The LD-PO algorithm computes absolute value of the sum of products to void discussing opposite situation in Fig. 1(b), in which situation the best response is a negative value.

After finding the best point m, we associate point $\tilde{m}$ to m and update association field array: $A_j[\tilde{m}] = m - \tilde{m}$ in scale 2^j. The size of binary matrix BP and line detection mask LD is a fixed value 9 and it needs to compute just 3 times to find the best orientation. To an image F with N samples, proposed algorithm LD-PO computes the JN values of the J association fields A_j with $O(27JN) = O(JN)$ operations, which has the same complexity as forward decomposition.

4 Experimental Results and Conclusions

We perform experiments to validate the efficiency of the proposed LD-PO algorithm and compare it with block matching algorithm used by Mallat in [3]. Standard test images in Fig. 3 are selected whose gray level is 256, including Lena of size 512×512 and Babar of size 128×128. Each image is transformed by tight frame grouplet respectively using LD-PO algorithm and block matching to compute association fields.

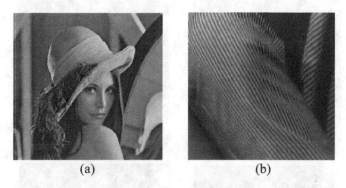

(a)   (b)

Fig. 3. Test image. (a) Lena, size of 512×512. (b) Babar, size of 128×128.

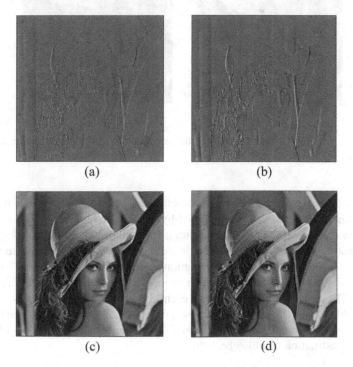

(a)   (b)

(c)   (d)

Fig. 4. Results of block matching. (a) Detail of scale 2^1. (b) Detail of scale 2^2. (c) The approximation. (d) Reconstructed image.

Figure 4 shows experimental results on image Lena by tight frame grouplet using block matching and results of proposed LD-PO algorithm are showed in Fig. 5. According to the comparison of (a) and (b) in Figs. 4 and 5, LD-PO algorithm can also describe detail information. Figure 5(d) is the result of inverse grouplet transform, which shows LD-PO algorithm's same ability to reconstruct image perfectly like block matching algorithm.

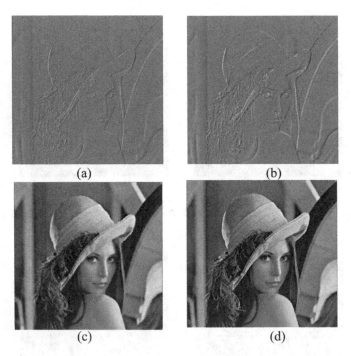

Fig. 5. Results of LD-PO algorithm. (a) Detail of scale 2^1. (b) Detail of scale 2^2. (c) The approximation. (d) Reconstructed image.

Figure 6 describes image Babar's geometric flow in scale 2^1, in which scale the flow is the finest. Geometric flow computed by block matching is showed in Fig. 6(a) and (c). Flow computed by LD-PO algorithm is showed in Fig. 6(b) and (d). According to the comparison of (a) and (b), although some of the arrows are a bit messy, geometric flow represents the texture orientation successfully in Fig. 6(b). The reason resulting messy arrows is that line detection masks respond strongly to lines on one pixel thick. These messy arrows well represent the edge of geometric flow.

From Tables 1 and 2, we can see that the proposed LO-PO algorithm need less time than block matching to compute association field coefficients with little loss of sparsity. Errors of reconstruction can also be ignored.

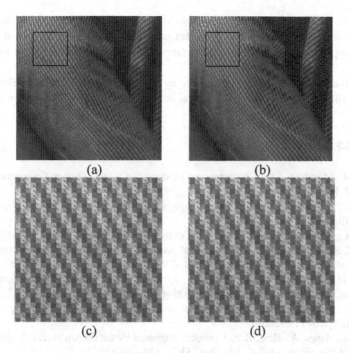

Fig. 6. Association field of image Babar in scale 2^1. (a) Association field computed by block matching. (b) Association field computed by LD-PO algorithm. (c), (d) is the area that shown in red rectangle of (a), (b) separately (Color figure online)

Table 1. Block matching for tight frame grouplet transform.

Image	Time (s)	Sparsity in scale 1 (%)	Sparsity in scale 2 (%)	Sum of errors
Lena	31.77	40.14	30.33	8.88e−14
Babar	1.90	20.10	16.49	2.13e−13

Table 2. LD-PO algorithm for tight frame grouplet transform.

Image	Time (s)	Sparsity in scale 1 (%)	Sparsity in scale 2 (%)	Sum of errors
Lena	20.38	37.69	25.00	3.48e−13
Babar	1.20	17.43	13.92	3.44e−13

Conclusion. In this paper, the computation of association field is improved by LD-PO algorithm. Compared with block matching, the experimental results show that the new method reflects a high efficiency in tight frame grouplet to compute association field coefficients. The tight frame grouplet using proposed algorithm will be applied widely in the future, such as image zooming based on geometric flow, SAR image road detecting, image compression based on texture and so on. How to use it to image processing application widely will be the emphasis of our research in the future.

Acknowledgments. This article was sponsored by the National Natural Science Foundation of China (No. 61672335) and the National Natural Science Foundation of China (No. 61772144).

References

1. Landy, M., Movshon, J.A.: Computational Modeling of Visual Texture Segregatio, pp. 253–271. MIT Press, Cambridge (1991)
2. Le Pennec, E., Mallat, S.: Bandelet image approximation and compression. Multiscale Model. Simul. **4**(3), 992–1039 (2005)
3. Mallat, S.: Geometrical grouplets. Appl. Comput. Harmon. Anal. **26**(2), 161–180 (2009)
4. Bressloff, P.C., Cowan, J.D.: The functional geometry of local and horizontal connections in a model of vl. J. Physiol.-Paris **97**(2), 221–236 (2003)
5. Heeger, D.J., Simoncelli, E.P., Movshon, J.A.: Computational models of cortical visual processing. Proc. Natl. Acad. Sci. **93**(2), 623–627 (1996)
6. Hess, R.F., Hayes, A., Field, D.J.: Contour integration and cortical processing. J. Physiol.-Paris **97**(2), 105–119 (2003)
7. Field, D.J., Hayes, A., Hess, R.F.: Contour integration by the human visual system: evidence for a local "association field". Vis. Res. **33**(2), 173–193 (1993)
8. Maalouf, A., Larabi, M.C., Fernandez-Maloigne, C.: A grouplet-based reduced reference image quality assessment. In: Quality of Multimedia Experience, QoMEx 2009, San Diego, pp. 59–63. IEEE (2009)
9. Lin, Z., Yan, J., Yuan, Y.: Algorithm for image fusion based on orthogonal grouplet transform and pulse-coupled neural network. J. Electron. Imaging **22**(3), 033028 (2013)
10. Yan, J., Wang, Z., Dai, L., et al.: Image denoising with Grouplet transform. In: 2010 2nd International Conference on Advanced Computer Control (ICACC), vol. 3, pp. 65–69. IEEE, Shen Yan (2010)
11. Peyré, G.: Texture synthesis with grouplets. IEEE Trans. Pattern Anal. Mach. Intell. **32**(4), 733–746 (2010)
12. Almeida, M.P.: Anisotropic textures with arbitrary orientation. J. Math. Imaging Vis. **7**(3), 241–251 (1997)
13. Ben-Shahar, O., Zucker, S.W.: The perceptual organization of texture flow: a contextual inference approach. IEEE Trans. Pattern Anal. Mach. Intell. **25**(4), 401–417 (2003)
14. Jain, A., Hong, L., Bolle, R.: Online fingerprint verification. IEEE Trans. Pattern Anal. Mach. Intell. **19**(4), 302–314 (1997)
15. Barjatya, A.: Block matching algorithms for motion estimation. IEEE Trans. Evol. Comput. **8**(3), 225–239 (2004)

Adaptive Coding for Compressed Video Sensing

Jian Wu[1] , Yongfang Wang[1,2(✉)], Yun Zhu[1], and Yuan Shuai[1]

[1] School of Communication and Information Engineering, Shanghai University,
Shanghai 200072, China
{wjgxw,yfw}@shu.edu.cn, wjtcw@hotmail.com
[2] Key Laboratory of Advanced Display and System Application,
Ministry of Education, Shanghai 200072, China

Abstract. In this paper, we propose an Adaptive Coding based Compressed Video Sensing (ACCS) scheme for Distributed Video Coding. Our scheme mimics the traditional video coding method and performs the mode decision both at the encoder and the decoder. At the encoder, the ACCS divides the frame blocks into three categories: the SKIP mode, INTER mode and COMBINED mode according to the residual of the blocks, and the adaptive sampling rate is chosen for these modes. At the decoder, we adopt different decoding methods for different modes. For the COMBINED mode, we apply adaptive decoding scheme by exploiting the intra-frame and inter-frame sparsity. Experimental results show that the proposed algorithm outperforms existing state-of-the-art video CS approaches at a very low sampling rate.

Keywords: Compressed sensing · Distributed video coding
Adaptive measurements · Sparse representations

1 Introduction

The resolution of today's video is much higher than before, and it brings huge challenges to the limited network. What's more, the attractive 3D videos have increasingly come into the public sight, which give people even better quality of experience. How to capture and compress the videos becomes a big problem. High Efficiency Video coding (HEVC) [1], as the latest video coding scheme, has a very high compression efficiency by exploiting the spatial and temporal structure for the video sequences, but it is not suited for the inexpensive video recording devices such as cellphones, wireless video cameras, which have limited computing capability and battery capacity.

Compressed sensing (CS) [2], as a novel signal processing theory, can acquire a signal at a sampling rate much lower than Nyquist rate via linear projection onto a random basis, and the original signal can be reconstructed through optimization method with high probability from some random measurements under certain conditions.

Given a signal $\mathbf{x} \in R^N$ with length N, it can be called K-sparse in a domain $\boldsymbol{\Psi}$ when K entries in its transform coefficients $\boldsymbol{\theta} = \boldsymbol{\Psi}^T \mathbf{x}$ are nonzero, and $\boldsymbol{\Psi}$ is an orthonormal basis here. CS attempts to reconstruct the K-sparse signal vector from a relatively small number of samples with linear projection $\mathbf{y} = \boldsymbol{\Phi}\mathbf{x}$, and the size of $\boldsymbol{\Phi}$ is

© Springer International Publishing AG 2017
Y. Zhao et al. (Eds.): ICIG 2017, Part II, LNCS 10667, pp. 197–205, 2017.
https://doi.org/10.1007/978-3-319-71589-6_18

M by N. The dimension of measurement vector $\mathbf{y}$ is M, and the values of the nonzero coefficients can be well recovered if $M \ll N$.

In CS, instead of encoding all the coefficients of a signal, we only encode the M measurements and the reconstruction problem can be solved with the following l_0 minimization method

$$\min \|\mathbf{\Psi x}\|_0, s.t. \quad \mathbf{y} = \mathbf{\Phi x} \tag{1}$$

where $\|\mathbf{x}\|_0$ is a pseudo-norm (l_0-norm), which equals the number of nonzero elements in vector $\mathbf{x}$. Minimizing the number of nonzero entries is difficult. Instead, the optimization problem can be solved with l_1 minimization method

$$\min \|\mathbf{\Psi x}\|_1, s.t. \quad \mathbf{y} = \mathbf{\Phi x} \tag{2}$$

This is a convex optimization problem and can be solved easily via subspace pursuit [3] or CVX toolbox [4] and so on.

CS has a great potential in image and video applications for its low complexity and low power consumption. In CS based image compression techniques, an image is divided into n small blocks, then each one is rearranged into a vector $\mathbf{x}$. Next, the vector is sampled with the measurement matrix $\mathbf{\Phi}$. Finally, the original image can be reconstructed by many state-of-the-art algorithms such as BCS-SPL [5], SGSR [6], GSR [7] and so on.

As for the application of CS to video compression [8–12], the sparsity between the successive frames with the classic transform domain (e.g. DWT, DCT) is exploited based on the adjacent frames' correlation in video sequences. In [8], authors proposed a reconstruction model based on the idea that the total variation (TV) norm of the residual between the frame and its prediction, TV norm of the frame, l_0-norm of the frame in a certain transform domain are all very small. The similar idea appeared again in [9] which introduced the forward and the backward motion-compensated residuals. The support (location of large valued entries) is estimated based on the idea that the large valued entries belonging to the adjacent frames are located in almost the same place [10]. A hierarchical frame structure was proposed to exploit the correlation between the current frames and the reference frames in [11].

Unlike above methods, Distributed Compressed Video Sensing (DISCOS) framework is introduced in [13], which present the idea that the sparsest representation of a block is a linear combination of a few temporal neighboring blocks of previous reconstructed frames or nearby key frames. The same method also can be found in [14]. However, if the blocks are non-rigid objects (dancer in Fig. 1) whose shapes change a lot. And their sparsest representation is not a linear combination of a few temporal neighboring blocks, which means that it is unable to be well recovered even at a very high sampling rate by using DISCOS algorithm. As the result illustrated in Fig. 1, most of the regions in the frame are decoded perfectly, except for the dander in the background. Because the regions near the dancer change a lot and cannot be represented by the reference ones no matter how high the sampling rate is. So these blocks should be recovered by the image CS algorithms (INTRA). Moreover in [14, 15], a feedback

Origin   DISCOS

Fig. 1. The performance of DISCOS (the 5th frame and the sampling rate is 0.08)

channel was used to allocate the different measurement rates to each block at the encoder. Although it improved the image quality, it may lower the efficiency of the encoder.

Traditional video coding techniques, as we all know, can achieve high compression ratio by making complicated mode decision in the encoder. And can we perform the mode decision both in the encoder and decoder in the framework of CS? Therefore, we propose a new CS based video coding framework based on mode decision in this paper. We employ different measurement rates for different block modes at the encoder, and perform mode decisions at the decoder side.

The paper is organized as follows. Section 2 proposes CS video scheme based on adaptive coding. Experimental results are given in Sect. 3, and we conclude this paper in Sect. 4.

2 Adaptive Coding Based on Video CS

Motivated by the above analysis, we propose the adaptive coding for compressed video sensing scheme (ACCS). The architecture of our proposed ACCS framework is depicted in Fig. 2, and we will show the details in the next subsections.

2.1 Adaptive CS Video Encoder

At the encoder, firstly, video sequences are divided into group of pictures (GOP), and each GOP contains two categories: key frames (K-frames) and non-key frames (CS frames), as shown in Fig. 3 (K stands for key frames, and CS stands for non-key frames). Be different from [14], the K-frames and CS-frames in the paper are both coded using CS principles. K-frames are sampled at a high sampling rate, while CS-frames are sampled at adaptive sampling rate.

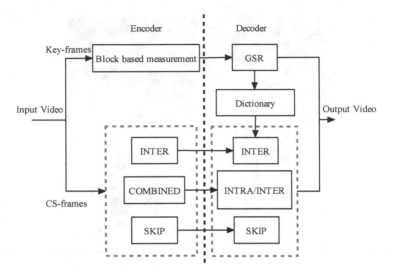

Fig. 2. Block diagram of the proposed CS scheme.

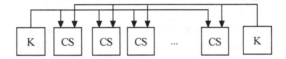

Fig. 3. GOP structure. Every CS-frame is recovered with two K-frames.

In this paper, we propose an adaptive sampling method for CS-frames by considering different characteristics of blocks in a frame. Firstly, we classify the blocks into three kinds of mode: SKIP, COMBINED and INTER based on the l_1 -norm of the residual between the current frame and the reference ones. If the residual is very small, which means the block changes very little with the co-located blocks in the reference frames, we only transmit a flag indicating the SKIP mode, which does not need any measurements so the sampling rate here is zero. If a block has very large change with respect to its co-located block, we will assign the COMBINED mode to it, which needs a high sampling rate and would be decoded both by INTRA and INTER. While the remainder blocks with minor change will take a small sampling rate, we refer to this coding mode as INTER mode, which decoded by INTER. The decoder schemes for three modes (SKIP, INTRA, INTER) will be explained in the next section. Figure 4 shows three kinds of mode of blocks in image, which is marked by different colors. The dark-red blocks show the COMBINED blocks, the light-red ones choose the INTER mode, and the rest blocks select the SKIP mode. The above description can be represented as follows

$$MODE = \begin{cases} SKIP, & difference < threshold1 \\ COMBINED, & threshold1 < difference < threshold2 \\ INTER, & difference > threshold1 \end{cases} \quad (3)$$

(a)   (b)

Fig. 4. The mode decision: (a) foreman (b) news.

where *difference* means the l_0 -norm of the difference between the blocks in current frame and the references. *thresholds1* and *threshold2* are thresholds, respectively, which are set by experimental results.

2.2   Adaptive CS Video Decoder

At decoder, we decode the K-frame by GSR, which can achieve the excellent performance in CS without using the information of the reference frames. For CS-frames, there are three kinds of blocks, and each of them will adopt different decoding schemes. The SKIP blocks can be decoded by copying the co-located block in the reference frames. The INTER blocks can be decoded by solving Eq. (2), whose redundant dictionary comes from the blocks near the co-located blocks in previously reconstructed frames. COMBINED blocks, which are the most complicated blocks, will perform the mode decision at the decoder. It recovered both by GSR (INTRA) and Eq. (2) (INTER). INTER blocks can be represented by the redundant dictionary sparsely, which is suitable for the blocks with complex local details but simple motion, while GSR cannot reconstruct the details finely at a low sampling rate, although it is a state-of-the-art scheme. As the blocks with complicated motion cannot be represented by the reference ones no matter how high the sampling rate is, they should be recovered by GSR. Then, we will decide which recovered block to be chosen by comparing the residual of the measurements based on the idea that the residual between the original ($\mathbf{x}$) and the prediction ($\hat{\mathbf{x}}$) is proportion to the residual of the measurements, as shown in (4). When the residual between the original measurements and the recovered measurements (by INTER) is smaller than the residual between the original and the recovered (by INTRA), we will choose block recovered by INTER and vice versa.

$$\mathbf{y} - \hat{\mathbf{y}} = \Phi(\mathbf{x} - \hat{\mathbf{x}}) \tag{4}$$

3   Experiment Results and Analysis

To evaluate the performance of our proposed scheme, several CIF video sequences are used: news, foreman, football, hall, coastguard, mobile, which represent for small, moderation and large movement videos. In our experiments, the CS measurements are obtained by using random matrix with Gaussian i.i.d entries at the block level, and the size of block (BS) is set to 32 * 32. *threshold*1 and *threshold*2 determine the coding modes for blocks. In order to determine the *threshold*1 and *threshold*2, we design a lot of experiments as follows. Firstly, we do not use the *threshold*2, and let the *threshold*1 vary from 0.05 * BS * BS to 5 * BS * BS. We can find from Fig. 5 that the PSNR is high when *threshold*1 < 3, and we choose *threshold*1 = 2 * BS * BS by considering all sequences. Secondly, in order to determine *threshold*2, we set the *threshold*1 to 2 * BS * BS and *threshold*2 varies from 1 * BS * BS to 10 * BS * BS. As shown in Fig. 6, we choose *threshold*2 = 8 * BS * BS by considering all sequences. In order to improve the compression ratio, the GOP size is set to 8, the first frame and the eighth frame are K-frames and others are CS-frames, as shown in Fig. 3. We assumed K-frames are losslessly available at the decoder in our experiments, as used in [14]. The high sampling rate (used in COMBINED mode) is five times the low one (used in INTER mode). We compare our proposed algorithm with two state-of-the-art image/ video CS methods including GSR [7] and DISCOS [13]. GSR is an excellent still-image CS approach but smooths the details of the image. DISCOS makes full use of the inter-frame sparsity but it will introduce the blocking artifacts. Coding efficiency is measured using PSNR and sampling rate.

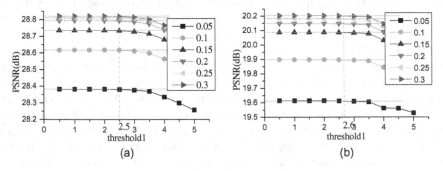

Fig. 5. Recovery performance changes with *threshold*1 in different sequences: (a) coastguard (b) football.

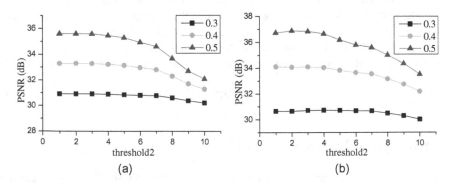

Fig. 6. Recovery performance changes with *threshold*2 in different sequences: (a) coastguard (b) football.

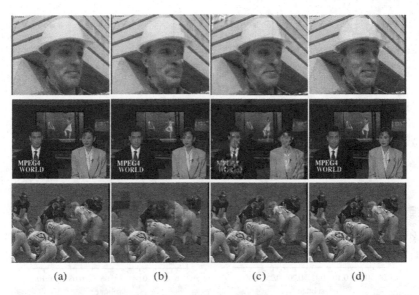

      (a)   (b)   (c)   (d)

Fig. 7. Visual quality comparison with different algorithm for sequences (the 5th frame): (a) origin, (b) DISCOS [13], (c) GSR [7], (d) Proposed.

Figure 8 shows the rate-distortion curves of the proposed and the other approaches of all the test sequences. We can see that the rate-distortion performance of our approach is superior to GSR and DISCOS in most cases. Especially, for news and hall sequences with non-rigid objects, the proposed method achieves better coding performance compared to other two methods. For football sequence with large/complicated movement, our scheme will choose the INTRA mode in most cases, so the performance is similar to GSR. For Mobile sequence with large movement, different to football sequence, DISCOS achieves the best performance when the sampling rate is very low. This is due to the fact that mobile sequence has large motion but little shape-changing. Our scheme may choose the wrong encoding mode when the sampling rate is very low. However with the increase of sampling rate, our method achieves better performance than DISCOS. Besides, PSNR gain for DISCOS is less with the sampling rate increased [14]. Because the blocks have simple motion can be recovered perfectly even at a very low sampling rate, while the blocks have complicated motion which are not sparse in redundant dictionary cannot be reconstructed well.

Figure 7 shows the visual quality comparison for the foreman and news at the average rate about 0.04 (the actual sampling rates of our proposed scheme are 0.044 and 0.043 in foreman and news respectively) and for football at the sampling rate about 0.2. From Fig. 7, we can see that the proposed algorithm provides better visual quality than others. Table 1 provides the corresponding average execution time of various algorithms for reconstructing a frame in different sequences. These data are obtained using Matlab on a computer with Intel i5-3230, 2.6G CPU and 4 GB memory. From Table 1, we can see that the complexity of the proposed algorithm can be the medium one in most cases. Therefore, the proposed method provides a good tradeoff between visual quality and complexity.

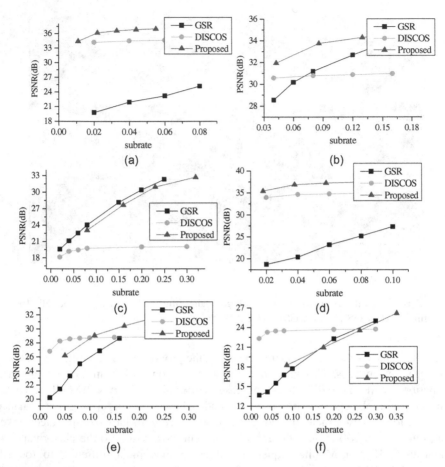

Fig. 8. Recovery performance comparison with different algorithms: (a) news, (b) foreman, (c) football, (d) hall, (e) coastguard, (f) mobile.

Table 1. Reconstruction time in minutes.

	Foreman (0.04)	News (0.04)	Football (0.2)
DISCOS	0.4	0.4	0.6
GSR	92.1	102.8	105.0
Proposed	13.3	3.0	42.5

4 Conclusion

In this paper, a new ACCS method has been proposed, which makes full use of the intra-frame and inter-frame sparsity. Our algorithm also exploits the fact that when the sequences have large or non-rigid motion, the sparsest representation of a block in video sequences is not a linear combination of a few temporal neighboring blocks that are in nearby key frames. Experimental results show that the proposed algorithm can achieve excellent performance even at a very low sampling rate, and outperforms existing state-of-the-art image/video CS approaches.

Acknowledgments. This work was supported by Natural Science Foundation of China under Grant Nos. 61671283 and 61301113, and Shanghai National Natural Science under Grant No. 13ZR14165.

References

1. Sze, V., Budagavi, M., Sullivan, G.J.: High Efficiency Video Coding (HEVC): Algorithms and Architectures. Integrated Circuit and Systems. Springer, Cham (2014)
2. Candès, E.J., Romberg, J., Tao, T.: Robust uncertainty principles: exact signal reconstruction from highly incomplete frequency information. IEEE Trans. Inf. Theory 52(2), 489–509 (2006)
3. Dai, W., Milenkovic, O.: Subspacepursuit for compressive sensing signal reconstruction. IEEE Trans. Inf. Theory 55(5), 2230–2249 (2009)
4. Grant, M., Boyd, S.: CVX: MATLAB software for disciplined convex programming, version 2.0 beta, September 2013. http://cvxr.com/cvx
5. Gan, L.: Block compressed sensing of natural images. In: 15th International Conference on Digital Signal Processing, pp. 403–406, Cardiff (2007)
6. Zhang, J., Zhao, D., Jiang, F., Gao, W.: Structural group sparse representation for image compressive sensing recovery. In: IEEE Data Compression Conference, pp. 331–340, Snowbird (2013)
7. Zhang, J., Zhao, D., Gao, W.: Group-based sparse representation for image restoration. IEEE Trans. Image Process. 23(8), 3336–3351 (2014)
8. Chang, K., Qin, T., Tang, Z.: Reconstruction of compressed-sensed video using compound regularization. In: 15th IEEE International Conference on Multimedia and Expo, pp. 1–6, Chengdu (2014)
9. Asif, M.S., Fernandes, F., Romberg, J.: Low-complexity video compression and compressive sensing. In: Asilomar Conference on Signals, Systems and Computers, pp. 579–583 (2013)
10. Mansour, H., Yilmaz, Ö.: Adaptive compressed sensing for video acquisition. In: IEEE International Conference on Acoustics, Speech and Signal Processing, pp. 3465–3468 (2012)
11. Che, W., Gao, X., Fan, X., et al.: Spatial-temporal recovery for hierarchical frame based video compressed sensing. In: IEEE International Conference on Image Processing, pp. 1110–1114 (2015)
12. Chang, K., Ding, P.L.K., Li, B.: Compressive sensing reconstruction of correlated images using joint regularization. IEEE Sig. Process. Lett. 23(4), 449–453 (2016)
13. Do, T.T., Chen, Y., Nguyen, D.T., et al.: Distributed compressed video sensing. In: IEEE International Conference on Image Processing, pp. 1393–1396 (2009)
14. Prades-Nebot, J., Ma, Y., Huang, T.: Distributed video coding using compressive sampling. In: Picture Coding Symposium, pp. 1–4 (2009)
15. Ran, L., Zongliang, G., Ziguan, C., Minghu, W., Xiuchang, Z.: Distributed adaptive compressed video sensing using smoothed projected landweber reconstruction. China Commun. 10(11), 58–69 (2013)

Deep Top Similarity Preserving Hashing for Image Retrieval

Qiang Li, Haiyan Fu, and Xiangwei Kong[(✉)]

School of Information and Communication Engineering,
Dalian University of Technology, Dalian 116024, China
`kongxw@dlut.edu.cn`

Abstract. As a kind of approximate nearest neighbor search method, hashing is widely used in large scale image retrieval. Compared to traditional hashing methods, which first encode each image through hand-crafted features and then learn hash functions, deep hashing methods have shown superior performance for image retrieval due to its learning image representations and hash functions simultaneously. However, most existing deep hashing methods mainly consider the semantic similarities among images. The information of images' positions in the ranking list to the query image has not yet been well explored, which is crucial in image retrieval. In this paper, we propose a Deep Top Similarity Preserving Hashing (DTSPH) method to improve the quality of hash codes for image retrieval. In our approach, when training the convolutional neural network, a top similarity preserving hashing loss function is designed to preserve similarities of images at the top of the ranking list. Experiments on two benchmark datasets show that our proposed method outperforms several state-of-the-art deep hashing methods and traditional hashing methods.

Keywords: Image retrieval · Deep hashing · Top similarity preserving

1 Introduction

Image retrieval [17–23] has received increasing attention in computer vision. With the rapid growth of large-scale image data, hashing has attracted more and more attention in image retrieval due to its fast search speed and low storage cost. The purpose of hashing is to learn a set of hash functions that map each image to binary codes while trying best to preserve the semantic similarities among images.

Based on whether using deep convolutional neural network to learn hash codes, hashing methods can be divided into two categories: traditional hashing and deep hashing. Traditional hashing methods first extract hand-crafted feature vectors of each image and then learn hash functions based on these feature vectors. Traditional hashing methods can be further categorized into unsupervised methods and supervised methods. In unsupervised methods, only unlabeled data

© Springer International Publishing AG 2017
Y. Zhao et al. (Eds.): ICIG 2017, Part II, LNCS 10667, pp. 206–215, 2017.
https://doi.org/10.1007/978-3-319-71589-6_19

is used during the training procedure. Representative unsupervised methods contain iterative quantization hashing (ITQ) [4] and topology preserving hashing (TPH) [14]. Supervised methods utilize label information to assist the learning of hash functions, which can improve the quality of hash codes. Representative supervised methods include minimal loss hashing (MLH) [10] and supervised hashing with kernels (KSH) [9].

Compared to traditional hashing methods, deep hashing [8,15,16] methods show their superior performance for image retrieval. Usually, deep hashing methods use CNNs [6] to extract discriminative image representations and learn hash functions simultaneously. For example, Xia *et al.* [13] proposed CNNH, which is a two stage learning method that first learns approximate hash codes from the pairwise similarity matrix and then utilizes CNN to learn image representations and hash functions. Lai *et al.* [8] proposed DNNH, in which the deep architecture used a triplet ranking loss function to preserve relative similarities. Zhang *et al.* [15] presented a novel bit-scalable deep hashing approach DRSCH.

Although the existing deep hashing methods have brought substantial improvements over traditional supervised hashing methods. Most of them mainly consider similarities among images. The information of images' positions in the ranking list to the query image has not yet been well explored. However, users always pay their most attention to the images ranked in the top. So whether images ranked in the top are similar to the query image or not is crucial to the quality of image retrieval.

In this paper, we propose deep top similarity preserving hashing (DTSPH) to generate high quality of hash codes for image retrieval. As shown in Fig. 1, we utilize CNN to extract discriminative image representations and learn hash functions directly from images. At the top of the CNN model, a top similarity preserving hashing loss function is designed to preserve the similarities in the top of the ranking list. Each time, a group of images are fed into the CNN model and then the stochastic gradient descent algorithm is used to train model parameters. Experimental results on two benchmark datasets show that our proposed method has superior performance over several other deep hashing methods including traditional hashing methods with CNN features. The rest of this paper is organized as follows. In Sect. 2, we introduce our deep top similarity preserving hashing method. Then experimental results are shown in Sect. 3. Finally, we give a conclusion in Sect. 4.

2   Deep Top Similarity Preserving Hashing

In this section, we first introduce our deep top similarity preserving hashing loss function. Then we give its gradients which are vital to back-propagation algorithm.

2.1   Deep Hash Model

We adopt the architecture of AlexNet [6] as our basic framework, which has five convolutional layers($conv_1 - conv_5$) with optional pooling layers, followed

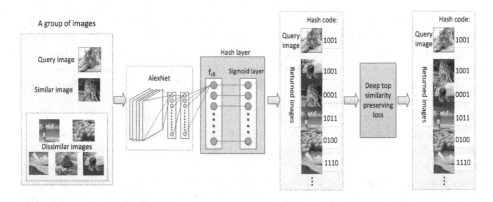

Fig. 1. Overview of DTSPH framework. During training stage, the input to the CNN model is a group of images, i.e., $\{I^q, I^s, \{I_k^d\}_{k=1}^n\}$, where I^q is the query image, I^s is similar to I^q and $\{I_k^d\}_{k=1}^n$ are dissimilar to I^q. Through the CNN model, each image is encoded into a hash code. Then these hash codes are used to calculate the deep top similarity preserving loss, which aims to optimize the parameters of the model to preserve the similarities at the top of the ranking list.

by two fully connected layers($f_{c6} - f_{c7}$) and the classification output layer. The activation function of the first seven layers of AlexNet is the rectified linear units (ReLUs), which is much faster than these saturating nonlinearities such as the logistic sigmoid and the hyperbolic tangent in terms of training time with gradient descent [3]. For more details about the configurations of the convolutional layers, pooling layers and fully connected layers, please refer to [6]. In order to adopt to learning hash functions, we replace the classification output layer in original AlexNet with a hash layer as shown in Fig. 1. The goal of hash functions is to encode feature representation into hash codes. As we can see from Fig. 1, our hash layer is a fully connected layer followed by a sigmoid layer, which transform the 4096-dimension feature of the layer f_{c7} into q-dimension output and the value is restricted to [0, 1]. Then the K-bit hash codes are obtained by quantifying the K-dimension output. Usually, the performance of deep hash method is related to two aspects. One is the deep model. Usually, the model is deeper, the performance is better. The other is the loss function, which is used to guide training the deep model. Here, we focus on the loss function, not the deep model. Please note that our DTSPH algorithm also could be easily applied to other models, such as VGG [2], and we will also test our method on VGG-F model [2].

2.2 Top Similarity Preserving

For an Information Retrieval, correctly ranking documents on the top of the result list is crucial [1]. While for an Image Retrieval, user usually pay most of their attentions to the results on the first few pages [16]. However, most of deep hash methods mainly consider similarities among images and few of them explore the information of images' positions in the ranking list. Considering it, we carefully design a top similarity preserving loss function, which mainly preserves the similarities in the top of ranking list to explore the information of positions.

Let $\mathcal{I}$ be the image space and $f_{c7}(I_i) \in \mathbb{R}^d$ denote the feature vector from the output of the layer f_{c7} by feeding the image $I_i \in \mathcal{I}$ into the CNN model. Then we can obtain the binary codes $b(I_i) \in \mathbb{H}^K \equiv \{0,1\}^K$ as follows:

$$b(I_i) = sgn(\mathbf{w}^T f_{c7}(I_i)) \tag{1}$$

where $\mathbf{w} \in \mathbb{R}^{d \times K}$ denotes the weights of hash layer. Here for the sake of conciseness, bias terms of hash layer and parameters of the first seven layers are omitted. $sgn(x)$ is a sign function that $sgn(x) = 1$ if $x > 0$ and 0 otherwise, and it performs element-wise operations.

Considering the information of images' positions in the ranking list, during training stage, each time, we feed a group of images to the CNN model, among which the query image is I^q, whose similar image is I^s and dissimilar images are $\{I_k^d\}_{k=1}^n$, where n is the number of dissimilar images. Then we get the corresponding hash codes, denoted as $b(I^q)$, $b(I^s)$, and $\{b(I_k^d)\}_{k=1}^n$ respectively. According to their Hamming distance to the query image, we can obtain a ranking list for the query image I^q. Intuitively, we expect that the similar image I^s will be in the top of the ranking list, which means that the Hamming distance between $b(I^q)$ and $b(I^s)$ is smaller than that between $b(I^k)$ and $b(I^s)$ for any $k \in \{1, n\}$. Then following [12], the "rank" of the similar image I^s with respect to the query image I^q is defined as following:

$$R(I^q, I^s) = \sum_{k=1}^n I\{(\|b(I^q) - b(I^s)\|_H - \|b(I^q) - b(I_k^d)\|_H) > 0\} \tag{2}$$

where $\| \cdot \|_H$ represents Hamming distance. $I(condition)$ is an indicator function that $I(condition) = 1$ if the $condition$ is true and 0 otherwise. The function $R(I^q, I^s)$ counts the number of the dissimilar images I^k, which are closer to the query image I^q than the similar image I^s in terms of Hamming distance. Obviously, $R(I^q, I^s)$ is relative small if the similar image I^q is ranked in the top of the ranking list and is relative large otherwise.

Usually, whether images ranked in the top of the ranking list are similar to the query image or not is crucial in image retrieval [16]. Considering that, we define a top similarity preserving loss function:

$$L(R(I^q, I^s)) = -\frac{\psi^2}{\psi + R(I^q, I^s)} \tag{3}$$

where the parameter ψ controls the decreasing speed of the first order derivative $L'(R)$ of $L(R)$. With the increase of R, the loss $L(R)$ increases relative quickly when R is small than that when R is large. The loss function penalizes the mistakes in the top of the ranking list more than those in the bottom, which means the similarity in top of the ranking list is more important than that in the bottom.

Then, the objective function is defined as following:

$$\mathcal{L} = \frac{1}{Z} \sum_q \sum_s -\frac{\psi^2}{\psi + R(I^q, I^s)} \quad (4)$$

where Z is the number of $\{I^q, I^s, \{I_k^d\}_{k=1}^n\}$.

Although the ranking loss in Eq. (3) is differentiable, the objective function in Eq. (4) is still not differentiable due to Eqs. (1) and (2). For ease of optimization, Eq.(1) is relaxed as:

$$f_h(I_i) = sigmoid(\mathbf{w}^T f_{c7}(I_i)) \quad (5)$$

where $sigmoid(\cdot)$ function is used to approximate $sgn(\cdot)$ function and $f_h(I_i)$ denotes the output of the hash layer for image I_i. Please note, as shown in Fig. 1, the hash layer of our model is a fully connected layer followed by a sigmoid layer essentially. Then we can get the hash codes with respect to the image I_i as following:

$$b(I_i) = sgn(f_h(I_i) - 0.5) \quad (6)$$

Next, in Eq. (2), the Hamming norm is replaced with the l_1 norm and the indicator function $I(\cdot)$ is approximated by the $sigmoid(\cdot)$ function. Accordingly, Eq. (2) can be written as:

$$\hat{R}(I^q, I^s) = \sum_{k=1}^n sigmoid(\|f_h(I^q) - f_h(I^s)\|_1 - \\ \|f_h(I^q) - f_h(I_k^d)\|_1) \quad (7)$$

Finally, the overall objective function is formulated as following:

$$\mathcal{L} = \frac{1}{Z} \sum_q \sum_s -\frac{\psi^2}{\psi + \hat{R}(I^q, I^s)} + \frac{\alpha}{2} \sum_i \|b(I_i) - f_h(I_i)\|_2 \\ + \frac{\beta}{2} \| \underset{i}{mean}(f_h(I_i) - 0.5)\|_2 + \frac{\lambda}{2} \|\mathbf{W}\|_2 \quad (8)$$

The second term is used to minimize the quantization error between the output of the hash layer and the corresponding hash codes, which could minimize the loss of information. The third term is used to make each bit averaged over the training data [11], which in some sense is to maximize the entropy of binary codes. So the binary codes would be compact and discriminative. The fourth term is regularizer term to control the scales of the weights so as to reduce the effect of the over-fitting. α, β and λ are three parameters to control the effect of above three terms.

2.3   Learning Algorithm

Stochastic gradient descent method is used to train the network parameters. Each time, we randomly select Z (during training stage, Z is the mini-batch) group of images from training set. Each group consists of $n+2$ images. One image as the query image I^q, one as the similar image I^s, and n images as dissimilar images $\{I_k^d\}_{k=1}^n$. We feed the network with these Z groups of images to get the corresponding output. The gradients of the objective function $\mathcal{L}$ with respect to $f_h(I^q)$, $f_h(I^s)$, $\{f_h(I_k^d)\}_{k=1}^n$ are as following:[1]

$$\frac{\partial \mathcal{L}}{\partial f_h(I^q)} = \frac{1}{Z} \frac{\psi^2}{(\psi + \hat{R}(I^q, I^s))^2} \frac{\partial \hat{R}(I^q, I^s)}{\partial f_h(I^q)}$$
$$+ \alpha(f_h(I^q) - b(I^q)) + \frac{\beta}{n+2}(\underset{i}{mean}(f_h(I_i)) - 0.5)) \quad (9)$$

$$\frac{\partial \mathcal{L}}{\partial f_h(I^s)} = \frac{1}{Z} \frac{\psi^2}{(\psi + \hat{R}(I^q, I^s))^2} \frac{\partial \hat{R}(I^q, I^s)}{\partial f_h(I^s)}$$
$$+ \alpha(f_h(I^s) - b(I^s)) + \frac{\beta}{n+2}(\underset{i}{mean}(f_h(I_i)) - 0.5)) \quad (10)$$

$$\frac{\partial \mathcal{L}}{\partial f_h(I_k^d)} = \frac{1}{Z} \frac{\psi^2}{(\psi + \hat{R}(I^q, I^s))^2} \frac{\partial \hat{R}(I^q, I^s)}{\partial f_h(I_k^d)}$$
$$+ \alpha(f_h(I_k^d) - b(I_k^d)) + \frac{\beta}{n+2}(\underset{i}{mean}(f_h(I_i)) - 0.5)) \quad (11)$$

where the *mean* operation is performed on Z groups of images. Then these gradient values would be fed into the network via back-propagation algorithm to update the parameters of each layer.

3 Experiments

3.1 Datasets and Settings

We validate our algorithm on two benchmark datasets: (1) The CIFAR10 dataset contains 60,000 32×32 color images of 10 classes; (2) The NUS-WIDE dataset consists of 269,648 images. Following [24], we use the subset of images annotated with the 21 most frequently happened classes. For CIFAR10, we use 10,000 images as the query samples, and the rest as the training samples. For NUS-WIDE, we randomly select 100 images from each of the 21 class labels as the query samples, and the rest as the training samples. Whether two images are similar or not depends on whether they share at least one common label.

We compare our method with five state-of-the-art hashing methods, including three traditional hashing methods KSH [9], MLH [10] and BRE [7], and two deep hashing methods, DSRH [16] and DRSCH [15].

---

[1] $\frac{\partial \hat{R}(I^q, I^s)}{\partial f_h(I^q)}$, $\frac{\partial \hat{R}(I^q, I^s)}{\partial f_h(I^s)}$, and $\frac{\partial \hat{R}(I^q, I^s)}{\partial f_h(I_k^d)}$ are easy to compute. Due to space limitations, we don't give the specific expressions of above terms here.

We implement our method by the open-source Caffe [5] framework. In all the experiments, the weights of layers F_{1-7} of our network are initialized by the weights of AlexNet [6] which has been trained on the ImageNet dataset, while the weights of other layers are initialized randomly. The mini-batch is set to 64. The parameter ψ, α and β are empirically set as 20, 0.01 and 0.1 respectively.

3.2   Results

We use four evaluation metrics for the performance comparison, which are mean average precision (mAP), precision within Hamming distance 2, precision at top 500 samples of different code lengths and precision curves with 64 bits with respect to different numbers of top returned samples.

Performance on CIFAR10. For CIFAR10, we follow [15] that the query image is searched within the query set itself. Table 1 shows the mAP values of CIFAR10 with different code lengths. From Table 1, we can find that DTSPH achieves better performance than other traditional hashing and deep hashing methods. Specially, DTSPH improves the mAP values of 48 bits to 0.805 from 0.631 achieved by DRSCH [15]. In addition, DTSPH shows an improvement of 34.7% compared to KSH [9] with CNN features. Figure 2 shows the comparison results of other three evaluation metrics on CIFAR10. As we can see, DTSPH has better performance gains over the other five methods.

Table 1. Accuracy in terms of mAP w.r.t. different number of bits on two datasets. For NUS-WIDE, the mAP value is calculated within the top 50,000 returned neighbors.

Method	CIFAR10(mAP)				NUS-WIDE(mAP)			
	16bits	24bits	32bits	48bits	16bits	24bits	32bits	48bits
DTSPH	**0.783**	**0.800**	**0.803**	**0.805**	**0.773**	**0.787**	**0.788**	**0.789**
DRSCH [15]	0.615	0.622	0.629	0.631	0.618	0.622	0.623	0.628
DSRH [16]	0.608	0.611	0.617	0.618	0.609	0.618	0.621	0.631
KSH-CNN [9]	0.401	0.430	0.444	0.458	0.607	0.619	0.625	0.626
MLH-CNN [10]	0.250	0.289	0.313	0.319	0.525	0.559	0.568	0.581
BRE-CNN [7]	0.198	0.206	0.206	0.216	0.538	0.558	0.566	0.576
KSH [9]	0.322	0.352	0.365	0.383	0.546	0.556	0.562	0.567
MLH [10]	0.133	0.158	0.163	0.180	0.487	0.507	0.511	0.524
BRE [7]	0.122	0.156	0.161	0.172	0.486	0.515	0.518	0.528

Performance on NUS -WIDE. Due to that NUS-WIDE is a relative big dataset, so we calculate mAP values within the top 50,000 returned samples. At the right of Table 1, the mAP values of different methods with different code lengths are shown. DTSPH shows superiority over other five methods again.

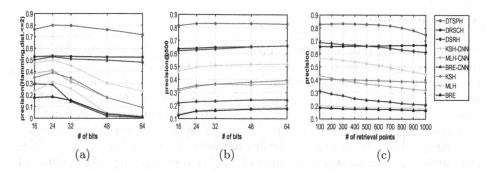

(a)   (b)   (c)

Fig. 2. The results on CIFAR10: (a) Precision curves within Hamming distance 2; (b) Precision curves within top 500 returned; (c) Precision curves with 64 bits w.r.t. different numbers of top returned samples.

Specially, DTSPH obtains a mAP of 0.789 with 48bits while the mAP value of DRSCH is 0.628 and the mAP value of KSH-CNN is 0.626. Figure 3(a) reports the precision curves within Hamming radius 2. Figure 3(b) shows the precision curves within top 500 returned. Figure 3(c) shows the precision curves of top 1000 returned samples with 64 bits. Our approach DTSPH shows better search accuracies than other five methods.

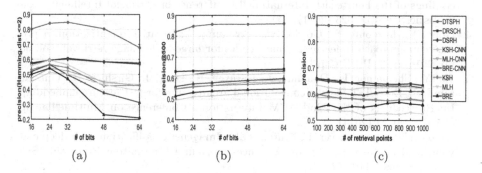

(a)   (b)   (c)

Fig. 3. The results on NUS-WIDE: (a) Precision curves within Hamming distance 2; (b) Precision curves within top 500 returned; (c) Precision curves with 64 bits w.r.t. different numbers of top returned samples.

Note that DRSCH and DSRH are deep hashing methods and they mainly consider the similarities among images. Experimental results on two benchmark datasets show that DTSPH is superior to DRSCH [15] and DSRH [16]. It demonstrates the effectiveness of DTSPH, which tries to preserve similarities of images in the top of the ranking list.

4   Conclusions

In this paper, we propose a deep top similarity preserving hashing (DTSPH) method to improve the quality of hash codes for image retrieval. We use CNN to extract discriminative image representations and learn hash functions simultaneously. At the top the CNN model, a deep top similarity preserving hashing loss function is designed to preserve the similarities at the top of the ranking list. The bigger dissimilarities at the top of the ranking list, the larger penalties are. Experimental results on two benchmark datasets show that DTSPH has superior performance against several state-of-the-art deep hashing and traditional hashing methods.

References

1. Cao, Y., Xu, J., Liu, T.Y., Li, H., Huang, Y., Hon, H.W.: Adapting ranking SVM to document retrieval. In: Proceedings of the 29th Annual International ACM SIGIR Conference on Research and Development in Information Retrieval, pp. 186–193. ACM (2006)
2. Chatfield, K., Simonyan, K., Vedaldi, A., Zisserman, A.: Return of the devil in the details: delving deep into convolutional nets. arXiv preprint arXiv:1405.3531 (2014)
3. Glorot, X., Bordes, A., Bengio, Y.: Deep sparse rectifier neural networks. In: Proceedings of the Fourteenth International Conference on Artificial Intelligence and Statistics, pp. 315–323 (2011)
4. Gong, Y., Lazebnik, S., Gordo, A., Perronnin, F.: Iterative quantization: a procrustean approach to learning binary codes for large-scale image retrieval, vol. 35, pp. 2916–2929. IEEE (2013)
5. Jia, Y., Shelhamer, E., Donahue, J., Karayev, S., Long, J., Girshick, R., Guadarrama, S., Darrell, T.: Caffe: convolutional architecture for fast feature embedding. In: Proceedings of the 22nd ACM International Conference on Multimedia, pp. 675–678. ACM (2014)
6. Krizhevsky, A., Sutskever, I., Hinton, G.E.: Imagenet classification with deep convolutional neural networks. In: Advances in Neural Information Processing Systems, pp. 1097–1105 (2012)
7. Kulis, B., Darrell, T.: Learning to hash with binary reconstructive embeddings. In: Advances in Neural Information Processing Systems, pp. 1042–1050 (2009)
8. Lai, H., Pan, Y., Liu, Y., Yan, S.: Simultaneous feature learning and hash coding with deep neural networks. In: Proceedings of the IEEE Conference on Computer Vision and Pattern Recognition, pp. 3270–3278 (2015)
9. Liu, W., Wang, J., Ji, R., Jiang, Y.G., Chang, S.F.: Supervised hashing with kernels. In: 2012 IEEE Conference on Computer Vision and Pattern Recognition (CVPR), pp. 2074–2081. IEEE (2012)
10. Norouzi, M., Blei, D.M.: Minimal loss hashing for compact binary codes. In: Proceedings of the 28th International Conference on Machine Learning (ICML 2011), pp. 353–360 (2011)
11. Norouzi, M., Fleet, D.J., Salakhutdinov, R.R.: Hamming distance metric learning. In: Advances in Neural Information Processing Systems, pp. 1061–1069 (2012)

12. Song, D., Liu, W., Meyer, D.A., Tao, D., Ji, R.: Rank preserving hashing for rapid image search. In: Data Compression Conference, DCC 2015, pp. 353–362. IEEE (2015)

13. Xia, R., Pan, Y., Lai, H., Liu, C., Yan, S.: Supervised hashing for image retrieval via image representation learning. AAAI **1**, 2156–2162 (2014)

14. Zhang, L., Zhang, Y., Tang, J., Gu, X., Li, J., Tian, Q.: Topology preserving hashing for similarity search. In: Proceedings of the 21st ACM International Conference on Multimedia, pp. 123–132. ACM (2013)

15. Zhang, R., Lin, L., Zhang, R., Zuo, W., Zhang, L.: Bit-scalable deep hashing with regularized similarity learning for image retrieval and person re-identification. TIP **24**(12), 4766–4779 (2015)

16. Zhao, F., Huang, Y., Wang, L., Tan, T.: Deep semantic ranking based hashing for multi-label image retrieval. In: Proceedings of the IEEE Conference on Computer Vision and Pattern Recognition, pp. 1556–1564 (2015)

17. Zheng, L., Wang, S., Liu, Z., Tian, Q.: Lp-norm IDF for large scale image search. In: Proceedings of the IEEE Conference on Computer Vision and Pattern Recognition, pp. 1626–1633 (2013)

18. Zheng, L., Wang, S., Liu, Z., Tian, Q.: Packing and padding: coupled multi-index for accurate image retrieval. In: Proceedings of the IEEE Conference on Computer Vision and Pattern Recognition, pp. 1939–1946 (2014)

19. Zheng, L., Wang, S., Tian, L., He, F., Liu, Z., Tian, Q.: Query-adaptive late fusion for image search and person re-identification. In: Proceedings of the IEEE Conference on Computer Vision and Pattern Recognition, pp. 1741–1750 (2015)

20. Zheng, L., Wang, S., Tian, Q.: Coupled binary embedding for large-scale image retrieval. IEEE Trans. Image Process. **23**(8), 3368–3380 (2014)

21. Zheng, L., Wang, S., Wang, J., Tian, Q.: Accurate image search with multi-scale contextual evidences. Int. J. Comput. Vis. **120**(1), 1–13 (2016)

22. Zheng, L., Wang, S., Zhou, W., Tian, Q.: Bayes merging of multiple vocabularies for scalable image retrieval. In: Proceedings of the IEEE Conference on Computer Vision and Pattern Recognition, pp. 1955–1962 (2014)

23. Zheng, L., Yang, Y., Tian, Q.: Sift meets CNN: a decade survey of instance retrieval. IEEE Trans. Pattern Anal. Mach. Intell. https://doi.org/10.1109/TPAMI.2017.2709749

24. Zhu, X., Zhang, L., Huang, Z.: A sparse embedding and least variance encoding approach to hashing. TIP **23**(9), 3737–3750 (2014)

A Fast CU Decision Algorithm in Inter Coding Based on Residual Analysis

Lanfang Dong$^{(\boxtimes)}$ and Li Wang

School of Computer Science and Technology,
University of Science and Technology of China, Hefei, China
lfdong@ustc.edu.cn, wanglia@mail.ustc.edu.cn

Abstract. Inter coding in HEVC can greatly improve video compression efficiency. However it also brings huge computational cost due to adaptive partition of Coding Tree Unit (CTU) with the quadtree technique. In this paper, a fast CU (Coding Unit) decision algorithm is proposed to alleviate the computational burden. This algorithm is fulfilled by analyzing the residual using mean and dispersion. And the optimal RQT (Residual Quad-tree Transform) depth is used innovatively to measure the residual dispersion. First, the optimal RQT depth and avgdis (defined in 3.3) is obtained after inter coding in 2N × 2N PU mode. Then the decision of CU partition is determined through comparing avgdis with the corresponding threshold. Thresholds are predicted based on the distribution of CU partition in the encoded pictures and they can be adaptively changed as the video content changes. Compared to HM13.0 (HEVC test model), the improved algorithm could save about 56% of encoding time on average, with 0.2034% increase of bitrate and the influence on the quality of reconstructed videos is negligible.

Keywords: HEVC · Inter coding · CU partition · Residual · Dispersion

1 Introduction

More and more popular video applications and the increasing video resolution have brought the huge bandwidth consumption and the high storage cost. The existing video compression standard H.264/AVC has been unable to satisfy the high-definition and ultra-high-definition video. Joint Collaborative Team on Video Coding (JCT-VC) [1], established by ITU-T/VCEG and ISO-IEC/MPEG, released the video coding standard HEVC (High Efficiency Video Coding), and the standard is still evolving.

Compared to H.264/AVC, under the similar video quality, HEVC can save 50% of the video stream [2]. However, different from the fixed macroblock of H.264, HEVC uses the quadtree technique to realize adaptive partitioning of CTU which will traverse all possible combinations to determine the best partitioning, greatly increasing the computational complexity of video coding.

HEVC coding techniques can be divided into intra prediction and inter prediction. The compression rate of inter prediction several times that of intra prediction, the main reason of which lies in that inter prediction requires finding the most matching block of PU (Prediction Unit) in the reference frame. According to the relevant statistics, inter

Y. Zhao et al. (Eds.): ICIG 2017, Part II, LNCS 10667, pp. 216–228, 2017.
https://doi.org/10.1007/978-3-319-71589-6_20

prediction accounts for more than 60% of the overall coding time. Therefore, the acceleration of inter prediction is of great significance.

In this paper, a fast CU decision algorithm for inter prediction based on residual analysis is proposed. The residual is analyzed by mean and dispersion, and its optimal RQT depth is used innovatively to measure the residual dispersion. At first we statistically analyze the relationship between mean and dispersion and CU partition. Then the determination threshold of the current frame is predicted based on the distribution of CU partition of the threshold image. At last unnecessary CU calculations are terminated by threshold comparison. Experiments show that the proposed algorithm can significantly reduce the computational complexity of inter prediction without losing the video quality and compression ratio.

The remainder of this paper is organized as follows. Section 2 gives a brief introduction of background knowledge. Section 3 describes the proposed algorithm in detail. Experimental results are shown in Sect. 4. At last Sect. 5 concludes this paper.

2 Background Knowledge

2.1 Brief Introduction of Inter Coding in HEVC

Inter coding can eliminate the redundancy in time domain to achieve the purpose of video compression. For inter coding, current block would find its best matching block by motion estimation in the reference frame as the prediction block. The difference between the matching block and the current block is called the residual.

By using the quadtree technique, the CU with depth d can be divided into four sub-CUs in depth d + 1. And decision-making for partition is determined by the rate distortion of the CU and the sub-CUs. The definition of RD (Rate Distortion) can be seen in Formula (1), where D represents the distortion in the current prediction mode and R is the number of bits required to encode the prediction mode. Figure 1(a) is an example of CTU partition, in which the white indicates that CU continues to be divided and the black stands for stopping CU partition.

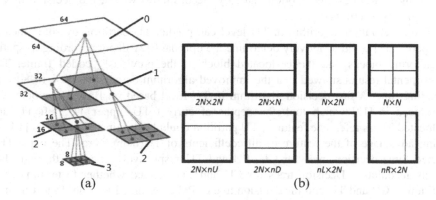

Fig. 1. (a) One example of CTU partition (b) PU partition modes

In HEVC the CU will be further divided into PUs which are basic units of inter prediction. There are eight types of PU partition, containing four types of symmetric partition and four types of asymmetric partition [3], as shown in Fig. 1(b). HEVC will test all the PU partition modes for CU, and ultimately select the optimal PU partition with the minimum RD cost.

$$RDCost = D + \lambda R \tag{1}$$

TU (Transform Unit) is the basic unit for transform and quantization. Similar to CU partition, TU partition can be flexibly fulfilled by quadtree technique in a recursive manner [4].

2.2 Related Work

HEVC inter coding can be accelerated in three aspects: CU level, PU level and TU level.

In the CU level, accelerating can be realized by skipping unnecessary CU partition tests or terminating CU partition earlier. The paper [5] first got the depth range of CU partition based on visual saliency map detection, and then CU partition was determined by the comparison of coding bits and the specific threshold. A RD cost based accelerative algorithm was proposed by [6], where the decision of CU partition was made by comparing RD cost of the current CU with the specific threshold. Paper [7] proposed a fast algorithm determining the depth range of CU partition, which made a comprehensive utilization of zero CU detection, standard deviation of statistic spatiotemporal depth information and edge gradient of CTU. Paper [8] introduced an accelerating algorithm of inter encoding aiming at surveillance videos. Inter-frame difference was utilized to segment out moving objects encoding in CU of small size from background encoding in CU of large size. Wu et al. presented a fast inter encoding algorithm aiming at H.264 in [9] which determined the size of the coding block according to spatial homogeneity based on edge information and temporal stationary characteristics judged by MB differencing. The paper [10] constructed a feature vector for each CU consisting of RD cost and motion category, according to which, the decision of CU partition was determined.

The acceleration algorithm in TU level can predict TU partition by some means. The paper [11] could adaptively determine the optimal RQT depth according to spatial neighboring blocks and the co-located block at the previously coded frame. The experimental results showed that the improved algorithm could save 60% to 80% of encoding time. A fast decision algorithm in TU level based on Bayesian model was introduced in [12] which took the depths of current TU, upper TU, left TU and co-located TU as reference features. TU partition could be terminated earlier in [13] by taking advantage of the feature of all coefficients of TU being zero. The paper [14] created three decision trees for CU, PU and TU respectively obtained through data mining techniques. Decision trees for CU and TU decided whether to terminate the partition of CU and TU and the decision tree of PU determined whether to test the rest of PU partition modes.

In paper [15], an improved algorithm in PU level for HEVC inter prediction was proposed whose core idea was to reduce motion estimation calls. The CU was divided into four blocks of the same size, and then the PU partition was determined by comparing the motion vectors of the four PU blocks. Gao et al. in [16] calculated a quadtree probability model based on a quantization parameter and a group of pictures and then a new quadtree was constructed by skipping low probability tree nodes.

Algorithms above have achieved a good acceleration effect with minimal impact on video quality and the increment of bitrate on average is also in a reasonable range. However, the increment of bitrate between different videos has a big difference in this paper, we propose a fast CU decision algorithm based on residual analysis in which no extra calculation is required and intermediate results are fully utilized. CU splitting decision is fulfilled by thresholds comparing and the thresholds can adaptively be adjusted as the video content changes. Experimental results prove that the improved method can significantly reduce encoding time.

3 Fast CU Decision Algorithm Based on Residual Analysis

3.1 Residual Analysis

Generally speaking, for the same image region, compared to encoding in large-size CU, small-size CU can achieve better matching effect with smaller prediction error but larger coding bits. If the matching performance of current CU in 2N × 2N PU mode is in good condition, coding bits become larger and prediction error reduces slightly after CU is divided, leading to larger RD cost. So current CU is not appropriate to be divided into smaller CUs. On the contrary, if the matching performance is too bad, current CU has significant reduction of prediction error after being divided, bringing smaller RD cost. Further CU partition should be performed.

The residual is the result after motion compensation which directly reflects the matching performance of the current block. Therefore the decision of CU partition can be made by analyzing the residual.

In this paper, dispersion and mean of residuals are utilized to analyze residuals. Dispersion refers to the degree of difference between values in residuals. And mean is the average of all data items in residuals.

3.2 How to Measure the Dispersion

There are two commonly used methods for measuring the dispersion:

- Standard deviation: Calculate standard deviation of data items in the residual.
- Edge detection: Edge detection such as Sobel operator or Canny operator is operated on the residual block to extract edges. And then calculate the number of nonzero values in the edge map.

Both of the two methods require additional computation, and they also need to set thresholds between uniform and non-uniform artificially. Here we make use of the optimal RQT depth of current CU to measure dispersion of residuals creatively.

After inter prediction, the residual block is imputed into the transform module for further compression. In the transform module, DCT (Discrete Cosine Transform) is performed on the residual block, which can remove the correlation between data items in the residual block.

If the residual block is in uniform distribution, DCT coefficients that have been quantized remain a small amount of larger value with most of them being zero, resulting in lower coding bits and smaller RD cost. Then current TU will not be divided into smaller TUs, as shown in Fig. 2(a). On the other hand, if the residual has rich texture, there are many larger values and a small amount of smaller values, leading to more coding bits and larger RD cost. Therefore current TU can get more zero DCT coefficients by further TU partition, as shown in Fig. 2(b). According to the local variation characteristics of the predicted residuals, TU can adaptively select the optimal TU partition.

2	6	5	2	2	-1	-2	-1
2	8	5	1	0	-5	-1	-1
5	1	4	2	1	-1	2	1
7	2	5	3	1	8	5	0
4	9	6	7	6	5	4	4
1	11	5	7	7	5	1	2
-5	8	6	2	3	5	1	1
-2	5	1	-1	6	3	4	4

(a)

137	125	35	-17	3	1	11	-7
136	133	34	-43	-52	15	22	-6
135	136	43	-38	-57	23	25	2
135	135	47	-17	-39	54	19	4
135	142	59	7	4	49	16	-11
135	139	58	5	-3	31	54	-14
135	139	63	2	11	21	69	4
132	136	57	-5	19	0	56	38

(b)

Fig. 2. (a) TU partition of residual block in uniform distribution (b) TU partition of residual block in rich texture

Based on the above analysis, we can see that the optimal RQT depth has a close relationship with dispersion. The deeper the optimal RQT depth is, the greater dispersion is. Thus the optimal RQT depth can be used to measure dispersion directly. The maximum depth of TU can be set in the configuration file, default as three. In this paper, the maximum partition depth of TU adopts the default value.

3.3   The Relationship Between CU Partition and Dispersion and Mean

As described in Sect. 3.2, dispersion is measured using optimal RQT depth denoted as opRdepth which has three cases: 0, 1 and 2. The optimal RQT depth doesn't require additional computation which is the intermediate result. In order to simplify the calculation, mean is replaced by average value of ssd (short for avgdis) produced by HEVC, which is the sum of the squared error of original pixels and reconstructed pixels.

$$D_{split} = f(\text{opRdepth}, \text{avgdis}, \text{CUsize}) \tag{2}$$

We can get opRdepth and avgdis of current CU after inter encoding in 2N × 2N PU mode is fulfilled. Then the splitting decision D_{split} can be represented as a function of opRdepth, avgdis and CU size.

In order to determine the mapping relationship f, we make a mass of statistics on opRdepth, avgdis and its corresponding CU splitting decision. Each video has 50 frames to participate in statistics. For example, detailed statistical results of BasketballDrill can be seen in Fig. 3, where the horizontal axis stands for the number of CU and the vertical axis is avgdis. The green dots mean the current CU need to be divided further while the red dots mean not. We can see that there is a boundary between red dots and green dots. According to statistical results of numerous videos, we propose a fast CU decision algorithm denoted as CUDecision which can be seen in Table 1. TH_bootom_{ij} and TH_up_{ij} is the threshold for CU splitting decision, where i represents the depth of current CU and j is opRdepth.

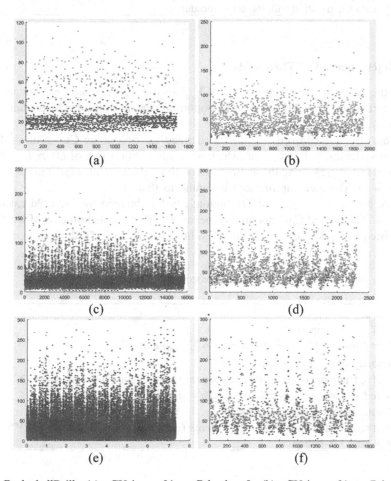

Fig. 3. BasketballDrill   (a)   CUsize = 64   opRdepth = 0   (b)   CUsize = 64   opRdepth = 2 (c) CUsize = 32 opRdepth = 0 (d) CUsize = 32 opRdepth = 2 (e) CUsize = 16 opRdepth = 0 (f) CUsize = 16 opRdepth = 2 (Color figure online)

Table 1. Detailed process of CUDecision

1. Perform inter coding in 2N×2N PU mode on the current CU, and then opRdepth and avgdis is obtained.
2. If opRdepth is zero, jump to 3. If not, jump to 5.
3. If avgdis<TH_bootom_{i0}, splitting of CU should be terminated.
4. If avgdis>TH_up_{i0}, skip calculation of current CU and calculate CUs in next depth. If not, jump to 7.
5. If opRdepth is two, jump to 6. If not, jump to 7.
6. If avgdis>TH_up_{i2}, skip calculation of current CU and calculate CUs in next depth.
7. Process CU partition with standard procedures.

3.4   Determination of Thresholds

Due to the similarity of image content, CU partition between adjacent images has a strong correlation. Thus TH_up and TH_bottom in current frame can be predicted from previous frames.

A data structure denoted as drawer is defined for describing CU partition. It contains two variables, red and green, which are arrays with a size of 60. red_i is the i-th element of red, representing the number of not divided CUs with avgdis in the range of 5i to 5(i + 1). The meaning of green is similar to that of red.

Given a drawer, TH_up and TH_bottom can be obtained by threshold calculating methods CalTHup and CalTHbottom respectively. The detailed process of CalTHbottom is listed in Table 2 and CalTHup has a flow similar to CalTHbottom.

Table 2. Detailed process of CalTHbottom

1. i=0.
2. If i>=60, jump to 9.
3. red_num = $\sum_{j=i}^{i+3} red_j$, green_num = $\sum_{j=i}^{i+3} green_j$.
4. total_num=red_num+green_num.
5. If red_num/total_num>=0.9, TH_bottom= (i+4)*5 and i=i+4 and jump to 2.
6. red_sub = $red_i + red_{i+1}$, green_sub = $green_i + green_{i+1}$.
7. total_sub=red_sub+green_sub.
8. If red_sub/total_sub>=0.9, TH_bottom= (i+2)*5. If not, TH_bottom= (i+1)*5.
9. Return TH_bottom.

The image that serves to predict TH_up and TH_bottom is called THimage. PredictSet is a set of THimages defined as follows where Pi is the POC (Picture Order

Count) of corresponding THimage. The size of PredictSet equals to GOP (Group Of Pictures) size which is set to four in our experiments.

$$PredictSet = \{P_i | i = 0, 1, 2, 3\} \tag{3}$$

Updating PredictSet. RD1 in Eq. (4) is RD cost of current CU which is not divided and RD2 in Eq. (5) is the corresponding RD cost of divided CU. With Eq. (4) and Eqs. (5) and (6) is deduced. What's more, λ is positively correlated with the QP (Quantization Parameter), as shown in Eq. (7) where α and W_k are weighting factors related to different configurations. Accordingly we can conclude that QPs will make a difference on distribution of CU partition. The HEVC encoder sets a series of QP values for each frame in a GOP, and each GOP has the same QP configuration. Therefore, THimages in PredictSet should contain all QP values in one GOP. In our experiments, QP values are set to be 35, 34, 35 and 33 in one GOP. A PredictSet updating algorithm named UpdatePed is proposed to initialize and update PredictSet, as shown in Table 3.

$$RD1 = D1 + \lambda R1 \tag{4}$$

$$RD2 = D2 + \lambda R2 \tag{5}$$

$$\lambda > = \frac{D2 - D1}{R1 - R2} \tag{6}$$

$$\lambda = \alpha \cdot W_k \cdot 2^{\frac{(QP-12)}{3}} \tag{7}$$

Table 3. Detailed process of UpdatePed

1. The first frame with POC=0 is encoded in intra coding.
2. CurPOC=1.
3. The frame is encoded in inter coding using initial TH_up and TH_bottom.
4. CurPOC= curPOC+1.
5. If curPOC<=4, jump to 3.
6. PredictSet = {1, 2, 3, 4} and TH_poc=5.
7. If CurPOC< TH_poc, the frame is encoded using updated TH_up and TH_bottom and jump to 12.
8. If (CurPOC = TH_poc), the frame is encoded using initial TH_up and TH_bottom.
9. The minimum value in PredictSet is replaced by TH_poc.
10. Update TH_up and TH_bottom using PredictSet.
11. TH_poc= TH_poc+5.
12. CurPOC= CurPOC+1.
13. Jump to 7.

Threshold Calculation. Each THimage $P_i(i = 0, 1, 2, 3)$ in PredictSet has its corresponding drawer set D_i defined in Eq. (8) where d_{ijk} is the drawer of CUs in depth j with opRdepth being k. Dsum is the sum of D_i, defined in Eq. (9). TH_up_{j0} and TH_up_{j2} can be obtained by inputting $dsum_{j0}$ and $dsum_{j2}$ into CalTHup respectively.

$$D_i = \{d_{ijk}|j = 0, 1, 2; k = 0, 2\} \tag{8}$$

$$\text{Dsum} = \{(dsum_{jk} = \sum\nolimits_{i=0}^{3} d_{ijk})|j = 0, 1, 2; k = 0, 2\} \tag{9}$$

TH_up_{j0} and TH_up_{j2} are predicted without considering the influence of QPs. Differing from prediction of TH_up, the calculation of TH_bottom takes QPs into consideration and each QP value has its corresponding prediction threshold. $TH\_GOPbottom_{ijk}$ and $TH\_QPbottom_{ijk}$ are defined for i-th QP value where j is the depth of CUs and k is opRdepth. In fact, we just need to calculate $TH\_GOPbottom_{ij0}$ and $TH\_OPbottom_{ij0}$.

Inputting $dsum_{j0}$ into CalTHbottom can get TH_bottom_{j0} and Inputting d_{ij0} can output $TH\_QPbottom_{ij0}$. $TH\_GOPbottom_{ijk}$ is the optimal threshold selected from them. In most cases, TH_bottom_{j0} is an appropriate prediction threshold. However if $TH\_QPbottom_{ij0}$ is greater more than TH_bottom_{j0}, maybe $TH\_QPbottom_{ij0}$ is more accurate (see Fig. 4.), which is caused by QP difference. According to derivation process of CU partition in last section, we can see the larger the QP value is, the greater the threshold is. Similarly the larger the QP value is, the more not divided TUs are. Therefore the QP value is measured by the number of CUs with opRdepth being zero denoted as $CUnum_i$. Thus the optimal threshold can be chosen through $CUnum_i$.

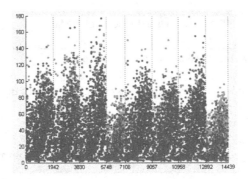

Fig. 4. CU partition of BQTerrace in depth one

Based on the above analysis, the method of threshold calculation denoted as CalTHpred describes the flow for calculating $TH\_GOPbottom_{ijk}$, shown in Table 4.

Table 4. Detailed process of CalTHpred

1. Compute TH_bottom_{j0} and $TH\_QPbottom_{ij0}$.
2. Calculate $CUnum_i$.
3. avgCUnum $= (\sum_{i=0}^{3} CUnum_i)/4$.
4. $TH\_GOPbottom_{ij0} = TH\_bottom_{j0}$.
5. If $TH\_OPbottom_{ij0} - TH\_bottom_{j0} \geq 10$ *and* $CUnum_i >$ avgCUnum, $TH\_GOPbottom_{ij0} = TH\_QPbottom_{ij0}$.

4 Experiments and Results

The proposed algorithm is implemented on HM13.0 and the coding performance can be evaluated by ΔPSNR (Peak Signal to Noise Ratio), ΔBR (Bitrate), and ΔET (Encoding Time) defined in (10) to (12) under lowdelay P configuration. PSNR is calculated by Eq. (13). In our experiments, 50 frames are tested for each video.

$$\Delta\text{PSNR} = \frac{PSNR_{proposed} - PSNR_{HM}}{PSNR_{HM}} \tag{10}$$

$$\Delta\text{BR} = \frac{BR_{proposed} - BR_{HM}}{BR_{HM}} \tag{11}$$

$$\Delta\text{ET} = \frac{ET_{proposed} - ET_{HM}}{ET_{HM}} \tag{12}$$

$$\text{PSNR} = (\text{PSNRY} \times 4 + \text{PSNRU} + \text{PSNRV})/6 \tag{13}$$

Table 5 shows the acceleration effect of the proposed algorithm. Through careful observation and analysis, we can get the following points.

1. The improved algorithm could save about 56% of encoding time on average, with 0.2034% increase of bitrate and 0.0423 reduction in PSNR.
2. If the video content changes slowly such as Flowervase, Mobisode2 and so on, the proposed method can reduce execution time by about 70% with a small change in bitrate and PSNR. In some cases, the bitrate is even reduced.
3. If the video content changes quickly such as BasketballDrill, Tennis and so on, the proposed algorithm can reduce execution time by 36%–50% and the increment of bitrate is a little higher than that of small changing videos.
4. The PSNR of SlideShow decreases by 0.1164% which is greatest in test sequences and the increment of bitrate reaches 1.4575%, a little higher than that of other videos.
5. The increment of bitrate is limited within 1.11%. This proves that the proposed algorithm can guarantee compression ratio when it realizes accelerating.

Table 5. Results of the proposed algorithm compared to HM13.0

Resolution	Video name	ΔBR (%)	ΔPSNR	ΔET (%)
832 * 480	BasketballDrill	1.1178	−0.0329	−48.4424
	BasketballDrillText	0.9064	−0.0466	−49.4051
	Flowervase	−1.0959	−0.0163	−70.7357
	Mobisode2	0.3659	−0.0402	−67.5394
	RaceHorsesC	0.5669	−0.0158	−39.2287
	BQMall	0.4097	−0.0331	−47.4201
	Keiba	0.6921	−0.0273	−43.8054
	PartyScene	0.2589	−0.0178	−36.2514
1024 * 768	ChinaSpeed	−0.5957	−0.0443	−50.0416
1280 * 720	FourPeople	−0.1044	−0.0323	−72.5145
	Johnny	−0.6339	−0.0479	−75.0793
	SlideShow	1.4575	−0.1164	−74.6874
	vidyo1	−0.3152	−0.0243	−74.6151
	KristenAndSara	−0.4875	−0.0456	−73.0945
1920 * 1800	Cactus	0.3813	−0.0202	−53.8501
	Kimono1	0.8674	−0.0174	−52.4435
	BQTerrace	−1.3989	−0.0231	−53.4527
	ParkScene	0.0071	−0.0206	−49.1677
	Tennis	0.9690	−0.0222	−49.8077
2560 * 1600	PeopleOnStreet	0.8509	−0.0145	−39.8343
	Traffic	0.0522	−0.0298	−57.8289
Average		0.2034	−0.0423	−56.1545

We can find that the video with small changes can achieve more reduction of computational complexity. That's because CUs in the small changing video can get good matching performance and then terminates CU partition earlier. For the video with fast content change, prediction of TH_up and TH_bottom is less accurate, leading to more bitrate increasing.

SlideShow has much more sudden changes and sometimes image content is completely different between adjacent frames. Under this circumstance, thresholds are not accurate, contributing to slightly larger image distortion and more bitrate increasing. In fact, due to big difference between adjacent frames, inter coding is not suitable for SlideShow to realize compression.

5 Conclusion

For one CTU, HEVC will traverse all possible divisions with the quadtree technique to make the coding efficiency optimized. However, the exhaustive search process greatly aggravates the computational burden. A fast CU decision algorithm based on residual analysis is proposed to predict whether current CU will be divided and then skip redundant computation process. The residual is analyzed by mean and dispersion, and then the measure of dispersion is fulfilled by the optimal RQT depth. When the optimal RQT depth equals to 0 or 2, the decision of CU partition will be determined by comparing avgdis with the corresponding threshold. What's more, the proposed algorithm could realize adaptive changes of thresholds for different videos.

Experimental results show that the proposed algorithm can achieve good performance on speeding up calculation without affecting compression ratio and the quality of reconstructed videos.

References

1. Duanmu, F., Ma, Z., Wang, Y.: Fast mode and partition decision using machine learning for intra-frame coding in HEVC screen content coding extension. IEEE J. Emerg. Sel. Topics Circuits Syst. **6**(4), 517–531 (2016)
2. Correa, G., Assuncao, P., Agostini, L., et al.: Performance and computational complexity assessment of high-efficiency video encoders. IEEE Trans. Circuits Syst. Video Technol. **22** (12), 1899–1909 (2012)
3. McCann, K., Rosewarne, C., Bross, B., et al.: High efficiency video coding (HEVC) test model 16 (HM 16) improved encoder description. JCT-VC, Technical report JCTVC-S 1002 (2014)
4. Sullivan, G.J., Ohm, J., Han, W.J., et al.: Overview of the high efficiency video coding (HEVC) standard. IEEE Trans. Circuits Syst. Video Technol. **22**(12), 1649–1668 (2012)
5. Qing, A., Zhou, W., Wei, H., et al.: A fast CU partitioning algorithm in HEVC inter prediction for HD/UHD video. In: Signal and Information Processing Association Annual Summit and Conference, pp. 1–5. IEEE Press, Pacific (2016)
6. Wang, J., Dong, L., Xu, Y.: A fast inter prediction algorithm based on rate-distortion cost in HEVC. Int. J. Sig. Process. Image Process. Pattern Recogn. **8**(11), 141–158 (2015)
7. Liu, J., Jia, H., Xiang, G., et al.: An adaptive inter CU depth decision algorithm for HEVC. In: Visual Communications and Image Processing, pp. 1–4. IEEE Press, Singapore (2015)
8. Wang, J., Dong, L.: An efficient coding scheme for surveillance videos based on high efficiency video coding. In: 10th International Conference on Natural Computation, pp. 899–904. IEEE Press, Xiamen (2014)
9. Wu, D., Wu, S., Lim, K.P., et al.: Block inter mode decision for fast encoding of H.264. In: IEEE International Conference on Acoustics, Speech, and Signal Processing, pp. iii–181. IEEE Press, Canada (2004)
10. Mallikarachchi, T., Fernando, A., Arachchi, H.K.: Fast coding unit size selection for HEVC inter prediction. In: IEEE International Conference on Consumer Electronics, pp. 457–458. IEEE Press, Taiwan (2015)
11. Wang, C.C., Liao, Y.C., Wang, J.W., et al.: An effective TU size decision method for fast HEVC encoders. In: International Symposium on Computer, Consumer and Control, pp. 1195–1198. IEEE Press, Taiwan (2014)
12. Wu, X., Wang, H., Wei, Z.: Bayesian rule based fast TU depth decision algorithm for high efficiency video coding. In: Visual Communications and Image Processing, pp. 1–4. IEEE Press, Chengdu (2016)
13. Fang, J.T., Tsai, Y.C., Lee, J.X., et al.: Computation reduction in transform unit of high efficiency video coding based on zero-coefficients. In: International Symposium on Computer, Consumer and Control, pp. 797–800. IEEE Press, Xi'an (2016)

14. Correa, G., Assuncao, P.A., Agostini, L.V., et al.: Fast HEVC encoding decisions using data mining. IEEE Trans. Circuits Syst. Video Technol. **25**(4), 660–673 (2015)
15. Sampaio, F., Bampi, S., Grellert, M., et al.: Motion vectors merging: low complexity prediction unit decision heuristic for the inter-prediction of HEVC encoders. In: IEEE International Conference on Multimedia and Expo, pp. 657–662. IEEE Press, Australia (2012)
16. Gao, Y., Liu, P., Wu, Y., et al.: Quadtree degeneration for HEVC. IEEE Trans. Multimedia **18**(12), 2321–2330 (2016)

Feature-Based Facial Image Coding Method Using Wavelet Transform

Chuxi Yang[1], Yan Zhao[1(✉)], Shigang Wang[1], and Yuanyuan Liu[2]

[1] Communication Engineering, Jilin University, Changchun 130012, China
zhao_y@jlu.edu.cn
[2] Information Technology, Jilin Agricultural University, Changchun 130118, Jilin, China

Abstract. This paper proposed a novel image coding scheme for facial images in the transform domain based on Scale Invariant Feature Transform (SIFT). With the characteristic of rotation scale invariability, SIFT descriptors are perfect to describe the details in an image. Our proposed coding scheme combine wavelet transform with SIFT algorithm. High frequency sub band images of the input image are encoded according to SIFT key points rather than pixel value on the encoder side. On the decoder side, we can get restoring patch from an image database according to key point matching. After clustering and transformation, the matching patches are used to restore the high frequency sub band images. Final reconstructed image was produced by wavelet inverse transform from low frequency sub band image and restored high frequency sub band images. Experimental results show that compared with HEVC and JPEG2000, the proposed algorithm can reach a higher compression ratio and a satisfactory reconstruction performance.

Keywords: Image coding · Wavelet transform · SIFT · Local feature
Database

1 Introduction

Now Internet is an inseparable part of our daily life. Almost every day, we get news from the news site, search information through the search engine and watch some pictures and videos on the Internet. In recent years, Internet, as a large scale information carrier, has a rapid-growing image database. Facial images become an important part of all kinds of images and are widely used in various applications. Therefore effective facial image coding is vital for storage and transmission of facial images.

From the earliest standard JPEG to recently proposed HEVC/H.265, the development of mainstream image coding method took more than two decades. Some classical coding algorithms emerged, including JPEG2000 [1], AVC/H.264 and HEVC (High Efficiency Video Coding) [2]. H.264 uses intra-frame prediction in the spatial domain to remove redundancy between adjacent image blocks. JPEG2000 is a representative transform domain oriented coding method, which transforms the image into wavelet domain and then compresses it by quantizing the wavelet coefficients. Since cloud database is huge, it is very likely to find some similar images from the cloud database. For facial image, even

© Springer International Publishing AG 2017
Y. Zhao et al. (Eds.): ICIG 2017, Part II, LNCS 10667, pp. 229–238, 2017.
https://doi.org/10.1007/978-3-319-71589-6_21

for different people, the face similarity can reach 70%. If we can use the database resource to help for image coding, we may get a higher compression ratio.

Currently, there are many visual feature extraction algorithms. For a facial image, we can extract some local features in the sense organs and hair areas. These local features can well reflect the portrait characteristics and can be invariant in some cases. Therefore we consider to encode facial images according to the local features, and try to keep the feature area and neglect the non-feature area appropriately.

In this paper, we propose a feature-based coding method for facial image in the transform domain. First of all, the input image is transformed by multi-layer wavelet transform. After transformation, we can get one low frequency sub band (LF sub band) and some high frequency sub bands (HF sub bands). We use local feature to describe the HF sub bands. The encoded bit stream is consists of encoded feature information and encoded LF sub band. On the decoded side, we use the decoded feature information to match features in a database and find similar patches to restore the HF sub bands, Final reconstructed image is obtained using wavelet inverse transform from decoded LF sub band and restored HF sub bands.

The rest of this paper is organized as follows: Sect. 2 introduces related works of proposed algorithm; Sect. 3 provides our coding method in detail; Sect. 4 shows our experimental results; Final conclusions are given in Sect. 5.

2 Related Works

In 2004, Lowe proposed SIFT algorithm [3]. SIFT features have the advantage of scale and rotation invariance. A scale space is established firstly, and extreme values are found in the scale space as feature key points in SIFT algorithm. There are three basic parameters for each key point: position, scale and orientation. Scale expresses the layer of the key points, and orientation gives the gradient orientation value of the neighborhood of the key point. The scale invariance of the SIFT feature can be used for matches between images at different scale, and rotation invariance can be used to adapt to the rotation transformation.

In this paper, we use SIFT algorithm to extract features of facial images. Each key point can be expressed by:

$$K_i = (Pt_i, s_i, o_i) \tag{1}$$

where Pt_i is the coordinate of the key point, s_i and o_i are the scale and orientation of the key point respectively.

After the feature extraction, the feature key points need to be described. In [3], Lowe used a 128-dimension descriptor to described each key point. According to the location of the key point, a neighborhood image block is selected, whose size is related to the scale of the key point. To realize the rotation invariance, the image block is rotated to its main orientation o_i Then the block is divided into 4×4 subblocks, and a 8-dimension vector is calculated for each subblock. Finally, a vector with $4 \times 4 \times 8 = 128$ dimensions is obtained. We can get the SIFT descriptor of one each point after normalization, which is expressed by D_i.

SIFT algorithm had immediately attracted a wide spread attention when proposed. It was widely used in image reconstruction [4], image classification [5], image detection and recognition [6, 7] and image search [8, 9]. The method of image reconstruction based on feature was first proposed in [4]. Weinzaepfel et al. extracted image features by SIFT algorithm, then did the sift-match with a big image database. However, the reconstructed image had a serious distortion. Based on this idea, Yue et al. proposed a cloud-based image coding algorithm in [10]. A down sampled image was transferred to the decoder side as a guide of image reconstruction. At the decoder side, matching patches could be found from the cloud according to the feature match. Patches was pasted to the up sampled image after processing. This method can achieve high compression ratio, as well as good restoration quality. However, as it said in [10], when the high similarity image was removed from the database, the reconstructed image becomes blurred. In 2014, Song et al. proposed an image reconstruction method based on thumbnail [11], which got better performance in compression ratio and PSNR comparing with JPEG.

3 The Proposed Coding Method

3.1 General Analysis

On the encoder side, the image is multi-level wavelet transformed first. After wavelet transformation, *LF* sub band and *HF* sub bands are produced. *LF* sub band is transmitted to the decoder side after being encoded. For *HF* sub bands, we just remain some features of *HF* sub bands, and transmit the feature key point information to the decoder side. The key points of *HF* sub bands are got from the difference set between key points of input image and key points of HF-missed inverse wavelet transform image. The coded bit stream is consist of coded *LF* sub band L_{en} and coded key point information K_{en}.

In the decoder, L_{en} and K_{en} are first decoded. Then HF-missed wavelet reverse transformation is done to get an inverse wavelet transform image which is as large as the input image. Then the decoded key point information is used to calculate the feature descriptor in the inverse wavelet transform image. After we get the descriptors, we can do SIFT match to a large image database. Each matching key points in the database corresponds a small image patch. These small patches are used to restore the *HF* sub bands. When all the *HF* sub bands are restored, we can do HF-restored inverse wavelet transform to get the reconstructed image (Fig. 1).

3.2 Encoder

STEP 1 Wavelet transform
After the image wavelet transform, the input image can be decomposed into 4 sub band images: low frequency *LL*, and high frequency sub bands *HL, LH, HH*. The structure and color information are included in the LF sub band, while the HF sub bands include the texture and detail information. In order to obtain a higher compression ratio, low frequency sub band can continue to be decomposed. For instance, LL_{n-1} can be divided into LL_n, LH_n, HL_n and HH_n. In our image coding scheme, we use 2-level wavelet

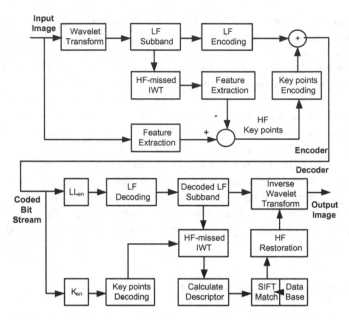

Fig. 1. System framework of proposed image coding scheme

transform, and totally produce 1 low frequency sub band LL_2, and 6 high frequency sub bands (HL_2, HH_2, HH_2, LH_1, HL_1, HH_1). We use L and H to represent low and high frequency parts for short respectively.

STEP 2 HF key point extraction

The goal of this step is to find effective information in the HF sub bands. SIFT algorithm can well detect the edges, corners and some texture. So the SIFT key points can well describe the effective information in an image. Therefore, effective information in HF sub bands can be described by HF key points. To get all the HF key points information, we first extract SIFT key point from the input image, denoted by K_I. Meanwhile, using LL_2 to do a 2-level inverse wavelet transform with HF sub bands are all zero, Each inverse transform level can be expressed by:

$$I_{iwt} = \frac{1}{2} \sum_{j,k} WT_f(j,k) \cdot \psi_{j,k}(t) \tag{2}$$

where, $\psi_{j,k}(t)$ is the wavelet basis. The inverse transform image is denoted by I_L. Then key point from I_L is extracted and denoted by K_L. It is obviously that K_L contains only low frequency information. The difference set of K_I and K_L is the HF key points. The information of HF feature key points can be described as:

$$K_H = \{(pt_1, s_1, o_1), (pt_2, s_2, o_2), \ldots, (pt_n, s_n, o_n)\} \tag{3}$$

where n is the number of key points.

STEP 3 LF sub band encoding

Since low frequency image includes most of the color and intensity information of the input image, we can use coding algorithm with low distortion to encode the LF sub band such as JPEG2000 and HEVC. In our coding scheme, we use HEVC to encode the low frequency image LL_2. The encoded LF sub band is expressed by LL_{en}.

STEP 4 Feature encoding

The locations of the key points are represented by a binary matrix M, which has the same size as the input image. If $k(x, y)$ is a feature key point, M_{xy} is set to 1, otherwise M_{xy} is set to 0. The binary matrix M is encoded using binary run-length coding. We use 14 bits to encode each sift key point, 7 bits for the scale and others for the orientation. $K_{en} = \{Pt_{en}, S_{en}, O_{en}\}$ is used to express the encoded feature points. The encoded bit stream is consist of LL_{en} and K_{en}.

3.3 Decoder

STEP 1 Bit stream decoding

The coded bit stream is first split into two parts—LL_{en} and K_{en}. HEVC decoder is used for low frequency decoding to get LL_{de}. And Pt_{de}, S_{de} and O_{de} are got by the corresponding key point decoding.

STEP 2 Feature descriptor calculation

After we get the location, scale and orientation of all the key points, we need to use these data to calculate the SIFT descriptor of each key point to do the match with image database. We take 2-level HF-missed inverse wavelet transform with LL_{de} and use Pt_{de}, S_{de} and O_{de} to calculate the SIFT descriptors in the IWT image I_{Lde}. Then we can get the descriptor $D_{de}\{d_1, d_2, \ldots, d_n\}$.

STEP 3 SIFT Key point matching

There is a large image database in the decoder. Images in the database are processed as the same way as for the input images. There are lot of features in the database images, making a key point set K^D, whose corresponding descriptor set is $D^D\{d_1^D, d_2^D, \ldots, d_m^D\}$. Assume that we have a certain HF key point k_i, we use its descriptor d_i to do the matching. If the Euclidean distance between d_i and d_j^D is the minimum value of all the database key point descriptors, k_i and k_j^D are a pair of matching points, which is denoted by M_i.

STEP 4 Optimizing and Clustering

In the encoder, the HF sub band key point K_H is the difference set of K_I and K_L. In the decoder, the SIFT descriptors are calculated in the I_{Lde}, which may have errors when calculating the descriptors, so as the matching process. Therefore we do not use all the matching points to restore the HF sub bands. A threshold value

$$Rs = 0.3 \times max\{dist(k_i, M_i)\} \tag{4}$$

is used to reduce mismatching points.

Where $\{dist(k_i, M_i)\}$ is the set of all the Euclidean distance between descriptors of k_i and M_i. For a certain key point k_i, if the Euclidean distance between k_i and its matching point M_i is smaller than Rs, We regard M_i as a good matching, and this matching pair will be reserved. Otherwise, we regard M_i as a mismatching, the matching pair will be ignored.

After optimization, we need to take features into cluster. One reason is that clustering can effectively avoid image patches overlapped closely to each other when pasting to the *HF* sub bands. The other reason is to calculate the transformation matrix more precisely—we can calculate different transformation matrix for different cluster. We use K-means algorithm to do the clustering, which can be expressed by:

$$Cluster_{mk} = \left\{ d_{kj} = min \sum_{j=1}^{K} \sum_{i=1}^{J} \parallel pt_i - \mu_j \parallel^2 \right\} \qquad (5)$$

where m is the index number of a database image, μ is the coordinate value of the cluster center.

STEP 5 HF sub bands restoration

When the cluster process is completed, for each cluster, we use RANSAC algorithm [12] to wipe off some mismatching points, and calculate the transformation matrix according to the rest of matching key points. Then we use the transformation matrix to all points in the cluster, make perspective transformation of the patches and paste them to the *HF* restoration sub bands to get the restored *HF* sub band images H_r.

STEP 6 Wavelet inverse transform

2-level inverse wavelet transform is used at this step. In the first level, LL_{1de} is got from LL_{de} and H_{r2}. Similarly, the final reconstructed image is produced by the second transform level.

4 Experimental Results

The facial database Utrecht ECVP [13] is used as our experimental image database. There are 131 images taken from 49 men and 20 women whose expression is usually natural or smile. The image resolutions is 900×1200 for all images. Each person has 1–3 pictures. The sense organs and hair cuts are different between different persons. We pick 6 images as the input image and the input image need to be removed from the database. After we get the reconstructed image, we compared it with HEVC and JPEG2000. The input images are shown in Fig. 2.

Fig. 2. Input images. From left to right marked "a" to "f".

Basic information of the input images are shown in Table 1.

Table 1. Basic information of input images

Image index	Size (KB)	LF size (KB)	No. of K_I	No. of K_L	No. of K_H
a	3164.06	198	301	102	258
b			766	292	648
c			638	252	536
d			220	128	163
e			175	107	122
f			306	125	256

Take image *b* as an example, the reconstructed image is shown in Fig. 3. The comparison of compress ratio and image quality is shown in Tables 2 and 3.

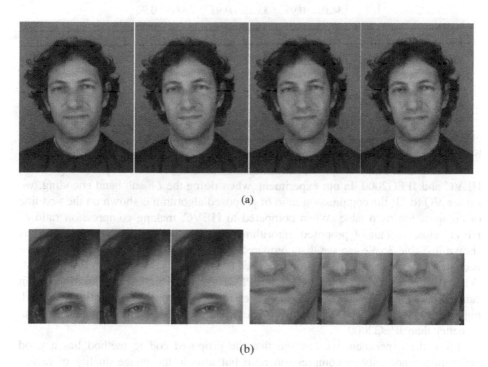

(a)

(b)

Fig. 3. The reconstructed results of image b. In the row (a), images from left to right: input image, proposed algorithm, HEVC, JPEG2000. The second row is the corresponding details. In the row (b), details from left to right: proposed algorithm, HEVC, JPEG2000.

Table 2. Comparison of compression ratio

Image	L_{en} (KB)	K_{en} (KB)	Compression ratio		
			Proposed	HEVC	JPEG2000
a	1.68	1.45	1011	1010	500
b	2.63	3.64	505	509	500
c	2.40	3.01	585	591	501
d	1.72	0.92	1198	1055	498
e	1.81	0.69	1265	1044	498
f	1.79	1.44	980	1014	508

Table 3. Comparison of image quality

Image	Proposed		HEVC		JPEG2000	
	PSNR	SSIM	PSNR	SSIM	PSNR	SSIM
a	36.31	0.93	35.68	0.93	38.2	0.93
b	34.01	0.91	33.86	0.91	33.08	0.90
c	33.13	0.91	34.48	0.91	33.62	0.90
d	36.67	0.93	36.18	0.92	36.37	0.92
e	36.19	0.93	36.36	0.92	34.59	0.91
f	35.55	0.94	36.21	0.93	36.15	0.93

From Fig. 3 we can see our coding scheme has a satisfactory subjective visual effect. Under high compression ratio, details of HEVC-coded images will become blurred, and JPEG2000 would appear blocking artifact.

Table 2 shows the comparison of compression ratio between proposed algorithm, HEVC and JPEG2000. In our experiment, when doing the *LF* sub band encoding, we set the VQ to 31, the compression ratio of proposed algorithm is shown on the first line of compression ratio table. When compared to HEVC, making compression ratio of HEVC close to that of proposed algorithm, the corresponding PSNR and SSIM is shown in Table 3. We can see that compared with HEVC, when the compression ratio is close to or higher than HEVC, the proposed algorithm has a higher PSNR and SSIM. When compared to JPEG2000, we set the JPEG2000 to the highest compression ratio it can reach. We can see that when the compression ratio of proposed algorithm is much higher than that of JPEG2000, the PSNR and SSIM of proposed algorithm can be equal or better than JPEG2000.

From the experiment we can see that the proposed coding method has a good performance not only in compression ratio but also in the image quality of reconstructive image. A further optimization will be used to the feature detection step to improve the coding performance.

5 Conclusions

This paper proposed a novel facial image coding scheme in the transform domain base on SIFT. The input image is first decomposed into low frequency sub band image and high frequency sub band images by wavelet transform. While the high frequency part is encoded according to SIFT descriptors rather than pixel value at the encoder side. SIFT-match is used at the decoder side to restore the high frequency images. Final reconstructed image is obtained by inverse wavelet transform. Experimental results show high compression ratio of our coding scheme. However, it still needs to be improved for processing edge information.

Acknowledgment. This work was supported by:

1. The State Key Program of National Natural Science Foundation of China (61631009);

2. The Jilin province science and technology development project of China (20150204006GX);

3. Graduate Innovation Fund of Jilin University.

References

1. Skodras, A., Christopoulos, C., Ebrahimi, T.: The Jpeg 2000 still image compression standard. IEEE Sig. Process. Mag. **18**(5), 36–58 (2001)
2. Sullivan, G.J., Ohm, J., Han, W.J., et al.: Overview of the high efficiency video coding (HEVC) standard. IEEE Trans. Circuits Syst. Video Technol. **22**(12), 1649–1668 (2012)
3. Lowe, D.G.: Distinctive image features from scale-invariant keypoints. Int. J. Comput. Vis. **26**, 91–110 (2004)
4. Weinzaepfel, P., Jegou, H., Perez, P.: Reconstructing an image from its local descriptors. In: Proceedings of the 2011 IEEE Conference on Computer Vision and Pattern Recognition, pp. 337–344. IEEE Computer Society (2011)
5. Xiao, X., Xu, C., Wang, J., et al.: Enhanced 3-D modeling for landmark image classification. Multimedia IEEE Trans. **14**(4), 1246–1258 (2012)
6. Kang, L.W., Hsu, C.Y., Chen, H.W., et al.: Secure SIFT-based sparse representation for image copy detection and recognition. In: 2010 IEEE International Conference on Multimedia and Expo (ICME), pp. 1248–1253 (2010)
7. Hsieh, S.L., Chen, Y.W., Chen, C.C., et al.: A geometry-distortion resistant image detection system based on log-polar transform and scale invariant feature transform. In: 2011 IEEE 13th International Conference on High Performance Computing and Communications (HPCC), pp. 893–897 (2011)
8. Wengang, Z., Houqiang, L., Richang, H., et al.: BSIFT: towards data-independent codebook for large scale image search. IEEE Trans. Image Process. **24**(3), 967–979 (2015)
9. Chimlek, S., Piamsa-Nga, P.: Landmark image searching with inattentive salient regions. In: 2014 International Conference on Information Science and Applications (ICISA), pp. 48–52. IEEE (2014)
10. Yue, H., Sun, X., Yang, J., Wu, F.: Cloud-based image coding for mobile devices—toward thousands to one compression. IEEE Trans. Multimedia **15**(4), 845–857 (2013)

11. Song, X., Peng, X., Xu, J., Wu, F.: Cloud-based distributed image coding. In: 2014 IEEE International Conference on Image Processing (ICIP), pp. 4802–4806 (2014)
12. Bolles, R.C., Fischler, M.A.: Ransac-based approach to model fitting and its application to finding cylinders in range data. In: International Joint Conference on Artificial Intelligence (1981)
13. Utrecht ECVP database. http://pics.psych.stir.ac.uk/2D_face_sets.htm

Video Content Caching and Delivery for Tri-Party Joint Profit Optimization

Congcong Zhai[1], Junni Zou[2(✉)], and Yunfei Zhang[3]

[1] Department of Communication Engineering, Shanghai University,
Shanghai 200072, China
yujiaerzong@t.shu.edu.cn
[2] Department of Computer Science and Engineering, Shanghai Jiao Tong University,
Shanghai 200240, China
zou-jn@cs.sjtu.edu.cn
[3] Yulong Computer Communication Technology, Shenzhen, China

Abstract. With the increasing demands for videos over wireless networks, the weak backhaul links can hardly provide desirable service. Caching, a technique to reduce peak traffic rates and improve the QoE of cellular users, has become quite popular. In this paper, we study the video caching and delivery problem from the point of maximizing the QoE of cellular users and the profits of both the network operator (MNO) and the video provider (VP). We consider a commercial cellular caching system consisting of a VP, a MNO and multiple cellular users. Generally, the VP may lose its users if the users are not getting their desired QoE. Meanwhile, by introducing the caching technique, the MNO can greatly reduce the accessing delay of the cellular users, thus improve their QoE performance. We formulate the profit maximization problem of the VP, MNO and cellular users as a tri-party joint optimization problem, and then solve it through primal dual decomposition method. Numerical results are provided for verifying the effectiveness of the proposed method.

1 Introduction

With the rapid development of mobile video applications, the mobile network operator (MNO) has been under great pressure and shown no sign of suspend. According to the cisco visual networking index mobile forecast for 2016–2021 [1], mobile data traffic is expected to grow at a CAGR of 47 percent to 49 exabytes (one million gigabytes) per month by 2021, among which the leading contributor is the video traffic generated by the mobile users. To cope with the tremendous traffic increase, some changes are required for the current cellular infrastructure. One effective solution is to introduce caching technique at the

J. Zou—This work has been partially supported by the NSFC grants No. 61622112 and No. 61472234, and Shanghai Natural Science Foundation grant No. 14ZR1415100.

base station (BS), i.e., to cache video content in advance to the BS that is geographically closer to the users [2,3]. As the caching-capable BS can enable high density spatial reuse of the wireless resources with high speed localized communication, which is usually assumed to be faster than the backhaul links connected to the VP. On the other hand, adaptive bit rate streaming has become a popular video delivery technique, guaranteed with improving QoE of videos delivered on wireless networks. Therefore, every video file can be delivery with different rate versions to accommodate different media terminal and network channel condition. Achieving the appropriate scheme of caching and delivery strategy is currently one of the most important challenges for the commercial cellular caching networks.

Generally, whenever a mobile user make a playback request for a video, it will first attempt to find an available version from the adjacent BS. If the local BS has cached the corresponding version, the mobile user will download from the BS and playback the video, otherwise it has to download the video file from the VP through weak and costly backhaul links. There are three issues should be considered: the mobile users will suffer a long access latency when the cellular network is congested. For the BS which belongs to the MNO has to use the expensive weak backhaul to retrieve video file from remote VP, when the video is not cached in the BS while the users request for it. For the VP who own all the video files, tries to earn profits by serving as many users as possible. In this work, we consider three interest groups consisting of users, MNO and VP. The VP may lose its users if the users cannot achieve the desired QoE, thus the proportion of attrition cost caused by user losses can be used as the measure of VP revenues. In the meanwhile, the congestion of wireless or backhaul links will inevitably increase the access delay of the users to the video streaming. Therefore, the access delay can be used to measure the QoE performance of the users. Further, the MNO, by storing popular videos at its BSs, can earn the profit from reducing the repetitive video transmissions over the backhaul link.

The challenge of catering to video file, as a dominant type of traffic, is critical for commercial cellular network system. Up to now, many researchers attempted to improve cache utilization with various caching strategies, such as uncoded caching and coded caching [4,5], transcoding [6] and so on. The authors of [7] present a novel strategy in ICNs for adaptive caching of variable video files, which is to achieve optimal video caching to reduce access delay for the maximal requested bit rate for each user. However, it only considered the profit of the user. In [8–10], the authors considered a commercial caching network, and solved the problem of maximizing the profit of both the VP and the MNO by Stackelberg game, but they did not consider the user's profit and the case in which each video can be encoded into multiple rate versions. The authors in [11] considered the joint derivation of video caching and routing policies for users with different quality requirements, but did not consider the VP's profit. There are some studies which have simultaneously considered the problem of video caching and delivery [12,13], but the problem of addressing video caching and delivery over different bit rates remains untouched.

In this paper, we propose a caching strategy to handle multirate video content caching and delivery in a commercial cellular network. Our objective is to maximize the overall profits of the cellular network, which includes the profits of the mobile users, the MNO, and the VP. We formulate the caching problem as a tri-party joint cost minimization problem, and use primal-dual decomposition method [14] to decouple the problem into two optimization problems, which are solved by the subgradient method and greedy algorithm, respectively. The main contributions of this article are summarized as follows:

1. We propose a multi-objective optimization problem, and then formulate it as a tri-party joint cost minimization (profit maximization) problem. Unlike the previous works which mostly focused either the MNO and the users, or the VP and MNO, or the users only, we consider together these three groups with conflicting interests, and model their profit maximization problem as a weighted tri-party joint optimization problem.
2. We use the Lagrange relaxation and primal-dual decomposition method to decompose the original optimization problem into two subproblems. The first subproblem, called as the delivery subproblem, decides the portion of the requests satisfied by the BSs. As it is a typical convex problem, we solve it by using the standard convex optimization methods. For the second subproblem, called as the caching subproblem, it decides whether a video should be cached in a BS. It can be viewed as a knapsack problem, and we can solve it through greedy algorithm.
3. Numerical results illustrate that the proposed caching strategy can significantly improve not only the users' profits but the profit of VP and MNO for a commercial cellular network.

The remainder of the paper is organized as follows. Section 2 presents the system model and the related specifications. In Sect. 3, we formulate the tri-party joint minimization problem and demonstrate the distributed solution. Our experiment setup and performance evaluation results are detailed in Sect. 4, and our conclusions are summarized in Sect. 5.

2   System Model

In this section, we detail the assumptions and definitions upon which our system model is built.

The system architecture is depicted in Fig. 1. We consider a MNO consisting of a set $I = \{1, 2, ...i..|I|\}$ of caching enabled BSs connected to a VP through backhaul links which is too weak to meet so much user requests. Under each BS, there are a number of user requests for video streaming service. When a user requests some video file j, it first asks its local BS (i.e. the BS in the neighborhood of the user). If the video file is available at the local BS, it handles the request directly. Otherwise, the request would be redirected to the VP. We study the system for a certain time period during which each BS $i \in I$ has an average capacity of $F_i \geq 0$ bps, while the capacity of the backhaul link is $G_i \geq 0$

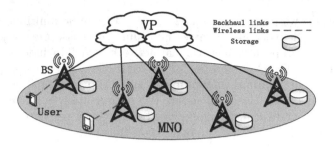

Fig. 1. A commercial cellular caching system

bps, and each BS is endowed with a certain storage capacity of $S_i \geq 0$ bytes. We assume that the BSs in the system cannot communicate with each other.

The VP contains all $J = \{1, 2, ...j.. |J|\}$ video files and each video can be delivered with different rate versions. We assume that for each video $j \in J$, there is a set $Q = \{1, 2, ...q.. |Q|\}$ of rate versions that can be offered. Each rate version $q \in Q$ corresponds to a certain playback rate R_{jq} and has size o_{jq} bytes which increases with the rate (i.e. $o_{jq} \geq o_{jr}$ if $q > r$). Moreover, the file size is assumed to be an affine function: $o_{jq} = aq + b$ [15]. The important notations are summarized in Table 1.

Table 1. List of important notations.

Symbol	Definition
λ_{ij}	The total demand for video j that must be served by BS i
x_{ijq}	Whether version q of video j will be cached in BS i
y_{ijq}	The portion of requests for video j will be satisfied with version q downloaded from BS i
z_{ijq}	The portion of requests for video j will be satisfied with version q downloaded from the VP through backhaul link
o_{jq}	The size of version q of video j
c^{bh}	The average backhaul cost for a video transmission
S_i	The storage capacity of BS i
F_i	The average wireless capacity of BS i
G_i	The average wireless capacity of the backhaul link from BS i to the VP
R_{jq}	The playback rate of video j (i.e. version q)

User Request Model. The rate version of video j requested by the user is characterized by R_{jq}. In this paper, we assume the rate versions requested by the users follow a uniform distribution. Due to the constrained wireless capacity, there must be some requests that can not be satisfied. Let $y_{ijq} \in [0, 1]$ represent the portion of the requests for video j with version q that can be served by the corresponding BS i. For the required video which is not cached at the BS will be turned to the VP through the backhaul link, and we denote the portion of such request served by the VP as $z_{ijq} \in [0,1]$.

Content Caching Model. Whether video j with version q will be cached in BS i is denoted by a binary matrix $x_{ijq} \in \{0,1\}$, where $x_{ijq} = 1$ means video j with version q is placed in BS i and 0 otherwise. In order to minimizing the average access latency, the content caching policy must be carefully designed based on the user requests.

3 Problem Formulation

In this section, we first define the profit of the users, the MNO and the VP respectively, and then formulate the tri-party joint optimization problem. Finally, we present out distributed solution.

3.1 Profit Modeling

Users Profits. We use the user access delay to measure the user profit. The average delay $\overline{d}_{ijq}$ experienced by the users at BS i for downloading video file j with version q depends on the path and the congestion of the respective links. In order to serve a user by a BS, the requested video should either be already cached there or retrieved via the backhaul link. This latter option adds delay and may be quite significant. Ideally, we want the objective function to reflect the congestion level of the link, so the caching strategy will avoid the congestion of corresponding link. A common option that meets this requirement is to use the average delay in a M/M/1 queue, expressed by $D(f) = \frac{1}{C-f}, f < C$, where C denotes the link capacity and f denots the load of correspond links. Therefore, the average delay for the users accessing to version q of video j at BS i can be defined as

$$\min : \overline{d}_{ijq} = \frac{y_{ijq}\lambda_{ij}o_{jq}}{F_i - A_i(y)} + \frac{z_{ijq}\lambda_{ij}o_{jq}}{G_i - B_i(z)} \tag{1}$$

s.t.

$$y_{ijq} \leq x_{ijq} + z_{ijq} \tag{2}$$

$$\sum_j \sum_q x_{ijq}o_{jq} \leq S_i \tag{3}$$

$$\sum_j \sum_q y_{ijq}\lambda_{ij}R_{jq} \leq F_i \tag{4}$$

$$\sum_j \sum_q z_{ijq}\lambda_{ij}R_{jq} \leq G_i \tag{5}$$

$$y_{ijq}, z_{ijq} \in [0,1], \forall i \in I, j \in J, q \in Q \tag{6}$$

$$x_{ijq} \in \{0,1\}, \forall i \in I, j \in J, q \in Q \tag{7}$$

where $A_i(y) = \sum_j \sum_q y_{ijq} \lambda_{ij} R_{jq}$ is the load of the wireless link of BS i, and for

the backhaul link we have $B_i(z) = \sum_j \sum_q z_{ijq} \lambda_{ij} R_{jq}$. Inequality (3) indicates the

storage capacity constraint of BS i. Inequality (4) and (5) indicate the capacity constraints of the wireless links and the backhaul links, respectively.

MNO Profit. The revenue gained by MNO is from the saved cost of the backhaul link due to local caching. Once a user downloads a required video from the local storage, the MNO can save a video transmission over the backhaul link. Therefore, we have the MNO profit defined as

$$\max : S_i^{BS} = \sum_j \sum_q (y_{ijq} - z_{ijq}) c^{bh} \lambda_{ij} o_{jq} \tag{8}$$

VP Profit. Users who are experiencing high delays or do not get the service he wants when streaming a video from one VP may switch to another. This will lead to the losses of the former VP. When it occurs we call the VP has a user attrition cost [16]. We use the user attrition cost to measure the VP's profit, and the user attrition cost is formulated as the penalty of the requests that are unserved.

$$\min : P_i = t \sum_j \sum_q (1 - y_{ijq}) \lambda_{ijq} \tag{9}$$

where t denotes the unit cost of user attrition. Our objective here is to serve as many users as possible through both local BSs and the remote VP.

Tri-party Joint Minimization Problem (TJM Problem). According to the foregoing analysis, we have three objective functions, which include maximizing the MNO profit, minimizing the user access delay, and minimizing the user attrition cost. We change this multiobjective optimization problem as a single objective optimization problem through the weighted method [17]. That is, we introduce a weighted system parameter $\alpha \in [0,1]$ and combine these three objective functions together into a single objective optimization problem [18] as follows:

$$\min : \alpha \left(\sum_j \sum_q \overline{d}_{ijq} - \sum_j \sum_q (y_{ijq} - z_{ijq}) c^{bh} \lambda_{ij} o_{jq} \right) + (1 - \alpha) P_i \tag{10}$$

s.t.

$$(2), (3), (4), (5), (6), (7)$$

3.2   Distributed Algorithm

To solve the above problem in a distributed manner, we relax the constraints (2), (4), (5) and formulate the Lagrange function as

$$L(\mathbf{u},\mathbf{v},\mathbf{w},\mathbf{x},\mathbf{y},\mathbf{z}) = \alpha(\sum_j\sum_q \bar{d}_{ijq} + \sum_j\sum_q (y_{ijq} - z_{ijq})\, c^{bh}\lambda_{ij}o_{jq})$$
$$-(1-\alpha)P_i + \sum_j\sum_q u_{ijq}(y_{ijq} - x_{ijq} - z_{ijq}) + v_{ijq}(\sum_j\sum_q y_{ijq}\lambda_{ij}R_{jq} \qquad (11)$$
$$-F_i) + w_{ijq}(\sum_j\sum_q z_{ijq}\lambda_{ij}R_{jq} - G_i)$$

where u_{ijq}, v_{ijq} and w_{ijq} are Lagrange multipliers. In addition, the corresponding Lagrange dual function is

$$g(u,v,w) = \inf_{x,y,z} L(u,v,w,x,y,z) \qquad (12)$$

The Lagrange dual problem of (10) is then defined as: $\max g(u,v,w)$, which can be solved in an iterative fashion, using a primal-dual Lagrange method. Notice that due to the discrete constraint set, we have to employ a subgradient method for updating the dual variables.

$$u_{ijq}^{(n+1)} = [u_{ijq}^{(n)} + \tau^{(n)}(y_{ijq} - x_{ijq} - z_{ijq})]^+ \qquad (13)$$

$$v_{ijq}^{(n+1)} = [v_{ijq}^{(n)} + \tau^{(n)}(\sum_j\sum_q y_{ijq}\lambda_{ij}R_{jq} - F_i)]^+ \qquad (14)$$

$$w_{ijq}^{(n+1)} = [w_{ijq}^{(n)} + \tau^{(n)}(\sum_j\sum_q z_{ijq}\lambda_{ij}R_{jq} - G_i)]^+ \qquad (15)$$

where $[*]^+$ denotes the projection onto the set of nonnegative real numbers, and $\tau^{(n)}$ is a positive step size.

The primal problem can be further decomposed into two subproblems, named P1 and P2, as follows:

$$P_1: \quad \min: \alpha(\sum_j\sum_q \bar{d}_{ijq} - \sum_j\sum_q (y_{ijq} - z_{ijq})\, c^{bh}\lambda_{ij}o_{jq}) + (1-\alpha)P_i$$
$$+ \sum_j\sum_q u_{ijq}(y_{ijq} - z_{ijq}) + v_{ijq}(\sum_j\sum_q y_{ijq}\lambda_{ij}R_{jq} - F_i) \qquad (16)$$
$$+ w_{ijq}(\sum_j\sum_q z_{ijq}\lambda_{ij}R_{jq} - G_i)$$

s.t.

$$(4),(5),(6)$$

$$P_2: \qquad\qquad \max: \sum_j\sum_q u_{ijq}x_{ijq} \qquad\qquad (17)$$

s.t.

$$(3),(7)$$

3.3   Implementation Problem

A decentralized solution procedure of the proposed primal-dual algorithm is summarized in Algorithm 1. For each BS i, subproblem P1 involves only the delivery decision variables y_{ijq} and z_{ijq}, we call it delivery subproblem. Since the objective function of P1 is convex and there exits strictly feasible solutions. Hence, it can be efficiently solved using standard convex optimization techniques [18]. By using the subgradient method, we have

---

Algorithm 1. Distributed Optimization Algorithm

Input: $S_i^{Bs}(*), d_{ijq}(*), P_i(*), \alpha, \lambda$
Output: x^*, y^*, z^*
Set $n = 0$ and $y_{ijq}^{(0)}, z_{ijq}^{(0)}, u_{ijq}^{(0)}, v_{ijq}^{(0)}, w_{ijq}^{(0)}$ to some nonnegative value for all i, j, q
$W_i \leftarrow S_i, U \leftarrow \emptyset, O \leftarrow \emptyset$
Repeat
Solve the caching problem
Receives $o_{ijq}, u_{ijq}^{(n)}$ from BS i
$O = O \cup o_{ijq}, U = U \cup u_{ijq}^n$
if $\sum O \leq S_i$ **then**
   $W_i = W_i - o_{ijq}, x_{ijq} = 1$
else
   Sorting values in decreasing order of U
   for k=1 to $|U|$ **do**
      if $u_k \leq W_i$ **then**
         $W_i = W_i - u_k, x_{ijq} = 1$
      else
         $x_{ijq} = 0$
      end if
   end for
end ifSolve the delivery problem
Receives $y_{ijq}^{(n)}, z_{ijq}^{(n)}$ from the BS i
Fetches $v_{ijq}^{(n)}, w_{ijq}^{(n)}$ stored in the BS i
Updates $v_{ijq}^{(n)}, w_{ijq}^{(n)}$ by (14), (15)
Updates $u_{ijq}^{(n)}$ by (13)
Updates $y_{ijq}^{(n)}, z_{ijq}^{(n)}$ by (18), (19)
Sends new $u_{ijq}^{(n+1)} v_{ijq}^{(n+1)}, w_{ijq}^{(n+1)}$ to the BS i
Until All variables converge to the optimums.

$$y_{ijq}^{(n+1)} = [y_{ijq}^{(n)} - \overset{\bullet}{y}_{ijq}]^{\pm} = [y_{ijq}^{(n)} - \tau^{(n)} \frac{\partial L(u, v, w, y, z)}{\partial y_{ijq}}]^{+} \qquad (18)$$

$$z_{ijq}^{(n+1)} = [z_{ijq}^{(n)} - \overset{\bullet}{z}_{ijq}]^{\pm} = [z_{ijq}^{(n)} - \tau^{(n)} \frac{\partial L(u,v,w,x,y,z)}{\partial z_{ijq}}]^{\pm} \qquad (19)$$

Subproblem P2 involves only the caching decision variables x_{ijq}, we call it caching subproblem. It can be separated into $|I|$ unidimensional knapsack problems, one for each $i \in I$. The optimal solution of each knapsack problem for $i \in I$ can be optimally solved using greedy algorithm in a distributed manner.

3.4 Convergence Analysis

Algorithm 1 converges asymptotically to the optimal solution x_{ijq}^*, y_{ijq}^*, z_{ijq}^*. A formal proof of the convergence directly follows from the properties of the decomposition principle [11]. In general, either constant step sizes or diminishing step sizes can be used for a subgradient algorithm [19]. A constant step size is more convenient for distributed implementation, whereas the corresponding subgradient algorithm will only converge to some suboptimal solution within any given small neighborhood around the optimum [14]. Using a diminishing step size, the convergence to the optimum can be guaranteed.

4   Numerical Analysis and Result

In this section, we present the numerical results for the performance evaluation of our proposed tri-party joint optimization policy. For the numerical analysis, we consider a commercial cellular caching network consisted of a VP and a MNO which contains $I = 100$ of BSs with 1000 mobile users are uniformly placed in random statistically independent positions in the cell. We use Zipf distribution [20] to model the popularity of video files.

In all simulations, we assume totally have $|J| = 100$ video files, each of which can be delivered in $|Q| = 2$ versions. The size of a version of a video o_{jq} is equal to 10 and 20 units of data in the low and the high quality level respectively and thus the playback rate R_j is equal to 9.5 and 19.5 respectively as we set $a = 1$ and $b = 0.5$ [15]. Within a certain period, each user requests a video file follows a Zipf distribution with a Zipf exponent $\gamma = 0.8$ and follows a uniform probability distribution for which version. Unless otherwise specified, The capacity of wireless links $F_i = 100$ and backhaul links $G_i = 50$. We also set $t = 1000$ and $c^{bh} = 200$ which can be a arbitrary constant in simulation and it can be set by the VP in reality.

We compare the percentage of users that can be served by our commercial cellular caching system which are shown in Fig. 2(a). Noted that all ratios of users that can be served are obtain under the condition of wireless and backhaul capacity constrained. In Fig. 2(a) we observe that the ratio of users that can be served is increased gradually with the size of the storage capacity. It is obvious that each local BS can cache more popularity video files with the increase of storage capacity, and thus, more user requests can be satisfied locally, the weak backhaul capacity can naturally be saved, therefore, under the same conditions, when one can't find the video he want in the local BS will be served by VP through the previously saved backhaul capacity. So, to a certain extent it is increased the proportion of users can be served by the proposed caching policy.

In Fig. 2(b) we observe that the total cost of the tri-party decreases with the size of storage capacity, this is because more user requests can be served by local BS with the increase of storage capacity, as more popularity videos can be cached in the storage of BS in advance and lead to great reduction of duplicated video transmission. On the other hand, there are lots of backhaul resources saved with the reduction of duplicated transmission that can be used to serve more user requests, which cannot get deserved service from local BS.

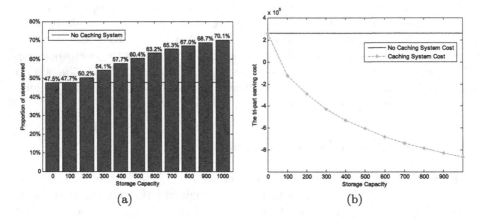

Fig. 2. Effect of the proposed caching strategy on (a) proportion of users served and (b) total serving cost of tri-party.

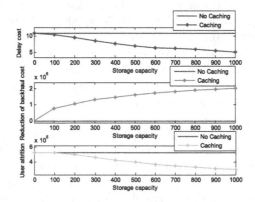

Fig. 3. Effect of storage capacity on tri-party utility respectively.

In upper Fig. 3 we can see that the cost of users (i.e. user access delay) decrease with the size of storage capacity, this is because more users can be served by the adjacent BS where is geographically closer to the users directly, and it's obviously faster than the backhaul links connected to VP with reduced access delay. Due to more users can download required video from the local storage, the MNO can save much video transmission over the backhaul link too. Therefore, from middle Fig. 3 we can see the profit of MNO (i.e. reduction of the backhaul cost) increases with the storage capacity. From lower Fig. 3 we can see the user attrition decreases with the size of storage capacity, this is because more user requests can be served by the local cache of BS and in the meanwhile the number of requests served by VP observably decreased, and with considerable saved backhaul resource, the VP can serve more users that can't get desired service from local BS. Therefore, with the increase of storage capacity the profit of the users, the MNO and the VP are increased dramatically.

The impact of Zipf parameter γ on the tri-party serving cost is illustrated in Fig. 4. We see that the average serving cost of our proposed scheme in certain caching system is obviously lower than in no caching system. We can observe that as the Zipf parameter γ increases (from 0.1 to 1.7) the corresponding optimal average tri-party serving cost decreases dramatically. This is because with the increase of Zipf parameter γ a few popular videos account for a large percentage of video traffic, and through our strategy most popular videos are cached in the local BSs despite the constrained of storage capacity.

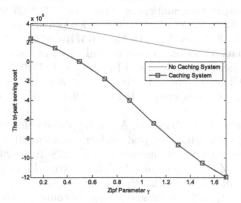

Fig. 4. Effect of Zipf parameter on the tri-party serving cost.

5   Conclusion

In this paper, we addressed the profit maximization problem of the tri-party joint, which consisting of mobile users, VP and MNO, by introducing a weighted coefficient to formulate our three object functions as one tri-party joint minimization problem. Then we solve the problem through prim dual decompose method. By observation, we discovering that we can decompose the primal profit maximization problem to a caching problem and a delivery problem, which can be solved by greedy algorithm and subgradient method, respectively. Finally, abundant simulation results are testified the proposed scheme.

References

1. Cisco Visual Networking Index: Global Mobile Data Traffic Forecast Update, 2016–2021 White Paper. http://www.cisco.com/c/en/us/solutions/collateral/service-provider/visual-networking-index-vni/mobile-white-paper-c11-520862.html. Accessed 09 July 2017
2. Molisch, A.F., Caire, G., Ott, D., et al.: Caching eliminates the wireless bottleneck in video-aware wireless networks. An Overview Paper Submitted to Hindawi's J. Adv. Electr. Eng. **2014**(9), 74–80 (2014)
3. Wang, X., Chen, M., Taleb, T., et al.: Cache in the air: exploiting content caching and delivery techniques for 5G systems. IEEE Commun. Mag. **52**(2), 131–139 (2014)
4. Shanmugam, K., Golrezaei, N., Dimakis, A.G., et al.: FemtoCaching: wireless content delivery through distributed caching helpers. IEEE Trans. Inf. Theory **59**(12), 8402–8413 (2013)
5. Maddah-Ali, M.A., Niesen, U.: Fundamental limits of caching. IEEE Trans. Inf. Theory **60**(5), 2856–2867 (2014)
6. Jin, Y., Wen, Y., Westphal, C.: Optimal transcoding and caching for adaptive streaming in media cloud: an analytical approach. IEEE Trans. Circuits Syst. Video Technol. **25**(12), 1914–1925 (2015)
7. Li, W., Oteafy, S.M.A., Hassanein, H.S.: Dynamic adaptive streaming over popularity-driven caching in information-centric networks. In: 2015 IEEE International Conference on Communications, pp. 5747–5752 (2015)
8. Li, J., Chen, W., Xiao, M., et al.: Efficient video pricing and caching in heterogeneous networks. IEEE Trans. Veh. Technol. **65**(10), 8744–8751 (2016)
9. Li, J., Sun, J., Qian, Y., et al.: A commercial video-caching system for small-cell cellular networks using game theory. IEEE Access **4**, 7519–7531 (2016)
10. Li, J., Chen, H., Chen, Y., et al.: Pricing and resource allocation via game theory for a small-cell video caching system. IEEE J. Select. Areas Commun. **34**(8), 2115–2129 (2016)
11. Poularakis, K., Iosifidis, G., Argyriou, A., et al.: Video delivery over heterogeneous cellular networks: optimizing cost and performance. In: 2014 IEEE International Conference on Computer Communications, pp. 1078–1086 (2014)
12. He, J., Zhang, H., Zhao, B., et al.: A Collaborative Framework for In-network Video Caching in Mobile Networks. Eprint Arxiv (2014)
13. Jiang, W., Feng, G., Qin, S.: Optimal cooperative content caching and delivery policy for heterogeneous cellular networks. IEEE Trans. Mob. Comput. **16**(5), 1382–1393 (2017)
14. Palomar, D., Chiang, M.: A tutorial on decomposition methods and distributed network resource allocation. IEEE J. Sel. Areas Commun. **24**(8), 1439–1451 (2006)
15. Zhang, W., Chen, Z., Chen, Z., et al.: QoE-driven cache management for HTTP adaptive bit rate streaming over wireless networks. IEEE Trans. Multimedia **15**(6), 1431–1445 (2013)
16. Gharaibeh, A., Khreishah, A., Ji, B., et al.: A provably efficient online collaborative caching algorithm for multicell-coordinated systems. IEEE Trans. Mob. Comput. **15**(8), 1863–1876 (2015)
17. Miettinen, K.: Nonlinear Multiobjective Optimization. Kluwer Academic Publishers, Norwell (1999)
18. Zou, J., Xiong, H., Li, C., et al.: Lifetime and distortion optimization with joint source/channel rate adaptation and network coding-based error control in wireless video sensor networks. IEEE Trans. Veh. Technol. **60**(3), 1182–1194 (2011)

19. Bertsekas, D.: 6.253 convex analysis and optimization. Athena Sci. **129**(2), 420–432 (2004). Spring 2004
20. Breslau, L., Cao, P., Fan, L., et al.: Web caching and Zipf-like distributions: evidence and implications. In: Proceedings of IEEE INFOCOM, vol. 1, pp. 126–134 (1999)

Information Gain Product Quantization for Image Retrieval

Jingjia Chen$^{(\boxtimes)}$, Yonghong Song, and Yuanlin Zhang

Xi'an Jiaotong University, Xi'an, China
ccncai00@gmail.com, songyh@xjtu.edu.cn

Abstract. Approximate nearest neighbor (ANN) research has become the key method of content-based image retrieval. Product quantization (PQ) is a popular method for approximate nearest neighbor search. However, the informativeness may not be uniformly distributed across the subspace in product quantization. Allocating the same number of bits for the subspace will bring large quantization loss. To address this issue, in this paper, we propose an improved product quantization method, which adaptively allocates different numbers of bits to subspace via information gain. The key of our method is to find the optimal bit allocation strategy. To this end, our method maximizes the summation of information gain for each subspace, and also takes the limited length of codes into account. Experimental results on two large-scale bench-marks GIST1M and 22K-LabelMe demonstrate that our approach significantly outperforms state-of-the-art methods in terms of accuracy.

Keywords: Product quantization · Approximate nearest neighbor
Adaptive bit allocation

1 Introduction

Approximate nearest neighbor search (ANN) has a wide range of applications including image retrieval [1], object detection [2] and image recognition [3]. However, thanks to the development of multimedia information, computer science and other technologies, image data is growing rapidly on a large scale. In addition, the dimensions of image feature can be very high. So the cost of computing will increase significantly, resulting in a sharp decline in image retrieval performance, which is called 'curse of dimensionality' [4]. It is of great significance to study the issue of finding nearest neighbors with good balance between retrieval performance and efficiency. Recently, many ANN search approaches are proposed including tree-based methods and hashing-based methods.

Hashing-based methods have become one of the most popular approaches to ANN search. These methods encode the original image features into compact binary codes in Hamming space which preserving the neighborhood structure of the original data. Practice shows that hashing-based methods are able to reduce the storage cost and improve the retrieval efficiency. The key to the hashing-based methods lies in formulating an effective hash function, mapping the high-dimensional data spaces to low-dimensional data spaces. LSH [5], as the pioneering work, uses random projection

Y. Zhao et al. (Eds.): ICIG 2017, Part II, LNCS 10667, pp. 252–261, 2017.
https://doi.org/10.1007/978-3-319-71589-6_23

to map the original data space to Hamming space. SH [6] introduces the graph partitioning theory into hash function formulation to get binary codes. ITQ [7] proposes an efficient alternating binary coding scheme for finding an optimal rotation matrix. Additionally, many supervised hashing [8] methods are proposed by utilizing the label information on data set.

Product quantization (PQ) [10] is an alternative compact encoding method, which quantizes the data by precomputed codebook. The PQ is designed to decompose the original data space and quantize decomposed low-dimensional subspace separately. Since the low-dimensional space can be encoded with a smaller sub-codebook, it can reduce the data storage space. The similarity between two vectors is calculated by the summation of distances in each subspace.

However, PQ uses a fixed-length bits to quantize subspace. When the informativeness contained between the subspaces is large, a large quantization loss will be generated. For the above issues, in this paper, we propose an adaptive bit allocation of subspace method based on information gain for ANN search. To summarize, our main contributions of this paper is as follows:

- We define the measure of information gain for each subspace, which is the important basis for subspace bit allocation.
- We propose a novel adaptive bit allocation strategy according to information gain of each subspace to minimize the quantization loss. Subspaces with larger value of information gain get more bits while subspaces with smaller value of information gain get less bits. Extensive experiments have verified the superiority of our method.

The remaining part of the paper is structured as follows: We first discuss related work in the immediately following section. In Sect. 3, we introduce the problem of the basis of our method. And we describe the details of our Information Gain Product Quantization (IGPQ) method. Experiments result and analysis follow in Sect. 4. The paper is concluded in Sect. 5.

2 Related Work

Product quantization (PQ) is a frequently used quantization method that compresses data and reduces the cardinality of space. Let $X \in R^D$ donate a D-dimensional vector, and the whole quantization process can be represented as:

$$q(X) \in C = \{c_i\} \tag{1}$$

Here, q is the mapping function and c_i is the ith element called codeword in codebook $C = \{c_i\}$.

It can be seen that quantization is the process of reconstructing eigenvectors using codeword. PQ methods typically use the mean squared error (MSE) to quantize the data point to the codeword with smallest error. The mean squared error (MSE) is defined as

$$\text{MSE} = \frac{1}{n} \sum_x ||q(x) - x||^2 \tag{2}$$

where vector x donates an input image.

But when the dimension of the features is large, the training process will be very time consuming. For example, in order to encode a vector to 64 bits, the size of codebook will be 2^{64}, which would be unaffordable. PQ is an effective solution to these issues by reducing the time complexity of quantizer training. Specifically, PQ decompose the input vector X into M disjoint sub-vectors u_j, $1 \le j \le M$. Hence, the dimension of each sub-vector is reduced to the previous $1/M$. Then each sub-vector is mapped by corresponding sub-quantizer separately. The feature vector X can be represented to the following form:

$$\underbrace{x_1, x_2, \cdots, x_{D/M}}_{u_1(x)}, \cdots, \underbrace{x_{D+1-D/M}, x_{D+2-D/M}, \cdots, x_D}_{u_M(x)} \tag{3}$$

$$\Rightarrow q(x) = [q_1(u_1(x)), q_2(u_2(x)), \cdots, q_M(u_M(x))]$$

where q_j is the jth sub-quantizer corresponding to the sub-codeword c^j. In this way, the codebook of the entire data space C will be the Cartesian product of decomposed sub-codebooks as follows:

$$c = c^1 \times c^2 \times \cdots \times c^M \tag{4}$$

Since the dimensions of each sub-vector will be greatly reduced, the spatial complexity of the algorithm to train each sub-quantizer is also greatly reduced.

3   Proposed Method

3.1   Problem Statement

Quantization loss and retrieval accuracy are closely related. There is a certain quantization loss in PQ. Recent works [11] point the impact of quantization. The problem of quantization loss becomes more serious in product quantization. PQ method does not take the distribution of data into account. The size of the codebook of each subspace generated by PQ is the same. But the informativeness in each subspace is not exactly the same, the number of clusters in different subspaces may be different. So it is unreasonable to allocate the same number of bits for the different subspaces. Figure 1 shows the different results of quantization using fixed bits and variable bits.

In Fig. 1, by using the spatial allocation of fixed bits, the data in the space is forcibly allocated to the unrelated cluster center because of the limited number of codes. This causes the large quantization loss between the original points and the quantized points. If a variable encoding allocation method is used, variable bits can be allocated so that similar data can be allocated to the same cluster. The quantization result is not accurate

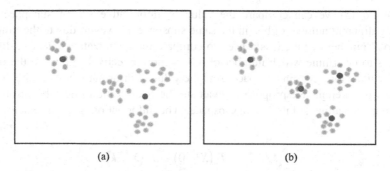

Fig. 1. Illustrating the different result of quantization using fixed bits and variable bits. (a) is an example of using fixed bits. (b) is an example of using variable bits

enough by allocating the same number of bits to each subspace. So the length of bits in each subspace should be determined by the informativeness of the subspace.

In this paper, according to the distribution of data in each subspace, we use the strategy that adaptively allocates different numbers of bits to subspace. Inspired by Adaptive Quantization for Hashing (AQH) [12], we calculate the information gain for each subspace. Then the exact number of bits allocation for each subspace is determined by comparing the information gain of the subspace.

3.2   Strategies of Bit Allocation for Subspace

Given a set of n data $X = \{x_1, x_2, \cdots, x_n\}$, $x_i \in R^D$, we follow the idea of PQ splitting the D-dimensional space into M subspaces: $X = \{X^1, X^2, \cdots, X^M\}$. And the subspaces have common number of dimensions D/M. If k bits are allocated for a subspace X^j, the subspace will generate 2^k clusters. Based on PQ, we use sub-codebook C^j to represent this set of clusters. The whole codebook C can be defined as the Cartesian product of its sub-codebooks: $C = C^1 \times C^2 \times \cdots \times C^M$.

According to the analysis of the previous section, it is unreasonable to quantize the subspace by using the same number of bits like PQ algorithm because of the different information distribution in each subspace. In this paper, we follow the norm that the larger the value of informativeness contained in the subspace is, the more bits are allocated. In order to allocate bits for each subspace reasonably, we first calculate the value of informativeness for each subspace when allocating k bits. Here we use the variance to measure the informativeness of subspace:

$$E_j(X^j, k) = \frac{1}{n} \sum_{b=0}^{2^k} \sum_{i=1}^{n} \left\| x_i^j - c_b^j \right\|^2 \tag{5}$$

where x_i^j represents the ith data of subspace and $c_b^j = c^j(x_i^j)$ indicates that c_b^j is the nearest sub-codeword for data x_i^j.

With Eq. (5) we can compare the value of informativeness of subspace when allocating different number of bits in the same subspace. However, due to the limitation of the total number of bits, it is a need to compare the quantization effect in different subspaces to determine which number of bits is more effectively improve the quantization accuracy for a certain subspace. And the value of informativeness in the different subspaces is different, we propose to evaluate the quantization effect by information gain when allocating k bits for a subspace. The information gain is calculated as follows:

$$G_j(X^j, k) = E_j(X^j, 0) - E_j(X^j, k) \tag{6}$$

Here, $E_j(X^j, k)$ is the value of informativeness of the subspace allocated k bits and $E_j(X^j, 0)$ can be thought of as the whole subspace only into one cluster when 0 bits is allocated for the subspace. So we can get $E_j(X^j, 0)$ according to Eq. (5):

$$E_j(X^j, 0) = \frac{1}{n} \sum_{i=1}^{n} \left\| x_i^j - c^j \right\|^2 \tag{7}$$

Here, c^j is the only one codeword for the subspace X^j.

Given a subspace X^j under the k_j bits encoding, we can obtain the total information gain for the entire data space X as follows:

$$G = \sum_{j=1}^{M} G_j(X^j, k_j) \tag{8}$$

We think that the larger the total information gain is, the better the quantification effect of the method would be.

3.3   Bit Allocation Optimization

Based on the strategy of adaptive bit allocation proposed in the previous section, the optimal bit allocation can be obtained for each subspace. However, the total number of bits is fixed, the combination of the best bit allocation results of each subspace may not accord with the total number of bits. So bit allocation optimization method is required to obtain the best bit allocation result under the total number of bits L. In order to get the optimal quantization effect in consideration of the total number of bits limit, we have the following objective function:

$$\{k_1, k_2, \ldots, k_M\} = \operatorname*{arg\,max}_{\{k_1, k_2, \ldots, k_M\}} \sum_{j=1}^{M} G(X^j, k_j)$$

$$s.t. \quad \sum_{j=1}^{M} k_j = L \tag{9}$$

Here, k_j is the number of bits allocation for the jth subspace, L is the total number of the binary code. $E_j(X^j, k_j)$ is the information gain when allocating k_j bits for the jth subspace X^j.

In order to solve the above objective function, we use the dynamic programmingmethod [13] to solve the optimal bit allocation problem. According to the k_j defined above, we allocatebits for the subspace by different combinations of k_j, so that it meets the total fixed number of bits L. Thus, the total information gain state formula under current combination can be obtained as follows:

$$Cost_M(L) = \sum_{j=1}^{m} G_i(X^j, k_j)$$

$$s.t. \quad \sum_{j=1}^{m} k_j = L \tag{10}$$

In the dynamic programming process, there is a natural connection between decision making and state transfer. State transition is based on the previous stage of the state and decision to get the status of this stage. According to the already defined state formula, the state transition equation can be deduced.

$$Cost_m(L) = \max(Cost_{m-1}(v_m), \; Cost_{m-1}(v_m) + G_m(X, \; L - v_m)) \tag{11}$$

Through the dynamic programming algorithm, we can obtain the global optimal coding bit allocation result of the divided subspace under the condition of the total length of the given binary codes.

4 Experiment Results and Comparison

4.1 Settings and Protocol

Our experiments compare IGPQ with the state-of-the-art methods on the following public datasets:

- GIST1M [14]: a set of one million 960 dimensional GIST descriptors.
- 22K-LabelMe [15]: a set of 22019 images represented as 512 dimensional GIST descriptors.

We follow the protocol in [16]. For the experiment on 22K-LabelMe and GIST1M, we use 1000 queries that do not have any overlap with the dataset. The ground truth is defined by the 100 nearest neighbors based on the Euclidean distance. We use Mean Average Precision (MAP) and Precision-Recall curve to measure the performance.

In order to verify the superiority of IGPQ, we compare the improved algorithm with the following state-of-the-art methods: Iterative quantization (ITQ) [7] and Product quantization (PQ) [10]. In the experiments, we set the iteration number t = 200 for

ITQ, and iteration number of the k-means in PQ and IGPQ is also 200. The experiment environment is Intel Xeon-2680 CPU and 16G memory.

4.2   Results

The bit allocation for each subspace is presented in Table 1. We can see that more bits are allocated to subspaces with more informativeness while fewer bits are allocated to subspaces with less informativeness.

Table 1. Bit allocation on 22K-LabelMe

Number of bits	Bit allocation for subspaces
32	{12,12,4,4}
64	{14,14,14,14, 2, 2, 2, 2}
128	{14,14,14,14, 5,14, 5, 14, 4, 6, 4, 6, 3, 4, 3, 4}

The MAP value on the 22K-LabelMe and the GIST1M comparisons presented in Fig. 2. We can see that as the number of binary code becomes larger, the MAP results of each quantization method are improved. And for the 64 bits and 128 bits, the MAP result for IGPQ is better than ITQ and PQ. Since the adaptive bits allocation strategy with information gain is added to the product quantization algorithm, the IGPQ algorithm is less than the PQ algorithm in quantization loss. So in the experiment, the retrieval accuracy has been improved, and the MAP results of each encoding bits IGPQ are higher than PQ.

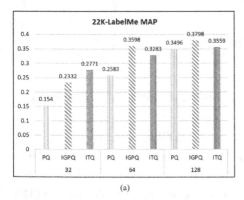 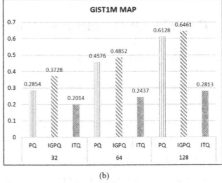

(a)   (b)

Fig. 2. The results of MAP of state-of-art methods on 22K-LabelMe and GIST1M at 32 bits, 64 bits and 128bits. (a) MAP on 22K-LabelMe. (b) MAP on GIST1M.

We also evaluate all the compared methods by precision and recall. The results on GIST1M960 and 22K-LabelMe are presented in Figs. 3, 4 and 5. In the experiments of three different coding bits, the precision of the three methods will decrease when the recall rate increased. However, the rate of descent of IGPQ is lower than that of PQ and

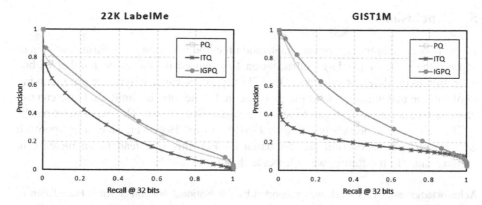

Fig. 3. Comparison of IGPQ to state-of-art methods on 22K-LabelMe and GIST1M at 32 bits.

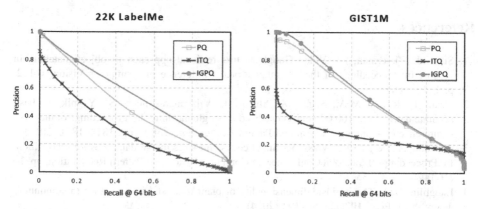

Fig. 4. Comparison of IGPQ to state-of-art methods on 22K-LabelMe and GIST1M at 64 bits.

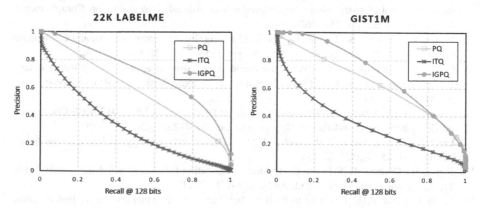

Fig. 5. Comparison of IGPQ to state-of-art methods on 22K-LabelMe and GIST1M at 128 bits.

ITQ in encoding of 32 bits, 64 bits, 128 bits. IGPQ is at the highest position, indicating the accuracy is higher than the other methods with different recall. So the accuracy of IGPQ is higher than the other two algorithms in different encoding bits.

5   Conclusions

In this paper, we propose a novel quantization method based on the information gain to address the issue of the large quantization loss caused by the same number of bits allocation to the different subspace. Our IGPQ approach can use dynamic programming to obtain the maximum information gain size under the total bit limit, and also can use variable bit allocation strategies to reduce the quantization loss. The experiment results indicate that our approach has achieved good results. However, since our approach adds adaptive bit allocation process based on PQ, this will lead to an increase in training time. In the future, we will tackle this issue.

Acknowledgment. This work was supported by the National Natural Science Foundation of China (91520301).

References

1. Sivic, J., Zisserman, A.: Video Google: a text retrieval approach to object matching in videos. In: Proceedings of the 9th International Conference on Computer Vision, vol. 2, p. 1470 (2003)
2. Dean, T., Ruzon, M.A., Segal, M., Shlens, J., Vijayanarasimhan, S., Yagnik, J.: Fast, accurate detection of 100,000 object classes on a single machine. In: Proceedings of the 2013 Conference on Computer Vision and Pattern Recognition, vol. 9, pp. 1814–1821 (2013)
3. Torralba, A., Fergus, R., Weiss, Y.: Small codes and large image databases for recognition. In: Proceedings of the 2008 Conference on Computer Vision and Pattern Recognition, pp. 1–8 (2008)
4. Laughlin, D.C.: The intrinsic dimensionality of plant traits and its relevance to community assembly. J. Ecol. **102**(1), 186–193 (2014)
5. Datar, M., Immorlica, N., Indyk, P., Mirrokni, V.S.: Locality-sensitive hashing scheme based on p-stable distributions. In: Proceedings of Annual Symposium on Computational Geometry, vol. 34, pp. 253–262 (2004)
6. Weiss, Y., Torralba, A., Fergus, R.: Spectral hashing. In: Proceedings of Annual Conference on Neural Information Processing Systems, pp. 1753–1760 (2009)
7. Gong, Y., Lazebnik, S.: Iterative quantization: a procrustean approach to learning binary codes. In: Proceedings of the 2011 Conference on Computer Vision and Pattern Recognition, pp. 817–824 (2011)
8. Chang, S.F.: Supervised hashing with kernels. In: Proceedings of the 2012 IEEE Conference on Computer Vision and Pattern Recognition, pp. 2074–2081 (2012)
9. Lin, G., Shen, C., Suter, D., Hengel, A.V.D.: A general two-step approach to learning-based hashing, pp. 2552–2559 (2013)
10. Jegou, H., Douze, M., Schmid, C.: Product quantization for nearest neighbor search. IEEE Trans. Pattern Anal. Mach. Intell. **33**(1), 117–128 (2011)
11. Li, W.J., Zhou, Z.H.: Learning to hash for big data: current status and future trends. Chin. Sci. Bull. **60**, 485–490 (2015)
12. Xiong, C., Chen, W., Chen, G., et al.: Adaptive quantization for hashing: an information-based approach to learning binary codes. In: Proceedings of International Conference on Data Mining, Society for Industrial and Applied Mathematics, pp. 172–180 (2014)

13. Richard, B.: On the theory of dynamic programming. In: Proceedings of the National Academy of Sciences of the United States of America, vol. 38, no. 8, p. 716 (1952)
14. Jégou, H., Douze, M., Schmid, C., Pérez, P.: Aggregating local descriptors into a compact image representation. In: Proceedings of the 2010 Conference on Computer Vision and Pattern Recognition, vol. 238, pp. 3304–3311 (2010)
15. Russell, B.C., Torralba, A., Murphy, K.P., Freeman, W.T.: Labelme: a database and web-based tool for image annotation. Int. J. Comput. Vis. **77**(1), 157–173 (2008)
16. Guo, Q.Z., Zeng, Z., Zhang, S., Zhang, Y., Wang, F.: Adaptive bit allocation hashing for approximate nearest neighbor search. Neurocomputing **151**, 719–728 (2015)

A Crop Disease Image Retrieval Method Based on the Improvement of Inverted Index

Yuan Yuan, Lei Chen$^{(\boxtimes)}$, Miao Li, and Na Wu

Institute of Intelligent Machines, Chinese Academy of Sciences, Hefei 230031, China
{yuanyuan,chenlei,mli}@iim.ac.cn, wuna@mail.ustc.edu.cn

Abstract. According to the characteristics of crop leaf disease images, we proposed a new image retrieval method based on the improvement of inverted index to diagnose crop leaf diseases. First of all, the input crop disease images were preprocessed, including compression, denoising, enhancement, etc. And then the features of disease in the whole image were extracted. Meanwhile, in order to reduce the storage space of inverted index feature vectors, the Hash method was adopted to map the inverted index feature vectors to binary values. Hamming distance was used in the similarity calculation between the obtained features data and the lesion features from the constructed disease images indexes. According the ranking of similarities, top 5 images were selected as the candidate diagnostic results list of the input crop disease image. And the results were evaluated by some standard criteria, such as precision, recall, etc. The experiments were conducted on cucumber disease images, including: downy mildew, powdery mildew and target spot disease, and rice disease images, including: rice blast, leaf spot and sheath blight. The results showed that the proposed method can achieve the higher retrieval accuracy than traditional SVM method both of cucumber and rice disease images.

Keywords: Image retrieval · Crop disease diagnosis · Inverted index
Image processing

1 Introduction

In recent years, in the field of crop disease prevention and control, the application of computer vision, digital image processing and artificial intelligence technology provided some new ways and ideas for non-destructive detection and intelligent diagnosis of crop diseases. Since 1980s, image processing technology was used to identify crop diseases [1]. And with the development of machine learning technologies, Support Vector Machine (SVM) and Artificial Neural Network (ANN) have become the most commonly used methods in the studies of crop diseases identification [2–6]. The results of these two methods are more dependent on the original training samples. In the conditions of simple image background or under laboratory environment, these two methods can achieve good results. However,

© Springer International Publishing AG 2017
Y. Zhao et al. (Eds.): ICIG 2017, Part II, LNCS 10667, pp. 262–273, 2017.
https://doi.org/10.1007/978-3-319-71589-6_24

the actual crop disease images captured in the field are easily affected by the surrounding environment, such as uneven illumination, color distortion, image noise and so on. which may easily cause the great differences among samples. For these crop disease images, SVM and ANN can not often achieve the desired classification results.

Due to the good fault tolerance of the samples, the content-based image retrieval [7] can avoid the above problems of SVM and ANN. However, when the training data is not large enough, the effect of this method is still not ideal. In recent years, the development of big data technology has overcome this shortcoming. The content-based image retrieval method has got a new attention and development in crop diseases classification. Especially with the popularity of smart phones, the real-time crop diseases diagnosis is expected to achieve. When a farmer or an agricultural technician takes a picture of crop disease and uploads it to the server, the crop disease image retrieval system can quickly match the image features of the disease and return the diagnosis result of the most similar disease images in time. Li et al. [8] proposed a wheat pest image retrieval system, which focused on image feature extraction, image similarity measurement and users' feedback technology. Song [9] and Pu [10] presented a method of disease image retrieval based on color and other spot features for eggplant and tobacco respectively.

These works have been successful in some crop disease image retrieval. However, we found that when the training data of crop disease images is large, there are two key issues need to be solved in the content-based image retrieval method, given as follows:

- How to select and extract the appropriate features of crop disease images is critical.
- How to set up the index to improve the retrieval efficiency is also a problem that needs to be further studied and solved.

In order to solve these two problems, this paper proposed a crop disease image retrieval method based on the improvement of inverted index. On the one hand, both global and local characteristics of crop diseases were considered for selecting and extracting the features of images. On the other hand, the inverted index approach was introduced to construct the index of feature vectors. Meanwhile, in order to reduce the storage space of inverted index feature vectors, a Hash function was adopted to map the inverted index feature vectors to further compressed binary values. In the experiments, the disease images of cucumber and rice were used to validate this method.

2 The Method

2.1 Method Overview

As Fig. 1 showing, the whole process of the proposed method mainly consists of the following two parts:

1. Constructing the index of features for the training set, the procedure is as
   follows:
   - Using the feature matching algorithm to extract the feature of each image
     in training set to form the feature database.
   - Constructing and purifying the feature descriptors and compressing the
     feature vectors.
   - Using Hash function and tree structure to build hierarchical index
     information.
2. Searching the candidate diagnostic results list of the input crop disease image,
   the procedure is as follows:
   - Extracting and compressing the features of the input crop disease image.
   - Using the fast matching technology to search the matching indexes in the
     feature database.
   - Calculating the Hamming similarity between the feature vectors and
     returning the top 5 images, as the final classification results according
     to the similarity ranking.

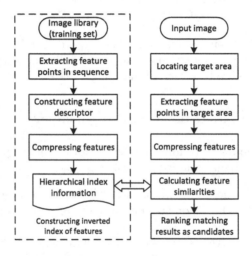

Fig. 1. The overview of system flow

2.2 Feature Extraction and Compression

Since some features of crop disease images, such as color, texture, etc., are easily
affected by the natural environment, this paper mainly focuses on the extraction of shape features. Besides, considering the characteristics of crop disease
images, the extracted shape features should have the good stability under the
conditions of rotation, uneven illumination, color distortion and affine transformation, which often occur during the process of image acquisition. Therefore, we
choose Scale-invariant Feature Transform (SIFT) [11] as the main method for

extracting features. As a local feature detection algorithm, the SIFT method can quickly find some interest points or corner points of the given image in spatial scale with their scale and orientation descriptors to get features.

In this paper, according to the SIFT method, we extract features of crop disease images as follows:

- Compressing the original captured image to the resolution $600*400$ pixels, denoted by i_0.
- Adopting the Different of Gaussian to find interest points or corner points in scale space of i_0.
- Locating the key points by comparing the adjacent layers of each Different of Gaussian space in the same group.
- Determining the distribution of gradient directions by the gradient histogram.
- Counting and describing gradient information of Gauss image in the neighborhood of feature points.

After feature extraction, the Gauss normalization method is adopted to normalize the obtained features. And then the feature database can be constructed.

Since the feature vectors takes up a lot of space while the image database is large, the feature vector should be compressed to improve the retrieval efficiency. Given a feature vector x_i, the difference matrix C of the specified crop disease type can be calculated. And according to the distribution pattern of C, the feature vector x_i can be converted to the binary code of length l, which is denoted by $B = (b_0, b_1, ..., b_{l-1})$. Since the value of l in SIFT is 128, the storage space of binary codes is very large and the computation efficiency of feature matching is low. So a compression method of feature descriptors is proposed. Given a feature descriptor $B = (b_0, b_1, ..., b_{l-1})$ and a threshold α, the compression is conducted by the following formula:

$$C(i,j) = \begin{cases} 11, & if \ b_j - b_i > \alpha \\ 10, & if \ -\alpha < b_j - b_i \leq \alpha \\ 00, & otherwise \end{cases} \tag{1}$$

After the feature compression, the storage space of the binary codes is significantly reduced. Meanwhile, the computational efficiency of feature matching can be improved. Figure 2 shows an example of feature extraction and compression.

Fig. 2. Feature extraction and compression

2.3 Image Retrieval

Since the inverted index method can meet the actual retrieval requirement, which finds records according to the value of the selected property, the image retrieval method based on inverted index has been widely studied in recent years [12–14]. The inverted index consists of a lexicon and corresponding inverted lists. The lexicon is a set of strings made up of all the words that appear in the document set. Each index entry records some information about the word itself and a pointer to the inverted list. And the inverted list uses a data structure of the form $(docid, wf, <p_1, ..., p_f>)$ to record the hit information of a word item in a document, where $docid$ is the ID of the document, wf is the word frequency and p_i indicates each position offset of the word appearing in this document. For each word item in a query, it is necessary to find out whether it appears in the lexicon, and the disk location of the corresponding inverted list. Since the speed of locating a word directly determines the retrieval efficiency, the efficient data structures including Hash table and tree structure are used to build the word lexicon and conduct the search. Besides, in the image retrieval tasks, the index storage space is usually larger because of the large number of image features. Besides, the retrieval efficiency is low when there are much more candidate retrieval results. Therefore, it is worthy of further study on index compression [15,16] and result filtering [17,18].

In this paper, in order to reduce the storage space, the following Hash function is trained to map the feature vector of the original space to binary codes,

$$h_k(x_i) = sgn(w_k^T x_i + a_k), \tag{2}$$

where x_i denotes the content feature vector of the image, w_k denotes the mapping vector that needs to be learned, a_k is the average vector of all content features that need to be mapped. And then the hierarchical index is constructed in tree structure. In the inverted index structure, each inverted list is represented by a visual word. Each list is equivalent to a cluster. And the corresponding cluster center is the visual word. When constructing an inverted index for image retrieval, the visual features of the image are inserted into the inverted list corresponding to the nearest visual word. The image retrieval procedure usually finds several visual words which have the nearest distance to the visual features of the query image. And the query results are all the visual features of the inverted list corresponding to these visual words. If the final query results only need KNN similar visual features, some distance such as Euclidean, Hamming, etc. needs to be calculated and sorted between the query feature and all the query results. Hamming distance is adopted in this paper. Given two feature vectors x_i and x_j with the length l, the Hamming distance between binary codes is calculated to measure the similarity of features as the following formula:

$$S(H(x_i), H(x_j)) = \sum_{n=1}^{l} (xor(H(x_i), H(x_j))). \tag{3}$$

In order to further reduce the search space, only the index values of the first half of the Hash table are used to quickly classify the query object. And then the retrieved files are ranked according to the final statistics of their hit frequencies. Hence, according to the similarity ranking, five candidate images with the highest similarities of the input image in the relative database can be obtained.

3   Experiments

3.1   Experimental Setup

We conducted experiments both on small scale and large scale samples. When the experimental sample scale is small, the proposed image retrieval method was compared with the traditional SVM method, which can achieve good performance on small scale samples. The traditional SVM method contains some main steps, such as image segmentation, feature extraction and classification recognition, etc. The experimental data includes six diseases of cucumber and rice which were captured in the field. More concretely, the images used in this paper were collected from 10:00am to 15:00pm on sunny days in Hefei, using the digital SLR camera of the model Canon EOS 6D, with the lens EF 17–40 mm f/4L USM for capturing the disease images of cucumber leaves in greenhouse and the macro lens EF 100 mm f/2.8L IS USM for capturing the disease images of rice leaves in field. The original image resolution is 5472 * 3648 pixels. The cucumber diseases include target spot, powdery mildew and downy mildew. The rice diseases include rice blast, sheath blight and brown spot.

In image preprocessing, first we selected and clipped the main diseased area from the original images. And then the clipped images were compressed to the resolution of 600 * 400 pixels for the consideration of time and space efficiency while preserving more image details. Some examples are shown in Fig. 3.

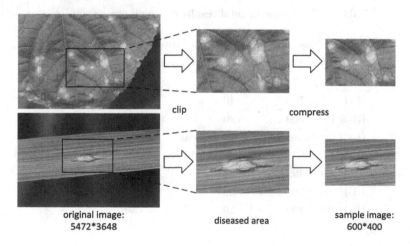

Fig. 3. Examples of main diseased area clipping and compressing

In the traditional SVM method, we adopted graph cuts fusing multiple features to segment the disease images [19]. And we conducted feature extraction and classification according to the early work [20].

In the proposed method, the training set was used to construct the inverted index. And the test set was used to verify the method. Hamming distance was adopted to measure the feature similarity. According the ranking of similarities, the top 5 images were selected as the candidate diagnostic results list of the input test image. And the results were evaluated by some standard criteria, such as precision, recall, that is: $P = h_1/S_t * 100\%, R = h_5/S_t * 100\%$, where h_1 is the number that the ranked first image in the candidate images is the correct matching, h_5 is the number that the top five candidate images contains the correct matching, S_t is the size of test set.

Besides, we further evaluated our method in large scale samples. In order to verify the robustness of this method, the inverted index is trained by using the original images without any preprocessing.

The experimental environment are as follows: Intel Core i7-4790@3.66 GHz, 4 GB RAM, Microsoft Windows 10 64-bit, Microsoft Visual Studio 2013, Open Source Computer Vision Library (OpenCV) 2.4.8, Matlab R2014b.

3.2   Experiments on Small Scale Samples

In the experiments on small scale samples, each disease set contains 60 images, where 50 images are randomly selected as the training set and the remaining 10 images are taken as the test set. Table 1 shows the experimental results, where SVM denotes the classification accuracy of the traditional SVM method, IR-P and IR-R are the evaluation criteria of the proposed method mentioned above.

Table 1. The experimental results on small scale samples

(a) The classification of cucumber diseases

	Target spot	Powdery mildew	Downy mildew
SVM (%)	37.9	93.5	23.6
IR-P (%)	70	40	50
IR-R (%)	100	90	90

(b) The classification of rice diseases

	Rice blast	Sheath blight	Brown spot
SVM (%)	89.6	37.9	63.9
IR-P (%)	70	90	10
IR-R (%)	100	100	30

It can be seen that our method is better than the traditional SVM method. Especially in the identification of cucumber target spot, downy mildew and rice sheath blight, the percentage that the first image of five candidates is the correct matching is obviously better than the traditional SVM method. For the classification of other diseases, although the proportion that the first candidate image is the correct matching is not high, the percentage of the correct matching occurring in five candidates is still better than SVM. However, in the identification task of rice brown spot, the effect of our method is not good, which indicates that our method needs to be further optimized. Figure 4 shows the more intuitive comparison of experimental results.

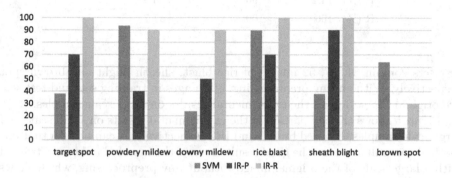

Fig. 4. Comparison between the traditional SVM method and the proposed method

3.3 Experiments on Large Scale Samples

In the experiments on large scale samples, the image database consists of 4338 images of cucumber and rice diseases. More details are shown in Table 2.

Table 2. The sizes of experimental training set and test set

Crop diseases		Training set	Test set	Total
Cucumber	Target spot	755	50	805
	Powdery mildew	794	52	846
	Downy mildew	1000	70	1070
Rice	Rice blast	471	31	502
	Sheath blight	266	17	283
	Brown spot	780	52	832
	Sum	4066	272	4338

The training set of cucumber diseases contains 2549 images, where the test sets contain 50, 52, 70 images of target spot, powdery mildew and downy mildew respectively. The training set of rice diseases contains 1517 images, where the

Table 3. The experimental results on large scale samples

(a) The classification of cucumber diseases

	Target spot	Powdery mildew	Downy mildew
P (%)	84	50	38.6
R (%)	96	92.3	75.7

(b) The classification of rice diseases

	Rice blast	Sheath blight	Brown spot
P (%)	74.2	90	5.8
R (%)	100	100	57.7

test sets contain 31, 17, 52 images of rice blast, sheath blight and brown spot respectively. Without any preprocessing, all images in training sets and test sets are original. Table 3 gives the experimental results on large scale samples.

Figure 5 shows the comparison of the experimental results on small scale and large scale samples, denoted by IR1 and IR2 respectively. It can be seen that our method can still achieved the good results even if the inverted index was trained with a large scale of the original image without any preprocessing, which shows that the proposed method has good robustness.

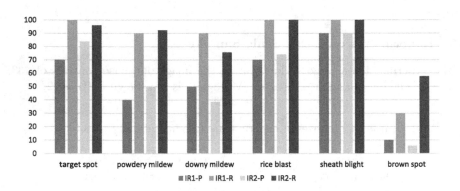

Fig. 5. Comparison between small scale and large scale samples

In addition, we conducted the experiment that the training set contains 4066 hybrid images of cucumber and rice diseases, where the test sets of cucumber and rice are the same as the above experiments. The experimental results are shown in Table 4. The stable results show that our method has good universality. For a variety of crop diseases, this method does not need to train multiple classifiers. All kinds of crop disease images can be trained together to improve computational efficiency.

Table 4. The experimental results of hybrid diseases

(a) The classification of cucumber in hybrid diseases

	Target spot	Powdery mildew	Downy mildew
P (%)	80	42.3	28.6
R (%)	96	86.5	51.4

(b) The classification of rice in hybrid diseases

	Rice blast	Sheath blight	Brown spot
P (%)	77.4	17.6	3.8
R (%)	100	76.5	19.2

4 Concluding Remarks

The paper proposed a content-based image retrieval method for the classification of crop disease images. Focusing on how to improve the construction of inverted index of feature vectors, the Hash function was adopted to map the inverted index feature vectors to further compressed binary values to reduce the storage space and improve the efficiency of feature matching.

We validated this method by using cucumber disease images and rice disease images. The experimental results show that:

1. Comparing with the traditional SVM method, our method can achieve the better results. And the accuracy that the correct matching image occurs in five candidates is higher than the accuracy that the first candidate is the correct matching image.
2. Since the cucumber leaves occupy a larger proportion in the whole image and the interference of the complex background is less, the experimental results of cucumber disease image retrieval are better than the results of rice.
3. The method has good robustness on large scale of original image without any preprocessing. And the accuracy decrease of hybrid disease image retrieval is not obvious.
4. The proposed method is general and it can also be applied to other crop diseases.
5. The method of feature extraction and similarity calculation in this paper still need to be further optimized to improve the efficiency and accuracy of image retrieval.

The proposed method needs to be further improved. Comparing with other related algorithms and validating on more crop disease images will be concerned in next works.

Acknowledgments. The authors would like to thank the anonymous reviewers for their helpful reviews. The work is supported by the National Natural Science Foundation of China under No. 31501223.

References

1. Wolfe, R.R., Sandler, W.E.: An algorithm for stem detection using digital image analysis. Trans. ASAE **28**(2), 641–644 (1985)
2. Rumpf, T., Mahlein, A.K., Steiner, U., Oerke, E.C., Dehne, H.W., Plümer, L.: Early detection and classification of plant diseases with support vector machines based on hyperspectral reflectance. Comput. Electron. Agric. **74**(1), 91–99 (2010)
3. Omrani, E., Khoshnevisan, B., Shamshirband, S., Saboohi, H., Anuar, N.B., Nasir, M.H.N.M.: Potential of radial basis function-based support vector regression for apple disease detection. Measurement **55**(9), 512–519 (2014)
4. Zhang, J., Kong, F., Li, Z., Wu, J., Chen, W., Wang, S., Zhu, M.: Recognition of honey pomelo leaf diseases based on optimal binary tree support vector machine (in Chinese). Trans. Chin. Soc. Agric. Eng. **30**(19), 222–231 (2014)
5. Zhu, L., Feng, Q., Yang, M., Zhang, Z.: Study on segmentation and diagnosis of wine grape disease based on image processing (in Chinese). J. Chin. Agric. Mech. **36**(1), 111–115 (2015)
6. Ma, X., Guan, H., Qi, G., Liu, G., Tan, F.: Diagnosis model of soybean leaf diseases based on improved cascade neural network (in Chinese). Trans. Chin. Soc. Agric. Mach. **48**(1), 163–168 (2017)
7. Liu, Y., Zhang, D., Lu, G., Ma, W.: A survey of content-based image retrieval with high-level semantics. Pattern Recogn. **40**(1), 262–282 (2007)
8. Li, Z., Liu, Y., He, D., Long, M., Liu, Q.: Investigation and implementation of content-based retrieval system for wheat pest images (in Chinese). Trans. Chin. Soc. Agric. Eng. **23**(11), 210–215 (2007)
9. Song, J.: Eggplant disease image search method based on color characteristics (in Chinese). J. Anhui Agric. Sci. **39**(19), 11920–11921, 11977 (2011)
10. Pu, Y.: Image searching method of tobacco disease based on disease spot feature fusion (in Chinese). J. Henan Agric. Sci. **44**(2), 71–76 (2015)
11. Lowe, D.G.: Distinctive image features from scale-invariant keypoints. Int. J. Comput. Vis. **60**(2), 91–110 (2004)
12. Sivic, J., Zisserman, A.: Video Google: a text retrieval approach to object matching in videos. In: 9th IEEE International Conference on Computer Vision (ICCV 2003), Nice, France, 14–17 October 2003, pp. 1470–1477 (2003)
13. Chen, Y., Guan, T., Wang, C.: Approximate nearest neighbor search by residual vector quantization. Sensors **10**(12), 11259–11273 (2010)
14. Jégou, H., Douze, M., Schmid, C.: Product quantization for nearest neighbor search. IEEE Trans. Pattern Anal. Mach. Intell. **33**(1), 117–128 (2011)
15. Anh, V.N., Moffat, A.: Inverted index compression using word-aligned binary codes. Inf. Retrieval **8**(1), 151–166 (2005)
16. Yan, H., Zhang, X., Shan, D., Mao, X., Zhao, X.: SIMD-based inverted index compression algorithms (in Chinese). J. Comput. Res. Dev. **52**(5), 995–1004 (2015)
17. Hwang, Y., Han, B., Ahn, H.: A fast nearest neighbor search algorithm by non-linear embedding. In: 2012 IEEE Conference on Computer Vision and Pattern Recognition (CVPR 2012), Providence, RI, USA, 16–21 June 2012, pp. 3053–3060 (2012)
18. Ai, L., Yu, J., Guan, T., He, Y.: Adaptively filtering query results for large scale image feature retrieval (in Chinese). Chin. J. Comput. **38**(1), 122–132 (2015)

19. Wu, N., Li, M., Chen, S., Yuan, Y., Zeng, X., Chen, L., Sun, X., Bian, C.: Automatic segmentation of plant disease images based on graph cuts fusing multiple features (in Chinese). Trans. Chin. Soc. Agric. Eng. **30**(17), 212–219 (2014)
20. Yuan, Y.: Research and application of image-based intelligent recognition for cucumber leaf diseases (in Chinese). Ph.D. thesis, Anhui Agricultural University (2013)

A Novel Self-adaptive Defog Method Based on Bionic

Shi-ping Ma$^{(\boxtimes)}$, Quan-He Li, Du-Yan Bi, and Ya-Yun Dong

Aeronautics and Astronautics Engineering College,
Air Force Engineering University, Xi'an 710038, China
simplexian@126.com

Abstract. Due to the weak robust and unsatisfied performance in the color natural index, color colorfulness index and brightness of some existing algorithms, a novel bionic based algorithm is proposed in this paper. In the proposed algorithm, the human visual contrast sensitivity is introduced in to set the threshold for external lightness calculation, and potential function in Markov random fields for calculating external lightness is built; color constancy is quantified as adjusting pixel values along the vertical grayline, so that the scene reflectance can be restored with changing color saturation only; function for adjusting image background brightness is proposed by simulating the human visual photosensitive adaptability, and then the enhancement result satisfying the human photopic vision is restored under the constraint of the adjusted background brightness. The experimental results yield that the proposed algorithm can get better color natural index and color colorfulness index than some existing algorithms, and the brightness of enhancement results is more suitable for the human photopic vision.

Keywords: Bionic · Contrast sensitivity · Color constancy
Brightness adaptive faculty · Image defog

1 Introduction

Human vision system has prominent faculty at apperceiving and processing scene's color, brightness, size, detail and the other information, therefore, bionic based image processing methods have been being explored by experts in this field. Some outstanding bionic based image enhancement methods have been proposed in recent years, including method proposed by Academician Wang of CAS, which proposed a novel bio-inspired algorithm to enhance the color image under low or non-uniform lighting conditions that models global and local adaptation of the human visual system [1], method proposed by Lu from Beijing Institute of Technology, which is based on the retinal brightness adaption and lateral inhibition competition mechanism of ganglion cells [2], Liu of CAS also proposed a novel image enhancement method simulating human vision system, which is based on the adjacency relation of image regions, a gray consolidation strategy is proposed to represent image using the least gray, and according to the Just Noticeable Difference (JND) curve, it signs a gray mapping relation for maximum perception of human eyes to enhance image [3].

© Springer International Publishing AG 2017
Y. Zhao et al. (Eds.): ICIG 2017, Part II, LNCS 10667, pp. 274–285, 2017.
https://doi.org/10.1007/978-3-319-71589-6_25

In this paper, we proposed a novel Self-adaptive defog method based on bionic. In the proposed algorithm, Retinex model is adopted to describe a haze degraded image [4], white balance is performed on the degraded image at first, then, human visual brightness adaption mechanism is introduced in to estimate background brightness, and then under the constraint of color constancy image contrast is enhanced based on human visual contrast sensitivity, and finally in order to make the enhancement result satisfy human vision better, the brightness of the restored image is adjusted directed by the brightness of the original image.

2   Image Enhancement Based on HVS

Retinex model is adopted here to describe a degraded image, whose expression is

$$I(x) = T(x) \cdot L(x), \tag{1}$$

where I is the obtained image, T is the reflectance image, and L is the external illumination. Under the weather condition of haze, L does not take the property of spatial smoothness as under weather condition of unbalanced illumination, because it is greatly disturbed by scene depth, therefore, L takes the property of local smoothness. In order to get Retinex model's solution T, and make the enhancement result be with better visual pleasure, the following steps are proposed to solute the problem: Firstly, white balance is put on I, then the background brightness of white-balanced I is calculated; Secondly, calculate the external illumination L, and then remove L from the white-balanced I under the constraint of color constancy to upgrade the image's contrast and restore the scene's real color; Finally, adjust the brightness of the reflectance image to the dynamic suitable to human visual system. The detail processes could be described as Fig. 1.

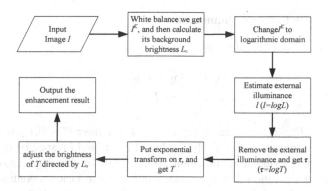

Fig. 1. Flow chat of the proposed defog algorithm

2.1   White Balance and the Calculation of Background Brightness

White balance is used to correct the external illumination's color and normalize the original image. The key process of white balance is to acquire the color of external illumination. White balance could be described as Eq. (2).

$$I^K(x) = L(x)/L_\infty \cdot T(x),$$ (2)

In Eq. (2) $L_\infty = (L_{\infty,r}, L_{\infty,g}, L_{\infty,b})$, it represents the color of external illumination. Generally, external illumination is estimated by sky area of an image, then we could calculate the color of external illumination through the following constraints:

No. 1, sky area locates at image's top, it could be described as $i \leq 2\%H$, where H is the total row of I, and i is the horizontal ordinate of pixels, the origin is located at the top left corner.
No. 2, the brightness of sky area is larger than almost all the other pixels, it could be described as $L_\infty \geq 99\%\max(I)$.

Through the research of human visual brightness adaption mechanism, we know that when perceiving the brightness of the central pixel, human vision always be disturbed by pixels around [5], therefore, we could calculate background brightness through Eq. (3),

$$L_O(x) = \frac{\sum\limits_{y \in N_0(x)} \varphi(y) I_V^K(y)}{\sum\limits_{y \in N_0(x)} \varphi(y)}$$ (3)

where $N_0(x)$ is a local patch centered at x except x, the patch size is 5×5 in this paper; $\varphi(y)$ is Gaussian weighted-coefficient; $I_V^K(y)$ is the lightness component of white-balanced image in HSV space.

2.2   Estimate the External Illumination

Transform I^K to logarithmic domain, we get

$$\log I^K = \log T + \log L,$$
$$\Rightarrow I^w = \tau + l$$ (4)

As $I^k \leq L$, so $I^w \leq l$, and because $0 \leq I^K, L \leq 1$, we have $I^w \leq 0, l \leq 0$, so $|I^w| \geq |l|$. Let $\sim I^w$, $\sim \tau$, $\sim l$ represent the absolute value of I^w, τ, and l respectively. In the haze weather conditions, external illumination could result in the degradation of image contrast and color saturation directly. According to human vision's contrast sensitivity mechanism, we designed the following steps to calculate external illumination:

When pixels in window Ω centralized with pixel x satisfies the condition $\frac{|\sim I_x^w - \sim l_o|}{\sim l_o} \geq N_\Omega$, we let the external illumination above pixel x to be 0, that is $\sim l = 0$, where $\tilde{l}_o$ is the average background brightness of the window, N_Ω is the corresponding just noticeable difference.

When pixels in window Ω satisfies the condition $\frac{|\tilde{I}_x^w - \tilde{l}_o|}{\tilde{l}_o} < N_\Omega$, we could calculate the external illumination above pixel j through Eq. (5),

$$\max F(\tilde{l}) = \sum_\Omega |\nabla(\tilde{I}_v^w - \tilde{l})| + \eta \sum_\Omega \left(1 - |\tilde{l}_x - \tilde{l}_y|\right)$$
$$s.t.\ 0 \leq \tilde{l} \leq \min_{c \in \{r,g,b\}} (\tilde{I}_c^w). \tag{5}$$

In the functional $F(\tilde{l})$, the data term $|\nabla(\tilde{I}_v^w - \tilde{l})|$ forces the reflectance image to have maximal contrast, and $\tilde{I}_v^w$ is the lightness component of image I^w in HSV space. The second penalty term $\left(1 - |\tilde{l}_x - \tilde{l}_y|\right)$ is smoothness term, which forces spatial smoothness on the external illumination. η is non-negative parameter and acts as the strength of the smoothness term here.

The above function is a potential function of Markov random fields (MRFs). Detailed implementation of the framework is described as the following steps:

    ① Compute the data term $|\nabla(\tilde{I}_v^w - \tilde{l})|$ from $\tilde{I}_v^w$;
    ② Compute the smoothness term $\left(1 - |\tilde{l}_x - \tilde{l}_y|\right)$;
    ③ Do the inference to get the external illumination $\tilde{l}$.

Detailed algorithm to calculate the data cost could be described as the following pseudocode:

    ① for $\tilde{l} = 0$ to $\omega \cdot \min_{c \in \{r,g,b\}} (\tilde{I}_c^w)$
    compute $|\nabla(\tilde{I}_v^w - \tilde{l})|$
    ② return $|\nabla(\tilde{I}_v^w - \tilde{l})|$ for all pixels in window Ω, and for each pixel, $|\nabla(\tilde{I}_v^w - \tilde{l})|$ is a vector with $\omega \cdot \min_{c \in \{r,g,b\}} (\tilde{I}_c^w)$ dimensions.

Where ω is introduced in to keep a very small amount of haze for the distance objects, to ensure the image seem natural, and it is fixed to 0.95 here [6].

By obtaining both data cost and smoothness cost, we have a complete graph in term of Markov random fields. In step 3, to do the inference in MRFs with number of labels equals to $\omega \cdot \min_{c \in \{r,g,b\}} (\tilde{I}_c^w)$, we use the graph-cut with multiple labels [7] or belief propagation.

2.3   Calculate the Reflectance Image

In Fig. 2, OA is gray scale line, on which pixels have the same intensity, and it ranges from black point O(0,0,0) to white point A(255,255,255). PH is the perpendicular from point P to line OA, and the less the |PH| is, the lower the color saturation of pixel P is [8]. Color constancy reflects in image is that pixel values in three different channels keep in order and move along the direction of HP. In addition, from Eq. (6), expression of color saturation, we know that the difference among the three channels is little,

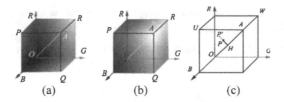

Fig. 2. RGB color space, (a) planes border upon origin O (b) planes apart from origin O (c) distance to gray scale line

which leads to the reduction of color saturation. In conclusion, removing haze from image and getting the scene reflectance under the constraint of color constancy is to move pixel p along the direction of HP, make pixel value of one channel tend to be 0, increase the difference between three channels and promote the color saturation.

$$S = 1 - 3 \times \frac{\min_{C \in \{r,g,b\}}(I_C)}{I_r + I_g + I_b}. \tag{6}$$

In which S represents the color saturation of image. Suppose that the coordinates of pixel P and H are (P_r, P_g, P_b) and (h_r, h_g, h_b) respectively, as PH$\perp$OA, and pixel in OA satisfies $h_r = h_g = h_b$, then there is $h_r = h_g = h_b = \frac{P_r + P_g + P_b}{3}$, so we get $\overrightarrow{HP} = (\frac{-2P_r + P_g + P_b}{3}, \frac{P_r - 2P_g + P_b}{3}, \frac{P_r + P_g - 2P_b}{3})$. After dehazing pixel P moves to P′, whose coordinate is $(P_r - q_r \cdot {}^\sim l, P_g - q_g \cdot {}^\sim l, P_b - q_b \cdot {}^\sim l)$, so $\overrightarrow{p'p} = (q_r \cdot {}^\sim l, q_g \cdot {}^\sim l, q_b \cdot {}^\sim l)$, in which q_r, q_g, q_b is the weight of step length in R, G, B channel respectively. Because $\overrightarrow{p'p}$ and $\overrightarrow{HP}$ are parallel to each other, so

$$\frac{q_r \cdot {}^\sim l}{-2P_r + P_g + P_b} = \frac{q_g \cdot {}^\sim l}{P_r - 2P_g + P_b} = \frac{q_b \cdot {}^\sim l}{P_r + P_g - 2P_b}. \tag{7}$$

In conclusion, the steps of recovering scene reflectance is concluded as following:

Step 1: set the step weight of the minimal channel of $^\sim I^w$ to be 1. For example, suppose $q_r = 1$, then the step weights of other two channels are

$$q_g = \frac{P_r - 2P_g + P_b}{-2P_r + P_g + P_b},$$
$$q_b = \frac{P_r + P_g - 2P_b}{-2P_r + P_g + P_b}. \tag{8}$$

Step 2: subtract the external illumination with different weight in three channels,

$$^\sim \tau_r = {}^\sim I_r^w - {}^\sim l,$$
$$^\sim \tau_g = {}^\sim I_g^w - q_g \cdot {}^\sim l,$$
$$^\sim \tau_b = {}^\sim I_b^w - q_b \cdot {}^\sim l. \tag{9}$$

From the hypothesis of Step 1 we know that $\sim I_r^w \leq \sim I_g^w$, $\sim I_r^w \leq \sim I_b^w$, and it is easy to demonstrate that $q_g \leq 1$, $q_b \leq 1$, while $q_r = 1$, thus the channel of minimum value takes the maximum step weight. Moreover, from $q_g - q_b = \frac{-3(\sim I_g^w - \sim I_b^w)}{-2 \sim I_r^w + \sim I_g^w + \sim I_b^w}$ it is we know that if $\sim I_g^w \leq \sim I_b^w$ then $q_g \geq q_b$, and if $\sim I_g^w \geq \sim I_b^w$, then $q_g \leq q_b$, therefore the channel of maximum value corresponds the minimum step weight. In conclusion Eq. (9) ensures that channel with the largest luminance value subtracts the smallest external illumination, while channel with the smallest luminance value subtracts the largest external illumination, so the relative size among three color channels keeps unchanged and the color saturation is enhanced.

Step 3: put exponential transform on τ, and get the finally dehazed scene reflectance,

$$T = e^\tau. \tag{10}$$

2.4   Brightness Emendation

The areas with dense haze will be dark after removing external illumination, so the brightness compensation of scene reflectance is necessary. It could be drawn from the curve describing human vision's Just Noticeable Difference (JND) that the best brightness for human vision to apperceive details is 125, so we rearrange the reflectance image brightness to around this value. The final result could be got through Eq. (11),

$$L_O^{adjust} = \mu - k \cdot \log(1/L_O - 1), \tag{11}$$

Where μ is the average brightness after correction, and it is set to be $125/255$ here, k is a non-negative parameter, deciding the dynamic range of brightness, and it is set to be 0.2 here. Curve of this function could be seen from Fig. 3(b), and it is clear that this function could heighten the brightness of dark area effectively and restrain the brightness of lightful area.

The final enhancement result could be got through Eq. (12),

$$T_{adjust} = L_O^{adjust} \Big/ L_{T,O} \cdot T \tag{12}$$

Where $L_{T,O}$ is the background brightness of T, and it could be calculated by Eq. 3.

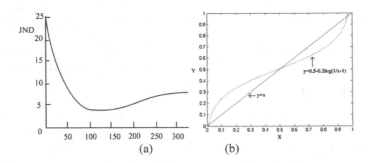

Fig. 3. (a) Human vision's JND curve. (b) Brightness adjusting curve

3   Experimental Results

To demonstrate the effectiveness of our method, we chose some classical images from representational papers [6, 9] for test, and compared our results with the other two distinguished algorithms, K. He's dark channel prior [10] and Tarel's fast visibility restoration [11], which were quoted vastly in recent years. We listed the key variables during enhancing visibility process in Fig. 4: external illumination L, the scene reflectance without brightness emendation T, the scene reflectance after brightness emendation T_{adjust}. We also tested some other images in Figs. 5, 6 and 7 are the comparative experimental results.

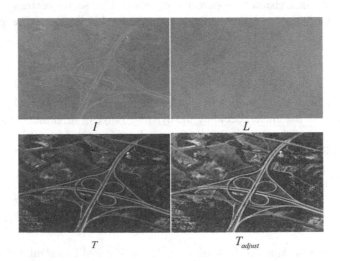

Fig. 4. Key variables during enhancing visibility process

- Comparing the original images with the enhancement results in Fig. 5, we confirmed that the proposed algorithm could improve images plagued by fog effectively, and it could recover the real color of scenes. From Figs. 6 and 7 we could

Fig. 5. Top: images plagued by fog. Bottom: the results of enhancing visibility using the method introduced in this paper.

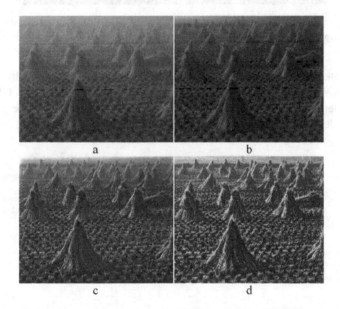

Fig. 6. Image "straw". a: original images. b: K. He's result. c: Tarel's result. d: our result

notice that the results of proposed approach have a higher contrast and vivid color. However the saturation overtops, the image luminance has a good balance and increase the image details. At the same time, objects far away from the camera become visible in our results, while K. He's results appear to be dim although the algorithm could reduce fog illusion effectively, and Tarel's results still have fog illusion.

Fig. 7. Image "rill" a: original images. b: K. He's result. c: Tarel's result. d: our result

To evaluate the results of enhancing visibility listed in Figs. 6 and 7 objectively, we adopted color natural index [11] (CNI), color colorfulness index [11] (CCI) and gradient based definition [4, 9] here. The gradient based definition could be got through Eq. (13). Table 1 shows these objective evaluation results.

Table 1. Measure CNI, CCI and definition

Images\Metrics	Figure 6 "straw"				Figure 7 "rill"			
	Origin (a)	K. He's result (b)	Tarel's result (c)	Our result (d)	Origin (a)	K. He's result (b)	Tarel's result (c)	Our result (d)
Color naturalness index (CNI: 1 is best)	0.491	0.672	0.396	0.905	0.512	0.933	0.317	0.893
Color colorfulness index (CCI: 16–20 is good)	4.346	11.367	9.613	12.834	7.204	18.997	9.351	19.372
Gradient based definition (Def:)	0.337	0.659	0.727	0.877	0.301	0.823	0.516	0.899

The CNI can be calculated by:

$$CNI_{im} = \frac{n_{skin} \cdot CNI_{skin} + n_{grass} \cdot CNI_{grass} + n_{sky} \cdot CNI_{sky}}{n_{skin} + n_{grass} + n_{sky}} \tag{13}$$

where S_{av_skin}, S_{av_grass} and S_{av_sky} represent the mean saturation of the three kinds pixels, the corresponding numbers of pixels are n_{skin}, n_{grass} and n_{sky}.

$$CNI_{skin} = e^{(-0.5\times((S_{av\_skin}-0.76)/0.52)^2)} \tag{14}$$

$$CNI_{grass} = e^{(-0.5\times((S_{av\_grass}-0.81)/0.53)^2)} \tag{15}$$

$$CNI_{sky} = e^{(-0.5\times((S_{av\_sky}-0.43)/0.22)^2)} \tag{16}$$

The definition of CCI is:

$$CCI_{im} = S_{av} + \sigma \tag{17}$$

where S_{av} is the mean of image saturation, σ is its standard deviation.

$$Def = \frac{1}{M}\sum_{x}^{M} \sqrt{(I_H(x))^2 + (I_V(x))^2} \tag{18}$$

We can compute the image definition by Eq. (18). In which M are the total rows and columns respectively; I_H, I_V are the gradients in horizontal and vertical direction respectively. The Table 1 indicates that our algorithm has a distinct superiority in color natural and abundance.

More statistical experiments are listed in Figs. 8, 9 and 10, 66 pictures with uniform fog are taken from Tarel's dataset: www.lcpc.fr/english/products/image-databases/article/frida-foggy-road-image-database.

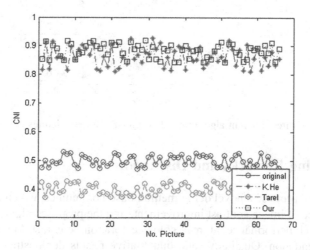

Fig. 8. CNI of three different algorithms' defog results for 66 pictures with uniform fog

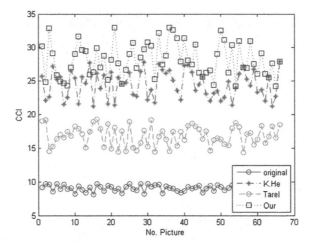

Fig. 9. CCI of three different algorithms' defog results for 66 pictures with uniform fog

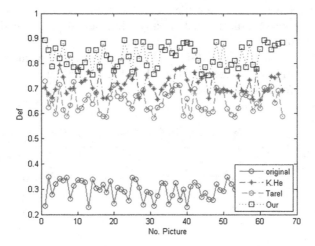

Fig. 10. Def of three different algorithms' defog results for 66 pictures with uniform fog

4   Concluding Remarks and Discussion

In this paper, we propose a novel defog method based on bionics, which is enlightened by the substance of image contrast improvement, and the proposed algorithm is proved to have a good performance at real color restoration, contrast improvement and brightness emendation. Qualitative and quantitative results demonstrate that the proposed method can get better color natural index and color colorfulness index than some existing algorithms, and it is robuster and more effective. However, scenes near the camera become over enhancement, and scenes far away from the camera appears a lot of noise after enhancing visibility. Therefore, for future work, we intend to concentrate on the above constraints of our method.

References

1. Wang, S.-J., Ding, X.-H., Liao, Y.-H., Guo, D.-H.: A novel bio-inspired algorithm for color image enhancement. Acta Electron. Sin. **36**(10), 1970–1973 (2008)
2. Lu, L.-L., Gao, K., Shao, X.-G., Ni, G.-Q.: An adaptive high dynamic range color image enhancement algorithm based on human vision property. Trans. Beijing Inst. Technol. **32**(4), 415–419 (2012)
3. Liu, X., Wu, J., Hao, Y.-M., Zhu, F.: Image enhancement method for human vision. J. Comput. Eng. **38**(2), 254–256 (2012)
4. Li, Q.-H., Bi, D.-Y., Ma, S.-P., He, L.-Y.: Non-uniform lightness image repeated exposure directed by visual mechanism. J. Acta Autom. Sin. **39**(9), 1458–1466 (2013)
5. Tan, R.T.: Visibility in bad weather from a single image. In: IEEE Conference on Computer Vision and Pattern Recognition, pp. 1–8, June 2008
6. He, K., Sun, J., Tang, X.: Single image haze removal using dark channel prior. IEEE Trans. Pattern Anal. Mach. Intell. **33**(12), 1–13 (2011)
7. Szeliski, R., Zabih, R., Scharstein, D., Veksler, O., Kolmogorov, V., Agarwala, A., Tappen, M., Rother, C.: A comparative study of energy minimization methods for Markov random fields. In: Leonardis, A., Bischof, H., Pinz, A. (eds.) ECCV 2006. LNCS, vol. 3952, pp. 16–29. Springer, Heidelberg (2006). https://doi.org/10.1007/11744047_2
8. Gan, J.-H., He, T.-L.: Pixel-level single image dehazing algorithm in color space. Appl. Res. Comput. **22**(9), 3591–3593 (2012)
9. Lan, X., Zhang, L.-P., Shen, H.-F., Yuan, Q.-Q., Li, H.-F.: Single image haze removal considering sensor blur and noise. EURASIP J. Adv. Sig. Process. (2013). http://asp.eurasipjournals.com/content/2013/1/86
10. Tarel, J.-P., Hautiere, N.: Fast visibility restoration from a single color or gray level image. In: Proceedings of IEEE International Conference on Computer Vision (ICCV), pp. 2201–2208, September 2009
11. Huang, K.-Q., Wang, Q., Wu, Z.-Y.: Natural color image enhancement and evaluation algorithm based on human visual system. In: Computer Vision and Image Understanding, pp. 52–63 (2006). http://www.elsevier.com/locate/cviu

Local Disparity Vector Derivation Scheme in 3D-AVS2

Qi Mao$^{(\boxtimes)}$, Shanshe Wang, and Siwei Ma

Institute of Digital Media, Peking University, Beijing, China
qimao@pku.edu.cn

Abstract. 3D-AVS2 is the 3D extension of AVS2 (audio video coding standard 2), which is under the development of AVS Working Group. Besides including all efficient techniques in AVS2, it has developed extensive 3D coding tools consist of disparity compensated prediction and the inter-view motion information inheritance. In these inter-view techniques, disparity vector (DV) plays a critical role to eliminate inter-view redundancy. Global disparity vector (GDV) is first proposed as the DV derivation method in 3D-AVS2, which is calculated by averaging all the disparity vectors of 16 × 16 block in the latest previous coded frame. The prediction accuracy of GDV may be however limited by the lack of local adaptivity. Thus we propose the local disparity vector (LDV) and its improved sub-candidate local disparity vector (SCLDV) derivation scheme to make full use of local information. In addition, utilizing depth map to refine DV can further improve our derivation scheme. Experimental results show that the proposed SCLDV derivation method can provide 1.34% and 0.92% BD-rate saving in low delay P (LDP), and 1.00% and 0.73% BD-rate saving in random access (RA) for the compressed views and synthesized views compared with the GDV scheme, respectively. It also shows that our LDV scheme can be further improved by depth refinement.

Keywords: 3D-AVS2 · Disparity vector · Local disparity vector
Depth refinement

1 Introduction

Driven by the enormous development of three-dimensional (3D) video techniques and increasing popularity in 3D video content, 3D video services such as 3D television [1] and free viewpoint television [2] (FTV) become more and more popular. To better support various 3D video applications, the working group of China audio video coding standard [3] (AVS) begins to develop a 3D or multi-view video oriented coding standard. In 2014, the 3D Ad hoc Group is established to develop 3D-AVS2 standard on top of AVS2 [4], which aims to provide high coding efficiency for multi-view plus depth (MVD) video data and support high quality depth-based image rendering for auto-stereoscopic.

© Springer International Publishing AG 2017
Y. Zhao et al. (Eds.): ICIG 2017, Part II, LNCS 10667, pp. 286–298, 2017.
https://doi.org/10.1007/978-3-319-71589-6_26

Since all cameras capture the same scene simultaneously from different views, compared with conventional 2D video compression, eliminating the statistical redundancy among different views in the same instant, i.e., inter-view redundancy, is a considerable and fundamental problem in multi-view and three-dimensional (3D) video coding. To exploit the inter-view correlation, disparity vector (DV) is required to identify pixels of the same object in two different views to utilize texture or motion information in coded view for the current. Such inter-view techniques can be employed as new modes to further improve the compression efficiency.

Besides including all efficient coding tools in 2D video, 3D-AVS2 has developed extensive 3D coding tools consist of disparity compensated prediction (DCP) and the inter-view motion information inheritance. Since the accuracy of DV has direct impact on the efficacy of these inter-view techniques, how to efficiently derive an effective DV needs to be carefully explored.

In 3D-AVS2, global disparity vector [5] (GDV) is first proposed as the DV derivation method, which is calculated by averaging all the disparity vectors of 16×16 block in the latest previous coded frame. The global disparity vector exploits the global information and a constant DV is used for the whole picture, however, the prediction accuracy of GDV may be limited by the lack of local adaptivity. Hence, we propose a novel local disparity vector (LDV) [6] derivation scheme fully utilizing the neighbouring information to replace the GDV in 3D-AVS2. Then the improved versions of sub-candidate LDV (SCLDV) [7] and depth refinement of LDV [10] are also considered to further improve the accuracy, which have been adopted by MV-AVS2 in 59th AVS meeting [7] and 3D-AVS2 in 60th AVS meeting [10], respectively.

In this paper, the DV derivation schemes especially local disparity vector (LDV) derivation schemes in 3D-AVS2 is fully explained. The rest of this paper is organized as follows. In Sect. 2, the global disparity vector (GDV) scheme is introduced. The technical details of the proposed local disparity vector (LDV) and its improved versions are described in Sect. 3. The experimental results are presented and analysed in Sect. 4. At last, Sect. 4 concludes the paper.

2   Global Disparity Vector Derivation Scheme

In 3D-AVS2, the global disparity vector (GDV) [5] derivation scheme is proposed by considering the inter-similarity between the current frame with the frame that coded before.

More specifically, there are three prediction modes in one coded frame, as shown in Fig. 1, intra prediction, motion compensation prediction (MCP) and disparity compensation prediction (DCP). If the block is disparity compensated, the disparity vector can be acquired. It is assumed that the disparity vectors are typically highly correlated in temporary direction. When coding the current frame, the previously coded frame's disparity vectors information can be used to derive current frame's disparity vector.

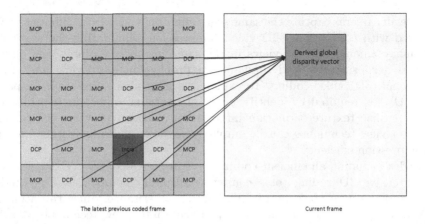

Fig. 1. Global disparity vector derivation scheme.

There are many ways to derive the global disparity vector (GDV) in current frame. In 3D-AVS2 standard, GDV [5] is calculated by averaging all disparity vectors of block 16×16 in the latest previous coded frame, performed as formula 1.

$$GDV = \frac{1}{N} \sum_{DV_i \in \Omega} DV_i, \tag{1}$$

where Ω indicates the set of all DVs in the 16×16 blocks of latest previously coded frame, and N is size of Ω.

It is a two dimensional vector that explicitly transmitted for each texture picture and all blocks in the same picture share this vector. The benefit of GDV lies in low coding complexity and it replaces zero-dv in following inter-view techniques in 3D-AVS2:

- The predictor of disparity vector (PDV) in inter prediction mode: When reference picture is an interview reference in inter prediction and the predictor of the disparity vector (PDV) is zero vector, replace the PDV with GDV.
- Inter-view motion information inheritance techniques: GDV instead of the zero vector is used to find a corresponding block in the reference view so that motion information of this block can be inherited by the current block.

3   Local Disparity Vector (LDV) Derivation Scheme

The GDV can be derived with low coding complexity and performs better than zero-disparity vector, however, the GDV exploits the global information and a constant DV is used for the whole picture. The prediction accuracy of GDV may be limited by the lack of local adaptivity. In order to further improve the coding efficiency of 3D-AVS2, a more accurate DV which adapts to the content is strongly desired.

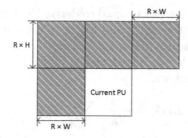

Fig. 2. Local-adapted neighboring region (LANR).

Algorithm 1. Algorithm of Local Disparity Vector (LDV) Derivation Based on LANR

Input:
- R_M : Given Maximum R
- **GDV** : Global Disparity Vector

Output:
- **LDV** : Local Disparity Vector

Initialization:
- **LDV** = 0
- **LDV**$_S$ = 0
- $R = 1$

while $(R \leq R_M)$ and (**LDV**== 0) **do**
  Find Ω_R in LANR;
  if Ω_R exists **then**
    for $DV_i \in \Omega_R$ **do**
      $\lfloor$ **LDV**$_S$=**LDV**$_S$+**DV**$_i$;
    $\lfloor$ **LDV**=**LDV**$_S$/N_R;
  $\lfloor$ $R = R + 1$;
if **LDV**== 0 **then**
  $\lfloor$ **LDV**=**GDV**;
return **LDV**;

3.1 LDV Derivation Based on LANR

Disparity vectors also present high spatial correlations, it can be easily inferred that if a block is coded by inter-view prediction, its neighboring blocks also coded by inter-view prediction may have a similar disparity vector. Based on this, we propose an improved local disparity vector [6] (LDV), where the local-adapted neighboring region (LANR) is defined to explore the content-based adaptivity.

As shown in Fig. 2, the LANR of current prediction unit (PU) is defined as its left, above left, above and above right blocks, which are already compressed and their coding information can be used to derive the DV for current PU. In the Fig. 2, W and H indicate the width and height of current PU. The parameter R is utilized to adaptively adjust the range of LANR.

Subsequently, the LDV can be calculated by averaging all the DVs of 4×4 blocks in the LANR as follows,

$$LDV = \frac{1}{N_R} \sum_{DV_i \in \Omega_R} DV_i, \tag{2}$$

where Ω_R indicates the set of all DVs in the LANR given R, and N_R is size of Ω_R.

Furthermore, the range of LANR can adaptively expand for maximum information utilization. The algorithm of the proposed method is shown in Algorithm 1. Firstly we examine whether a non-zero LDV is derived by initializing $R = 1$. If not, R would be continually increased by a step of 1 to expand the LANR until a non-zero LDV is acquired or the R reaches the maximum fixed R_M. R_M is a parameter which can be defined by users in configuration file and suggested to be 4 in 3D-AVS2. Finally, if the derived LDV is non-zero, it will replace the GDV in 3D-AVS2.

3.2 Sub-candidate LDV (SCLDV) Derivation Scheme

Averaging all DVs in the whole neighboring region can be inaccuracy when the parameter R becomes larger. In order to fully use the statistical similarity, the neighboring region has been expanded and divided into five spatial neighbouring candidate region. We introduce them as the sub-candidate local-adapted neighboring regions [7] (SCLANR), which include the left ($a1$), above left ($b1$), above

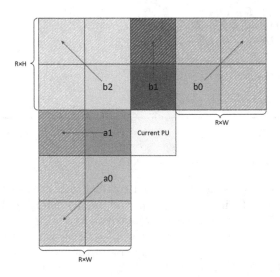

Fig. 3. Sub-candidate local-adapted neighboring region (SCLANR)

Algorithm 2. Algorithm of Local Disparity Vector (LDV) Derivation Based on SCLANR

Input:

- R_M : Given Maximum R
- GDV : Global Disparity Vector

Output:

- LDV : Local Disparity Vector

Initialization:

- $LDV_R = 0$
- $LDV_S = 0$
- $R = 1$

while $(R \leq R_M)$ and $(LDV == 0)$ **do**

    Search SCLANR one by one in defined order and Find Ω_R;

    if Ω_R exists **then**

        for $DV_i \in \Omega_R$ **do**

            $LDV_S = LDV_S + DV_i$;

        $LDV = LDV_S / N_R$;

    $R = R + 1$;

if $LDV == 0$ **then**

    $LDV = GDV$;

return LDV;

($b2$), above right ($b0$) and below left ($a0$) coded blocks of current prediction unit (PU), as shown in Fig. 3. W and H also indicate the width and height of current PU. The parameter R is utilized to adaptively adjust the range of SCLANR.

Unlike deriving LDV using all the neighboring regions, we advance a priority search method where each candidate region is checked in a certain defined order to decide whether the dvs are derived or not within it. If dvs can be acquired in one candidate region, the search processing will terminate. Otherwise, the five candidate areas are automatically expanded by increasing the parameter R to continue searching until the dvs are found or the maximum area size is reached. And all the dvs we find in this candidate region are averaged to derive the final LDV, presented as formula 3.

$$LDV = \frac{1}{N_R} \sum_{DV_i \in \Omega_{SC_R}} DV_i, \tag{3}$$

where Ω_{SC_R} indicates the set of all DVs in one sub-candidate local-adapted region (SCLANR) given R, and N_R is size of Ω_{SC_R}.

The searching-order can be arranged in many ways. In 3D-AVS2, the scheme of $a1$, $b1$, $b2$, $b0$, $a0$ is employed. The algorithm is similar with Algorithm 1, but we only averaging the dvs in one candidate region, as shown in Algorithm 2. In this way, the non-zero sub-candidate LDV (SCLDV) is derived and it will replace GDV in all inter-view techniques such as inter-view motion information inheritance.

3.3 Depth Refinement of LDV

Utilizing depth information, our proposed LDV derivation scheme can be further improved. In the current multi-view or three-dimensional (3D) system, 1D linear camera arrangement scenario is most commonly used, as shown in Fig. 4. Depth to disparity mapping can be defined as formula 4 in which f means focal length of two cameras, c means the translation between two cameras, d means the depth value of current point, and the function DV_{Depth} means depth to DV conversion.

$$DV_{Depth}(d) = \frac{f \cdot c}{d}.$$

(4)

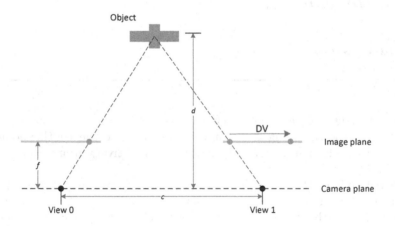

Fig. 4. Depth to disparity vector mapping in 1D linear camera arrangement

In 3D-AVS2, texture layer is coded before depth layer for each view. The true depth value d is not available yet when coding current texture block, thus an estimated depth value derived from the corresponding depth picture of the reference view is required in formula 4 to obtain the DV. Depth oriented neighbouring block based disparity vector [8] (DoNBDV) is proposed in 3D-HEVC by using the derived NBDV to locate the corresponding depth block in the reference view. Converting the max depth of four corners in derived depth block into refined disparity can further improve the accuracy of NBDV. Motivated by this, the derived LDV in Sect. 3.2 can also be used to locate the depth block in base view and refined [9,10] by utilizing the depth map information.

In details, for current block B in the current picture, first employing the derived LDV locates the depth block DB_1 in the corresponding depth picture of the reference view shown in Fig. 5. The maximum value of four corners of DB_1 is considered as the estimated depth to derive the DV (donated as DV_1) as shown in formula 5.

$$DV_1 = DV_{Depth}(dm_1),\tag{5}$$

dm_1 is the max value of four corners of DB_1. Then the depth refinement of LDV is derived.

The performance can be promoted by more steps refinement using depth map. Take two-step depth refinement as an example, after deriving the one-step depth refinement dv DV_1, another depth block DB_2 is re-located in the corresponding depth picture of reference view by DV_1 as shown in Fig. 5. And we use the maximum value of four corner of DB_2 to derive the two-step depth refinement of LDV (denoted as DV_2) as shown in formula 6 where dm_2 is the max value of four corners of DB_2.

$$DV_2 = DV_{Depth}(dm_2).\tag{6}$$

The derived depth-refined LDV can enhance the accuracy of DV and be applyed in techniques such as the disparity vector predictor, inter-view motion information inheritance to further improve the compression efficiency of 3D-AVS2.

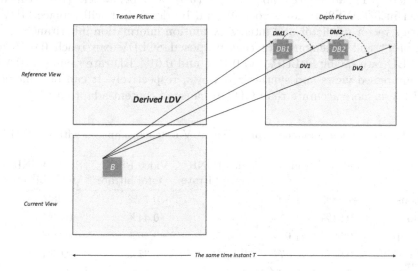

Fig. 5. One step refinement derives DV_1, then using DV_1 can re-derive DV_2.

4 Experimental Results

To verify the efficiency of our proposed LDV derivation schemes, all of them have been implemented on RFD8.0 [11], the latest reference software of 3D-AVS2. And it is tested strictly in accordance with the common test conditions [12] of 3D-AVS2, where the low delay P (LDP) and random access (RA) configurations are used for simulation.

The commonly used BD-rate index [13] is utilized for comparing the performance of two different schemes. A negative value of the BD-rate indicates coding gains over the anchor. In following tables, the first and second column represent the BD-rate performance considering Y-PSNR of view 1 and 2 (dependent view). The third and fourth column represent the BD-rate performance considering Y-PSNR of the coded texture views over the bitrates of texture data and over the bitrates of texture data and depth data. The last column represents the BD-rate performance considering Y-PSNR of the synthesized texture views over the bitrates of texture data and depth data.

It should be noted that since GDV and SCLDV have been involved in RFD8.0. In Sect. 4.1, we close SCLDV and set GDV as anchor. In Sect. 4.2, the anchor is RFD8.0 with GDV and SCLDV opening.

4.1 Results of Sub-candidate LDV (SCLDV) Derivation

In this section, LDV derived in SCLANR [7] in Sect. 3.2 is tested. R_M is defined in suggested value 4. The searching order of candidate region is the left ($a1$), above left ($b1$), above($b2$), above right ($b0$), and below left ($a0$), which is advised in 3D-AVS2. If non-zero LDV can be derived, it will replace GDV in disparity vector predictor and inter-view motion information inheritance.

Tables 1 and 2 demonstrate that proposed SCLDV can reach 0.61% and 0.37% BD-rate saving in LDP, and 0.73% and 0.61% BD-rate saving in RA for the compressed views and synthesized views, respectively. It can be concluded that LDV is more accurate than GDV because of content-adaptivity.

Table 1. BD-rate performance of proposed LDV scheme compared with GDV (LDP)

Sequence	Video1	Video2	Video PSNR \video bitrate	Video PSNR \total bitrate	Synth PSNR \total bitrate
Balloons	−1.88%	−1.50%	−0.86%	−0.78%	−0.48%
Kendo	−0.91%	−1.16%	−0.52%	−0.44%	−0.30%
Newspaper	−0.99%	−1.01%	−0.51%	−0.46%	−0.29%
PoznanHall	−0.92%	−0.57%	−0.50%	−0.37%	−0.07%
PoznanStreet	−2.47%	−2.32%	−1.04%	−0.97%	−0.70%
1024 × 768	−1.26%	−1.22%	−0.63%	−0.56%	−0.36%
1920 × 1088	−1.69%	−1.44%	−0.77%	−0.67%	−0.39%
Average	−1.44%	−1.31%	−0.69%	−0.61%	−0.37%

4.2 Results of Depth Refinement of LDV

Depth map can be utilized to further improve the DV accuracy, depth refinement of SCLDV in this section is tested. RFD8.0 is the anchor, where GDV and SCLDV have already involved. Furthermore, we consider both one step and second step refinement.

Tables 3 and 4 illustrate that one step depth-based refinement can reach 1.34% and 0.92% BD-rate saving in LDP, and 1.00% and 0.73% BD-rate saving in RA for the compressed views and synthesized views, respectively. Tables 5 and 6 show that two step depth-based refinement can reach 1.37% and 0.97% BD-rate saving in LDP, and 1.05% and 0.78% BD-rate saving in RA for the compressed views and synthesized views, respectively.

From the results above, it can be confirmed that depth information does help to improve the accuracy of LDV and brings a appealing gain. It can also be noticed that more steps of depth refinement are employed, the better the performance improvements obtained. However, these improvements taper off as

Table 2. BD-rate performance of proposed LDV scheme compared with GDV (RA)

Sequence	Video1	Video2	Video PSNR \video bitrate	Video PSNR \total bitrate	Synth PSNR \total bitrate
Balloons	−2.52%	−2.61%	−0.98%	−0.86%	−0.74%
Kendo	−2.42%	−1.82%	−0.83%	−0.63%	−0.57%
Newspaper	−2.27%	−2.29%	−0.82%	−0.68%	−0.73%
PoznanHall	−2.97%	−1.55%	−0.97%	−0.84%	−0.56%
PoznanStreet	−1.91%	−2.22%	−0.70%	−0.66%	−0.44%
1024 × 768	−2.40%	−2.24%	−0.88%	−0.72%	−0.68%
1920 × 1088	−2.44%	−1.88%	−0.84%	−0.75%	−0.50%
Average	**−2.42%**	**−2.10%**	**−0.86%**	**−0.73%**	**−0.61%**

Table 3. BD-rate performance of one-step depth-based refinement compared with RFD 8.0 (LDP)

Sequence	Video1	Video2	Video PSNR \video bitrate	Video PSNR \total bitrate	Synth PSNR \total bitrate
Balloons	−4.92%	−6.02%	−2.56%	−2.12%	−1.68%
Kendo	−2.20%	−2.39%	−1.11%	−0.93%	−0.54%
Newspaper	−2.31%	−2.86%	−1.25%	−1.07%	0.72%
PoznanHall	−3.34%	−1.92%	−1.34%	−1.24%	−0.88%
PoznanStreet	−3.12%	−2.77%	−1.44%	−1.35%	−0.78%
1024 × 768	−3.14%	−3.76%	−1.64%	−1.37%	−0.98%
1920 × 1088	−3.23%	−2.34%	−1.39%	−1.30%	−0.83%
Average	**−3.18%**	**−3.19%**	**−1.54%**	**−1.34%**	**−0.92%**

Table 4. BD-rate performance of one-step depth-based refinement compared with RFD 8.0 (RA)

Sequence	Video1	Video2	Video PSNR \video bitrate	Video PSNR \total bitrate	Synth PSNR \total bitrate
Balloons	−3.62%	−3.95%	−1.54%	−1.32%	−1.04%
Kendo	−2.96%	−2.65%	−1.18%	−1.02%	−0.66%
Newspaper	−2.01%	−3.00%	−0.95%	−0.83%	0.65%
PoznanHall	−3.78%	−2.20%	−1.31%	−1.19%	−0.82%
PoznanStreet	−1.85%	−1.85%	−0.66%	−0.63%	−0.46%
1024 × 768	−2.86%	−3.20%	−1.22%	−1.06%	−0.78%
1920 × 1088	−2.82%	−2.03%	−0.99%	−0.91%	−0.64%
Average	**−2.84%**	**−2.73%**	**−1.13%**	**−1.00%**	**−0.73%**

Table 5. BD-rate performance of two-step depth-based refinement compared with RFD 8.0 (LDP)

Sequence	Video1	Video2	Video PSNR \video bitrate	Video PSNR \total bitrate	Synth PSNR \total bitrate
Balloons	−5.01%	−5.90%	−2.54%	−2.12%	−1.75%
Kendo	−2.19%	−2.41%	−1.12%	−0.94%	−0.62%
Newspaper	−2.30%	−3.26%	−1.33%	−1.13%	0.94%
PoznanHall	−3.70%	−2.37%	−1.56%	−1.41%	−0.67%
PoznanStreet	−2.87%	−2.80%	−1.35%	−1.24%	−0.84%
1024 × 768	−3.17%	−3.86%	−1.66%	−1.40%	−1.11%
1920 × 1088	−3.29%	−2.58%	−1.46%	−1.33%	−0.75%
Average	**−3.22%**	**−3.35%**	**−1.58%**	**−1.37%**	**−0.97%**

Table 6. BD-rate performance of two-step depth-based refinement compared with RFD 8.0 (RA)

Sequence	Video1	Video2	Video PSNR \video bitrate	Video PSNR \total bitrate	Synth PSNR \total bitrate
Balloons	−3.74%	−4.21%	−1.64%	−1.41%	−1.11%
Kendo	−2.93%	−2.97%	−1.25%	−1.02%	−0.66%
Newspaper	−2.47%	−3.55%	−1.14%	−0.98%	0.75%
PoznanHall	−4.02%	−2.14%	−1.35%	−1.18%	−0.78%
PoznanStreet	−1.89%	−1.80%	−0.65%	−0.61%	−0.44%
1024 × 768	−3.05%	−3.58%	−1.34%	−1.15%	−0.90%
1920 × 1088	−2.95%	−1.97%	−1.00%	−0.89%	−0.61%
Average	**−3.01%**	**−2.93%**	**−1.21%**	**−1.05%**	**−0.78%**

more steps are used, which can be easily inferred that the DV may be accurate enough with ample depth refinement.

5   Conclusion

In this paper, we have discussed different disparity vector derivation schemes in 3D-AVS2. Disparity vector plays a fundamental and crucial role in all inter-view techniques, how to derive an efficient DV is essential. Global disparity vector (GDV) can be derived with low coding complexity, the prediction accuracy of GDV may be however limited by the lack of local adaptivity. Therefore, we propose the local disparity vector (LDV) to fully utilize local information and further put forward sub-candidate local disparity vector (SCLDV) to achieve higher accuracy. Depth value can be converted into disparity vector using camera parameters. Derived local disparity vector (LDV) can locate the corresponding depth block in reference view to obtain estimated depth value to refine itself. The experimental results show that proposed LDV performs better than GDV with 0.61% and 0.37% BD-rate saving in low delay P configuration, 0.73% and 0.61% BD-rate saving in random access configuration for the compressed vies and synthesized views, respectively. It can be further improved by depth refinement and more steps of refinement can achieve better results.

Acknowledgement. This research was supported by grants from NVIDIA and the NVIDIA DGX-1 AI Supercomputer.

References

1. Fehn, C., Cooke, E., Schreer, O., Kauff, P.: 3D analysis and image-based rendering for immersive TV applications. Sig. Process. Image Commun. **17**(9), 705–715 (2002)
2. Tanimoto, M.: Overview of free viewpoint television. Sig. Process. Image Commun. **21**(6), 454–461 (2006)
3. Fan, L., Ma, S., Wu, F.: Overview of AVS video standard. In: 2004 IEEE International Conference on Multimedia and Expo (ICME), Taipei, Taiwan, pp. 423–426. IEEE Press (2004)
4. AVS Workgroup: Information Technology - Advanced Media Coding Part2: Video 3D Extension WD, AVS Doc. AVS-M2245 (2015)
5. Ma, J., Zhang, Y., Zhang, N., Fan, X., Zhao, D.: An effective method for obtaining disparity vector. In: Document M3582. 51st AVS Meeting, Fuzhou, China (2014)
6. Mao, Q., Wang, S., Su, J., Zhang, X., Zhang, X., Ma, S.: A local-adapted disparity vector derivation scheme for 3D-AVS. In: 2016 Visual Communications and Image Processing (VCIP), Chengdu, pp. 1–4. IEEE Press (2016)
7. Mao, Q., Su, J., Cui, J., Wang, S., Luo, F., Ma, S.: CE: a local-adapted disparity vector derivation scheme. In: Document M4072. 59th AVS Meeting, Haikou, China (2016)
8. Chang, Y.-L., Wu, C.-L., Tsai, Y.-P., Lei, S.: CE1.h: Depth-Oriented Neighboring Block Disparity Vector (DoNBDV) With Virtual Depth Retrieval. In: Document JCT3V-C0131. The Third JCT-3V Meetings, Geneva, Switzerland (2013)
9. Zhang, J., Chen, J., Lee, J.Y., Park, M.W.: Depth based two-step disparity vector derivation for AVS2-3D. In: 2016 Visual Communications and Image Processing (VCIP), Chengdu, pp. 1–4. IEEE Press (2016)

10. Mao, Q., Su, J., Cui, J., Wang, S., Luo, F., Ma, S.: CE: a local-adapted disparity vector derivation scheme. In: Document M4125. 60th AVS Meeting, Beijing, China (2017)
11. Wang, S.: AVS2-P2-3D: Describe of the RFD 8.0 platform. In: Document N2385. 59th AVS Meeting, Haikou, China (2017)
12. Wang, S.: AVS2-P2-3D: RFD Common Test Condition and Software reference configuration. In: Document N2247. 55th AVS Meeting, Beijing, China (2015)
13. Bjontegaard, G.: Calculation of average PSNR differences between RD-curves. In: Document VCEG-M33 ITU-T Q6/16, Austin, TX, USA (2001)

A Feature-Based Coding Algorithm for Face Image

Henan Li[1], Shigang Wang[1], Yan Zhao[1(✉)], Chuxi Yang[1],
and Aobo Wang[2]

[1] College of Communication Engineering,
Jilin University, Changchun 130012, China
zhao_y@Jlu.edu.cn
[2] Department of Communication and Signal Processing,
University of Maryland-College Park, College Park 20740, USA

Abstract. Face images have great significance in machine vision field especially like face recognition and tracking. Considering the similarity of face images, this paper proposes a face image coding scheme based on Scale Invariant Feature Transform (SIFT) descriptor. The SIFT descriptor, which is a kind of local feature descriptor, characterizes an image region invariant to scale and rotation. The facial features are combined with the SIFT descriptor to make use of the external image contents to improve the coding efficiency in this paper. We segment an image into certain regions according to the facial features and get SIFT features in these regions. Then the SIFT features are used to find the corresponding patches from a large-scale face image database. Experimental results show that the proposed image coding method provides a better visual quality of reconstructed images than the intra-frame coding in HEVC under the similar compression ratio.

Keywords: SIFT · Face image compression · Feature descriptor

1 Introduction

Some offices and organizations (e.g. customs, police office, institution for academic research) need a large-scale face image database for research or logging information. Face image database is different from other because of the similarity between facial features. If the database is large enough, we can always find the very similar facial features in it [1]. When transmitting such large amount of face images by using conventional image coding scheme like JPEG which compresses images pixel by pixel, it will waste precious power and network bandwidth. Therefore if the similarity between different face images can be used, the coding efficiency could be improved.

Conventional image or video coding schemes (e.g. JPEG [2], AVC/H.264 [3], HEVC [4]) only utilize the information from intra frame and hardly consider the external images. JPEG uses DCT (Discrete Cosine Transform), quantization, run–length encoding and entropy encoding. Intra frame compression takes advantage of the spatial correlation between neighbor macro-blocks. So when encode an image via conventional coding schemes, we will find it may not so appropriate for the face image.

© Springer International Publishing AG 2017
Y. Zhao et al. (Eds.): ICIG 2017, Part II, LNCS 10667, pp. 299–309, 2017.
https://doi.org/10.1007/978-3-319-71589-6_27

One of the main reasons is the conventional coding scheme does not search for the highly correlated images in database. The other reason is it hardly utilizes the facial features in the face images.

Recent researches on image processing have made it clear how to reconstruct an image from the large-scale image database. Weinzaepfel et al. are the first to propose that we can use the local SIFT descriptors to reconstruct images [1]. For getting a visually pleasing result, Huanjing Yue et al. propose the cloud-based image coding [5]. Their scheme no longer compressed image by utilizing only the correlation between pixels from the input image. They extract the local features from image and encode the features. This scheme shows that the feature-based coding is not only feasible, but also efficient. However, SIFT descriptors extracted from the full image are too many and SIFT descriptors which are only extracted from certain regions of details will result in fewer matched regions from external images.

To solve the above problems, we proposed a face image coding method based on local feature descriptors. In our scheme, the regions of facial features along with SIFT descriptors are extracted from the input image. They are both to find the most similar patches and calculate the homographic matrixes between the patches and the input image. There is a down-sampled image of the original face image to be generated at the same time. This down-sampled image is encoded and decoded by conventional coding scheme then it is up-sampled to be a target for the matched patches to patch on. Finally a residual image of the input image and the local reconstruction is generated.

The rest of this paper is organized as follows. Section 2 gives a brief overview of the related work. Section 3 shows and discusses the frameworks of the feature-based face image encoder and decoder. Section 4 presents and analyzes the experimental results. Finally, Sect. 5 concludes this paper and discusses the future work.

2 Related Work

2.1 Local Feature Descriptor

SIFT descriptor, proposed by Lowe in [6], is one of the most popular local feature descriptors. SIFT descriptor provides a solution which characterizes an image region invariantly to the scale, rotation, perspective and luminance. So it is often used to perform robust matching between different views of an object. In this paper, we use SIFT descriptor to describe the local feature.

When extracting SIFT descriptors from an image I, we denote r_i as one of the SIFT descriptors associated with a region.

$$r_i = \{v_i, x_i, s_i, o_i\} \tag{1}$$

where v_i is a 128-dimension vector which represents the gradients of the local image region around the key-point x_i, and $x_i = (x_i, y_i)$, s_i and o_i represent the coordinate, scale and dominant gradient orientation of the key-point, respectively.

To generate SIFT descriptors, we have to firstly build the scale space. The locations of key-points are defined as maxima and minima from difference of Gaussians function applied in scale space to a series of smoothed and resampled images. Therefore, SIFT descriptor characterizes an image region invariant to scale and rotation

2.2 Interest Region Location

In a face image, there are a lot of details in the regions of facial features like eyes, mouth, ears, and so on. To improve the accuracy of matching, we divide the whole SIFT descriptors into certain clusters so that the SIFT descriptors from one region (like eyes) of an image will match the same region (eyes) in face image from database. Therefore, the regions with facial features are regarded as the interest regions.

To complete the above idea, we have to recognize face region and the facial features. There are many organizations such as CMU and MIT which are working on face recognition [7]. Active Shape Models (ASM) and Active Appearance Models (AAM) based on Point Distribution Models (PDM) proposed by Cootes et al. are the typical techniques for face recognition [8, 9]. There are also some methods based on the statistical features in image like Principal Component Analysis (PCA) [10], Artificial Neural Network (ANN) [11], Support Vector Machine (SVM) [12], AdaBoost [13], and so on. Among all the methods, AdaBoost has a wonderful performance of recognizing speed and accuracy. Therefore, the Haar-like features based on AdaBoost are used to recognize the facial features in our paper [14, 15].

3 Feature-Based Face Image Compression

The encoder and decoder of the proposed feature-based face image compression scheme are shown in Figs. 1 and 2.

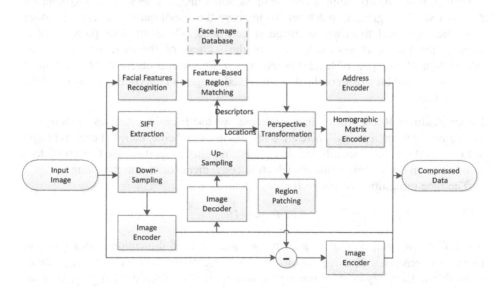

Fig. 1. The block diagram of the proposed feature-based face image encoder

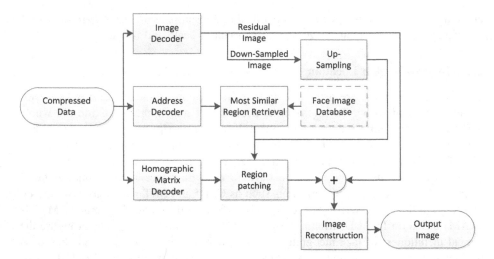

Fig. 2. The block diagram of the proposed feature-based face image decoder.

3.1 Encoder

On the encoder side, the regions of facial features are recognized in the original image firstly. Secondly, the SIFT descriptors are extracted from the feature regions and used to find the most similar regions from the face image database. Then, the homo-graphic matrix is calculated between the feature regions of the input image and the corresponding feature regions of the matched image. Thirdly, the down-sampled image of the input face image is encoded and decoded by conventional image coding scheme. After that, it will be up-sampled and the up-sampled image is set as a back-ground for the most similar regions to patch on. To improve the visual quality, a residual image from the input and the patched image is generated. There are four parts together forming the final compression bit-stream: the address of the matched region, the information of four pair of feature points which are used to obtain the homographic matrix, the coded bit stream of the down-sampled image and the coded bit stream of the residual image.

Facial Features Recognition. In our scheme, we use Haar-like features to recognize the regions of facial features. There are 8 regions in our scheme: hair, left eye, right eye, left ear, right ear, nose, mouth and neck. Every region has its database (set up by face recognition in our current solution) which is convenient for region matching.

The face recognition of image $I(x, y)$ is defined as

$$P_i = L(I) \tag{2}$$

where $P_i = \{p_h, p_{leye}, p_{reye}, p_{lear}, p_{rear}, p_{no}, p_m, p_{ne}\}$ is an 8-dimention vector that represents the positions of 8 regions and $L(\cdot)$ represents the process of facial features recognition. Each segment of the region is a rectangle. Take the hair region as an example. p_h is its position and $p_h = \{(x_{h1}, y_{h1}), (x_{h2}, y_{h2})\}$ where (x_{h1}, y_{h1}) is the top left corner of this region and (x_{h2}, y_{h2}) is the bottom right corner. The 8 positions got by facial feature recognition will play an important role in the process of region matching.

Local Descriptors Extraction and Matching. According to the above introduction, we adopt SIFT descriptors in this process. In our scheme, the SIFT descriptors used in matching module come from the recognized regions of input image I and all the external database images. Let R denote the set of SIFT descriptors and C denote the external face image database. According to (1), $r_j = \{v_j, x_j, s_j, o_j\}, (j \in C)$ is one of the SIFT descriptors associated with a region of one face image in database. The sets of the SIFT descriptors for the input image and the external image are denoted as R_I and R_J $(r_i \in R_I, r_j \in R_J)$.

For each SIFT descriptor r_i, its matching SIFT descriptor r_m in R_C is retrieved if the condition of distance ratio is satisfied. We define the ratio between the Euclidean distances of v_{m1} and v_{m2} is the distance ratio, where v_{m1} and v_{m2} are the 128-dimension vectors of the nearest point and the second nearest point away the key-point. Let α denotes the distance ratio, then

$$\alpha = \frac{\sqrt{\sum_{k=0}^{128}(v_{m1}(k) - v_i(k))^2}}{\sqrt{\sum_{k=0}^{128}(v_{m2}(k) - v_i(k))^2}} \tag{3}$$

$0.4 < \alpha < 0.6$ is generally considered the satisfied range. We set α as 0.49 in our scheme. If $\alpha < 0.49$, the pair of SIFT descriptors is considered matching with each other. In general cases, the set of descriptors got in this way still have a number of wrong matching. Therefore, the wrong matching pairs are discarded by using RAN-SAC [16]. Then the remaining pairs of SIFT descriptors are considered as the correct matching pairs.

We define the most similar patch from the face image database is the one which gets the maximum correct matching pairs. After the extraction and matching process for local descriptors, the path of the most similar patch along with the number of its type is encoded by address value encoder. We adopt entropy encoding to encode the address value. The locations $x(x, y)$ in SIFT descriptors from the correct matching pairs between the input image and the most similar one are used in the process of region stitch.

Local Reconstruction and Residual Generation. According to the above introduction, the background of the local reconstructed image is defined as a sub-sampled version I' of the input image. So

$$I' = D(E(I)) \tag{4}$$

where $D(\cdot)$ is the decoding process and $E(\cdot)$ is the encoding process of the local reconstructed image. The down-sampling ratio is 4 in our scheme. Then the cost of encoding bit-stream will be greatly reduced, and the quality of the reconstructed image will still be pretty good. In the current research of image compression, JPEG2000 and HEVC can perform wonderfully in image encoding. The down-sampled image is encoded using the intra coding scheme of HEVC.

According to the above section, the most similar region and the locations of the correct matching pairs are used in the process of region stitch. Firstly, the sub-sampled image I' is set as the target for the most similar regions to stitch on. Secondly, every matched patch from database subscribes the average gray value of it and adds the average gray value of the matched region in original image. The 8 average gray values are encoded by the entropy coding in the address encoder. Thirdly, the most similar regions will be stitched by perspective transform. The transformations H of the most similar regions are calculated by the locations $x(x, y)$ of the matched point-pairs and estimated by RANSAC. H is a 3×3 matrix and will be encoded by entropy encoding at the homographic matrix encoder. Finally, the local reconstructed image is generated in the encoder for obtaining the following residual image.

To improve the visual quality of the reconstructed image in the decoder, we transmit a residual to the decoder. This residual is an image which is the difference between the input image and the local reconstructed image.

3.2 Decoder

On the decoder side, the compressed bit-stream is decoded into three groups. The conventional image decoder, which is HEVC in our scheme, decompresses the down-sample image and the residual image. The address of the most similar region is from the address decoder and the homographic matrix of the perspective transform between the matched region and the input image is decoded by the homographic matrix decoder. The matrix is used to patch the most similar region on the up-sampled image. Finally, the patched image and the decompressed residual image are combined to reconstruct the high-quality image.

Image Decoder, Address and Homographic Matrix Decoder. We adopt the HEVC intra decoding scheme in image decoder. The sub-sampled image and the residual image are decoded after intra decoding. The address decoder and the homographic matrix decoder use the decoding scheme corresponding to the encoder. When the addresses of the most similar patches are decoded, the most similar patch will be found in the face image database by these pieces of information. And the decoded homographic matrixes are used to patch the most similar patches on the up-sampled image.

Region Retrieval and Patching. According to the type of the most similar region, database will be selected. Then if we have the address of the matched region, we will find the patch of the most similar region in the database. The process of up-sampling is the same module as that in encoder. Clearly the up-sampling ratio is 4. Then there will be 8 patches found to patch on the up-sampled image. The homographic matrixes are used to set up the perspective transform between the 8 patches and the original image. Finally, the 8 most similar patches are patched on the up-sampled image by perspective transformation.

Image Reconstruction. The final reconstruction is a summation image of the patched un-sampled image and the decoded residual image.

All the modules before image reconstruction are processing the gray image of the original one. The color information is extracted from the sub-sampled image. This process is completed based on the YUV color space.

4   Experimental Results and Analyses

We use Utrecht ECVP from the 2D face sets of Psychological Image Collection at Stirling (PICS) dataset for our experiments in this paper [17]. There are 131 images in total and the resolution of every image is 900×1200 pixels. We select 5 images as input images and the rest 126 images are used as a face image database. The input images are denoted from "1" to "5" in this paper. HEVC is one of the best coding standards now so we select the intra-frame coding in HEVC to compare with our scheme.

4.1   Size and Compression Ratio

In our proposed scheme, the compressed data consists of 4 parts: the address, the homographic matrixes of perspective transformation between the input image and the matched patches, down-sampled image, residual image. We try to keep the size and compression ratio of our proposed scheme and HEVC to be nearly the same. So the quantization step of HEVC compression for down-sampled image is set as 32–35 and for residual image is set as 33–36 and for original image is set as 38–43.

The experimental results of size and compression ratio are listed in Table 1. As we see, the average size of our proposed scheme is slightly smaller and the compression ratio is a little bit higher than HEVC. There are 80% images get the higher compression ratio in our proposed scheme.

Table 1. Size and compression ratio for HEVC and the proposed scheme.

Image number	HEVC		Proposed	
	Size (byte)	Ratio	Size (byte)	Ratio
1	3347	968.047206	3661	885.018847
2	4694	690.254367	4431	731.224103
3	3942	821.931507	3855	840.480934
4	4262	760.219146	4113	787.759300
5	3662	884.777171	3691	877.825522
Ave.	3981.4	813.797659	3950.2	820.225305

4.2   Visual Quality

For the 5 input images, we use Peak Signal to Noise Ratio (PSNR) and Structural Similarity Index (SSIM) as the visual quality. For the compression ratios listed in Table 1, their corresponding PSNR and SSIM of the reconstructed image are shown in Table 2. For example, when compression ratio of image "1" by HEVC is 968.047206, its corresponding PSNR and SSIM are 35.683951 and 0.9195 respectively.

Table 2. PSNR of gray image and SSIM of color image for HEVC and the proposed scheme (full image).

Image number	HEVC		Proposed	
	PSNR (dB)	SSIM	PSNR (dB)	SSIM
1	35.683951	0.9195	36.998547	0.9268
2	31.475868	0.8206	33.186162	0.8692
3	36.051083	0.9184	36.072498	0.9148
4	33.503461	0.9077	34.184705	0.9084
5	36.907650	0.9349	36.325349	0.9229
Ave.	34.7244026	0.90022	35.3534522	0.90842

The experimental results of visual quality are listed in Table 2 which calculates the full image. The average PSNR of gray image by our proposed scheme is 0.63 dB higher than HEVC and the average SSIM of color image by our proposed scheme is also a little bit higher.

According to Tables 1 and 2, when the average compression ratio of the results in our coding method is higher than HEVC, the corresponding average PSNR and SSIM of the results in our coding method are both higher than HEVC too.

The curves of PSNR and SSIM of image "1" are also shown in Figs. 3 and 4.

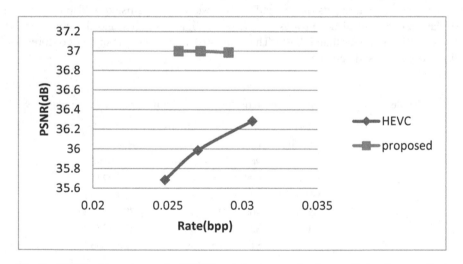

Fig. 3. PSNR of gray image for HEVC and the proposed scheme. (Color figure online)

According to Figs. 3 and 4, the curves of PSNR and SSIM in the proposed method are always higher than the visual quality in HEVC.

The experimental results of visual quality which are listed in Table 3 calculate only the face region. The average PSNR of gray image by our proposed scheme is 0.79 dB higher than HEVC and the average SSIM of color image by our proposed scheme is

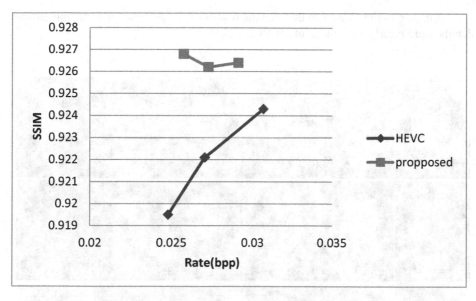

Fig. 4. SSIM of color image for HEVC and the proposed scheme. (Color figure online)

Table 3. PSNR of gray image and SSIM of color image for HEVC and the proposed scheme (the face region).

Image number	HEVC		Proposed	
	PSNR (dB)	SSIM	PSNR (dB)	SSIM
1	33.489484	0.8796	35.146772	0.9009
2	30.836050	0.8000	32.673850	0.8627
3	33.974071	0.8849	34.112579	0.8907
4	31.375075	0.8562	32.214286	0.8695
5	35.105115	0.9076	34.598943	0.8938
Ave.	32.955959	0.86566	33.749286	0.88352

0.018 higher. There are 80% reconstructed images getting better visual quality when the compression ratio is nearly the same. Because our coding scheme for face image is based on the facial features, the visual quality of face region improves more than that of full image. According to the experimental results, our coding scheme for face image is feasible.

The reconstructed results of image "2" are shown in Fig. 3. This group of results consists of three rows. In the first row, images from left to right are the color input image and the color results of HEVC and the proposed scheme, then the gray input image and the gray results of HEVC and the proposed scheme. The second row shows the results of face region indicated by the red rectangle. The third row shows the results of the details in a corresponding region indicated by yellow rectangle.

According to Fig. 5 we can find that the results of the proposed scheme present the details more clearly than those of HEVC.

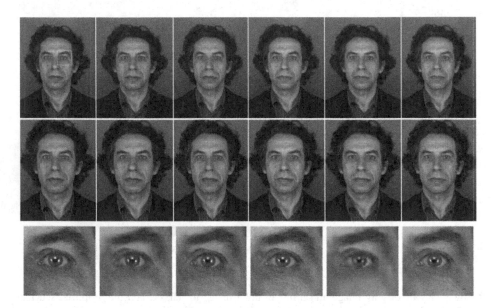

Fig. 5. The reconstructed results of image "2".

When the compression ratio of HEVC and our scheme are almost the same, the visual quality of our scheme is better and the details of using our scheme are presented more clearly.

5　Conclusion and Future Discussion

This paper proposes a novel face image coding scheme based on local feature descriptors. Experimental results show that our feature-based face image coding scheme provides a better visual quality of the reconstructed images than the intra-frame coding of HEVC when the compression rate is almost same. Even so, our scheme still has some processes to be improved. For example, we can use some seamless stitching methods like Poisson Seamless Cloning when stitch the matched patches on the sub-sampled image. We will improve our scheme and the reconstruction image quality in the future work.

Acknowledgement. This work was supported by the State Key Program of National Natural Science Foundation of China (61631009) and the Jilin province science and technology development project of China (20150204006GX).

References

1. Weinzaepfel, P., Jégou, H., Pérez, P.: Reconstructing an image from its local descriptors. In: IEEE Conference on Computer Vision and Pattern Recognition, pp. 337–344. IEEE Computer Society (2011)
2. Pennebaker, W.B., Mitchell, J.L.: JPEG Still Image Data Compression Standard. Van Nostrand Reinhold, New York (1992)
3. Wiegand, T., Sullivan, G.J., Bjontegaard, G., et al.: Overview of the H.264/AVC video coding standard. IEEE Trans. Circ. Syst. Video Technol. 13(7), 560–576 (2003)
4. Sullivan, G.J., Ohm, J.R.: Recent developments in standardization of high efficiency video coding (HEVC). In: Proceedings of SPIE, vol. 7798, no. 1, pp. 731–739 (2010)
5. Yue, H., Sun, X., Yang, J., et al.: Cloud-based image coding for mobile devices—toward thousands to one compression. IEEE Trans. Multimedia 15(4), 845–857 (2013)
6. Lowe, D.G.: Distincitive image features from scale-invariant keypoints. Int. J. Comput. Vis. 60(2), 91–110 (2004)
7. Yang, M.H., Kriegman, D.J., Ahuja, N.: Detecting faces in images: a survey. IEEE Trans. Pattern Anal. Mach. Intell. 24(1), 34–58 (2002)
8. Cootes, T.F., Taylor, C.J., Cooper, D.H., et al.: Active shape models-their training and application. Comput. Vis. Image Underst. 61(1), 38–59 (1995)
9. Cootes, T.F., Edwards, G.J., Taylor, C.J.: Active appearance models. IEEE Trans. Pattern Anal. Mach. Intell. 23(6), 681–685 (2001)
10. Wang, J., Yang, H.: Face detection based on template matching and 2DPCA algorithm. In: Image and Signal Processing (CISP 2008), pp. 575–579 (2008)
11. Rowley, H.A., Baluja, S., Kanade, T.: Neural network-based face detection. IEEE Trans. Pattern Anal. Mach. Intell. 20(1), 23–38 (1998)
12. Waring, C.A., Liu, X.: Face detection using spectral histograms and SVMs. IEEE Trans. Syst. Man Cybern. Part B Cybern. 35(3), 467–476 (2005)
13. Viola, P., Jones, M.J.: Robust real-time face detection. Int. J. Comput. Vis. 57(2), 137–154 (2004)
14. Viola, P., Jones, M.: Rapid object detection using a boosted cascade of simple features. In: Proceedings of the 2001 IEEE Computer Society Conference on Computer Vision and Pattern Recognition (CVPR 2001), vol. 1, pp. 511–518. IEEE (2001)
15. Lienhart, R., Maydt, J.: An extended set of haar-like features for rapid object detection. In: Proceedings of the International Conference on Image Processing, vol. 1, pp. 900–903. IEEE (2002)
16. Fischler, M.A., Bolles, R.C.: Random sample consensus: a paradigm for model fitting with applications to image analysis and automated cartography. Commun. ACM 24(6), 381–395 (1981)
17. 2D face sets. http://pics.psych.stir.ac.uk/2D_face_sets.htm

5G Multimedia Communications

Video Quality Assessment Based on the Improved LSTM Model

Qiuxia Bao[1], Ruochen Huang[1], and Xin Wei[1,2(✉)]

[1] Nanjing University of Posts and Telecommunications, Nanjing 210003, China
ml8351925305@163.com, huangruochen@outlook.com,
xwei@njupt.edu.cn
[2] National Engineering Research Center of Communications and Networking,
Nanjing University of Posts and Telecommunications, Nanjing, China

Abstract. With the development of computer and network technologies, video service and content will continue to dominate while comparing to all other applications. It is particularly important to build a real-time and effective video quality assessment system. Video content, network status, viewing environment and so on will affect the end user quality of experience (QoE). In this work, we evaluate the prediction accuracy and code running time of Support Vector Machine (SVM), Decision Tree (DT) and Long Short Term Memory (LSTM). Moreover, we try to further improve the prediction accuracy from two aspects. One is to introduce some new input features to change the characteristic parameters. The other is to combine the LSTM with traditional machine learning algorithms. Experimental results show that the QoE prediction accuracy can be improved with the increased characteristic parameters. It is worth mentioning that the prediction accuracy can be increased by 8% with the improved LSTM algorithm.

Keywords: Quality of experience (QoE) · Feature preprocessing
Decision tree · Long Short Term Memory (LSTM)

1 Introduction

With the development of multimedia technology, life becomes more rich and convenient. Compared with newspaper, radio and other one-way media, multimedia has a better information feedback channel and higher service experience. The 39th China Internet Development Statistics Report shows that the size of Chinese Internet users is about 711 million as of December 2016 and the number of new users throughout this year is 42.99 million [1]. Internet penetration rate is 53.2% in 2016, which is 50.3% in 2015. The Cisco report predicts that IP traffic will grow nearly three times than that of the current by 2020. Video service and content will continue to dominate. By 2020, Internet video will account for 79% of global Internet traffic, with a proportion of 63% in 2015 [2].

The market share of video traffic is growing. So for service providers and end users, the establishment of a real-time and effective video quality assessment system is particularly important. Initially the researchers use Quality of Service (QoS) to measure video quality. Evaluation indexes of QoS include network throughput, jitter, delay,

Y. Zhao et al. (Eds.): ICIG 2017, Part II, LNCS 10667, pp. 313–324, 2017.
https://doi.org/10.1007/978-3-319-71589-6_28

packet loss rate and other network layer parameters [3]. QoS mainly considers the distortion caused during the video transmission process. It can only reflect the impact of network technology, while ignoring the end user's subjective factors. Thus quality of experience (QoE) is proposed later defined as the overall consecutive quality of an application or service by ITU-T. It is commonly used to represent user's true perception [4]. Compared with QoS, QoE takes into account factors that contribute to the perceived quality of the overall user. These factors include codec algorithms, resolution of user's terminal devices, viewing environment, user's expectation and video content.

Video quality assessment method has gone through four stages. Table 1 gives a comparison of these stages [5].

Table 1. Comparison of video quality assessment stages

Heading level	Direct measure	Objective or subjective	Real-time	Cost
QoS monitoring	No	Objective	Yes	Not sure
Subjective test	Yes	Subjective	No	High
Objective quality model	No	Objective	Yes/No	Low
Data-driven analysis	Yes	Objective	Yes	Not sure

The first stage is a simple measurement of QoS. Now the measurement of network simply cannot show the overall experience of end user, which is also the reason why QoE is proposed later. The second stage is subjective test. Results of methods in this stage are the most direct and practical. The defect is the requirement of several man-power and material resources. The third stage is objective quality model. The general idea is to establish a mapping relationship between QoS and QoE. It is classified basing on that if the establishment of the model needs to depend on the source video. Mapping relationship can be linear, exponential, polynomial, and so on. After an objective quality model is established, it is necessary to combine the results of the subjective test to analyze the credibility. The methods in the last stage are data-driven analysis, which are proposed in the backend of big data. Data-driven analysis method can obtain the user's subjective parameters such as viewing time, viewing type and viewing date. It is different from the objective quality model which simply depends on the network service. This method is also the choice of our subject.

The rest of the paper is organized as follows. Section 2 describes previous related works. Section 3 describes our process of generating new features. Section 4 is the main part of this paper. It describes the base algorithms we use and how we improve it for our work. Experimental results and analysis are in Sect. 5. Finally, we summarize the work in Sect. 6.

2 Related Work

There are several research works on prediction of user QoE. Data-driven evaluation method tries to obtain the mapping relationship between input characteristics and output results by computer simulation. The computing method chosen in this paper is machine learning. In [6], an adapted ANN model is proposed based on video stream QoE prediction. In this paper, the author evaluates the performance of the ANN-based QoE prediction model under mismatched condition. Then they develop a feature transformation to adapt the model from one condition to another. The result shows that the QoE prediction accuracy under mismatched condition can be improved substantially using as few as five data samples under the new condition. PNN (probabilistic neural network) based QoE model is proposed in [7]. In this paper, the author describes a QoE measuring model for video applications over LTE system. With the help of the equipment of video quality evaluation model, they establish the relationship between network parameters and Mean Opinion Score(MOS). By using PNN, there is no need to study the complex relationship between affecting parameters of QoE and user's perceived quality. In [8], the author presents a new objective method based on neural network. This model has six input parameters. The author compares the combination of different input parameters and different neural network layers to get the best performance and finally finds that it works best with all six features and twelve hidden neurons. We are also concerned with the impact of data-driven metrics on QoE. In [9–12], the researchers focus on the relationship between network security, watch time and QoE. The impact of network framework and delayed announcement is taken into account in [13–15]. In [16], the author establishes the relationship between viewing time and video quality.

It shows that the prediction accuracy of the experiment can be improved by changing the combination of input parameters or improving the learning algorithms [17–20]. The idea of our work is based on these two points. On one hand, we enhance the model effect by adding new input features. On the other hand, we improve the algorithm for a better model performance with no new input features.

3 Feature Preprocessing

3.1 Description of Dataset

Our experimental data is obtained from the operator. It is the real data of users, so our experimental results have a certain reference.

Specifically, data comes from IPTV box. A box in the open state and with no other operation returns a data message to the data center every five minutes. When there is an operation such as a click, it reports to the data center immediately. When the box is in the closed state, there is no feedback information during this time.

Our experiment selects the most active 1100 users' data from August 4 to August 31 of 2016. The scale of data is large enough for the requirement of training process and the experimental results have a high degree of universality.

Each data record has 42 values, including data id, user id, playtime, end time, multimedia address and other information. Some data values such as program id, multimedia address, etc. have no influence on end user QoE. We just need to think about packet loss rate, the average network bit rate, viewing time and so on.

3.2 Basic Features

- *Delay factor (DF): DF* indicates the delay and jitter status of the tested video stream. DF changes the concept of jitter in the video stream to the setting of the buffer space for the decoding device.
- *Media loss rate (MLR): MLR* indicates the number of lost media packets per unit time. Occasional data loss in voice and video content does not cause much impact. As the retransmission mechanism will greatly increase the network burden, we do not set it in these systems.
- *Jitter: Jitter* is caused by the uneven transmission of the network.
- *Number of overflows: Number of overflows* indicates the number of packets abandoned during transmission. The number of overflows depends on the arrival number of the node, the size of the cache space and the transmission efficiency.

3.3 New Features

Non-technical factors also affect the end user's viewing experience. This paper focuses on the influence of viewing date and viewing time on QoE. Although the impact of these parameters is proposed before, there is no actual experimental test of their influence level.

Viewing Date

Figure 1 shows the average viewer request strength of different date. We can see that the strength of viewing request from Monday to Friday is not the same. But the strength of request on Saturday and Sunday is significantly higher than those of work days. Although the gap is not particularly large, it actually indicates that viewing date has influence on users. After analyzing the data, we find that the experimental data selected is in August 2016. It is the summer vacation in China. Therefore, the children's impact on the viewing request has not been demonstrated.

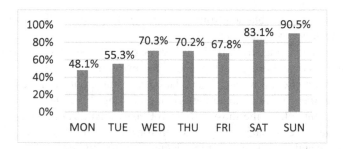

Fig. 1. Viewer request strength of different date

Viewing Time

Figure 2 shows the statistical results of the number of viewing requests on different time points. The horizontal axis is the 24 time points in a day, and the vertical axis is the number of viewer requests. From 0:00 to 5:00, the number of viewer requests closes

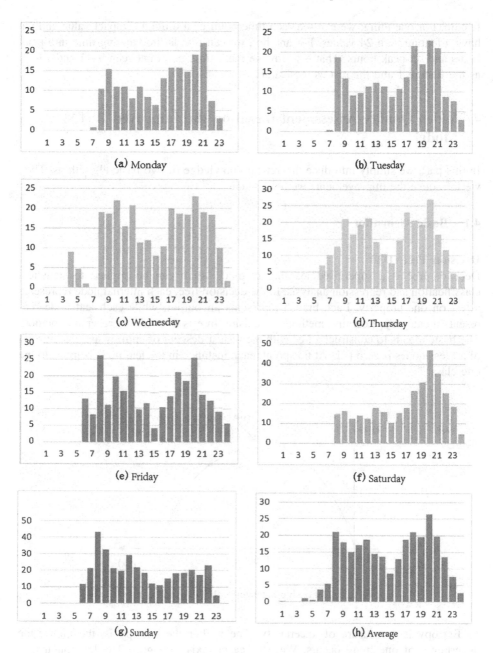

Fig. 2. Viewer requests on different time point

to zero. During this period, users are asleep. In general, user's viewing date and daily viewing time are of no contact. As to one day, we can conclude that there are two daily peak hours, which are respectively 10 point and 20 point. Thus, we can add the viewing time as a new feature to the experimental model. There are two methods to express this feature. For one thing, we can see each time point as a different impact value and we have a feature with 24 values. For another, we can divide the viewing time into peak hours and off-peak hours. That is to say we mark time point between 9–11 and 19–21 as the feature 1 and the rest as the feature 0.

4 Video Quality Assessment Based on the Improved LSTM Model

In this part, we simply introduce theoretical knowledge of two basic algorithms. Then we introduce the improvements we have made.

4.1 Basic Algorithm

Decision Tree (DT)
Decision tree is a supervised learning method which can be applied to statistical classification and regression analysis. In the decision tree, each internal node represents a test on one property. Each branch represents an output, while each leaf node represents a category. Learning method of decision tree is a top-down recursive method. The basic idea is to construct a tree with the fastest descent of entropy and the entropy of all leaf nodes is zero [21].At this point, each instance in the leaf node belongs to the one class.

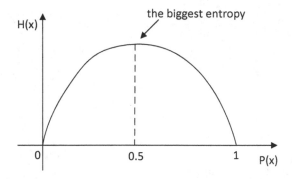

Fig. 3. Relationship between probability and entropy

Entropy is a measure of uncertainty. The higher the entropy is, the higher the uncertainty of one thing occurs. We can see an axis in Fig. 3. The horizontal axis represents the probability of occurrence of one thing, and the vertical axis represents the uncertainty of this thing. When the probability is 0, it can be determined that this thing will not happen. And the entropy is 0. When the probability is 1, it can be determined that this thing will happen. Also the entropy is zero. Only when the probability of occurrence is 0.5, the event entropy is the largest.

Long Short Term Memory (LSTM)

LSTM is a kind of recurrent neural network. Recurrent neural network (RNN) mainly takes into account the timing of the input data. Apart from the vertical input-output relationship at the computational level, there is a time-dependent causal relationship. The change in LSTM relative to the underlying RNN is that LSTM improves the memory cell. The information that should be recorded always passes, and the information that should not be recorded is effectively truncated by the door. Figure 4 shows the illustration of a memory cell.

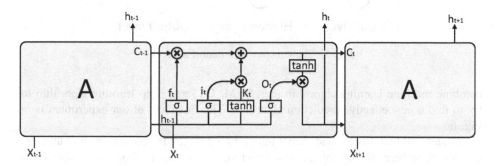

Fig. 4. Memory cell of LSTM

As the time interval increases, the RNN will lose the ability to learn the information of nodes that are relatively distant. When the capacity of memory cell is limited, stored information need to be cut off as needed. The memory cells of LSTM can excavate the long-term dependency in the information, so LSTM can predict the output better.

4.2 Improved Algorithm

Deep learning neural network can arbitrarily set the number of layers and the number of neurons. The initial input characteristics will experience a weight handling process after each nerve layer to get the output dimension. Observing the neural network in Fig. 5, we can find that the output of each layer will have a certain dimension. Each dimension has its certain characteristic significance.

The weight handling procedure is shown in Eq. (1). W is the weight matrix. X is the input matrix. Y is the output matrix of each layer. B is a bias term.

$$Y = X \cdot W + B \tag{1}$$

The layer processing of the deep learning neural network behaves the function of data feature preprocessing. Feature preprocessing can generate new features of certain dimension. Unfortunately, the physical meaning of output of each layer cannot be explained at present. However, we can still use the characteristics of the neural network layer to deal with the problem of feature dimension. On the basis of this idea, we

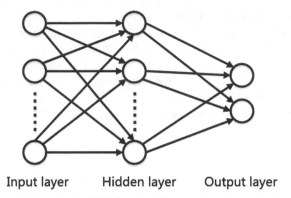

Input layer   Hidden layer   Output layer

Fig. 5. The structure of a neural network

combine machine learning algorithm (e.g. SVM, DT) and deep learning algorithm to try to find a new effective prediction algorithm. The flowchart of our experiment is in Fig. 6.

Model building process and model training process are the basic steps and they are not described here. We talk about how to get the output feature from the middle layer and retrain it as input to get the machine learning predictive output. Our code runs in python condition. With the help of an integrated deep learning framework 'Keras', we build a neural network model easily. Keras has a function that can save the weight matrix and certain layer output after training process. So the thing that we need to do is marking the layer that we want and saving the function output. We need to change the data format so that we can handle it with a machine learning algorithm.

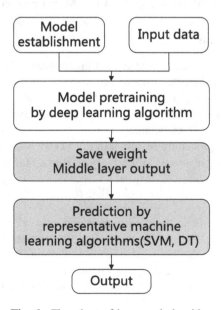

Fig. 6. Flowchart of improved algorithm

5 Result Analysis

5.1 Comparison of Algorithm

Our experiment includes three basic algorithms, Support Vector Machine (SVM), DT and LSTM. There are also two improved algorithms based on the underlying algorithm. We have five comparison algorithms in the end. Figure 7 is generated based on the basic data set with a comparison of prediction accuracy and running time. In terms of prediction accuracy, LSTM is not superior to SVM and DT, whereas DT is doing well on this data set. The improved algorithm LSTM + DT is excellent. It improves the accuracy of 13% points on the basis of LSTM and 8% points on the basis of DT. Although SVM performs well on accuracy aspect, it takes too much time calculating. So it is not suitable in real time system.

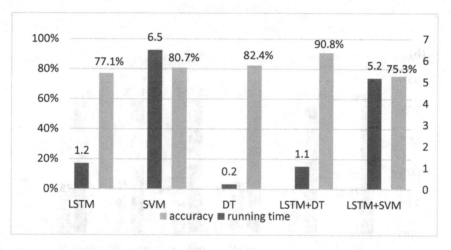

Fig. 7. Comparison of prediction accuracy and running time between the proposed algorithm and competing algorithms

In conclusion, the improved algorithm LSTM + DT is fast and the prediction accuracy is high. This result proves the theoretical correctness of the combination of the feature preprocessing based on deep learning with the prediction based traditional machine learning models. It also shows the advantage of LSTM algorithm in performing feature dimensional reduction.

5.2 Comparison of Dataset

In the data feature preprocessing phase, two new features are added: viewing date and viewing time. Experimental results are discussed based on six data sets, as shown in Fig. 8. We draw the comparison of basic algorithms in Fig. 8(a) and comparison of improved algorithms in Fig. 8(b). We can see that LSTM + DT algorithm has the highest accuracy, followed by DT. The result is consistent with the discussion in the previous section. Actually, the increase of the input characteristics does bring about the

(a)

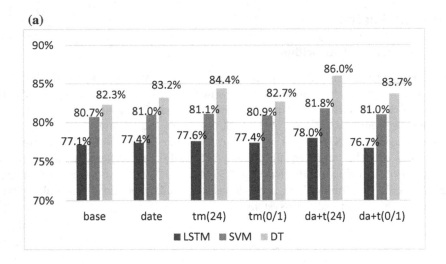

(b)

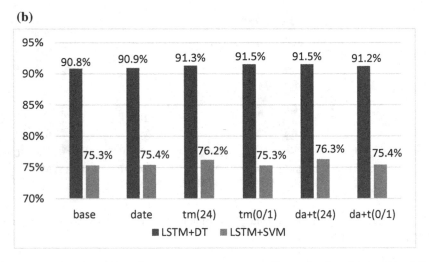

Fig. 8. (a) Comparison of prediction accuracy among LSTM, SVM and DT with different dataset, (b) Comparison of prediction accuracy between LSTM + DT and LSTM + SVM with different dataset

improvement of the prediction accuracy. However, the promotion is not obvious. In general, the 24-h viewing characteristic is better than 0/1. And the combination of date + time (24) is the best.

6   Conclusion

Considering the prediction accuracy of different algorithms and different datasets, we can find that the improvement on algorithm has obvious advantage. The LSTM + DT improved algorithm on the basic data set can improve the prediction accuracy of 13%

on the basic of LSTM algorithm. In the feature preprocessing stage, we increase two new input features, which are more correlated with user's experience. The addition of new features can increase the final accuracy of the experiment by a maximum of 3%.

Acknowledgements. This work is partly supported by the State Key Development Program of Basic Research of China (Grant No. 2013CB329005), the National Natural Science Foundation of China (Grant Nos. 61322104, 61571240), the Priority Academic Program Development of Jiangsu Higher Education Institutions, the Natural Science Foundation of Jiangsu Province (Grant No. BK20161517), the Qing Lan Project, the Postdoctoral Science Foundation of China (Grant No. 2017M611881), the Scientific Research Foundation of NUPT (Grant No. NY217022).

References

1. China Internet Network Information Center. http://www.cnnic.net.cn/hlwfzyj/hlwxzbg/hlwtjbg/201701/t20170122_66437.html. Accessed 22 Jan 2017
2. Cisco Systems, Inc. http://www.cisco.com/c/zh_cn/about/press/corporate-news/2017/02-08.html. Accessed 08 Feb 2017
3. ITU-T Recommendation E.800: Definition of terms of Quality of service (2008)
4. ITU-T Recommendation P.10/G.100 (2006) Amendment 1 (01/07), P.10: New Appendix I – Definition of Quality of Experience (QoE) (2001)
5. Chen, Y., Wu, K., Zhang, Q.: From QoS to QoE: a tutorial on video quality assessment. IEEE Commun. Surv. Tutor. **17**, 1126–1165 (2015)
6. Deng, J., Zhang, L., Hu, J., He, D.: Adaptation of ANN based video stream QoE prediction model. In: Ooi, W.T., Snoek, C.G.M., Tan, H.K., Ho, C.-K., Huet, B., Ngo, C.-W. (eds.) PCM 2014. LNCS, vol. 8879, pp. 313–322. Springer, Cham (2014). https://doi.org/10.1007/978-3-319-13168-9_35
7. He, Y., Wang, C., Long, H., Zheng, K.: PNN-based QoE measuring model for video applications over LTE system. Presented at the August 2012
8. Menor, D.P.A., Mello, C.A.B., Zanchettin, C.: Objective video quality assessment based on neural networks. Procedia Comput. Sci. **96**, 1551–1559 (2016)
9. Li, Y., Chen, M.: Software-defined network function virtualization: a survey. IEEE Access **3**, 2542–2553 (2015)
10. Chen, M., Ma, Y., Li, Y., Wu, D., Zhang, Y., Youn, C.-H.: Wearable 2.0: enabling human-cloud integration in next generation healthcare systems. IEEE Commun. Mag. **55**, 54–61 (2017)
11. Chen, M., Yang, J., Zhu, X., Wang, X., Liu, M., Song, J.: Smart home 2.0: innovative smart home system powered by botanical IoT and emotion detection. Mob. Netw. Appl. 1–11 (2017)
12. Liu, C., Dong, Z., Xie, S., Pei, L.: Human motion recognition based on incremental learning and smartphone sensors. ZTE Commun. **14**, 59–66 (2016)
13. Zhou, L., Wu, D., Zheng, B., Guizani, M.: Joint physical-application layer security for wireless multimedia delivery. IEEE Commun. Mag. **52**, 66–72 (2014)
14. Zhou, L.: On data-driven delay estimation for media cloud. IEEE Trans. Multimedia **18**, 905–915 (2016)
15. Zhou, L.: QoE-driven delay announcement for cloud mobile media. IEEE Trans. Circ. Syst. Video Technol. **27**, 84–94 (2017)
16. Zhou, L., Yang, Z., Wang, H., Guizani, M.: Impact of execution time on adaptive wireless video scheduling. IEEE J. Sel. Areas Commun. **32**, 760–772 (2014)

17. Zheng, K., Zhang, X., Zheng, Q., Xiang, W., Hanzo, L.: Quality-of-experience assessment and its application to video services in LTE networks. IEEE Wirel. Commun. **22**, 70–78 (2015). Estimation of video QoE from MAC parameters in wireless network: a random neural network approach

18. Zhou, L.: Specific versus diverse computing in media cloud. IEEE Trans. Circ. Syst. Video Technol. **25**, 1888–1899 (2015)

19. Paudel, I., Pokhrel, J., Wehbi, B., Cavalli, A., Jouaber, B.: Estimation of video QoE from MAC parameters in wireless network: a random neural network approach. Presented at the September 2014

20. Anchuen, P., Uthansakul, P., Uthansakul, M.: QOE model in cellular networks based on QOS measurements using neural network approach. Presented at the June 2016

21. Quinlan, J.R.: Induction of decision trees. Mach. Learn. **1**, 81–106 (1986)

GECKO: Gamer Experience-Centric Bitrate Control Algorithm for Cloud Gaming

Yihao Ke[1,2], Guoqiao Ye[1,2], Di Wu[1,2(✉)], Yipeng Zhou[1,3], Edith Ngai[4], and Han Hu[5]

[1] Department of Computer Science, Sun Yat-sen University, Guangzhou, China
wudi27@mail.sysu.edu.cn
[2] Guangdong Province Key Laboratory of Big Data Analysis and Processing, Guangzhou, China
[3] Institute for Telecommunications Research, University of South Australia, Adelaide, Australia
[4] Department of Information Technology, Uppsala University, Uppsala, Sweden
[5] School of Computer Engineering, Nanyang Technological University, Singapore, Singapore

Abstract. Cloud gaming considered as the future of computer games enables users to play high-end games on resource-constrained heterogeneous devices. Games are rendered on remote clouds and delivered to users via the Internet in the form of video streaming, which can dramatically reduce the consumption of client-side resources. However, such service needs high bandwidth connections to make the game streaming smooth, which is already a major issue to hamper the prevalence of cloud gaming. In this paper, we propose a gamer experience-centric bitrate control algorithm called GECKO, to reduce the consumption of bandwidth resources for cloud gaming while only slightly impairing user quality-of-experience (QoE). Through measurement studies, we find that user QoE is mainly determined by the ROI (Region of Interest) size and QP offset. Hence, in order to save bandwidth consumption without severely impairing user QoE, we can lower the quality of the region outside of ROI. Our proposed GECKO algorithm is designed to adaptively tune the size of ROI and the quality of the outside region. We implement the GECKO algorithm on a real cloud gaming platform. The experiment results show that over 15.8% bandwidth can be saved compared with state-of-the-art approaches.

Keywords: Cloud gaming · Region of Interest · H.264 · Video coding Controller

1 Introduction

Cloud gaming as a fast-growing technology enables users to play high-end games with resource-constrained devices. Game scenes are rendered by remote clouds

© Springer International Publishing AG 2017
Y. Zhao et al. (Eds.): ICIG 2017, Part II, LNCS 10667, pp. 325–335, 2017.
https://doi.org/10.1007/978-3-319-71589-6_29

and delivered via the Internet in the form of video streaming. Technavio [1] predicted that the global cloud gaming market to grow exponentially at a compound annual growth rate (CAGR) of more than 29% during 2016–2020. However, high-speed bandwidth connections are required for smooth game streaming, which could severely restrict the prevalence of cloud gaming. Chen *et al.* [6] indicated that the bitrate of StreamMyGame varies between 9 Mbps and 18 Mbps, whereas Akamai [3] stated that the global average connection speed was 6.3 Mbps in the first quarter of 2016. In particular, the average speed of 65% countries is lower than 10 Mbps. The situation is worse for mobile users. There are only 18 countries serving mobile users with an average speed at or exceeding 10 Mbps.

Given the challenge of limited bandwidth, our work aims to propose a rate control algorithm on top of existing game streaming encoders to reduce bandwidth consumption without impairing user QoE. As stated in [11], major cloud gaming providers, e.g., Gaikai and Onlive, use H.264/AVC to encode gaming videos. To reduce bandwidth consumption, several rate control algorithms, e.g., CRF and ABR [4], have been implemented on H.264 by tuning parameters with the cost to harm user QoE. Different from the above works, our proposed GECKO algorithm tries to only lower the bitrate of the region that will not affect users' subjective feeling based on the fact that the human visual system (HVS) receives most of the visual information from the fixation points and around, regarded as Region-of-Interest (ROI) [15]. On the contrary, HVS's resolution falls rapidly from the point of gaze, hence we can propose a rate control algorithm to lower the quality of the region outside of ROI without harming user QoE much. Specifically, we first decide the size of ROI based on bandwidth conditions before we degrade the quality of the outside region. Intuitively speaking, the ROI size is enlarged if the bandwidth is not tight, otherwise it is shrunk.

Our contribution of this work is summarized as follows. We first conduct an in-depth measurement study to quantify the impacts of the ROI size and QP offset on the video bitrate and user QoE. The results indicate that it is feasible to lower down video bitrate with only slightly impairing user QoE by dynamically adjusting the ROI size and QP offset. We further propose a control-theoretic gamer experience-centric bitrate control algorithm for cloud gaming named GECKO, which can adaptively tune parameters according to video bitrate requirements. Finally, we implement our algorithm on top of x264, and use GamingAnywhere [8] for implementation and experiment to verify the effectiveness our algorithm.

2   Related Work

Different rate control or bit location schemes have been proposed in previous works. Sun and Wu [13] proposed a bit allocation scheme on macroblock layer based on Region of Interest (ROI). Their work assumed that the ROI of every frame is already known and then we can allocate different weights and bits to each macroblock. After getting the target bit of each MB, the QP of each MB can be computed by using the R-Q model proposed by JVT-G012.

Ahmadi et al. [5] introduced a conceptual Game Attention Model which determines the importance level of different regions of game frames according to user's attention. Subjective quality assessment showed that Game Attention Model helps to decrease the bitrate while maintaining the users' quality of experience (QoE). In cloud gaming, *Xue et al.* [18] found that delay and bandwidth played the important roles while improving the satisfaction of users. In order to improve the QoE of users, Some studies focused on which game server to connect [14], reducing the latency [22], improving the efficiency of transcoding [21] and streaming with minimal cost [17], or reducing the bandwidth consumption [7]. In this paper, we would explore control scheme associated with the bitrate of the ROI and reduce the bandwidth overload.

Shen et al. [12] proposed a novel rate control algorithm that takes into account visual attention. This work spent more efforts on ROI extraction and allocated bits for each macroblocks by local motion activity, edge strength and texture activity. *Yang et al.* [19] proposed a ROI-based rate control algorithm for video communication systems, in which the subjective quality of ROI can be adjusted according to users' requirements. In the proposed scheme, a Structural Similarity Index Map—quantization parameter (SSIM-QP) model is established.

3   Measurement Analysis of Bitrate Control for Game Streaming

To visualize how parameters affect streaming bitrate and user QoE and show the tradeoff between bitrate and QoE, we conduct a series of measurements in this section to quantitatively study the impacts of ROI size and QP offset.

3.1   Measurement Methodology

The game streaming is delivered to users in a sequence of frames, and each is composed by multiple macroblocks. The video quality (or bitrate) of the original game streaming is determined by quantization parameter (QP) of each macroblock. Larger QP value implies a larger step size in quantization and lower quality (or bitrate), and vice versa. Thus, by tuning the parameter QP, one can control the bitrate of the game streaming, which is a prevalent approach adopted by existing solutions. However, such trivial parameter tuning solution unavoidably harms user QoE.

In contrast, our control algorithm only adjusts QP for the region out of user interests to minimize the influence caused by lowering bitrate. We introduce one more parameter ROI size, which is defined as the ratio of the size of ROI compared with the size of the whole frame in the range from 0% to 100%. For simplicity, we assume that the ROI is a rectangular area located at the center of the frame. To control the bitrate, our algorithm will tune both ROI size and the QP for region outside ROI. In other words, only QP for the region out of ROI will be increased if it is necessary to reduce bitrate. For convenience, we define QP offset as the difference of QPs between macroblocks in and outside the ROI.

Note that QP offset and ROI size are two parameters irrelevant with the original streaming quality, and can be easily tuned by our proposed GECKO algorithm. For example, a QP offset of two means that the QP of each macroblock outside of ROI is increased by two compared with its original value; while the QP within ROI remains unchanged.

It is worth to mention that our approach is friendly for implementation since we only need to add a few auxiliary functions to existing streaming encoders, which will be introduced later.

In our measurements, we use the library x264 to generate the game streaming, which is a widely used software library for video streams encoding. The standard of the generated game streaming by x264 is H.264/AVC. According to the previous work [11], H.264/AVC is a *de facto* standard for cloud gaming.

The *pic_in* is one of the core data structure of x264 storing the properties and data of the input frame. In *pic_in→prop*, there is an array *quant_offsets* that controls the QP offsets for each macroblocks to be applied to this frame during encoding.

We control the streaming bitrate by altering the QP offsets stored in the array *quant_offsets*. Intuitively, QP offset value is set as zero for ROI and a positive value for region outside.

3.2 Metrics

We use game streaming bitrate as the main metric to evaluate bandwidth consumption. We assume that more bandwidth is consumed if the game streaming with higher bitrate is delivered.

DSSIM (structural dissimilarity index) [10] is used as the metric to evaluate user QoE in this study. DSSIM can indicate how much distortion is incurred after we tune parameters with the rate control algorithm. DSSIM is defined as follows, $DSSIM = \frac{1}{SSIM} - 1$, where SSIM is the structural similarity index. SSIM is designed as the metric [16] to measure the similarity between two different images and DSSIM measures the dissimilarity instead. Thus, DSSIM is just computed by comparing the frame with altered parameters and the original frame. SSIM ranges from 0 to 1, thus DSSIM ranges from 0 to infinity. Higher DSSIM means lower QoE. The DSSIM depends on SSIM and it has been proved that SSIM is more consistent with human visual perception and significantly outperforms traditional measures, e.g., peak signal-to-noise ratio (PSNR) and mean squared error (MSE) [20].

There is a tradeoff between bandwidth consumption and user QoE. In spite that enlarging ROI size or decrease QP offsets for non-ROI will improve user QoE, the cost is more bandwidth consumption. In practice, due to limited bandwidth resources, we have to consider how to balance the tradeoff continuously.

3.3 Insights from Measurement Analysis

In principles, bandwidth consumption and user QoE can be expressed as functions of the ROI size and QP offset, namely *bitrate = f(ROI size, QP offset)*

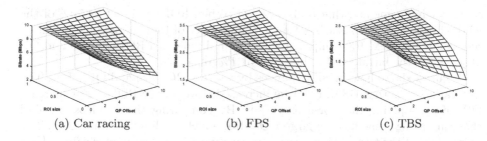

Fig. 1. Bitrate of each type of game.

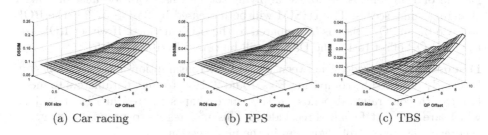

Fig. 2. DSSIM of each type of game.

and $QoE = g(ROI\ size, QP\ offset)$. It is not difficult to accurately tune ROI size and QP offset, if we have exact expressions of functions f and g. However, unfortunately it is difficult to derive general expressions for f and g, which are affected by game type, gaming scene and so on. Specially, for game streaming with a sequence of frames, it becomes a tedious job because we have to create functions f and g for each frame in the worst case. Consequently, we turn to develop a control-theoretic gamer experience-centric bitrate control algorithm for cloud gaming to automatically tune parameters without the need explicitly derive f and g.

We select three most representative game types for numerical analysis by varying parameter values, including car racing game, first-person shooting (FPS) game and turn-based strategy (TBS) game. We generate a 30-s gaming video clip encoded by x264 encoder for each type of game. For each video clip, the ROI size varies from 0 to 100%, with a step of 5%; while the QP offset varies from 1 to 10, with a step of 1. We calculate the bitrate and DSSIM for each pair of parameter values.

Figure 1 shows how bitrate changes by varying ROI size and QP offset for each game video. x and y axes are parameter values, while z axis is the tuned video bitrate. In general, the trend is that the video bitrate will be lowered if the ROI size is shrunk or the QP offset is raised. By comparing different video types, we notice that the car racing game has the largest bitrate, due to the fast moving scenes with rich content. The TBS game has the lowest bitrate because the game scene changes slowly. The bitrate of FPS game is just in between that of car racing game and that of TBS game. When ROI size is set as 50% of the whole frame and QP offset is set as 5, the bitrates of these game videos will be reduced by 9.3%–21.9% compared with original videos. If ROI size is 0 and QP offset is 10, the bitrate will reduced by 51.1%–62.4%.

Figure 2 shows how DSSIM changes by varying ROI size and QP offset. The general trend is that DSSIM will be increased if we reduce ROI size or increase QP offset implying the worse user QoE. By comparing three videos, we find that car racing game has the largest DSSIM, which implies the worst QoE. The reason is that the fast moving scenes are very sensitive to parameter values. User QoE will drop sharply even if the bitrate is lowered a little bit. In contrast, the DSSIM of TBS game is the lowest implying the best user QoE because of slowly changing game scenes. The DSSIM will be increased by 25.1%–37% if the ROI size is 50% and QP offset is 5 compared to the original video. If we set ROI size to 0 and QP offset to 10, the DSSIM will be raised by 106%–156.5%.

Discussion: The tradeoff between bandwidth consumption and user QoE can be clearly observed by comparing Figs. 1 and 2. How to tune parameters to meet bandwidth constraints depends on the curve shapes plotted in Figs. 1 and 2, which are different for all three videos. This inspires us to propose a control-theoretic bitrate control algorithm in the next section.

4   GECKO—A Gamer Experience-Centric Bitrate Control Algorithm for Cloud Gaming

In this section, we turn to use control-theoretic algorithm that will automatically tune parameters by taking into account the feedback from the last time slot so that the long term average bandwidth constraints can be satisfied.

4.1   Problem Formulation

We assume that the Internet access services purchased by users will give them a certain bandwidth for streaming, which will not change in a short term. Then, our problem is how to control the video bitrate to meet the average downloading rate constraint as much as possible.

Define b^* as the target bitrate, i.e., the maximum tolerable bandwidth cost of cloud gaming. In this study, we can focus on the case of single gamer.

Consider a time-slotted system with time slot length of τ s. Define $D(k)$ and $R(k)$ as the QP offset and ROI size for time slot k respectively. Let b_k be the average bitrate in time slot k. We use DSSIM to represent the user QoE. Let q_k be the average DSSIM in time slot k.

By taking the tradeoff between the bandwidth (bitrate) cost and the QoE into account, we can define a generic utility function $\Phi(\cdot)$ to capture the impact of user preferences on the cloud gaming video bitrate. In this paper, we define the utility function $\Phi(\cdot)$ as a concave function of b_k. In general, the value of the utility function increases concavely with the increase of b_k. This property captures the fact that the marginal utility will decrease more significantly when b_k becomes larger.

4.2   Algorithm Design

Control theory [9] is an efficient methodology to solve our problem without the need to know the exact functions of f and g. The bitrate in the previous time slot can be used as a feedback signal for adjusting ROI size and QP offset. The value of b_k and q_k can be obtained at the end of each time slot k. Consequently, we can design an gamer experience-centric bitrate control algorithm for cloud gaming based on control theory [9] to optimize bandwidth cost. In this work, this proposed algorithm is named as **GECKO**. By controlling the update of ROI size and QP offset, we can approach the target control objective b^* gradually.

Although proportional-integral-derivative (PID) controller may have a better controlling performance, it relies heavily on the tuning of K_p, K_i and K_d, which are the coefficients for the proportional, integral, and derivative terms respectively. However, tuning these coefficients is not so easy. The coefficient of proportional controller has an intuitive interpretation—if the current bitrate is larger than the target bitrate, the coefficient of controlling ROI size should be a fraction to reduce the ROI size and vice versa. Thus, we adopt a proportional controller to solve the ROI size and QP offset allocation problem.

Let $\Delta_b(k)$ be the marginal utility incurred by the difference between the current state and the target state, which is defined as below:

$$\Delta_b(k) = \Phi(b_k) - \Phi(b^*). \tag{1}$$

We define two separate proportional control factors $G_R(k)$ and $G_D(k)$, where ψ_r and ψ_d are two positive constants which determine the smoothness of two control factors.

$$G_R(k) = \frac{1 + e^{\psi_r \cdot \Delta_b(k)}}{2e^{\psi_r \cdot \Delta_b(k)}} \quad , \quad G_D(k) = \frac{2e^{\psi_d \cdot \Delta_b(k)}}{1 + e^{\psi_d \cdot \Delta_b(k)}}. \tag{2}$$

If $b_k > b^*$, we should decrease the ROI size or increase the QP offset and vice versa. From the above definitions, the $\Delta_b(k)$ is positive value at this time, and $e^{\psi_r \cdot \Delta_b(k)}$ is a value larger than 1, consequently $G_R(k)$ is a fraction between 0 and 1, which satisfies our requirements. The $G_D(k)$ works in a similar manner. The properties of exponent function and the above control factor definitions also ensure the amplitude of adjustment will not be too large when b_k has a large difference with b^*, because the large amplitude of ROI size or QP offset adjustment may deteriorate user QoE.

The update of ROI size and QP offset can be governed by the following controllers:

$$R(k+1) = G_R(k) \cdot R(K) \quad , \quad D(k+1) = G_D(k) \cdot D(K). \tag{3}$$

The detailed description of our proposed algorithm is given in Algorithm 1.

5   Implementation and Performance Evaluation

In this section, we describe how to implement our proposed GECKO algorithm on x264 and GamingAnywhere [8] and conduct a set of experiments to evaluate the effectiveness of GECKO algorithm.

Algorithm 1. GECKO algorithm

Input:
    Target bitrate b^*;
    Time slot length τ;
    User utility function $\Phi(\cdot)$;
1: Initialize: $k = 0$, $R(0)$ and $D(0)$ as the default values in cloud gaming server;
2: **repeat**
3:    Obtain the value of b_k from the H.264 encoder.
4:    Use b_k as the feedback signal to calculate control factors $G_R(k)$ and $G_D(k)$.
5:    Calculate ROI size and QP offset according to $R(k+1) = G_R(k) \cdot R(K)$ and
    $D(k+1) = G_D(k) \cdot D(K)$.
6:    Update ROI size and QP offset of the next time slot.
7:    Wait for a time slot τ.
8:    Increase the slot index: $k = k + 1$.
9: **until** Quit playing cloud gaming.

5.1   Implementation on x264 and GamingAnywhere

The key point on the implementation of GECKO algorithm is how to obtain the bitrate and DSSIM for each frame. Obtaining the bitrate can be transformed into obtaining the frame size and then we can calculate the bitrate by the frame size and the number of frame-per-second (fps). Correspondingly, the return value of the core encoding function *x264_encoder_encode* is the encoded frame size. DSSIM is calculated by SSIM and we can obtain SSIM of each frame in x264. To enable SSIM computation, we set *param.analyse.b_ssim* = 1 when creating the encoder. After that, the SSIM of each frame is retrieved by *pic_out.prop.f_ssim* after encoding. After getting the bitrate and SSIM, we derive the average bitrate and DSSIM. Then we apply the GECKO algorithm to obtain the control factors $G_R(k)$ and $G_D(k)$ and update the $R(k+1)$ and $D(k+1)$. Finally, the new *quant_offset* array is produced and used in the encoding phase.

GamingAnywhere [8] is the first open source cloud gaming platform. From the version of *0.8.0*, it divides different functions into modules. Each module has several interfaces, such as *init*, *start* and *stop*. In this paper, we modified the *encoder_x264* module to implement our ROI rate control algorithm.

The modifications are listed as below:

- Add several variables in global states, including b^*, ψ_r, ψ_d, $G_R(k)$, $G_D(k)$, $R(k)$, $D(k)$ and *quant_offset* array.
- Add a controller function, which performs computation of $G_R(k)$ and $G_D(k)$ and update of $R(k)$, $D(k)$ and *quant_offset* array.
- Modify the *init* interface. In the initialization phase, we set $R(0)$ and $D(0)$ as the default values and retrieve the corresponding *quant_offset*. We also enable the flag of SSIM computation.
- Modify the *reconfigure* interface. The modified *reconfigure* interface calls the controller function to update the ROI size, QP offset and *quant_offset*.

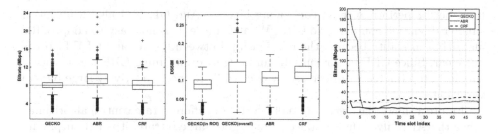

Fig. 3. Distribution of bitrate.

Fig. 4. Distribution of DSSIM.

Fig. 5. Bitrate of first 50 time slots.

- Modify the *threadproc* interface, which calls the x264's encoding function. We assign *quant_offset* array to the *pic_in* struct before encoding and retrieve the frame size and SSIM.
- Add a *reconfigure* thread in *ga-server-periodic* core module which generates a *GA_IOCTL_RECONFIGURE* event every time slot and calls the *ioctl* interface of encoder module. The *ioctl* interface will later call the *reconfigure* interface.

5.2   Experimental Settings

We record a user's input of car racing game for 5 min. The input is then re-played into the GamingAnywhere to ensure the same input. The bitrate and DSSIM are retrieved during video encoding in GamingAnywhere. We adopt different rate control algorithms in the encoder module, including our proposed GECKO algorithm, ABR and CRF [4]. The ABR (Average Bit Rate) algorithm is a rate control algorithm targeting a specific bitrate on average. CRF (Constant Rate Factor) is the default rate control algorithm of x264, which aims to get the bitrate it needs to keep the requested quality level. The range of the factor is 0–51 and a lower value is a higher quality.

We define the utility function as a concave function like $\Phi(b_k) = \ln(b_k + 1)$. With the increase of b_k, the utility of a user will be increased but the marginal utility gain will decrease when b_k becomes larger. Note that other concave functions that have the similar properties can also be adopted. The time slot length τ is 0.1 s in following experiments. We set $b^* = 8$ Mbps. As for CRF algorithm, it is difficult to know the exact bitrate when we set the CRF factor. Thus, we experiment with several CRF factors and choose the best result whose bitrate is mostly closed to b^*. For GECKO algorithm, we set $\psi_r = 1$ and $\psi_d = 1$.

5.3   Experiment Results

In Fig. 3, it shows the ABR algorithm has the largest average bitrate. When setting the same bitrate target, GECKO algorithm can save about 15.8% of bandwidth compared with ABR. The result of CRF algorithm with a factor of 25 is the best one among all settings. The CRF algorithm and GECKO algorithm have better performance on controlling bitrate. And GECKO algorithm has a smaller deviation compared to CRF. What is more, it is not easy to adopt CRF algorithm in reality because the relationship between bitrate and CRF factor is not clear. Since CRF factor must be an integer, even tuning CRF factor with a smallest step (increase or decrease by one) will produce a relatively large bitrate variation.

Figure 4 shows the distribution of DSSIM of different rate control algorithms. Since the ABR algorithm produces a relatively large bitrate, it is not surprising to see its DSSIM is smaller than CRF and GECKO algorithms. The overall DSSIM of GECKO algorithm is worse than ABR and CRF, but the GECKO algorithm produces a lower DSSIM in the ROI, which confirms well with our assumption about lowering down video bitrate with only slightly impairing user QoE by dynamically adjusting the ROI size and QP offset.

Figure 5 shows the bitrate of each rate control algorithm in the first 50 time slots. The result indicates that our proposed GECKO algorithm converges to the target bitrate quickly while the other two algorithms converge slowly and have a large deviation from the target bitrate.

6 Conclusion

In this paper, we first conduct an in-depth measurement study to quantify the impacts of the ROI size and QP offset on the video bitrate and user QoE. The results indicate that it is feasible to lower down video bitrate with only slightly impairing user QoE by dynamically adjusting the ROI size and QP offset. We further propose a control-theoretic gamer experience-centric bitrate control algorithm for cloud gaming named GECKO, which can adaptively tune parameters according to video bitrate requirements. Finally, we implement our algorithm on GamingAnywhere and conduct a series of experiments to verify the effectiveness of our algorithm. The experiment results show that over 15.8% bandwidth can be saved compared with state-of-the-art approaches. In the future work, we will utilize low-cost gaze tracking devices, such as Intel RealSense [2] camera, to extract users' ROI and build a complete ROI-enabled cloud gaming platform.

Acknowledgement. This work was supported by the National Key Research and Development Program of China under Grant 2016YFB0201900, the National Science Foundation of China under Grant 61572538, the Fundamental Research Funds for the Central Universities under Grant 17LGJC23.

References

1. Global Cloud Gaming Market 2016–2020 (2016). http://www.technavio.com/report/global-gaming-cloud-market
2. Intel RealSense Technology (2016). http://www.intel.com/content/www/us/en/architecture-and-technology/realsense-overview.html

3. Q1 2016 State of the Internet Report (2016). https://goo.gl/wS6wl2
4. Rate control definition in x264 (2016). https://goo.gl/rn80ct
5. Ahmadi, H., Zad Tootaghaj, S., Hashemi, M.R., Shirmohammadi, S.: A game attention model for efficient bit rate allocation in cloud gaming. Multimed. Syst. **20**(5), 485–501 (2014)
6. Chen, K.T., Chang, Y.C., Hsu, H.J., Chen, D.Y., Huang, C.Y., Hsu, C.H.: On the quality of service of cloud gaming systems. IEEE Trans. Multimed. **16**(2), 480–495 (2014)
7. He, J., Wu, D., Xie, X., Chen, M., Li, Y., Zhang, G.: Efficient upstream bandwidth multiplexing for cloud video recording services. IEEE Trans. Circuits Syst. Video Technol. **26**(10), 1893–1906 (2016)
8. Huang, C.Y., Hsu, C.H., Chang, Y.C., Chen, K.T.: Gaminganywhere: an open cloud gaming system. In: Proceedings of the 4th ACM Multimedia Systems Conference, MMSys 2013, pp. 36–47. ACM (2013)
9. Lee, E.B., Markus, L.: Foundations of optimal control theory. Technical report, DTIC Document (1967)
10. Loza, A., Mihaylova, L., Canagarajah, N., Bull, D.: Structural similarity-based object tracking in video sequences. In: 2006 9th International Conference on Information Fusion, pp. 1–6. IEEE (2006)
11. Shea, R., Liu, J., Ngai, E.C.H., Cui, Y.: Cloud gaming: architecture and performance. IEEE Netw. **27**(4), 16–21 (2013)
12. Shen, L., Liu, Z., Zhang, Z.: A novel H.264 rate control algorithm with consideration of visual attention. Multimed. Tools App. **63**(3), 709–727 (2013)
13. Sun, K., Wu, D.: Video rate control strategies for cloud gaming. J. Vis. Commun. Image Represent. **30**, 234–241 (2015)
14. Tian, H., Wu, D., He, J., Xu, Y., Chen, M.: On achieving cost-effective adaptive cloud gaming in geo-distributed data centers. IEEE Trans. Circuits Syst. Video Technol. **25**(12), 2064–2077 (2015)
15. Wandell, B.A.: Foundations of Vision. Sinauer Associates, Sunderland (1995)
16. Wang, Z., Bovik, A.C., Sheikh, H.R., Simoncelli, E.P.: Image quality assessment: from error visibility to structural similarity. IEEE Trans. Image Process. **13**(4), 600–612 (2004)
17. Wu, D., Xue, Z., He, J.: iCloudAccess: cost-effective streaming of video games from the cloud with low latency. IEEE Trans. Circuits Syst. Video Technol. **24**(8), 1405–1416 (2014)
18. Xue, Z., Wu, D., He, J., Hei, X., Liu, Y.: Playing high-end video games in the cloud: a measurement study. IEEE Trans. Circuits Syst. Video Technol. **25**(12), 2013–2025 (2015)
19. Yang, L., Zhang, L., Ma, S., Zhao, D.: A ROI quality adjustable rate control scheme for low bitrate video coding. In: 2009 Picture Coding Symposium, pp. 1–4. May 2009
20. Zhang, L., Zhang, L., Mou, X., Zhang, D.: A comprehensive evaluation of full reference image quality assessment algorithms. In: 2012 19th IEEE International Conference on Image Processing, pp. 1477–1480. September 2012
21. Zheng, Y., Wu, D., Ke, Y., Yang, C., Chen, M., Zhang, G.: Online cloud transcoding and distribution for crowdsourced live game video streaming. IEEE Trans. Circuits Syst. Video Technol. (IEEE TCSVT) **27**(8), 1777–1789 (2017)
22. Zhou, L.: QoE-driven delay announcement for cloud mobile media. IEEE Trans. Circuits Syst. Video Technol. **27**(1), 84–94 (2017)

A QoE-Aware Video Quality Guarantee Mechanism in 5G Network

Ruyan Wang, Yan Yang[⊠], and Dapeng Wu

Key Laboratory of Optical Communication and Networks,
Chongqing University of Posts and Telecommunications,
Chongqing 400065, China
425504592@qq.com

Abstract. Future Fifth-Generation networks are expected to predominantly carry multimedia traffic. Video consume an enormous amount of scarce resources in mobile devices and cellular wireless networks due to the demand for high data rates of video streaming. The limited resource of wireless media and unreliable nature of wireless channels in cellular networks make challenging to deliver videos at high quality of experience. Therefore, this paper proposed an a QoE-aware video quality guarantee Mechanism. Considered link state information and scalable video coding structure, established a QoE evaluation mode, and used the particle swarm optimization algorithm to select optimal video transmission rate. The results show that the proposed method can effectively improve the utilization rate of network resources and reduce network congestion while improving the quality of the user experience.

Keywords: 5G network · Scalable video coding · Quality of experience
Particle swarm algorithm

1 Introduction

In the future Fifth-Generation (5G) mobile communication network, the extensive promotion of mobile Internet applications, and the extensive use of intelligent terminals, such as smart phones, tablet PCs, which will make video business to further rapid growth [1, 2]. Therefore, the network carrying capacity has put forward higher requirements due to its high bandwidth and delay sensitive characteristics. The user needs to communicate with the Internet through the mobile communication network constantly, and the entire mobile communication network carries the data traffic become extremely large [3], which bring the huge challenge for the mobile communication network data transmission and distribution ability. Faced with such a massive amount of data traffic, as the core technology of the next generation mobile communication system, the development of 5G key technology needs to support the massive data business effectively [4, 5].

Research shows that the number of user clicks on video is closely related to the popularity of the video. In the large video site, the top 20% of the prevailing video occupies nearly 80% of the click-through rate, both of which follow the Zipf distribution [6]. According to Cisco's latest networking forecast, mobile video will account

© Springer International Publishing AG 2017
Y. Zhao et al. (Eds.): ICIG 2017, Part II, LNCS 10667, pp. 336–352, 2017.
https://doi.org/10.1007/978-3-319-71589-6_30

for about 75% of all mobile data traffic by 2019, 13-fold as much as that in 2014 [7]. In 5G network, the base station(BS) needs to allocate resources for each demand user in the time domain and frequency domain, and send the same content to different users repeatedly. Obviously, the large data volume of multimedia services cause a great waste of network resources, resulting in a rapid decline in user service experience (QoE) [8]. Multicast transmission mechanism can effectively alleviate this phenomenon, according to the downlink broadcast characteristics of BS. transmits the same video stream to multiple users at the same time. However the differentiated channel and link resources between BS and users can not guarantee that all users successfully receive. Therefore, in order to meet the demand of different users for video services and dynamic changes in the network environment, scalable video coding (SVC) is widely used in video multicast transmission [9]. SVC coding technology divides video content into a base layer (BL) and several enhancement layers (EL). In general, an EL cannot be decoded unless all its requisite lower layers have been successfully received and decoded [10].

In addition to the increasing consumer expectations in terms of service quality, the persistent growth in the volume of video traffic traversing both public and private computer networks, has brought challenges to the multimedia traffic engineering, quality of service (QoS) model constraints [11], and efficient QoE metric measurements for video clients in traditional networks. In [12], proposed a capacity and delay-aware routing algorithm, using the link packet arrival rate for the link capacity calculation, allocates the resources reasonably to support a higher load with low latency, but its resource utilization is low. In [13], using the worst play delay as the video transmission quality evaluation index, it proposes a batch processing broadcast mechanism for non-hot users to ensure that there are enough resources to serve hot users. In multi-hop mechanism, the utilization of available videos cached in the femtocells can be maximized compared to single-hop [14] although it may cause multi-hop delay problem. However, the above mechanism mainly uses the network throughput, packet loss rate and network delay as the video service transmission quality evaluation standard, it do not necessarily equate to the end users' perception of delivered content.

In this paper, we propose a QoE-aware video quality guarantee Mechanism (QAVGM). Firstly, according to the wireless link status and user requests, it quantifies the user's subjective experience during business interaction. Secondly, the vector particle swarm algorithm is proposed to allocate the appropriate transmission rate for each layer of video service. Thirdly, considering multi-user situations, we extend a management for multi-user situation. Using the user's signal to interference plus noise ratio (SINR) to assigns a specific number of service layer to each user.

2 Video Quality Assessment

QoE represents the user's integrated subjective feelings on the application or multimedia business quality [15]. Statistics found that t viewing duration can indirectly reflect the user's satisfaction with regardless the video content and length. Therefore, using the viewing duration to adjust the video transmission rate adaptively, it can effectively guarantee the user QoE [16]. In this section, we first select the main factors that affect the continuous viewing time based on the link state information and the transmission characteristics of the SVC video stream. Next, we obtain a user satisfaction function aiming at the continuous viewing time to evaluate QoE.

2.1 Estimation of QoE Metrics

To estimate the QoE metrics, we encode raw video into the SVC format with one BL and $N - 1$ ELs. In this paper, using the MCS_k to denote the modulation and coding schemes (MCS) of kth layer. The research shows that when the cache data stored of the receiver below the play threshold, the video can produce a rebuffer event, causing the playback interrupt. This situation can seriously affect the user experience. Furthermore, if the quality of the video provided can not meet the user's expectation, the user experience also decreases rapidly. So we use buffering ratio (BR) and playback quality acceptance to *estimate* the QoE. A part of the symbols used in our derivation is provided in Table 1.

Table 1. The symbol definition

Symbol	Definition
ζ_k	Packet loss rate of kth layer
BW_k	required bandwidth of kth layer
C	Video playback threshold
∂	Video interrupt threshold
$Play_T$	Average playback time
$Buff_T$	buffering duration

(1) Buffering Ratio

For the kth Layer of video in the ith Link, the transmission of this layer is interfered by other layers, because different layers with SVC coding method use different MCS. And the transmission of different links also has an impact on this link. Thus the interference noise of this layer mainly comes from three aspects: link interference, interlayer interference and white Gaussian noise. Note that, $H_{i,k}$ and $L_{i,k}$ denote the transmit power of the kth layer data in the ith link and the pass loss of the kth layer data in the ith link, respectively. Then the Signal to Interference plus Noise Ratio (SINR) of the data in the k layer is computed as follows:

$$SINR_{i,k} = \frac{H_{i,k}/L_{i,k}}{\sum\limits_{j \neq i}\sum\limits_{k} H_{j,k}/L_{j,k} + \sum\limits_{z \neq k} H_{i,z}/L_{i,z} + N_0} \tag{1}$$

According to Shannon's theorem, the bandwidth required for the kth layer data is shown in Eq. (2). Where r_k indicates the transmission rate of the kth layer video traffic and it depends on the MCS selected.

$$BW_k = \frac{r_k}{\log_2(1 + SINR_k)} \tag{2}$$

The transmission of video stream requires the terminal to steadily review the received video content. Packet loss makes the terminal continue to apply for retransmission constantly, which not only needs additional network resources, but also causes redundant data transmission and reduces the effective data reception rate. Due to the lack of transmission capability, the BS will cache data exceeding the processing capability of the front-end device, until there is available resources to re-transmission, which can avoid unnecessary packet loss and network congestion. Therefore, the packet loss rate of the kth layer service is shown in Eq. (3). Where B_k indicates the size of the kth layer data cached at the BS and λ_k denotes the input stream code rate of the kth layer.

$$\zeta_k = \frac{\lambda_k t - r_k t - B_k}{\lambda_k t} \tag{3}$$

And then the average video reception rate can be acquired, as shown in Eq. (4).

$$Data_{avg} = \sum_{k=1}^{N} r_k \cdot (1 - \zeta_k) \tag{4}$$

The transmission capacity of the link is limited. When the packet is larger than the maximum transmission unit of the link, it can be fragmented into small enough packets. The fragmentation threshold of the link is represented as TH_{frag}, which determined by the connection type of the link and the processing capability of the node. In order not to make the data transmission efficiency of the wireless link too low, it is generally set to 1500 bytes. So the data of the kth layer will be divided into $\left\lceil \frac{r_k}{TH_{frag}} \right\rceil$ fragments in unit time. Considering the particularity of video services, the video data can be properly received after all the fragments is received successfully. Hence, the success probability of the kth layer data is shown in Eq. (5).

$$S_k = (1 - \zeta_k)^{\left\lceil \frac{r_k}{TH_{frag}} \right\rceil} \tag{5}$$

The quality of video encoded by SCV depends on the number of video layers that the terminal can decode. The upper-level data is dependent on the lower-level data. If the EL data is to be decoded successfully, the BL data must be received correctly. The playback rate PL_{avg} reflects the quality of the video that the user can view or the consumption rate of the video data at the cache. Therefore, considered the effect of network state on it, the average playback rate of the video is shown in Eq. (6).

$$PL_{avg} = r_1 \cdot (1 - \zeta_1)^{\left\lceil \frac{r_1}{TH_{frag}} \right\rceil} + r_2 \cdot (1 - \zeta_1)^{\left\lceil \frac{r_1}{TH_{frag}} \right\rceil} \cdot (1 - \zeta_2)^{\left\lceil \frac{r_2}{TH_{frag}} \right\rceil} + \cdots$$

$$+ r_k \cdot (1 - \zeta_1)^{\left\lceil \frac{r_1}{TH_{frag}} \right\rceil} \cdots (1 - \zeta_k)^{\left\lceil \frac{r_k}{TH_{frag}} \right\rceil} \tag{6}$$

$$= \sum_{k=0}^{N} r_k \cdot \prod_{j=0}^{k} S_j$$

When the terminal buffer data is below the playback threshold, the video will interrupt playback and convert to the rebuffering state. Until the data rebuffers to the video playback condition, then it can playback again. The study shows that the amount of data in the buffer is not exactly equal to zero when the interruption happen, but about 0.5 s of video data (represented as ∂, $\partial = 0.5PL_{avg}$); When the amount of buffer data accumulate to 1.9 s of video data (represented as C, $C = 1.9PL_{avg}$), video can resume playback [17]. $Buff_T$ denotes the interrupt buffer times from interrupt to replay, as shown in Eq. (7)

$$Buff_T = \frac{C - \partial}{Data_{avg}} = \frac{1.4PL_{avg}}{Data_{avg}} \tag{7}$$

At the beginning of the video playback, the user caches the video data firstly. The video playback process is started until the cache capacity reaches the playback threshold C required for playback. During playback times, the terminal receives video data from the network at the rate of $Data_{avg}$ and provides video services to the user at the rate of PL_{avg}. If the video reception rate is less than the average playback rate, the video data in buffer will be reduced continuously during the video playback. When the buffer capacity decreases at the interrupt threshold ∂, the user incurs playback interruption and returns to the rebuffering state (i.e., video lag). If the playback rate is much greater than the receiving, it will continue to enter the playback – interruption process, which must increase the video interrupt buffer time. Instead, if the network provides a higher transmission rate than the playback rate, cache capacity is sufficient enough to avoid rebuffering, so the user can continue to accept the video service. Hence, during the period from playback to interruption, the average play time $Play_T$ of the video service can be expressed as the time that the cache capacity is consumed from C to the interrupt threshold ∂, as shown in Eq. (8).

$$Play_T = \begin{cases} \frac{C-\partial}{PL_{avg}-Data_{avg}} & Data_{avg} \leq PL_{avg} \\ \infty & Data_{avg} > PL_{avg} \end{cases} \tag{8}$$

Video services need to occupy a larger network bandwidth continuously. In the 5G network with multi-service, it is difficult to guarantee the resource of video services. If the playback rate of the terminal is greater than the transmission rate, the buffered data will be consumed, and the playback will be interrupted when satisfies the interrupt condition. Let interrupt buffering ratio indicates the ratio of the video playback duration and the interrupt buffer duration, which reflects the percentage of time the user incurs interruption during the viewing process. As shown in Eq. (9).

$$BR = \frac{Buff_T}{Play_T + Buff_T} = \begin{cases} 1 - \frac{Data_{avg}}{PL} & Data_{avg} \leq PL_{avg} \\ 0 & Data_{avg} > PL_{avg} \end{cases} \tag{9}$$

(2) Video Quality Acceptance

The playback rate provided by network is related to the current network load, link quality and other physical factors. If there is a large difference between the playback rate and the user's expected playback rate, his viewing experience will be declined. Let r denotes the user's request rate. Generally, the request rate can be represented by a specific probability density function $f(r)$ [18], where $r \in [r_0, r_{max}]$. r_0, r_{max} denotes the minimum and maximum values of the requested rate, respectively. The user's request rate reflects the subjective expectation of the video quality and not be affected by other users and network factors, so the request rate obeys the uniform distribution in this interval [18]. Then, $f(r)$ satisfy the probability density function as shown in Eq. (10)

$$f(r) = \frac{1}{r_{max} - r_0}, r \in [r_0, r_{max}] \tag{10}$$

Weber-Fickner's Law points out that the user's evaluation of the external environment is a logarithmic function of subjective expectation [19], which is generally applicable to the fields of vision, hearing, touching and so on. So we can use this law to evaluate the user viewing experience. Because of the user's sense is non-linear, it is difficult to quantify from the number. But it is feasible to quantitative determinate the user's satisfaction by his requesting. In order to make the playback rate and the request rate to meet an approximate monotonic change relationship, and reduce the absolute value difference between the two rates. A logarithmic function $Q(PL_{avg}, r)$ is formulated to denote the acceptance of video quality, as shown in Eq. (11).

$$Q(PL_{avg}, r) = \alpha \ln \frac{\beta PL_{avg}}{r} \tag{11}$$

where α, β is the adjustment factor. α is in the range of 0.5–1, which is related to the type of video. β represents the average amount of data per unit frame, as shown in Eq. (12).

$$\beta = \frac{\sum_{i=1}^{N} r_k}{FPS} \tag{12}$$

2.2   User Satisfaction Assessment

The BS, as the wireless network access point, completes the wireless service transmission. it assigns the appropriate link resources for each user according by the user's request information. Let BW_j denotes the total link bandwidth of BS_j, and as described in the formula (2), it can acquire the required link bandwidth for transmission the kth layer of video stream under different MCS. With the actual situation of the network, the required bandwidth should be less than or equal to the total bandwidth of the sender. In order to save network resources as much as possible, the importance of different layers can be utilized to select an appropriate MCS for them. For example, we choose a slower MCS for the base layer to ensure reliable transmission of the video, while select a faster MCS for enhanced layers to save the network resource.

As mentioned above, The video will be interrupted for a long time with high buffering ratio, thus it will make his viewing experience decline rapidly. And if the playback rate fails to meet his expected, which will also have an impact on viewing. This paper establishes a user satisfaction function to evaluate his acceptance, as shown in Eq. (13).

$$U_i = T_{\text{full}} \cdot e^{-BR} \cdot \alpha \ln \frac{\beta PL_{avg}}{r}$$

$$s.t \sum_{k=1}^{N} BW_{ik} \leq BW_{ji} \tag{13}$$

The constraint function indicates that the bandwidth of the video service should be less or equal to the total bandwidth of the BS allocated. T_{full} indicates the maximum viewing duration, depending on the video content. The user's viewing duration can be an indirect response to his satisfaction about this video, i.e. The more longer viewing time he is, it mean that he has a higher experience degree.

3   Link Adaptive Algorithm

To make the playback rate to meet the requirements of users as much as possible, BS also should choose a more reasonable MCS in addition to improve the reliability of each layer. However, according to Shannon's theorem, the faster transmission rate, the more bandwidth resources are consumed. In the case of limited resources, transmission rate of different video layer is mutual restriction and conflict, that is, the increase of one will lead to the reduction of another, which has a great impact on satisfaction. Each layer of SVC video resources deployment is a discrete solution set. As the particle swarm algorithm has the advantages of fast calculation speed and easy portability, it can avoid the local optimal solution and produce a high-performance solution. In this paper, we use the Vector Particle Swarm Optimization Algorithm (VPSO) to select a optimal MCS under the condition of limited network resources, which makes the user's QoE performance to reach the optimal state.

3.1 Single User Link Adaptive Control

Each of the available solutions in VPSO is represented by a particle. Each particle is an N-dimensional vector with two characteristics of position and velocity, the objective function value corresponding to the current position of the particle is the fitness value of the particle. An SVC video service has a total of N layer data, the current position $X_i = (x_{i1}, x_{i2}, \ldots x_{iN})$ of the ith particle represents a video distribution scheme in which each element x_{ik} represents the MCS selected by the kth layer video service; The optimal position of the ith particle current search is represented by $PB_i = (pb_{i1}, pb_{i2} \ldots pb_{iN})$, and the optimal position of the entire particle swarm search is denoted by $GB = (gb_1, gb_2 \ldots gb_N)$. The particle velocity at the next moment in the iteration is affected by the current position of the particle, the optimal position searched by the particle, and the optimal position of the particle swarm search. The update rate and the next time position of particle are calculated as shown in Eqs. (14) and (15).

$$v_{ik}(t+1) = \mu \times v_{ik}(t) + \tau_1 \times rand \times (pb_{ik}(t) - x_{ik}(t)) + \tau_2 \times rand \times (gb_{ik} - x_{ik}(t))$$
(14)

$$x_{ik}(t+1) = x_{ik}(t) + v_{ik}(t+1) \tag{15}$$

where μ is the inertia constant of the particle, τ_1 τ_2 is the weight parameter, which is used to adjust the weight relationship between the best position searched by itself and the global optimal position, and rand is a random constant with a range of [0, 1].

In the scheduling process, the computational complexity is exponentially increasing considering multiple user requests at the same time due to the difference of link quality and the request status between users. Therefore, firstly this paper considers the single-user video scheduling strategy, using the formula (13) as a fitness function to evaluate each particle in the particle group, and the optimal allocation combination is selected by iteratively to optimize the function. However, the fitness function is limited by the link bandwidth, and the direct use of Eq. (13) produces many cases where the particle fitness is high but does not satisfy the constraint condition. Therefore, the fitness function needs to be relaxed. Considering the influence of the restriction condition, this paper designs a dynamic penalty function P. After the particle chooses MCS for each layer of video, BS calculates the bandwidth BW_1 consumed by all the video layers. If it is larger than the link bandwidth of the user, the fitness function after relaxation is defined as the difference between the original fitness function and the nonnegative penalty function term $P(BW_1 - BW_{ji})$, and if $BW_1 - BW_{ji}$ is less than 0, the penalty function is 0, that is, no penalty; As the gap between the consumed network bandwidth and the link bandwidth increases, the penalty function increases proportionally. In this section, the penalty function and the fitness function are given by (16), (17), respectively.

$$P(BW_1 - BW_{ji}) = \begin{cases} 0 & BW_1 - BW_{ji} < 0 \\ e^{(BW_1 BW_{ji})} & BW_1 - BW_{ji} \geq 0 \end{cases} \tag{16}$$

$$C_i = T_{\text{full}} \times e^{-\text{BR}} \times \alpha \ln \frac{\beta PL_{avg}}{r} - P(BW_1 - BW_{ji}) \tag{17}$$

According to the above algorithm and fitness function selection, the deployment steps are as follows:

1. Deployment strategy initialization.
To determine the selected MCS, we selects four different MCSs: BPSK,QPSK,16-QAM, 64-QAM. The corresponding numbers are 1, 2, 3, and 4, respectively. We assumes that no transmission is also a modulation strategy with the number 0, then the data of each layer can choose five kinds of modulation mode. Each modulation scheme represents a different transmission rate and reliability. Then, it can randomly generate O particles, each particle is an N-dimensional vector, and the number of iterations is limited to L.

2. Particle sequence update.
The particles in the population are evaluated by using the generated fitness function (17), and the larger fitness value indicates the better performance of the user under this deployment scheme. According to the inter-layer dependency of the SVC video, if the enhancement layer is successfully decoded, it means that the video layer data lower than this layer must be successfully received. If the lower layer is not transmitted (that is, the policy number is 0), the higher layer cannot be successfully decoded even if it is received. In this paper, it is assumed that this is the same as in the case of no transmission. For example, the sequence of a particle is (1, 0, 2 ... 4) in the iteration process. Since the first enhancement layer is not sent, the subsequent layer cannot be decoded even if the data is received. Therefore, it should adjust the particle sequence to (1, 0, 0 ... 0). And then recalculate the fitness of the particle.

3. To achieve the optimization of particle swarm.
In this paper, we use the formulas (14) and (15) to change the position and velocity of the particles to obtain a better video scheduling strategy. In the process of iteration, the individual extremum PB_i is used to represent the optimal position of the particle i under the current iteration. If the fitness value of the iteration is larger than the fitness value of the individual extremum, the individual extremum is replaced by the position of the iteration; otherwise, the individual extremum is not updated. Similarly, the whole extremum GB of the whole particle group represents the optimal position under current iteration. If the individual extremum of the ith particle under the iteration is larger than the whole extremum, the whole extremum is replaced by the position of the particle; otherwise, the extreme value is not updated.

4. Optimal solution selection.
With the change of the velocity and position of the particle, the velocity and the move trajectory of the particle are influenced by the individual extremum and the global extremum of the whole particle group. It makes all the particles move towards the direction of the objective function. If the variation between the global extremum fitness $U_i(GB_k)$ of the particle after the kth iteration and the global extremum before the iteration is less than a certain predetermined range, it means that the extremum is very close to the optimal extremum and the iteration should be stopped. The stop expression is shown in (18).

$$GB^* = GB_k \qquad if \, \frac{U_i(GB_k)}{U_i(GB)} \le \Delta \qquad (18)$$

If the iterative process satisfies the above process, the iteration is stopped. GB^* is the optimal position of the particle at the time of the stopped iteration, that is, the optimal video hierarchical scheduling scheme chosen in this paper. If the above situation does not occur, it should repeat the above steps until the maximum number of iterations is reached.

The proposed SVC video deployment strategy pseudo-code is as follows:

Algorithm1 (A Single User Link Adaptive Control, SLAC)
1:Initialization   O   N   L
2:for($i=1;i<=M;\ i++$)
3:{
4:for($j=1;k<=N;\ k++$)
5:{
6:Generate the initial population
7:}
8:}
9:while(iteration<=L ;iteration++)
10:{
11:Evaluate $C_i = T_{full} \cdot e^{-BR} \cdot \alpha \ln \frac{\beta PL_{avg}}{r} - P(BW_1 - BW_{ji})$
12:Update particle sequence
13:Calculate population individual extremum and the extremum(PB,GB)
14:Update the particle velocity(v_{ik})
15:Update the particle position(x_{ik})
16:Update the particle fitness
17:if($\frac{U_i(GB_k)}{U_i(GB)} \le \Delta$)
18:$GB^* = GB_k$
19:end
20:else
21:Update C and repeat procedure 12
22:end
23: }

3.2 Multicast User Link Adaptive Control

In the case of multicasting an SVC video stream, our goal is to give every group member the ability to receive an acceptable QoE from the video stream. Since these users have different link quality and request status, the traditional method is to select the user with the worst link quality as the transmission standard of this multicast group to meet the needs of multicast group users. This method can ensure that every users can receive video successfully, but it will result in part of the waste of resources for the people with better quality of the link. Figure 1(a) shows an example of multicast an SVC video stream, layers are fragmented into small packets and each of the three

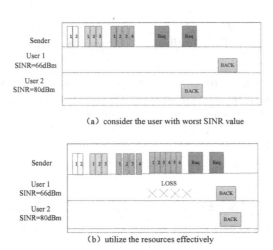

(a) consider the user with worst SINR value

(b) utilize the resources effectively

Fig. 1. Multicast users video transmission model

receivers has a different SINR value. If we consider the receiver with the lowest SINR value, only three layers of video services can be received for this group, but for user 2 with better link quality, he needs to wait for the user 1 to receive completely, then he can receive follow-up video business. This can cause serious waste of resources, while reducing the quality of the video that users can receive.

We propose a multicast users link adaptive control to solve the above problems. the BS collects the SINR values of all of its group members, it sorts the user in an increasing order of each of their SINR values. The SLAC algorithm, shown in Algorithm 1, starts from the user i with the lowest SINR value to obtain the optimal solution set of the user and the number of video layers K and Calculate the bandwidth used in this state, shown as $\sum_{k=1}^{K} BW_k$. Then, considering the next user $i + 1$, if the user's remaining link bandwidth is met $BW_{ji+1} - \sum_{k=1}^{K} BW_k > BW_{K+1}$, it indicates that the link can transmit a higher layer of video. Therefore, in the case of ensuring that the data transfer mode of the former K layer is unchanged, the SLAC algorithm is used to allocate the remaining link bandwidth for user $i + 1$. This algorithm stops loop this process until all layers are assigned an MCS, or the algorithm has completed for all users. As shown in Fig. 2(b), When the remaining bandwidth of user 2 can meet the transmission of layer 4, the sender will transmit 4 layers of video for the multicast group. Although the user 1 can not receive the layer data due to the limited transmission capability, the user 2 can successfully receive and improve the viewing experience of the user 2. The deployment strategy pseudo-code is as follows.

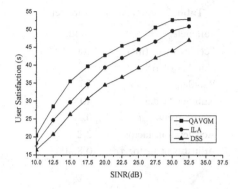

Fig. 2. The user satisfaction under various SINR

Algorithm2(A Multicast Users Link Adaptive Control)
1:Initialization   GRP_SIZE MAX_LAYER
2:K=0
3:Collect SINR values from receivers
4:Sort receivers in increasing order of SINR values
5:for(r=the worst receiver;(r<GRP_SIZE&&K<MAX_LAYER);r++)
6:{
7:Run SLAC for rth receiver
8: K=the highest layer that has been assigned an MCS
9:calculate $\sum_{k=1}^{K} BW_k$ BW_{K+1}
10:if($BW_{r+1} - \sum_{k=1}^{K} BW_k > BW_{K+1}$)
11:{
12:repete 6
13:else
14:end
15:}
16:service_layer[r]=K
17:}

4 Performance Evaluation

In this section, we present the performance evaluation of our proposed mechanism by Network Simulator 2. Then, we compare the proposed mechanism (QAVGM) with ILA mechanism [15] and DSS mechanism [20]. The ILA algorithm uses the fairness constraint to adjust the video transmission rate and ensures the transmission performance of the video service when the link state changes. And the DSS designs to maximize the number of service recipients by effectively conserving bandwidth consumption. The simulation parameters are given in Table 2.

Table 2. Simulation parameters

Parameter	Value
Scenario size (m²)	500 × 500
Number of BS	4
Population size (w)	20
Number of iterations	40
Inertia weight μ	0.5
Acceleration factor $\tau_1\tau_2$	2,2
Adjustment factor $\alpha\beta$	0.8,400

The SVC video has an average bit rate of 10 Mbps with total playback duration of 60 s, its specification is given in Table 3. the peak signal-to-noise ratio (PSNR) is an objective evaluation of image quality, it is computed for the difference between the decoded frame and the original frame. So we use PSNR as a standard to evaluate video quality. In order to simulation, we assume that the user request rate corresponds to the transmission rate of the video layer, for example, if a user expects to view two layers of video content, his request rate is 2656 kpbs.

Table 3. SVC video specification

Layer	Resolution	Frame rate (fbps)	Bitrate (kbps)
0	700 * 500	30	1177
1	700 * 500	30	1479
2	700 * 500	30	2845
3	700 * 500	30	5103

4.1 Performance of Different Link Quality

Figure 2 reflects the relationship between link quality and user satisfaction. Obviously, customer satisfaction has a whole upward trend with the improvement of link quality. Increasing the quality of the link will enhance the user satisfaction when SINR is poor. From the results, we can see that the performance of the QAVGM mechanism is higher than those of ILA and DSS mechanisms by 22.5 and 38.3%, respectively. This is mainly because of QAVGM dynamically adjusts the transmission rate of different layer services according to SVC service characteristics and link quality. It can allocate bandwidth resources more rationally, improve the efficiency of video buffer and reduce the impact of interruption play caused by insufficient buffer.

The available video quality under different link quality is shown in Fig. 3. As can be seen, when SINR is lower than 17.5 dB, improving the quality of the link will make the video business improved significantly. Because of the link packet loss rate, which is the main factor affecting video performance, will increase greatly when the SINR decreases rapidly. While at SINR is higher than 30 dB, the increase in video quality

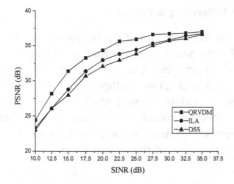

Fig. 3. The relationship between the video quality and the link quality

tends to be smooth. The proposed mechanism can effectively enhance the user viewing quality, improve the transmission efficiency, and avoid the packet loss during the video distribution.

4.2 Performance Analysis Under Different Loads

Business delay is also an important indicator of user QoE. The business delay under various loads is shown in Fig. 4. The results show that the network delay increases with the lowing network load but it is not obvious. Because the available bandwidth of the node is relatively abundant, and the increasing load has a limited influence on the delay. Therefore, the three mechanisms have the similar performance. However, when the node load is large, QAVGM mechanism can decrease the amount of redundant data transmission, thus it reduces the impact of network congestion on video services. It can be seen from the figure that the delay performance of proposed mechanism is 25.7% and 33.1% higher than those of the video distribution mechanism when the load is large.

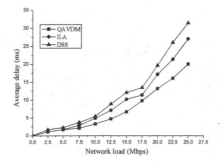

Fig. 4. The average delay under various network load

4.3   Performance at Different User Sizes

We simulate the multicast user size from 2–10 business performance. The relationship between the number of users and the average user satisfaction is shown in Fig. 5. The average satisfaction has a downward trend with the number of users increase. This is because increasing number will allow multiple users to share network bandwidth, thereby it will reduce the availability of individual user. The proposed mechanism can effectively enhance the video transmission performance of low SINR users, ensure that they can successfully receive business, improve the transmission efficiency. Thus also increasing the average satisfaction of the overall users.

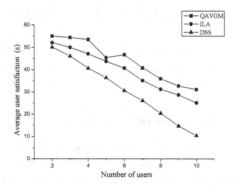

Fig. 5. The average user satisfaction in different number of users

Besides, to validate the efficacy of the proposed mechanism, the average PSNR value for the video service under various users is simulated in Fig. 6. the growing number of users indicates more and more users apply for the same video business. When the number is large, the performance in QAVGM is higher than others mechanism while the overall performance has declined. In order to ensure the users' experience whose link state is poor, QAVGM mechanism takes consideration of the

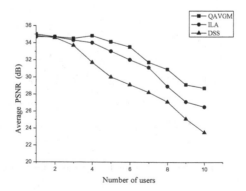

Fig. 6. The average video quality in different number of users

physical conditions of different users and the advantages of SVC video structure. Then use the available bandwidth to improve the video quality gradually. So this mechanism can maintain better video quality when the number of users is large.

5   Conclusions

To solve the problem in delivering high-demanding multimedia applications in 5G mobile networks, we have proposed a QoE-aware video quality guarantee Mechanism. With the mechanism, the link status and user request are used to establish the appropriate QoE evaluation system. Besides, to maximize the user satisfaction, SLAC assigns MCSs on the basis of the buffering ratio, the average playback bitrate, and SINR of each of the users. Finally, considering an SVC video stream over multicast, we designed an MLAC which extends our SLAC scheme by adding a method which allows us to optimize the average users experience. Simulation results show that the proposed mechanism have high performance in video distribution and bandwidth resource efficiency.

References

1. Eiza, M.H., Ni, Q., Shi, Q.: Secure and privacy-aware cloud-assisted video reporting service in 5G-enabled vehicular networks. IEEE Trans. Veh. Technol. **65**(10), 7868–7881 (2016)
2. Beyranvand, H., Levesque, M., Maier, M., et al.: Toward 5G: FiWi enhanced LTE - a hetnets with reliable low-latency fiber backhaul sharing and wifi offloading. IEEE/ACM Trans. Netw. **PP**(99), 1–18 (2016)
3. Qiao, J., Shen, X.S., Mark, J.W., et al.: Video quality provisioning for millimeter wave 5G cellular networks with link outage. IEEE Trans. Wirel. Commun. **14**(10), 5692–5703 (2015)
4. Qiao, J., He, Y., Shen, X.S.: Proactive caching for mobile video streaming in millimeter wave 5G networks. IEEE Trans. Wirel. Commun. **15**(10), 7187–7198 (2016)
5. Wu, D.P., Yan, J.J., Wang, H.G., et al.: Social attribute aware incentive mechanisms for video distribution in device-to-device communications. IEEE Trans. Multimed. **19**, 1908–1920 (2017). https://doi.org/10.1109/TMM.2017.2692648
6. Tu, W.: Efficient wireless multimedia multicast in multi-rate multi-channel mesh networks. IEEE Trans. Sig. Inf. Process. Over Netw. **2**(3), 376–390 (2016)
7. Wang, S., Chen, S., Ge, L., et al.: Distributed generation hosting capacity evaluation for distribution systems considering the robust optimal operation of OLTC and SVC. IEEE Trans. Sustain. Energy **7**(3), 1111–1123 (2016)
8. Kuo, W.H., Kaliski, R., Wei, H.Y.: QoE-based link adaptation scheme for H.264/SVC video multicast over IEEE 802.11. IEEE Trans. Circuits Syst. Video Technol. **25**(5), 812–826 (2015)
9. Staehle, B., Hirth, M., Pries, R., et al.: YoMo: a Youtube application comfort monitoring tool. In: New Dimensions in the Assessment and Support of Quality of Experience for Multimedia Applications (2010)
10. Reaz, A., Ramamurthi, V., Sarkar, S., et al.: CaDAR: an efficient routing algorithm for a wireless-optical broadband access network (WOBAN). J. Opt. Commun. Netw. **1**(5), 392–403 (2009)

11. Li, Y., Dai, S.F., Chang, X.M.: Delay guaranteed VoD services over group-based integrated fiber-wireless (FiWi) access networks with energy efficiency. Opt. Fiber Technol. **24**, 100–105 (2015)
12. Shanmugam, K., Golrezaei, N., Dimakis, A.G., et al.: Femtocaching: wireless content delivery through distributed caching helpers. IEEE Trans. Inf. Theory **59**(12), 8402–8413 (2013)
13. Ren, D.P., Li, H., Ji, Y.F.: Demonstration of QoS-aware wireless protection scheme for video service in fiber-wireless access network. Optik **124**(14), 1827–1831 (2013)
14. Akyildiz, I.F., Wang, P., Lin, S.C.: SoftAir: a software defined networking architecture for 5G wireless systems. Comput. Netw. **85**, 1–18 (2015)
15. Fallah, Y.P., Mansour, H., Khan, S., et al.: A link adaptation scheme for efficient transmission of H.264 scalable video over multirate WLANs. IEEE Trans. Circuits Syst. Video Technol. **18**(7), 875–887 (2008)
16. Mitola, J., Guerci, J., Reed, J., et al.: Accelerating 5G QoE via public-private spectrum sharing. IEEE Commun. Mag. **52**(5), 77–85 (2014)
17. Aissioui, A., Ksentini, A., Guerou, A.M., et al.: Toward elastic distributed SDN/NFV controller for 5G mobile cloud management systems. Access IEEE **3**, 2055–2064 (2016)
18. Zhang, W., Wen, Y., Chen, Z., et al.: QoE-driven cache management for HTTP adaptive bit rate streaming over wireless networks. IEEE Trans. Multimed. **15**(6), 1431–1445 (2013)
19. Reichl, P., Tuffin, B., Schatz, R.: Logarithmic laws in service quality perception: where microeconomics meets psychophysics and quality of experience. Telecommun. Syst. **52**(2), 587–600 (2013)
20. Kuo, W.H., Lee, J.F.: Multicast recipient maximization in IEEE 802.16j WIMAX relay networks. IEEE Trans. Veh. Technol. **59**(1), 335–343 (2010)

Energy-Aware Fast Interest Forwarding
for Multimedia Streaming over ICN 5G-D2D

Xingyan Chen[1(✉)], Mu Wang[1(✉)], Shijie Jia[2], and Changqiao Xu[1(✉)]

[1] State Key Laboratory of Networking and Switching Technology,
Beijing University of Posts and Telecommunications, Bejing 100876, China
cqxu@bupt.edu.cn
[2] Academy of Information Technology, Luoyang Normal University,
Luoyang 471022, China

Abstract. By providing extremely low delivery latency, very high data rate and significant improvement on network capacity, 5G wireless communications have paved the way for introducing high quality multimedia services such ultra HD videos into mobile Internet. The new emerging multimedia applications further spurs the ever growing mobile data traffic and diverse quality of service requirements, which has motivated the need to explore new data delivery paradigms and network architectures. Recently, the combined use of device-to-device (D2D) and information-centric networking (ICN) has been shown to be a promising approach for wide range of multimedia applications in 5G. However, a critical issue is how to select appropriate *Interest* forwarders in order to fast discover nearby content provider while remains low energy consumption. In this paper, we propose an energy-aware fast *Interest* forwarding scheme (EAFF) for multimedia streaming over ICN 5G-D2D. We firstly formulate the *Interest* forwarding problem to jointly optimize the energy consumption and forwarding coverage, and prove it to be NP-hard but submodular and monotonous. Then we propose a greed-based distributed forwarder selection algorithm which enables each node individually determines the next-hop forwarders during the *Interest* forwarding process. We also conduct a series of simulation tests to show that our proposed method achieves dramatically performance improvement with the respect to state-of-art solutions.

1 Introduction

The increasing wireless bandwidth and ubiquitously network accessing provided by the incoming of 5G [1–3] have further spurred the explosive growth of high quality video streaming applications such as ultra HD video [4] in mobile Internet. According to the VNI report of CISCO [5], the traffic of mobile video will conquered the 70% of the total mobile traffic. Due to the on-demand and bandwidth hogging features of video streaming, the rapid expanding of video traffic greatly challenges the backhaul capacity and require new technologies to further improve the backhaul efficiency. Device-to-Device (D2D) communications [6–8]

© Springer International Publishing AG 2017
Y. Zhao et al. (Eds.): ICIG 2017, Part II, LNCS 10667, pp. 353–365, 2017.
https://doi.org/10.1007/978-3-319-71589-6_31

enable mobile node directly communicate with other to offload traffics to edge and alleviate the pressures of backhaul networks, hence becoming a promising technology to cope with the growing demand of multimedia applications over future 5G networks.

However, if we still use the IP network as our underly architecture, which is originally designed for host communication instead of content distribution, current solutions such as traditional P2P [9] requires building overlays to distribute the video content, which introduces extra computation and communication costs. Besides, with the increasing scale of end users, P2P system also face the scalability issues due to the overlay maintenance cost. To handle the shifting of network function and provide efficient content sharing in future 5G network, recently emerged information-centric networks (ICNs) [10] redesign the network architecture by addressing the content rather than host, which not only provides efficient data sharing but also enables 5G-D2D targets including mobility, heterogenous accessing and multihoming. Hence, ICN has become a promising technologies for 5G-D2D scenarios [11,12]. As Fig. 1 shows, in ICN 5G-D2D, each nodes equips with D2D communication interface and maintains three data structures: content store (CS), pending interest table (PIT) and forwarding information base (FIB). The receiving node of interest message firstly checks its CS which contains the local caching content. If *Interest* hits in CS, the receiving node returns the content directly, otherwise, it will checks the PIT. For *Interest* hits in PIT, the node will record incoming interface of *Interest* in PIT and then discard it. Otherwise, a new entry in PIT will be created for this *Interest* and node sends out *Interest* according to FIB (maintains the mapping between name prefix and next-hop). When the requested content flows back, the intermitted nodes can proactively cache the passing data into local CS in order to serve future same requests, which intuitively reduce the deliver latency as the content is already cached nearby.

As multimedia streaming requests (referred as *Interests*) in ICN is routed by name, the content lookup efficiency heavily relies on *Interest* forwarding strategy. Current solutions in D2D environment can be classified into unicast/broadcast-based methods. Unicast-based methods forward the *Interest* message to single next-hop node by maintaining the routing information. For instance, mobile nodes in RUFS [13] exchange the recent searching success information and use it to construct the neighbor satisfied list (NSL). For *Interest* receiving node that the requested content in not in its CS, it will forward *Interest* to next hop according to the maintained NSL. Our previously work PaFF [14] defines nodes with similar playback and movement behavior as cooperative partners and build high preferred content table (HPCT) by collecting the caching status of cooperative partners. Based on HPCT, a unicast forwarding strategy is proposed to fast locate user demand content. However, due to the high dynamic of mobile environment, mobile nodes in unicast-based methods need to frequently exchange routing information about content in order to maintain the validation of routing information, which quickly exhausts the battery life of energy constraint mobile device. Mobile nodes in broadcast-based methods broadcast *Interest* message to all one-hop neighbors. For instance, VNDN proposed in [15] employs a geo-based forwarding strategy which choose the neighbors with farthest distance as the forwarders to broadcast *Interest*. However, this solution requires mobile nodes wait a random delay before sending *Interest*, which results in extra delivery latency and it is difficult to discover the nearby content provider due to the limited broadcast coverage. As a consequence, to enable ICN in mobile environment with high dynamic and energy constraints, it is necessary to design light weight *Interest* forwarding strategy with fast content lookup low energy consumption.

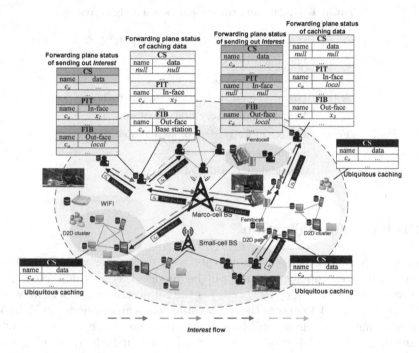

Fig. 1. An illustration of content sharing over information centric 5G-D2D

In this paper, we propose an energy-aware *Interest* forwarding strategy (EAFF) for ICN 5G-D2D, which select limited numbers of nodes as forwarders in order to fast routing interest to provider while saving energy costs. Specifically, the main contributions of this paper are:

First, we model and formulate the *Interest* forwarding problem to jointly minimize the energy consumption and searching coverage. And we prove the problem is NP-hard and corresponding objective function is submodular and non-decreasing.

Second, based on the forwarding problem we formulated, we further propose a greedy-based distributed forwarder selection algorithm to choose forwarders with higher probability discover the requested content and larger residual battery lifetime.

Third, we also conduct a series of simulation test to validate the superiority of EAFF in terms of the delay in finding data, energy consumption and number of disseminated *Interest* with respect to state-of-art solutions.

The rest of the paper is organized as follows, Sect. 2 formulates the forwarder selection problem. Section 3 present the detail design of forwarder selection algorithm. Section 4 conduct a series simulation tests to validate the superiority of proposed algorithm. Section 5 concludes the paper and discuss the future works (Table 1).

Table 1. Update and conversion rate among states

$\mathcal{G}$	The network topology of 5G D2D ICN
$\mathcal{E}$	The link set of $\mathcal{G}$
$\mathcal{V}$	The node set of $\mathcal{G}$
$\mathcal{N}(v_i)$	The neighbour node set of mobile node v_i
r_v	The residual battery lifetime of node v
V_{f_i}	The set of forwarders of source node i
D_v	*weightcoverage* of node v
$C(v)$	Candidate forwarder of node v

2   Problem Formalization

We consider N mobile nodes communicate with each other via 5G-D2D connections with given topology, which can be modeled as an undirected graph $\mathcal{G} = (\mathcal{V}, \mathcal{E})$, where $\mathcal{V} = \{v_1, v_2, v_3, \ldots, v_n\}$ is the set of mobile nodes in networks. $\mathcal{E} = \{(v_i, v_j) \mid v_i, v_j \in \mathcal{V}\}$ denotes the set of connections among nodes in $\mathcal{V}$. In 5G-D2D environment, two nodes will have connection, i.e., $(v_i, v_j) \in \mathcal{V}$ only when they are in the communication range of each other, namely $v_i \in \mathcal{N}(v_j)$ and $v_j \in \mathcal{N}(v_i)$, where $\mathcal{N}(v_j)$ and $\mathcal{N}(v_i)$ denote the set of one hop neighbours of v_i and v_j, respectively. By leveraging the broadcasting feature of wireless channel, the interest packets can be received by all neighbors, i.e., $\mathcal{S}(v_i)$ the receiving node set of v_i is equal to $\mathcal{N}(v_i)$. In this context, we define the *forwarding cover* relationship between two nodes and *forwarding coverage* of one node as follows:

Definition 1. *We say node v_i forwarding covers v_j if $v_j \in \mathcal{N}(v_i)$. Hence, the forwarding coverage of v_i is $\mathcal{N}(v_i)$ and the size of forwarding coverage of v_i is defined by $|\mathcal{N}(v_i)|$ the cardinality of $\mathcal{N}(v_i)$. Accordingly, $\mathcal{N}(\mathcal{V}_m)$ the forwarding coverage of node set $\mathcal{V}_m$ ($\mathcal{V}_m \subset \mathcal{V}$) can be also defined as union set of $\mathcal{N}(v_j)$ ($v_i \in \mathcal{V}_m$), i.e., $\mathcal{N}(\mathcal{V}_m) = \cup_{v_i \in \mathcal{V}_m} \mathcal{N}(\mathcal{V}_i)$.*

2.1 Optimization Problem

The main goal of *Interest* forwarding is to fast discover the potential provider while maintains low network resource consumption. According to the Definition 1, as the relay nodes of *interest* message *forwarding covers* all its one-hop neighbours and data can be returned immediately when relay nodes *forwarding covers* a content provider of corresponding data. Intuitively, the more forwarders chosen, the higher probability of discovering the requested content in next hop. And the content can be definitely found once the *forwardingcoverage* of forwarder set $\mathcal{V}_{f_i}$ of source i equal to the whole node set, namely $\mathcal{N}(\mathcal{V}_{f_i})$, as Fig. 2(a) shows. However, one mobile node may receive repetitive interest message from same source when it covered by multiple forwarders, as Fig. 2(b) illustrates. According to the design idea of NDN, such redundancy interest will be discard, which not only makes no contribution to efficiency of content lookup but also consumes precious energy resource of mobile devices. Therefore, it is necessary to limit the size of forwarder set while *forwarding covers* as much node as possible. Another critical issue is mobile nodes in 5G-D2D consume their own battery life to forward the receive *Interest* message, choosing node with low remaining battery lifetime may accelerate the battery running out, which may not preferred by mobile users. Therefore, it is also necessary to take the remaining battery lifetime into consideration when design forwarding strategies.

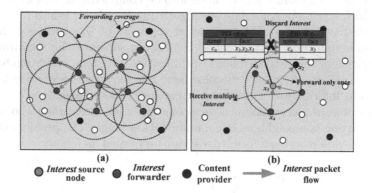

(a)   **(b)**

⬤ *Interest* source   ⬤ *Interest*   ⬤ Content   ➡ *Interest* packet
   node   forwarder   provider   flow

Fig. 2. (a) The *forwarding coverage* equals to the whole networks; (b) One node receives redundancy *Interest* from multiple forwarders

Based on above discussions, the optimization problem of interest forwarding in 5G D2D scenarios can be formulated as follows

$$\min \quad \sum_{v \in \mathcal{V}_{f_i}} \frac{1}{r_v} \tag{1}$$

$$\text{s.t} \quad \cup_{v \in \mathcal{V}_{f_i}} \mathcal{N}(v) = \mathcal{V} \tag{2}$$

where r_v denotes the residual battery lifetime of mobile node v. The reason of forming optimization problem in such way can be explained as follows: r_v can be considered as the cost of choosing node v as the forwarder. As a result, node with lower battery lifetime will have higher cost, and the objective function of (1) indicates the total cost of choosing set $\mathcal{V}_{f_i}$ as the forwarding set. Hence, in order to minimize the Eq. (1) under the constraints Eq. (2), forwarding set $\mathcal{V}_{f_i}$ should contains fewer nodes which has higher battery lifetime and *forwarding coverage*.

According to the form of above optimization problem, we have following proposition:

Proposition 1. *The proposed optimization problem (1)(2) is NP-hard.*

Proof. We consider a special case of Eq. (1) when all r_v $(r_v \in V_f)$ are equal to 1, this special case can be formed as follows:

$$\min \quad |\mathcal{V}_{f_i}| \tag{3}$$

$$\text{s.t} \quad \cup_{v \in \mathcal{V}_{f_i}} \mathcal{N}(v) = \mathcal{V} \tag{4}$$

where the $|\mathcal{V}_{f_i}|$ is the cardinality of $\mathcal{V}_{f_i}$. The optimization problem (3)(4) is a set cover problem, which has already been proved as NP-hard [16]. Therefore, the NP-hardness of (1)(2) is proven.

To solving this NP-hard problem (1)(2), a possible way is traversing all subset of $\mathcal{V}$, as there are $2^{\mathcal{V}}$ subsets and therefore the complexity of this algorithm is $O\left(2^{\mathcal{V}}\right)$, which is not a polynomial-time algorithm. Besides, it is also require each source node have the knowledge of global topology of $\mathcal{G}$, which is unrealistic in D2D communication environments. Hence, we separate the forwarding set selection problem into a distributed optimization problem which enable each selected forwarders individually choosing next-hop forwarders according to the 2-hop neighbors information. This is mainly because two-hop neighbor information can be easy obtained since mobile device constantly broadcast the Hello message to detect the one-hop neighbors in communication range. The problem of select next-hop forwarders at each forwarder e can be formed as follows:

$$\min \quad \sum_{v \in \mathcal{V}_{f_e}} \frac{1}{r_v} \tag{5}$$

$$\text{s.t} \quad \cup_{v \in \mathcal{V}_{f_e}} \mathcal{N}(v) = \mathcal{N}(\mathcal{N}(e)) \tag{6}$$

where $\mathcal{V}_{f_e}$ is the next-hop forwarder set of e, $\mathcal{N}(\mathcal{N}(e))$ denotes the two-hop neighbours of e. The optimization problem (5)(6) indicates each forwarder should choose a number of nodes as forwarders that forwarding covers its two-hop neighbors. Intuitively, the solution of optimization problem (1)(2) can be approximated by the recursion of optimization (5)(6).

Although similar to the optimization problem (1)(2), the distributed forwarder selection problem (5)(6) is still NP-hard as the two-hop cover set problem can be considered as a special case of this problem, a near optimal solutions still can be derived in polynomial time due to the submodularity and monotonicity of (5).

Theorem 1. *The objective function of optimization problem (5)(6) is submodular and nondecreasing.*

Proof. Let two set $\mathcal{V}_a, \mathcal{V}_b \in \mathcal{V}$, $z\left(\mathcal{V}_a\right) = \sum\limits_{v \in \mathcal{V}_a} \frac{1}{r_v}$ and $z\left(\mathcal{V}_b\right) = \sum\limits_{v \in \mathcal{V}_b} \frac{1}{r_v}$, we consider following two cases:

Case 1: If $\mathcal{V}_a \bigcap \mathcal{V}_b = \emptyset$, namely $z\left(\mathcal{V}_a \bigcap \mathcal{V}_b\right) = 0$, we have

$$z\left(\mathcal{V}_a\right) + z\left(\mathcal{V}_b\right) = \sum_{v \in \mathcal{V}_a} \frac{1}{r_v} + \sum_{v \in \mathcal{V}_b} \frac{1}{r_v} = \sum_{v \in \mathcal{V}_a \bigcup \mathcal{V}_b} \frac{1}{r_v} = z\left(\mathcal{V}_a \bigcup \mathcal{V}_b\right)$$
$$= z\left(\mathcal{V}_a \bigcup \mathcal{V}_b\right) + z\left(\mathcal{V}_a \bigcap \mathcal{V}_b\right) \tag{7}$$

Case 2: If $\mathcal{V}_a \bigcup \mathcal{V}_b \neq \emptyset$, according to the inclusion-exclusion principle of two sets, we have

$$z\left(\mathcal{V}_a \bigcup \mathcal{V}_b\right) = \sum_{v \in \mathcal{V}_a \bigcup \mathcal{V}_b} \frac{1}{r_v} = \sum_{v \in \mathcal{V}_a} \frac{1}{r_v} + \sum_{v \in \mathcal{V}_b} \frac{1}{r_v} - \sum_{v \in \mathcal{V}_a \bigcap \mathcal{V}_b} \frac{1}{r_v}$$
$$= z\left(\mathcal{V}_a\right) + z\left(\mathcal{V}_b\right) - z\left(\mathcal{V}_a \bigcap \mathcal{V}_b\right) \tag{8}$$

Therefore, for both cases, we have

$$z\left(\mathcal{V}_a\right) + z\left(\mathcal{V}_b\right) = z\left(\mathcal{V}_a \bigcup \mathcal{V}_b\right) + z\left(\mathcal{V}_a \bigcap \mathcal{V}_b\right)$$

which satisfies the definition of submodular set function [17] and therefore prove the submodularity of Eq. (5).

For $\forall \mathcal{V}_a \subseteq \mathcal{V}$ and $\forall k \in \mathcal{V}/\mathcal{V}_a$, we have

$$z\left(\mathcal{V}_a \bigcup \{k\}\right) - z\left(\mathcal{V}_a\right) = \sum_{v \in \mathcal{V}_a \bigcup \{k\}} \frac{1}{r_v} - \sum_{v \in \mathcal{V}_a} \frac{1}{r_v} = \sum_{v \in \mathcal{V}_a} \frac{1}{r_v} + \frac{1}{r_k} - \sum_{v \in \mathcal{V}_a} \frac{1}{r_v}$$
$$= \frac{1}{r_k} > 0 \tag{9}$$

hence, Eq. (5) is nondecreasing.

3   Distributed Energy-Aware Fast Forwarding Algorithm

According to the discussion above, the forwarding set selection problem of a given source i can be solved by a decentralized fashion, namely, forwarders in each hop can decide the next-hop by solving the optimization problem (5)(6), which only require two-hop neighbor information. Since Eq. (5) is submodular and monotonous according to Theorem 1, a 1-ε optimal solution that can be found in polynomial time by greed-based method [17]. Therefore, we propose a greed-based distributed energy-aware fast forwarding algorithm as following.

Algorithm 1. Energy oriented forwarder selection algorithm performed at each forwarder s

---

Input: forwarder s, candidate next-hop forwarder set $C(s)$, CFIB of $C(s)$,
        $C(t)$'s neighbor node set $\mathcal{N}(C(s))$.
Output: next hop forwarder array $\mathcal{V}_{f_s}$ of each forwarder e.
1   sort the elements in $C(s)$ in the descending order of $\mathcal{D}_v$;
2   $i = 0$;
3   **while** $\mathcal{N}(\mathcal{V}_{f_s})$ *is not equal to* $\mathcal{N}(\mathcal{N}(s))$ **do**
4      $\mathcal{V}_{f_s}[i] \leftarrow C(s)[1]$;
5   **while** $j \in \mathcal{N}(\mathcal{V}_{f_e}[i])$ **do**
6   **while** $k \in C(s)$ **do**
7   **if** $j \in \mathcal{N}(k)$ **then**
8   omit j from $\mathcal{N}(k)$;
9   **else**
10   **continue**;
11   **end**
12   **end**
13   **end**
14   Omit $C(s)[1]$ from $C(s)$;
15   sort the elements in $C(s)$ in the descending order of value $\mathcal{D}_v$;
16      $i++$;
17 **end**
18 **final** ;
19 **return** $\mathcal{V}_{f_s}$;

To be aware of the two-hop neighbours and residual battery lifetime of one-hop neighbors, mobile nodes periodically exchange the set of neighbours and residual battery lifetime by smuggling such information into hello message. Once a mobile node is selected as the forwarder[1], it will individually select forwarders from one-hop neighbors in order to minimize the objective (5) with constraint (6). To search the next-hop forwarder by greed method, we first introduce the concept of *weighted coverage* as follows:

$$\mathcal{D}_v = r_v |\mathcal{N}(v)|$$

each node calculate the $\mathcal{D}_v$ by collecting the "hello" message of its neighbour nodes and rank its neighbours according to the descending of value of $\mathcal{D}_v$. Let $C(i)$ as the candidate forwarder set of i and a candidate forwarder information base (CFIB) will be created, which maintains the neighbour nodes information of one-hop nodes.

Mobile node i first select the one-hop neighbour v with maximum value of $\mathcal{D}_v$ and update CFIB and $C(i)$ according to following process: (1) Omit v from CFIB and $C(i)$; (2) Omit all nodes in $\mathcal{N}(v)$ from the neighbor node set of other nodes in CFIB; (3) Re-sort the node in $C(i)$ according to $\mathcal{D}_v$.

---

[1] As our forwarding scheme can be performed recursively, the source node also can be equivalently as forwarder.

Then the forwarder will continue select the node with maximum value from $C(i)$ and update the CFIB and $C(i)$ again. The above process will repeat until the constraint (6) satisfied, and the selected nodes will be considered as the forwarders. The pseudo code of the algorithm is given as Algorithm 1.

Table 2. Simulation parameter setting

	Parameter	Value
MAC layer	Channel	Channel/Wireless channel
	Data rate	300 Mbps
	Bandwidth frequency	3.5 GHz
	Multiple access	OFDM
	Transmission power	33 dBm
	Wireless transmission range	250 m
	Interface queue type	Queue/DropTail/PriQueue
	Interface queue length	50 packets
	Access control	CSMA/CA
	Antenna type	Antenna/OmniAntenna
NDNSim	Caching size	10000MTU
	Interest size	5 KB
	Interest generating rate	0.1/s

3.1 Complexity Analysis

According to the pseudo code of algorithm, the time complexity partially depends on number of selected forwarders $|\mathcal{V}_{f_e}|$ as the algorithm will execute in loop to select the forwarders. The node sort process also influences the time complexity of the algorithm. For the case of using heap sort, the time complexity of this sort step is ranging from $O(|\mathcal{N}(i)|\log|\mathcal{N}(i)|)$ to $O(1)$, since the number of pending sort nodes is decreased by one in each iteration of forward selection. Paralleled with sorting process, node will also performs the delete operation to omit the neighbors CFIB, whose time complexity is $O(|\mathcal{N}(i)\mathcal{N}(v)|)$. Based on above discussion, the overall time complexity of the algorithm is

$$O(|\mathcal{V}_{f_e}|\max(|\mathcal{N}(i)|\log|\mathcal{N}(i)|,|\mathcal{N}(i)\mathcal{N}(v)|))$$

4 Performance Evaluation

Our simulation is based on NDNSIm, which is an open source ICN simulation tools based on network simulator 3 (NS-3). We consider a $1500 * 1000 \left(m^2\right)$ scenarios which is extracted from digital map of Beijiing and 300 mobile nodes are moving in this scenarios according to the real mobility trace in T-Drive [18].

The movement speed of each node is set in the range of $[20, 40]$ km/h. Each mobile node is equipped with 5G-D2D modular in order to communicate with each other and the parameter setting of MAC layer is given as Table 2.

Figure 3 compares the delay in finding data (DFD), which is measured by the time span between sending *Interest* and receiving data. As figure shows, the EAFF achieves better performance in terms of DFD than other two solutions, and the superiority of EAFF expands when number of mobile nodes growing. Figure 4 shows the energy consumption of forwarding *Interest* packets, where the number of mobile nodes varies from 150 to 300. From the figure, we observe that EAFF achieves the lowest energy consumption among three solutions when the system scale is small (before number of nodes increasing to 200). With the increasing of number of mobile nodes, the energy consumption of EAFF is slightly higher than VNDN but far more lowest than flooding-based strategy. Figure 5 compares the number of generated *Interest* packet during the simulation process, the number of mobile node is set to 200. As figure shows, the number of *Interest* generated per-second in EAFF is lower than that of VNDN and flooding-based method. Figure 6 compares the playback freeze during the simulation time, which is one of the important performance indexes for video streaming service. As figure shows, EAFF achieves the lowest the playback freeze times among three solutions. The curves corresponding to the VNDN is higher than the one of EAFF at stable phase (i.e., after 250 s). The flooding-based method reveals a linear increasing trend, which reaches 9 after 900 s.

EAFF leverages a greed-based distributed forwarder selection method to select nodes with higher *forwarding coverage* and residual battery lifetime as next-hop forwarders. As nodes with higher *forwarding coverage* also have higher probability of discovering asked content in one-hop range, which therefore speeds up the content searching process. Besides, EAFF also limits the number of forwarders and selects nodes with higher residual battery lifetime as forwarders. Hence, avoid broadcast storm and alleviate the consumption of forwarding *Interest*. Therefore, EaFF achieves low DFD, energy consumption and number of generated *Interest* as Figs. 3, 4 and 5 show. Since the EAFF has the lowest DFD, or equivalently, has the lowest delivery latency, hence it has the

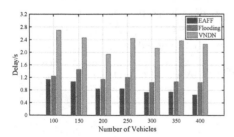
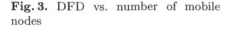

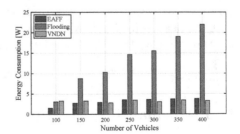

Fig. 3. DFD vs. number of mobile nodes

Fig. 4. *Interest* forwarding energy consumption vs. number of mobile nodes

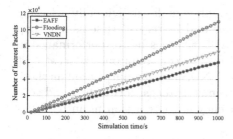
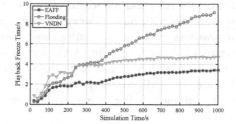

Fig. 5. Number of disseminated *Interest* vs. simulation time

Fig. 6. Playback freeze vs. simulation time

minimum number of playback freeze times. VNDN select the farthest node as *Interest* forwarder in each hop. VNDN selects one node in each hop to forward *Interest* in order to mitigate the consumption of *Interest* forwarding. However, due to the limited *forwarding coverage* in each hop, the probability of locating a nearby content provider is low, namely lengthen the content searching delay. In addition, because each node requires waiting a random delay to detect whether a farther node exists, which introduces extra delay when forwarding the *Interest*. Besides, due to the randomness searching feature of VNDN, the performance of playback freeze experiences a vibration at the beginning of simulation due to the variation of delay in finding data, as Fig. 6 depicts. Consequently, although VNDN has low energy consumption and number of *Interest* generated, this is at the cost of content delivery latency, which bring huge negative effects to the QoE of end users, hence also result in high frequency of playback freeze. In flooding-based method, all mobile nodes that receiving the *Interest* will broadcast this *Interest* in one-hop range, which discover the content providers by fast traversing the network. However, flooding-based method results in *Interest* broadcasting storm which not only consume huge bandwidth but also higher the energy consumption of mobile nodes. As a result, flooding-based method has highest energy consumption and number of *Interest* as Figs. 4 and 5 show. Besides, flooding-based method also higher the risk of network congestion. Hence, with the simulation time increasing, the network congestion is becoming more and more serve when using flooding-based method and therefore higher the playback freeze frequency.

5 Conclusion

In this paper, we focus on video sharing in information centric 5G-D2D networks and proposed EAFF, a energy-aware fast *Interest* forwarding to support fast content sharing in ICN 5G-D2D which aims to fast search demand content with low energy consumption. We firstly formulate the *Interest* forwarding in ICN 5G-D2D as an optimization problem which is NP-hard but submodular and monotonous, namely a $1-\varepsilon$ approximation solution can be found within polynomial time by greedy method. Then, we proposed a greed-based distributed forwarder selection algorithm which enable mobile nodes individually selecting neighbours with higher *forwardering coverage* and battery lifetime as next-hop forwarders. Simulation results show how EAFF achieves better performance in terms of delay in finding data, forwarding energy consumption, *Interest* cost and playback freeze than sate-of-art solution VNDN and flooding-based method. Future work will consider how to jointly optimize *Interest* forwarding and content caching in order to achieve higher efficiency of content sharing in ICN 5G-D2D.

Acknowledgment. This work was partially supported by the National Natural Science Foundation of China (NSFC) under Grant Nos. 61372112, 61522103 and 61232017.

References

1. Ge, X., Yang, J., Gharavi, H., Sun, Y.: Energy efficiency challenges of 5G small cell networks. IEEE Commun. Mag. **55**(5), 184–191 (2017)
2. Huang, J., Wang, C.-X., Feng, R., Sun, J., Zhang, W., Yang, Y.: Multi-frequency MmWave massive MIMO channel measurements and characterization for 5G wireless communication systems. IEEE J. Sel. Areas Commun. **99**, 1 (2017)
3. Shafi, M., Molisch, A.F., Smith, P.J., Haustein, T., Zhu, P., Silva, P.D., Tufvesson, F., Benjebbour, A., Wunder, G.: 5G: a tutorial overview of standards, trials, challenges, deployment and practice. IEEE J. Sel. Areas Commun. **99**, 1 (2017)
4. Hayward, S.S., Palacios, E.G.: Multimedia resource allocation in mmWave 5G networks. IEEE Commun. Mag. **53**(1), 240–247 (2015)
5. Cisco visual networking index: Forecast and methodology, 01 June 2016
6. Cao, W., Feng, G., Qin, S., Yan, M.: Cellular offloading in heterogeneous mobile networks with D2D communication assistance. IEEE Trans. Veh. Technol. **66**(5), 4242–4255 (2017)
7. Jiang, L., Tian, H., Xing, Z., Wang, K., Zhang, K., Maharjan, S., Gjessing, S., Zhang, Y.: Social-aware energy harvesting device-to-device communications in 5G networks. IEEE Wirel. Commun. **23**(4), 20–27 (2016)
8. Zhou, L.: D2D communication meets big data: from theory to application. Mob. Netw. Appl. **20**(6), 783–792 (2015)
9. Xu, C., Zhao, F., Guan, J., Zhang, H., Muntean, G.M.: QoE-driven user-centric VoD services in urban multihomed P2P-based vehicular networks. IEEE Trans. Veh. Technol. **62**(5), 2273–2289 (2013)
10. Jacobson, V., Smetters, D.K., Thornton, J.D., et al.: Networking named content. In: Proceedings of ACM the 5th International Conference on Emerging Networking Experiments and Technologies (CoNEXT), pp. 1–12, December 2009
11. Ravindran, R., Chakraborti, A., Amin, S.O., Azgin, A., Wang, G.: 5G-ICN: delivering ICN services over 5G using network slicing. IEEE Wirel. Commun. **55**(5), 101–107 (2017)
12. Liang, C., Yu, F.R., Zhang, X.: Information-centric network function virtualization over 5G mobile wireless networks. IEEE Netw. **29**(3), 68–74 (2015)
13. Ahmed, S.H., Bouk, S.H., Kim, D.: RUFS: RobUst forwarder selection in vehicular content-centric networks. IEEE Commun. Lett. **19**(9), 1616–1619 (2015)
14. Wang, M., Xu, C., Jia, S., Guan, J., Grieco, L.A.: Preference-aware fast interest forwarding for video streaming in information-centric VANETs. In: Proceeding of IEEE Conference on Communications, May 2017

15. Grassi, G., Pesavento, D., Pau, G., Vuyyuru, R., Wakikawa, R., Zhang, L.: VANET via named data networking. In: Proceedings of the IEEE Conference Computer Communications Workshops, pp. 410–415, July 2014
16. Cormen, T.H., Leiserson, C.E., Rivest, R.L., et al.: Introduction to Algorithms, 3rd edn. The MIT Press, Cambridge (2009)
17. Nemhauser, G.L., Wolsey, L.A., Fisher, M.L.: An analysis of approximations for maximizing submodular set functions. Math. Program. $14(1)$, 265–294 (1978)
18. Brampton, A., et al.: Characterising user interactivity for sports video-on-demand. In: ACM NOSSDAV, Urbana-Champaign, IL, USA, pp. 1–6, April 2007

Artificial Intelligence

Stability Analysis of ECOC Kernel Machines

Aijun Xue, Xiaodan Wang[(✉)], and Xiaolong Fu

Department of Computer Science, Air Force Engineering University,
Changle East Road, Xi'an 710051, China
Wang_afeu@126.com

Abstract. Error correcting output codes kernel machines (ECOC kernel machines) are ensemble of kernel machines based on ECOC decomposition methods. How to improve the generalization capability of this framework is an open problem. In this paper, we discussed the condition for generalization in terms of the stability property of ECOC kernel machines. Here we provide a proof for the result that an ECOC kernel machine has the pointwise hypothesis stability. This stability property can be calculated by training on the training dataset once and has clear and meaningful formulation. It can be applied to tune the kernel parameters in model selection and design good matrixes for ECOC kernel machines.

Keywords: Error correcting output codes (ECOC) · Kernel machines
Pointwise hypothesis stability · Generalization error bound

1 Introduction

Many real-world pattern recognition applications are aim to map the instances into a set of classes. To deal with such problems, the efficient way is to decompose the multiclass problems into a set of binary classification problems [1]. In this case, many techniques addressing the binary classification task can be used to solve the complex multiclass problems. There are many different approaches for recasting the multiclass problem into a series of smaller binary classification tasks, such as one-versus-all (OVA), one-versus-one (OVO) [2, 3], and error correcting output codes (ECOC) [4, 5]. One-versus-all which is the simplest approach considers the comparison between each class and the others, and takes the maximum output as the final classification decision. One-versus-one approach addresses the comparison of all possible pairs of classes, and obtains the final classification result by means of a voting procedure. Error correcting output codes (ECOC) is a general framework to achieve this decomposition, which was presented by Dietterich and Bakiri [4]. Due to the error correcting capability [6–8], ECOC has been successfully applied to a wide range of applications [9–12].

When the ECOC framework is applied in practice, we expect that this framework will have an accuracy classification result. Generally speaking, training the learning algorithms on the empirical datasets to predict the unlabeled samples precisely is one of the key points for machine learning. The ECOC framework can be seen as a special learning algorithm, which is an ensemble of some binary classifiers. How to improve and evaluate the generalization capability of this framework is an open problem and

© Springer International Publishing AG 2017
Y. Zhao et al. (Eds.): ICIG 2017, Part II, LNCS 10667, pp. 369–384, 2017.
https://doi.org/10.1007/978-3-319-71589-6_32

some works have been done. Masulli and Valentini [13] attempted to analyze the main factors affecting the effectiveness of ECOC methods experimentally, and their analysis showed that all these factors concurred to the effectiveness of ECOC methods in a not straightforward way and interacted between them. Garcia-Pedrajas and Fyfe [14] proposed an evolutionary approach to the design of output codes, which took five different aspects into account, but it was difficult to define an apparent relationship between these aspects and the generalization ability of ECOC methods. These results underscore the difficulty of this problem.

On the other hand, some works focused on just one or two aspects that were related to generalization performance of ECOC methods. Pujol and Radeva [15] focused on obtaining the partitions which had the maximum class discrimination. Escalera and Tax [16] used the subclass information to guarantee that the base classifier can split each subgroup of classes. Ali-Bagheri [17, 18] aimed to improve independency among base classifiers using different feature subsets for each base classifiers. Angel-Bautista and Escalera [19] presented a novel genetic strategy to obtain the better dichotomizers. These works provide us some new ways to the ECOC framework research. However, it is a pity that there is little formal justification to support these improvements. The previous works show that it is difficult to determine what is the intrinsic factors affecting the effectiveness of ECOC methods.

To improve the generalization capability of ECOC framework, what we need to do is to go back to the nature of ECOC framework. The nature is it is just a special learning algorithm. Note that in this case, we do not discuss the decoding strategy. A central question for machine learning is to determine conditions under which a learning algorithm will generalize from its finite training set to novel samples [20]. A milestone in learning theory was empirical risk minimization (ERM) based on minimizing the training error. Furthermore, Valentini [21] proposed the upper bounds on the training error of ECOC kernel machines. In this case, the problem is changed to how to minimize the difference between the training error and the generalization error. Fortunately, Poggio and Rifkin [20] discussed the conditions for generalization in terms of a precise stability property of the learning process. Bousquet and Elisseeff [22] showed how to use the stability to derive bounds on the generalization error based on the training error. The stability of a learning algorithm can be a bridge between the training error and the generalization error, and as a powerful tool in ECOC framework research.

In other word, if the learning algorithm has minimization training error and is more stable, the learning algorithm can have better generalization capability. It is our purpose in this paper to discuss the stability of ECOC framework with kernel machines. The most contribution of our work is that we obtain the result that ECOC kernel machines have pointwise hypothesis stability. This stability can be calculated by training on the training dataset once, and has clear and meaningful formulation. It can be applied to tune the kernel parameters in model selection and design good matrixes for ECOC kernel machines.

The rest of this paper is organized as follows: Sect. 2 provides a brief introduction to the ECOC decomposition methods and background on kernel machines. The pointwise hypothesis stability of ECOC kernel machines is explained in detail in

Sect. 3. In Sect. 4, some applications of pointwise hypothesis stability are presented. Finally, Sect. 5 draws the main conclusions of the paper.

2 ECOC Kernel Machines

2.1 ECOC

The ECOC framework consists of two stages: encoding and decoding. At the coding stage, the main task is to construct a coding matrix. Each column of the coding matrix is the bipartition (groups of classes), which indicates one binary problem. Each row of the coding matrix is the codeword for each class, where the bit implies the label of the class for a binary problem [23]. The base classifier is obtained by training the binary problem. Binary ECOC is the original framework. It has two symbols $\{+1, -1\}$ in the coding matrix, which represent the negative class and the positive class in one binary problem. When the coding step attracted special attention, Allwen et al. [5] introduced zero as the third symbol, which indicated that the corresponding class would be ignored for a binary problem. The classical ECOCs are shown in Fig. 1.

In Fig. 1, the white, black and gray regions of the coding matrix stand for the symbol "1", "−1" and "0" respectively. For example, in Fig. 1(c) when classifier f_1 is

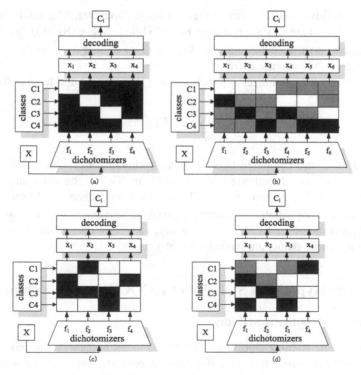

Fig. 1. Four classical ECOCs, binary ECOC: (a) one-versus-all; (c) dense random; ternary ECOC: (b) one-versus-one; (d) sparse random

trained, classes C_1 and C_4 are seen as the positive class and classes C_2 and C_3 as the negative class. In the same way, finally, we obtain a classifier vector $\{f_1, f_2, f_3, f_4\}$.

Given a test sample, the base classifiers output a codeword. Note that the obtained codeword cannot take the value zero since the output of the base classifier is "+1" or "−1". At the decoding stage, this codeword is compared with the codewords defined in the coding matrix, and the test sample is assigned to the class corresponding to the closest codeword. Usually, this comparison is implemented by the Hamming and the Euclidean decoding distance. Specially, Allwen et al. [5] showed the advantage of using a loss-based function of the margin of the output of the base classifier. For example, in Fig. 1(c) given the test sample X, the classifier vector output a codeword $\{x_1, x_2, x_3, x_4\}$. Then, the final classification result is obtained by a given decoding strategy.

2.2   Kernel Machines

We assume that the training set is $Z^m = \left\{(x_i, y_i)_{i=1}^m \in \{X \times \{-1, 1\}\}^m\right\}$ and $\ell : R \to R$ is a loss function. Kernel machines are the minimizers of functionals of the form

$$F[f; Z^m] = \frac{1}{m} \sum_{i=1}^m \ell(y_i f(x_i)) + \lambda \|f\|_K^2 \tag{1}$$

where λ is a positive constant named regularization parameter. The minimization of functional in (1) is done in a Reproducing Kernel Hilbert Space (RKHS) $\mathcal{H}$ defined by a symmetric and positive definite kernel $K : X \times X \to R$, and $\|f\|_K^2$ is the norm of a function $f : X \to R$ belonging to $\mathcal{H}$.

If ℓ is convex, the minimizer of functional in (1) is unique and has the form

$$f(x) = \sum_{i=1}^m \alpha_i y_i K(x_i, x) \tag{2}$$

The coefficients α_i are computed by solving an optimization problem whose form is determined by the loss function ℓ. For example, in SVMs, the soft-margin loss is $\ell(y f(x)) = |1 - y f(x)|_+$, where $|x|_+ = x$ if $x > 0$ and zero otherwise. In this case, the α_i is the solution of a quadratic programming problem with constraints $\alpha_i \in [0, 1/2m\lambda]$. A peculiar property of an SVM is that, usually, only few data points have nonzero coefficients α_i. These points are named support vectors.

3   Pointwise Hypothesis Stability of ECOC Kernel Machines

3.1   Pointwise Hypothesis Stability

The stability of one learning algorithm can be used to get bounds on the generalization error [22]. Here we focus on the stability with respect to changes in the training set. Firstly, we introduce some notations.

A training dataset is given as follows

$$S = \{z_1 = (x_1, y_1), \ldots, z_m = (x_m, y_m)\} \tag{3}$$

By removing the ith element, the changed training dataset is given as:

$$S^{\backslash i} = \{z_1, \ldots, z_{i-1}, z_{i+1}, \ldots, z_m\} \tag{4}$$

Then, we denote by f the function trained on the set S, and $f^{\backslash i}$ the function trained on the set $S^{\backslash i}$. The definition of pointwise hypothesis stability is given in Definition 1.

Definition 1 (Pointwise Hypothesis Stability). An algorithm A has pointwise hypothesis stability δ with respect to the loss function ℓ if the following holds

$$\forall S \in Z^m, \forall i \in \{1, \cdots, m\}, \mathrm{E}_S\left[\left|\ell(f, z_i) - \ell\left(f^{\backslash i}, z_i\right)\right|\right] \leq \delta \tag{5}$$

3.2 Multiclass Loss Function

Based on Definition 1, the loss function of ECOC kernel machines is needed. Let the coding matrix be $M \in \{-1, 0, 1\}^{k \times l}$, where k is the number of class and l is the number of binary classifier. m_{ps} is the code bit which indicates the label of class p in the s th binary classifier. The vector function formed by the binary classifiers is $f(x) = \{f_1(x), \cdots, f_l(x)\}$.

The multiclass margin of a sample $(x_i, y_i) \in X \times \{1, \cdots, k\}$ can be written as [24]

$$g(x_i, y_i) = d_L(m_p, f(x_i)) - d_L(m_{y_i}, f(x_i)) \tag{6}$$

where $d_L(m_p, f(x_i)) = \sum_{s=1}^{l} L(m_{ps} f_s(x_i))$ is the linear loss-based decoding function with $L(m_{ps} f_s(x_i)) = -m_{ps} f_s(x_i)$, and $p = \arg\min_{q \neq y_i} d_L(m_q, f(x_i))$.

Note that the multiclass margin is positive when sample x_i is classified correctly. Considering a loss function is typically a nondecreasing function of the margin, the linear-margin loss function can be defined as $\ell(f, z) = -g(x, y)$.

3.3 Pointwise Hypothesis Stability of ECOC Kernel Machines

In this section, we present the proof of pointwise hypothesis stability of ECOC kernel machines. To this end, we first need the following lemma [24].

Lemma 1. Let f be the kernel machine as defined in (2) obtained by solving (1). Let $f^{\backslash i}$ be the solution of (1) found when the data point (x_i, y_i) is removed from the training set. We have

$$y_i f(x_i) - \alpha_i G_{ii} \le y_i f^{\backslash i}(x_i) \le y_i f(x_i) \tag{7}$$

where $G_{ij} = K(x_i, x_j)$.

By applying Lemma 1 simultaneously to each kernel machine used in the ECOC procedure, Inequality (7) can be rewritten as

$$f_s^{\backslash i}(x_i) = f_s(x_i) - \lambda_s m_{y_i s}, \quad s \in \{1, \cdots, l\} \tag{8}$$

where λ_s is a parameter in $\left[0, \alpha_i^s G_{ii}^s\right]$.

Theorem 1. Let $M \in \{-1, 1\}^{k \times l}$ be the code matrix and $f_s(x) = \sum_{i=1}^m \alpha_i^s m_{y_i s} K^s(x_i, x)$ be the s th binary classifier, where $\alpha_i \in [0, C]$ with $C = 1/(2m\lambda)$. The multiclass loss function is $\ell(f, z) = -g(x, y)$. Let $\kappa = \max_s \max_i G_{ii}^s = \max_s \max_i K^s(x_i, x_i)$. f is the vector function derived by the ECOC kernel machines based on the coding matrix M. Decoding strategy is set as linear loss-based decoding function. $\theta(\cdot)$ is the Heavyside function: $\theta(x) = 1$ if $x > 0$ and zero otherwise. Thus, ECOC kernel machines have pointwise hypothesis stability with

$$\mathrm{E}_S\left[\left|\ell(f, z_i) - \ell\left(f^{\backslash i}, z_i\right)\right|\right] \le \frac{2\kappa C}{m} \sum_{i=1}^m \sum_{s=1}^l \theta(\alpha_i^s) \tag{9}$$

Proof. In order to prove that ECOC kernel machines has pointwise hypothesis stability, we have to find the bound for $\mathrm{E}_S\left[\left|\ell(f, z_i) - \ell(f^{\backslash i}, z_i)\right|\right]$. Firstly, for $\forall S \in Z^m$, $\forall z_i = (x_i, y_i) \in S$, we have

$$\mathrm{E}_S\left[\left|\ell(f, z_i) - \ell\left(f^{\backslash i}, z_i\right)\right|\right] = \frac{1}{m} \sum_{i=1}^m \left|\ell(f, z_i) - \ell\left(f^{\backslash i}, z_i\right)\right| = \frac{1}{m} \sum_{i=1}^m \left|g(x_i, y_i) - g^{\backslash i}(x_i, y_i)\right|$$

So, if we want to bound $\mathrm{E}_S\left[\left|\ell(f, z_i) - \ell(f^{\backslash i}, z_i)\right|\right]$, firstly we can bound $\left|g(x_i, y_i) - g^{\backslash i}(x_i, y_i)\right|$.

The above problem can be divided into two parts. On one hand, from the definition of $g(x, y)$ and linear loss-based decoding function, we have

$$g^{\backslash i}(x_i, y_i) = m_{y_i} f^{\backslash i}(x_i) - m_{p \backslash i} f^{\backslash i}(x_i) \tag{10}$$

where $p^{\backslash i} = \arg\max_{q \ne y_i} m_q f^{\backslash i}(x_i)$.

$$g(x_i, y_i) = m_{y_i} f(x_i) - m_p f(x_i) \tag{11}$$

where $p = \arg\max_{q \ne y_i} m_q f(x_i)$.

Moreover, from the definition of p, we can get

$$m_p f(x_i) \geq m_{p \backslash i} f(x_i) \tag{12}$$

(11) minus (10), there is

$$g(x_i, y_i) - g^{\backslash i}(x_i, y_i) = \sum_{s=1}^{l} \left[m_{y_i s} f_s(x_i) - m_{ps} f_s(x_i) - m_{y_i s} f_s^{\backslash i}(x_i) + m_{p \backslash i s} f_s^{\backslash i}(x_i) \right] \tag{13}$$

Now, applying (8), we can get

$$g(x_i, y_i) - g^{\backslash i}(x_i, y_i) = \sum_{s=1}^{l} \left[m_{y_i s} f_s(x_i) - m_{ps} f_s(x_i) - m_{y_i s} \left(f_s(x_i) - \lambda_s m_{y_i s} \right) + m_{p \backslash i s} \left(f_s(x_i) - \lambda_s m_{y_i s} \right) \right]$$

$$= \sum_{s=1}^{l} \left[\left(m_{p \backslash i s} - m_{ps} \right) f_s(x_i) + \left(m_{y_i s} - m_{p \backslash i s} \right) \lambda_s m_{y_i s} \right] \tag{14}$$

Considering (12), we can write the following inequality

$$g(x_i, y_i) - g^{\backslash i}(x_i, y_i) \leq \sum_{s=1}^{l} \left(m_{y_i s} - m_{p \backslash i s} \right) \lambda_s m_{y_i s} \leq \sum_{s=1}^{l} 2\lambda_s \leq \sum_{s=1}^{l} 2\alpha_i^s G_{ii}^s \leq 2\kappa \sum_{s=1}^{l} \alpha_i^s \tag{15}$$

Note that the second inequality is just because of $m_{y_i s} \in \{-1, 1\}$, and then

$$0 \leq \left(m_{y_i s} - m_{p \backslash i s} \right) m_{y_i s} \leq 2 \tag{16}$$

Considering $\alpha_i^s \in [0, C]$, and $\alpha_i^s > 0$ indicates z_i is a support vector, for $\forall (x_i, y_i) \in S$,

$$g(x_i, y_i) - g^{\backslash i}(x_i, y_i) \leq 2\kappa \sum_{s=1}^{l} \alpha_i^s \leq 2\kappa C \sum_{s=1}^{l} \theta(\alpha_i^s) \tag{17}$$

On the other hand, due to (16) and $\lambda_s \geq 0$, we have

$$\sum_{s=1}^{l} \left(m_{y_i s} - m_{p \backslash i s} \right) \lambda_s m_{y_i s} \geq 0 \tag{18}$$

From (14), we can get

$$g(x_i, y_i) - g^{\backslash i}(x_i, y_i) \geq \sum_{s=1}^{l} \left(m_{p\backslash i_s} - m_{ps} \right) f_s(x_i)$$

$$= \sum_{s=1}^{l} \left[m_{p\backslash i_s} f_s(x_i) - m_{p\backslash i_s} f_s^{\backslash i}(x_i) \right] + \sum_{s=1}^{l} \left[m_{p\backslash i_s} f_s^{\backslash i}(x_i) - m_{ps} f_s(x_i) \right]$$

$$\geq \sum_{s=1}^{l} \left[m_{p\backslash i_s} f_s(x_i) - m_{p\backslash i_s} f_s^{\backslash i}(x_i) \right] + \sum_{s=1}^{l} \left[m_{ps} \left(f_s^{\backslash i}(x_i) - f_s(x_i) \right) \right] \qquad (19)$$

$$= \sum_{s=1}^{l} \left[m_{p\backslash i_s} \left(f_s(x_i) - f_s^{\backslash i}(x_i) \right) \right] - \sum_{s=1}^{l} \left[m_{ps} \left(f_s(x_i) - f_s^{\backslash i}(x_i) \right) \right]$$

$$= \sum_{s=1}^{l} \left(m_{p\backslash i_s} - m_{ps} \right) \lambda_s m_{y_i s}$$

Moreover, $\lambda_s \geq 0$ and $\left(m_{p\backslash i_s} - m_{ps} \right) m_{y_i s} \geq -2$, the following inequalities are given

$$g(x_i, y_i) - g^{\backslash i}(x_i, y_i) \geq \sum_{s=1}^{l} \left(m_{p\backslash i_s} - m_{ps} \right) \lambda_s m_{y_i s} \geq -2 \sum_{s=1}^{l} \lambda_s \geq -2\kappa \sum_{s=1}^{l} \alpha_i^s \qquad (20)$$

So, for $\forall (x_i, y_i) \in S$,

$$g(x_i, y_i) - g^{\backslash i}(x_i, y_i) \geq -2\kappa \sum_{s=1}^{l} \alpha_i^s \geq -2\kappa C \sum_{s=1}^{l} \theta(\alpha_i^s) \qquad (21)$$

And then, we get the bound

$$\forall i \in \{1, \cdots, m\}, \quad \left| g(x_i, y_i) - g^{\backslash i}(x_i, y_i) \right| \leq 2\kappa C \sum_{s=1}^{l} \theta(\alpha_i^s) \qquad (22)$$

Finally, we prove that ECOC kernel machines has pointwise hypothesis stability with

$$E_S \left[\left| \ell(f, z_i) - \ell\left(f^{\backslash i}, z_i \right) \right| \right] \leq \frac{2\kappa C}{m} \sum_{i=1}^{m} \sum_{s=1}^{l} \theta(\alpha_i^s) \qquad \blacksquare$$

Remark. *The parameters α_i^s indicate if point x_i is a support vector for the sth kernel machine, which depend on the solution of the machines trained on the full dataset (so training the machines once will suffice). Our result indicates that pointwise hypothesis stability δ is related with all samples in the training set. For binary ECOC the number of training samples of every dichotomy is the same, thus, there exists parameter α_i for every z_i. But, for ternary ECOC the number of training samples of every dichotomy is different, thus, many training samples are not considered in the training phase of a kernel machine. Considering the parameters α_i indicate if point x_i is a support vector, so, the parameters α_i for these ignored points can be seen as zero just as that these*

*points are not support vectors for kernel machines. This hypothesis is an open problem
and will be discussed in our future work.*

4 Application of Pointwise Hypothesis Stability

In this section, we introduce two aspects of application of pointwise hypothesis stability: model selection and good coding matrixes design for ECOC kernel machines.

4.1 Model Selection

When a coding matrix M is given, in order to have a better generalization performance we should tune the kernel parameters to find the better binary classifiers. Importantly, we need to evaluate the generalization error to check if the tuned kernel parameter is the best one. However, it is difficult to calculate the generalization error, due to the unknown distribution of the data. We have to estimate the generalization error from the available dataset. This available dataset is often defined as the training dataset. On the training dataset we can only obtain the training error or the empirical error. Previously, the better classifier is selected by empirical error minimization, which is known as empirical risk minimization (ERM). But this always leads to an overfitting problem, which means that although the classifier has the minimum empirical error, it has a bad generalization performance. There must be a gap between the empirical error and the generalization error. Fortunately, Bousquet and Elisseeff [22] have given the relation between stability and generalization. They give the generalization error bound in Theorem 2. That is to say the difference between the empirical error and the generalization error can be measured by the stability of a learning algorithm.

Theorem 2. For any learning algorithm A with pointwise hypothesis stability δ with respect to a loss function ℓ such that $0 \leq \ell(f, z) \leq B$, we have

$$R(A, S) \leq R_{emp}(A, S) + \sqrt{\frac{B^2 + 12Bm\delta}{2m}} \tag{23}$$

where $R(A, S)$ is the generalization error and $R_{emp}(A, S)$ is the empirical error.

Note that for a loss function we can always find a suitable upper bound, for example, a large enough bound. Considering we tune the kernel parameters with the same loss function, the upper bound can be seen as a constant argument. In this case, the generalization error bound is just affected by the empirical error on the training dataset and the pointwise hypothesis stability of the learning algorithm.

In order to present the application of pointwise hypothesis stability in model selection, we carry out the experiments on the UCI datasets [25]. Table 1 shows a summary of the datasets used in the experiments. We take the experiment on the vowel dataset as an instance. To reduce the computational complexity, we use 10-fold cross validation to split the whole dataset into 10 parts, and select one part as the training dataset and another part as the test dataset. Moreover, we do not discuss the parameter C which is related to the regularization parameter λ, and treat it as a constant argument.

Table 1. Summary of the used datasets.

Dataset	#Instances	#Features	#Classes
glass	214	9	6
vehicle	846	18	4
zoo	101	18	7
ecoli	336	8	8
vowel	990	13	11
letter	1214	16	26
iris	150	4	3

SVMs are trained on a Gaussian kernel $K(x, x_i) = \exp\left\{ -|x - x_i|^2 / \sigma^2 \right\}$. So, we have $\kappa = \max_s \max_i G_{ii}^s = \max_s \max_i K^s(x_i, x_i) = 1$. In this case, computing the pointwise hypothesis stability means computing the average number of support vectors for each sample on all binary classifiers. Note that we focus on searching for the best value of the kernel parameter σ of the Gaussian kernel. Finally, the parameters are set as $C = 10$ and $\sigma \in [0.1, 4]$ sampled with step 0.1. The used coding strategy is one-versus-all. Figure 2 shows the experimental result.

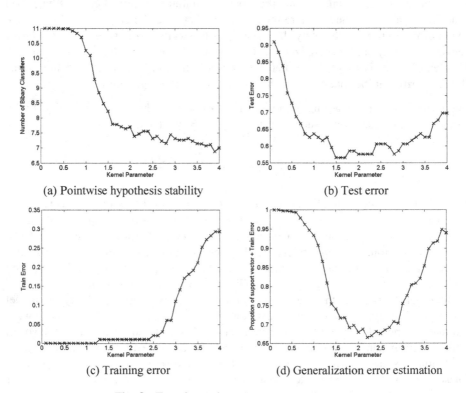

(a) Pointwise hypothesis stability

(b) Test error

(c) Training error

(d) Generalization error estimation

Fig. 2. Experimental result on the vowel dataset

Figure 2(c) plots the training error against different kernel parameter σ. We can observe that when the kernel parameter σ is smaller than 1.3, the training error is the minimum value, equal to zero. However, in Fig. 2(b) the test error is not at the least level, although there is a downward trend. This is just the overfitting problem. In other word, the minimum training error not always leads to the minimum test error. Intuitively, if we combine two figures together [Fig. 2(a) and (c)], the combination will have the same trend with the test error, which is just a validation to Theorem 2. To finish this combination, we calculate the proportion that the number of support vectors for each sample takes on the number of binary classifiers, which can be seen as the possibility of being a support vector for each sample, and regard it as the pointwise hypothesis stability. Refer to Theorem 2, Fig. 2(d) shows the estimation of generalization error against different kernel parameter σ. We can observe that the minimum of the generalization error estimate is very close to the minimum of the test error, although there is a slight deviation. Moreover, Fig. 3 shows the comparison between the generalization error and the test error on several UCI datasets. The comparison result shows that the generalization error estimated by pointwise hypothesis stability can be used to select the better value of kernel parameter in the model selection.

4.2 Good Coding Matrixes Design

On the other hand, the coding matrix design problem is that given a set of binary classifiers, finding a matrix which has better generalization performance. Crammer and Singer [26] have proven that this problem is NP-complete. As an alternative way, many works have focused on the problem dependent design for coding matrixes, such as, Discriminant ECOC [15] and Subclass ECOC [16], which can be a promising approach in the future. For the moment, these problem dependent designs are implemented to achieve a specific criterion. For example, Discriminant ECOC is designed to maximize a discriminative criterion, and Subclass ECOC is designed to guarantee that the base classifier is capable of splitting each subgroup of classes. In this case, the key point for problem dependent design is to find a criterion, which will lead to a better generalization performance. However, there is less formal justification to find it. The difficulty for the problem dependent design is that there is no an apparent relationship between the generalization performance and the property of coding matrix. That is to say if we know which property of coding matrix will lead to a better generalization performance, we can take this property as the criterion in the problem dependent design, such as, the discriminative criterion.

Fortunately, we think that pointwise hypothesis stability will make a certain process for the problem dependent design. Theorem 2 shows the difference between the generalization error and the empirical error. It is sure that if we reduce this difference, we will obtain the better generalization performance. Note that in this paper we do not discuss how to get minimum empirical error, because this problem needs a more detailed work. Just as in Sect. 4.1, we also take the upper bound for the loss function as the constant argument. So, the difference is just affected by pointwise hypothesis stability of the learning algorithm. In this case, the minimization for this difference is equal to the minimization for pointwise hypothesis stability.

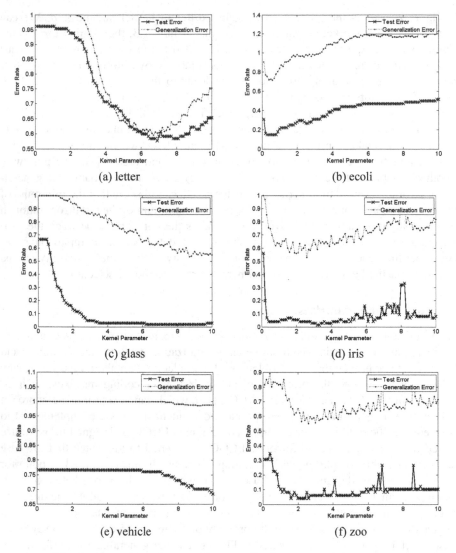

Fig. 3. Comparison between the generalization error and the test error

Refer to Theorem 1, pointwise hypothesis stability for ECOC kernel machines can be written as follows:

$$\delta = \frac{2\kappa C}{m} \sum_{i=1}^{m} \sum_{s=1}^{l} \theta(\alpha_i^s) \qquad (24)$$

Considering that we just take care the coding matrix design, parameters, such as, κ, C, m, can be seen as the constant arguments. So, pointwise hypothesis stability is determined by $\sum_{s=1}^{l} \theta(\alpha_i^s)$.

Note that l is the codeword length or the number of binary classifiers. Now we discuss that when the codeword length is given, what we should do to minimize the pointwise hypothesis stability. In this case, $\sum_{s=1}^{l} \theta(\alpha_i^s)$ can be seen as the possibility for one sample (x_i, y_i) to be support vectors among all binary classifiers. Reducing the pointwise hypothesis stability means to reduce the possibility for all samples in the training dataset. On the other hand, the support vectors are the samples on the separating surface. In other word, the separating surface is represented by the support vectors. Complex separating surface needs more support vectors, which often means that the two class groups are difficult to be split. If two class groups have maximum class discrimination, the separating surface will be simple and the possibility for one sample to be a support vector will be reduced. That is to say if we want to reduce the pointwise hypothesis stability and have a better generalization performance for ECOC kernel machines, we should design the coding matrix which has high discrimination power. This also validates that the Discriminant ECOC has the advantage to have better generalization performance.

In order to validate the relationship between the discriminative criterion in problem dependent design of coding matrix and the pointwise hypothesis stability, we carry out a simple experiment on the synthetic dataset. The synthetic dataset generated randomly has four classes. There are 100 samples for each class. The feature vector of each class has two dimensions: Feature1 and Feature2. The probability density function for each class is defined as follows:

$$p(x|class_i) = \frac{1}{2\pi|\Sigma_i|^{1/2}} \exp\left[-\frac{1}{2}(x - \mu_i)^T \Sigma_i^{-1}(x - \mu_i)\right] \quad i = 1, 2, \cdots 4 \quad (25)$$

where the parameters are shown in Table 2. Figure 4 shows the distribution of four classes.

Table 2. Parameters for synthetic dataset

Class	Mean vectors	Covariance matrices
C_1	$\mu_1 = (2,2)^T$	$\Sigma_1 = \begin{pmatrix} 2 & 0 \\ 0 & 2 \end{pmatrix}$
C_2	$\mu_2 = (2,4)^T$	$\Sigma_2 = \begin{pmatrix} 2 & 0 \\ 0 & 2 \end{pmatrix}$
C_3	$\mu_3 = (8,2)^T$	$\Sigma_3 = \begin{pmatrix} 2 & 0 \\ 0 & 2 \end{pmatrix}$
C_4	$\mu_4 = (8,4)^T$	$\Sigma_4 = \begin{pmatrix} 2 & 0 \\ 0 & 2 \end{pmatrix}$

Simply, we take the design of one column of the coding matrix into consideration. In this experiment, we compare two columns with different discrimination power. Intuitively, in Fig. 4 we can observe that the class groups $\{\{Class1, Class2\}, \{Class3, Class4\}\}$ can be split more easily than the class groups $\{\{Class1, Class3\},$

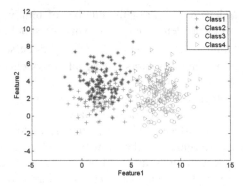

Fig. 4. The synthetic dataset with four classes

$\{Class2, Class4\}\}$. So, one column is set as $P1 = [1, -1, 1, -1]^T$ and the other column is set as $P2 = [1, 1, -1, -1]^T$, with more class discrimination. The pointwise hypothesis stability for each column is calculated by the proportion that the support vectors take up all the samples in the synthetic dataset, which is proportional to the possibility of one sample to be a support vector. Figure 5 shows the fluctuation curves of pointwise hypothesis stability of two columns against different experiment times. We can see that the pointwise hypothesis stability of $P2$ is smaller than that of $P1$. This experiment proves that the maximization of discriminative criterion can lead to have smaller pointwise hypothesis stability, which may lead to a better generalization performance finally.

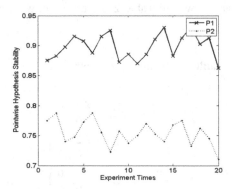

Fig. 5. Pointwise hypothesis stability of two columns

However, the design of good coding matrix is a complex problem, which is determined by many different factors, such as, the codeword length and the minimum hamming distance. Furthermore, these factors may work in an intersectant way. For example, if we only achieve the minimum pointwise hypothesis stability, maybe we will get a bad training error rate. So, the design of good coding matrix needs a tradeoff among several factors or criterions.

5   Conclusion

We provide a proof for the result that an ECOC kernel machines has the pointwise hypothesis stability. In our proof, the stability is determined by the coefficients which can be calculated by training the machines once on the training dataset, and it is easy to be applied in practice. Note that the stability can be seen as the difference between the training error and the generalization error. Minimizing this gap can help to reduce the generalization error. Finally, the applications of this stability in model selection and good coding matrixes design for ECOC kernel machines are presented. How to take both the training error and pointwise hypothesis stability into consideration in good coding matrixes design will be a meaningful direction to get better generalization capability, which will be discussed in our future research works.

Acknowledgments. This work is supported by National Science Foundation of China under grant 61273275.

References

1. Garcia-Pedrajas, N., Ortiz-Boyer, D.: An empirical study of binary classifier fusion methods for multiclass classification. Inf. Fusion **12**(2), 111–130 (2011)
2. Anand, R., Mehrotra, K., Mohan, C.K., Ranka, S.: Efficient classification for multiclass problems using modular neural networks. IEEE Trans. Neural Netw. **6**(1), 117–124 (1995)
3. Clark, P., Boswell, R.: Rule induction with CN2: some recent improvements. In: Kodratoff, Y. (ed.) EWSL 1991. LNCS, vol. 482, pp. 151–163. Springer, Heidelberg (1991). https://doi.org/10.1007/BFb0017011
4. Dietterich, T., Bakiri, G.: Solving multiclass learning problems via error-correcting output codes. J. Artif. Intell. Res. **2**, 263–268 (1995)
5. Allwein, E.L., Schapire, R.E., Singer, Y.: Reducing multiclass to binary: a unifying approach for margin classifiers. J. Mach. Learn. Res. **1**, 1113–1141 (2001)
6. Kong, E., Dietterich, T.: Error-correcting output coding corrects bias and variance. In: Prieditis, A., Lemmer, J. (eds.) Machine Learning: Proceedings of the Twelfth International Conference on Machine Learning, pp. 313–321 (1995)
7. Kong, E., Dietterich, T.: Why error-correcting output coding works with decision trees. Technical report, Department of Computer Science, Oregon State University, Corvallis, OR (1995)
8. Windeatt, T., Ghaderi, R.: Coding and decoding strategies for multi-class learning problems. Inf. Fusion **4**(1), 11–21 (2003)
9. David, A., Lerner, B.: Support vector machine-based image classification for genetic syndrome diagnosis. Pattern Recogn. Lett. **26**(8), 1029–1038 (2005)
10. Ubeyli, E.D.: Multiclass support vector machines for diagnosis of erythematosquamous diseases. Expert Syst. Appl. **35**(4), 1733–1740 (2008)
11. Kittler, J., Ghaderi, R., Windeatt, T., Matas, J.: Face verification via error correcting output codes. Image Vis. Comput. **21**(13–14), 1163–1169 (2003)
12. Bagheri, M.A., Montazer, G.A., Escalera, S.: Error correcting output codes for multiclass classification: application to two image vision problems. In: 2012 16th CSI International Symposium on Artificial Intelligence and Signal Processing (AISP), Shiraz, Iran, pp. 508–513 (2012)

13. Masulli, F., Valentini, G.: Effectiveness of error correcting output coding methods in ensemble and monolithic learning machines. Pattern Anal. Appl. **6**, 285–300 (2003)
14. Garcia-Pedrajas, N., Fyfe, C.: Evolving output codes for multiclass problem. IEEE Trans. Evol. Comput. **12**(1), 93–106 (2008)
15. Pujol, O., Radeva, P., Vitria, J.: Discriminant ECOC: a heuristic method for application dependent design of error correcting output codes. IEEE Trans. Pattern Anal. Mach. Intell. **28**(6), 1007–1012 (2006)
16. Escalera, S., Tax, D.M.J., Pujol, O., Radeva, P., Duin, R.P.W.: Subclass problem-dependent design for error-correcting output codes. IEEE Trans. Pattern Anal. Mach. Intell. **30**(6), 1041–1053 (2008)
17. Ali-Bagheri, M., Ali-Montazer, G., Kabir, E.: A subspace approach to error correcting output codes. Pattern Recogn. Lett. **34**, 176–184 (2013)
18. Ali-Bagheri, M., Gao, Q., Escalera, S.: A genetic-based subspace analysis method for improving Error-Correcting Output Coding. Pattern Recogn. **46**, 2830–2839 (2013)
19. Angel-Bautista, M., Escalera, S., Baro, X., Pujol, O.: On the design of an ECOC-Compliant Genetic Algorithm. Pattern Recogn. **47**, 865–884 (2014)
20. Poggio, T., Rifkin, R., Mukherjee, S., Niyogi, P.: General conditions for predictivity in learning theory. Nature **428**(25), 419–422 (2004)
21. Valentini, G.: Upper bounds on the training error of ECOC SVM ensembles. Technical report DISI-TR-00-17, Dipartimento di Informatica e Science dell' Informazione, Universita di Genova (2000)
22. Bousquet, O., Elisseeff, A.: Stability and generalization. J. Mach. Learn. Res. **2**, 499–526 (2002)
23. Escalera, S., Pujol, O., Radeva, P.: Separability of ternary codes for sparse designs of error-correcting output codes. Pattern Recogn. Lett. **30**(3), 285–297 (2009)
24. Passerini, A., Pontil, M., Frasconi, P.: New results on error correcting output codes of kernel machines. IEEE Trans. Neural Netw. **15**(1), 45–54 (2004)
25. Asuncion, A., Newman, D.: UCI Machine Learning Repository. University of California, Irvine, School of Information and Computer Sciences (2007)
26. Crammer, K., Singer, Y.: On the learnability and design of output codes for multiclass problems. Mach. Learn. **47**, 201–233 (2002)

Deep Convolutional Neural Network for Emotion Recognition Using EEG and Peripheral Physiological Signal

Wenqian Lin$^{(\boxtimes)}$, Chao Li, and Shouqian Sun

College of Computer Science of Zhejiang University, Hangzhou, China
linwq@zju.edu.cn

Abstract. Emotions play an important role at our day-to-day activities such as cognitive process, communication and decision making. It is also very essential for interaction between human and machine. Emotion recognition has been receiving significant attention from various research communities and capturing user's emotional state such as facial expressions, voice and body language, all of which are emerging way to find the human emotions. In recent years, physiological signals based emotion recognition has drawn increasing attention. Most of the physiological signals based methods use well-designed classifiers with hand-crafted features to recognize human emotions. In this paper, we present an approach to perform emotional states classification by end-to-end learning of deep convolutional neural network (CNN), which is inspired by the breakthroughs in the image domain using deep convolutional neural network. The approach is tested using the database "DEAP" including electroencephalogram (EEG) and peripheral physiological signals. We transform EEG into images combine extract hand-crafted features of other peripheral physiological signals, and classify emotions into valence and arousal. The results show this approach is possible to improve classification accuracy.

1 Introduction

Emotion playing a significant role in human's daily activities. It is an psychological expression of affective reaction and mental state based on human subjective experience [1]. Emotion is critical aspect of the human interpersonal relationship and essential to the human communication and behaviors. Psychologists often used discrete and dimensional emotion classification systems. Eight basic emotion states (anger, fear, sadness, disgust, surprise, anticipation, acceptance, and joy) proposed by Plutchik [2] and six basic emotion states based on facial expressions (anger, disgust, fear, happiness, sadness and surprise) proposed by Ekman [3] both belong to discrete emotion classification system. And the most widely used valence and arousal emotion classification model, proposed by Russell [4] belongs to dimensional system. In this model, the valence axis represents the quality of an emotion and the arousal axis refers to the emotion activation level.

© Springer International Publishing AG 2017
Y. Zhao et al. (Eds.): ICIG 2017, Part II, LNCS 10667, pp. 385–394, 2017.
https://doi.org/10.1007/978-3-319-71589-6_33

In order to improve human-machine interaction (HMI), emotion recognition began to attract increasing attention. In the past few decades, various sensory data have been used to identify human emotion, including facial expression, auditory signals, text, body language, peripheral physiological signals and electroencephalogram (EEG) [5,6]. The last two, especially EEG, can provide more objective and comprehensive information for emotion recognition in comparison with other sensory data, because they can detect the body dynamics in response to emotional states directly.

Existing EEG based emotion recognition methods can be roughly grouped into two main categories: hand-crafted features based methods with well-designed classifiers [7,8] and recurrent neural network (RNN) [9]. Inspired by [10,11], where deep CNN is successfully in some fields of identification, we transform processed EEG data into images based on different frequency bands which contains time and frequency domain information, and then the generated images and hand-crafted features extracted from peripheral physiological signals were fed into CNN models to perform fine-tuning and emotion recognition. Experiments were conducted for cross-subject evaluation on the DEAP dataset [12] to validate the effectiveness of our proposed method. Our purpose was to affirm if the classification results of our method could obtain better average accuracy and F1 score on valence and arousal classification compares with several studies on the same database before.

The rest of this paper is organized as follows. Section 2 presents the descriptions of DEAP database. Section 3 presents the proposed method. The results are discussed in Sect. 4 and we conclude the paper in Sect. 5.

2   DEAP Database

DEAP dataset, which we conduct our experiment is a multimodal dataset for emotion analysis, contains both electroencephalogram (EEG) (recorded over the scalp using 32 electrodes and the positions of the electrodes are according to 10–20 International System: Fp1, AF3, F3, F7, FC5, FC1, C3, T7, CP5, CP1, P3, P7, PO3, O1, Oz, Pz, Fp2, AF4, Fz, F4, F8, FC6, FC2, Cz, C4, T8, CP6, CP2, P4, P8, PO4, and O2) and peripheral physiological signals (8 channels, include electromyogram (EMG) collected from zygomaticus major and trapezius muscles, horizontal and vertical electrooculograms (EOGs), skin temperature (TMP), galvanic skin response (GSR), blood volume pulse (BVP), and respiration (RSP)) of 32 subjects (aged between 19 and 37), as each subject watched 40 one-minute music video clips, which were carefully selected to evoke different emotional states according to the dimensional valence-arousal emotion model of subjects, and played in a random order.

After watching each music video, participants were required to report their emotion using Self-Assessment Manikins (SAM) questionnaire, rating their tastes level of five dimensions (valence, arousal, dominance, liking, and familiarity), the first four scales range from 1 to 9 and the fifth dimension range between 1 and 5. In this paper, identifications the dimensions of valence (ranging from negative to positive) and arousal (ranging from calm to active) are addressed as two independent tasks according to valence-arousal emotion model proposed by Russell [4]. Both two tasks posed as binary classification problems.

3 Proposed Method

Figure 1 shows the overall architecture of our proposed method. We first perform data preprocessing to normalize all the physiological signals. Secondly, every sample of electroencephalogram (EEG) signals is transformed into six gray images according to different frequency bands. Thirdly, we extract the 81-dimensional hand-crafted features of other peripheral physiological signals. Finally, the generated images and hand-crafted features are fed into four pretrained AlexNet models [15] to perform fine-tuning and emotion recognition.

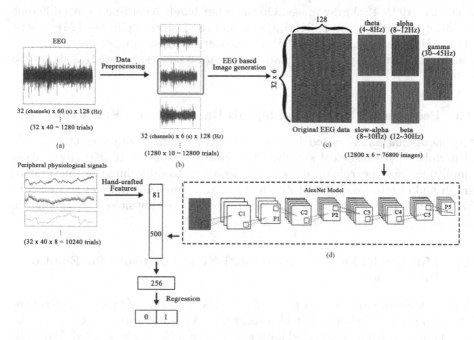

Fig. 1. An illustration of the proposed emotion recognition process. (C: convolution, P: max-pooling.)

3.1 Data Preprocessing

For all 40 channels of physiological signals in DEAP dataset, the preprocessing included down sampling the data from 512 Hz to 128 Hz. Especially for EEG data, a band-pass filter with cutoff frequencies of 4.0 and 45.0 Hz is first used to remove the unwanted noises and averaged to the common reference, as in [13,14]. The data was segmented into 60 s trials and a 3 s pre-trial baseline removed, then we divide the 60 s data of each trial into 10 clips to perform emotion recognition as in Sect. 3. Additionally, we perform data normalization for each channel of physiological signals as follows:

$$I_{i,j} = (I_{i,j} - min_i)/(max_i - min_i) \tag{1}$$

where $I_{i,j}$ is the value of channel i at time j, max_i and min_i are, respectively, the maximum value and the minimum value of the channel i during $T = 60s$.

3.2 Electroencephalogram Signals Based Image Generation

After data preprocessing, the size of original EEG data for one sample is 32 × 6 × 128, where 32 stands for the channels, 6 stands for the time of one clip, and 128 stands for the sampling rate and we rearrange the EEG data into a fixed size (192 × 128) gray image. On the other hand, according to five different frequency bands (theta (4~8 Hz), slow-alpha (8~10 Hz), alpha (8~12 Hz), beta (12~30 Hz), and gamma (30~45 Hz)), another five gray images are generated. Finally, for each sample of EEG data, we obtain 6 images. Figure 1(a) shows the details.

3.3 Peripheral Physiological Signals Based Feature Extraction

81-dimensional hand-crafted features are extracted from other eight channels of peripheral physiological signals: GSR, electrooculogram (EOG), respiration amplitude, electrocardiogram, skin temperature, blood volume by plethysmograph and electromyograms of Zygomaticus and Trapezius muscles as shown in Table 1. Before feature extraction, all the peripheral physiological signals are separately normalized to mean = 0 and s.d. = 1.

3.4 Multimodal Deep Convolutional Neural Network for Emotion Recognition

Network Structure. In this paper, the partial structure of famous deep convolutional model (AlexNet) [15] which consists of 8 parameterized layers (5 convolutional layers, 1 fully connected layer and 1 softmax layer) is adopted. We make some changes with AlexNet: (1) we encode the 81-dimensional hand-crafted feature into our CNN model by concatenating it with the hidden fully connected layer. (2) The number of hidden units in the fully connected layer is 500 and the output layer has only two neurons, which represents the two classes of the problem. Figure 1(d) shows our model's structure.

End-to-End Fine-Tuning. In order to fine-tune the pre-trained AlexNet model, the size of input skeleton sequence based image must be compatible with AlexNet's input size which is known as 227 × 227 pixel size. We first rescale each image to 256 × 256 pixel size and then randomly cropping and mean-subtracting

Table 1. Description for the hand-crafted features of peripheral physiological signals

Feature name	Feature index	Feature details
EOG & EMG frequency-domain features	1~5	Eye blink rate Average PSD of vertical Horizontal EOG Trapezius EMG Zygomaticus EMG
EOG and EMG time-domain features	6~21	Mean, Variance Zero-crossing rate The approximate entropy of 4 EOG and EMG channels
Skin temperature features	22~27	Average PSD in the frequency bands (0~0.1 Hz) and (0.1~0.2 Hz) Mean, Variance Approximate entropy Mean of derivative
GSR features	28~52	Mean Mean of derivative Mean of negative derivative values Proportion of negative values in all Derivative values Number of local minima Mean of rising time 15 PSD values in frequency band (0~2.4 Hz) Zero-crossing rates and means for the bands of (0~0.2 Hz) and (0~0.8 Hz)
Blood volume pressure features	53~59	Power ratio between the frequency bands of (0.04~0.15 Hz) and (0.15~0.5 Hz) Average PSD in the frequency bands of (0.1~0.2 Hz), (0.2~0.3 Hz), (0.3~0.4 Hz),(0.01~0.08 Hz), (0.08~0.15 Hz) and (0.15~0.5 Hz)
Respiration features	60~81	Power ratio between frequency bands of (0.05~0.25 Hz) and (0.25~0.5 Hz) Mean Mean of derivative Centroid of PSD Respiration rate 15 values of PSD in frequency band (0~2.4 Hz) peak-to-peak time

are adopted. For the last softmax layer (i.e., the output layer), the number of the unit is the same as the number of the emotion classes. Each sample of EEG signals is transformed into 6 images, which are separately fed into the proposed multimodal CNN with the same label for fine-tuning. Regarding the hyper-parameter setting, we empirically selected the size of mini-batches for the SGD as 200. Moreover, we set the initial learning rate to 0.001, which is decreased by multiplying it by 0.1 at every 500th iteration. The fine-tuning is stopped after 50 epochs.

Emotion Recognition. In this study, we separately focus on valence and arousal scales because Koelstra et al. [12] finds that there is a significant difference between low and high among these two emotions. For each trial, two labels were generated. The affective level in valence space described HV (high valence) or LV (low valence), and the affective level in valence space described HA (high arousal) or LA (low arousal). The label 1 indicates high valence/arousal and the label 0 indicates low valence/arousal. Considering subject-specificity of the subjective ratings, the binary emotional classes could be much proper generated based on personal threshold, which determine the target classes by clustering subjective rating data for each subject using classical k-means clustering algorithm [14]. The threshold is computed by the midpoint of two cluster centers as examples shown in Fig. 2 of subject 1, and all threshold values for 32 subjects summarized in Table 2. The classification performances based on them.

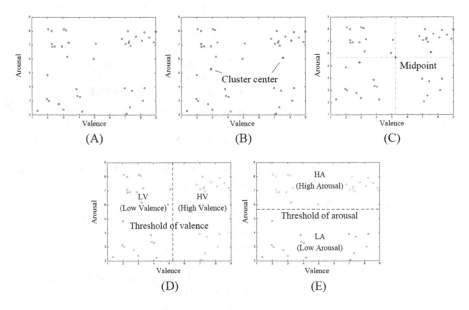

Fig. 2. The target emotion classes generated based on personal threshold. (A) Ratings of all 40 one-minute music videos by subject 1. (B) Two cluster centers based on results of k-means clustering. (C) Midpoint of two cluster centers. (D) The low and high valence states discretized by the threshold. (E) The low and high arousal states discretized by the threshold.

Table 2. All threshold values for 32 subjects.

Subject	Arousal	Valence	Subject	Arousal	Valence
1	5.6803	5.2342	17	5.1932	5.0815
2	5.6126	6.0166	18	5.5781	5.5596
3	3.7776	5.5513	19	5.4990	5.3685
4	4.5916	4.6503	20	5.6172	5.8185
5	5.1736	4.9791	21	6.0432	5.6618
6	4.6612	5.7579	22	5.3251	4.2624
7	5.0705	4.8358	23	3.6487	6.1354
8	5.6286	5.8466	24	5.8675	4.9634
9	5.6759	5.4592	25	5.9870	5.3552
10	5.6759	5.0015	26	3.8795	4.8234
11	5.1886	4.0322	27	4.6934	5.8161
12	6.3644	4.9731	28	4.7856	5.3817
13	6.6635	4.8578	29	4.3479	4.5732
14	5.4360	4.9597	30	5.1283	5.5714
15	4.7245	5.8538	31	5.6703	4.6661
16	4.7233	4.2413	32	5.6419	5.1586

Because each sample of EEG signals is transformed into 6 images, during testing, the class scores of all images are averaged to form the final prediction of the action class i as follows:

$$P = (\sum_{i=1}^{6} O_k)/6 \qquad (2)$$

and

$$i = arg \max_{i \in [0,1]} P_i \qquad (3)$$

where O represents the output vector of our proposed CNN model and P is the final probability of high/low emotion.

3.5 Evaluation Criteria

As our analysis of emotion is a binary classification, we adopt mean classification accuracy and F1-score as the final evaluation criteria. The mean classification accuracy is calculated as follows:

$$Mean\_Acc = (n_{TP} + n_{TN})/(n_{TP} + n_{TN} + n_{FP} + n_{FN}) \qquad (4)$$

where n_{TP}, n_{TN}, n_{FP} and n_{FN} denote the numbers of correct classified $label : 1$ instance, the numbers of correctively classified $label : 1$ instance, the numbers of correctly classified *label* : 0 instance, the numbers of incorrectly classified *label* : 1 instance and the numbers of incorrectly classified *label* : 0 instance, respectively.

The precision for recognizing the high-class (1) instances is defined as p_1,

$$p_1 = (n_{TP})/(n_{TP} + n_{FP}) \tag{5}$$

The precision for recognizing the low-class (0) instances is defined as p_0,

$$p_0 = (n_{TN})/(n_{TN} + n_{FN}) \tag{6}$$

Finally, the F1-score is calculated:

$$p_f = 2p_0p_1/(p_0 + p_1) \tag{7}$$

4 Results

Experiments of valence and arousal classification were conducted. We divide the last 60 s data of each trial into 10 clips to perform emotion recognition and the 10-fold cross validation technique was carried out to evaluate the performance. Which partitioned samples into 10 disjoint subsets. One of the subsets was used as test sample at each fold, rest subsets were used as training samples and repeated 10 times till all the subsets were used as test sample ones. The average classification accuracy and F1-score values for all subjects were computed at each fold and were averaged at the end of the experiment. The classification results of the method we proposed was further compared with results obtained by other methods in Table 3.

Table 3. Experimental results on DEAP Dataset

Methods	Arousal		Valence	
	Accuracy [%]	F1-score [%]	Accuracy [%]	F1-score [%]
Koelstra et al. [12]	62.00	63.10	62.70	65.20
Liu and Sourina [16]	76.51	–	50.80	–
Naser and Saha [17]	66.20	–	64.30	–
Yoon and Chung [18]	70.10	–	70.90	–
Wang and Shang [19]	51.20	–	60.90	–
Chen et al. [20]	69.09	68.96	67.89	67.83
Li et al. [21]	64.20	–	58.40	–
Atkinson and Campos [22]	73.06	–	73.14	–
Yin et al. [13]	84.18	77.98	83.04	79.50
Our proposed method	**87.30**	**78.24**	**85.50**	**80.06**

It shows our proposed method could obtain better average accuracy and F1 score on valence and arousal classification compares with several studies on the same database before. More specifically, separately with respect to arousal and valence, the performance is improved by 3.12% and 2.46%, and F1 score also enhanced 0.26% and 0.56%.

5   Conclusion

In this paper, we proposed to transform different frequency band of EEG signals into six gray images which contains time and frequency domain information, and extracted hand-crafted features of other peripheral physiological signals. These images and features were then fed into a AlexNet model to perform end-to-end fine-tuning. To achieve better performances, data preprocessing of the original signal was also adopted. The provided experimental results prove the effectiveness and validate the proposed contributions of our method by achieving superior performance over the existing methods on DEAP Dataset.

References

1. Mauss, I.B., Robinson, M.D.: Measures of emotion: a review. Cogn. Emot. **23**(2), 209–237 (2009)
2. Plutchik, R.: Emotions and Life: Perspectives from Psychology, Biology, and Evolution, 1st edn. American Psychological Association, Washington (2003)
3. Ekman, P.: Basic Emotions. Handbook of Cognition and Emotion. Wiley, New York (1999)
4. Russell, J.: A circumplex model of affect. J. Pers. Soc. Psychol. **39**(6), 1161–1178 (1980)
5. Nie, D., Wang, X.W., Shi, L.C., et al.: EEG-based emotion recognition during watching movies. In: International IEEE/EMBS Conference on Neural Engineering, pp. 667–670. IEEE Xplore (2011)
6. Liu, Y., Sourina, O., Nguyen, M.K.: Real-time EEG-based human emotion recognition and visualization. In: International Conference on Cyberworlds, pp. 262–269. IEEE Computer Society (2010)
7. Heraz, A., Razaki, R., Frasson, C.: Using machine learning to predict learner emotional state from brainwaves. In: IEEE International Conference on Advanced Learning Technologies, ICALT 2007, July 18–20 2007, Niigata, Japan, DBLP, pp. 853–857 (2007)
8. Wang, X.-W., Nie, D., Lu, B.-L.: EEG-based emotion recognition using frequency domain features and support vector machines. In: Lu, B.-L., Zhang, L., Kwok, J. (eds.) ICONIP 2011. LNCS, vol. 7062, pp. 734–743. Springer, Heidelberg (2011). https://doi.org/10.1007/978-3-642-24955-6_87
9. Ishino, K., Hagiwara, M.: A feeling estimation system using a simple electroencephalograph. In: IEEE International Conference on Systems, Man and Cybernetics, vol. 5, pp. 4204–4209. IEEE Xplore (2003)
10. Shiraga, K., Makihara, Y., Muramatsu, D., et al.: GEINet: view-invariant gait recognition using a convolutional neural network. In: International Conference on Biometrics, pp. 1–8. IEEE (2016)

11. Li, C., Min, X., Sun, S., Lin, W., Tang, Z.: DeepGait: a learning deep convolutional representation for view-invariant gait recognition using joint Bayesian. Appl. Sci. **7**(3), 210 (2017)
12. Koelstra, S., Muhl, C., Soleymani, M., et al.: DEAP: a database for emotion analysis; using physiological signals. IEEE Trans. Affect. Comput. **3**(1), 18–31 (2012)
13. Yin, Z., Zhao, M., Wang, Y., et al.: Recognition of emotions using multimodal physiological signals and an ensemble deep learning model. Comput. Methods Programs Biomed. **140**, 93–110 (2017)
14. Yin, Z., Wang, Y., Liu, L., Zhang, W., Zhang, J.: Cross-subject EEG feature selection for emotion recognition using transfer recursive feature elimination. Front. Neurorob. **11** (2017)
15. Krizhevsky, A., Sutskever, I., Hinton, G.E.: ImageNet classification with deep convolutional neural networks. In: International Conference on Neural Information Processing Systems, pp. 1097–1105. Curran Associates Inc. (2012)
16. Liu, Y., Sourina, O.: EEG-based valence level recognition for real-time applications. In: International Conference on Cyberworlds, pp. 53–60 (2012)
17. Naser, D.S., Saha, G.: Recognition of emotions induced by music videos using DT-CWPT. In: Medical Informatics and Telemedicine, pp. 53–57. IEEE (2013)
18. Yoon, H.J., Chung, S.Y.: EEG-based emotion estimation using Bayesian weighted-log-posterior function and perceptron convergence algorithm. Comput. Biol. Med. **43**(12), 2230–2237 (2013)
19. Wang, D., Shang, Y.: Modeling physiological data with deep belief networks. Int. J. Inf. Educ. Technol. **3**(5), 505–511 (2013)
20. Chen, J., Hu, B., Moore, P., et al.: Electroencephalogram-based emotion assessment system using ontology and data mining techniques. Appl. Soft Comput. **30**, 663–674 (2015)
21. Li, X., Zhang, P., Song, D., Yu, G., Hou, Y., Hu, B.: EEG based emotion identification using unsupervised deep feature learning. In: SIGIR2015 Workshop on Neuro-Physiological Methods in IR Research, 13 August 2015
22. Atkinson, J., Campos, D.: Improving BCI-based emotion recognition by combining EEG feature selection and kernel classifiers. Expert Syst. Appl. **47**, 35–41 (2015)

Incremental Active Learning Method
for Supervised ISOMAP

Guopeng Zhang, Rui Huang$^{(\boxtimes)}$, and Junli Chen

Shanghai University, Shanghai, China
huangr@shu.edu.cn

Abstract. The supervised Isomap (S-Isomap), a supervised version of Isomap, can achieve better recognition performance by considering the class label information. However, S-Isomap usually suffers from heavy computation burden especially when new data arrive and re-computation of distance matrix is needed. To address the limitation, an incremental strategy is applied to update the geodesic distances using the previous results. Meanwhile, informative samples are selected through active learning to exploit the added data information with less human labeling effort on incremental process. Therefore, an incremental active learning S-Isomap (IALSI) is proposed. Image retrieval and classification experiments are conducted to evaluate the performance of IALSI. The results show that the proposed method can improve the accuracy meanwhile reducing the running time greatly.

Keywords: Dimension reduction · Supervised Isomap (S-Isomap)
Manifold learning · Incremental learning · Active learning

1 Introduction

With the rapid growth of information technology, massive data sets, such as human gene distribution, human healthy report, climate patterns, commercial record, have been created. Dimension reduction (DR), as a key technique to extract the important formation from the high-dimensional data, has increasingly attracted considerable attentions and studies.

The major task of DR is to find a projection to map the high dimension data into a lower dimensional space according to some criterion. So far, many DR methods have been proposed, and they can be divided into linear and nonlinear groups. PCA and LDA [1] are most popular linear methods, which try to obtain linear projection matrices. In contrast to the linear DR methods, nonlinear approaches are able to discover the nonlinear structure data in real world. Most incremental DR methods are based on kernel function. For example, kernel principal component analysis (KPCA) [2] has been widely used to get an implicit nonlinear mapping. But the result may be worse once the inappropriate kernel function is chosen. Recently, some methods based on manifold learning, such as laplacian eigenmaps (LE) [3], locally linear embedding (LLE) [4] and Isomap [5] have drawn much concern. In particular, Isomap, which can

Y. Zhao et al. (Eds.): ICIG 2017, Part II, LNCS 10667, pp. 395–404, 2017.
https://doi.org/10.1007/978-3-319-71589-6_34

reveal the intrinsic geometric structure of manifold by preserving geodesic distance of all similarity pairs, has presented some encouraging results. Therefore, a series of Isomap methods have occurred, such as supervised Isomap (S-Isomap) [6], orthogonal constrained marginal Isomap (M-Isomap) [7] and multi-manifold discriminant Isomap (MMD-Isomap) [8]. Among them, S-Isomap has shown good performances in visualization, image retrieval and classification by modifying the distances between the pairwise points with the same and different class labels. Despite the good performances achieved by Isomap family, they suffer from heavy computation burden that is caused by calculating the geodesic distances of all point pairs. In particular, distance recalculation has to be done when new data arrive [9] and leads to more computational load.

Incremental learning, as a family of efficient of scalable machine learning methods, has been proposed to operate on a sequence of data instance. At each step, the incremental learning algorithms process an incoming example and update the learner through the instance. An incremental version of Isomap has been proposed, which can efficiently update the geodesic distances and re-estimate the eigenvectors using the previous computation results [10]. On the other hand, for supervised learning, the number of labeled samples is limited in practice due to cost and time. This issue has motivated the recent study of active learning [11], which queries only a subset of informative incoming instances to update the learner and aims to maximize learner performance using minimal human labeling effort at each iteration.

In order to cut down the computation amount of S-Isomap and use the most informative labeled samples, we present an incremental active learning S-Isomap, called by IALSI. The proposed method modifies the original S-Isomap to the incremental version and reduces the computational cost greatly. Furthermore, active learning is applied for high efficiency and scalability towards large-scale learning tasks.

The remainder of this paper is organized as follows: Sect. 2 describes our proposed incremental active learning S-Isomap. The experimental results are shown in Sect. 3. Finally, Sect. 4 gives the conclusion and future work.

2 Incremental Active Learning S-Isomap

In this section, we will elaborate our method. Before that, we first give a brief review of S-Isomap. Then we introduce the details of our method.

2.1 S-Isomap

Given a data set $\mathbf{X} = [\mathbf{x}_1, \mathbf{x}_2, \ldots, \mathbf{x}_N] \in \mathbf{R}^{r \times N}$ with N points, DR is to find a mapping function that maps these points to a new data set $\mathbf{Y} = [\mathbf{y}_1, \mathbf{y}_2, \ldots, \mathbf{y}_N] \in \mathbf{R}^{r' \times N}$ in a lower dimensional space $(r' \ll r)$. $d(\mathbf{x}_i, \mathbf{x}_j)$ denotes the Euclidean distance between points $\mathbf{x}_i$ and $\mathbf{x}_j$.

S-Isomap is a supervised version of Isomap. Considering the class label information of samples, it defines the distance metric as follows:

$$\tilde{d}(\mathbf{x}_i, \mathbf{x}_j) = \begin{cases} \sqrt{1 - \exp(-d^2(\mathbf{x}_i, \mathbf{x}_j)/\beta)} & \text{if } l(\mathbf{x}_i) = l(\mathbf{x}_j) \\ \sqrt{\exp(d^2(\mathbf{x}_i, \mathbf{x}_j)/\beta)} - \alpha & \text{if } l(\mathbf{x}_i) \neq l(\mathbf{x}_j) \end{cases} \tag{1}$$

where the parameters of α and β are used to control the range of $d(\mathbf{x}_i, \mathbf{x}_j)$. Actually, α is set to be a small positive value, and β is set to be the average Euclidean distance between all pairs of data points. $l(\mathbf{x}_i)$ is the class label of $\mathbf{x}_i$. After the modification of point distances, the same steps as Isomap are used to obtain the lower dimensional representations of samples. It can be summarized as follows:

1. Construct neighborhood graph $\mathbf{D}_G$. For every pair of data points, if $\tilde{d}(\mathbf{x}_i, \mathbf{x}_j)$. is smaller than the fixed us radius $\in$ or $\mathbf{x}_j \in \text{KNN}(\mathbf{x}_i)$ ($\text{KNN}(\mathbf{x}_i)$ means $\mathbf{x}_j$ is the K-nearest neighbors of $\mathbf{x}_i$), set edge with weight of $\tilde{d}(\mathbf{x}_i, \mathbf{x}_j)$.
2. Compute the shortest geodesic distances. Initial the distance $d_G(\mathbf{x}_i, \mathbf{x}_j) = \tilde{d}(\mathbf{x}_i, \mathbf{x}_j)$. if $\mathbf{x}_j$ and $\mathbf{x}_i$ are neighbors, otherwise, put $d_G(\mathbf{x}_i, \mathbf{x}_j) = \infty$. Estimate the geodesic distances between all pairs of points by computing their shortest path distances in $\mathbf{D}_G$ using Dijkstra's or Floyd's algorithm.
3. Construct r'-dimensional embedding. Define the optimization problem as follows:

$$\min_{\mathbf{Y}} \sum_{\mathbf{x}_i, \mathbf{x}_j} \left(d(\mathbf{y}_i, \mathbf{y}_j) - d_G(\mathbf{x}_i, \mathbf{x}_j) \right)^2 \tag{2}$$

Let $\mathbf{H} = \mathbf{I} - (1/N)\mathbf{e}\mathbf{e}^T$, where $\mathbf{I}$ is an $N \times N$ identity matrix, and $\mathbf{e}$ is the vector of all ones. Let $\mathbf{Q}$ is an $N \times N$ matrix with elements $\mathbf{Q}_{ij} = d_G^2(\mathbf{x}_i, \mathbf{x}_j)$. The lower-dimensional embedding $\mathbf{Y}$ is obtained as $[\sqrt{\lambda_1}\mathbf{v}_1, \sqrt{\lambda_2}\mathbf{v}_2, \ldots, \sqrt{\lambda_{r'}}\mathbf{v}_{r'}]^T$., where $\{\mathbf{v}_i\}_{i=1}^{r'}$ denotes the eigenvectors corresponding to the first r' leading eigenvalues of $\mathbf{R} = -\mathbf{H}\mathbf{Q}\mathbf{H}/2$.

2.2 Proposed IALSI

In IALSI, incremental learning is applied to update the shortest distance matrix based on Floyd's algorithm en new training data arrive in each iteration. These new incoming samples are chosen by active learning according to a given criterion.

The main task of active learning is to select information and representative samples for classification. According to different criteria for sample selection, active learning methods can be roughly divided into two groups: committee-based approaches and uncertainty-based approaches. Committee-based approaches, based on committee of classifiers, select the data whose classification results have the greatest disagreements among the classifiers. While in the uncertainty-based approaches, the most uncertain samples determined by some uncertainty scheme are chosen and labeled.

In the proposed IALSI, the uncertainty of sample $\mathbf{x}_i$ are measured as follows:

$$w(\mathbf{x}_i) = \max_{1 \leq c \leq C} d(\mathbf{x}_i, \bar{\mathbf{x}}_c) - \min_{1 \leq c \leq C} d(\mathbf{x}_i, \bar{\mathbf{x}}_c), \tag{3}$$

where $\bar{\mathbf{x}}_c$ is the mean value of samples belonging to class c, and C is the number of classes. A smaller $w(\mathbf{x}_i)$ means that the distances between sample $\mathbf{x}_i$ and each class center are comparable and thus there is ambiguity to label $\mathbf{x}_i$ based on the distances. Therefore, $\mathbf{x}_i$ is more informative and to be labeled and added to the training set.

Suppose the available training data set is $\{\mathbf{x}_i, l(\mathbf{x}_i)\}_{i=1}^N$, the unlabeled data set is $\{\mathbf{x}_j\}_{j=1}^M$. We will select m samples from the unlabeled set through active learning. The details of active learning algorithm are summarized in Table 1.

Table 1. Active learning

Input: Training data set $\{\mathbf{x}_i, l(\mathbf{x}_i)\}_{i=1}^N$, unlabeled data set $\{\mathbf{x}_j\}_{j=1}^M$, m.

Output: $\{\mathbf{x}_j, l(\mathbf{x}_j)\}_{j=1}^m$.

1. Compute $w(\mathbf{x}_i)$ $(i = 1, 2, ..., M)$ using Eq. (3).
2. Rank $w(\mathbf{x}_i)$ in an ascend order.
3. Choose first m smallest samples from $\{\mathbf{x}_j\}_{j=1}^M$ and assign them true class labels to get $\{\mathbf{x}_j, l(\mathbf{x}_j)\}_{j=1}^m$.

In the beginning of IALSI, distances between points in $\{\mathbf{x}_i, l(\mathbf{x}_i)\}_{i=1}^N$. are calculated using Eq. (1), and the shortest distance matrix $\mathbf{D}_0$ is obtained. In the t th iteration, m samples selected by active learning algorithm are added to the training set as $\{\mathbf{x}_j, l(\mathbf{x}_j)\}_{j=1}^m$, and used to update the geodesic distances between points $(1 \leq t \leq T)$. The extended distance matrix is given as:

$$\mathbf{D}_t = \begin{bmatrix} \mathbf{D}_{t-1} & \mathbf{D}_E \\ \mathbf{D}_E^T & \mathbf{D}_A \end{bmatrix} \tag{4}$$

where $\mathbf{D}_A$ denotes the distance matrix among the new arriving data $\{\mathbf{x}_j, l(\mathbf{x}_j)\}_{j=1}^m$, $\mathbf{D}_E$ denotes the distances between $\{\mathbf{x}_i, l(\mathbf{x}_i)\}_{i=1}^N$ and $\{\mathbf{x}_j, l(\mathbf{x}_j)\}_{j=1}^m$. Instead of re-computing the shortest distances for all points, only new data points are considered. For new point $\mathbf{x}_i$, the distance between it and point $\mathbf{x}_j \in \{\mathbf{x}_i, l(\mathbf{x}_i)\}_{i=1}^{N+m}$. is initialized as $d_G(\mathbf{x}_i, \mathbf{x}_j) = \tilde{d}(\mathbf{x}_i, \mathbf{x}_j)$ if $\mathbf{x}_j$ and $\mathbf{x}_i$ are neighbors, otherwise, put $d_G(\mathbf{x}_i, \mathbf{x}_j) = \infty$. Then Floyd's algorithm is adopted to dynamically update the shortest distance matrix in all-pairs data. Hence, for each value of $p = N+1, \cdots, N+m$. in turn, replace all entries $d_G(\mathbf{x}_i, \mathbf{x}_j)$ by $\min\{d_G(\mathbf{x}_i, \mathbf{x}_j), d_G(\mathbf{x}_i, \mathbf{x}_p) + d_G(\mathbf{x}_p, \mathbf{x}_j)\}$. After the iteration, the final matrix is denoted $\mathbf{D}_t$. At last, we use the classic MDS algorithm to construct r'-dimensional embedding. During the iterations, the k value in neighborhood graph changes allows

$$k(t) = k_0 + k_1 t \tag{5}$$

where k_0 is the initial value and k_1 acts as a factor controlling the change range. Table 2 lists the details of IALSI.

Table 2. IALSI

Input: $\{\mathbf{x}_i, l(\mathbf{x}_i)\}_{i=1}^{N}$, unlabeled data set $\{\mathbf{x}_j\}_{j=1}^{M}$, m, k_0, k_1

Output: $\mathbf{Y}$

1. Initialization: $k := k_0$; compute $\mathbf{D}_0$.

2. Incremental active learning loop:

for $t = 1$ to T

   Obtain $\{\mathbf{x}_j, l(\mathbf{x}_j)\}_{j=1}^{m}$ using algorithm in Table 1

   $k := k(t)$ using Eq. (5)

   Compute $\mathbf{D}_A$ and $\mathbf{D}_E$;

   Construct $\mathbf{D}_t$ using Eq. (4);

   $\{\mathbf{x}_i, l(\mathbf{x}_i)\}_{i=1}^{N+m} := \{\mathbf{x}_i, l(\mathbf{x}_i)\}_{i=1}^{N} \cup \{\mathbf{x}_j, l(\mathbf{x}_j)\}_{j=1}^{m}$;

   $\{\mathbf{x}_j\}_{j=1}^{M-m} := \{\mathbf{x}_j\}_{j=1}^{M} - \{\mathbf{x}_j\}_{j=1}^{m}$;

   $N := N + m$; $M := M - m$;

   $\mathbf{D}_{t-1} := \mathbf{D}_t$;

   end for

3. Obtain $\mathbf{Y}$ using Eq. (2).

Remark on computational complexity. We focus on the space complexity of construction of distance matrix and neighborhood graph, as the steps is the major computing load in practice. The space complexity of original S-Isomap algorithm is $O(N^2)$ [8]. When the new data points are added, the space complexity of batch algorithm reaches to $O\left((N+m)^2\right)$. In IALSI, only the shortest distances involving new data need to be computed. Hence, the space complexity of IALSI is simply $O(2N \times m + m^2)$.

3 Experiments and Discussions

In this section, experiments are carried out to evaluate the performance of IALSI. Three publicly available image data sets, including Corel [12], UC Merced LULC [13], and MNIST [14], are used for image retrieval and classification. Two batch methods including original Isomap and S-Imap, two incremental methods including incremental S-Isomap (ISI) and IALSI are compared. It is noted that, in ISI, samples to be added into training set are randomly selected. All the algorithms are implemented in MATLAB and run on an Intel(R) core(TM) i5-3470 PC at 3.2 GHz with 12 GB RAM.

3.1 Data Sets and Experimental Setting

Two datasets, the UC Merced LULC and Corel, are used for image retrieval. The LULC data set, obtained from aerial imagery, consists of images from 20 classes, with a pixel resolution of 30 cm. Each class contains 100 images of size 256 by 256 pixels. The Corel data set is from the real-world photo from COREL Photo Gallery. It has 20 categories with 500 images per category. We extract basic color features and wavelet texture features to describe images [15]. The features include color histogram (32 dimensions), color moment (64 dimensions), color auto correlogram (6 dimensions), wavelet moment (40 dimensions) and Gabor transform where the number of scales was set 4 and orientation was set 6 (48 dimensions). All the features are concatenated into a long vector as an image feature and each image is represented by a 190-dimensional vector. The new feature is normalized to zero mean and unit variance. The MNIST handwritten digit database is used for classification. It has 70000 handwritten digit images with size of 28×28 pixels. We randomly choose 4000 images from digits "0–9" for evaluation. Figure 1 gives some example images of the three data sets.

In our experiments, each dataset is randomly divided into three partitions: training set, candidate set and test set. Among them, the candidate set is for sample selection where the informative samples are selected and added into the training set in each iteration. For the LUCL, Corel and MNIST data sets, the numbers of training and test samples are 200 and 300, 500 and 500, 500 and 500, respectively. The rest acts as candidate samples. For supervised DR methods, a BP neural network is constructed to approximate the mapping from the high-dimensional space to the lower-dimensional space. In the reduced dimension space, L_2 distance metric is employed for image retrieval to measure the similarities between the query image in the test set and the training images. For classification task, KNN $(K = 1)$ classifier is used to predict their class labels for the test samples.

In our experiments, the dimension of data is reduced to the number of classes of each data set. The parameters of each method are carefully adjusted to get the best performance. In particular, for Isomap and S-Isomap, the k value in KNN is assigned to 25 for LULC, 80 for COREL, 60 for MNIST. For the incremental learning methods, k_0 is set 15 for LUCL, 60 for Corel and MNIST, k_1 is 30 for the three data sets. Besides, we set $m = 300$ for all datasets, $T = 3$ for LULC and $T = 6$ for others.

3.2 Experimental Results and Analysis

Table 3 summarizes the retrieval precisions of 4 different methods when top 5 to 25 (with 5 step intervals) images are retrieved. In addition, classification accuracies on MNIST are also listed. It can be seen: (1) supervised methods perform better than unsupervised Isomap; (2) more training samples help to improve the performance; (3) IALSI with active learning outperforms the other methods, as more informative samples are chosen.

(a) Corel dataset

(b) LULC dataset

(c) MNIST dataset

Fig. 1. Example images of the three datasets used in our experiments.

Table 3. Performance comparison of different methods

		Isomap	S-Isomap	ISI	IALSI
COREL	5	0.2335	0.3639	0.4367	**0.4628**
	10	0.2159	0.3553	0.4252	**0.4464**
	15	0.2036	0.3412	0.4154	**0.4335**
	20	0.1939	0.3400	0.4073	**0.4199**
	25	0.1852	0.3312	0.3996	**0.4043**
	AVE	0.2064	0.3463	0.4168	**0.4334**
LULC	5	0.1593	0.2680	0.4240	**0.4607**
	10	0.1333	0.2653	0.4037	**0.4374**
	15	0.1153	0.2238	0.3936	**0.4211**
	20	0.1055	0.2033	0.3863	**0.4077**
	25	0.0967	0.1777	0.3789	**0.3921**
	AVE	0.1220	0.2274	0.3973	**0.4238**
MNIST		0.7940	0.7660	0.8840	**0.8920**

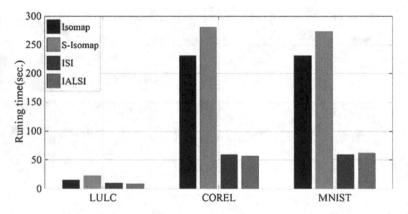

Fig. 2. Running time comparison of different methods

The running time of different methods are shown in Fig. 2. Compared with the batch methods, incremental learning methods are more efficient. Figure 3 takes the Corel data set as an example, and further depicts the running time during iterations. For the batch methods, re-computation of distance matrix is necessary when new samples are added and thus the computation amount rises dramatically while a smooth increase can be observed in the incremental methods.

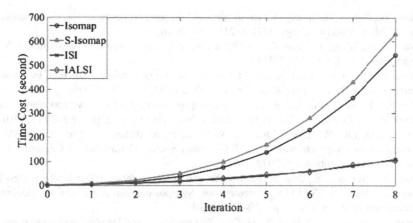

Fig. 3. Running time during iterations on Corel data set

4 Conclusions

An incremental active learning method for S-Isomap, IALSI, is proposed in the paper. IALSI aims to modify the original S-Isomap into incremental learning version meanwhile selecting informative samples through active learning in each iteration. The core idea of IALSI is to update the geodesic distance matrix based on the existing computation results and select informative samples according to an uncertainty criterion. The encouraging experimental results show that IALSI not only achieves better performance in image retrieval and classification tasks, but reduces the running time greatly.

References

1. Cai, D., He, X., Han, J.: Training linear discriminant analysis in linear time. In: 24th IEEE International Conference on Data Engineering, Cancun, pp. 209–217 (2008)
2. Zhang, D., Zhou, Z.H., Chen, S.: Adaptive kernel principal component analysis with unsupervised learning of kernels. In: 6th International Conference on Data Mining, Hong Kong, pp. 1178–1182 (2006)
3. Belkin, M., Niyogi, P.: Laplacian eigenmaps and spectral techniques for embedding and clustering. Adv. Neural Inf. Process. Syst. **14**(6), 585–591 (2002)
4. Roweis, S.T., Saul, L.K.: Nonlinear dimensionality reduction by locally linear embedding. Science **290**(5500), 2323–2326 (2000)
5. Tenenbaum, J.B., De, S.V., Langford, J.C.: A global geometric framework for nonlinear dimensionality reduction. Science **290**(5500), 2319–2323 (2000)
6. Geng, X., Zhan, D.C., Zhou, Z.H.: Supervised nonlinear dimensionality reduction for visualization and classification. IEEE Trans. Syst. Man Cybern. B Cybern. **35**(6), 1098–1107 (2005)
7. Zhang, Z., Chow, T.W., Zhao, M.: M-Isomap: orthogonal constrained marginal Isomap for nonlinear dimensionality reduction. IEEE Trans. Syst. Man Cybern. B Cybern. **43**(1), 180–191 (2012)

8. Yang, B., Xiang, M., Zhang, Y.: Multi-manifold discriminant Isomap for visualization and classification. Pattern Recogn. **55**(11), 215–230 (2016)
9. Hoi, S.C.H., Wang, J., Zhao, P.: LIBOL: a library for online learning algorithms. J. Mach. Learn. Res. **15**(1), 495–499 (2014)
10. Law, M.H.C., Jain, A.K.: Incremental nonlinear dimensionality reduction by manifold learning. IEEE Trans. Patter Anal. Mach. Intell. **28**(28), 377–391 (2006)
11. Huang, S.J., Jin, R., Zhou, Z.H.: Active learning by querying informative and representative examples. In: Advance in Neural Information Processing System, pp. 892–900 (2010)
12. Hoi, S.C.H, Liu, W., Lyu, M.R., Ma, W.Y.: Learning distance metrics with contextual constraints for image retrieval. In: IEEE Computer Society Conference on Computer Vision and Pattern Recognition, pp. 2072–2078 (2006)
13. Yang, Y., Newsam, S.: Bag-of-visual-words and spatial extensions for land-use classification. In: ACM SIGSPATIAL International Symposium on Advances in Geographic Information Systems, USA, pp. 270–279 (2010)
14. Lecun, Y., Bottou, L., Bengio, Y., Haffner, P.: Gradient-based learning applied to document recognition. Proc. IEEE **86**(11), 2278–2324 (1998)
15. Xia, H., Hoi, S.C., Jin, R.: Online multiple kernel similarity learning for visual search. IEEE Trans. Pattern Anal. Mach. Intell. **36**(3), 536–549 (2013)

USTB-Helloear: A Large Database of Ear Images Photographed Under Uncontrolled Conditions

Yi Zhang[1], Zhichun Mu[1(✉)], Li Yuan[1], Chen Yu[2], and Qing Liu[1]

[1] School of Automation and Electrical Engineering,
University of Science and Technology Beijing, Beijing 100083, China
mu@ies.ustb.edu.cn
[2] Xi'an Musheng Electronic Technology Co., LTD., Xi'an 710061, China

Abstract. The capabilities of biometric systems, such as face or fingerprint recognition systems, have recently made extraordinary leaps by the emergence of deep learning. However, due to the lack of enough training data, the applications of deep neural network in the ear recognition filed have run into the bottleneck. Therefore, the motivation of this paper is to present a new large database that contains more than 610,000 profile images from 1570 subjects. The main distinguishing feature of the images in this USTB-Helloear database is that they were taken under uncontrolled conditions with illumination and pose variation. In addition, all of individuals were required to not particularly care about ear occlusions. Therefore, 30% of subjects had the additional control groups with different level of ear occlusions. The ear images can be utilized to train a deep learning model of ear detection and recognition; moreover, the database, along with pair-matching tests, provides a benchmark to evaluate the performances of ear recognition and verification systems.

Keywords: Biometrics · Deep learning · Ear recognition
Uncontrolled conditions · Ear database

1 Introduction

Ear based human recognition technology is an important research field in biometric identification. Compared with classical biometric identifiers such as fingerprints, faces, and irises, using an ear has its distinctive advantages. An ear has a stable and rich structure that changes little with age and does not suffer from changes in facial expressions at the same time [1]. Moreover, it is easy and non-intrusive to collect ear images in the application scenarios. As such, ear biometrics has recently received some significant attention.

Researchers have developed several 2D ear recognition approaches in the early years [2–4]. Most of existing ear recognition techniques are based on manually designing features or shallow learning algorithms. However, researchers found that most of these techniques performed poorly when the test images were photographed under uncontrolled conditions. Nevertheless, occlusion, pose and illumination variation are very common in practical application. Therefore, this puts forward a challenging problem, which must be addressed.

© Springer International Publishing AG 2017
Y. Zhao et al. (Eds.): ICIG 2017, Part II, LNCS 10667, pp. 405–416, 2017.
https://doi.org/10.1007/978-3-319-71589-6_35

In the last decade, the algorithms based on deep learning have significantly advanced the performance of state-of-the-art in computer vision. Numbers of vision tasks such as face recognition [5–12], image classification [13–19] and object detection [20–22] have obtained a series of breakthroughs via deep learning models. Face recognition and verification as an example, Facebook trained a deep CNN model utilizing 4.4 million labeled face images. They achieved the best performance on the Labeled Faces in the Wild (LFW) benchmark [23] at the time. [24] proposed a VGG-Face model which was trained on 2.6 million images. Furthermore, the Google FaceNet [12] utilized 200 million labeled face images for its training. Some researchers turned to propose lightened deep models with less labeled data [25] or transfer learning methods [26] to solve the small sample size problem. However, as to the human ear recognition, the existing labeled ear images are so limited that even insufficient for the transfer learning.

To solve this problem, a new large database that contains more than 610,000 profile images from 1570 subjects is present in this paper. These images are extracted from video sequence. The main characteristic of this ear database is all of the images were photographed under uncontrolled conditions with illumination and pose variation. Furthermore, 30% of subjects in this database had an additional control groups with different level of ear occlusions. The ear images can be utilized to train a deep learning model of ear detection or recognition; moreover, the proposed database, along with pair-matching tests, provides a benchmark to evaluate the performances of ear recognition and verification systems.

The rest of this paper is structured as follows: a review of related work is given in Sect. 2, and Sect. 3 overviews the existent databases of ear images. In Sect. 4, a detailed description of the USTB-Helloear database is present. A series of experiments and comparisons can be found in Sect. 5. Finally, Sect. 6 provides the conclusions.

2   Related Works

Current ear recognition approaches exploited 2D images (including range images) or 3D point cloud data. In this section, we discuss some well known or recent 2D ear recognition methods utilizing 2D images or range images.

The existing ear recognition methods can be categorized into the holistic methods and the local feature based methods. The holistic methods utilized global features or statistical measures to classify ears. A force field transformation based technique was developed by Hurley et al. [27]. They generated the force field from ear images utilizing the Gaussian function. The directional properties of the force field were exploited to locate potential energy wells, which form the basis of the characteristic vector. Arbab-Zavar and Nixon [28] utilized the log-Gabor filter to exploit the frequency content of the ear boundary curves. A specific aim of this approach was to obtain the information in the ear's outer structures. Abate et al. [29] proposed a rotation invariant descriptor, namely GFD (Generic Fourier Descriptor), to extract features from ear images. This descriptor was robust to both ear rotations and illumination changes.

Researchers also proposed several ear recognition methods utilizing local feature descriptors. Kisku et al. [30] utilized the SIFT feature descriptors for the ear structural representation. The SIFT key points were extracted and an augmented vector of extracted SIFT features were created for matching. In [31], the SURF feature extraction was carried out on ear images to obtain three sets of local features, three nearest neighbor classifiers were trained on these three sets of features. Matching scores generated from all the three classifiers were fused for the final decision. Yuan and Mu [32] proposed a 2D ear recognition approach based on local information fusion to deal with ear recognition under partial occlusion. They separated the whole image to sub-windows and extracted local feature on each sub-windows. Finally, a sub-classifier fusion approach was used for recognition with partially occluded images. Chen and Mu [33] proposed a weighted multi key point descriptor sparse representation-based classification method to use local features of ear images. By adding adaptive weights to all the key points on a query image, the intra-class variations were reduced.

It is worth noting that most of the mentioned ear recognition works were tested on images that were photographed under controlled conditions. The recognition rates may have sharply dropped when those systems were applied in a realistic scenario, which contains occlusion, illumination variation, scaling, and rotation.

3   Related Databases

Most widely-used standard image databases for ear recognition systems are described in brief below.

3.1   USTB Databases

The USTB ear database contains 4 subsets which were collected by University of Science and Technology, Beijing. The USTB database I, II, and III are available under license. All of the databases were collected under controlled condition with single background. The presented USTB-Helloear database in this paper is the fifth database.

USTB database I: There are 180 ear images from 60 subjects in this database. Every volunteer was shot three different images. They are normal frontal image, frontal image with trivial angle rotation and image under different lighting condition.
USTB database II: This collection contained 308 right ear images from 77 volunteers. For each subject, there were 4 images with pose and lighting variation.
USTB database III: In this dataset, 79 subjects were photographed in different poses. There were total 785 images in this dataset, and some of the ears were occluded by hair.
USTB database IV: This database contained 500 subjects. 17 CCD cameras placed round the individual at every 15° and images of the face and ear were captured.

3.2   UND Databases

Those databases were collected by University of Notre Dame. All of the UND databases are available to the public (free of charge). All of the UND databases were collected under controlled condition with a single background.

Collection E: There were 942 profile images of 302 people in 3D and 2D images.
Collection F: This collection total consisted of 464 side face 3D and 2D images of 114 subjects.
Collection G: This collection had 738 side face images of 235 peoples in 3D and corresponding 2D images.
Collection J2: The collection had 1800 profile images from 415 subjects in 3D and corresponding 2D images.

3.3 WPUT Database

This database was collected by The West Pomeranian University of Technology. The database consisted of 2071 images from 501 subjects. For each subject, the database contains 4 to 8 images, which were taken under different lighting conditions. Moreover, there were earrings and hair occlusions in some images.

3.4 UBEAR Database

This database consisted of 9121 profile images from 242 subjects. The images in this database were taken under varying lighting conditions while subjects were moving. In addition, no particular care was required regarding ear occlusions and poses. The ground truth of the ear's location was provided, which made it particularly convenient for researchers to study the accuracy of ear detection.

4   USTB-Helloear Database

In cooperation with Xi'an Musheng Electronic Technology Co., LTD., we present a large scale collection of ear images along with labels and pair-matching tests. In this section, a detailed description of the USTB-Helloear database is provided. The images in this database are extracted from video sequence. The entire database is divided into two subsets. There are 336,572 profile images from 1104 subjects in subset A and 275,909 profile images from 466 subjects in subset B. The more detailed description is provided in Tables 1 and 2.

Table 1. Detailed description of video and images in USTB-Helloear database.

Video acquisition parameters	
Camera	Iphone 6s
Focal length	29 mm
Aperture	f/2.2
Video resolution	1980 * 1080 pixels
Frames per second	30
Videos codec	MOV
Details of the images	
Image resolution	1980 * 1080 pixels
Image codec	JPG

Table 2. Overview of the ear database.

Attribute	Range
No. of subjects	1570 (34.7% female, 65.3% male)
No. of photos	612,661
Age of subjects	11–18 (32.9%)
	19–21 (46.8%)
	22–26 (13.5%)
	27 and above (4.8%)
Occlusions in subset B	Minor (37.4%)
	Normal (42.9%)
	Major (19.7%)
Type of occlusions in subset B	Earphones (13.7%)
	Hair (86.3%)

Ear images in subset A only contain pose variations. For every subject in subset A, about 150 images on average per one ear are extracted from a 10 s video. Both left and right ears of every subject are photographed so that there are about 300 images from one person on average in subset A. As shown in Fig. 1, for each 10 s video, the camera moves around the ear to get ear pictures from different views. In the first 5 s, the camera moves from the front to back (Fig. 1(a)); In the rest 5 s, the camera moves from the top to bottom (Fig. 1(b)). In this 10 s video, We utilize the relative movement between the camera and ear to simulate the pose variations of the human ear under uncontrolled conditions. Therefore, the profile images in subset A extracted from the videos can be utilized to evaluate the performance of ear detection and recognition systems with pose variations. Some examples in subset A are illustrated in Fig. 2(a).

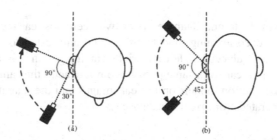

Fig. 1. The camera shoots the ear from different views. (a) The camera moves from the front to back. (b) The camera moves from the top to bottom.

Among all the 1570 volunteers, 30% of them had different level of ear occlusions. As mentioned above, all of individuals were required to not particularly care about ear occlusions. Therefore, we collected subset B of USTB-Helloear database which contained 466 subjects with pose variations and ear occlusions.

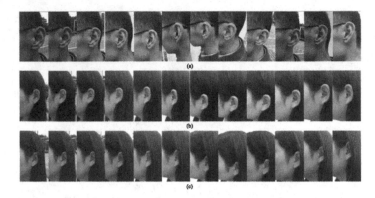

Fig. 2. Some example of images in the USTB-Helloear database. (a) Images in subset A. (b) Images without ear occlusion in subset B. (c) Images with ear occlusions in subset B.

For every subject in subset B, two 10 s videos were shot per one ear. Firstly, in the first video, the natural occluded ear pictures were photographed with different poses. Then we take the second video of the same ear without occlusion from different views. Finally, 150 images are extracted from each video sequence. It's worth noting that, the way of camera move around the ear in subset A and subset B are all the same (as shown in Fig. 1). Therefore, each of the ears in subset B consists of two sets of images, one set with pose variations, and another set with both pose variations and hair or earphone occlusions. This subset of USTB-Helloear database can be utilized for training and evaluating ear detection and recognition models. Examples of images in subset B are illustrated in Fig. 2(b) and (c).

5 Experiments

In this section, we evaluate our database under two scenarios: ear recognition and ear verification. Several deep learning models are trained and tested to evaluate the proposed database. Every subject has left and right ear images in this database. As we know, The left and right ears of a same person are not exactly the same. Therefore, we train and test ear recognition models on left ear images and the matching pairs for ear verification are generated from right ear datasets.

5.1 Ear Recognition

The images in the USTB-Helloear database are 2D profile images. The ear regions have to be detected and extracted from the profile images before recognition procedure. In this paper, the Multiple Scale Faster RCNN algorithm which we proposed in [35] is utilized to detect ears. Examples of extracted ear regions from subset A subset B are shown in Fig. 3.

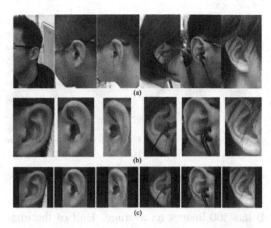

Fig. 3. Examples of extracted ear regions from subset A subset B. (a) Original profile images in USTB-Helloear database. (b) The extracted ear regions from subset A subset B. (c) The normalized ear images.

We train several deep learning models utilizing ear images from the USTB-Helloear database to evaluate the database. As we know, the input size of CNN architecture must be unified. As showed in Fig. 3(b), the image size and the aspect ratio of the extracted ear regions are varied due to the different shape and pose of the ears. Therefore, before we input the images into the CNN, we fill the images to square images and then resize them to 256 * 256 (Fig. 3(c)).

We fine-tune the VGG-Face pre-trained model [24] on subset A and subset B successively. Firstly, the pre-trained model is trained on subset A. We divide all of the images in the subset A into 5 parts, then we train 5 models utilizing the 5-fold cross validation method. During every training process, 4 parts are utilized as training data and the last part is used as test data. After 5 times training, all of the images are trained and tested, then the average recognition rate of 5 models is reported as the final recognition rate. Because the ear images in the presented database are extracted from video sequence, the neighboring images are similar to each other. If we divide all of the images into 5 subsets randomly, the trained model might be over-fitting. Therefore, The 5 subsets are divide in sequence.

The experiments are based on Caffe framework [36] and implemented on a work station with four Titan X GPUs. A batch size of 64 and initial learning rate of 0.001 are used. The last layer is trained from scratch, so that the learning rate of this layer is 0.01. During training, we randomly crop a 224 * 224 pixel square patch and feed it into the network to ameliorate the diversity of training data. The recognition rates are given in Fig. 4.

It is shown that, the average recognition rate of 5 models is 98.18%. The trained deep models are robust to ear recognition with pose variation. Therefore, we then fine-tune this pre-trained model on subset B to get deep models which are both robust to pose variation and occlusions. One of the trained models with the highest recognition rate is utilized to be fine-tuned on subset B. The parameters of this network are the same as previous networks. As mentioned above, different from the images in subset A,

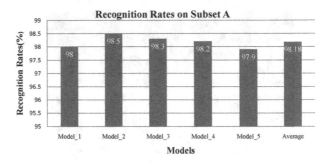

Fig. 4. The recognition rates on subset A.

every ear in subset B has 300 images on average. Half of the images are ear images with pose variation, and another half part of the images are control groups with different level of ear occlusions. We divide all of the images in subset B into 5 parts in sequence. In every part, half of the data are ear images with pose variation and another half are control groups. Then we also train 5 models utilizing 5-fold cross validation method. Finally, the average recognition rate of 5 models is reported as the final recognition rate. The recognition rates are 97.9% (Fig. 5). In the next section of this paper, we will discuss the ear feature representation capacity of the models mentioned above.

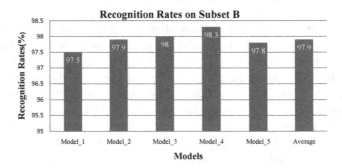

Fig. 5. The recognition rates on subset B.

5.2   Ear Verification

The CNN deep model can be utilized as a feature extractor to get the ear feature representation vector. In [9], Sun et al. used the Joint Bayesian technique for face verification based on the face feature representation vector extracted from a CNN. In this paper, two images are fed in to the trained model and the last layers are extracted as feature vectors. The cosine distance is utilized to measure the similarity of two ear feature vectors.

As a benchmark for comparison, we present pair-matching tests rules, which provide benchmarks to evaluate the performances of ear verification systems.

3000 match pairs and 3000 mismatch pairs are randomly generated from subset A. We also randomly generate 3000 match pairs and 3000 mismatch pairs on subset B which both contain pose variation and occlusions. Lists of pair-matching test will be provided along with the USTB-Helloear database. Researchers can test and compare their ear verification algorithm on those pairs. Some challenging examples are shown in Fig. 6.

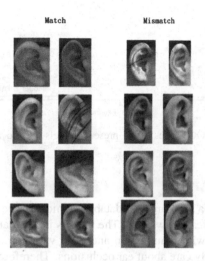

Fig. 6. Some challenging examples in the validation set.

In this section, we evaluate the two trained deep models with highest recognition rate on subset A and subset B. For convenience, we call them *Model_A* and *Model_B* respectively. The lists of pair-matching test are called *Pairs_A* and *Pairs_B* as well. The ear verification results are presented in Table 3. The ROC curves are also showed in Fig. 7.

Table 3. The ear verification results.

	Pairs_A	Pairs_B
Model_A	92.6%	82.83%
Model_B	94.67%	88.5%

It is shown that, The *Model_B* has achieved the best ear verification result both on benchmarks of *Pairs_A* and *Pairs_B*. The stronger capacity of ear feature representation can be obtained via feeding the net with the more challenging training data in subset B. In addition, The fact of the *Model_B* perform better than *Model_A* on the benchmark of *Pairs_A* indicate that the trained deep models don't over-fit the training data. Therefore, we can draw the conclusion that, the ear images in the proposed USTB-Helloear database can satisfy the meet of training and testing ear recognition systems.

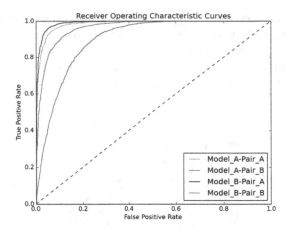

Fig. 7. The ROC curves of the present models on two validation set.

6   Conclusions

In this paper, we present a new large ear database which can be utilized to train and test ear recognition and verification systems. The images in this database were taken under uncontrolled conditions with illumination and pose variation. All of individuals were required to not particularly care about ear occlusions. Therefore, researchers can utilize the images to train a deep learning model to represent ear feature. The experiments demonstrate that, the capacity of ear feature representation can be obtained via feeding the CNN with images in this database. This database will be public and freely available from our web site: http://www1.ustb.edu.cn/resb/en/index.htm.

Acknowledgement. This article is supported by the National Natural Science Foundation of China (Grant No. 61472031). The authors would like to thank the Xi'an Mu sheng Electronic Technology Co., LTD. for their cooperation.

References

1. Jain, A., Flynn, P., Ross, A.A.: Handbook of Biometrics, pp. 131–150. Springer Science & Business Media, Berlin (2007). https://doi.org/10.1007/978-0-387-71041-9
2. Yuan, L., Mu, Z., Xu, Z.: Using ear biometrics for personal recognition. In: Li, S.Z., Sun, Z., Tan, T., Pankanti, S., Chollet, G., Zhang, D. (eds.) IWBRS 2005. LNCS, vol. 3781, pp. 221–228. Springer, Heidelberg (2005). https://doi.org/10.1007/11569947_28
3. Yuan, L., Mu, Z.C.: Ear recognition based on local information fusion. Pattern Recogn. Lett. **33**(2), 182–190 (2012)
4. Zhang, B., Mu, Z., Li, C., et al.: Robust classification for occluded ear via Gabor scale feature-based non-negative sparse representation. Opt. Eng. **53**(6), 061702 (2014)
5. Taigman, Y., Yang, M., Ranzato, M.A., et al.: Deepface: closing the gap to human-level performance in face verification. In: Proceedings of the IEEE Conference on Computer Vision and Pattern Recognition, pp. 1701–1708 (2014)

6. Zhou, E., Cao, Z., Yin, Q.: Naive-deep face recognition: touching the limit of LFW benchmark or not? arXiv preprint arXiv:1501.04690 (2015)
7. Yi, D., Lei, Z., Liao, S., et al.: Learning face representation from scratch. arXiv preprint arXiv:1411.7923 (2014)
8. Sun, Y., Chen, Y., Wang, X., et al.: Deep learning face representation by joint identification-verification. In: Advances in Neural Information Processing Systems, pp. 1988–1996 (2014)
9. Sun, Y., Wang, X., Tang, X.: Deep learning face representation from predicting 10,000 classes. In: Proceedings of the IEEE Conference on Computer Vision and Pattern Recognition, pp. 1891–1898 (2014)
10. Sun, Y., Wang, X., Tang, X.: Deeply learned face representations are sparse, selective, and robust. In: Proceedings of the IEEE Conference on Computer Vision and Pattern Recognition, pp. 2892–2900 (2015)
11. Sun, Y., Liang, D., Wang, X., et al.: Deepid3: face recognition with very deep neural networks. arXiv preprint arXiv:1502.00873 (2015)
12. Schroff, F., Kalenichenko, D., Philbin, J.: FaceNet: a unified embedding for face recognition and clustering. In: Proceedings of the IEEE Conference on Computer Vision and Pattern Recognition, pp. 815–823 (2015)
13. Krizhevsky, A., Sutskever, I., Hinton, G.E.: Imagenet classification with deep convolutional neural networks. In: Advances in Neural Information Processing Systems, pp. 1097–1105 (2012)
14. Lin, M., Chen, Q., Yan, S.: Network in network. arXiv preprint arXiv:1312.4400 (2013)
15. Szegedy, C., Liu, W., Jia, Y., et al.: Going deeper with convolutions. In: Proceedings of the IEEE Conference on Computer Vision and Pattern Recognition, pp. 1–9 (2015)
16. Simonyan, K., Zisserman, A.: Very deep convolutional networks for large-scale image recognition. arXiv preprint arXiv:1409.1556 (2014)
17. He, K., Zhang, X., Ren, S., et al.: Deep residual learning for image recognition. In: Proceedings of the IEEE Conference on Computer Vision and Pattern Recognition, pp. 770–778 (2016)
18. Szegedy, C., Vanhoucke, V., Ioffe, S., et al.: Rethinking the inception architecture for computer vision. In: Proceedings of the IEEE Conference on Computer Vision and Pattern Recognition, pp. 2818–2826 (2016)
19. Szegedy, C., Ioffe, S., Vanhoucke, V., et al.: Inception-v4, Inception-ResNet and the impact of residual connections on learning. arXiv preprint arXiv:1602.07261 (2016)
20. Girshick, R., Donahue, J., Darrell, T., et al.: Rich feature hierarchies for accurate object detection and semantic segmentation. In: Proceedings of the IEEE Conference on Computer Vision and Pattern Recognition, pp. 580–587 (2014)
21. Girshick, R.: Fast R-CNN. In: Proceedings of the IEEE International Conference on Computer Vision, pp. 1440–1448 (2015)
22. Ren, S., He, K., Girshick, R., et al.: Faster R-CNN: towards real-time object detection with region proposal networks. In: Advances in Neural Information Processing Systems, pp. 91–99 (2015)
23. Huang, G.B., Ramesh, M., Berg, T., et al.: Labeled faces in the wild: a database for studying face recognition in unconstrained environments. Technical report 07-49, University of Massachusetts, Amherst (2007)
24. Parkhi, O.M., Vedaldi, A., Zisserman, A.: Deep face recognition. BMVC 1(3), 6 (2015)
25. Wu, X., He, R., Sun, Z.: A lightened cnn for deep face representation. In: 2015 IEEE Conference on IEEE Computer Vision and Pattern Recognition (CVPR) (2015)
26. Yosinski, J., Clune, J., Bengio, Y., et al.: How transferable are features in deep neural networks? In: Advances in Neural Information Processing Systems, pp. 3320–3328 (2014)

27. Hurley, D.J., Nixon, M.S., Carter, J.N.: Force field energy functionals for image feature extraction. Image Vis. Comput. **20**(5), 311–317 (2002)
28. Arbab-Zavar, B., Nixon, M.S.: Robust log-Gabor filter for ear biometrics. In: International Conference on Pattern Recognition, pp. 1–4. IEEE (2008)
29. Abate, A.F., Nappi, M., Riccio, D., et al.: Ear recognition by means of a rotation invariant descriptor. In: International Conference on Pattern Recognition, pp. 437–440. IEEE (2006)
30. Kisku, D.R., Mehrotra, H., Gupta, P., et al.: SIFT-based ear recognition by fusion of detected keypoints from color similarity slice regions. In: 2009 International Conference on Advances in Computational Tools for Engineering Applications, ACTEA 2009, pp. 380–385. IEEE (2009)
31. Prakash, S., Gupta, P.: An efficient ear recognition technique invariant to illumination and pose. Telecommun. Syst. **52**, 1435–1448 (2013)
32. Yuan, L., Mu, Z.C.: Ear recognition based on local information fusion. Pattern Recogn. Lett. **33**(2), 182–190 (2012)
33. Chen, L., Mu, Z.: Partial data ear recognition from one sample per person. IEEE Trans. Hum.-Mach. Syst. **46**, 799–809 (2016)
34. Frejlichowski, D., Tyszkiewicz, N.: The West Pomeranian university of technology ear database – a tool for testing biometric algorithms. In: Campilho, A., Kamel, M. (eds.) ICIAR 2010. LNCS, vol. 6112, pp. 227–234. Springer, Heidelberg (2010). https://doi.org/10.1007/978-3-642-13775-4_23
35. Zhang, Y., Mu, Z.: Ear detection under uncontrolled conditions with multiple scale faster region-based convolutional neural networks. Symmetry **9**(4), 53 (2017)
36. http://caffe.berkeleyvision.org/

Survival-Oriented Reinforcement Learning Model: An Effcient and Robust Deep Reinforcement Learning Algorithm for Autonomous Driving Problem

Changkun Ye[1], Huimin Ma[1(✉)], Xiaoqin Zhang[1],
Kai Zhang[1], and Shaodi You[2,3]

[1] Tsinghua University, Beijing, China
mhmpub@tsinghua.edu.cn
[2] Data61-CSIRO, Sydney, Australia
[3] Australian National University, Canberra, Australia

Abstract. Using Deep Reinforcement Learning (DRL) algorithm to deal with autonomous driving tasks usually have unsatisfied performance due to lack of robustness and means to escape local optimum. In this article, we designs a Survival-Oriented Reinforcement Learning (SORL) model that tackle these problems by setting survival rather than maximize total reward as first priority. In SORL model, we model autonomous driving task as Constrained Markov Decision Process (CMDP) and introduce Negative-Avoidance Function to learn from previous failure. The SORL model greatly speed up the training process and improve the robustness of normal Deep Reinforcement Learning algorithm.

Keywords: Reinforcement learning · Robustness · Local optimum
Negative-avoidance

1 Introduction

Deep Reinforcement learning (DRL), an approach using deep neural networks in Reinforcement Learning (RL) methods has been very successful in control problems in recent years. With a well designed reward, programs can learn to tackle complex tasks such as play Atari games using image as input [1], play the game of Go [2] and achieve human level performance. Subsequently, a number of new reinforcement learning algorithms [3–5] have been developed and step further to improve performance and robustness of the learning program. With inspiration of success of DRL in virtual field [1,2] and the widely developed DRL control algorithms, it seems promising to apply similar method on real world problems such as autonomous driving tasks.

Autonomous driving is a challenging and complicate task for program to learn. With camera and sensor data as inputs, the program needs to learn to select appropriate driving policy that can stay on the right track and avoid accidents. Several progress have been made in this field. Shalev-Shwartz et al. [6]

© Springer International Publishing AG 2017
Y. Zhao et al. (Eds.): ICIG 2017, Part II, LNCS 10667, pp. 417–429, 2017.
https://doi.org/10.1007/978-3-319-71589-6_36

uses reinforcement learning to maximize the "desire" of abstract driving policy choice like overtaking or merging. Sallab et al. [7] use Deep Deterministic Actor Critic algorithm and Deep Q-Network to learn Lane Keeping.

However, there are several challenges still lie in the way. **Problem 1.** DRL training is highly sensitive to the noise and reward function, the converging time maybe significantly varies depend on the reward function designed and random noise. To train the algorithm efficiently, one needs to carefully select reward function and control random noise. **Problem 2.** DRL algorithms have a poor mechanism of exploring state-action space and are easily trapped in local optimum. Actually, RL algorithms are usually gradients based and cannot guarantee global maximum unless the data from global maximum regions are well treated. Therefore, in order to teach agent the right driving policy, one not only needs to accurately define the global optimum but carefully avoid other undesired local optimum.

In this article, we proposed a Survival-Oriented Reinforcement Learning (SORL) model to tackle the sensitivity problem and local optimum problem. The core idea of the model is: optimized policy should prefer to survive in given time steps than "die" somewhere between with better total reward. In other words, the DRL algorithm should try other policy if current policy cannot reaches the max-allowed-step.

In SORL model, the DRL learning process is modelled as a Constrained Markov Decision Process (CMDP) with continuous state-action space. We introduce a new structure called Negative-Avoidance Function (NA Function) to DRL algorithm that can learn from failure from previous training. The SORL model combines normal DRL algorithm aim at optimize total reward with the NA Function, using NA Function as a constraint and can helps normal DRL algorithms escape faster from undesired local optimum. Because the structure is independent of normal DRL algorithms, the SORL model can use different DRL algorithms for different situations.

We test the model for lane keeping tasks on TORCS – a car racing game simulator. The training procedure and time of the DRL algorithm Deep Deterministic Policy Gradient (DDPG) [3] and our Survival-Oriented DDPG (SO-DDPG), the SORL model using DDPG as DRL algorithm are compared. Our SO-DDPG algorithm shows a significant increase in speed and robustness: For the same environment parameter, the number episodes takes for convergence for DDPG varies from 1000 to more than 2000, while SO-DDPG needs only 600 episodes with about a max of 400 episode deviation. The SO-DDPG also shows it's insensitivity to design of NA Function, which makes NA Function easy to designed.

2 Background

In this section, some basic mechanisms for Reinforcement Learning and Deep Reinforcement Learning are introduced. Those mechanisms are useful for our Survival-Oriented Reinforcement Learning (SORL) model.

Most of Reinforcement Learning algorithm are based on **Markov Decision Process (MDP)**. A normal MDP is a 5-tuple $(S, A, P(.|.,.), R(.,.), \gamma)$, where the S is a set of continuous states, A is a set of continuous actions, $P(s_{+1}|s, a)$ denotes the probability of environment transit to new state s_{+1} given state s and the action a and $R(s, a)$ is the set of reward assigned for the action a taken under state s.

The formal learning setup is: The agent acquires the state s from the environment Using policy $\pi : S \times A$; Agent select an action $a = \rho_\pi(s)$ and apply this action a to the environment; the environment returns a reward $r(s, a)$ and new state s_{+1} according to $P(s_{+1}|s, a)$; Using the (s, a, r, s_{+1}) pairs, agent train itself and get a new action $a_{+1} = \rho_\pi(s_{+1})$ to be applied in the environment.

The goal of the algorithm is to find a optimized policy π that can maximize the long-run total reward $R_{total} = \sum_{t=t_0+1}^{\infty} \gamma^t r(s, a)$ given initial state s_{t_0}. The $\gamma \in [0, 1]$ is the discount factor that restrict the summation to finite value. Many reinforcement learning algorithms like DDPG and RDPG adopt the action value function $Q(s, a)$ as a mean to represent total reward. The Q-function gives the expectation value of long-run total reward with respect to given state and the action corresponding to the policy and state. It can be written as follows:

$$Q^\pi(s_{t_0}, a_{t_0}) = E_{a=\rho_\pi(s), s_{t+1}=P(s,a)} \left[\sum_{t=t_0}^{\infty} \gamma^t r(s_t, a_t) \right] \tag{1}$$

The Q-function, like other function used to represent value of long-run total reward, obeys the recursive relation called Bellman Equation:

$$Q^\pi(s_{t_0}, a_{t_0}) = E_{s_{t+1}=P(s,a)} \left[r(s_{t_0}, a_{t_0}) + \gamma Q^\pi(s_{t_0+1}, a_{t_0+1}) \right] \tag{2}$$

If the Q-function is well-known, one can directly get the optimum policy by looking for the action that maximize Q-function in given state:

$$\rho_\pi(s) = \arg\max_a Q^\pi(s, a) \tag{3}$$

For **Deep Reinforcement Learning (DRL)** algorithms, deep neural networks are used as function approximators for values in the RL algorithms. For example, the total reward and policy can be rewritten as function approximators as

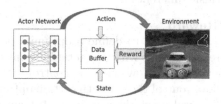

Fig. 1. The structure of the agent-environment interaction process of actor-critic setup of DRL algorithms. The Actor Network is an approximator of policy $a = \rho_\pi(s)$. Action, reward, state are saved in the Data Buffer for training the neural networks.

$Q(s, a; \theta)$. We consider a type of DRL algorithms [3–5] equipped with similar actor-critic architectures, with function approximators for long-run total reward function and policy function. The common structure is shown on the Figs. 1 and 2 below.

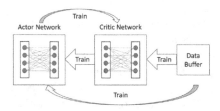

Fig. 2. The structure of the training process of actor-critic setup of DRL algorithms. The Critic Network is an neural network approximator of Q-function $Q(s, a)$. Critic Network is trained using data in Data Buffer, while Actor Network is trained using Critic Network and data in Data Buffer.

3   Autonomous Driving Problem Analysis

In this section, we analyses autonomous driving problem in detail. We show the reason that DRL tending to converge in local optimum matters in training the model. It's also shown that extra structure to help escape local optimum is also needed to avoid danger condition. Then several methods in related works that may get over these problems are examined, which help justify construction of Survival-Oriented Reinforcement Model in next section.

Considering the lane keeping task in autonomous driving, the program is required to learn to keep in lane with a rational speed. This control process can be modelled as a Markov Decision Process. Every time step, the driver obtain a state of outside and some information of car itself. Base on the state, the driver make a decision of turning left or right, step on brake or throttle. The reward is designed to award action and state that keep car follow the track while penal others.

But like other similar real-world control problem, this lane keeping tasks have characteristics that simple MDP-based DRL model cannot take account for. There are two intrinsic differences.

– **Hard-to-defined Reward**
  First of all, it's not a good idea to define a optimum policy for autonomous driving tasks. The reason is that what we actually want the program to learn is a large set of policy aim at follow the lane, control the speed, not follow the lane in certain position, control the car with certain optimum speed. Although [8] have shown that neural networks can learn abstract rules, these progress haven't been developed enough to use in the control problems.

– **Safety Issues**

Finally, for autonomous driving problem, safety is absolutely the first concern. It appears possible to solve this issue by assign a low or negative reward to the actions and states that leads to the accident. But Shalev-Shwartz et al. [6] have proved that, for rare accident with few sample available, the reward should be set extremely low for the program to learn to avoid.

Apart from the difficulties that model autonomous driving problem as a MDP process, there are problems with MDP-based algorithm themselves. DRL algorithms like DDPG, RDPG and A3C don't have a good architecture to escape from local optimum. The γ discount factor using in the algorithm prefers local optimum to global ones.

Some RL algorithms have been raised to avoid these problems. [9,10] provides a way directly learning global optimum from demonstration. [11] suggest dividing reward into multiple ones for different RL programs to learn and give the action base on the combination of different learned policies. [12,13] provide an approach to learn from teachers or demonstrations to avoid the local optimum to some aspect.

To let problem avoid constraint like danger condition or local optimum, one apparent approach is model problems as Constrained Markov Decision Process (CMDP). CMDP has been widely studied in RL regime [14–16] for constrained optimization problem. [15] raised an actor-critic RL algorithm for problems with discrete state. But non-of those approach uses non-linear function approximators like neural network.

To balance between exploration and exploitation and avoid local optimum, appealing method would be ϵ - greedy approach where the algorithm accept temporal worse policy with a possibility to better explore the space. This requires some non-gradient based settings in the algorithm.

In order to add some structure to normal DRL algorithm to let the program learn to avoid danger condition as well as better explore the state-action space, we designs a Survival-Oriented Reinforcement Learning Model. The detail will be described in the next section.

4   Survival-Oriented Reinforcement Learning Model

In order to allow the DRL learning algorithm escape local optimum and moreover, detect and avoid danger condition or accidents, we introduce Survival-Oriented Reinforcement Learning (SORL) model. Unlike the normal DRL model that aims simply at maximize the total designed reward function, we consider the real world environment where the program should value safety as first priority. For this reason, we raise a proposition:

Proposition 1 (Survival Proposition). *For the program, learns to survive in the environment (agent reaches max allowed step) is more important than maximize total reward.*

To achieve this, we add a new function called Negative-Avoidance Function (NA Function) $D(s,a)$ to the DRL algorithm in order to help program learns to survive. The CMDP system is designed then as a 6-tuple $(S, A, P(.|.,.), R(.,.), \gamma, D(s,a))$. The extra $D(s,a)$ gives danger index of given state and action, which assess whether the action chosen by policy π is "safe" enough under state s.

Like reward the NA Function is not given directly by the environment, but there are clues – early termination means danger. If the environment terminates at some time step $n < n_{max}$, then there should be some reason that causes the early termination. The cause may come from series of action under certain states, hence one can use a NA Function $D(s,a)$ to assess the aptitude of danger.

Some characters of NA Function can be inferred easily. At the start (s_0, a_0), it's rational to set $D(s_0, a_0) = 0$. When the agent takes action and goes further, the danger may increase or decrease. Finally at termination, the danger reaches maximum $D(s_n, a_n) = 1$, which cause the environment terminates. Hence, we use the proposition:

Proposition 2 (NA Function Proposition). *For a n steps interaction episodes, where the agent gets states $\{s_0, s_1, ..., s_n\}$, have action $\{a_0, a_1, ..., a_{n-1}\}$, the aptitude of danger should start from zero, statistically increase as the agent goes further until reaches max when the environment terminated, which can be defined as:*

$$D(s_k, a_k) = f_d(k, n) \tag{4}$$

Which satisfy:

$$D(s_0, a_0) = f_d(0) = 0, D(s_n, a_n) = f_d(n) = 1 \tag{5}$$

If the DRL algorithm can learn a good NA function, the program can detect danger situation and avoid them uses a simple mechanism – if the NA Function reaches some threshold $D(s_k, a_k) \leq D_{threshold}$ and is higher than the temporal reward environment provides $D(s_k, a_k) > r(s_k, a_k)$, one can change policy to some $a_k = f(a_k)$ to avoid early termination.

Neural networks are used as function approximators for policy $a = \rho_\pi(s|\theta^1)$, Q-function $Q(s,a) = Q(s, a|\theta^2)$ and danger assess function $D(s,a) = D(s, a|\theta^3)$. Then under the MDP setting, the survival proposition mathematically add negative avoidance constraint requirement and MDP optimization problem become CMDP problem:

Lemma 1 (Survival Proposition for CMDP). *For the DRL algorithm, it's more important to reach max-allowed-step than maximize Reward, the optimized policy should choose action that maximize total reward with temporal reward larger than temporal danger. The optimized policy written as:*

$$\begin{cases} \rho_\pi(s) = \arg\max_a Q(s, a|\theta^2) \\ D(s, a|\theta^3) < r(s, a) \\ D(s, a|\theta^3) < D_{threshold} \end{cases} \tag{6}$$

The learning process of the model different from simple MDP, which can be written as:

1. The agent observes a state s_{t_0} from the environments.
2. The normal learning program (DDPG, RDPG, etc.) gives a reward-based action $r_{t_0}^{action}$.
3. Danger assess function gives the danger index for the previous state and action $d_{t_0} = D(s_{t_{-1}}, ar_{t_{-1}})$.
4. If the danger index is larger than the reward in previous time step $d_{t_0} > r(a_{t_{-1}}, s_{t_{-r}})$, consider the agent as in "danger" and choose the danger avoidance action as real action $a_{t_0} = f(ar_{t0})$ base on certain function $f(a)$, else use reward-based action as real action $a_{t_0} = ar_{t_0}$.
5. The environment receives the action a_{t_0}, returns the reward $r(s_{t_0}, a_{t_0})$, next state st_1. If the environment terminates, we assign each s, a pair a danger index $D(s, a)$ according to certain rule.
6. The learning program uses $r(s, a), s, a, s_{+1}$ to train the learning program, uses $D(s, a)$ to train danger assess program with supervised training.

If use this model to modify actor-critic structure, the adjusted structure of the system can be shown in Figs. 3 and 4 below.

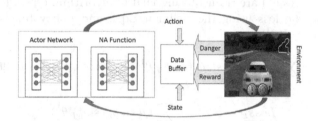

Fig. 3. The structure of the agent-environment interaction process of SORL Model. Unlike normal actor-critic algorithm, the action goes into environment is decided by policy and NA function

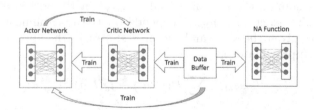

Fig. 4. The structure of the training process of SORL Model. State, action and danger data saved in data buffer are used to train NA function.

There are several advantages for define an extra NA Function. First, the NA function can help deal with the problem where the optimum is hard to defined.

By using different types of NA Function, one can adjust the DRL algorithms' sensitivity to danger condition.

Besides, if the DRL algorithm temporally converges at optimum with early termination, as the $D(s, a)$ is learned, the early termination will finally been assigned a high NA Function value, which leads the DRL algorithm to try other policy. This help the DRL algorithm to move out from early termination, since early termination is defined in this model as a worse choice than finish max-allowed-step.

Finally, the extra-structure of NA function does not depend on specific DRL algorithm. From the adjust learning process one can see that, the SORL Model doesn't have a specific requirement on which DRL algorithm to use. One can change different DRL algorithm in the model to deal with different tasks. The SORL model using DDPG as reward-based DRL algorithm will be described in detail in the next section.

5   Survival-Oriented DDPG Algorithm

The SORL model can built on different DRL algorithms that aims at maximize total reward. The SORL model built on DDPG is described in Algorithm 1. The $Q(s, a|\theta^1)$ and $\rho_\pi(s|\theta^2)$ are trained using DDPG algorithm. $Q(s, a|\theta^1)$ is trained by minimizing the loss using the Bellman Eq. 2 and policy function $\rho_\pi(s|\theta^2)$ using gradient of $J(\theta^2)$:

$$Loss_Q = \sum_i \left[r_i + \gamma Q(s_i, \rho_\pi(s_i|\theta^2)|\theta^1) - Q(s_{i+1}, \rho_\pi(s_{i+1}|\theta^2)|\theta^1) \right]^2 \quad (7)$$

$$Loss_P = J(\theta^2) = \sum_i Q(s_i, \rho_\pi(s|\theta^2)|\theta^1) \quad (8)$$

We also uses Ornstein-Uhlenbeck noise ϵ added to action $a = \rho_\pi(s) + \epsilon$ as DDPG does for the purpose of exploring stae-action space and robustness of DRL algorithm.

As for the NA function approximator, the $D(s_i, a_i|\theta^3)$ is trained using supervise learning assuming the predefined $f_d(n, n_{max})$ in Proposition 2 is the true distribution. The exact $f_d(n, n_{max})$ depends on the environment like reward does. Therefore given the s_i, a_i and the max step n in the episode, the loss of NA Function Approximator is:

$$Loss_D = \sum_i (D(s_i, a_i) - f_d(i, n))^2 \quad (9)$$

Apart from loss function, another thing is needed to be concerned. If the NA Function give a high danger index, it's required to change original action $a = \rho_\pi(s) + \epsilon$ into $a = f(\rho_\pi(s) + \epsilon)$ that helps the agent escape local optimum and explore state-action space. This function is also depend on the environment and needed to be defined according to the environment.

Algorithm 1. SO-DDPG algorithm

Initialize function approximator $Q(s, a|\theta^1)$, $\rho_\pi(s|\theta^2)$ and $D(s, a|\theta^3)$ with neural networks parameters θ^1, θ^2 and θ^3, set target network $\theta^1 = \theta^{1'}, \theta^2 = \theta^{2'}, \theta^3 = \theta^{3'}$
Initialize Replay Buffer R, Episode Buffer R_E
for episode=1, M **do**
  Initialize the environment, receive state s_0
  for t=1,t_{max} **do**
    Get noise action $ar = \rho_\pi(s|\theta^3) + \epsilon$ where ϵ is the noise
    if Agent goes far enough, $t > t'$ **then**
      Calculate danger index for previous action and state $d(s_t, a_t) = D(s_{t-1}, a_{t-1}|\theta^3)$
      if = **then**$d(s_t, a_t|\theta^3) > r_{t-1}$
        Use new policy, put $a = f(ar)$ as real action
      else
        Use $a = ar$ as real action
      end if
    end if
    Input a into the environment, get $\{s_{t+1}, r_t, IfTermination\}$ pair
    Store a_t, s_t, s_{t+1}, r_t into the episode buffer R_E
    if Replay Buffer large enough **then**
      Sample a minibatch of N pairs $\{s_i, a_i, r_i, s_{i+1}, d_i\}_{i=1,...,N}$ from R
      Set $y_i = r_i + \gamma Q(s_i, \rho_\pi(s_i|\theta^{2'})|\theta^{1'})$
      Update critic,actor and NA function by minimizing the losses:
      $Loss_Q, Loss_P, Loss_D$ which defined previously
      Update the target networks:
      $\theta^{1'} \leftarrow \tau\theta^1 + (1-\tau)\theta^{1'}$
      $\theta^{2'} \leftarrow \tau\theta^2 + (1-\tau)\theta^{2'}$
      $\theta^{3'} \leftarrow \tau\theta^3 + (1-\tau)\theta^{3'}$
    end if
    if $IfTermation = True$ **then**
      Break the loop, terminate the environment
    end if
  end for
  Assign danger index $d_t = D(s_t, a_t)$ for each $\{s_t, a_t, r_t, s_{t+1}\}$ pairs in Episode Buffer R_E, save new $\{s_t, a_t, r_t, s_{t+1}, d_t\}$ pairs into Replay Buffer R
end for

---

6   Experiment and Results

In this section, we first use SO-DDPG and DDPG algorithm to learn lane keeping task. For the purpose of test if SORL model can increase the learning speed, SO-DDPG and DDPG algorithms are trained with same environment parameter. After that, we use different NA Function for SO-DDPG algorithm to test the sensitivity of SORL model to NA Function.

We use The Open Racing Car Simulator (TORCS) as the environment to learning lane keeping tasks with SO-DDPG algorithm and DDPG algorithm. [17] provides a Application Programming Interface (API) for translating data between the DRL learning algorithm and TORCS. DRL algorithm takes a feature vector as input, including sensor data like obstacle distance and position of car in the track. The action available including brake, throttle and turn.

We set the environment to terminate if collision happens or the car get stuck, which is more close to real world driving problem. Termination condition is necessary for SORL model, since NA-Function $D(s_i, a_i) = f_d(i, n)$ needs the termination step. Hence unlike [7], condition of termination is always activated in the learning process.

As mentioned in SORL model, the NA Function $D(s_i, a_i) = f_d(i, n)$ and avoid policy $a = f(\rho_\pi(s) + \epsilon)$ are like reward and needed to be defined according to the environment. Here we use: $D(s_i, a_i) = Exp\left(\frac{-(n-i)^2}{2\min(20, n/5)^2}\right)$ and $f(\rho_\pi(s) + \epsilon) = -\rho_\pi(s) - \epsilon$. The $D(s_i, a_i)$ function make use of the form of normal distribution, which is just for convenient. There are some reason to set avoidance policy as $f(a) = -a$. If policy have converged at local optimum, then the action are designed to approach towards local optimum. A rational policy that tries to escape local minimum would be choose the opposite action.

6.1 Efficiency and Robustness of SORL Model

The SO-DDPG using the equations above and normal DDPG algorithm are tested on TORCS. Using the same environment setting, reward function and NA Function, We choose the track CG Speedway Number 1 for test. We trains the SO-DDPG and DDPG for a number of times. Four results are selected and shown in Fig. 5.

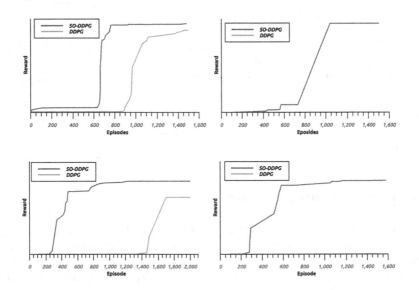

Fig. 5. Our SO-DDPG algorithm compare with baseline DDPG algorithm

Figure 5 shows how max achieved total reward is changed during the learning process. The four experiments are done using slightly different reward functions.

The left two figure uses reward $r = v_x \cos(\theta_x)$ and right two figure we use $r = 70 \tanh(\frac{v_x \cos(\theta_x)}{70})$, where v_x is speed of car towards it's heading direction and θ_x is the angle between this direction and direction of track. The NA Functions and avoid policy are kept unchanged. We can see the DDPG algorithm is highly sensitive to the reward function and noise that used to explore state-action space. In the left two sub-figure in Fig. 5, DDPG algorithm escape the local optimum. But as shown in the right side of the figure, the DDPG get trapped in local optimum and can't escape.

In contrast, we can see that although our method SO-DDPG also get trapped in local optimum for some time, it can escape the local optimum faster despite the reward function is adjusted.

6.2   SORL Model Sensitivity to NA Function

Different choice of NA Function and avoid policy may influence the converging speed of algorithm. In order to test if SORL model is sensitive to NA Function, in this section, we compare SO-DDPGs that using different NA Function with DDPG. The NA Functions selected are:

$$D(s_i, a_i) = Exp \left(\frac{-(n-i)^2}{2 \min(20, n/5)^2} \right) \tag{10}$$

$$D(s_i, a_i) = u \left[(n-i) - min(20, n/5)^2 \right] \tag{11}$$

where $u(x)$ is the unit step function. Two NA Functions both assume the final $\frac{1}{5}$ of the s_i, a_i pairs may be the real cause for early termination.

Figure 6 also shows how max achieved total reward is changed during learning process. From Fig. 6 we can see that, also the NA Function changes a lot, it doesn't prevent the SO-DDPG to converge fast and stable to global optimum. Hence SORL model is not sensitive to NA Function.

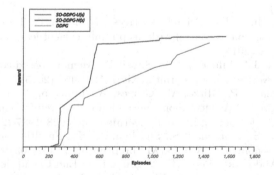

Fig. 6. Algorithm comparison for SO-DDPG with N(0,1) like and U(x) like NA functions and DDPG

7 Conclusion

In this article, we analyses the difficulties that DRL algorithms faces when learning real world control problem. The DRL algorithm needs to develop a structure that can escape from local optimum and being robust to reward function and noise.

To tackle this problem, we introduces the Survival-Oriented Reinforcement Learning model that model autonomous driving problem as a Constrained Markov Decision Process. The SORL model introducing Negative-Avoidance Function and danger avoidance mechanism into normal DRL model so that the adjusted DRL structure can learn from previous failure in training process. The SORL model is not model-based and can uses different DRL algorithms like DDPG as normal DRL model.

The experiments of learning lane keep tasks in TORCS for SO-DDPG and DDPG algorithm shows proves that our SORL model is not sensitive to reward function and may speed up the converging of DRL algorithm. Besides, the experiments of SO-DDPG using different NA Functions also shows that SORL model is no sensitive to NA Functions design.

Acknowledgements. This work was supported by National Key Basic Research Program of China (No. 2016YFB0100900), National Natural Science Foundation of China (No. 61171113), and Science and Technology Innovation Committee of Shenzhen (No. 20150476).

References

1. Mnih, V., Kavukcuoglu, K., Silver, D., Rusu, A.A., Veness, J., Bellemare, M.G., Graves, A., Riedmiller, M., Fidjeland, A.K., Ostrovski, G., et al.: Human-level control through deep reinforcement learning. Nature **518**(7540), 529–533 (2015)
2. Silver, D., Huang, A., Maddison, C.J., Guez, A., Sifre, L., Van Den Driessche, G., Schrittwieser, J., Antonoglou, I., Panneershelvam, V., Lanctot, M., et al.: Mastering the game of go with deep neural networks and tree search. Nature **529**(7587), 484–489 (2016)
3. Lillicrap, T.P., Hunt, J.J., Pritzel, A., Heess, N., Erez, T., Tassa, Y., Silver, D., Wierstra, D.: Continuous control with deep reinforcement learning, arXiv preprint arXiv:1509.02971 (2015)
4. Heess, N., Hunt, J.J., Lillicrap, T.P., Silver, D.: Memory-based control with recurrent neural networks, arXiv preprint arXiv:1512.04455 (2015)
5. Mnih, V., Badia, A.P., Mirza, M., Graves, A., Lillicrap, T., Harley, T., Silver, D., Kavukcuoglu, K.: Asynchronous methods for deep reinforcement learning. In: International Conference on Machine Learning, pp. 1928–1937 (2016)
6. Shalev-Shwartz, S., Shammah, S., Shashua, A.: Safe, multi-agent, reinforcement learning for autonomous driving, arXiv preprint arXiv:1610.03295 (2016)
7. Sallab, A.E., Abdou, M., Perot, E., Yogamani, S.: End-to-end deep reinforcement learning for lane keeping assist, arXiv preprint arXiv:1612.04340 (2016)
8. Graves, A., Wayne, G., Reynolds, M., Harley, T., Danihelka, I., Grabska-Barwińska, A., Colmenarejo, S.G., Grefenstette, E., Ramalho, T., Agapiou, J., et al.: Hybrid computing using a neural network with dynamic external memory. Nature **538**(7626), 471–476 (2016)

9. Abbeel, P., Ng, A.Y.: Apprenticeship learning via inverse reinforcement learning. In: Proceedings of the Twenty-First International Conference on Machine Learning, p. 1. ACM (2004)
10. Ho, J., Ermon, S.: Generative adversarial imitation learning. In: Advances in Neural Information Processing Systems, pp. 4565–4573 (2016)
11. Laroche, R., Fatemi, M., Romoff, J., van Seijen, H.: Multi-advisor reinforcement learning, arXiv preprint arXiv:1704.00756 (2017)
12. Zhan, Y., Ammar, H.B., et al.: Theoretically-grounded policy advice from multiple teachers in reinforcement learning settings with applications to negative transfer (2016)
13. Hester, T., Vecerik, M., Pietquin, O., Lanctot, M., Schaul, T., Piot, B., Sendonaris, A., Dulac-Arnold, G., Osband, I., Agapiou, J., et al.: Learning from demonstrations for real world reinforcement learning, arXiv preprint arXiv:1704.03732 (2017)
14. Altman, E.: Constrained Markov Decision Processes, vol. 7. CRC Press, Boca Raton (1999)
15. Borkar, V.S.: An actor-critic algorithm for constrained Markov decision processes. Syst. Control Lett. **54**(3), 207–213 (2005)
16. Chow, Y., Ghavamzadeh, M., Janson, L., Pavone, M.: Risk-constrained reinforcement learning with percentile risk criteria, arXiv preprint arXiv:1512.01629 (2015)
17. Loiacono, D., Cardamone, L., Lanzi, P.L.: Simulated car racing championship: competition software manual, arXiv preprint arXiv:1304.1672 (2013)

Edge Detection Based on Primary Visual Pathway

Chao Lv[1](✉), Yuelei Xu[1], Xulei Zhang[2], Shiping Ma[1], Shuai Li[1],
Peng Xin[1], Mingning Zhu[1], and Hongqiang Ma[1]

[1] Aeronautics and Astronautics Engineering College,
Air Force Engineering University, Xi'an 710038, China
lvchao1112@163.com
[2] Training Base of Xinjiang Border Defense Corps,
Changji Hui Autonomous Prefecture 831100, China

Abstract. Edge is an important feature and edge detection matters a lot to image processing and pattern recognition. In consideration of high properties of human visual system in image perception, a brain-inspired edge detection model based on primary visual pathway was raised. According to the mechanism of lateral geniculate nucleus (LGN) cells and simple cells in primary visual cortex (V1), first, the difference of Gaussian function was adopted to model the concentric receptive field (RF) of a LGN cell; then, cell groups were created by the union of LGN cells with same property; next, RFs of simple cells with a certain preferred orientation were created by combining those of cell groups; finally, the responses of all V1 simple cells were gained by integrating the responses of different simple cells. The proposed model reflects orientation selectivity of simple cells. Results on the USF database indicate that it has better anti-noise performance and robustness in edge detection compared with the previous methods. It effectively combines brain-inspired intelligence with computer vision.

Keywords: Edge detection · Primary visual pathway
Simple cell · Receptive field

1 Introduction

Since American and Europe began their 'Brain Project' in 2013 respectively, brain-inspired intelligence has drawn a lot of attention all around the world. China has carried out its brain project titled "Brain Science and Brain-inspired Intelligence" since 2016 [1]. How to apply brain-inspired intelligence into pattern recognition and image processing? It becomes a research frontier. Edge is a basis feature of object. Human visual system, the most important sensory system, processes over 80% of the information that our brain receives [2]. Exploring the information processing mechanism of human visual system, and constructing a brain-inspired visual perception model are of great significance to the development of artificial intelligent. A large number of biological experiments show that the primary visual pathway, containing retina, lateral geniculate nucleus (LGN) and primary visual cortex (V1), can detective the edges [3]. It plays a

© Springer International Publishing AG 2017
Y. Zhao et al. (Eds.): ICIG 2017, Part II, LNCS 10667, pp. 430–439, 2017.
https://doi.org/10.1007/978-3-319-71589-6_37

key role in the overall perception. On the basis of mechanism in primary visual pathway, we propose a feedforward LGN-V1 model, which can effectively detect the edge, and lay the foundation for further research.

When recognizing objects, the human brain first detective the edges. The edges are formed by such factors as discontinuity in intensity and changes of surface direction. It is a basic visual feature and plays a key role in object recognition [4]. Edge detection can retain important structural information of images as well as reduce the amount of data greatly. Edge detection, as a basic subject of image perception and pattern recognition, has been widely used in unmanned driving and military target detection. At present, differential operator method are used for edge detection. And the edge is obtained by convolution of image and template [5]. The common operators include Canny-operator, Prewitt-operator and so on. Although methods of computer vision are effective in edge detection to some degree, it is far from the high property of human brain. With the exploration of brain, people have a preliminary understanding of human visual system. To build brain-inspired models for image processing has become a new direction in the field of computer vision.

In view of this, we establish a brain-inspired model with the mechanism of primary visual pathway. Compared with Canny-operator [6] and Prewitt-operator [7], our model has better performance and robustness in edge detection.

2 Primary Visual Pathway

Biological experiments have shown that human visual system possesses a multi-layered complex neural structure. It perceives most of the external information. The visual pathways are divided into dorsal stream and ventral stream. They are responsible for perceiving motion information and static information respectively [8]. The primary visual pathway, consisting of retina, LGN and V1, is in the early stage of visual system.

In primary visual pathway, firstly, the retina receives optical signals, and transforms those into bio-electrical signals to sends to LGN; then LGN processes the obtained information, and finally passes those to V1, the beginning of visual cortex. Primary visual pathway senses a lot of static information. LGN has a 6-layers structure: 2 magnocellular layers and 4 parvocellular layers. Magnocellular layers, the dorsal area of LGN, deal with the motion information; while parvocellular layers, the ventral area, are sensitive to color and contour [9]. The vast majority of LGN cells have a center-surround receptive field (RF), which shows a concentric antagonism at different areas of the RF. If the center of RF is sensitive to visual stimulus and surround causes the inhibition of response, a cell is called a 'center-on' cell, as shown in Fig. 1(a); else, we call it a 'center-off' cell, as shown in Fig. 1(b). Experiments indicate that RFs of LGN cells are under Gaussian distribution. Such LGN cells can detect contrast changes easily [10].

V1, sensitive to both static and dynamic visual stimulus, is the beginning of visual cortex [11]. Similar to LGN, V1 is also divided into six layers. Cells in V1 are generally divided into simple cells, complex cells and Hypercomplex cells [12]. Hubel and Wiesel found that the RFs of simple cells are small, long and narrow [13]. The RFs of simple cells have a property called orientation selectivity, which means that a cell is

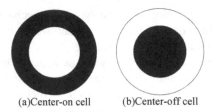

(a)Center-on cell   (b)Center-off cell

Fig. 1. LGN cells of different polarity

sensitive to the contrast of bright and dark at its preferred orientation [14]. If the stimulus' orientation is not consistent with the preferred orientation, the response decreases and is almost zero when the displacement is 45° or more. This property determines the high sensitivity to the edge at preference orientation. The RFs of complex cells and super complex cells are far broader and wider than the ones of simple cells. They are more sensitive to the bar stimulus. Simple cells receive visual stimulus from LGN, and their RFs are integration of ones of LGN cells. The size is positively correlated with the number of LGN cells in the local area. The feedforward model based on primary visual pathway is called the Hubel-Wiesel model, which lays the foundation for our edge detection model.

3   Brain-Inspired Computational Model

3.1   The Model Based on Bio-Visual System

According to the mechanism of LGN and V1 in primary visual pathway, we put forward a brain-inspired model as shown in Fig. 2.

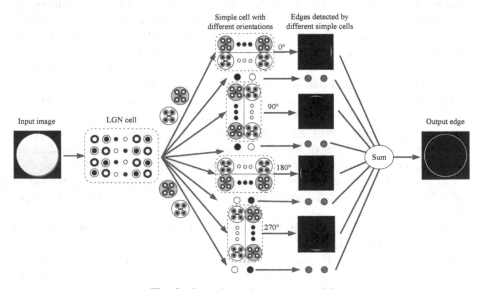

Fig. 2. Procedure of proposed model

Figure 2 illustrates the procedure the computational model with the mechanism of LGN and V1 simple cells in primary visual pathway.

Response of a cell group is got by computing the sum of the weighted responses of the LGN cells with same polarity and RF size. Similar to a single LGN cell, a cell group can detect contrast changes as well, but it does so in a broader and wider RF. A group can be seen as a branch of a simple cell which obtained input from a pool of adjacent LGN cells.

As illustrated in Fig. 2, by combining the responses of cell groups with appropriate spatial alignment of their RFs, a V1 simple cell possessing orientation selectivity is got. By calculating the weighted geometric mean of the group responses, the response of the all V1 simple cells is got, and that's the output of our model.

Because of the opposite polarity between center-on LGN cells and center-off ones, we define a property parameter δ and property function h. For a center-on cell, δ is '$+$' and $h(x) = x$; else, δ is '$-$' and $h(x) = -x$. No matter a center-on LGN cell and a center-off one, its RF is under Gaussian distribution, so a difference of Gaussian functions is adopted. That is expressed as:

$$DoG_\sigma^\delta(x,y) \overset{\text{def}}{=} h\left[\frac{1}{2\pi\sigma^2}e^{\left(-(x^2+y^2)/2\sigma^2\right)} - \frac{1}{2\pi(k\sigma)^2}e^{\left(-(x^2+y^2)/2(k\sigma)^2\right)}\right] \tag{1}$$

where σ is the standard deviation of the outer Gaussian function, which means the range of surround RF. k, the ratio of the standard deviations, means the ratio of the ranges RF shows excitation or inhibition. $DoG_\sigma^+(x,y)$, $DoG_\sigma^-(x,y)$ represent the RFs of a center-on cell and a center-off one respectively.

For a LGN cell with a RF centered at image coordinates (x,y), its response can obtained by calculating the convolution of intensity distribution function and RF of a cell.

$$l_\sigma^\delta(x,y) \overset{\text{def}}{=} I * DoG_\sigma^\delta \tag{2}$$

where $l_\sigma^\delta(x,y)$ may be negative because of the difference of δ, however, a firing rate of a cell should be positive. Inspired by simoncelli [15] and Zou [11], we adopted a rectification. So the response of a single cell is as followed:

$$D_\sigma^\delta(x,y) = \max\langle 0, l_\sigma^\delta(x,y)\rangle \tag{3}$$

A cell group is consisted of some cells with the same polarity. That is:

$$S = \{(\delta_i, \sigma_i, \rho_i, \phi_i)|i = 1, 2, \cdots, m\} \tag{4}$$

where the parameter m is the number of cells in a cell group. Parameter δ represents the polarity; σ means the range of RF; ρ reflects the radius and ϕ means the polar angle.

For a cell group, the center of whose RF is at coordinates (x,y), we compute the convolution of $D_\sigma^\delta(x,y)$ and RF of its center so that its response is worked out:

$$Z_{\delta_i,\sigma_i,\rho_i,\phi_i}(x,y) \stackrel{\text{def}}{=} \sum_{x'}\sum_{y'}\left\{D_{\sigma_i}^{\delta_i}(x-\Delta x_i - x', y - \Delta y_i - y')G_{\sigma'}(x',y')\right\} \qquad (5)$$

In the equation above,

$$\begin{aligned}\Delta x_i = -\rho_i\cos\phi_i; \Delta y_i = -\rho_i\sin\phi_i\\ -3\sigma' \le x'; y' \le 3\sigma'\end{aligned} \qquad (6)$$

where $\sigma' = b + \lambda\sigma$.

We define Q_{S,ϕ_i}, the response of a V1 simple cell whose preferred orientation is ϕ_i. It is determined by all cell groups it receives input from. According to the biological experiments by Hubel and Wiesel, only if all groups' responses are exited, can V1 simple cell be excited at visual stimulus. In order to represent the biological property, we compute the product of all groups' responses, and then work out the weighted geometric mean to get the responses of all simple cells. That is:

$$Q_{S,\phi_i}(x,y) \stackrel{\text{def}}{=} \left(\prod_{i=1}^{|S|}\left(Z_{\delta_i,\sigma_i,\rho_i,\phi_i}(x,y)\right)^{\omega_i}\right)^{1/\sum_{i=1}^{|S|}\omega_i} \qquad (7)$$

where

$$\begin{aligned}\omega_i = e^{-\rho_i/2\sigma^2}\\ \sigma' = \frac{1}{3}\max_{i\in\{1...|S|\}}\{\rho_i\}\end{aligned} \qquad (8)$$

We define orientation function $\beta = \{2\pi i/n | 0 \le i < n\}$. 0 to 2π is averagely divided into n, to represent different preferred orientation of V1 simple cells. While $i = 0,1,2.\ldots\ldots$n, we calculate the integration of responses of all simple cells, and the whole response is got:

$$Q_{all}(x,y) = \sum_{\phi\in\beta}Q_{S,\phi}(x,y) \qquad (9)$$

3.2   Related Parameters Setting

To qualitatively match the physiological data [14, 16], the parameters' values are as followed: $\sigma = 2.5$, $k = 0.5$, $b = 0.33$, $\lambda = 0.15$. Based on control variable method, we set $m = 16$ to get better orientation selectivity. Tuning curves of simple cells (preferred orientation is 0°) are shown in Fig. 3.

From Fig. 3, we can see that the model simple cells have biological properties of real cells, which demonstrates the validity of the model.

With parameters above determined, we need to find the best value of n to detect edge better and reduce the data amount. We take the image named mainbuilding in

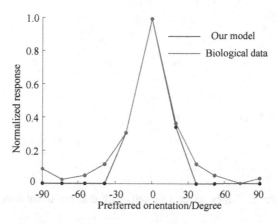

Fig. 3. Tuning curves of simple cells (preferred orientation is 0°)

USF (University of South Florida) database as an example. As shown in Fig. 4 (a) is original image; (d) is ground truth of edge; (b), (c) (e), (f) are edge detected by proposed model while n = 4, n = 8, n = 12, n = 16, respectively.

From Fig. 4, we can see that, our model exist missing detection greatly while n = 4. The detected edges are incomplete and we can hardly have a satisfied identification with them; while n = 8, our model improves its property of edge to some degree. It detects more edges but the result is far from satisfactory; while n = 12, our model detect more edge, with which we can recognize the picture well. The edges detected achieve the expected effect; while n = 16, we achieve nearly the same property of edge detection as n = 12. So, in order to get expected result and reduce the data amount at the same time, we set n = 12. It means with 12 simple cells with different preferred orientations together, we can achieve the properties of all cells while detecting edges. Edges detected by 12 model simple cells are as shown in Fig. 5. From

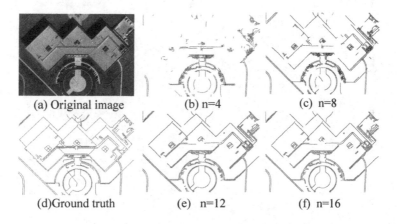

Fig. 4. Edge detected by the model with different values of n

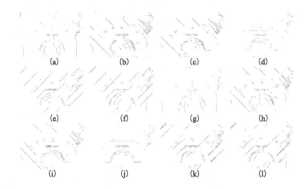

Fig. 5. Edges detected by cells with different orientation

Fig. 5, we can see a model cell is only sensitive to the visual stimulus at its preferred orientation, which reflect the real orientation selectivity in biology.

Generally speaking, this set of values above was retained for all of simulation results later, except where specifically noted.

4   Analysis of Experimental Results

To examine the effectiveness of our model, we take images in the USF (University of South Florida) database as examples. We get the results as shown in Fig. 6.

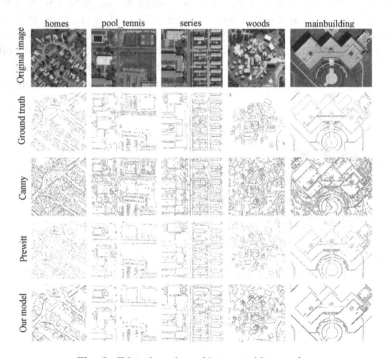

Fig. 6. Edge detection of images with no noise

From Fig. 6, we can see that the model preserves the complete edges of the image, and the object can be identified from the extracted result. Canny-operator can extract the basic edges. But it also regards some non-edge as the edges, which causes some false detection. The property of Prewitt-operator is between our model and Canny-operator. In a word, our model is better than Canny-operator and Prewitt-operator.

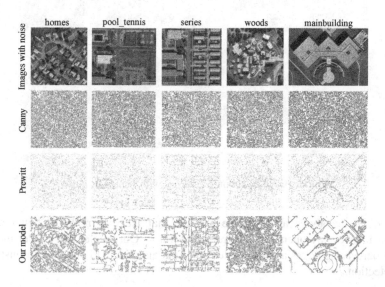

Fig. 7. Edge detection of images with salt & pepper noise

Anti-noise performance and robustness is an important indicator of edge detection performance. In order test the robustness of our model, we analyze the detected edges of three methods after adding salt and pepper noise (density is 0.1), Gaussian noise (mean value is 0 and variance is 0.1) into the original images, respectively. The results are as shown in Figs. 7 and 8.

It can be seen from Fig. 7 that after the adding salt and pepper noise, the images have a large number of pixel points with gray mutation, so that the edges are weakened. And the edge detection becomes more difficult because most methods utilize sudden changes of pixel values in images. The Canny-operator and Prewitt-operator have a large number of false detections in this case. It is difficult to identify the objects. Instead, our model can extract most edges and contain the basic appearance at the same time.

From Fig. 8, we find that after adding Gaussian noise, there is a certain gray gradient everywhere. The noise created blurring at the edge. Detecting edge has become more difficult as well. In this case, Canny-operator is more sensitive to Gaussian noise and brings a lot of noise into the edges detected. And we can hardly identify the basic shape of the object. The Prewitt-operator and our model both have good performance in detecting edges in images with Gaussian noise. But Prewitt-operator regards some obvious edges as discontinuous points, and our model is better than it.

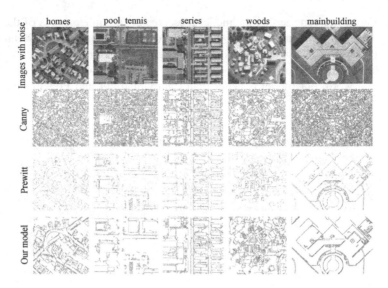

Fig. 8. Edge detection of images with Gaussian noise

Based on the above analysis, we can see that the our model is better at edge detection than Canny-operator and Prewitt-operator. Our model can model the properties in perceiving edges as V1 simple cells. It is effective and has good robustness in edge detection.

5   Conclusion

In this paper, a brain-inspired edge detection model is established based on the receptive fields of LGN and V1 simple cells in the brain's primary visual pathway. The model reflects the real biological properties of LGN and V1 simple cells. We created mathematical model to simulate visual system, and bring it into edge detection, a important part in image processing. By comparing with the traditional edge detection operators, the robustness of the model proposed is demonstrated.

The model proposed in this paper simulates the primary visual pathway. It realizes the ability of perception of static edge information, and explores the application of brain cognitive mechanism in image processing. In view of the fact that the human brain vision system can perceive complex static and dynamic information, we will continue to explore the visual system for further research. Next, We are going to explore the mechanisms of V1 complex cells, and building spatial and temporal model to simulate more properties of primary visual pathway. With brain-inspired intelligence and motivation from 'Brain Project', pattern recognition and image processing will achieve greater development in the future.

Acknowledgements. This work is supported by the National Natural Science Foundation of China (NSFC) (No. 61372167, No. 61379104).

References

1. Poo, M., Du, J., Ip, N.Y., et al.: China brain project: basic neuroscience, brain diseases, and brain-inspired computing. Neuron **92**(3), 591–596 (2016)
2. Shou, T.D.: Neuronal basis of vision. Chin. J. Nature **37**(1), 17–25 (2015)
3. Bednar, J.A.: Building a mechanistic model of the development and function of the primary visual cortex. J. Physiol.-Paris **106**(5), 194–211 (2012)
4. Dollar, P., Zitnick, C.L.: Fast edge detection using structured forests. IEEE Trans. Pattern Anal. Mach. Intell. **37**(8), 1558–1570 (2015)
5. Gunen, M.A., Civicioglu, P., Beşdok, E.: Differential search algorithm based edge detection. In: ISPRS-International Archives of the Photogrammetry, Remote Sensing and Spatial Information Sciences, pp. 667–670 (2016)
6. Ding, L., Goshtasby, A.A.: On the canny edge detector. Pattern Recogn. **34**(3), 721–725 (2001)
7. Garcialamont, J.: Analogue CMOS prototype vision chip with prewitt edge processing. Analog Integr. Circ. Sig. Process. **71**(3), 507–514 (2012)
8. Mercier, M.R., Schwartz, S., Spinelli, L., et al.: Dorsal and ventral stream contributions to form-from-motion perception in a patient with form-from motion deficit: a case report. Brain Struct. Funct. **222**(2), 1093–1107 (2016)
9. Rucci, M., Edelman, G.M., Wray, J., et al.: Modeling LGN responses during free-viewing: a possible role of microscopic eye movements in the refinement of cortical orientation selectivity. J. Neurosci. **20**(12), 4708–4720 (2000)
10. Piscopo, D.M., Eldanaf, R.N., Huberman, A.D., et al.: Diverse visual features encoded in mouse lateral geniculate nucleus. J. Neurosci. **33**(11), 4642–4656 (2013)
11. Zou, H.Z., Xu, Y.L., Ma, S.P., et al.: Motion feature extraction of random-dot video suquences based on V1 model of visual cortex. J. Comput. Appl. **36**(6), 1677–1681 (2016)
12. Pettigrew, J.D., Daniels, J.: Gamma-aminobutyric acid antagonism in visual cortex: different effects on simple, complex, and hypercomplex neurons. Science **182**(4107), 81–83 (1973)
13. Constantinepaton, M.: Pioneers of cortical plasticity: six classic papers by Wiesel and Hubel. J. Neurophysiol. **99**(6), 2741–2744 (2008)
14. Hubel, D.H., Wiesel, T.N.: Receptive fields, binocular interaction and functional architecture in the cat's visual cortex. J. Physiol. **160**(1), 106–154 (1962)
15. Simoncelli, E.P., Heeger, D.J.: A model of neural responses in visual area MT. Vis. Res. **38** (5), 743–761 (1998)
16. Xu, X., Bonds, A.B., Casagrande, V.A., et al.: Modeling receptive-field structure of koniocellular, magnocellular, and parvocellular LGN cells in the owl monkey (*Aotus trivigatus*). Vis. Neurosci. **19**(06), 703–711 (2002)

Multi-channel Satellite Cloud Image Fusion in the Shearlet Transform Domain and Its Influence on Typhoon Center Location

Changjiang Zhang[1(⊠)], Yuan Chen[1], and Leiming Ma[2]

[1] College of Mathematics, Physics and Information Engineering,
Zhejiang Normal University, Jinhua 321004, China
zcj74922@zjnu.edu.cn
[2] Laboratory of Typhoon Forecast Technique/CMA,
Shanghai Typhoon Institute, Shanghai 200030, China

Abstract. A multi-channel satellite cloud image fusion method by the shearlet transform is proposed. The Laplacian pyramid algorithm is used to decompose the low frequency sub-images in the shearlet domain. It averages the values on its top layer, and takes the maximum absolute values on the other layers. In the high frequency sub-images of the shearlet domain, fusion rule is constructed by using information entropy, average gradient and standard deviation. Next, a nonlinear operation is performed to enhance the details of the fusion high frequency sub-images. The proposed image fusion algorithm is compared with five similar image fusion algorithms: the classical discrete orthogonal wavelet, curvelet, NSCT, tetrolet and shearlet. The information entropy, average gradient and standard deviation are used objectively evaluate the quality of the fused images. In order to verify the efficiency of the proposed algorithm, the fusion cloud image is used to determine the center location of eye and non-eye typhoons. The experimental results show that the fused image obtained by proposed algorithm improve the precision of determining the typhoon center. The comprehensive performance of the proposed algorithm is superior to similar image fusion algorithms.

Keywords: Shearlet transform · Multi-channel satellite cloud image
Laplacian pyramid · Image fusion · Typhoon center location

1 Introduction

At present, the automatic location of the typhoon center is still in at an early stage. Regarding typhoon center location technology based on satellite data, Dvorak proposed the Dvorak technique (DT) [1]. Recently, many improved Dvorak technology were subsequently developed that aim to determine the typhoon center. The main typhoon center location methods currently used include: the mathematical morphology/feature extraction method [2], the intelligent learning method [3], wind field analysis [4], temperature/humidity structure inversion [5], tempo-spatial movement matching [6] and the objective tropical cyclones location system [7]. Although these methods have certain advantages, they have some problems. For example, the subjectivity of DT is

© Springer International Publishing AG 2017
Y. Zhao et al. (Eds.): ICIG 2017, Part II, LNCS 10667, pp. 440–451, 2017.
https://doi.org/10.1007/978-3-319-71589-6_38

stronger. Mathematical morphology is suitable for tropical cyclones for which the morphology characteristics can be easily identified. The intelligent learning method requires a lot of experimental data and accumulated experience. It is suitable for recognizing the particular structures. The wind field analysis method is applicable for locating the centers of a tropical cyclones that are weak and do not have a clear circulation center. When the intensity level of a tropical cyclone is strong, the center location is not accurate, because it is affected by the resolution and heavy rain [7]. The temperature/humidity structure inversion method is also only applied to locate tropical cyclone centers that have a strong intensity. The tempo-spatial movement matching method mainly uses the implied movement information of the time series image which is combined with the characteristics and movement to track the tropical cyclone center [7]. However, the computational complexity of the method is very large. Other center location methods are not often used and are still in the early stages of developmental. Meanwhile, the existing typhoon center location system based on the satellite material mainly uses a single channel satellite cloud image or time sequence cloud images; therefore, the amount of the information obtained is not very large.

Considering that it can improve the accuracy of the location of the typhoon center if the multi-channel cloud images are fused. Recently, many researchers have made significant contributions in multi-channel satellite cloud image fusion. Among them, wavelet analysis has been successfully used in image fusion [8]. However, it can only capture three directions. Recently multi-scale geometric analysis tool is not only the same as the wavelet transform which has multi-resolution, but also has good time-frequency local features and a high degree of directionality and anisotropy [9]. They have been successfully applied in satellite image fusion (curvlet [10], contourlet [11], NSCT [12], tetrolet [13]). In 2005, Labate et al. proposed the shearlet transform [14]. It can realize the decomposition of images in different directions. It can not only detect all singular points, but can also follow the direction of the singular curve. In addition, it overcomes the shortcomings of the wavelet transform which loses the information in the process of image fusion. Compared with the contourlet transform, it eliminates the limited directions in the process of filtering [15]. Recently, researchers are paying more and more attention to the shearlet transform [16]. In this paper, we aim to introduce the shearlet transform into multi-channel satellite cloud images. We use the fusion cloud image to locate and explore its influence on the typhoon center position. In order to verify the performance of the proposed algorithm, the proposed algorithm is compared with five other types of image fusion algorithms that are designed by multi-scale decomposition.

2 The Proposed Image Fusion Algorithm

2.1 Fusion Rule for the Low Frequency Component of the Shearlet Transform

After implementing the shearlet transform to an image, the low frequency component mainly includes the large-scale information of the image. The low frequency component contains less detail, but it has most of the energy of the image. Thus, the information fusion for the low frequency component is also very important. An adaptive fusion algorithm is designed to fuse the low frequency sub-images in the shearlet domain. The Laplacian pyramid algorithm is used to decompose the low frequency sub-images. It has been reported that the image fusion algorithm based on Laplacian pyramid decomposition is stable and reliable [17].

In this paper, the Laplacian pyramid decomposition algorithm is used to decompose the low frequency component in the shearlet domain. The fusion rules and specific steps of the low frequency component in the shearlet domain are designed as follows:

Step 1. The low frequency coefficients SL_A and SL_B of the source images A and B are decomposed by the Laplacian pyramid algorithm, respectively. The number of decomposition layers is Q. The decomposed images are written as LA and LB. The qth ($1 \leq q \leq Q$) layer sub-images can be written as LA_q and LB_q;

Step 2. An averaging method is used to fuse the top layer sub-images LA_Q and LB_Q of the Laplacian pyramid. Then, the fusion result LF_Q is written as:

$$LF_Q(i,j) = \frac{LA_Q(i,j) + LB_Q(i,j)}{2} \tag{1}$$

where $1 \leq i \leq CL_Q$, $1 \leq j \leq RL_Q$, CL_Q is the number of rows of the Q th layer image and RL_Q is the number of columns of the Q th layer image;

Step 3. The fusion rule that chooses the greatest gray absolute value is designed to fuse the image LA_q and LB_q ($1 \leq q \leq Q - 1$). The fusion result LF_q is written as:

$$LF_q(i,j) = \begin{cases} LA_q(i,j), & |LA_q(i,j)| \geq |LB_q(i,j)| \\ LB_q(i,j), & |LA_q(i,j)| < |LB_q(i,j)| \end{cases} \tag{2}$$

Step 4. Reconstruct the Laplacian pyramid and obtain the fusion result TL_F of the low frequency components.

2.2 Fusion Rule for the High Frequency Component of the Shearlet Transform

For the satellite cloud images which are used for locating the typhoon center, the information amount, spatial resolution and definition of the satellite cloud images are very important. The details and texture feature of the fusion image should be more abundant. Therefore, the fusion rule of the high frequency components in the shearlet domain should be designed by above the evaluation indexes.

Here, we select information entropy to evaluate the amount of information of the high frequency components in the shearlet domain. The larger the information entropy, greater the average amount of information contained in the fusion image. The standard deviation reflects the discrete degree of the gray level values relative to the average value of the gray values of the image. The greater the standard deviation, the better the contrast of the fusion image. On the other hand, the smaller the standard deviation σ, the more uniform the gray level distribution of the image. Also, the contrast of the image is not obvious. It is not easy to identify the details of the fusion image. Image definition can be evaluated by the average gradient. The average gradient can sensitively reflect the expression ability in the minute details of the image. Generally, the greater the average gradient, the larger the rate of the gray values in the image changes and the clearer the image. Hence, we choose to use information entropy, average gradient and standard deviation to construct the fusion rule of the high frequency components in the shearlet domain.

For the high frequency components of the source images A and B in the shearlet domain, we have designed the fusion rule as follows:

Step 1. Firstly, we calculate the information entropy, average gradient and standard deviation of each layer in every direction of the sub-images separately. The high frequency coefficients whose layer is w $(0 < w \leq W)$ and direction is t $(0 < t \leq T)$ are written as $(SH_A)_w^t$ and $(SH_B)_w^t$. Their sizes are $M \times N$ which is the same as the original image. Information entropy E can be written as:

$$E = -\sum_{i=0}^{L-1} P_i \log_2 P_i \tag{3}$$

where P_i is the probability of the gray value i in the pixel of the sub-images and L is the number of the gray level. The average gradient of the high frequency sub-image is expressed as:

$$\bar{G} = \frac{\sum_{ii=1}^{M-1} \sum_{jj=1}^{N-1} \sqrt{\frac{\left(\frac{\partial SH_w^t(x_{ii},y_{jj})}{\partial x_{ii}}\right)^2 + \left(\frac{\partial SH_w^t(x_{ii},y_{jj})}{\partial y_{jj}}\right)^2}{2}}}{(M-1)(N-1)} \tag{4}$$

where $SH_w^t(x_{ii}, y_{jj})$ is the pixel point whose position is (x_{ii}, y_{jj}) in the high frequency sub-image $(SH_A)_w^t$ or $(SH_B)_w^t$. Here, $0 < ii \leq M$ and $0 < jj \leq N$. The standard deviation of the high frequency sub-image is shown as:

$$\sigma = \sqrt{\sum_{ii=1}^{M} \sum_{jj=1}^{N} \frac{(SH_w^t(x_{ii}, y_{jj}) - \bar{h})^2}{M \times N}} \tag{5}$$

where $\bar{h}$ is the average value of gray levels in the high frequency sub-image.

Step 2. The information entropy E, average gradient $\bar{G}$ and standard deviation σ of the high frequency sub-images $(SH_A)_w^t$ or $(SH_B)_w^t$ are normalized. Then, we will obtain the normalization of information entropy E_g, average gradient $\bar{G}_g$ and standard deviation σ_g. The high frequency sub-image whose product of these three values is the greatest is chosen as the fusion sub-image. Namely,

$$(SH_F)_w^t = \begin{cases} (SH_A)_w^t, & (E_g)_A \times (\bar{G}_g)_A \times (\sigma_g)_A \geq (E_g)_B \times (\bar{G}_g)_B \times (\sigma_g)_B \\ (SH_B)_w^t, & (E_g)_A \times (\bar{G}_g)_A \times (\sigma_g)_A < (E_g)_B \times (\bar{G}_g)_B \times (\sigma_g)_B \end{cases} \tag{6}$$

Step 3. The nonlinear enhancement operation is performed on the high frequency sub-images [18]. We assume that the maximum absolute value of all gray pixel points is *mgray*. Then, the enhanced high frequency sub-image $(E\_SH_F)^t_w$ is written as:

$$(E\_SH_F)^t_w(ii,jj) = a \cdot \text{max}h\{sigm[c(Sh^t_w(ii,jj) - b)] - sigm[-c(Sh^t_w(ii,jj) + b)]\} \tag{7}$$

Here, $b = 0.35$ and $c = 20$. They are used to control the size of the threshold and enhance the rate. $a = 1/(d_1 - d_2)$, where $d_1 = sigm(c \times (1 + b))$, $d_2 = sigm(-c \times (1 - b))$, $sigm(x) = \frac{1}{1+e^{-x}}$ and $Sh^t_w(ii,jj) = (SH_F)^t_w(ii,jj)/mgray$.

2.3   Fusion Algorithm of the Satellite Cloud Image

The registered source images are written as A and B. The detail steps of the proposed image fusion algorithm are shown as follows:

Step 1. The registered image A and B (the size is $M \times N$) are decomposed by the shearlet transform. The number of decomposition layers is W. The direction of decomposition is T ($T = 2^r, r \in Z^*$), and Z^* means the positive integer. Then, the following coefficients can be obtained: the high coefficients SH_A and SH_B and the low coefficients SL_A and SL_B;

Step 2. According to Sect. 3.1 which introduces the fusion rule of the low frequency part, we fuse the low frequency sub-image, and we obtain the low frequency fusion coefficient TL_F;

Step 3. According to Sect. 3.2 which explains the fusion rule of the high frequency part, we fuse the high frequency sub-image, and we obtain the high frequency fusion coefficient E_SH_F;

Step 4. The inverse shearlet transform is implemented to the fused shearlet coefficients to obtain the final fusion image F.

3   Experimental Results and Discussion

Two groups of satellite cloud images captured by the Chinese meteorological satellite FY-2C are used to verify the proposed fusion algorithm. There are one group of eye typhoon cloud images and one group of non-eye typhoon cloud images: 1. Infrared channel 2 cloud image and water vapor channel cloud image of the No. 0513 typhoon "Talim" which were obtained at 12:00 am on August 31, 2005; 2. Infrared channel 1 cloud image and water vapor channel cloud image of the No. 0713 typhoon "Wipha" which were obtained at 6:00 am on September 16, 2007. In order to verify the efficiency of the proposed fusion algorithm, it is compared with five similar image fusion algorithms: the classical discrete orthogonal wavelet transform [19], the curvelet transform [10], NSCT [12], the tetrolet transform [13] and the shearlet transform [15]. The number of the decomposed layers is two. In order to express the diagram conveniently, the image fusion algorithm based on the classical discrete orthogonal wavelet is labeled as "DWT". The curvelet image fusion algorithm is labeled as "Curvelet". The NSCT image fusion algorithm is labeled as "NSCT". The tetrolet image fusion algorithm is labeled as "Tetrolet". The shearlet image fusion algorithm in Ref. [15] is labeled as "Shearlet" and the proposed image fusion algorithm is labeled as "S_Lap".

3.1 Experimental Results for the Multi-channel Satellite Cloud Image Fusion

Example 1 for Eye Typhoon Cloud Image Fusion

The first group of experimental images is the infrared channel 2 cloud image and water vapor cloud image for typhoon "Talim" which were obtained at 12 o'clock on August 31, 2005. They are shown in Fig. 1(a) and (b) respectively. Figure 1(c)–(h) respectively represents the fusion images obtained by the DWT, Curvelet, NSCT, Tetrolet, Shearlet and S_Lap, respectively.

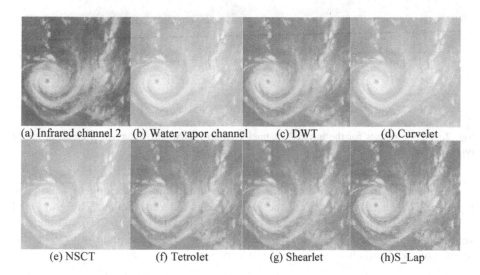

(a) Infrared channel 2   (b) Water vapor channel   (c) DWT   (d) Curvelet

(e) NSCT   (f) Tetrolet   (g) Shearlet   (h)S_Lap

Fig. 1. Fusion results for the infrared channel 2 cloud image and water vapor cloud image of typhoon "Talim" in 2005.

We can see from Fig. 1 that the gray level values of the fusion image by the curvelet transform (Fig. 1(d)) and the fusion image by NSCT (Fig. 1(e)) are a little larger, and the difference between the typhoon eye and the surrounding of the clouds is small. They are close to that of the water vapor cloud image (Fig. 1(b)). In Fig. 1(f), some edge details are fuzzy in the fusion image by tetrolet transform which is influenced by the block effect. The visual qualities of the other fusion images are similar.

Example 2 for Non-Eye Typhoon Cloud Image Fusion

The second group experimental images are infrared channel 1 cloud image and water vapor channel cloud image of the No. 0713 typhoon "Wipha" which were obtained at 6 o'clock on September 16, 2007. They are shown in Fig. 2(a) and (b) respectively. Figure 2(c)–(h) respectively represents the fusion images by DWT, Curvelet, NSCT, Tetrolet, Shearlet and S_Lap respectively.

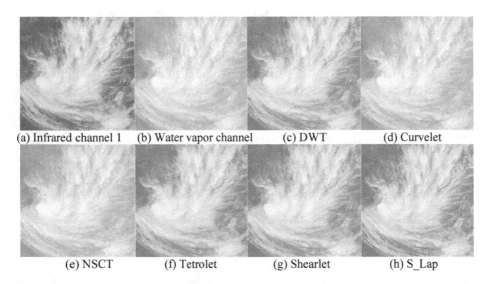

(a) Infrared channel 1   (b) Water vapor channel   (c) DWT   (d) Curvelet

(e) NSCT   (f) Tetrolet   (g) Shearlet   (h) S_Lap

Fig. 2. Fusion results for the infrared channel 1 cloud image and water vapor cloud image of typhoon "Wipha" in 2007.

We can see from Fig. 2 that this group of cloud images belong to a non-eye typhoon. The visual quality of all the fusion images is very similar. The gray level values of the fusion images obtained by the NSCT transform (Fig. 2(e)) and the curvelet transform (Fig. 2(d)) are a little larger than those of other transforms. The difference of the details between them is not very larger.

3.2   Evaluation Parameters for the Fusion Images

In order to objectively evaluate the quality of these fusion images, information entropy E, average gradient $\bar{G}$ and standard deviation σ are used to evaluate these fusion images. The larger these parameters values are, better the visual quality of the fusion image is. The evaluation parameters of the fusion images in Figs. 1 and 2 are shown in Tables 1 and 2, respectively.

We can see from Tables 1 and 2 that the information entropy, average gradient and standard deviation of the fusion image by the proposed algorithm are better than those of the other fusion algorithms. The fusion images obtained by the proposed algorithm contain more information on the multi-channel cloud images and have good contrast.

Table 1. Evaluation parameters for Fig. 2 with different fusion algorithms.

Fusion algorithm	E	$\bar{G}$	σ
DWT	6.33	1.77	23.44
Curvelet	5.99	1.19	16.00
NSCT	5.93	1.39	15.47
Tetrolet	6.29	1.42	22.93
Shearlet	6.33	1.50	23.33
S_Lap	6.34	2.00	23.87

Table 2. Evaluation parameters for Fig. 4 with different fusion algorithms.

Fusion algorithm	E	$\bar{G}$	σ
DWT	6.78	2.65	31.50
Curvelet	6.44	1.75	23.08
NSCT	6.42	2.20	22.90
Tetrolet	6.80	2.14	31.60
Shearlet	6.78	2.28	31.69
S_Lap	6.79	3.03	32.37

The proposed algorithm can extrude the details of the cloud images well. The comprehensive visual quality of the fusion images by the proposed algorithm is optimal.

Typhoon Center Location Test based on the Fusion Cloud Images
In order to further verify the performance of the proposed image fusion algorithm, fusion images which are obtained by various algorithms are used to locate the center position of the typhoon. In this paper, the typhoon center location algorithm in [20] is used. In order to compare the accuracy of the center position by the various fusion images, we use the typhoon center position in the "tropical cyclone yearbook" which is compiled by Shanghai typhoon institute of China meteorological administration as the reference typhoon center position. In addition, the single infrared channel satellite cloud image and the water vapor channel satellite cloud image are used to locate the center position of a typhoon to verify the performance of the proposed algorithm. This is because the existing typhoon center location systems are based on a single infrared channel satellite cloud image or time series images.

Example 1 for Eye Typhoon Center Location
The typhoon center location algorithm in [20] is used to locate the center position based on the fusion typhoon cloud images. The center location results based on different fusion images are shown in Fig. 3.

We can see from Fig. 3 that the center locations in Fig. 3(b)–(e) are far away from the center of the typhoon. The center location in Fig. 3(a) is close to the reference center position of the typhoon. The center locations based on the fusion images by the tetrolet transform in Fig. 3(f) and by the shearlet transform in Fig. 3(g) are very close to the reference center position. The center location based on the fusion image by the proposed algorithm in Fig. 3(h) is almost the same as the reference center position of the typhoon. The center location errors based on Fig. 3 are shown in Table 3.

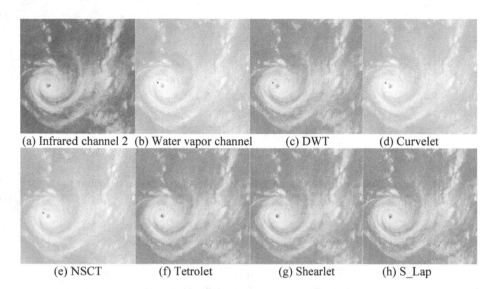

(a) Infrared channel 2 (b) Water vapor channel   (c) DWT   (d) Curvelet

(e) NSCT   (f) Tetrolet   (g) Shearlet   (h) S_Lap

Fig. 3. The center location results by using fusion images for typhoon "Talim" obtained at 12:00 am on August 31, 2005.

Table 3. The center location errors of the various fusion images for typhoon "Talim" (12:00 am, August 31, 2005).s

Fusion algorithm	North latitude (°)	East longitude (°)	Error (km)
Infrared channel 2	23.78	122.87	13.73
Water vapor channel	24.87	122.11	138.86
DWT	24.87	122.11	138.86
Curvelet	24.87	122.11	138.86
NSCT	24.87	122.11	138.86
Tetroelet	23.99	122.65	29.49
Shearelet	23.99	122.65	29.49
S_Lap	23.83	122.91	7.85
Reference values	23.90	122.90	

From Table 3, we can find that the error of the typhoon center location based on the fusion image obtained by the proposed algorithm is 7.85 km. The location error by the proposed algorithm is less than that of the five other the fusion algorithms, the single infrared channel 2 cloud image and single water vapor channel cloud image.

Example 2 for Non-Eye Typhoon Center Location
We use the typhoon center location algorithm in [20] to locate the center position based on the fusion typhoon cloud images in Fig. 4. The center location results are shown in Fig. 4.

We can see from Fig. 4 that the center locations of the fusion images obtained by the tetrolet transform in Fig. 4(f) and by the shearlet transform in Fig. 4(g) are far away from the reference center position of the typhoon. The center locations based on other fusion images are very close to the reference center position of the typhoon. Especially, the center locations based on the fusion images by the NSCT transform in Fig. 4(e) and the proposed algorithm in Fig. 4(h) are almost the same as the reference center position of the typhoon. The center location errors based on Fig. 4 are shown in Table 4. In Table 4, we can find that the center location error based on the fusion image obtained by the proposed algorithm is 15.46 km. The location error of the proposed algorithm is less than that of the five other the fusion algorithms, the single infrared channel 1 cloud image and the single water vapor channel cloud image.

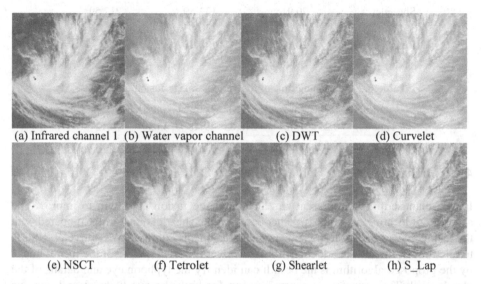

(a) Infrared channel 1 (b) Water vapor channel   (c) DWT   (d) Curvelet

  (e) NSCT   (f) Tetrolet   (g) Shearlet   (h) S_Lap

Fig. 4. The center location results by using fusion images for typhoon "Wipha" obtained at 6:00 am on September 16, 2007.

Computing Complexity of the Algorithm

In order to verify the performance of the proposed image fusion algorithm, the computing complexities of all the image fusion algorithms above are analyzed in this manuscript. The image fusion algorithms are run in MatLab R2009a software on a Dell OptiPlex 780 desktop computer with an Intel® Core™ 2 processor and four nuclear Q9400 at 2.66 GHz. The memory of this computer is 2 GB (JinShiDun DDR3 1333 MHz) and the operating system is Windows XP professional edition 32-bit SP3 (DirectX 9.0c). The running time of the different image fusion algorithms is tested by the image fusion experiment for the eye typhoon group. The running time of all of the image fusion algorithms are shown in Table 5.

From Table 5, we can see that the DWT has the smallest image fusion algorithm running time. The running time of the proposed image fusion algorithm is shorter than the running time of other multi-scale image fusion algorithms. Thus, the computing complexity of the proposed image fusion algorithm is acceptable.

Table 4. The center location errors of the various fusion image for typhoon "Wipha" (6:00 am, September 16, 2007).

Fusion algorithm	North latitude (°)	East longitude (°)	Error (km)
Infrared channel 1	20.35	131.05	47.74
Water vapor channel	20.41	131.31	70.92
DWT	20.67	131.13	48.36
Curvelet	20.47	131.31	69.23
NSCT	20.81	130.75	23.96
Tetroelet	19.63	132.29	206.74
Shearelet	20.91	132.59	212.59
S_Lap	20.65	130.83	15.46
Reference values	20.60	130.70	

Table 5. The running time of the various image fusion algorithms.

Algorithm	DWT	Curvelet	NSCT	Tetrolet	Shearlet	S_Lap
Time (s)	0.25	13.27	246.65	49.48	45.50	10.12

4 Conclusions

In this manuscript, we represent an efficient image fusion algorithm to improve the accuracy of locating the typhoon center based on the shearlet transform. Compared with the fusion images based on five similar image fusion algorithms (DWT, curvelet, NSCT, tetrolet transform and shearlet transfrom), the overall visual quality of the fusion image by the proposed algorithm is the best. It can identify the typhoon eye and details of the clouds well. The accuracy of center location for both the eye typhoon and non-eye typhoon can be improved by using the fusion image obtained by the proposed algorithm. It is superior to the center location methods based on the single channel satellite cloud image and other fusion images by other image fusion algorithms. Further work is needed to improve the fusion rule by combining some meteorological knowledge and practical forecasting experience. In addition, the work of this paper can be used to retrieve the typhoon wind field and to improve the prediction accuracy of typhoon intensity.

Acknowledgments. The part of work in this paper is supported by Natural Science Foundation of China (Nos. 41575046, 41475059), Project of Commonweal Technique and Application Research of Zhejiang Province of China (No. 2016C33010).

References

1. Dvorak, V.F.: Tropical cyclone intensity analysis and forecasting from forecasting from satellite imagery. Mon. Weather Rev. **103**(5), 420–430 (1975)
2. Li, H., Huang, X.-Y., Qin, D.-Y.: Research the artificial intelligent algorithm for positioning of eyed typhoon with high resolution satellite image. In: Proceedings of the 2012 5th International Joint Conference on Computational Sciences and Optimization, pp. 889–891 (2012)

3. Li, Y., Chen, X., Fei, S.-M., Mao, K.-F., Zhou, K.: The study of a linear optimal location the typhoon center automatic from IR satellite cloud image. In: Proceedings of SPIE - The International Society for Optical Engineering, vol. 8193 (2011)
4. Yang, J., Wang, H.: Positioning tropical cyclone center in a single satellite image using vector field analysis. In: Sun, Z., Deng, Z. (eds.) Proceedings of 2013 Chinese Intelligent Automation Conference. Lecture Notes in Electrical Engineering, vol. 256, pp. 37–44. Springer, Heidelberg (2013). https://doi.org/10.1007/978-3-642-38466-0_5
5. Fan, Z.Y.: Application of satellite SSM/I data in the typhoon center location and maximum wind speed estimation, pp. 1–2. National Central University in Taiwan, Taoyuan (2004)
6. Wei, K., Jing, Z., Li, Y., Liu, S.: Spiral band model for locating tropical cyclone centers. Pattern Recogn. Lett. 32(6), 761–770 (2011)
7. Yang, H.-Q., Yang, Y.-M.: Progress in objedctive position methods of tropical cyclone center using satellite remote sensing. J. Top. Oceanogr. 31(2), 15–27 (2012)
8. Yang, W., Wang, J., Guo, J.: A novel algorithm for satellite images fusion based on compressed sensing and PCA. In: Mathematical Problems in Engineering, pp. 1–10 (2013)
9. Miao, Q.G., Shi, C., Xu, P.F., Yang, M., Shi, Y.B.: Multi-focus image fusion algorithm based on shearlets. Chin. Opti. Lett. 9(4), 1–5 (2011)
10. Li, S., Yang, B.: Multifocus image fusion by combining curvelet and wavelet transform. Pattern Recogn. Lett. 29(9), 295–1301 (2008)
11. Miao, Q.G., Wang, B.S.: A novel image fusion method using contourlet transform. In: 2006 International Conference on Communications, Circuits and Systems Proceedings, vol. 1, pp. 548–552 (2006)
12. Lu, J., Zhang, C.-J., Hu, M., Chen, H.: NonSubsampled contourlet transform combined with energy entropy for remote sensing image fusion. In: 2009 International Conference on Artificial Intelligence and Computation Intelligence, vol. 3, pp. 530–534 (2009)
13. Yan, X., Han, H.-L., Liu, S.-Q., Yang, T.-W., Yang, Z.-J., Xue, L.-Z.: Image fusion based on tetrolet transform. J. Optoelectron. Laser 24(8), 1629–1633 (2013)
14. Easley, G., Labate, D., Lim, W.-Q.: Sparse directional image representations using the discrete shearlet transform. Appl. Comput. Harmonic Anal. 25(1), 25–46 (2008)
15. Miao, Q., Shi, C., Xu, P., Yang, M., Shi, Y.: A novel algorithm of image fusion using shearlets. Opt. Commun. 284(6), 1540–1547 (2011)
16. Liu, X., Zhou, Y., Wang, J.: Image fusion based on shearlet transform and regional features. Int. J. Electron. Commun. 68(6), 471–477 (2014)
17. Moria, I.S., Jamie, P.H.: Review of image fusion technology in 2005. In: Thermosense XXVII, vol. 5782, pp. 29–45 (2005)
18. Zhang, C.J., Wang, X.D., Duanmu, C.J.: Adaptive typhoon cloud image enhancement using genetic algorithm and non-linear gain operation in undecimated wavelet domain. Eng. Appl. Artif. Intell. 23(1), 61–73 (2010)
19. Lewis, J.J., O'Callaghan, R.J., Nikolov, S.G., Bull, D.R., Canagarajah, N.: Pixel-and region-based image fusion with complex wavelets. Inf. Fusion 8(2), 119–130 (2007)
20. Zhang, C.J., Chen, Y., Lu, J.: Typhoon center location algorithm based on fractal feature and gradient of infrared satellite cloud image. In: International Conference on Optoelectronic Technology and Application, pp. 92990F-1–92990F-6 (2014)

Biological and Medical Image Processing

Parallel Regional Growth Marching Cubes: Efficient Surface Reconstruction Based on MPI

Xiaohui Wei[1], Xinyan Bao[1], Xiaoli Pang[2(✉)], and Haolong Cui[1]

[1] College of Computer Science and Technology, Jilin University,
Changchun 130012, People's Republic of China
weixh@jlu.edu.cn, xybao15@mails.jlu.edu.cn,
cuihaolongjacky@foxmail.com
[2] The First Clinical Hospital, Jilin University,
Changchun 130012, People's Republic of China
px10811@126.com

Abstract. Three-dimensional surface reconstruction from medical images is an important task in clinical medical practice. Of all the methods for extracting surfaces from scalar fields, marching cubes algorithm is most popular due to its simplicity. In this contribution, we developed a robust and efficient algorithm for reconstructing surfaces from tomography images such as CT and MRI, in which we combine the regional growth marching cubes algorithm with message passing interface to highly parallelize the extracting process. The scalar field is first partitioned into parts and for each part, a process is created to run the regional growth marching cubes on the part. The parallel processing is implemented using MPI. Experiments show that the method has a higher efficiency in time than both marching cubes and regional growth marching cubes algorithms.

Keywords: Marching cubes · Regional growth marching cubes
3D reconstruction · Parallel computing · MPI

1 Introduction

The medical image data acquired using tomography imaging machines such as CT and MRI typically forms a regular distribution data field in 3D space, which is also referred to as volume data. Three-dimensional surface reconstruction from the volume data is usually performed for visualization, feature computing and computer-aided design. The cost of rendering and manipulating surface models is much less than that of volume models, and the surface rendering process can be highly accelerated with modern graphic hardware which is critical in real-time application. Therefore, surface model is a widely used tool for data visualization [1]. In addition, surface model is necessary for some modern industrial manufacture such as 3D printing.

Several algorithms have been proposed on surface reconstruction. Ekou [2] developed a contour-connecting method in which closed contours in each slice are first

© Springer International Publishing AG 2017
Y. Zhao et al. (Eds.): ICIG 2017, Part II, LNCS 10667, pp. 455–465, 2017.
https://doi.org/10.1007/978-3-319-71589-6_39

generated, then the whole surface is reconstructed by connecting the contours between adjacent slices. Yang [3] proposed an SMC method which connects the triangular facets in each cube through estimating state value of each vertex of the cube. Among all the surface reconstruction algorithms, the marching cubes (MC) algorithm proposed by Lorensen in 1987 is the most commonly used one due to its simplicity on understanding and implementation [4]. The algorithm proceeds through all elements (voxel) in the volume data, taking eight neighbor voxels at a time to define a cube, then computing the polygons which are the local surface in the cube. After processing all cubes, the polygons are merged to form a whole surface.

The original MC algorithm needs scan all cubes in the volume data, and much time is wasted on empty cubes where no polygon exists. This promotes some improved versions of MC algorithm aiming to accelerate the surface generating process by ignoring empty cubes. One of those is regional growth MC (RGMC) algorithm, which first selects a seed cube exactly intersects the target surface, then extract polygons in the cubes adjacent to the seed. These new cubes are queued as new seeds and the operations are repeated on these new cubes until the queue becomes empty. Since only cubes intersect the target surface would be considered during this process, the time is highly saved.

Parallel processing is another powerful way to speed up the extraction process by dividing the computation into several parts and process each part with a single core in CPU. This promotes the work in this paper. Among all the parallel computing frameworks, message passing interface (MPI) has become a de facto standard for communication among processes that model a parallel programming due to its openness and portability. In this work, we choose MPICH as the implementation of MPI for its high performance and easiness to use.

In this paper, we combine parallel computing and RGMC to further accelerate the process of surface extraction. The volume data is partitioned into several parts, and a single seed is initially selected manually for each part. Then RGMC is applied on each part in a single process started using MPICH. After extracting, the whole surface is smoothed to make a better visual effect.

2   Related Work

2.1   Marching Cubes

Marching cubes is a classical algorithm of surface extracting in 3D data visualization field. The algorithm assumes that the original data is a discrete three-dimensional regular data field defined on a volume data. When a cube intersects the surface, the algorithm first computes the intersecting vertices of the surface and cube edges using linear interpolation technique, then connects the vertices to form triangles which are the approximation of the surface in the cube. After traversing all the cubes, a whold surface is extracted.

Let $f(x, y, z)$ be a scalar function defined on the 3D volume data $V = \{v_{i,j,k}\}_{i,j,k=0,0,0}^{M,N,K}$, with $v_{i,j,k}$ to be voxel at (i, j, k). The MC algorithm divides the space of the volume data into a series of small cubes whose eight points are the voxels on each pair of adjacent slices along z direction. Mathematically, the surface corresponding to a given isovalue c_0 is the point set defined in the following way [5]:

$$\{(x, y, z)|f(x, y, z) = c_0\} \tag{1}$$

In discrete case, the surface is represented as a set of polygons which are the intersection of the surface and the cubes. Thus the basic question is how to determine whether a single edge of any cube intersects the surface. A simple answer to this question is: when the function value at one end of the edge is greater than or equal to c_0 (+), and the function value at the other end is less than c_0 (−), the edge intersects the surface. Since each point of a cube has two states (±), there are altogether 256 cases for any cube which forms a case table. There is a single index of any cube in the case table and from the index we can easily determine the states of the points in the cube. For more details, please refer to [4]. After finding the index of a cube in the case table, the coordinates of the vertices on an edge can be computed by the following linear interpolation process. Let e be the edge of a cube and S be the surface, the intersection of S and e is:

$$\mathbf{X} = \mathbf{P_1} + (c_0 - V_1)(\mathbf{P_2} - \mathbf{P_1})/(V_2 - V_1) \tag{2}$$

where $\mathbf{X}$ is the intersection vertex of e and S, $\mathbf{P_1}$, $\mathbf{P_2}$ are the two endpoints of e, $V1 = f(\mathbf{P_1})$ and $V2 = f(\mathbf{P_2})$ are the values of the scalar function f at the two endpoints. After obtaining the intersection of S and all the edges in each cube, the polygons in that cube can be determined considering the index of the states of the cube [6].

The normal vector at $\mathbf{X}$ is also required in the surface rendering tasks, the normal vector can be computed at the same time when computing the coordinate of $\mathbf{X}$. Central difference is used to calculate the normal vectors at each point of e, and the normal vector of $\mathbf{X}$ is computed by linear interpolating the normal vectors at $\mathbf{P_1}$ and $\mathbf{P_2}$. For any voxel $v_{i,j,k} = (x_i, y_j, z_k)$, the gradient of f at $v_{i,j,k}$ is:

$$g_x = \frac{[f(x_{i+1}, y_j, z_k) - f(x_{i-1}, y_j, z_k)]}{2\Delta x} \tag{3}$$

$$g_y = \frac{[f(x_i, y_{j+1}, z_k) - f(x_i, y_{j-1}, z_k)]}{2\Delta y} \tag{4}$$

$$g_z = \frac{[f(x_i, y_j, z_{k+1}) - f(x_i, y_j, z_{k-1})]}{2\Delta z} \tag{5}$$

where Δx, Δy, Δz are the lengths of the edges of the cube respectively. Then the normal vector of S at $v_{i,j,k}$ is:

$$\mathbf{g} = (g_x, g_y, g_z) \tag{6}$$

After normalizing $\mathbf{g}$ to a unit vector, the normal vector of S at $\mathbf{X}$ can be computed using the following linear interpolation:

$$\mathbf{N} = \mathbf{N}_1 + (c_0 - V_1)(\mathbf{N}_2 - \mathbf{N}_1)/(V_2 - V_1) \tag{7}$$

Where $\mathbf{N}_1 = \mathbf{g}(\mathbf{P}_1)$ and $\mathbf{N}_2 = \mathbf{g}(\mathbf{P}_2)$ are the normal vectors of S at $\mathbf{P}_1$ and $\mathbf{P}_2$ respectively.

Marching cubes algorithm flow:

1. Read the three-dimensional discrete data field and construct state table;
2. Scan each two layers of the data to construct cubes whose eight points are taken from two adjacent layers;
3. Scan all cubes. For each cube, the function value of each point of the cube is compared with the given isovalue of the surface, and the values are used to determine the index of current cube in case table;
4. Compute the intersection of the cube edge and the surface by linear interpolation method using (2) and generate polygons in the cube;
5. Compute the normal vectors of intersection vertices using (7);
6. Combine polygons in all cubes into a whole surface mesh.

2.2 Regional Growth MC Algorithm

The classic MC algorithm traverses all the cubes in the volume data, however, in general most cubes do not intersect the surface thus much time is wasted on empty cubes. To solve this problem, Kai [7] proposed a regional growth MC algorithm. First, a seed cube, which is a cube intersects the surface, is searched among all the cubes. The seed cube is immediately pushed into a queue and marked as visited. Then a loop process is applied on the queue. While the queue is not empty, the head cube will be popped out to compute the polygons inside it. Then its neighbors that have not been marked as visited and intersect the surface are pushed into the queue. This pop-compute-push process is repeated until the queue becomes empty. This way, traversing empty cubes is avoided and much time is saved. The workflow of RGMC is shown in Fig. 1.

2.3 MPI Programming

As a de facto standard, MPI has been widely accepted in high-performance computing systems [8, 9] for it provides a language independent platform. It provides bindings with C, C++ and Fortran languages which makes it a feasible tool in programming practice. MPI has the advantages of good portability and high efficiency, and can be used in heterogeneous environments. There are many different free, efficient and practical versions of MPI [10].

In most parallel programming, there are six most commonly used basic interfaces of MPI, and we only need four of them [11, 12].

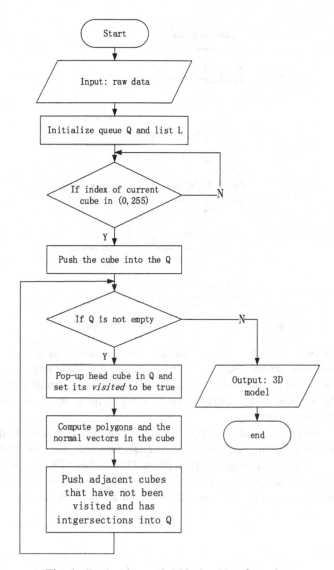

Fig. 1. Regional growth MC algorithm flow chart

3   Method

In this section, we will explain the details of our method of surface extracting from volume data, combined RGMC and MPI. The process is based on VTK/ITK pipelines and can be divided into the following steps: read, reconstruct, post-process and output.

The flow chart of this article is shown in Fig. 2.

3.1   Read Data

Digital Imaging and Communications in Medicine (DICOM) is a standard for handling, storing, printing, and transmitting information in medical imaging. DICOM is widely

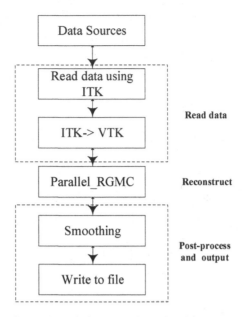

Fig. 2. A pipeline for three-dimensional reconstruction

used in radiotherapy, cardiovascular imaging and radiation diagnostic equipment (X-ray, CT, nuclear magnetic resonance, ultrasound, etc.). It has a large data dictionary, which contains almost all the medical environment under the common data, and can be a complete description of a variety of medical equipment, image format data and patient-related information.

Many software can read DICOM files, of which ITK and VTK are taken as the best combination for they can not only read and write DICOM files, but also provide a lot of useful medical image processing functionalities. That makes ITK and VTK a widely used set of tools for manipulating medical images and creating medical applications.

In this work, we use ITK to read DICOM data and use itk::ImageToVTKImage Filter to prepare data for VTK.

3.2 Reconstruct

For processing the volume data in parallel, the volume data is divided into multiple parts and the RGMC procedure described in Sect. 2.2 is applied on each part separately, with a single process created and assigned to each part using MPICH.

There are two basic MPI parallel programming modes: peer-to-peer and master-slave. We use peer-to-peer mode because each process is responsible for the processing of different parts of the same data space.

MPI will start multiple processes and call the following MAIN procedure in each process. The number of processes and the id of current process could be extracted from the arguments passed to the MAIN procedure, based on MPI mechanism. Let *imwidth* and *iheight* be the width and height of the volume data along x-y direction, the reconstruct process is shown in the following algorithm:

Algorithm 1.MAIN

Input: set *nproc* as the value of number of processes, set *rank_mpi* as the id of current process
1. **If** (rank_mpi>=0)
2.   Read image data using ITK as IM
3.   Pass IM to VTK
4.   Set size=IM.dimZ/nproc
5.   Generate CubeList from IM
6.   Perform Parallel_RGMC(size,rank_mpi,CubeList)
7. **End If**

Algorithm 2.Parallel_RGMC

Input: set *size* as the value of number of layers of cubes to be processed, set *rank_mpi* as the id of current process, set *CubeList* as the Cubes generated from the volume data
1. Build case table:CT
2. Set *visited=0* for all cubes in CubeList
3. **For** k=(rank_mpi*size),k<((rank_mpi+1)*size),k++
4.   **For** j=0,j<(imheight-1),j++
5.   **For** i=0,i<(imwidth-1),i++
6.   Index=index of cube in CT (refer to 2.1)
7.   **If** Index!=0 and Index!=255
8.   CubeQueue.push(cube)
9.   **End If**
10.   **Goto** SeedFound
11.   **End For**
12.   **End For**
13. **End For**
14. **SeedFound:**
15.   **While**!CubeQueue.empty()
16.   cube=CubeQueue.pop()
17.   find the cube that has not been visited
18.   Perform a linear interpolation calculation
19.   Generates triangles
20.   **For** nbcube in neighbor cubes
21.   **If** nbcube.visited==1 **Continue**
22.   **End If**
23.   Index=index of cube in CT
24.   **If** Index!=0 and Index!=255
25.   CubeQueue.push(nbcube)
26.   **End If**
27.   **End For**
28. **End While**

In VTK, the classic MC algorithm is implemented in class VtkMarchingCubes. Since there is no RGMC implementation in VTK, we must extent VTK to realize this functionality. We wrote a class named vtkRGMarchingCubes, in which most code comes from VtkMarchingCubes except that some functions are modified to implement the parallel RGMC algorithm.

3.3   Post-Process and Output

Before outputting the result surface, some further operations are needed for achieving a better visual effect. If the CT slices along the z-axis are not fine enough, the surface obtained will produce terraces (see Fig. 3(a)).

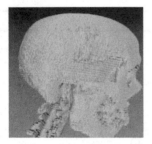
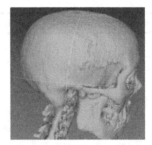

(a) Surface before smoothing   (b) Surface after smoothing

Fig. 3. Meshes before and after smoothing. The original surface has terrace effect (a), and a surface smoothing process is applied on the surface using vtkSmoothPolyDataFilter (b).

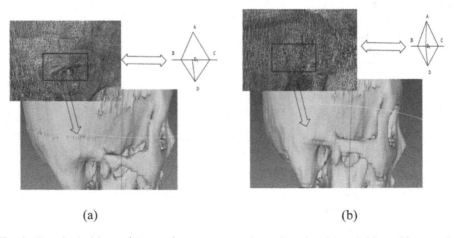

(a)   (b)

Fig. 4. Topological inconsistency along common edges of meshes (a) and this problem can be solved using triangular refinement techniques

In order to solve this problem, we use the vtkSmoothPolyDataFilter to smooth the result data, which is a filter that adjusts point coordinates using Laplacian operation. We took the default settings of vtkSmoothPolyDataFilter, of which the iteration number is 20 and relaxation factor is 0.01. The smoothing result is shown in Fig. 3(b). ·

Since the meshes in different part are generated separately, there might be topology inconsistency along the common boundary of adjacent meshes (see Fig. 4(a)). This topological problem can be corrected using triangular refinement techniques (see Fig. 4 (b)). For two parallel regions, look at their demarcation line (z-axis at k) for isolated nodes (e.g. point D_1). Then connect D_1 to a point that is not connected, which belongs to a triangle that has a common edge on another region.

4   Experimental Results

4.1   Programming Environment

CPU: Intel(R) Core(TM)2 Quad CPU Q9400 @2.66 GHz 2.67 GHz
RAM: 5.00 GB
Operating System: Windows7 64bit
Application software: ITK VTK
Development environment: Microsoft Visual Studio 2013

4.2   Results and Discussion

Three cases (skull, femur, forearm bone) were tested. The comparison of running time using MC, RGMC and our method 2 processes is shown in Table 1. As can be seen from the table that our method overcomes the other two significantly.

Table 1. Running time in seconds of MC, regional growth MC and our method

		MC algorithm	RGMC	Our method
Reconstruction	Skull	9.917	9.296	4.778
	Femur	4.011	3.861	1.912
	Forearm bones	2.762	2.653	1.388

Table 2 lists the experimental results under different number of processes.

Table 2. Experiments under different number of processes

Number processes	Running time (s)		
	Skull	Femur	Forearm bones
1	9.296	3.861	2.653
2	4.778	1.912	1.388
3	3.478	1.206	0.903

Figure 5(a) (b) (c) is the result of the RGMC algorithm, Fig. 5(d) (e) (f) is the result of our method with 2 processes. The reconstruction results of each process is colored in red and gray respectively.

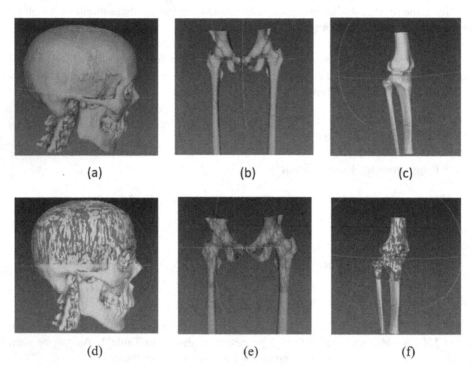

Fig. 5. The reconstruction result of RGMC and our method (Color figure online)

4.3   Evaluation

In order to assess the similarity between our reconstructed results and the RGMC reconstruction results, we used the hausdorff distance.

The hausdorff distance is a measure of the degree of similarity between two sets of point sets, which is a definition of the distance between two sets of points:

Assuming that there are two sets of sets $A = \{a_1, \ldots, a_p\}$, $B = \{b_1, \ldots b_q\}$, then the hausdorff distance between the two points is defined as:

$$H(A,B) = \max[h(A,B), h(B,A)] \tag{8}$$

where: $h(A,B) = \max_{a \in A} \min_{b \in B} ||a - b||$, $h(B,A) = \max_{b \in B} \min_{a \in A} ||b - a||$, $|| \bullet ||$ is the distance between the A and B points (e.g., L2 or Euclidean distance), h(A,B),h(B,A) are called the one-way hausdorff distance from A set to B set and from set B to set A, respectively. That is, h(A,B) actually first sorts the distance $||a_i - b_j||$ between each point a_i in point set A to the point b_j closest to this point a_i, and then take the maximum value in the distance as the value of h(A,B).h(B,A) is equally available. From the formula (1), the bidirectional hausdorff distance H (A, B) is the larger of the two-way distance h (A, B) and h (B, A), which measures the interval between two points maximum degree of mismatch.

Here we evaluate the results of these three datasets separately are 0.79511, 0.59136, 0.601142.

5 Conclusions

A parallel regional growth MC algorithm is presented which significantly overcomes the classic and regional growth MC algorithms in time efficiency. The scalar field is partitioned into several parts and the RGMC is applied for each part in different processes using MPI. Experiment illustrates that about 50% of time will be saved compared with classical MC algorithm and RGMC algorithms.

References

1. Gong, F., Zhao, X.: Three-dimensional reconstruction of medical image based on improved marching cubes algorithm. In: 2010 International Conference on Machine Vision and Human-Machine Interface (MVHI), pp. 608–611. IEEE (2010)
2. Yang, X.D., Liu, B.H., Wang, Y.: Triangular surface reconstruction of CT images by using isosurface construction. In: 6th International Conference on e-Engineering and Digital Enterprise Technology, pp. 503–507 (2008)
3. Herman, G.T., Liu, H.K.: Three-dimensional display of human organs from computed tomograms. Comput. Graph. Image Process. 9(1), 1–21 (1979)
4. Lorensen, W.E., Cline, H.E.: Marching cubes: a high resolution 3D surface construction algorithm. In: ACM Siggraph Computer Graphics, vol. 21, no. 4, pp. 163–169. ACM (1987)
5. Malagis. http://malagis.com/marching-cubes-algorithm.html. Accessed 28 Mar 2017
6. Wang, X., Wang, Z.: 3D reconstruction of medical images via nearest neighbor-based marching cubes algorithm. Comput. Eng. Appl. 48(18), 154–158 (2012)
7. Kai, Z., Lingzhong, F., HaiFang, L.: 3D reconstruction of brain atlas based on modified marching cubes algorithm. J. Comput. Appl. Softw. 33(4), 177–182 (2016)
8. Yu, X., Ge, H., He, J., et al.: MPI-based parallel medical image processing. Comput. Eng. Sci. 31(3), 32–34 (2009)
9. Jia, R.: Research on CT filtered back projection algorithm of image reconstruction based on MPI parallel computing. J. Inner Mongolia Agric. Univ. Nat. Sci. Ed. 2, 131–136 (2015)
10. Du, Z., Li, S., Shen, Y., et al.: Parallel programming technique for high performance computation - MPI parallel programming. Tsinghua University Press, Beijing (2001)
11. Chen, G.: Parallel Computing: Structure, Algorithm, Programming. Higher Education Press (2011)
12. Zhou, E.-Q., Zhao, J.-Q.: Efficient implementation of MPI and MPI. Comput. Eng. Sci. 21(5), 47–51 (2010)

Shape Registration and Low-Rank for Multiple Image Segmentation

Wei Hua and Fei Chen[✉]

College of Mathematics and Computer Science, Fuzhou University, Fuzhou, China
chenfei314@fzu.edu.cn

Abstract. Shape similarity is a useful cue for multiple image segmentations. In this paper, a shape registration and low rank based active contour model is developed to segment similar shapes. Under the assumption that the object shapes have similar contours, shape registration is quite helpful to object segmentation and the matrix formed by the shapes of object has a low-rank property. Given a group of multiple test images, normalization and circulant shift are used to register the shapes of objects, and a low-rank constraint is employed during the evolution of object contours. The proposed method could handle complex transformations of image group well, such as large-angle rotation. Experiments on the synthesized and real multiple images show that the proposed approach consistently improves the performance of active contour model and yields more accurate contours than previous methods.

Keywords: Active contours · Segmentation · Registration
Group similarity · Low-rank

1 Introduction

Image segmentation is a fundamental problem in computer vision, and has been widely used in medical analysis, remote sensing and video surveillance, etc. Among various applications, active contours model is popular in image segmentation. Active contours with edge-detection [4,13,14] and region information [6,16,17] are two classical methods for image segmentation by minimizing certain energies to match the object boundary. In real applications, the performance of active contour method is unsatisfactory because of the misleading or missing feature in images, therefore, researchers have developed many ways to model the prior of shapes and use the shape prior to restrict evolvement of contours.

The addition of shape prior information has significantly improve object segmentation results. Chan and Zhu [5] inspired by the work of [8] introduces a labelling function which together with the level set function for object segmentation. In [19], shape prior is used to simultaneously segment multiple, possible overlapping objects. In addition to single shape prior, statistical information of given shapes could be used for accurate segmentation results. In [1], using active contour method, a geometric shape prior and the Mumford-Shah functional as

ⓒ Springer International Publishing AG 2017
Y. Zhao et al. (Eds.): ICIG 2017, Part II, LNCS 10667, pp. 466–475, 2017.
https://doi.org/10.1007/978-3-319-71589-6_40

complementary terms to segment an object. Jiang et al. [12] incorporated the generic knowledge of object and object boundary information into salient object segmentation. Recently, leaning methods are the attractive topic because of the excellent ability to cope with image noise and clutter. [7] use deep Boltzmann machine to learn shape priors from a training set of shapes. [20] employed the sparse shape composition to represent object shapes and proposed an effective shape prior modeling for segmentation.

An unsupervised approach of shape prior modeling [23] was proposed, which used the group similarity of shapes to segment objects from multiple images and utilized low-rank to restrain the evolution of contour. However, the method could not perform well when the contours of similar objects in multiple images are transformed with large rotation or scaling. In other words, the different pose of objects contour would limit the performance of low-rank.

It is reasonable to assume that the vectorized object shapes in multiple images form a low-rank matrix. However, similar shapes without registration will increase the rank of matrix, therefore it would lead a poor constraint on group similarity during the curve evolution. In order to enforce low-rank on similar shapes further, a shape registration is introduced for collaborative segmentation. The contributions of this paper are as follows:

1. A generic framework for joint object segmentation and shape registration is developed. By minimizing the proposed energy functional, segmentation and registration procedures are carried out simultaneously.
2. Circulant structure is adopted to shape registration, and it could be effectively solved by using Fast Fourier Transform (FFT).
3. Note that the matrix which contains vectors of similar shapes would be low-rank. Collaborative segmentation in multiple images is well performed by using SVD based low-rank matrix approximation, and it is robust to various disturbing factors such as noises, partial occlusions, missing information, etc.

The rest of the paper is organized as follows: Sect. 2 introduces the basic theory of our method and describes the algorithm to solve our method. Section 3 demonstrates experimental results. Finally, Sect. 4 gives some conclusions.

2   The Proposed Method

2.1   Necessity of Registration

Given a set of shapes $C_1 \cdots, C_n$, each shape could be represented by using a set of land-marks, $C_i = [x_{i,1}, \cdots, x_{i,p}, y_{i,1}, \cdots, y_{i,p}]^T$, where $(x_{i,j}, y_{i,j})$ is a landmark on the outline of the shape. It is assumedthat the object shapes have similar contours, C_i could be approximately generated from C_1 by certain affine transformation. Given a landmark $q = (x, y)$, we have coordinate transformation $q' = Mq + \tau$, where M and τ are the transformation matrix and translation, respectively. Usually, M consists of rotation θ and scale σ. Therefore, for each point, the affine transformation can be represented as follows:

$$\begin{bmatrix} x' \\ y' \end{bmatrix} = \begin{bmatrix} \cos\theta & -\sin\theta \\ \sin\theta & \cos\theta \end{bmatrix} \begin{bmatrix} \sigma & 0 \\ 0 & \sigma \end{bmatrix} \begin{bmatrix} x \\ y \end{bmatrix} + \begin{bmatrix} \tau_x \\ \tau_y \end{bmatrix}$$
$$= \begin{bmatrix} \sigma\cos\theta & -\sigma\sin\theta \\ \sigma\sin\theta & \sigma\cos\theta \end{bmatrix} \begin{bmatrix} x \\ y \end{bmatrix} + \begin{bmatrix} \tau_x \\ \tau_y \end{bmatrix} \tag{1}$$

For simplicity, we can represent C_i as $C_i = \Phi w_i$, where

$$\Phi = \begin{bmatrix} C_1^x & 0 & C_1^y & 0 & 1 & 0 \\ 0 & C_1^x & 0 & C_1^y & 0 & 1 \end{bmatrix}$$
$$w_i = \begin{bmatrix} \sigma_i\cos\theta_i, \sigma_i\sin\theta_i, -\sigma_i\sin\theta_i, \sigma_i\cos\theta_i, \tau_{ix}, \tau_{iy} \end{bmatrix}^T$$

Since Φ only depends on C_1, we have $\mathbf{C} = \Phi[w_1, w_2, \cdots, w_n]$, where $\mathbf{C} = [C_1, C_2, \cdots, C_n]$. Obviously, $Rank(C) \leq 6$. This implies that the rank of transformational matrix $[w_1, w_2, \cdots, w_n]$ is at most 6. The lower the rank of $\mathbf{C}$, the higher the level of the correlation or structure similarity among shapes in $\mathbf{C}$.

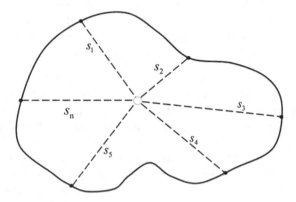

Fig. 1. The diagram of the vector **p**. Let s_i be the distance from landmark (solid circle) to centroid (hollow circle), and d is the maximum of s_i which could be used for normalization, therefore $p_i = s_i/d$.

Minimization of the rank of $\mathbf{C}$ has two principal effects. One encourages shape registration from multiple images, and the other is shape regularization that eliminates the difference between different shapes and keeps the main parts of structure similarity among shapes. Due to various disturbing factors such as noises, occlusion, etc., it is difficult to balance shape registration and regularization by using low-rank matrix approximation. Note that similar shapes without registration would increase the rank of $\mathbf{C}$. When some dissimilar shapes which could not generated from C_1 through transformation, the rank of shape matrix starts to mushroom, even more than 6, thereby it could not constrain the curve evolution well. To handle this, we propose an algorithm for joint shape registration and low-rank for object segmentation. Inspired by the work of Yezzi et al. [21, 22], object segmentation and registration are closely related problems, and it is widely accepted that registration is helpful to object segmentation and vice versa.

After shape alignment, the original vector C_i is transformed into a new vector $g(C_i)$, where g is the registration function. Therefore, the low-rank of aligned shape matrix $[g(C_1), g(C_2), \cdots, g(C_n)] \in \mathbb{R}^{2p \times n}$ would encourage shape regularization and it could be used as a shape constraint.

2.2 Shape Registration

The role of registration is to eliminate the deformations of unaligned shapes, therefore it needs to cope with affine transformations, such as rotation, stretching and displacement. Here, an unadorned ideal is used to deal with displacement and stretching. First, the centroid of shape C_i is calculated and denoted by O_i. Second, we compute the distance to the centroid of shape for each landmark, and use the maximum d_i to normalize all distances. As shown in Fig. 1, all nomalized distances are denoted by $p_0, p_1, \cdots, p_n$, where p_i denotes the nomalized distance from its centroid to ith landmark (x_i, y_i). The first step is to eliminate the effect of displacement and second one for the stretching.

The main observation in this work is that rotation invariance can be solved by circulant shift. Let $\mathbf{p} = [p_0, p_1, \cdots, p_n]$ denote the vector formed by all nomalized distances of shape. An $n \times n$ circulant matrix $U(\mathbf{p})$ is obtained from the vector $\mathbf{p}$ by concatenating all possible cyclic shifts of $\mathbf{p}$:

$$
U(\mathbf{p}) = \begin{bmatrix}
p_0 & p_1 & p_2 & \cdots & p_{n-1} \\
p_{n-1} & p_0 & p_1 & \cdots & p_{n-2} \\
p_{n-2} & p_{n-1} & p_0 & \cdots & p_{n-3} \\
\vdots & \vdots & \vdots & \cdots & \vdots \\
p_1 & p_2 & p_3 & \cdots & p_0
\end{bmatrix} \tag{2}
$$

Clearly, the first row is vector $\mathbf{p}$, and the second row is $\mathbf{p}$ shifted one element to the right. Given a vector $\mathbf{v}$, the product $U(\mathbf{p})\mathbf{v}$ represents convolution of vectors $\mathbf{p}$ and $\mathbf{v}$ [10], and it can be computed in the Fourier domain, using

$$
U(\mathbf{p})\mathbf{v} = \mathcal{F}^{-1}(\mathcal{F}(\mathbf{p}) \odot \mathcal{F}(\mathbf{v})) \tag{3}
$$

where $\odot$ denotes the element-wise product, while $\mathcal{F}^{-1}$ and $\mathcal{F}$ is the Fourier transform and its inverse, respectively. Because the circulant matrix U is defined by $\mathbf{p}$ and the element of $U(\mathbf{p})$ can be represented as $u_{ij} = p_{(j-i) \bmod n}$, we never should explicitly store and compute the entire matrix U.

Rotation alignment between C_i and C_j can be represented as circulant shift of the curve, namely, C_i can be approximately generated from C_j through circulant shifting z elements, where z is the number of elements shifted. Therefore, the problem of rotation invariance is converted to find the accurate value of z. Let $\mathbf{p}_i$ and $\mathbf{p}_j$ denote the distance vectors of C_i and C_j, respectively. Due to the circulant convolution of $\mathbf{p}_i \star \mathbf{p}_j$, we can quickly evaluate all locations of curve C_j according to reference curve C_i by using FFT [10,11], with $\star$ denoting the complex-conjugate,

$$
\mathbf{k}^{gauss} = \exp(-\frac{1}{\phi}(\|\mathbf{p}_i\|^2 + \|\mathbf{p}_j\|^2 - 2\mathcal{F}^{-1}(\mathcal{F}(\mathbf{p}_i) \odot \mathcal{F}^*(\mathbf{p}_j)))) \tag{4}
$$

Here the Gaussian kernel function is used and ϕ is the corresponding constant, and $\mathbf{k}^{gauss}$ measures the similarity between the curve C_i and C_j. Obviously, the optimal z is the index of the maximum of $\mathbf{k}^{guass}$. In shape registration, there are 3 parameters: the shape centroid O, the maximum distance d, and the shifted number z. More details about registration are shown in Algorithm 1.

Algorithm 1. Registration based on circulant matrix

---

1 **Input**: Unregistered $C_1, \cdots, C_n$

2 **Output**: Registered $\hat{C}_1, \cdots, \hat{C}_n$ and corresponding registration parameter
$$\delta_1, \cdots, \delta_n$$

3 **Initialization:**Initialize m the number of landmarks

4 **Registration:**

Loop: for $i = 1 : n$ do:

(1) For C_i, its centroid $O_i = (O_i^x, O_i^y)$ and maximum distance d_i is calculated:

$$(O_i^x, O_i^y) = \frac{1}{m} \sum_{j}^{m} (x_j, y_j)$$

$$d_i = \max_{1 \leq j \leq m} (\|(x_j - O_i^x, y_j - O_i^y)\|)$$

where (x_j, y_j) is the landmark of C_i

(2) Move C_i to the coordinate system whose origin is the centroid, and normalize the distance:

$$C_i^* = (C_i - (O_i^x, O_i^y))/d_i$$

(3) Compute $\mathbf{k}^{gauss}$ via Eq. (4) then find the index z_i of maximum value. After shifting z_i element, C_i is be registered with C_1

$$\hat{C}_i = circshift(C_i^*, z_i)$$

Lastly, $\delta_i = \{O_i, d_i, z_i\}$, circshift is a MATLAB function.

End for

2.3   Segmentation with Shape Registration and Low-Rank

Given a group of images $I_1, \cdots, I_n$, we want to find corresponding curves $C_1, \cdots, C_n$ to segment their objects. By using shape similarity during curve evolution, an energy function based on shape registration and low-rank is proposed:

$$\min_{\{\delta_i\}, \{C_i\}} \sum_{i=1}^{n} f_i(C_i) + \lambda \|\mathbf{Y}\|_* \tag{5}$$

where $\mathbf{Y} = [g(C_1), g(C_2), \cdots, g(C_n)]$, and $\|\mathbf{Y}\|_*$ is the nuclear norm, λ is a regularization parameter, the larger the λ the higher similarity, the smaller the λ the greater change. In registration of shape C_i, the corresponding transformation parameters $\delta_i = \{O_i, d_i, z_i\}$ could be calculated for each curves. Here, $f_i(C_i)$ is the energy of active contour model, such as CV model [6], snake model [14], geodesic active contour [3,9]. For simplicity, CV model is adopted as data term in the proposed model:

$$f_i(C_i) = \int_{\Omega_1} (I_i(\mathbf{x}) - u_1)^2 dx + \int_{\Omega_2} (I_i(\mathbf{x}))^2 dx$$
$$+ \beta \text{length}(C_i)$$

where Ω_1 and Ω_2 denote the regions inside and outside. u_1 and u_2 are the mean intensities of Ω_1 and Ω_2, respectively. β is a constant.

To optimize the energy function in (5), the proximal gradient method [15] is used for the following category of problems:

$$\min_{\mathbf{C}} F(\mathbf{C}) + \lambda \mathcal{R}(\mathbf{Y}) \tag{6}$$

where $\mathcal{R}(\mathbf{Y})$ is $\|\mathbf{Y}\|_*$. Therefore, the following iteration is applied:

$$\mathbf{Y}^{k+1} = \arg\min_{\mathbf{Y}} \frac{1}{2} \|\mathbf{Y} - [\mathbf{Y}^k - \frac{1}{\mu} \nabla F(\mathbf{Y}^k)]\|_F^2 + \frac{\lambda}{\mu} \mathcal{R}(\mathbf{Y}) \tag{7}$$

It could be solved by the singular value thresholding algorithm, and the final $\mathbf{C}^{k+1}$ can be obtained by the inverse function of g:

$$\mathbf{C}^{k+1} = g^{-1}(\mathcal{D}_{\frac{\lambda}{\mu}}(\mathbf{Y} - \frac{1}{\mu} \nabla F(\mathbf{Y}^k))) \tag{8}$$

where $\mathcal{D}_{\frac{\lambda}{\mu}}$ is a singular value thresholding operator introduced by Cai et al. in [2].

3   Experimental Results

In this section, we evaluate our method on Heart image sequence as the synthesized dataset and on the real images of notebook. In our implementation, we also found that parameters λ in (6) is easier to choose than [23], because the effect of λ is reduced by shape registration.

To certify that registration can reduce the rank of shape matrix and improve the accuracy of segmentation, we rotate some images of Heart with different angles as shown in Fig. 2. The results of [9] without the similarity constraint aren't correctly segmented. We select the regularization parameter $\lambda = 25$ which products fairly good results. However, the method of [23] fails to segment the shapes accurately and its rank of shape matrix is 8. With a high $\lambda = 50$, the resulting shapes of [23] are more similar to each other, and their object shapes lost some important detail. Our results with the registration are more robust compared to the results without such constraint and the rank of output is 6. The proposed method is also applied to the images of notebook with distinct rotations, scaling and misleading information. As shown in the bottom of Fig. 3,

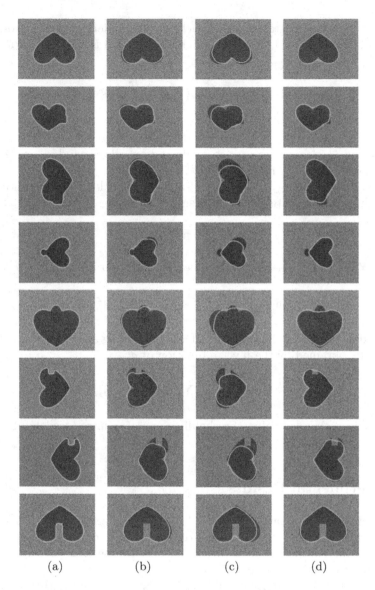

(a)   (b)   (c)   (d)

Fig. 2. Segmentation results on Heart with various rotation. (a) Results of [14], the rank is 8. (b) Results of [23] with a low λ, the rank is 8. (c) Results of [23] with a high λ, the rank is 6. (d) Results of the proposed model with registration, the rank is 6.

the rank of results is 3, much lower than [23] and [14]. It is clear that the proposed method is robust to deal with complex transformation of object shapes.

As shown in Table 1, Dice coefficient (Dice) and Hausdorff Distance (HD) [18] are used to quantitatively evaluate the segmentation results. We can see that [23] could not yields satisfactory result neither low λ nor high λ. Our method has a better segmentation result both in Dice and HD.

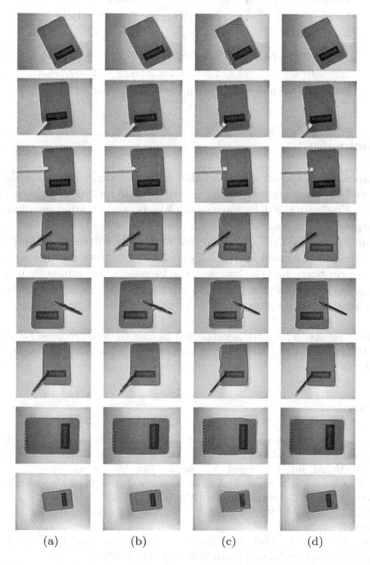

(a)   (b)   (c)   (d)

Fig. 3. Segmentation results on Heart with various rotation. (a) Results of [14], the rank is 8. (b) Results of [23] with a low λ, the rank is 8. (c) Results of [23] with a high λ, the rank is 6. (d) Results of the proposed model with registration, the rank is 6.

Table 1. Quantitative comparison. The values in each cell imply means/standard deviations of all frames in each image sequence.

Dataset	Heart		Notebook	
Metrics	Dice (%)	HD (px)	Dice (%)	HD (px)
Snake [14]	95.7/1.2	18.3/7.9	97.4/0.1	20.4/20.3
[23] with low λ	92.9/2.8	18.9/8.4	97.6/0.6	16.5/14.5
[23] with high λ	88.8/3.3	24.3/8.3	92.8/4.3	17.7/6.4
Proposed method	96.2/1.2	9.1/4.0	97.8/0.4	4.5/1.4

4 Conclusion

In this paper, we proposed a method that simultaneously estimates shape registration and object segmentation for group similar images. Shape registration was used to eliminate the deformations of objects, and rotation invariance could be represented by circulant convolution. Owe to the well-established theory of circulant matrices, rotation alignment was efficiently solved by using FFT. The shape matrix which formed by the curves of objects from multiple test images has low-rank property, and the low-rank can be used to regularize shapes. Experimental results show that the proposed method is able to cope with the group similar images more robustly.

Acknowledgments. This work is supported by the National Natural Science Foundation of China (61401098), and the Natural Science Foundation of Fujian Province (2017J0106).

References

1. Bresson, X., Vandergheynst, P., Thiran, J.P.: A variational model for object segmentation using boundary information and shape prior driven by the Mumford-Shah functional. Int. J. Comput. Vis. **68**(2), 145–162 (2006)
2. Cai, J.F., Candès, E.J., Shen, Z.: A singular value thresholding algorithm for matrix completion. SIAM J. Optim. **20**(4), 1956–1982 (2008)
3. Caselles, V., Kimmel, R., Sapiro, G.: Geodesic active contours. Int. J. Comput. Vis. **22**(1), 61–79 (1997)
4. Caselles, V., Catt, F., Coll, T., Dibos, F.: A geometric model for active contours in image processing. Numer. Math. **66**(1), 1–31 (1993)
5. Chan, T., Zhu, W.: Level set based shape prior segmentation. In: Proceedings of the IEEE Conference on Computer Vision and Pattern Recognition, vol. 2, pp. 1164–1170 (2005)
6. Chan, T.F., Vese, L.A.: Active contours without edges. IEEE Trans. Image Process. **10**(2), 266–277 (2001)
7. Chen, F., Yu, H., Hu, R., Zeng, X.: Deep learning shape priors for object segmentation. In: Proceedings of the IEEE Conference on Computer Vision and Pattern Recognition, pp. 1870–1877 (2013)

8. Cremers, D., Sochen, N., Schnörr, C.: Towards recognition-based variational segmentation using shape priors and dynamic labeling. In: Griffin, L.D., Lillholm, M. (eds.) Scale-Space 2003. LNCS, vol. 2695, pp. 388–400. Springer, Heidelberg (2003). https://doi.org/10.1007/3-540-44935-3_27

9. Goldenberg, R., Kimmel, R., Rivlin, E., Rudzsky, M.: Fast geodesic active contours. IEEE Trans. Image Process. **10**(10), 1467–75 (2001). A Publication of the IEEE Signal Processing Society

10. Gray, R.M.: Toeplitz and Circulant Matrices: A Review. Now Publishers Inc., Breda (2006)

11. Henriques, J.F., Caseiro, R., Martins, P., Batista, J.: Exploiting the circulant structure of tracking-by-detection with kernels. In: Fitzgibbon, A., Lazebnik, S., Perona, P., Sato, Y., Schmid, C. (eds.) ECCV 2012. LNCS, vol. 7575, pp. 702–715. Springer, Heidelberg (2012). https://doi.org/10.1007/978-3-642-33765-9_50

12. Jiang, H., Wang, J., Yuan, Z., Liu, T., Zheng, N., Li, S.: Automatic salient object segmentation based on context and shape prior. In: BMVC, vol. 6, p. 9 (2011)

13. Yezzi Jr., A., Kichenassamy, S., Kumar, A., Olver, P., Tannenbaum, A.: A geometric snake model for segmentation of medical imagery. IEEE Trans. Med. Imaging **16**(2), 199–209 (1997)

14. Kass, M., Witkin, A., Terzopoulos, D.: Snakes: active contour models. Int. J. Comput. Vis. **1**(4), 321–331 (1988)

15. Nesterov, Y.: Gradient methods for minimizing composite objective function. Core Discuss. Pap. **140**(1), 125–161 (2007)

16. Paragios, N., Deriche, R.: Geodesic active regions for supervised texture segmentation. In: The Proceedings of the Seventh IEEE International Conference on Computer Vision, p. 926 (1999)

17. Ronfard, R.: Region-based strategies for active contour models. Int. J. Comput. Vis. **13**(2), 229–251 (1994)

18. Taha, A.A., Hanbury, A.: Metrics for evaluating 3D medical image segmentation: analysis, selection, and tool. BMC Med. Imaging **15**(1), 29 (2015)

19. Vu, N., Manjunath, B.: Shape prior segmentation of multiple objects with graph cuts. In: Proceedings of the IEEE Conference on Computer Vision and Pattern Recognition, pp. 1–8. IEEE (2008)

20. Wang, G., Zhang, S., Xie, H., Metaxas, D.N., Gu, L.: A homotopy-based sparse representation for fast and accurate shape prior modeling in liver surgical planning. Med. Image Anal. **19**(1), 176–186 (2015)

21. Yezzi, A., Zöllei, L., Kapur, T.: A variational framework for integrating segmentation and registration through active contours. Med. Image Anal. **7**(2), 171–185 (2003)

22. Yezzi, A., Zollei, L., Kapur, T.: A variational framework for joint segmentation and registration. In: Proceedings of the IEEE Conference on Mathematical Methods in Biomedical Image Analysis, pp. 44–51. IEEE (2001)

23. Zhou, X., Huang, X., Duncan, J.S., Yu, W.: Active contours with group similarity. In: Proceedings of the IEEE Conference on Computer Vision and Pattern Recognition, pp. 2969–2976 (2013)

Efficient Statistical Shape Models-Based Image Segmentation Approach Using Deformable Simplex Meshes

Jinke Wang[1,3(✉)], Hongliang Zu[2], and Shinichi Tamura[3]

[1] Department of Software Engineering, Harbin University of Science and Technology,
Rongcheng, China
jkwang@hitwh.edu.cn
[2] School of Computer Science and Technology,
Harbin University of Science and Technology, Harbin, China
[3] Institute of Scientific and Industrial Research, Osaka University, Suita, Japan

Abstract. Principal component analysis (PCA) based statistical shape models (SSMs) are widely employed to incorporate high-level a priori shape knowledge of the structure to be segmented to achieve robustness. In this paper, a novel mesh-to-volume registration based shape correspondence establishment method was proposed to improve the accuracy and reduce the computational cost. Specifically, we present a greedy algorithm based deformable simplex mesh that uses vector field convolution (VFC) as the external energy. Furthermore, we develop an automatic shape initialization method by using a Gaussian mixture model (GMM) based registration algorithm, to derive an initial shape that has high overlap with the object of interest, such that the deformable models can then evolve more locally. We apply the proposed deformable surface model to the application of femur statistical shape model construction to illustrate its accuracy and efficiency. The experimental results suggest that our method can be employed for effective statistical shape model construction.

Keywords: Femur segmentation · Statistical shape model
Deformable models · VFC energy

1 Introduction

In the last few decades, lots of medical image segmentation methods have been proposed. Among these presented approaches, active shape model method has achieved state-of-the-art segmentation accuracy [5]. For achieving robustness, ASM utilizes principal component analysis-based statistical shape models to incorporate high level a priori shape knowledge of the structure to be segmented. A key step of building SSMs is to establish shape correspondence between all training shapes. So far various methods have been proposed to establish shape correspondence, and these approaches can be roughly divided

© Springer International Publishing AG 2017
Y. Zhao et al. (Eds.): ICIG 2017, Part II, LNCS 10667, pp. 476–486, 2017.
https://doi.org/10.1007/978-3-319-71589-6_41

into five major categories: mesh-to-volume registration, mesh-to-mesh registration, parameterization-to-parameterization registration, volume-to-volume registration, and population-based optimization. In particular, Gollmer et al. [4] proposed a evaluation of different groupwise correspondence approaches, including their re-parameterization strategies, objective functions, and optimization methods. However, a main limiting of current shape correspondence establishment approaches, is that the structure to be modeled has to be of the same topology as the sphere, besides they are much computationally intensive.

In mesh-to-volume registration based methods, a landmarked deformable surface model is fitted to all the segmented training images. After the convergence of the evolution of deformable model, the point correspondence is determined by the final landmark locations of the deformable template [5]. Kaus et al. [7] proposed a 3D elastically deformable model for the automated establishment of shape correspondence from segmented images, Their scheme can approximate and predict unseen shapes well. Shang and Dossel [9] then improved the above-mentioned method by utilizing the force equilibrium concept of deformable surface model. Shen et al. [10] presented an adaptive-focus deformable model to establish shape correspondence based on the hand-labeled 3-D brain images. An attribute vector for each landmark of the deformable template was introduced to preserve its geometric shape while evolution. Later, Zhao and Teoh [12] modified the AFDM method by exploiting a "bridge over" framework and made use of it to construct SSMs of brain ventricles. Clogenson et al. [1] raised a model-fitting based method to establish shape correspondence from manually segmented CT images. For getting accurate and robust results, we exploit an automatic shape initialization approach to derive an initial shape that has high overlap with the object of interest, such that the deformable models can then evolve more locally, and the proposed model was utilized for the construction of femur statistical shape model to demonstrate its accuracy and efficiency.

2   Method

In this section, we describe the details of the proposed statistical shape models construction process based on deformable surface model. The whole procedure is shown in Fig. 1.

2.1   Initialization of Deformable Surface Model

Providing with the training samples with ground truth segmentation, their simplex mesh representations are obtained firstly, which are defined as the dual of the triangular mesh derived via Marching Cubes algorithm and mesh smoothing methods. We then select the training sample that is similar to an average femur shape as the template mesh for the deformable models.

For purpose of obtaining a fine initial shape for the deformable models, the Gaussian mixture model (GMM) based point set registration method [6] was employed by aligning the template mesh with other training meshes via an affine

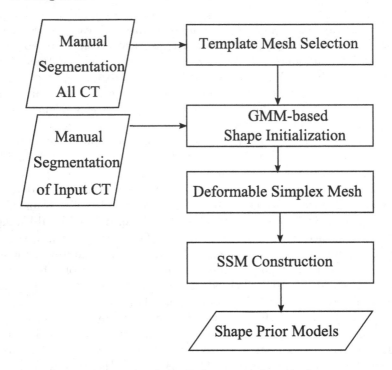

Fig. 1. Flowchart of the proposed method.

transformation. Specifically, we depict the point sets of the template mesh as a Gaussian mixture $f(\mathbf{x}) = \sum_{i=1}^{m} \alpha_i \phi(\mathbf{x} \,|\, \mu_i, \Sigma_i)$, the point sets of other training meshes are denoted by $g(\mathbf{x}) = \sum_{j=1}^{n} \beta_j \phi(\mathbf{x} \,|\, \nu_j, \Gamma_i)$. An affine transformation can be indicated by a 3×3 matrix $\mathbf{A}$, and a translation vector $\mathbf{t}$. For the purpose of convenience, the matrix $\mathbf{A}$ is factorized as an orthogonal matrix $\mathbf{Q}$ and a symmetric positive definite matrix $\mathbf{S}$, i.e., $\mathbf{A} = \mathbf{QS}$ [6]. Then the affine transformation can be obtained by minimizing the following L_2 distance between Gaussian mixtures $f(\mathbf{x})$ and $g(\mathbf{x})$ [6]:

$$d_{L_2}(f, g, \mathbf{A}, \mathbf{t}) = \int (g - f_{\mathbf{A},\mathbf{t}})^2 dx = \int (f_{\mathbf{A},\mathbf{t}}^2 - 2f_{\mathbf{A},\mathbf{t}}g + g^2) dx, \qquad (1)$$

Since $\int g^2$ is independent of the affine transformation, only $\int f_{\mathbf{A},\mathbf{t}}^2$ and $\int f_{\mathbf{A},\mathbf{t}}g$ are needed to consider. For the latter term:

$$\int f_{\mathbf{A},\mathbf{t}}g\, dx = \sum_{i=1}^{m} \sum_{j=1}^{n} \alpha_i \beta_j \phi(\mathbf{x} \,|\, \mu_i - \nu_j, \mathbf{Q}(\Sigma_i)\mathbf{Q}^T + \Gamma_i). \qquad (2)$$

Considering that the gradients associated with affine transformation have analytical solutions [6], fast gradient-based numerical optimization techniques can be deployed to minimize the objective function.

After deriving the affine transformation it was used to transform the template mesh to the space of other training meshes.

2.2   Evolution Method

The greedy algorithm was utilized as evolution method to conduct deformable 2-simplex meshes to the object of interest. Let V_i be the voxel in the volumetric image containing vertex P_i. In each iteration, a $w \times w \times w$ cubic window around V_i is searched, and the energy is computed at each voxel within the window (see Fig. 2a). The energy at vertex P_i is defined as a combination of both external and internal energy normalized within the window:

$$E(P_i) = \alpha E_{int}(P_i) + \beta E_{ext}(P_i)$$
$$= \alpha \left(E_{Tangent}(P_i) + E_{Normal}(P_i) \right) + \beta E_{VFC}(P_i), \tag{3}$$

where $E_{Tangent}$ and E_{Normal} are internal energy, E_{VFC} is the VFC external energy,

N_i^t is defined as the $w \times w \times w$ cubic window around voxel V_i. The position Q_i^t with minimum energy within the window N_i^t is selected as:

$$Q_i^t = \arg \min_{P_j \in N_i^t} E\left(P_j\right). \tag{4}$$

The vertex P_i is moved only along its normal direction $\mathbf{n}_i$, rather than directly moved to Q_i^t as in the classical greedy algorithm (see Fig. 2b):

$$P_i^{t+1} = P_i^t + \left((Q_i^t - P_i^t) \cdot \mathbf{n}_i\right) \mathbf{n}_i. \tag{5}$$

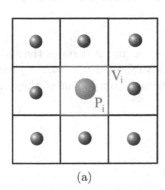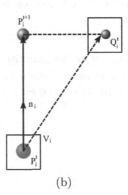

(a)   (b)

Fig. 2. The greedy algorithm: (a) The energy function is calculated at vertex P_i and voxels in the $w \times w \times w$ cubic window around V_i, and the point with the smallest energy is selected as the target position of P_i. (b) The vertex P_i is moved only along its normal direction $\mathbf{n}_i$.

2.3   Internal Energy Computation

The original internal force proposed in [3] is utilized as internal energy, which is decomposed into tangential energy and normal energy:

$$E_{int}(P_i) = E_{Tangent}(P_i) + E_{Normal}(P_i)$$

$$= \left\| \frac{1}{3}(P_{N_1(i)} + P_{N_2(i)} + P_{N_3(i)}) - F_i \right\|^2 + \left\| L(r_i, d_i, \tilde{\phi}_i) - L(r_i, d_i, \phi_i) \right\|^2, \tag{6}$$

2.4   VFC External Energy Computation

Vector field convolution (VFC) field [8] is largely used to solve the problems associated with traditional external force and can conduct the active contour into thin boundary. Besides, comparing with the classical GVF external force, VFC force shows superior stability to noise and initialization, and takes less computational time [8]. The 3D VFC field $\mathbf{v} = [u, v, w]$ is defined as the convolution of a vector field kernel $\mathbf{k}$ with the edge map f generated from the input image I:

$$\mathbf{v} = f \otimes \mathbf{k}, \tag{7}$$

where $\otimes$ indicates linear convolution.

Generally the edge map f for gray-level input images is defined as the gradient magnitude of the blurred image:

$$f = |\nabla[G_\sigma] \otimes I|, \tag{8}$$

where G_σ is a 3D Gaussian function with standard deviation σ, and ∇ is the gradient operator. The vector field kernel $\mathbf{k} = [u_k, v_k, w_k]$ can be computed as follows:

$$\mathbf{k} = m\mathbf{n}, \tag{9}$$

where m represents the magnitude of the vector and $\mathbf{n}$ denotes the unit vector.

In the practical implementation, the 3D VFC field $\mathbf{v} = [u, v, w]$ can be calculated by convolving the edge map f with each component of the vector field kernel $\mathbf{k} = [u_k, v_k, w_k]$ [8]:

$$u = f \otimes u_k, \tag{10}$$
$$v = f \otimes v_k, \tag{11}$$
$$w = f \otimes w_k. \tag{12}$$

The continuous vector field kernel $\mathbf{k}$ is approximated by a discrete matrix

$$\{\mathbf{k}(x, y, z) \,|\, x, y, z = -R, \ldots, -1, 0, 1, \ldots, R\}, \tag{13}$$

where R is the chosen kernel radius.

To handle with the major issues of the external energy, we modified it for greedy algorithm as external potential energy, and the following enhancements was made to the original VFC method:

1. The magnitude of the VFC field $\|\mathbf{v}\|$ is used as external energy instead of the force field itself.

2. The edge map is normalized before the computation of VFC energy,

Therefore, the VFC energy at vertex P_i can be defined as:

$$E_{VFC}(P_i) = \|\mathbf{v}(P_i)\|. \tag{14}$$

When vertex P_i is within the volumetric image, its external energy can be derived through a trilinear interpolation of the external energy at its neighboring image grid points; otherwise, its VFC energy is set to be the maximal value of the external energy in the volumetric image.

2.5   Statistical Shape Model Construction

Firstly, all training shapes are spatially aligned into a common coordinate frame using the generalized Procrustes analysis. The corresponding covariance matrix is defined as:

$$\mathbf{S} = \frac{1}{K-1} \sum_{i=1}^{K} (\mathbf{x}_i - \bar{\mathbf{x}})(\mathbf{x}_i - \bar{\mathbf{x}})^T, \tag{15}$$

where $\bar{\mathbf{x}}$ is the mean shape vector of all subjects: $\bar{\mathbf{x}} = \frac{1}{K}\sum_{i=1}^{K} \mathbf{x}_i$. Then the principal component analysis-based statistical shape model can be established by an eigen-decomposition on the covariance matrix $\mathbf{S}$:

$$\mathbf{S} = \mathbf{U}\mathbf{D}\mathbf{U}^T, \tag{16}$$

Then any valid shapes of femur structure can be approximated by a linear combination of the first c modes of variation:

$$\mathbf{x} = \bar{\mathbf{x}} + \sum_{m=1}^{c} b_m \phi_m, \tag{17}$$

b_m is the shape parameter constrained to $\left[-3\sqrt{\lambda_m}, 3\sqrt{\lambda_m}\right]$.

3   Experimental Results

3.1   Datasets and Parameters

To evaluate the performance of our the proposed method, we applied it to construct the femur statistical shape models based on a local database. The database consists of 5 femur CT scans from 5 different patients (3 males, 2 females) with ground truth segmentation manually segmented by radiology expert. These CT scans were provided by the Weihai Municipal Hospital, and were acquired by use of a 64-row multidetector CT scanner (Brilliance 64; Philips) with resolution between 0.58 mm and 0.67 mm, and a slice thickness of 1.5 mm.

3.2   Qualitative and Quantitative Analysis

Our proposed method was compared with the spherical harmonics (spharm) shape correspondence method [11]. Considering that the spharm method requires the input shape to be of spherical topology, all holes in the training images must be filled firstly. The spharm method maps all the input shapes to a common parameter domain through an area-preserving spherical parameterization. Finally we derived the corresponded training shapes by sampling the rotated spherical parameterization via icosahedron subdivision.

Figure 3 illustrates the first principal modes of variation for the constructed femur shape model, with the variation of a specific mode between -3σ and $+3\sigma$. It can be seen that the first mode accounts for the whole volume size of the femur structure.

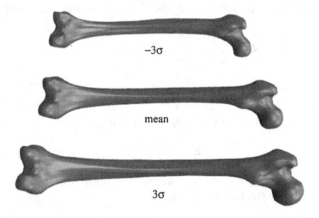

Fig. 3. The first principal mode of variation for the constructed femur shape model.

In this section, by using our proposed method, two metrics (compactness and generalization ability) are used to quantitatively evaluate the quality of the constructed femur shape model.

Compactness. The compactness is defined as the cumulative variance of the Mth mode used in the shape reconstruction [2]:

$$C(M) = \sum_{m=1}^{M} \lambda_m, \tag{18}$$

where λ_m is the mth eigenvalue. For the compactness, the smaller the value is, the better the constructed shape model.

Figure 4 shows the compactness for both spharm and our proposed method with varying number of modes of variation. For all the employed number of modes, our method achieves better compactness than the spharm method.

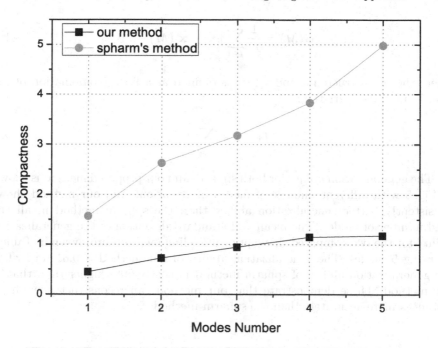

Fig. 4. Compactness for both spharm and our proposed method.

Table 1 shows the compactness for the two compared shape prior modeling methods with 5 modes. Specifically, the compactness of our method is 1.34 mm, and spharm method's compactness is more than three times that of our method. Therefore, the shape model constructed by our method is more compact than that of the spharm method.

Table 1. The compactness for the two compared shape prior modeling methods with 5 modes.

Method	*Compactness* [mm]
Spharm's method	4.31
Our method	1.34

Generalization Ability. The generalization ability quantifies the ability of the constructed shape model to represent new shape instances of the same structure class. It is measured based on the training data by performing leave-one-out tests. Specifically, a shape model is built by using all but one training shape x_i, and then the constructed model is employed to reconstruct the excluded shape x_i. The approximation error is defined as the distance between the excluded shape x_i and its reconstructed shape x_i'. The generalization ability is the average approximation error of all the performed K tests [2]:

$$G(M) = \frac{1}{K} \sum_{i=1}^{K} \left\| \mathbf{x}_i - \mathbf{x}_i'(M) \right\|^2, \tag{19}$$

where the reconstructed shape $\mathbf{x}_i'(M)$ is defined as a linear combination of the first M modes of variation:

$$\mathbf{x}_i'(M) = \bar{\mathbf{x}} + \sum_{m=1}^{M} b_m \phi_m. \tag{20}$$

The generalization ability for both spharm and our proposed method is shown in Fig. 5 with different number of modes of variation. And our method shows consistently better generalization ability than the spharm method in all the used number of modes. The mean and standard deviation of the generalization ability for the two compared shape prior modeling methods are shown in Table 2 by using 5 modes. The generalization ability of our method is 0.81 mm, while the generalization ability of spharm method is nearly 50% higher than that of our method. These demonstrate that our method can reconstruct new shape instances more accurately than the spharm method.

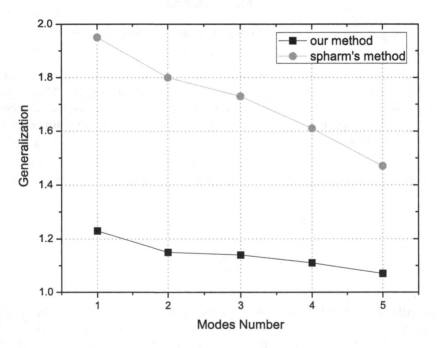

Fig. 5. Generalization ability for both spharm and our proposed method.

Table 2. The mean and standard deviation of the generalization ability for the two different shape prior modeling methods with 5 modes.

Method	Generalization [mm]
Spharm's method	1.13 ± 0.44
Our method	0.81 ± 0.22

Computational Time. The presented scheme was implemented in C++ and tested on a computer of GB RAM. In our experiment, an average of about 12.6 min is taken to establish shape correspondence for each shape. For comparison, the time taken by the spharm method for the same task is about 1 h in average, and it thus proved the superiority of our proposed method on computational efficiency.

4 Conclusion

In this paper, a novel mesh-to-volume registration based method was proposed for automatically establishing shape correspondence. It integrates the computational simplicity of simplex meshes, speed of the greedy algorithm, and robustness of VFC in a unified system. Through extensive experiments on 5 femur CT scans from 5 different patients, we demonstrate that the quality of the constructed femur shape models by using the proposed method is much better than that of the classical spharm method. Moreover, the proposed approach achieves much higher computational efficiency than the spharm method.

Acknowledgments. This work was supported by the Nature Science Foundation of Heilongjiang Province of China (No. QC2016090).

References

1. Clogenson, M., Duff, J.M., Lüthi, M., Levivier, M., Meuli, R., Baur, C., Henein, S.: A statistical shape model of the human second cervical vertebra. Int. J. Comput. Assist. Radiol. Surg. **10**(7), 1097–1107 (2015)
2. Davies, R.H.: Learning shape: optimal models for analysing natural variability. Ph.D. thesis, University of Manchester, Manchester, UK (2002). http://academy.bcs.org:8080/sites/academy.bcs.org/files/rhodri-davies.pdf
3. Delingette, H.: General object reconstruction based on simplex meshes. Int. J. Comput. Vis. **32**(2), 111–146 (1999)
4. Gollmer, S., Kirschner, M., Buzug, T.M., Wesarg, S.: Using image segmentation for evaluating 3D statistical shape models built with groupwise correspondence optimization. Comput. Vis. Image Underst. **125**, 283–303 (2014)
5. Heimann, T., Meinzer, H.P.: Statistical shape models for 3D medical image segmentation: a review. Med. Image Anal. **13**(4), 543–563 (2009)
6. Jian, B., Vemuri, B.C.: Robust point set registration using Gaussian mixture models. IEEE Trans. Pattern Anal. Mach. Intell. **33**(8), 1633–1645 (2011). http://gmmreg.googlecode.com

7. Kaus, M.R., Pekar, V., Lorenz, C., Truyen, R., Lobregt, S., Weese, J.: Automated 3-D PDM construction from segmented images using deformable models. IEEE Trans. Med. Imag. **22**(8), 1005–1013 (2003)
8. Li, B., Acton, S.T.: Active contour external force using vector field convolution for image segmentation. IEEE Trans. Image Process. **16**(8), 2096–2106 (2007)
9. Shang, Y., Dossel, O.: Statistical 3D shape-model guided segmentation of cardiac images. In: 2004 Proceedings of Computers in Cardiology, Chicago, Illinois, USA, pp. 553–556 (2004)
10. Shen, D., Herskovits, E., Davatzikos, C.: An adaptive-focus statistical shape model for segmentation and shape modeling of 3-D brain structures. IEEE Trans. Med. Imag. **20**(4), 257–270 (2001)
11. Styner, M., Oguz, I., Xu, S., Brechbühler, C., Pantazis, D., Levitt, J.J., Shenton, M.E., Gerig, G.: Framework for the statistical shape analysis of brain structures using SPHARM-PDM. In: Proceedings of Insight Journal - ISC/NA-MIC Workshop on Open Science at MICCAI 2006, Copenhagen, Denmark (2006)
12. Zhao, Z., Teoh, E.K.: A novel framework for automated 3D PDM construction using deformable models. In: Proceedings of SPIE Medical Imaging, San Diego, CA, USA, pp. 303–314 (2005)

An Artery/Vein Classification Method Based on Color and Vascular Structure Information

Dongmei Fu[1(✉)], Yang Liu[1], and Haosen Ma[2]

[1] University of Science and Technology Beijing,
30 Xueyuan Road, Haidian District, Beijing, China
fdm_ustb@ustb.edu.cn
[2] UC MOBILE CO., LTD.,
12F, No. 28 Chengfu Road, Haidian District, Beijing, China

Abstract. Identifying arteries and veins from fundus images plays an important role in human health census. Fundus images have the characteristics of uneven brightness, complexly staggered vessels, tiny difference between the arteries and veins, and so on. These characteristics lead to difficulties in distinguishing arteries and veins from fundus images. Therefore, it is a challenge for object extraction and classification in images. According to the prior knowledge, such as arteries are often brighter than the veins, arteries and veins have connectivity and are usually accompanied by each other, this paper proposes a recognition algorithm based on color and structure information to classify retinal vessels within 1DD— 1.5DD where is of particular interest in medicine. Experimental results show that the accuracy of this method has reached 93%, which proved that distinguishing arteries and veins based on color and structure information is valid.

Keywords: Fundus images · Artery/vein classification · Prior knowledge

1 Introduction

Medical practice shows that retinal vascular arteriovenous diameter ratio, shape and other changes are the basis for the early diagnosis of many diseases, such as cardio-vascular disease [1], diabetic retinopathy [2], hypertension [3] and so on. Medical experience shows that the region of 1DD-1.5DD (disc diameter) from the disc center is an important area to extract the biological information of retina [4, 5]. AVR (Arteriole to Venule Ratio) in this area is a commonly used characteristic signal for disease prediction and assessment. The paper [6] clearly pointed out: If the middle-aged people have a smaller AVR, then they are more likely to suffer from stroke. An important prerequisite for obtaining AVR values is to correctly distinguish the arteries and the veins. Therefore, achieving the automatic classification of arteries and veins is the key to obtaining AVR values before predicting and assessing the disease, it is of great practical significance. But the fundus images have the following characteristics: Illumination is not uniform, the blood vessels stagger with each other complexly, and the difference between arteries and veins is small. These characteristics result in difficulties in distinguishing arteries and veins.

In recent years, there are many research achievements on retinal vessels segmentation at home and abroad. However, there are just few researches focusing on

© Springer International Publishing AG 2017
Y. Zhao et al. (Eds.): ICIG 2017, Part II, LNCS 10667, pp. 487–495, 2017.
https://doi.org/10.1007/978-3-319-71589-6_42

automatic classification of arteries and veins. Vázquez proposed a localized arteriovenous classification method based on K-means clustering algorithm [7]. Relan
automatically classified retinal vessels as arteries or veins based on color features using
GMM-EM (Gaussian Mixture Model, Expectation-Maximization) unsupervised classifier and a quadrant-pairwise approach [8]. Niemeijer proposed a global artery/vein
classification method [9]. [10, 11] proposed an approach for artery/vein classification
based on the analysis of a graph extracted from the retinal vasculature. The proposed
method classified the entire vascular tree deciding on the type of each intersection point
(graph nodes) and assigning one of two labels to each vessel segment (graph links).
Vijayakumar proposed a classification method based on Random Forest and SVM
(Support Vector Machines) [12]. All of the above methods rely on color information
heavily, which leads to a relatively low classification accuracy for fundus images with
complex background and uneven brightness. Mirsharif divided the vessel tree into
several subsets, and then integrated vascular tracking techniques and color information
to classify the global vessels [13]. Vázquez used the minimal path approach [7, 14] to
revise the results of classification mentioned above [7]. Estrada proposed a novel,
graph-theoretic framework for distinguishing arteries from veins in a fundus image, and
made use of the underlying vessel topology to better classify small and midsized
vessels [15]. These three methods take the vascular structural properties into account,
but the use of vascular color information is not enough.

In summary, many of the current studies on artery/vein classification are mainly
based on color information or part of the vascular structural information, but there are
just few researches taking the color and structural information into account simultaneously. The paper comprehensively utilizes the prior knowledge of fundus color and
vessels structure, and proposes a retinal artery/vein classification algorithm to further
improve the accuracy of classification. As shown in Fig. 1, we first integrate the
FSFDP (Clustering by fast search and find of density peaks) algorithm [16] into the
CRCFV (Classification by Rotary Cutting on Fundus Vessels) focus points classification algorithm designed in this paper. Then we use the vascular connectivity and the
structural information that arteries and veins are usually accompanied by each other to
classify the blood vessels, and proposes a local retinal artery/vein classification method
based on color and structure of retinal vessels.

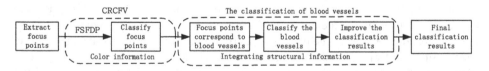

Fig. 1. The overall flow chart of the proposed algorithm.

2   FSFDP

The FSFDP algorithm is a new clustering method proposed by Alex Rodriguez, which
can quickly determine the clustering center and solve the nonlinear classification
problem. It is much more efficient than the traditional clustering algorithm. The FSFDP
algorithm was published in Journal Science, 2014.

The basic principle of FSFDP: for a set of data points $Q = \{q_1, q_2, \cdots, q_n\}$ where n is the number of data points, we will calculate the local density ρ_i of each data point q_i and the minimum distance δ_i' from this point to a point with a higher local density.

$$\rho_i = \sum_{j=1}^{n} \varphi(d_{ij} - d_c), \quad \varphi(m) = \begin{cases} 1, & m < 0 \\ 0, & m \geq 0 \end{cases} \tag{1}$$

$$\delta_i = \frac{\delta_i'}{\max_{i=1\cdots n}(\delta_i')}, \quad \delta_i' = \begin{cases} \min_{j:\rho_j > \rho_i}(d_{ij}), & \rho_i < \rho_{max} \\ \max_{j=1\cdots n}(d_{ij}), & \rho_i = \rho_{max} \end{cases} \tag{2}$$

And then $\rho = \{\rho_1, \rho_2, \cdots, \rho_n\}$ and $\delta = \{\delta_1, \delta_2, \cdots \delta_n\}$ will be obtained. In the above formula, d_{ij} is the distance between two points q_i and q_j, d_c is the threshold for calculating the local density, ρ_{max} is the maximum in the local density set ρ, and δ_i is the normalization of δ_i'. According to the formulas (1) and (2), the only points with higher δ and higher ρ are the clustering centers. As can be seen from Fig. 2, points 26, 27 and 28 have relatively higher δ and lower ρ, because they are isolated and can be considered as clusters composed of a single point. Points 1 and 10 have both higher δ and higher ρ, they can be judged as clustering centers. While the other data points have higher ρ and lower δ, they are judged to be the points near the clustering centers.

The FSFDP algorithm can be used to solve the nonlinear classification problem. Because there is no iterative and complex computation in the algorithm, the clustering centers can be found quickly. The keys of the algorithm are to reasonably describe the data set Q according to the actual problem and to define the correct and proper distance d_{ij}.

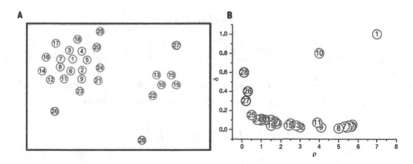

Fig. 2. The algorithm in two dimensions. (A) Point distribution. Data points are ranked in order of decreasing density. (B) Decision graph for the data in (A). Different colors correspond to different clusters. (Color figure online)

3 CRCFV

In this paper, we consider the non-uniformity of the light in the fundus images and the difference in the color of the adjacent arterial and venous blood vessels, and propose a CRCFV algorithm for the classification of arteries and veins in the local area. We extract the focus points within the region of 1DD – 1.5DD, which is of particular interest in medicine, and define the data set Q and the distance d_{ij} based on the color features.

3.1   Focus Points and Color Features

In Fig. 3(a), we draw three concentric circles R_1, R_2, R_3 with the radius $r_{R_1} = 1DD$, $r_{R_2} = 1.25DD$, $r_{R_3} = 1.5DD$. And then we define the points where the circles intersect the center lines of the blood vessels as the focus points, denoted as $Q = \{q_1, q_2, \cdots, q_n\}$. The position of each point $q_i(i = 1, 2, \cdots, n)$ in the image is represented as (x_{q_i}, y_{q_i}), as shown in Fig. 3(b).

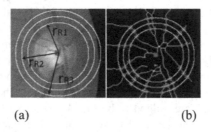

(a)   (b)

Fig. 3. Extraction of the focus points

In the fundus retinal images, arteries are often brighter than the veins. In this paper, we use formula (3) to obtain its color feature vector for each focus point.

$$I_{q_i} = \left[R_{q_i}, G_{q_i}, B_{q_i} \right]_{1*3} \tag{3}$$

where $R_{q_i} = \dfrac{\sum_{m=-1}^{1} \sum_{n=-1}^{1} I_r\left(x_{q_i}-n, y_{q_i}-m\right)}{9}$, $G_{q_i} = \dfrac{\sum_{m=-1}^{1} \sum_{n=-1}^{1} I_g\left(x_{q_i}-n, y_{q_i}-m\right)}{9}$, $B_{q_i} = \dfrac{\sum_{m=-1}^{1} \sum_{n=-1}^{1} I_b\left(x_{q_i}-n, y_{q_i}-m\right)}{9}$, and $I_k(x, y)(k = r, g, b)$ is the gray value of each color channel. Thus, the feature matrix of the focus points can be obtained.

$$I = \left[I_{q_1}, I_{q_2}, \cdots, I_{q_i}, \cdots I_{q_n} \right]_{n*3}^{T} \tag{4}$$

3.2   CRCFV Algorithm

There is a general problem that the color and brightness are uneven in the fundus images. The color and the brightness of arteries and veins vary widely in different regions. In this section, we propose a CRCFV algorithm to achieve the artery/vein classification of the focus points. The specific steps are as follows:

1. Divide the image into four parts by creating a coordinate system with the center of the disc as the origin, thus the set of focus points Q are separated into four subsets $Q_1^{(k)}, Q_2^{(k)}, Q_3^{(k)}, Q_4^{(k)} (k = 1, 2, \cdots, 9)$, and k represents the kth division of Q.

2. For each subset $Q_i^{(k)}(i = 1 \cdots 4, k = 1 \cdots 9)$, the color difference between the points q_i and q_j is defined as:

$$d_{ij} = \sqrt{\left(R_{q_i} - R_{q_j}\right)^2 + \left(G_{q_i} - G_{q_j}\right)^2 * \gamma + \left(B_{q_i} - B_{q_j}\right)^2} \tag{5}$$

where $\gamma > 1$, because the Green channel has stronger color information [17].

3. The FSFDP algorithm is used to calculate the two clustering centers of the focus points in each subset $Q_i^{(k)}$. And then we classify the other focus points to arterial point or venous point based on the color difference, which is recorded as the first classification result.

4. Rotate the coordinate axis counter-clockwise by 20°, and repeat step 3 until the coordinate axis is rotated nine times to return to the initial state. Then we will get nine kinds of division results of the focus points.

5. In step 4, nine classification results are obtained. For each point, the final classification result is determined by voting.

$$R_e^{(1)} = \left[r_{q_1}^{(1)}, r_{q_2}^{(1)}, \cdots, r_{q_i}^{(1)}, \cdots r_{q_n}^{(1)}\right]_{1*n} \tag{6}$$

4 The Improvement of the CRCFV Algorithm

The CRCFV algorithm only uses the color information of the arterial and venous blood vessels. Compared with other methods that use only color information to distinguish arteries and veins, the accuracy of this method is also limited. The simulation is carried out for 40 pictures of the public database DRIVE. But the average accuracy rate is only 77.05%. According to medical knowledge that the blood vessels have connectivity, in the same blood vessels, the classification results of the focus points are consistent. In addition, arteries and veins are usually accompanied by each other, there can not be all arteries or all veins in a region. This section summarizes and quantifies these medical prior knowledges. First, we determine the correspondence between the focus points and the blood vessel. On the basis of CRCFV algorithm, we propose an artery/vein classification method that integrates arteriovenous vascular structure information.

4.1 Vascular Connectivity

Vascular connectivity indicates that all focus points on the same vessel belong to the vein or belong to the artery. The classification of focus points is only dividing the set of focus points Q into two categories according to the color and the brightness information, not for blood vessels yet. In order to make the classification results of focus points consistent with vascular connectivity, and then to classify the blood vessels, we must firstly solve the problem of how to obtain the correspondence relationship between the set of focus points Q and the set of blood vessels $1 = \{l_1 \cdots l_i \cdots l_k\}$, where l_i represents the vessel, and k represents the number of blood vessels. This paper uses the connectivity determination method to solve the above problems.

The connectivity determination method: Fig. 4(b) shows the basic process of connectivity determination. Suppose that $q_i \in R_n (n = 1, 2, 3)$ and $q_j \in R_m (m \neq n)$, which means that q_i and q_j are not in the same circle. In Fig. 4(b):

$$D_f = r_3 - r_1 + c \tag{7}$$

Determine a local image with q_i as the center and D_f as the radius. In the local image, the connected domain set $L = \{L_1 \cdots L_i \cdots L_k\}$ is determined by 8 neighborhood rules, where L_i denotes the ith connected domain in the region and n denotes the number of connected domains. If q_i and q_j belong to the same connected domain L_i, then q_i and q_j belong to the same vessel l_i.

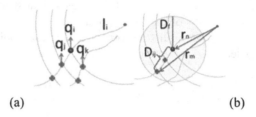

(a)   (b)

Fig. 4. The relationship between the focus points and the blood vessels

4.2   Artery/Vein Classification with Vascular Structural Information

After the analysis of Sect. 4.1, the corresponding relationship between the set of blood vessels l and the set of focus points Q was determined. Assuming $q_i \in l_i$, we can correct the classification of the focus points on the same vessel according to the following rules, and then achieve the classification of blood vessels:

$$r_{q_i}^{(2)} = \begin{cases} a & \sum_{q_i \in l_i} J_{q_i} > 0 \\ v & \sum_{q_i \in l_i} J_{q_i} < 0 \\ u & \sum_{q_i \in l_i} J_{q_i} = 0 \end{cases}, \quad r_{l_i} = \begin{cases} a_l & \sum_{q_i \in l_i} J_{q_i} > 0 \\ v_l & \sum_{q_i \in l_i} J_{q_i} < 0 \\ u_l & \sum_{q_i \in l_i} J_{q_i} = 0 \end{cases} \tag{8}$$

In the above formula, $J_{q_i} = (+1, -1, 0)$ indicates that the classification result of point q_i before correcting is artery, vein or uncertain point, respectively. And $r_{q_i}^{(2)}$ is the result of point q_i after correcting. a, v, u respectively indicates that the classification result is arterial, venous and uncertain. r_{l_i} represents the classification result of blood vessel l_i. We can get the matrix of the corrected classification results, as follows:

$$R_e^{(2)} = \left[r_{q_1}^{(2)}, r_{q_2}^{(2)}, \cdots, r_{q_i}^{(2)}, \cdots, r_{q_n}^{(2)} \right]_{1*n}, \quad R_{el} = [r_{l_1}, r_{l_2}, \cdots, r_{l_i}, \cdots, r_n]_{1*k} \tag{9}$$

Although the formula (9) gives the classification result of the blood vessels, but a large number of simulation results show that if several adjacent blood vessels are all identified as veins, this is likely to be wrong. Because this classification result violates the structural characteristics that arteries and veins are usually accompanied by each other. In the implementation of the above classification method, we have to follow the following rules:

1. If the classification results of two or more adjacent points on the same circle are all arteries or are all veins, all the focus points on the corresponding vessels are reclassified according to steps 2–3 in Sect. 3.2.
2. If the classification result obtained in the above step is changed, the classification result is corrected according to the formula (8).

5 Experimental Results Analysis

This method is applied to the public database DRIVE. DRIVE is a fundus image database that is widely used to research the related problems of retinal images. It is taken from 400 different individuals aged 25–90 years, and forty of all images are randomly selected, seven of which are fundus images with early diabetic retinopathy. Each image contains 565 * 584 pixels, and each pixel contains 8 bits of color information. In order to determine the accuracy rate of automatic classification results, we invite an ophthalmologist to determine the results of artery/vein classification. In this paper, the simulation results of all the images in DRIVE are used for statistical calculation. The final results of artery/vein classification are shown in Fig. 5, where "o" and "+" respectively indicate the classification of focus points as veins and arteries.

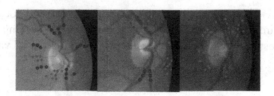

Fig. 5. Examples of artery/vein classification results

The accuracy of this method is calculated as follows:

$$\text{Accuracy} = \frac{n_c}{n_c + n_i + n_n} * 100\% \tag{10}$$

where n_c represents the number of focus points that are correctly classified, n_i represents the number of focus points that are misclassified, and n_n represents the number of focus points that can not be classified by the computer.

Table 1 shows some artery/vein classification methods published in recent years. Compared with other methods, our method can achieve more accurate classification.

Table 1. Comparison about the accuracy of several classification algorithms

Algorithms	Papers	Database	Accuracy
A supervised method	Paper [9]	DRIVE	88% (ROC)
Graph-based	Paper [10]	DRIVE	87.4%
Post processing	Paper [13]	DRIVE	84.05%
Our method	This paper	DRIVE	93%

6 Conclusion

In this paper, all 40 images in the DRIVE database are used for simulation, and 1531 focus points are extracted. The results of artery/vein classification are judged by an ophthalmologist. By comparing the final results of this paper with the methods published by other scholars in recent years, the accuracy rate of this paper is 93%, which is at a high level. The main contents and achievements of this paper are summarized as follows:

1. Based on the color information of blood vessels and the FSFDP algorithm, we propose a CRCFV algorithm to achieve the artery/vein classification of focus points under the condition of color and brightness unevenness.
2. Considering the structural features of vascular connectivity and companion, we propose an artery/vein classification method of blood vessels that integrates vascular structure information, which is a progressive fundus arteries and veins recognition algorithm.

In further research, we will consider using vascular color and location information simultaneously to improve the accuracy of classification and solving the problem that the classification result depends on the results of the extraction of vascular trees.

References

1. Wong, T., Mitchell, P.: The eye in hypertension. Lancet **369**(9559), 425–435 (2007)
2. Ng, D.S.K., Chiang, P.P.C., Tan, G., et al.: Retinal ganglion cell neuronal damage in diabetes and diabetic retinopathy. Clin. Exp. Ophthalmol. **44**(4), 243–250 (2016)
3. Mirsharif, Q., Tajeripour, F., Pourreza, H.: Automated characterization of blood vessels as arteries and veins in retinal images. Comput. Med. Imaging Graph. **37**(7), 607–617 (2013)
4. Wong, T.Y., Knudtson, M.D., Klein, R., et al.: Computer-assisted measurement of retinal vessel diameters in the Beaver Dam eye study: methodology, correlation between eyes, and effect of refractive errors. Ophthalmology **111**(6), 1183–1190 (2004)
5. Li, H., Hsu, W., Lee, M.L., et al.: Automatic grading of retinal vessel caliber. IEEE Trans. Bio-Med. Eng. **52**(7), 1352 (2005)
6. Lesage, S.R., Mosley, T.H., Wong, T.Y., et al.: Retinal microvascular abnormalities and cognitive decline the ARIC 14-year follow-up study. Neurology **73**(11), 862–868 (2009)
7. Vázquez, S.G., Cancela, B., Barreira, N., et al.: Improving retinal artery and vein classification by means of a minimal path approach. Mach. Vis. Appl. **24**(5), 919–930 (2013)

8. Relan, D., MacGillivray, T., Ballerini, L., et al.: Retinal vessel classification: sorting arteries and veins. In: 2013 35th Annual International Conference of the IEEE Engineering in Medicine and Biology Society (EMBC), pp. 7396–7399. IEEE, Osaka (2013)
9. Niemeijer, M., Ginneken, B.V.: Automatic classification of retinal vessels into arteries and veins. In: Proceedings of SPIE - The International Society for Optical Engineering, pp. 7260:72601F–72601F–8 (2009)
10. Dashtbozorg, B., Mendonca, A.M., Campilho, A.: An automatic graph-based approach for artery/vein classification in retinal images. IEEE Trans. Image Process. Publ. IEEE Sig. Process. Soc. 23(3), 1073–1083 (2014)
11. Joshi, V.S., Reinhardt, J.M., Garvin, M.K., et al.: Automated method for identification and artery-venous classification of vessel trees in retinal vessel networks. PLoS ONE 9(2), e88061 (2014)
12. Vijayakumar, V., Koozekanani, D.D., White, R., et al.: Artery/vein classification of retinal blood vessels using feature selection. In: International Conference of IEEE Engineering in Medicine and Biology Society, pp. 1320–1323. IEEE (2016)
13. Mirsharif, Q., Tajeripour, F., Pourreza, H.: Automated characterization of blood vessels as arteries and veins in retinal images. Comput Med. Imaging Graph. Off. J. Comput. Med. Imaging Soc. 37(7), 607–617 (2013)
14. Vázquez, S.G., Cancela, B., Barreira, N., et al.: On the automatic computation of the arterio-venous ratio in retinal images: using minimal paths for the artery/vein classification. In: International Conference on Digital Image Computing: Techniques and Applications, pp. 599–604. IEEE Computer Society (2010)
15. Estrada, R., Allingham, M.J., Mettu, P.S., et al.: Retinal artery-vein classification via topology estimation. IEEE Trans. Med. Imaging 34(12), 2518–2534 (2015)
16. Rodriguez, A., Laio, A.: Clustering by fast search and find of density peaks. Science 344 (6191), 1492–1496 (2014)
17. Vázquez, S.G., Barreira, N., Penedo, M.G., et al.: Improvements in retinal vessel clustering techniques: towards the automatic computation of the arteriovenous ratio. Computing 90(3), 197–217 (2010)

Improved U-Net Model for Nerve Segmentation

Houlong Zhao and Nongliang Sun[✉]

College of Electronics, Communication and Physics,
Shandong University of Science and Technology, Qingdao 266590, China
zhaohoulong@outlook.com, nl-jackson@vip.163.com

Abstract. Noticeable gains in computer vision have been made as a result of the large-scale datasets and deep convolutional neural networks (CNNs). CNNs have been used in a wide variety of tasks, for instance, recognition, detection, and segmentation. Recently, due to the open medical images datasets, CNNs have been used in Computer Aided Detection (CADe) to help doctors diagnose lesion. In this work, we present an end-to-end method based on CNNs for automatical segmentation from medical images. The proposed network architecture is similar to U-Net, which consists of a contracting path and an expansive path. However, we take advantage of inception modules and batch normalization instead of ordinary convolutional layers, which reduce the quantity of parameters and accelerate training without loss of accuracy. In addition, we confirm Dice coefficient as loss function rather than binary cross entropy. We use this model to segment nerve from ultrasound images and achieve a better performance.

Keywords: Nerve · Segmentation · Ultrasound Images · Inception
Dice coefficient

1 Introduction

Since 2012 krizhevsky et al. [16] won the ImageNet competition [6], deep convolutional neural networks [17] have been the mainstream to create the state of the art in computer vision and pattern recognition, in which there have been a series of breakthroughs among large lots of tasks, for example to classification [11,26,27], object-detection [7,21], and segmentation [23]. A series of success is credited on the ability of CNNs to self-educate from the raw input without manual intervention.

Benefited from the large open datasets about medical-images, computer aided detection (CADe) making use of deep learning has become a reality. Up to now, CADe has been used in clinical environments for over 40 years [1], but it usually can't replace the doctor or become the role in diagnosing. However, ResNet designed by He et al. [11] has 3.57% top-5 error on the ImageNet test set excelling human beings, which provides a possibility that machine can substitute for the doctors in some tasks, for instance, detecting cancer metastases [22], and diabetic retinopathy [9] etc.

© Springer International Publishing AG 2017
Y. Zhao et al. (Eds.): ICIG 2017, Part II, LNCS 10667, pp. 496–504, 2017.
https://doi.org/10.1007/978-3-319-71589-6_43

In this paper, we specifically consider of the problem of automatic segmentation for nerves: given an ultrasound image of neck, some with nerve, we want to fully automatically end-to-end segment the nerves. Recently, most approaches rely on deep convolutional neural networks of medical image segmentation have achieved great success, in view of which, we tested some foundational methods based on CNNs and attempted to raise our own architecture.

The proposed architecture is inspired by U-Net [4] that has a good performance in biomedical image segmentation but with too many parameters. In order to improve the performance, we adopted inception modules and batch normalization. Through some efforts we have done, the model has fewer parameters and less time for training. In addition, we confirmed Dice coefficient as loss function, which compares the pixel-wise agreement with a predicted segmentation and ground truth.

2 Related Work

Early medical image segmentation methods mostly based on statistical shape, gray level and texture collected in [12]. Recently, level set [18], graph cut [19] have been employed as approaches in biomedical image segmentation. However, these methods are not widely used owing to their speed and complex operation.

Through the rapid development in recent years, deep Convolutional Neural Networks (CNNs) have been exploited to improve the ability of machine to achieve state-of-art goals [10,11,28] in computer vision. More stirring, CNN seems to be widely-used, which prompted us to employ it to automatically segment nerves from ultrasound images.

Semantic segmentation methods based on convolutional neural networks got a big development. [23] is the first model to use fully convolutional networks that produce corresponding output as same size as input and skip architecture that combines semantic information from a deep layer with appearance information from a shallow layer, SegNet [2] uses encoder-decoder structures restore the feature maps from higher layers with spatial information from lower layers. DeepLab [3] combines the responses at the final CNN layer with a fully connected Conditional Random Field (CRF) to improve localization accuracy. PSPNet [28] proposes a pyramid scene parsing network to combine local and global features.

As for medical image segmentation, U-Net [25] can be trained end-to-end from very few medical images, [24] proposes V-Net to 3D image segmentation. [5] uses cascaded fully convolutional neural networks for liver and tumor segmentation, which firstly trains an FCN to segment the liver as input for the second FCN, secondly uses the second FCN solely segment tumor.

3 Dataset

The dataset we used to evaluate our model is provided by Kaggle[1], which contains a collection of nerves called the Brachial Plexus in ultrasound images. The

---

[1] https://www.kaggle.com.

training data is a set of 5635 images (580 × 420 pixels) and its corresponding masks where nerve (white) and background (black) have been manually annotated (Fig. 1). And the testing set with 5508 ultrasound images is publicly available, but its segmentation maps are kept secret. The main purpose of accurately segmenting the nerve structures in ultrasound images is to help doctors to effectively insert a patients pain management catheter that mitigate pain at the source in order to decrease the intake of narcotic drug and speed up patient recovery.

Fig. 1. The left image is the raw ultrasound image containing nerve structure, the middle image is the corresponding mask manually annotated by experts, and the right image is the ultrasound image overlaid with ground truth segmentation map (red border). (Color figure online)

4   Improved U-Net Model

The network architecture is illustrated in Fig. 2. There are two paths in this architecture, similar to U-Net [25], which are a contracting path and an expansive path. In this network, we combine the two paths with inception module [20,27] and batch normalization [14]. The contracting path (Fig. 2 left) is a normal convolutional neural network for recognition, it involves 3 basic convolutional units (Fig. 4) and 4 inception modules (Fig. 3), besides these, there are 5 max pooling operations with stride of 2 for downsampling. Between the contracting path and expansive path, there also have an inception module. In expansive path (Fig. 2 right), there are 5 upsample layers followed basic convolutional units or inception modules, generally symmetrical to the contracting path. At the final layer, a 1 × 1 convolution and a sigmoid activation function are used to output 2 class segmentation images which have the same size as inputs. We also used skip architectures [23], which concatenate features of shallower layers from contracting path with the features of deeper layers from expansive path. We concatenate the features in the inception modules with the 4 convolutional paths.

Each inception module has 4 paths, which act together on one input and are concatenated as an output following the practice in [27]. Before every expansive 3 × 3 and 5 × 5 convolution, 1 × 1 convolution layer is used to reduce computation. In total, the inception module has 6 convolutional layers and an average pooling layer. Besides the final layer, all of the convolutional operations are followed by a batch normalization and a rectified linear unit (ReLU), which make

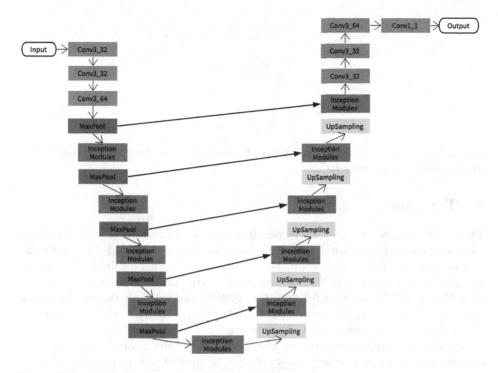

Fig. 2. The proposed architecture. The blue and green box represent the basic convolutional units and the inception modules respectively. And what the red and yellow box signify are downsampling (max pooling) and upsampling. Simultaneously, there are 5 skip architectures. (Color figure online)

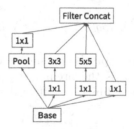

Fig. 3. Inception modules where four convolutional paths act on one input and connect to one output with average pooling as pooling layer.

up a basic convolutional unit (Fig. 4). We employed sample linear interpolation as the upsample operation to make the size of output segmentation maps to reach the size of the input image rather than using deconvolutional layers as in [23], which demand supernumerary computation.

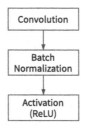

Fig. 4. The basic convolutional unit we used, where the convolutional layer followed a batch normalization and a ReLU.

5   Training

The input images and their corresponding masks are resized to 64 × 64 so as to reduce the computational cost. We adopt batch normalization [14] after each convolution and before activation. We use Adam [15] with a mini-batch size of 30. The learning rate is 0.001 and the models are trained for up to 78 epochs with Keras [4]. We use β_1 of 0.9 and β_2 of 0.999 following [15]. We set the initial random weights using Xavier normal initializer [8]. We have not used dropout [13] and any other approach for regularization.

In medical image segmentation, the interested region is more essential than background. If we use binary cross entropy to predict the probability of each pixel to belong to foreground or to background, all the pixels in input images are equally important. However, the interested region (white) just accounts for a smaller proportion of the area than background (black) as shown in Fig. 1, as a result, the interested region will be often missed. Binary cross entropy defined as

$$L = -\frac{1}{n} \sum_{i=1}^{n} [t_i \ log(o_i) + (1 - t_i) \ log(1 - o_i)] \tag{1}$$

where the sums run over the n pixels, i denotes the pixel position, t_i is the ground truth value, and the o_i is the predicted pixel value. In this paper, we employed Dice coefficient as loss function followed the practice in [24]:

$$L = -\frac{2 \sum_{i=1}^{n} o_i t_i}{\sum_{i=1}^{n} o_i^2 + \sum_{i=1}^{n} t_i^2} \tag{2}$$

where n, i, o_i, t_i denote same meaning as binary cross entropy.

6   Experiments and Analysis

The model is trained end-to-end on the 5635 training ultrasound images, and tested on the 5508 testing images. An evaluated score can be obtained by submitting the predicted segmentation maps to the Kaggle's sever. The result is evaluated on the mean Dice coefficient:

$$L = \frac{2|X \cap Y|}{|X| + |Y|} \tag{3}$$

where X is the set of predicted pixel values and Y is the set of ground truth values, correspondingly $|X|$ and $|Y|$ are the numbers of elements in them. We trained and evaluated our method and U-Net [25] (Fig. 5), which inspired our idea and was used widely in biomedical image segmentation. Same as our model, the U-Net we tested in this paper adopt Dice coefficient as the loss function and use basic convolutional units (Fig. 4) to replaced original convolutional layers without any dropout and other regularization.

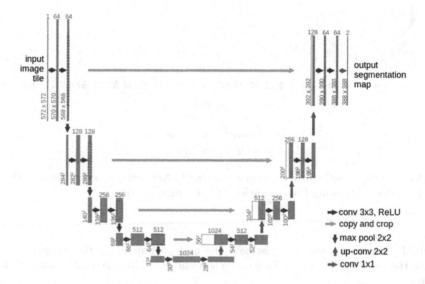

Fig. 5. U-Net [25] used to compare with our model, which totally has 23 convolutional layers. In our work, batch normalization is used after each convolution and before activation instead of the original model.

In Fig. 6 we compare Dice coefficient of our model with U-Net [25] during the training procedure. We have observed that our model reached 0.34 after first epoch and 0.80 after 32th epoch, faster than U-Net, which just reached 0.05 after first epoch and 0.80 after 50th epoch. The much faster convergence proves that the inception modules we adopted can accelerate training procedure.

The results in Table 1 show that our model achieves a score of 0.653, roughly equals to the score of 0.658 from U-Net. However, our model has fewer parameters, only 16% of the parameters of U-Net. The reason for parameters' reduction is that the 1×1 convolution does not care the correlation of information in same feature map and leads to dimension reduction. Figure 7 shows a testing result using our model.

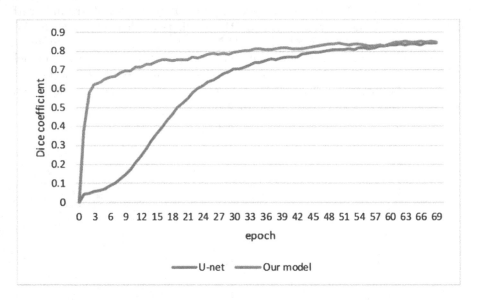

Fig. 6. Training on 5635 ultrasound images using U-Net (orange) and our model (blue). The lines denote training Dice coefficient. (Color figure online)

Table 1. The results from the test set. The first column shows the models we have tested, the second column their Dice coefficient and the third the total number of these models

Model	Dice coeff.	Total param.
Our model	0.653	5M
U-Net	0.658	31M

Fig. 7. One result of the test data, the left image is the testing ultrasound image containing nerve structure, the middle image is the predicted segmentation map, and the right image is the ultrasound image overlaid with segmentation map (green border). (Color figure online)

7 Conclusion

We present an approach based on convolutional neural networks, which achieves a good performance on ultrasound images segmentation and possesses fewer parameters thanks to inception modules. We adopted an efficacious loss function, Dice coefficient between the predicted segmentation maps and ground truth. Our model has satisfactory training time of 54 h on a Intel CORE i7 vPro and 16 GB of memory. Future work will aim at different biomedical segmentation applications and train our model over GPUs.

Acknowledgements. This work was supported by Leading talent development program of Shandong University of Science and Technology.

References

1. Computer-aided diagnosis. https://en.wikipedia.org/wiki/Computer-aided_ diagnosis
2. Badrinarayanan, V., Kendall, A., Cipolla, R.: SegNet: a deep convolutional encoder-decoder architecture for image segmentation. arXiv preprint arXiv:1511.00561 (2015)
3. Chen, L.C., Papandreou, G., Kokkinos, I., Murphy, K., Yuille, A.L.: DeepLab: semantic image segmentation with deep convolutional nets, atrous convolution, and fully connected CRFs. arXiv preprint arXiv:1606.00915 (2016)
4. Chollet, F., et al.: Keras (2015). https://github.com/fchollet/keras
5. Christ, P.F., Ettlinger, F., Grün, F., Elshaera, M.E.A., Lipkova, J., Schlecht, S., Ahmaddy, F., Tatavarty, S., Bickel, M., Bilic, P., et al.: Automatic liver and tumor segmentation of CT and MRI volumes using cascaded fully convolutional neural networks. arXiv preprint arXiv:1702.05970 (2017)
6. Deng, J., Dong, W., Socher, R., Li, L.J., Li, K., Fei-Fei, L.: ImageNet: a large-scale hierarchical image database. In: 2009 IEEE Conference on Computer Vision and Pattern Recognition, CVPR 2009, pp. 248–255. IEEE (2009)
7. Girshick, R., Donahue, J., Darrell, T., Malik, J.: Rich feature hierarchies for accurate object detection and semantic segmentation. In: Proceedings of IEEE Conference on Computer Vision and Pattern Recognition, pp. 580–587 (2014)
8. Glorot, X., Bengio, Y.: Understanding the difficulty of training deep feedforward neural networks. In: AISTATS, vol. 9, pp. 249–256 (2010)
9. Gulshan, V., Peng, L., Coram, M., Stumpe, M.C., Wu, D., Narayanaswamy, A., Venugopalan, S., Widner, K., Madams, T., Cuadros, J., et al.: Development and validation of a deep learning algorithm for detection of diabetic retinopathy in retinal fundus photographs. JAMA **316**(22), 2402–2410 (2016)
10. He, K., Gkioxari, G., Dollár, P., Girshick, R.: Mask R-CNN. arXiv preprint arXiv:1703.06870 (2017)
11. He, K., Zhang, X., Ren, S., Sun, J.: Deep residual learning for image recognition. In: Proceedings of IEEE Conference on Computer Vision and Pattern Recognition, pp. 770–778 (2016)
12. Heimann, T., Van Ginneken, B., Styner, M.A., Arzhaeva, Y., Aurich, V., Bauer, C., Beck, A., Becker, C., Beichel, R., Bekes, G., et al.: Comparison and evaluation of methods for liver segmentation from CT datasets. IEEE Trans. Med. Imaging **28**(8), 1251–1265 (2009)

13. Hinton, G.E., Srivastava, N., Krizhevsky, A., Sutskever, I., Salakhutdinov, R.R.: Improving neural networks by preventing co-adaptation of feature detectors. arXiv preprint arXiv:1207.0580 (2012)

14. Ioffe, S., Szegedy, C.: Batch normalization: accelerating deep network training by reducing internal covariate shift. arXiv preprint arXiv:1502.03167 (2015)

15. Kingma, D., Ba, J.: Adam: a method for stochastic optimization. arXiv preprint arXiv:1412.6980 (2014)

16. Krizhevsky, A., Sutskever, I., Hinton, G.E.: ImageNet classification with deep convolutional neural networks. In: Advances in Neural Information Processing Systems, pp. 1097–1105 (2012)

17. LeCun, Y., Bengio, Y., Hinton, G.: Deep learning. Nature **521**(7553), 436–444 (2015)

18. Li, C., Wang, X., Eberl, S., Fulham, M., Yin, Y., Chen, J., Feng, D.D.: A likelihood and local constraint level set model for liver tumor segmentation from CT volumes. IEEE Trans. Biomed. Eng. **60**(10), 2967–2977 (2013)

19. Li, G., Chen, X., Shi, F., Zhu, W., Tian, J., Xiang, D.: Automatic liver segmentation based on shape constraints and deformable graph cut in CT images. IEEE Trans. Image Process. **24**(12), 5315–5329 (2015)

20. Lin, M., Chen, Q., Yan, S.: Network in network. arXiv preprint arXiv:1312.4400 (2013)

21. Liu, W., Anguelov, D., Erhan, D., Szegedy, C., Reed, S., Fu, C.-Y., Berg, A.C.: SSD: single shot MultiBox detector. In: Leibe, B., Matas, J., Sebe, N., Welling, M. (eds.) ECCV 2016. LNCS, vol. 9905, pp. 21–37. Springer, Cham (2016). https://doi.org/10.1007/978-3-319-46448-0_2

22. Liu, Y., Gadepalli, K., Norouzi, M., Dahl, G.E., Kohlberger, T., Boyko, A., Venugopalan, S., Timofeev, A., Nelson, P.Q., Corrado, G.S., et al.: Detecting cancer metastases on gigapixel pathology images. arXiv preprint arXiv:1703.02442 (2017)

23. Long, J., Shelhamer, E., Darrell, T.: Fully convolutional networks for semantic segmentation. In: Proceedings of IEEE Conference on Computer Vision and Pattern Recognition, pp. 3431–3440 (2015)

24. Milletari, F., Navab, N., Ahmadi, S.A.: V-Net: fully convolutional neural networks for volumetric medical image segmentation. In: 2016 4th International Conference on 3D Vision (3DV), pp. 565–571. IEEE (2016)

25. Ronneberger, O., Fischer, P., Brox, T.: U-Net: convolutional networks for biomedical image segmentation. In: Navab, N., Hornegger, J., Wells, W.M., Frangi, A.F. (eds.) MICCAI 2015. LNCS, vol. 9351, pp. 234–241. Springer, Cham (2015). https://doi.org/10.1007/978-3-319-24574-4_28

26. Simonyan, K., Zisserman, A.: Very deep convolutional networks for large-scale image recognition. arXiv preprint arXiv:1409.1556 (2014)

27. Szegedy, C., Liu, W., Jia, Y., Sermanet, P., Reed, S., Anguelov, D., Erhan, D., Vanhoucke, V., Rabinovich, A.: Going deeper with convolutions. In: Proceedings of IEEE Conference on Computer Vision and Pattern Recognition, pp. 1–9 (2015)

28. Zhao, H., Shi, J., Qi, X., Wang, X., Jia, J.: Pyramid scene parsing network. arXiv preprint arXiv:1612.01105 (2016)

ECG Waveform Extraction from Paper Records

Jian Wang[1,2(✉)], Yanwei Pang[1], Yuqing He[1], and Jing Pan[3]

[1] School of Electrical and Information Engineering,
Tianjin University, Tianjin 300072, China
jianwang@tju.edu.cn
[2] National Ocean Technology Center, Tianjin 300112, China
[3] School of Electronic Engineering,
Tianjin University of Technology and Education, Tianjin 300222, China

Abstract. Electrocardiogram (ECG) is one of the most practiced methods to detect any abnormalities in human heart function. ECG waveforms are usually recorded as paper form. However, ECG paper records are inconvenient for storage and retrieval of the patient records. In this paper, an improved ECG waveform extraction algorithm from paper records is proposed. It is used to get accurate ECG trajectory information with a serious of adaptive image processing techniques, including skew correction, waveform segmentation, and tracking. The presented algorithm is tested with a number of ECG records printed from different equipment. Furthermore, three metrics are adopted for quantitative measurement between reconstructed signals and original waveforms. The comparison result shows an average accuracy of 95.5%, which proves the effectiveness of the method.

Keywords: ECG · Skew correction
ECG waveform segmentation and extraction

1 Introduction

The electrocardiogram (ECG) is a graphical representation of the electrical activity of the heart. It is obtained by connecting specially designed electrodes to the surface of the body [1]. Normally, ECG has to be printed on a thermal paper for further physical inspection by medical practitioner. This leads to archival and retrieval of patient's paper ECG records as a common way for diagnosis of ailments. This process requires large storage space and extensive manual effort. In addition, these large number of ECG records are difficult to share among doctors. Therefore, the process of extracting ECG waveforms and converting them into digital forms will help people to solve storage and retrieval problem.

The general ECG waveform digitalization process usually consists of three steps, that is, visual quality improvement, waveform segmentation and waveform extraction. Previous research work in the field of ECG waveform signal extraction is referred in [2–8]. In Ref. [3], a morphological approach is applied to remove background grids from ECG records. And the XOR operation is performed on the binary image's first periodic distance vertical direction (PDVD). In this method, correct estimation of

Y. Zhao et al. (Eds.): ICIG 2017, Part II, LNCS 10667, pp. 505–512, 2017.
https://doi.org/10.1007/978-3-319-71589-6_44

PDVD is necessary which strongly depends on the resulting binarization image. Gomes et al. [3] extract the ECG waveform signals by removing the axis and performing a median filtering operation on the resulting image. However, the removal of the axis leads to the additional difficulty in obtaining the ECG waveform details, which are essential for diagnosis. Chebil et al. [5] obtain binary scanned image by using appropriate global thresholds. Since the thresholds are not selected based on the statistical property of the image, there is a loss of information in extracted signals. Shi et al. [6] proposed a *k-means* based algorithm to extract ECG data from paper recordings. With the combination of Sobel edge operator and morphological closed operation, most background grids are discarded. The ECG waveform pixels are distinguished from background by using the *k-means* method. But our simulation results show that this method is invalid for inhomogeneous illumination case. In Ref. [7], Hough transform is used for de-skewing the scanned images. A color based segmentation technique is applied to remove background grids. And then, the ECG waveforms are segmented by region analysis. But the computational complexity of this algorithm is very high. In addition, if ECG records are scanned and saved as gray-scale images, this method is invalid. Badilini et al. [8] design software named as *ECG Scan* to convert ECG recorders into digital forms. But it requires some manual intervention in selecting ECG signal regions. Moreover, ECG records printed on the pure black and white background grids can result in incorrect results.

This paper proposes an improved ECG waveform extraction algorithm from scanned ECG paper records, which consists of three steps, that is, visual quality improvement, waveform segmentation, and waveform extraction. This paper makes two main contributions. First, skew correction is considered in ECG waveform digitization process for the first time, which significantly improve the accuracy of the extracted signal. Second, only edge points are used for waveform segmentation and extraction, which making the proposed works method very fast. In addition, our algorithm can be especially useful for scanned paper ECG records, as well as ECG pictures captured by digital cameras.

The paper is organized as follows. Section 1 gives introduction to the research topic. Section 2 discusses details of proposed method. In Sect. 3, simulation results are given and discussed. Finally, Sect. 4 presents conclusion and future work of this research.

2 Methodology

In this section, we describe our algorithm in detail. The proposed method includes three major steps: visual quality improvement, ECG waveform segmentation, and waveform extraction. First, scanned ECG images are enhanced by applying a serious of pre-processing steps, include spatial filtering, contrast stretching, and skew correction. And then, the edge map is obtained and used to calculate a global threshold, which is employed to distinguish ECG waveform from background. Finally, a compound technique combining region analysis and morphology operation is performed to extract precise ECG waveform signals.

The overall algorithmic steps are shown in Fig. 1 below. The detailed explanation of various steps in the algorithm is described as follows.

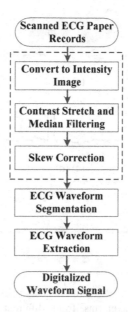

Fig. 1. Diagram of proposed algorithm.

2.1 Visual Quality Improvement

A typical ECG paper record includes several black ECG waveforms that appear on the white background together with horizontal and vertical red grid lines, as shown in Fig. 2(a). In addition, some label characters are also printed in the paper. In order to obtain good waveform extraction results, background grids and label texts must be removed.

The proposed algorithm uses grayscale information for waveform extraction. The maximum value among three color channels (represented by I_R, I_G, I_B) is selected as the grayscale value, which is denoted it as V, that is

$$V(x, y) = max(I_R, I_G, I_B) \tag{1}$$

In order to increase the gray-scale difference between the ECG waveform pixels and background, image V is enhanced by using contrast stretch technique. Figure 2(b) shows the grayscale and enhancement result of Fig. 2(a).

The edge information is needed for waveform segmentation step. Therefore we use a cross-shaped template for spatial median filtering. The radius of filter is set to be 3 pixels.

Skew is a kind of distortion frequently occurred in ECG records scanning processes, which is either due to human error or faulty scanners. This distortion makes hard of ECG waveform extraction and increases the complexity of analysis and classification. In order to extract faithfully the ECG signal from images, the skew has to be eliminated. To achieve skew correction, the skew angle is required. Here, in our work, we have proposed a *Horizontal Edge Project* (HEP) based technique to obtain the skew angle.

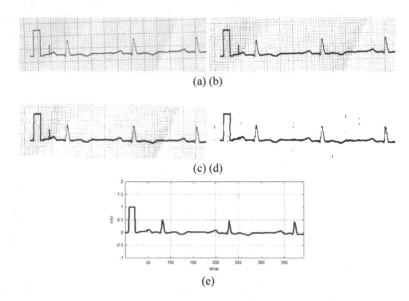

(a) (b)

(c) (d)

(e)

Fig. 2. Illustration of various waveforms from different stages of proposed algorithm. (a) Original color scanned ECG record image, (b) enhanced intensity image, (c) skew correction result, (d) segmentation result, (e) extraction result. (Color figure online)

The proposed HEP-based method consists of three steps. The horizontal edge map is first extracted by using 'Sobel' horizontal edge operator. We use **B** represents the edge map. Then **B** is rotated clockwise with a specific angle θ. The horizontal projection is performed using θ, and row projected values are computed. Next, a statistic metric (denoted as F_θ) is obtained using projected values. The angle (denoted as φ) which corresponds to maximum of F_θ is considered as the skew angle.

The details of our *HEP* algorithm are shown below:

Algorithm 1: horizontal edge project (HEP) based skew correction	
Input:	Intensity image
Output:	Intensity image after skew correction
Parameters:	The initial value of the rotation angle $\theta = -22$.
Step 1:	A horizontal edge binary map is extracted from input image by using 'Sobel' horizontal operator. The edge map is denoted as **B**.
Step 2:	Rotate **B** in degrees θ with clockwise. The horizontal project is performed using rotated map. The projected value of j-th row is represented by H_j.
Step 3:	Compute the *Mean* and *Variance* of H_j, then the statistic metric (F_θ) is obtained as follow: $F_\theta = \mathrm{var}(H_j)/\mathrm{mean}(H_j)$.
Step 4:	Update value of θ as $\theta+1$, and determine whether the condition of $\theta<23$ is met or not. If it is true, move to Step 2; otherwise, go to Step 5.
Step 5:	Find the angle corresponding to the maximum value of F_θ, which is denoted as φ. And φ is considered as the skew angle.
Step 6:	The skew correction is done by rotating the input image φ degrees with counter-clockwise.

Figure 2(c) shows the output of skew correction. For the convenience of waveform segmentation and extraction, those blank regions appears in the rotated image is filled with white.

2.2   ECG Waveform Segmentation

As shown in Fig. 2(c), the intensity values of background, grids and waveforms have obvious differences. In addition, the edge points usually appear near ECG waveforms or label characters, while the background and grid points have higher intensity value than waveform pixels. Therefore, the intensity value can be used to distinguish between waveforms and background. In our scheme, a threshold based ECG waveform segmentation algorithm is presented. Only edge points are chosen to determine the threshold used for waveform segmentation.

The details of proposed segmentation algorithm are shown below:

Algorithm 2: edge points based ECG waveform segmentation	
Input:	Intensity image after visual quality improvement (**E**)
Output:	Binary image of ECG waveform
Parameters:	Morphology *dilation* structure element
Step 1:	The binary edge image of input intensity image (**E**) is extracted by using 'Sobel' edge operator, which is denoted as **S**.
Step 2:	Apply morphological dilatation operation to **S**, and the result is denoted as **D**. It is considered that the dilatation operation is isotropic. Therefore the structure element set to be the 'disk' shape, where radius is set to 2.
Step 3:	According to **D**, the edge points in **E** are selected and sorted according to the intensity value from low to high. Then the median value is chosen as the global threshold (represented by *TH*) for ECG waveform segmentation.
Step 4:	Only edge points in **D** are considered as potential ECG waveform points. We use the follow formula to distinguish waveform points from backgrounds, $$S(x,y) = \begin{cases} 1 & E(x,y) < TH \\ 0 & \text{otherwise} \end{cases}$$ where **S** denotes the segmentation results.

Some edge points detected in Step 1 may be missed, which are caused by improper global threshold. For this situation, we employ the morphological dilation operation in Step 2 to connect the broken edge points.

2.3   ECG Waveform Extraction

Due to noise in recordings as well as the stylus speed in the ECG recorder, there are some gaps in the segmented ECG waveform which cause problems in curve extraction. Figure 2(d) gives a typical ECG the waveform segmentation result. As shown in Fig. 2 (d), some fragments of waveform are broken. In addition, these recording waveforms can be considered as time series of lead-voltage vs time. And there is more than one *y*-value for each *x* position in image coordinates. Therefore, we perform the tracking step to fill these gaps and choosing between multiple values of y for a particular value of *x*.

In our scheme, a predict-based technique is adopted to perform the waveform extraction. The morphology close operation and region analysis are combined to connect breaks. Then the ECG waveform is reduced to single pixel width by using vertical scanning analysis. Finally, missing points are interpolated by proximity points.

The details of proposed algorithm are show as follows:

Algorithm 3: ECG waveform extraction	
Input:	Segmented ECG waveform image(**S**)
Output:	Waveform extraction result
Parameters:	Morphology close structure element, Minimum area (S_{min})
Step 1:	Apply morphology *close* operation to input binary map **S**. The result is denoted by **W**. The close structure element is the same as the dilation operator used in Algorithm 2.
Step 2:	The connectivity analysis is performed for **W**. Those regions whose area is less than S_{min} are discarded. The result is denoted as **C**.
Step 3:	For each *x* position, calculate the upper and lower boundary of the each separated ECG waveform, which are depicted as $y_u(x)$ and $y_l(x)$. Then, the average value $(y_u(x)+y_l(x))/2$ is computed and regarded as the waveform trajectory value in *x* position. After above process, the trace of waveform is reduced to a single pixel width.
Step 4:	Missing points of waveform trajectory are reconstructed by linear interpolation operation by using proximity points.

Figure 2(e) gives the waveform extraction result, where the ECG trajectory is draw by solid blue line.

3   Results and Discussions

The database used in experiment consists of ECG paper records of 35 individuals. The data were obtained from different level of hospital in China. And the ECG records are printed and scanned by different equipment with various thermal papers made by different manufacturers.

Most the ECG signals are printed at 25-mm/s speed, 10 mm/mV-gain, scanned resolution of 300/600 DPI and stored as TIFF image format. Each ECG record has 12 leads of information and ECG lead traces are segmented manually. All the procedures will be implemented using OpenCV2.4.9 together with Visual C++ 2010 software platform.

To evaluate the performance of proposed scheme, three metrics are employed to measure the difference between original signals and reconstructed signals, that is, *Heart Rate (HR)*, *Average R-wave Amplitude (ARA)*, and *R-R peak Interval (RPI)*. Part of results are shown in Table 1, where M_O represents metrics that computed using original waveforms, M_E denotes metrics obtained from reconstructed waveforms.

The error of original waveforms and reconstructed waveforms can be measured by the normalized difference of M_O and M_E. As shown in Table 1, the largest error is only

4.5%, which demonstrate the validity of the proposed method. In addition, the error is proportional to the value of the skew angle. The larger the skew angle, the greater the error occurs. For instance, the skew angle of *ECG5* is 4 times larger than the skew angle of *ECG3*. As a result, errors of *ECG5* are also larger than *ECG3*.

Table 1. Comparison based on ECG features.

ECG lead waveform	Skew angle (φ)	Metrics	HR (times/min.)	AWA (mv)	RPI (ms)
ECG1	4°	M_O	78	1.65	853
		M_E	77	1.63	849
ECG2	−3°	M_O	59	1.78	729
		M_E	57	1.74	732
ECG3	2°	M_O	108	1.53	910
		M_E	106	1.51	904
ECG4	−6°	M_O	68	1.65	630
		M_E	65	1.60	635
ECG5	8°	M_O	112	1.80	803
		M_E	108	1.72	787

One limitation of presented scheme is not effective for the situation of strong noise. It particular, the waveform tracking will be failed when more than two lead waveforms are intersected. Figure 3 gives more experimental results of extracted ECG waveforms, where the left column indicates scanned ECG waveform segments and the right column

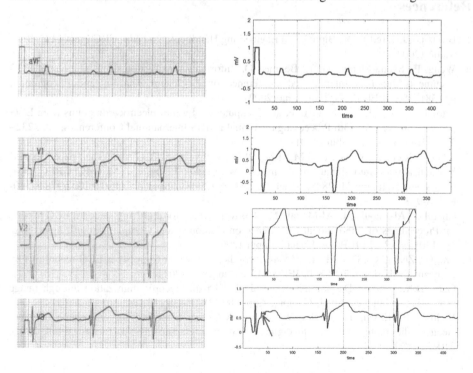

Fig. 3. More experimental results. (Color figure online)

represents reconstructed ECG signals by our method. The last row in Fig. 3 shows incorrect results. Some label characters and ECG waveforms are intersected, resulting in the error of the extracted waveform, as indicated by the red arrow in the Fig. 3.

4   Conclusion and Future Works

The conversion of ECG papers into digital form is very essential since it can be easily stored, accessed, exchanged and analyzed. This paper proposes some improvements to the existing ECG waveform digitalization process by using a HEP based skew correction technique, together with an edge points based ECG waveform segmentation and extraction algorithms. Experimental results show that extracted ECG waveform data keep the essential information of original ECG waveforms. In addition, our method can be easily extended to color/gray ECG pictures captured by digital cameras.

Further work is in progress to improve the accuracy of digitalized ECG signal for different backgrounds and resolutions. The final aim of our project is design the algorithm that can report and identify possible heart diseases automatically by using the estimated parameters of ECG waveform.

Acknowledgment. This work was supported in part by the National Natural Science Foundation of China (Grant Nos. 61002030 and 61472274) and Tianjin Postdoctoral Innovation Project.

References

1. Bronzino, J.D. (ed.): The Biomedical Engineering Handbook, 2nd edn. CRC Press LLC, Boca Raton (2000)
2. Wang, F., Syeda-Mahmood, T., Beymer, D.: Information extraction from multimodal ECG documents. In: 10th International Conference on Document Analysis and Recognition, pp. 381–385. IEEE Press, Barcelona (2009)
3. Kao, T., Hwang, L.J., Lin, Y.H., et al.: Computer analysis of electrocardiograms from ECG paper recordings. In: 23th Proceeding of Annual EMBS International Conferences, pp. 3232–3234. IEEE Press, Istanbul (2001)
4. Silva, A.R.G., de Oliveira, H.M., Lins, R.D.: Converting ECG and other paper legated biomedical maps into digital signals. In: Liu, W., Lladós, J., Ogier, J.-M. (eds.) GREC 2007. LNCS, vol. 5046, pp. 21–28. Springer, Heidelberg (2008). https://doi.org/10.1007/978-3-540-88188-9_3
5. Chebil, J., Al-Nabulsi, J., Al-Maitah, M.: A novel method for digitizing standard ECG papers. In: Proceedings of International Conference on Computer and Communication Engineering, pp. 1308–1312. IEEE Press, Kuala Lampur (2008)
6. Shi, G., Zheng, G., Dai, M.: ECG waveform data extraction from paper ECG recordings by K-means method, pp. 797–800. IEEE Press, Hangzhou (2011)
7. Garg, D.K., Thakur, D., Sharma, S., et al.: ECG paper records digitization through image processing techniques. Int. J. Comput. Appl. **48**(13), 35–38 (2012)
8. Badilini, F., Erden, T., Zareba, W., et al.: ECGscan: a method for conversion of paper electrocardiographic printouts to digital electrocardiographic files. J. Electrocardiol. **38**(4), 310–318 (2005)

Automatic Classification of Focal Liver Lesion in Ultrasound Images Based on Sparse Representation

Weining Wang[1], Yizi Jiang[1], Tingting Shi[1], Longzhong Liu[2(✉)],
Qinghua Huang[1], and Xiangmin Xu[1]

[1] School of Electronic and Information Engineering,
South China University of Technology, Guangzhou, China
[2] Department of Ultrasound, Sun Yat-Sen University Cancer Center, State Key
Laboratory of Oncology in South China, Collaborative Innovation Center for
Cancer Medicine, Guangzhou, China
Liulzh@sysucc.org.cn

Abstract. Early detection and accurate diagnosis for liver disease are very important. Due to the defects inherent in the ultrasound images and the complexity appearance of diseases, automatic classification for liver diseases in ultrasound images is a challenging task. In this paper, we introduce a novel method to classify focal liver lesions in ultrasound images. At first, we use an automatic image segmentation algorithm to delineate the lesion region. Then, according to the characteristics of liver lesions, we design a new image feature which is discriminative to liver lesions. Finally, six image features are processed by an improved sparse representation classifier to identify the diseases. We expand the sparse representation dictionary to optimize the classifier. Experimental results have shown that the proposed method could improve the classification accuracy in comparison with other state-of-the-art classifiers. It should be capable of assisting the physicians for liver disease diagnosis in the clinical practice.

Keywords: Focal liver lesion · Image classification · Sparse representation

1 Introduction

Liver cancer is the sixth most common cancer and the third leading cause of death in the word [1]. Early detection and accurate diagnosis for liver disease are very important, which are helpful to increase the chances for survival [2]. Currently, Ultrasound (US) imaging is the most widely spread imaging method because it is noninvasive, low cost and easy to operate.

Generally, the clinical diagnosis of liver diseases in ultrasound images is decided by specialized physicians' visual interpretation. The diagnosis is time-consuming and depends on the physicians' clinical experience. Hence, the demand for computer-aided diagnosis (CAD) in ultrasound images increased rapidly. CAD is able to assist the physicians and improve the diagnostic accuracy.

© Springer International Publishing AG 2017
Y. Zhao et al. (Eds.): ICIG 2017, Part II, LNCS 10667, pp. 513–527, 2017.
https://doi.org/10.1007/978-3-319-71589-6_45

With the development of computer technology, pattern recognition, and machine learning methods, researchers have done some effort on computer aided diagnosis of ultrasound images. In liver diseases diagnosis, most studies focused on diffused liver diseases [3–5] and focal liver diseases [6, 7]. Diffused liver diseases always attach to the whole liver. Hepatic adipose infiltration and cirrhosis are the most common diffused liver diseases. Focal liver diseases are concentrated over a quite small area of the tissue and it is very difficult to identify. Therefore, focal liver diseases classification is a more challenging task. Hepatic cyst (cyst), hemangioma (Hem) and hepatocellular carcinoma (HCC) are the most common focal liver diseases.

Typically, there are three main stages for liver diseases classification systems, including selection of region-of-interests (ROI), feature extraction and diseases classification by classifier.

For diffused liver diseases, Sabih and Hussain [3] and Owjimehr et al. [4] proposed automatic classification methods to diagnose liver steatosis in levels of Normal, Fatty and Heterogeneous. Sabih and Hussain [3] chose lesion regions as region-of-interests (ROI) and then used Wavelet Packet Transform (WPT) to extract regional statistical features. They finally achieve automatic classification by using a multi-class linear Support Vector Machine (SVM). Owjimehr et al. [4] mainly extracted Completed Local Binary Pattern (CLBP) features, and used SVM to do classification. In Alivar et al. [5], the ROI was cropped manually in ultrasound images and then extracted Wavelet Packet energy features, Gabor filter energy features and Gray Level Co-occurrence Matrix (GLCM) features. At last, normal, fatty and cirrhotic liver ultrasound images were classified by using K Nearest Neighbor (KNN) classifier.

For focal liver diseases, Jeon et al. [6] proposed an approach to recognize three kinds of focal liver lesions, including cysts, hemangiomas, and malignancies. They selected multiple different ROI, and then extracted five types of feature sets, containing GLCM features, First Order Statistics (FOS) features, Algebraic Moment Invariant (AMI) features, Auto-correlation (AC) features and Laws' texture energy measure (LTEM) features. In the end, Support Vector Machine (SVM) was used to reach the final goal. Raghesh Krishnan and Radhakrishnan [7] employed isocontour segmentation method for ROI segmentation. Then they put GLCM features and fractal features extracted from ROI into Artificial Neural Networks (ANN), achieving the classification on ten types of diffused and focal liver diseases.

In order to improve the accuracy of classification for liver lesions, most researches made efforts on extracting effective feature. Because various liver diseases have their own texture expressions in ultrasound images [8], texture feature has been widely used in classification. However, it is not enough to borrow the existing features that were designed for general image classification. We should carefully observe the characteristic of the lesions in ultrasound images to design specific image features.

On the other hand, current researches used common classifiers, such as SVM, ANN, KNN, to do classification. Most of these classifiers need training stages and large samples. However, as we know, it is hard to get plenty of medical images.

In recent years, Sparse Representation-based Classification (SRC) has been successfully used to solve problems in computer vision area, such as face recognition [9]. Different from other classifiers, the SRC is a nonparametric learning method which does not need a training process. SRC only uses the training data to construct an over-complete dictionary.

The SRC is just attracting attention in medical image recognition nowadays. Currently we find seldom papers of applications in ultrasound image, including classification for breast ultrasound image [10] or echocardiography [11]. In the work of [10, 11], researchers constructed the dictionary just by extracting the image feature vectors from training samples without considering the efficiency of features. On the one hand, in order to make the dictionary over-complete, the number of training samples should be far larger than the dimensions of features. It means that plenty of training samples are needed to construct such an over-complete dictionary. Meanwhile, the quality of dictionary may be effected by an incompact structure. The atoms of different classes in the dictionary are too similar to be partitioned, due to the intrinsic defects in ultrasound images like the speckle noise, artifacts and low contrast, and the diversity of different liver diseases. This problem will lead to false classification for liver diseases. In order to solve this problem, K-SVD based algorithm [12] is the most common method used for dictionary optimization. However, K-SVD based algorithms are computationally complex and need extra training samples because it contains complex singular value decomposition in iterative procedure.

In this paper, we propose a new method for focal liver lesion classification, including hepatic cyst (cyst), hepatic hemangioma (Hem), and hepatocellular carcinoma (HCC). Our main contributions are: (1) We use automatic image segmentation algorithm to acquire the lesion region, and select both normal region and lesion region in the ultrasound image, as our region of interests (ROI), to reduce the impact of individual differences; (2)According to the pathological characteristics of lesions and their diversity appearances in ultrasound images, we design a specific image feature named mutation ratio. Combining with GLCM and fractal features, the features in our method have a good discriminative ability for focal liver lesions classification; (3) We propose an effective dictionary optimization method named dictionary expansion based on sparse reconstruction (DESR) for SRC to classify lesions. The experimental result shows that our proposed method has an excellent performance in the focal liver lesion classification. The overall accuracy of the method is 97.76%.

This paper is organized as follows: Sect. 2 introduces the proposed method. Section 3 presents experimental results and performance analysis. Finally we draw a conclusion in Sect. 4.

2 Methods

In this paper, we propose an automatic classification method of liver ultrasound images based on sparse representation. It involves multiple ROI selection, feature extraction, and classification based on sparse representation. The architecture overview is shown in Fig. 1.

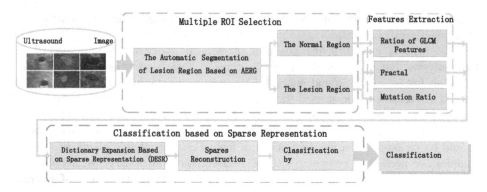

Fig. 1. Overview of the proposed focal liver lesion classification approach.

2.1   Multiple ROI Selection

In this paper, we choose the lesion and normal region as two ROIs considering the contrast between the lesion and normal region.

Automatic lesion region selection. We use an automatic energy-based region growing method (AERG) [13] of our previous work to get the lesion region automatically.

The lesion region is the focus in the ultrasound image of focal liver lesion. At present, most of the methods manually or semi-automatically select a fixation of the ROI that includes the lesion region [5, 7]. It is arduous and time-consuming. In this work, we use an automatic method to select the lesion region as ROI. The method makes the segmentation procedure timesaving and laborsaving. And the segmentation result is more accurate.

The specific steps are as follows.

(1) Delineating the boundary of focal liver lesion by AERG.
     At first, the seed point of lesion region is automatically selected by sparse reconstruction algorithm. Then the region growing process is controlled by a novel energy function including both internal and external energy, so as to make the edge of the region converge to the contour of the lesion accurately and keep a small internal difference at the same time. The details of this method can be found in reference [13].
(2) Getting a minimum enclosing rectangle of the focal liver lesion region.
(3) Cutting the rectangle area as a lesion image R_1.

Figure 2(a) is the original liver ultrasound images. The first line is an example of Hem image, the second line is cyst image and the last line is HCC image. Figure 2(b) shows the segmentation results of Fig. 2(a) using AERG. The green rectangle in Fig. 2(c) is the enclosing rectangle of lesion region.

Normal region selection. In order to describe the comparison of lesions and normal area, we also select the normal region as a ROI.

In ultrasonic diagnosis, the descriptors of echoes, such as hyperechogenicity, hypoechogenicity, echoless, echo enhancement etc., are often used for diseases

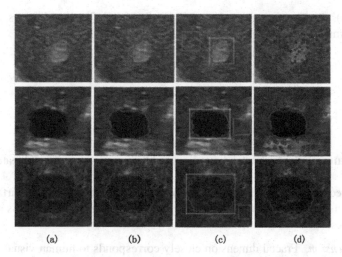

Fig. 2. Examples of liver ultrasound images. (a) The original liver ultrasound images, (b) segmentation results by AERG, (c) multiple ROI selection, (d) key points distribution. (Color figure online)

identification in ultrasound image. Due to the diversity of ultrasonic equipments and manipulators, the same region may have different appearances in different equipments and manipulators. Therefore, the absolute value of a single area is not comparable in ultrasound images. The descriptors should be given under comparison between the lesion and normal region of the same image to reduce such individual differences.

We extract a rectangle region outside the lesion region as the normal region. The normal region should lie in the liver parenchyma with uniform texture and don't contain blood vessels and bile stores. As shown in Fig. 2(c), the blue rectangle region is selected as the normal region R_2.

2.2 Feature Extraction

Generally, lesion disrupts uniform and regular texture distribution of the normal liver. The texture in lesion region has heterogeneous and distinctive characteristics in the ultrasound image. Therefore, the texture features play an important role in classification of ultrasound images [14]. According to the characteristics of the lesion region, we deliberately design a new feature called mutation ratio. Along with the GLCM and fractal features, we use 6 dimensional features for the following image classification.

GLCM feature ratio. The GLCM is a common and useful method for texture feature analysis [15, 16]. In order to eliminate the influence of different equipments or operators, we use the GLCM feature ratios of the lesion region R_1 and normal region R_2.

The specific method is as follows. (1) Lesion region R_1 and normal region R_2 are respectively computed three features (correlation, energy and homogeneity) of the GLCM at four directions $[0°, 45°, 90°, 135°]$. (2) Then the averages of features in four directions are computed to get the six features, namely correlation of $R_1(COR\_R_1)$ and $R_2(COR\_R_2)$ energy of $R_1(EN\_R_1)$ and $R_2(EN\_R_2)$, homogeneity of $R_1(Hom\_R_1)$ and

R_2(Hom_R_2). (3) The features ratios of R_1 to R_2 are defined as features of GLCM, listed in formula (1):

$$g_1 = COR\_R_1/COR\_R_2 \tag{1a}$$

$$g_2 = EN\_R_1/EN\_R_2 \tag{1b}$$

$$g_3 = Hom\_R_1/Hom\_R_2 \tag{1c}$$

Fractal features. We use fractal dimension and lacunarity as the fractal features in this paper.

Fractal geometry can effectively describe the roughness of nature surface. It has been successfully applied in ultrasound images to distinguish the roughness and texture characteristics.

Fractal dimension. Fractal dimension closely corresponds to human visual perception of roughness. It is invariant to image scale and rotation. Generally, the image surface is rougher, the fractal dimension value is bigger.

We use the differential Box-Counting approach proposed by Sarkar and Chaudhuri [17] to compute fractal dimension of image. It is calculated as:

$$N_r = \sum_{i,j} n_r(i,j) \tag{2}$$

N_r is counted for different values of r.

As we can see from Fig. 2(a), the appearances of the three lesion regions are various. The cyst is composed of clear fluid and its inner structure is very simple. Therefore, the appearance cyst area is smooth with minimum fractal dimension. Hem is a vascular coil and its structure is very complex, so its appearance is rough with the maximum fractal dimension. The pathological conditions of HCC are various, so the roughness of its appearance is fluctuant.

Lacunarity. Lacunarity is a feasible feature to measure textures in terms of gap distribution. Due to the fact that different texture may have the same or similar fractal dimension values, the fractal dimension can't determine the image alone. The notion of lacunarity, which is related to the degree of translational invariance, makes it possible to distinguish the images with the same fractal dimension values [18].

We adopt the box-counting method [18] to compute the lacunarity and set $t = 2$. which is performed:

$$L(t) = \frac{\sum_M M^2 P(M,t)}{[\sum_M MP(M,t)]^2} \tag{3}$$

Mutation ratio. We design a specific texture feature of mutation ratio based on the texture characteristics of different lesion regions in ultrasound images. The mutation

ratio is defined to describe the density of key points, which can represent the complexity of the lesion inner structure effectively.

Those pixels that have the obvious difference with the neighboring pixels are
defined as key points. Cyst is just clear fluids, whose structure is very simple. It is an
echoless area in ultrasound image, so its texture is uniform and there is almost no key
point. Hem which is filled with blood cells and blood vessels has large internal changes
inside. Therefore, a lot of key points can be detected in Hem images. HCC appearance
is mixed echogenicity and the number of key points stands between the Cyst and Hem.
As shown in Fig. 2(d), the blue circles are the key points detected in the images. The
key point distributions of the three images are very different.

The main stages of computing the mutation ratio are as follows. (1) Detecting key
points of liver ultrasound image. We use the method in [19] to extract the key points.
(2) Counting the total number φ of key points in the lesion region R_1. (3) A ratio φ to
the area $Area$ of the lesion' enclosing rectangle are defined as the mutation ratio.

Experiments in Sect. 3 will show the effectiveness of this feature in classification.
Equation (4) shows the specific definition mutation ratio d:

$$d = \varphi/Area \tag{4}$$

Feature normalization. In summary, the final feature vector f is composed of
3-dimensional GLCM feature ratios, 2-dimensional fractal features and 1-dimensional
mutation ratio feature. Then a normalization is done on vector f to normalize all
features to (0, 1).

2.3   The Improved Sparse Representation Classification

The core of Sparse Representation-based Classification (SRC) is that the test image can
be presented as a linear combination of those training samples from the same class. If
we represent the test sample in an over-complete dictionary whose base elements are all
the training samples, the representation is naturally sparse, involving only a small
fraction of the overall training database [9]. Different from other classifiers, SRC does
not need a train process but only need the training data [11].

Sparse representation-based classification [9]. Suppose that $D = [D\_1, D\_2, \ldots,$
$D\_i, \ldots, D\_c]$ is a matrix of the entire training set with n training samples of c classes,
where $D_i = [f_{i1}, f_{i2}, \ldots, f_{in_i}]$ is the sub-set of the training samples from class i and f_{ig} is
its gth feature vector.

A new test sample y is from one of the classes in the training set. It can be expressed
as a linear combination of the representation dictionary D:

$$y = Dx \tag{5}$$

where $x = [0, \ldots, 0, x_1^i, x_j^i, \ldots, x_n^i, 0, \ldots, 0]^T \in R^{n \times 1}$ is a coefficient vector, whose
coefficients are remarkable for the class the test sample belongs to, while for the other
classes, the coefficients are almost equal to zeros. x is obtained by solving the linear
Eq. (6):

$$\hat{x} = \arg \min\|x\|_1 \ s.t \ y = Dx \tag{6}$$

Where $\|\bullet\|_1$ is l1-norm, $\|\bullet\|_2$ is l2-norm.

Ideally, if the test sample y belongs to a certain class, the coefficients in the estimated $\hat{x}$ not within this class should all be zeros. However, noise and modeling error may lead to small nonzero entries associated with multiple object classes.

The noisy model is modified as:

$$\hat{x} = \arg \min\|x\|_1 \ s.t \ \|y - Dx\|_2 \le \varepsilon \tag{7}$$

where ε is a noise term.

We Define $\delta_i(x)$ as a classification vector, whose entries are zeros except for those associated with the class i. Using only the coefficients associated with the ith class, we can reconstruct the given test sample y as:

$$\hat{y}_i = D\delta_i(x) \quad i = 1, 2, \ldots, c \tag{8}$$

We then compute the residual $r_i(y)$ between y and $\hat{y}_i$:

$$r_i(y) = \|y - \hat{y}_i\|_2 \quad i = 1, 2, \ldots, c \tag{9}$$

The smaller $r_i(y)$ is, the more similar the true sample y and reconstructed sample $\hat{y}_i$ are. Therefore, we classify y based on these reconstruction samples by assigning it to the object class that minimizes the residual $r_i(y)$ between y and $\hat{y}_i$:

$$identity(y) = \arg \min_i\{r_i(y)\} \quad i = 1, 2, \ldots, c \tag{10}$$

Dictionary expansion based on sparse reconstruction. In this section, we propose a method of Dictionary Expansion based on Sparse Reconstruction (DESR) to construct a good dictionary for SRC, and then improve the classification accuracy of SRC.

Generally, by using sparse representation method, one image can be presented as a linear combination of a small number of atoms from predefined redundant dictionary. Therefore, the good or bad of the dictionary determinates the performance of sparse representation, and influences the final classification results. Hence, it is really necessary to construct a good redundant dictionary.

Traditional SRC does not get an ideal sparse representation which leads to an unsatisfied classification result. Traditional SRC directly simply uses the samples in the training set as atoms to construct dictionary. However, in order to get a redundant dictionary, a lot of training samples should be involved to make the number of training samples far more than the dimensions of the features. Nevertheless, we can't get so many training samples in medical image classification.

On the other hand, a good dictionary is supposed to have compact inner structure. It means that the difference between samples in the same class should be small, while be big between different class so as to make the reconstruction error small enough to classify the test samples correctly. However, due to the intrinsic defects and the complexity appearances of ultrasound image, sometimes the textures of the image appearances are very similar in different focal liver lesions. The dictionary gets an incompact structure when it is constructed by only using the samples in the training set as atoms directly.

Aiming to solve the problem in dictionary construction, we propose a method for Dictionary Expansion based on Sparse Reconstruction to construct a good dictionary.

In order to get an over-complete dictionary with good discriminative capability, we add a lot of new atoms to expand the dictionary. The dictionary is redundant and has a compact structure after expanding, which lead to a better performance in classification.

The details of DESR are shown as follows: (1) Constructing the initial dictionary $D = [f_1, f_2, \ldots, f_k, \ldots, f_n]$ by using the entire training set with n training samples of c classes, where f_k is the kth training sample. (2) Taking out atom f_k which belongs to the ith class from dictionary D in turn. Using the rest of atoms in D to sparsely

Table 1. The SRDE method

Dictionary Expansion based on Sparse Reconstruction

Input: initial dictionary D, maximum authorized residual error τ

Output: Optimized dictionary D_s

Initialization: extract features from training samples as dictionary atoms, namely $D = [f_1, f_2, \ldots, f_k, \ldots, f_n], D_s = D, k = 1$.

1) Take out every atom f_k from dictionary D in turn, then the original dictionary D changes to be D^* because the atom f_k is removed, namely $D^* = [f_1, \ldots, f_{k-1}, f_{k+1}, \ldots, f_n]$. Compute the sparse coefficients x of atom f_k using the new dictionary D^*:

$$\hat{x} = \arg\min \|x\|_1 \quad s.t \ \|y - D^* x\|_2 \le \varepsilon$$

2) Reconstruct the atom f_k:

$$\hat{f}_{kj} = D^* * \delta_j(x) \quad j = 1, 2, \ldots, c$$

3) Calculate residuals:

$$r_j(f_k) = \|f_k - \hat{f}_{kj}\|_2 \quad j = 1, 2, \ldots, c$$

4) If

$$\min(r_j(f_k)) \in label(f_k) \text{ and } \min(r_j(f_k)) \prec \tau$$

Then

$$D_s = [D_s, \hat{f}_{kj}]$$

5) Let $k=k+1$

If

$$k <= n$$

then

return back to step 1)

else

Output the dictionary D_s

represent f_k, and obtaining the sparse coefficients via (7). (3) Respectively using only the coefficients associated with the jth class ($j = 1, 2, \ldots, c$) to reconstruct f_k via (8). We can get c reconstruction samples $\{\hat{f}_{k1}, \ldots, \hat{f}_{kj}, \ldots, \hat{f}_{kc}\}$. (4) Computing all the residuals between f_k and each class-based reconstruction samples $\{\hat{f}_{k1}, \ldots, \hat{f}_{kj}, \ldots, \hat{f}_{kc}\}$. We can find the reconstruction sample $\hat{f}_{kj}$ which corresponds to the minimum residual. If j is equal to i (namely, reconstruction sample is in the same class with original sample) and the minimum residual is less than a predefined value, we think the reconstruction sample $\hat{f}_{kj}$ is small within-class scatter but big between-class scatter. Then, the reconstruction sample $\hat{f}_{kj}$ will be added to the original dictionary D to improve redundant and discriminative capability (Table 1).

Classification of focal liver lesions. We randomly select a certain number of samples as training samples and the rest as testing samples in the dataset. Training samples are used to construct the dictionary. And testing samples are classified through spare representation.

Figure 3 indicates the residual errors of a cyst and HCC ultrasound image which is correctly classified by our method and misclassified by traditional SRC.

As shown in Fig. 3, by using our method, the smallest residual error of a test image lies in the correct class. However, by using traditional SRC method, the smallest residual error of a test image lies in the incorrect class. It leads to the incorrect classification for this sample. For example, the smallest residual error of the cyst image lies in the cyst class in our method, while lies in HCC in traditional SRC method.

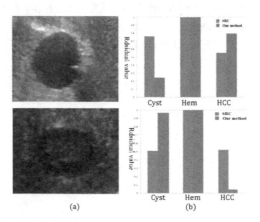

Fig. 3. Examples of cyst and HCC images. (a) The original liver ultrasound images, (b) residual diagram. The first line is an example of cyst image, the second line is HCC image.

The above analysis shows that SRC with DESR is more effective, and get better classification performance than the traditional SRC dictionary.

3 Experimental Results and Comparison

In this work, the dataset is comprised of 108 ultrasound image including 36 HCC, 36 Hem and 36 Cysts. All these liver lesions' categories were identified through the clinical pathological detection.

We employ leave-one-out cross validations in experiments. That is to say, we do the experiments with a training set formed from all but one case of the total data set. The single remaining sample is tested and compared with its labeled class. This process has been repeated 108 times until all samples were tested.

We extract GLCM features, fractal features and mutation ratio to make up six dimensional features, and then accomplish the Sparse Representation-based Classification with DESR to classify the three common focal liver diseases.

Five indices based on the true positive (TP), the false positive (FP), the true negative (TN), and the false positive (FP) are used to evaluate the performance of classifiers, which are the overall accuracy (ACC), the sensitivity (SEN), the specificity (SPE), the positive predicative value (PPF), and the negative predictive value (NPV) [20].

$$ACC = (TP + TN)/(TP + FN + FP + TN) \tag{12a}$$

$$SEN = TP/(TP + FN) \tag{12b}$$

$$SPE = TN/(FP + TN) \tag{12c}$$

$$PPV = TP/(TP + FP) \tag{12d}$$

$$NPV = TN/(FN + TN) \tag{12e}$$

Table 2 presents the classification results on three types of focal liver lesions by our method. The classification accuracy is up to 97.76% and the rest indices are also higher than 97%, which means our algorithm is indeed effective to classify focal liver diseases.

Table 2. The performance of proposed method in five indices

	ACC	SEN	SPE	PPV	NPV
Cyst	98.07%	97.22%	98.76%	99.07%	98.63%
Hem	98.07%	100%	98.61%	97.30%	100%
HCC	97.15%	97.22%	98.61%	97.22%	98.61%
Average	97.76%	98.15%	98.66%	97.86%	99.08%

Figure 4 lists some examples correctly classified by the proposed method.

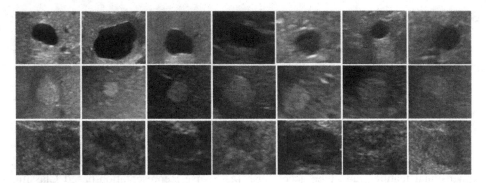

Fig. 4. The correct classification of examples. The first line is an example of Cyst image, the second line is Hem image and the last line is HCC image.

3.1   Comparison of Features Subsets

In order to further validate the effectiveness of our features, we compare the performance of three different feature sets by using SRC of DESR. The results are shown in Table 3.

Table 3 illustrates the following conclusion. (1) Compared with the feature set including only GLCM features and fractal features, the performance is greatly enhanced after adding feature of mutation ratio. It proves the effectiveness of mutation ratio feature. (2) We extract the best seven dimensional features in paper [8] to be a comparison on our dataset. The feature set contains Spatial Gray Level Co-occurrence Matrix, Fourier Power Spectrum, the Statistical Feature Matrix (SFM) texture, the Texture Energy Measures (TEM) suggested by Laws, and the fractal-based features. The results show that our features perform better and using GLCM Ratios is effectual, especially in SEN and PPV, which are the most important indexes in clinical diagnosis.

Table 3. The performance of the proposed classification method on different feature sets

	ACC	SEN	SPE	PPV	NPV
Features in paper [8]	91.98%	87.96%	93.98%	88.53%	94.08%
GLCM ratios and fractal features subset	93.83%	90.74%	95.37%	90.75%	95.40%
All features	97.76%	98.15%	98.66%	97.86%	99.08%

3.2   Comparison of Different Classifiers

In this section, the performance of our proposed classifier is compared with some state-of-the-art classifiers, including the traditional SRC, the SVM and the BPNN. The six features proposed in this paper is applied to all classifiers. We use the function provided by neural network tools in MATLAB for BPNN and SVM classifier provided by LIBSVM [21] to accomplish these classifiers. For BPNN, we select ten nodes as hidden layers and for SVM, we choose linear function as our kernel function.

Table 4. Comparative evaluation of four different classifiers

	ACC	SEN	SPE	PPV	NPV
BPNN	91.98%	88.89%	93.06%	89.77%	94.45%
SVM	94.44%	91.67%	95.83%	92.33%	95.92%
SRC	95.06%	92.59%	96.29%	92.69%	96.42%
The proposed method	**97.76%**	**98.15%**	**98.66%**	**97.86%**	**99.08%**

Table 4 shows the performances of different classifiers. It shows that our method gets the best results and all indexes are better than those in other outstanding methods.

Moreover, all classifiers achieved the overall correct percent over 90. It means that the proposed six dimensional features have a discriminative description to classify the liver diseases.

3.3 Comparison of Different Methods

We also make comparisons with current classification methods for liver ultrasound image [3, 6]. Sabih [3] chose liver lesion regions as ROI. This ROI was analyzed using Wavelet Packet Transform (WPT) and a number of statistical features were obtained. A multi-class linear SVM was then used for classification.

According to the advantages of existing ROI selection methods, Jeon [6] selected multiple ROI to represent well various ultrasonic appearances of liver lesions. In their view, multiple ROI could effectively hold a lot of used information and achieve good classification performance, regardless of features being used. We used five dimensional features from gray-level co-occurrence matrix, which achieved best classification results in paper [6].

As shown in Table 5, our method outperforms these two algorithms.

Table 5. Comparative evaluation of three different methods

	ACC	SEN	SPE	PPV	NPV
Method in paper [6]	90.12%	85.19%	92.59%	86.14%	92.93%
Method in paper [3]	90.74%	86.11%	93.06%	86.50%	93.05%
The proposed method	**97.76%**	**98.15%**	**98.66%**	**97.86%**	**99.08%**

4   Conclusion

In this paper, we propose an innovate method to classify the focal liver lesions in ultrasound images. This method can automatically and accurately extract the lesion region to save time and labor. In feature extraction, we employ ultrasonic appearances of liver lesions. Specially, we design the mutation rate feature based on key point distribution. Combined with the GLCM and fractal features, we obtain 6 dimensional features which have a discriminative capability to distinguish focal liver lesions. Furthermore, we propose an improved SRC of DESR, which can expand and optimize the dictionary of sparse representation. Experimental results show that the proposed method can improve the classification performance significantly. The better accuracy and simple implementation make the proposed method beneficial to help physicians make a diagnosis, providing a realistic performance benchmark for further research efforts.

Acknowledgements. This work was supported by the Natural Science Foundation of Guangdong Province #2015A030313212, Natural Science Foundation of China (NSFC) #61372007, #61171142, and the Science and Technology Planning project of Guangdong Province of China #2014B010111003, #2014B010111006, and the National Engineering Technology Research Center of Mobile Ultrasonic Detection #2013FU125X02. It was also supported in part by the National Natural Science Founding of China (U1636218), and Guangzhou Key Lab of Body Data Science (201605030011).

References

1. <http://www.cancer.gov/cancertopics/factsheet/Sites-Types/metastatic>
2. Santos, C.A., Brennan, D.C., Chapman, W.C., Fraser, V.J., Olsen, M.A.: Delayed-onset cytomegalovirus disease coded during hospital readmission in a multicenter, retrospective cohort of liver transplant recipients. Liver Transpl. **21**, 581–590 (2015)
3. Sabih, D., Hussain, M.: Automated classification of liver disorders using ultrasound images. J. Med. Syst. **36**, 3163–3172 (2012)
4. Owjimehr, M., Danyali, H., Helfroush, M.S.: Fully automatic segmentation and classification of liver ultrasound images using completed LBP texture features. In: Proceedings of Iranian Conference on Electrical Engineering (ICEE), pp. 1956–1960 (2014)
5. Alivar, A., Daniali, H., Helfroush, M.S.: Classification of liver diseases using ultrasound images based on feature combination. In: Proceedings of International Conference on Computer and Knowledge Engineering (ICCKE), pp. 669–672 (2014)
6. Jeon, J.H., Choi, J.Y., Lee, S., Ro, Y.M.: Multiple ROI selection based focal liver lesion classification in ultrasound images. Expert Syst. Appl. **40**, 450–457 (2013)
7. Raghesh Krishnan, K., Radhakrishnan, S.: Focal and diffused liver disease classification from ultrasound images based on isocontour segmentation. IET Image Process. **9**, 261–270 (2015)
8. Singh, M., Singh, S., Gupta, S.: An information fusion based method for liver classification using texture analysis of ultrasound images. Inf. Fusion **19**, 91–96 (2014)
9. Wright, J., Yang, A.Y., Ganesh, A., Sastry, S.S., Ma, Y.: Robust face recognition via sparse representation. IEEE Trans. Pattern Anal. Mach. Intell. **31**, 210–227 (2009)
10. Al Helal, A., Ahmed, K.I.: Rahman, M.S., Alam, S.K.: Breast cancer classification from ultrasonic images based on sparse representation by exploiting redundancy. In: Proceedings of International Conference on Computer and Information Technology (ICCIT), pp. 92–97 (2014)
11. Guo, Y., Wang, Y., Kong, D., Shu, X.: Automatic classification of intracardiac tumor and thrombi in echocardiography based on sparse representation. IEEE J. Biomed. Health Informat. **19**, 601–611 (2015)
12. Aharon, M., Elad, M., Bruckstein, A.: K-SVD: an algorithm for designing over complete dictionaries for sparse representation. IEEE Trans. Sig. Process. **54**, 4311–4322 (2006)
13. Wang, W., Li, J., Jiang, Y., Xing, Y., Xu, X.: An automatic energy-based region growing method for ultrasound image segmentation. In: Proceedings of International Conference on Image Processing (ICIP), pp. 1553–1557 (2015)

14. Mohanty, A.K., Beberta, S., Lenka, S.K.: Classifying benign and malignant mass using GLCM and GLRLM based texture features from mammogram. Int. J. Eng. Res. Appl. **1**, 687–693 (2011)
15. Suganya, R., Rajaram, S.: Feature extraction and classification of ultrasound liver images using haralick texture-primitive features: application of SVM classifier. In: Proceedings of International Conference on Recent Trends in Information Technology (ICRTIT), pp. 596–602 (2013)
16. Kumar, S.S., Moni, R.S., Rajeesh, J.: Liver tumor diagnosis by gray level and contourlet coefficients texture analysis. In: Proceedings of International Conference on Computing, Electronics and Electrical Technologies (ICCEET), pp. 557–562 (2012)
17. Sarkar, N., Chaudhuri, B.B.: An efficient differential box-counting approach to compute fractal dimension of image. IEEE Trans. Syst. Man Cybern. **24**, 115–120 (1994)
18. Allain, C., Cloitre, M.: Characterizing the lacunarity of random and deterministic fractal sets. Phys. Rev. A **44**, 3552–3558 (1991)
19. Witkin, A.P.: Scale-space filtering: a new approach to multi-scale description. In: Proceedings of International Conference on Acoustics, Speech, and Signal Processing, pp. 150–153 (1984)
20. Alvarenga, A.V., Infantosi, A.F.C., Pereira, W.C.A., Azevedo, C.M.: Assessing the performance of morphological parameters in distinguishing breast tumors on ultrasound images. Med. Eng. Phys. **32**, 49–56 (2010)
21. Chang, C.C., Lin, C.J.: LIBSVM: a library for support vector machines. ACM Trans. Intell. Syst. Technol. **2**, 27 (2011)

Simultaneous Segmentation of Multiple Regions in 3D Bladder MRI by Efficient Convex Optimization of Coupled Surfaces

Xiao-pan Xu[1], Xi Zhang[1], Yang Liu[1], Qiang Tian[3],
Guo-peng Zhang[1], Zeng-yue Yang[4], Hong-bing Lu[1(✉)],
and Jing Yuan[2(✉)]

[1] School of Biomedical Engineering,
Fourth Military Medical University, Xi'an, China
luhb@fmmu.edu.cn
[2] Mathematics and Statistics School, Xidian University, Xi'an, China
jyuan@robarts.ca
[3] Department of Radiology, Tangdu Hospital, Xi'an, China
[4] Department of Urology, Tangdu Hospital, Xi'an, China

Abstract. Urinary bladder cancer (BC) is a severe common cancer that threatens human health worldwide. The muscle-invasive depth of BC penetrating the bladder wall is a key factor for clinical diagnosis and treatment decision. To quantitatively calculate the invasive depth of BC from three-dimensional (3D) magnetic resonance (MR) images, first of all, an accurate and efficient segmentation algorithm other than manual segmentation is desirably needed to accurately and efficiently extract the wall region from bladder images. However, this is a challenging task due to the artifacts inside bladder urine, weak wall region, and complicated background intensity distributions. To deal with these challenges, in this paper we propose an efficient convex optimization based 3D multi-region continuous max-flow algorithm (MR-CMF) for bladder T2-weighted MR images (T2WI). It partitions a bladder dataset into three regions like wall region, the urine region and the background region by simultaneously generating two coupled surfaces: the inner-wall boundary (IB) and the outer-wall boundary (OB) of bladder, basing on the continuous max-flow model with anatomical inter-surface constraint and bladder wall thickness prior for efficient convex relaxation optimization. Primary experiments with five datasets of 3.0T T2WI indicate that the proposed algorithm obtains an average DSC of 87.28% and an average time span of 6.0 min without parallelized computation, obviously outperforming the other existing methods for bladder segmentation.

Keywords: Bladder cancer · MRI · T2WI · Image segmentation · MR-CMF
Convex relaxation optimization

1 Introduction

Urinary bladder cancer (BC) is the fourth most common cancer and ranks ninth as a cause of cancer related deaths among males globally [1, 2]. Accurate identification of tumor involvement, especially muscle-invasive depth (MID), is of paramount

© Springer International Publishing AG 2017
Y. Zhao et al. (Eds.): ICIG 2017, Part II, LNCS 10667, pp. 528–542, 2017.
https://doi.org/10.1007/978-3-319-71589-6_46

significance for treatment strategy [1, 3–5]. In recent years, optical cystoscopy (OCy) with transurethral biopsies is the standard reference for monitoring BC, muscle invasiveness prediction, MID determination as well as staging diagnosis [1–5]. However, it is an invasive manner with high expenses and large time consumption, bringing great pain to the patients and ascending the risk of urinary tract bleeding and infection [1–5]. Non-invasive imaging-based biomarkers may provide a direct evaluation of the disease. For example, the local-part thickening of bladder wall in medical images has become a useful indicator for non-surgical detection and extraction of suspected BC regions [1, 6–9].

Excellent resolution of soft tissues, non-invasive procedures and easy performance of three-dimensional (3D) magnetic resonance imaging (MRI) make it ideally suitable for in vivo bladder imaging, as well as observing and detecting BC with non-surgical imaging-based biomarkers [1, 2, 6–9]. In order to quantitatively compute such biomarkers from bladder images, it is required to accurately delineate the outer-wall boundary (OB) and inner-wall boundary (IB) of bladder to separate the whole bladder wall from urine and background regions [2, 6–9]. At present, the segmentation of bladder wall in MRI is manually performed by experts [6, 9]. However, it is a tedious and time-consuming process. An accurate and efficient segmentation algorithm, other than the manual segmentation, is in desirable need to extract the whole bladder wall region from bladder MR images.

The main objective of this paper is to explore an accurate 3D multi-region segmentation method for separating bladder wall from urine and outer background regions on T2-weighted MR images (T2WI) efficiently and robustly, which may greatly help the computer assisted detection and diagnosis of bladder cancer in clinical researches and applications.

Imaging-based segmentation of bladder wall is a difficult work full of challenges, including bladder shape variation, artifacts in the urine region, weak boundary of bladder wall and complicated background intensity distributions [6, 9]. So far, very a few bladder wall segmentation methods have been proposed. Duan et al. developed a coupled level-set framework, which adopted a modified Chan-Vese model to locate the inner and outer surfaces of bladder wall, and then generated a coupled model for segmenting both surfaces of bladder wall on T1-weighted MR images (T1WI) [6, 9]. However, it is difficult to locate the outer-wall boundary (OB) due to the complicated outside intensity distribution. Qin et al. proposed an adaptive shape prior (ASP) constrained coupled directional level-set algorithm, to fully exploit the shape prior information like directional gradient, inter-slice and regional shape variation, minimum thickness and so on, to obtain a robust segmentation result [2, 6–9]. Cha et al. incorporate the deep learning convolutional neural network (DL-CNN) with conjoint level-set analysis and segmentation system (CLASS) to realize the bladder segmentation on CT images [10]. These methods are either easily influenced by the initialized contours of OB and inner-wall boundary (IB) manually delineated on the middle bladder slice, or limited by time-consuming and complicated procedures [11]. Moreover, their core mathematical schemes are based on local optimization techniques, which are susceptible to image quality [11].

Apart from the level-set based algorithms mentioned above, Ukwatta and Yuan proposed a novel 3D multi-region segmentation algorithm based on coupled continuous max-flow (CMF) and convex relaxation optimization methods to simultaneously segment the wall region of carotid from the outer background region and inner lumen region [11]. Distinct from the discrete global optimization methods like graph-cuts, the convex relaxation methods are employed in a spatially continuous setting, providing sub-pixel accuracy while avoiding metrication artifacts [11–16].

Inspired by their work, in this study we try to develop an efficient convex optimization based 3D multi-region segmentation algorithm for bladder T2-weighted MR images (T2WI), basing on the continuous max-flow (CMF) model with anatomical inter-surface constraint and bladder wall thickness (BWT) prior for efficient convex relaxation optimization.

2   Methods

In this section, an accurate *multi-region continuous max-flow* (MR-CMF) segmentation method is proposed, which separates a dataset of 3D bladder image V into three regions: the urine region R_u, the bladder wall region R_w and the outer background region R_b, by simultaneously evolving two coupled surfaces including the inner-wall boundary (IB) S_{IB} and the outer-wall boundary (OB) S_{OB} to their globally optimized positions, as illustrated in Fig. 1.

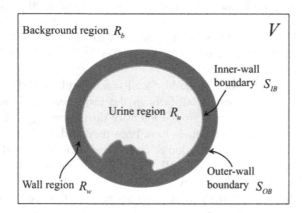

Fig. 1. Major regions and surfaces to be delineated in bladder image V

These three regions should strictly meet such conditions:

$$\begin{cases} R_b \cup R_w \cup R_u = V, \\ R_b \cap R_w = \varnothing \\ R_w \cap R_u = \varnothing \\ R_b \cap R_u = \varnothing \end{cases} \tag{1}$$

Considering the prior knowledge of the anatomic information, the inner-wall surface S_{IB} always remains incapsuled by the outer-wall surface S_{OB}, namely the anatomic inter-surface constraint:

$$S_{IB} \subset S_{OB} \tag{2}$$

In the process of segmentation, when the two surfaces S_{IB} and S_{OB} are evolved in each iteration, the generated three regions R_u, R_w and R_b are determined as:

$$R_u := \Omega_{S_{IB}}, \quad R_w := \Omega_{S_{OB}} \backslash \Omega_{S_{IB}}, \quad R_b := V \backslash \Omega_{S_{OB}} \tag{3}$$

where $\Omega_{S_{IB}}$ and $\Omega_{S_{OB}}$ are the regions enclosed by S_{IB} and S_{OB}, respectively.

Then, we introduce a convex optimization based approach with a novel and efficient continuous max-flow (CMF) based algorithm to accurately segment the whole bladder wall region R_w from the input 3D bladder MR images. Distinct from the previous bladder segmentation algorithms, such as level-set that bases on the techniques of local optimization for contour evolution, in this method, the two surfaces S_{IB} and S_{OB} can be evolved to their globally optimal locations, while enforcing the anatomic inter-surface constraint (2). Moreover, the intensity probability density functions (PDF) of the three regions R_u, R_w and R_b are exploited as global descriptors to guide the evolvement of the coupled surfaces S_{IB} and S_{OB} [11, 13–16].

2.1 Optimization Model and Convex Relaxation

Let $L_r := \{u, w, b\}$ be the label set representing the three independent regions of image V, and $L_s := \{IB, OB\}$ represent the label set of two surfaces to be calculated in this work. Here, we adopted PDF of intensity distributions in the region R_k to describe the probabilities of allocating each element $x \in V$ to the optimal region.

The PDF of intensities like intensity histogram is a kind of global descriptors of the objects of interest, such that matching the intensity PDF models of the object regions provides a robust mechanism to guide the evolvement of the surfaces [11, 13–16]. Let $I(x) \in Z$ be a given 3D bladder MR image, where Z is the set of image intensity values. According to the Parzen method, the intensity PDF $h_k(z)$, where $z \in Z, k \in L_r$, for the respective three regions can be computed as [11, 13, 16]

$$h_k(z) = \frac{\int_V K(z - I(x)) u_k(x) dx}{\int_V u_k(x) dx}, k \in L_r \tag{4}$$

where $K(\cdot)$ is the Gaussian kernel function described in Eq. (5) and $u_k(x)$ is the labeling function of the corresponding region R_k which is enclosed by the surface S_m, $m \in L_s$, respectively.

$$K(x) = \frac{1}{\sqrt{2\pi\sigma^2}} \exp(-x^2/2\sigma^2) \tag{5}$$

$$u_k(x) := \begin{cases} 1, x \in R_k \\ 0, otherwise \end{cases}, k \in L_r \tag{6}$$

In computation, we define $u_1(x)$ and $u_2(x)$ to be the binary region labeling functions of the regions enclose by S_{IB} and S_{OB}, respectively.

$$u_1(x) := \begin{cases} 1, & x \in \Omega_{S_{IB}} \\ 0, & otherwise \end{cases} \tag{7}$$

$$u_2(x) := \begin{cases} 1, & x \in \Omega_{S_{OB}} \\ 0, & otherwise \end{cases} \tag{8}$$

Considering the anatomic inter-surface constraint (2), the binary region labeling functions must satisfy the following equations:

$$u_1(x) \le u_2(x), \quad \forall x \in V \tag{9}$$

$$\begin{cases} u_u(x) = u_1(x), \\ u_w(x) = u_2(x) - u_1(x), \\ u_b(x) = 1 - u_2(x) \end{cases} \tag{10}$$

Therefore, we define the cost function $C_k(x)$, $k \in L_r$, of labeling each element $x \in V$ to be in the region R_k, $k \in L_r$ by log-likelihoods of the PDF value of x [13, 15, 16], i.e.

$$C_k(x) = -\log(h_k(z)), \quad k \in L_r \tag{11}$$

With the combination of the global optimization of the intensity PDF models $h_k(z)$ and their corresponding cost functions $C_k(x)$ with geometric constraint (9)–(10) on the labeling functions, we formulate the following energy function to segment the given image V by achieving both the minimum total labeling costs and the minimum total regions/volumes of segmented surfaces [15, 16], such that

$$\min_{u_{1,2}(x) \in \{0,1\}} \sum_{k \in L_r} \int_{R_k} C_k(x)dx + \sum_{k \in L_s} \int_{\partial R_k} ds \tag{12}$$
$$s.t. \quad u_1(x) \le u_2(x), \quad \forall x \in V$$

Considering the minimum geodesic length should be used to constrain the segmentation results, the proposed optimization model (12) can be equally written as follows:

$$\min_{u_{1,2}(x) \in \{0,1\}} \sum_{k \in L_r} <u_k, C_k> + \sum_{k \in L_s} \int_{\Omega} g(x)|\nabla u_k(x)|dx \tag{13}$$
$$s.t. \quad u_1(x) \le u_2(x), \quad \forall x \in V$$

where the weighted function $g(x) \ge 0$ and can be computed as follows [11, 13, 15, 16]

$$g(x) = \lambda_1 + \lambda_2 \exp(-\lambda_3 |\nabla \tilde{I}(x)|), \quad \lambda_{1,2,3} \ge 0 \tag{14}$$

Here, we introduce the image smoothing process with a 5×5 Gaussian kernel and $\sigma = 1$ to filter the original image data $I(x)$ in the spatial domain and obtain a more smoothing image data $\widetilde{I}(x)$ for further gradient calculation, which could diminish the influence of complicated background intensity distributions to the segmentation results.

In this work, we solve the challenging combinatorial optimization problem (14) by its convex relaxation [11, 13, 14]

$$\min_{u_{1,2}(x)\in[0,1]} \sum_{k\in L_r} <u_k, C_k> + \sum_{k\in L_s} \int_\Omega g(x)|\nabla u_k(x)|dx$$
$$s.t. \quad u_1(x) \leq u_2(x), \quad \forall x \in V \tag{15}$$

subject to the geometric constraints (9)–(10).

Obviously, the binary-valued labeling functions $u_{1,2}(x) \in \{0,1\}$ are relaxed into the convex constraints $u_{1,2}(x) \in [0,1]$ in (15). Given the convex energy function of (15) and the geometric constraints (9)–(10), the challenging combinatorial optimization problem (13) is reduced to the convex relaxation optimization problem [11, 13–16], as shown in (15).

2.2 Dual Formulation: Continuous Max-Flow Model

In this section, we introduce a new spatially continuous flow maximization model, namely the continuous max-flow (CMF) model [11, 13–16], which is mathematically equivalent or dual to the proposed convex relaxation model (15). Particularly, it results in an efficient algorithm to compute the optimum labeling functions of (15) while avoiding tackling its challenging non-smoothing function terms and constraints directly [11, 15, 16].

The proposed CMF model can be visually explained by means of streaming the maximum flow from a source through the specified graph, as shown in Fig. 2, and mathematically formulated as follows [11, 15, 16]

$$\max_{p,q} \int_V p_b(x)dx \tag{16}$$

subject to:

- *Flow capacity constraints* [11, 15, 16]: the sink flows $p_k(x), k \in L_r$ suffice:

$$p_k(x) \leq C_k(x), \quad k \in L_r, \tag{17}$$

and the spatial flows $q_k(x), k \in L_s$ suffice [11, 15, 16]:

$$|q_k(x)| \leq g(x), \quad k \in L_s, \tag{18}$$

- *Flow conservation constraints* [11, 15, 16]: the total flow residue vanishes at each x within the image domain Ω_k:

$$G_{IB}(x) := (divq_{IB} - p_w + p_u)(x) = 0;$$
$$G_{OB}(x) := (divq_{OB} - p_b + p_w)(x) = 0; \tag{19}$$

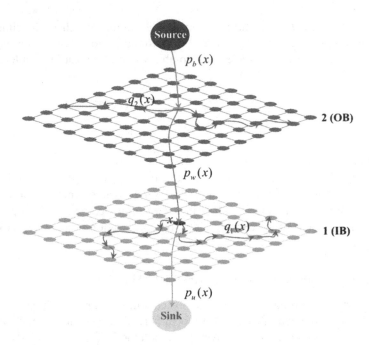

Fig. 2. The flow configuration of the proposed *CMF* model: links between terminals and the image regions, the source flow $p_b(x)$ and the sink flow $p_k(x)$, $k \in L_r$.

As defined above, the source flow function $p_w(x)$ is free of constraints. Through analysis, we can prove the duality between the *CMF formulation* (16) and the *convex relaxation model* (15), i.e.

Proposition 1. The *CMF model* (16) and the *convex relaxation model* (15) are dual (equivalent) to each other, namely

$$(15) \Leftrightarrow (16)$$

2.3   Duality-Based CMF Algorithm

According to **Proposition** 1, it is easy to see that the *convex relaxation model* (15) can be solved equally by computing the *CMF model* (16), which derives the new duality-based CMF algorithm proposed in this section through the state-of-the-art global convex optimization techniques. In addition, the introduced CMF algorithm enjoys great numerical advantages [11, 13–16]: (1) it successfully avoids directly tackling non-smoothing total-variation functions in the energy of convex minimization problem (15) by the projections to some simple convex sets instead; (2) it implicitly applies the anatomic inter-surface prior (2) and geometric constraints (9)–(10) into the introduced flow-maximization scheme (as depicted in Fig. 2).

With reference to the theory of augmented multiplier algorithms [11, 13–16], an efficient hierarchical CMF algorithm can be derived, which iteratively optimizes the following augmented Lagrangian function,

$$\max_{p,q} \quad \min_{u} L_c(u;p,q) := L(u;p,q) - \frac{c}{2} \sum_{k \in Ls} \|G_k\|^2, \quad where \quad u = u_i(x), i \in \{1,2\}.$$

(20)

subject to the flow capacity constraints (17) and (18). The coefficient c is positive constant [11, 15, 16]. The $L(u;p,q)$ above is the Lagrangian function associated with the CMF model, which is defined as

$$L(u;p,q) = \int_V p_b(x)dx + <u_1, divq_{IB} - p_w + p_u> + <u_2, divq_{OB} - p_b + p_w>$$

(21)

Therefore, the CMF algorithm explores the following steps at the n-th iteration:

- Maximize $L_c(u;p,q)$ over the spatial flows $|q_k(x)| \leq g(x), k \in L_s$, while fixing the other variables $(u;p)^n$, which amounts to

$$q_k^{n+1} := \arg\max_{|q_k(x)| \leq g(x)} -\frac{c}{2} \|divq_k - F_k^n\|^2$$

(22)

where $F_k^n(x)$, $k \in L_s$, are fixed. This can be computed by the gradient-projection iteration:

$$q_k^{n+1} = \text{Pr oj}_{|q_k(x)| \leq g(x)}(q_k^n + \tau\nabla(divq_k^n - (F_k^n)));$$

(23)

where $\tau > 0$, represents the step size for convergence [15, 16].
- Maximize $L_c(u;p,q)$ over the source flows $p_b(x)$, while fixing the other variables $(u;p_k,q)^n$, which amounts to

$$p_b^{n+1} := \arg\max_{p_b} \int_V p_b dx - \frac{c}{3} \sum_{k \in L_r} \|p_b - J_k^n\|^2$$

(24)

where $J_k^n(x)$, $k \in L_r$, are fixed. This can be solved exactly by

$$p_b^{n+1}(x) = (J_b^n(x) + J_w^n(x) + J_u^n(x) + 1/c)/3$$

(25)

- Update the labeling functions $u_{1,2}(x)$

$$u_{1,2}^{n+1}(x) = u_{1,2}^n - cG_{1,2}^n(x)$$

(26)

where $G_{1,2}^n(x)$ stand for the representative flow residue functions.

3 Experiments and Results

3.1 Study Population and Image Acquisition

The database consists of five sets of 3D bladder MR images respectively from five patients. They were consecutively selected for this study at Tangdu Hospital. All of them were postoperative pathologically confirmed bladder cancer and underwent preoperative bladder MRI examination.

Subjects were scanned by a clinical whole body scanner (GE Discovery MR 750 3.0T) with a phased-array body coil. A high-resolution 3D Axial Cube T2-weighted MR sequence was used due to its high soft tissue contrast and relatively fast image acquisition [2, 9]. Before MRI scan, each subject was instructed to drink enough mineral water, and waited for an adequate time period so that the bladder was fully distended. The scanning parameters are listed in Table 1.

Table 1. Principal parameters used for MRI acquisition

Parameter name	Corresponding value
Series description	Ax Cube T2
Acquisition type	3D
Acquisition time (ms)	160456
TR (ms)	2500
TE (ms)	135
Slice thickness (mm)	1
Spacing between slices (mm)	1
Pixel size (mm)	1.0×1.0
Image size	512×512

3.2 User Interaction

The user interaction in our method was choosing some nodes of urine region, bladder wall region and outer background region, respectively, on a single transverse slice of 3D MR image, as shown in Fig. 3(a). The nodes were chosen by the user with polygonous box interface tool, as shown in Fig. 3(b). With the nodes of these three regions delineated, the corresponding PDF functions of these regions were derived to conduct the 2D bladder multi-region CMF segmentation. Figure 3(c) shows the PDF curves calculated of the corresponding regions.

3.3 2D Multi-region Segmentation

With the PDF functions of three regions, the cost function $C_u(x)$, $C_w(x)$ and $C_b(x)$ were calculated based on (11). Here, we introduce the hard constraints [11, 15, 16]:

$$\begin{cases} C_w(x) = +\infty, & C_b(x) = +\infty, x \in N_u \\ C_l(x) = +\infty, & C_b(x) = +\infty, x \in N_w \\ C_l(x) = +\infty, & C_w(x) = +\infty, x \in N_b \end{cases} \tag{27}$$

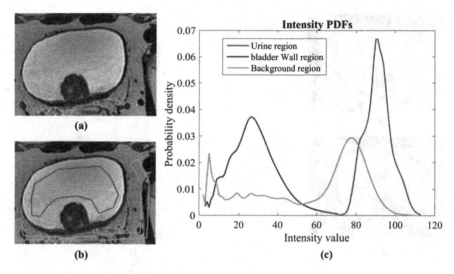

Fig. 3. Example of user initialization process for PDF functions calculation. (a) Is the single transverse slice of the 3D MR image. (b) Is the initialization contours manually depicted by the user. (c) Is the calculated PDF functions of the corresponding regions.

where N_u, N_w and N_b denote the nodes manually delineated from the urine, bladder wall and background regions, respectively.

In order to further reduce the cause of the complicated intensity distributions in the background region, we define a bounding box that roughly removes the sub-background regions with certain range of distance from the bladder wall region, as shown in Fig. 4(a).

$$C_l(x) = +\infty, \quad C_w(x) = +\infty, x \in N_{Boundingbox} \tag{28}$$

The urine region usually appears to be homogenous in intensity distributions and has more differentiable edges at IB, whereas the bladder wall is somewhat heterogeneous in intensity distribution and even has overlapping intensities with the background region. Consequently and empirically, we adopt the minimum bladder wall thickness (BWT) prior d_{minBWT} as 3 mm, such that the minimum distance between IB and OB should be larger than d_{minBWT} to maintain the separation of these two surfaces globally.

$$C_w(x) = +\infty, \quad s.t. \quad \min d(x, R_u) < d_{minBWT} \tag{29}$$

The 2D segmentation results exhibit in Fig. 4(b), and the convergence error curve during the entire iterations is shown in Fig. 4(c).

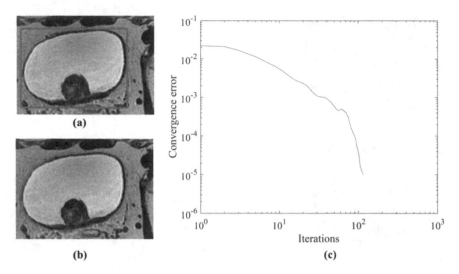

Fig. 4. 2D multi-region segmentation results. (a) Is bounding box placed around the outer-wall. (b) Shows the segmentation results. (c) Illustrates the convergence curve during iterations.

3.4   3D Multi-region Segmentation

With the single slice segmentation results, a region growing segmentation [11, 17] algorithm can be applied to obtain an initial 3D IB surface. To obtain the initial 3D surface of OB, the initial 3D IB surface can be dilated empirically by 8 mm. Finally, the two initial surfaces were simultaneously evolved using the proposed 3D multi-region segmentation approach for 3D bladder wall segmentation. Figures 5 and 6 show the final 3D segmentation results.

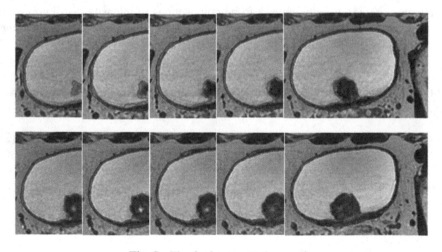

Fig. 5. The final segmentation results

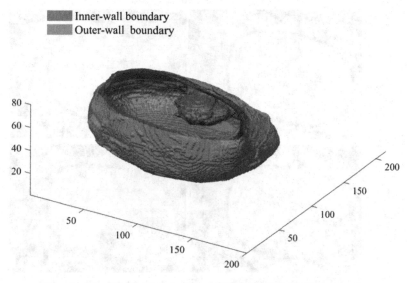

Fig. 6. The 3D bladder constructed with the segmentation results

3.5   Validation

The Dice's similarity coefficient (DSC) is used to quantitatively evaluate the accuracy of the algorithm with manual segmentation as the ground truth [11]. Besides, the performance of using the 3D coupled CMF algorithm is compared with that of level-set method [6, 9]. The results are shown in Table 2. From the table, we can find that the proposed MR-CMF algorithm outperforms Level-set method in bladder wall segmentation. Figure 7 is the results comparison of these two methods.

Table 2. Accuracy and efficiency of MR-CMF and level-set in bladder segmentation

Dataset ID	DSC (%)	
	MR-CMF	Level-set
No. 1	89.5	81.1
No. 2	84.3	80.6
No. 3	87.5	82.6
No. 4	86.8	78.8
No. 5	88.3	84.5
Average	87.28 ± 1.94	81.52 ± 2.15

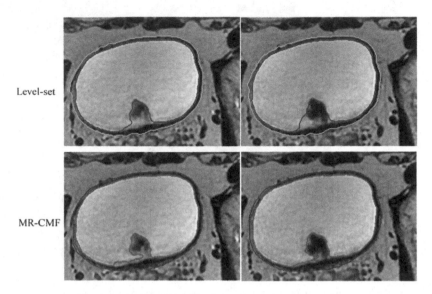

Fig. 7. The result comparison of using Level-set and MR-CMF for bladder segmentation

4 Discussions and Conclusions

We described and verified a novel global optimization-based approach for simultaneously segmenting the multiple regions of 3D bladder MR images by constructing two coupled surfaces of IB and OB via 3D MR-CMF algorithm, incorporating the anatomic inter-surface constraints with minimum BWT prior to jointly enhance the segmentation accuracy, efficiency and robustness, especially in the wall region that has overlapping intensity values with the background.

One of the obvious advantages of this new approach over the previous bladder wall segmentation algorithms is that it is not very sensitive to the initialization process, especially the background initialization [11, 15, 16]. The main reason is that the PDF model generated from the background nodes initially delineated from the 2D slice is just used for 2D segmentation of IB and OB. When these two boundaries are obtained, the PDF model corresponding to the current background is iteratively computed, eliminating the initial model.

Another advantage is that the mathematical schemes of MR-CMF are based on globally optimization techniques [11, 13–16], whereas the previous bladder segmentation algorithms are based on local optimization techniques, which are more sensitive to the user initialization and image quality.

The results in Table 2 and Fig. 7 demonstrate that the proposed 3D MR-CMF algorithm outperforms the Level-set based 3D methods in bladder MR image segmentation, which both has a higher accuracy and a faster calculation speed to meet the need for clinical applications. The proposed method was running on a platform with Intel (R) Core (TM) i5-6400 CPU @ 2.7 GHz, 8.00 GB RAM, equipped with 64-bit Windows 7, and MATLAB 2015 b. The average time expense of five datasets is

6.0 min per each, whereas the average time consumption that of using Level-set approach is 37.9 min.

However, the datasets used to verify this new algorithm is very sparse, more datasets need to be enrolled to revalidate the approach and come up with more objective and convincible results. Besides, in current version of MR-CMF algorithm, we only adopt the manually defined cost functions derived from the PDF functions of the intensity distributions in each targeted region. In the future work, we'll consider incorporating deep learning convolutional neural network (DL-CNN) into cost functions determination process to dig out some more useful factors as cost functions to further enhance the segmentation results.

Acknowledgements. This work was partially supported by the National Nature Science Foundation of China under grant No. 81230035.

References

1. Society, A.C.: Cancer Facts and Figures 2016. American Cancer Society (2016)
2. Xu, X., et al.: Three-dimensional texture features from intensity and high-order derivative maps for the discrimination between bladder tumors and wall tissues via MRI. Int. J. Comput. Assist. Radiol. Surg. **12**(4), 645–656 (2017)
3. Jakse, G., et al.: A second-look TUR in T1 transitional cell carcinoma: why? Eur. Urol. **45**(5), 539–546 (2004). Discussion 546
4. Miladi, M., et al.: The value of a second transurethral resection in evaluating patients with bladder tumours. Eur. Urol. **43**(3), 241–245 (2003)
5. Stein, J.P., et al.: Radical cystectomy in the treatment of invasive bladder cancer: long-term results in 1,054 patients. J. Clin. Oncol. **19**(3), 666–675 (2001)
6. Duan, C., et al.: A coupled level set framework for bladder wall segmentation with application to MR cystography. IEEE Trans. Med. Imaging **29**(3), 903–915 (2010)
7. Duan, C., et al.: Volume-based features for detection of bladder wall abnormal regions via MR cystography. IEEE Trans. Biomed. Eng. **58**(9), 2506–2512 (2011)
8. Duan, C., et al.: An adaptive window-setting scheme for segmentation of bladder tumor surface via MR cystography. IEEE Trans. Inf. Technol. Biomed. **16**(4), 720–729 (2012)
9. Qin, X., et al.: Adaptive shape prior constrained level sets for bladder MR image segmentation. IEEE J. Biomed. Health Inf. **18**(5), 1707–1716 (2014)
10. Cha, K.H., et al.: Urinary bladder segmentation in CT urography using deep-learning convolutional neural network and level sets. Med. Phys. **43**(4), 1882 (2016)
11. Ukwatta, E., et al.: 3-D carotid multi-region MRI segmentation by globally optimal evolution of coupled surfaces. IEEE Trans. Med. Imaging **32**(4), 770–785 (2013)
12. Guo, F., et al.: Globally optimal co-segmentation of three-dimensional pulmonary (1)H and hyperpolarized (3)He MRI with spatial consistence prior. Med. Image Anal. **23**(1), 43–55 (2015)
13. Qiu, W., et al.: Automatic segmentation approach to extracting neonatal cerebral ventricles from 3D ultrasound images. Med. Image Anal. **35**, 181–191 (2017)
14. Sun, Y., et al.: Three-dimensional nonrigid MR-TRUS registration using dual optimization. IEEE Trans. Med. Imaging **34**(5), 1085–1095 (2015)

15. Yuan, J., Bae, E., Tai, X.-C.: A study on continuous max-flow and min-cut approaches. In: IEEE Conference on Computer Vision & Pattern Recognition, vol. 238, no. 6, pp. 2217–2224 (2010)
16. Yuan, J., Bae, E., Tai, X.-C., Boykov, Y.: A continuous max-flow approach to potts model. In: Daniilidis, K., Maragos, P., Paragios, N. (eds.) ECCV 2010. LNCS, vol. 6316, pp. 379–392. Springer, Heidelberg (2010). https://doi.org/10.1007/978-3-642-15567-3_28
17. Adams, R., Bischof, L.: Seeded region growing. IEEE Trans. PAMI **16**(6), 641–647 (1994)

Color and Multispectral Processing

Background Self-adapted Digital Camouflage Pattern Generation Algorithm for Fixed Target

Qin Lei[1(✉)], Duan Ze-wei[2], Hu Jiang-hua[3], Xu Wei-dong[3], and Zhang Xiang[1]

[1] Xi'an Communications Institute, Xi'an 710106, China
qinleinust@126.com
[2] AVIC Xi'an Aeronautics Computing Technique Research Institute, Xi'an 710056, China
[3] PLA University of Science and Technology, Nanjing 210007, China

Abstract. Digital pattern painting is currently a hot topic in camouflage research. This paper presents a modified digital camouflage pattern generation algorithm for fixed target. The color characteristics of the background were extracted by K-means clustering algorithm and the characteristics of the background spots were counted. By filling the dominant color image with colors and blocks, digital pattern paintings were automatically generated. The characteristics such as the dominant color and the size of the digital unit were extracted from the background image, so the constraints of the algorithm can be automatically changed according to the background image. The experimental results show that the digital camouflage pattern generated by the presented algorithm fits the background image in color and spots with good camouflage effect.

Keywords: Image processing · Camouflage pattern · Self-adapted algorithm

1 Introduction

Pattern painting camouflage is not only an important part of the camouflage techniques 1, but also a commonly used method against high-tech reconnaissance. Digital pattern painting, also known as digital camouflage were made up by multicolor blocks and designed with image processing technology 2. In the current study, the spatial resolution of the human eye was often used as the basis for determining the size of the digital unit 3, supposed that the digital units were visible (or invisible) in a given distance. However, the digital pattern painting design is based on the optical background image, the sizes of the spots were counted by pixels and easily changed in different images. Meanwhile, the resolution of the human eye is a subjective parameter. It can't objectively represent the characteristics of the color and spots of the background image. To solve this problem, this paper presents a modified camouflage pattern generation algorithm for fixed target based on the characteristics of the background image. The color characteristics of the background were extracted by K-means clustering algorithm and the characteristics of the background spots were counted. By filling the dominant color image with colors and blocks, digital pattern paintings were automatically generated. The constraints of the algorithm such as the color, percentage

Y. Zhao et al. (Eds.): ICIG 2017, Part II, LNCS 10667, pp. 545–551, 2017.
https://doi.org/10.1007/978-3-319-71589-6_47

of the color in the pattern and size of the digital unit were extracted from the background image. So they can be automatically changed with the background in the process. So this modified pattern painting design algorithm was background adapted.

2   The Technological Process of the Algorithm

The modified camouflage pattern generation algorithm for fixed target was constituted of three main parts. They are the Color Feature Analyzing Module (1), the Spots Feature Analyzing Module (2) and the Pattern Painting Generating Module (3). The technological process of the algorithm was shown in Fig. 1.

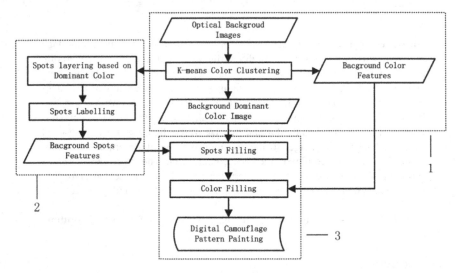

Fig. 1. Technological process of the algorithm

2.1   Color Feature Analyzing Module

K-means clustering, Median-cut method, Octree method, Uniform quantization method and Sequence frequency method were the commonly used color clustering methods in camouflage 45. The advantages such as high accuracy and speed makes the K-means clustering the most widely used color clustering method in analyzing the color features and extracting the camouflage dominant color 678. Using the K-means clustering the Color Feature Analyzing Module were designed. It constitutes three main steps.

Step 1: Color space conversion. The image is converted from sRGB color space to the $L^*a^*b^*$ color space.
Step 2: K-means clustering. The color difference formula in CIE1976 color space (shown in Eq. 1) was used as the function of cluster value in K-means clustering.

$$\Delta E_{lab} = \sqrt{\left(L_1^* - L_2^*\right)^2 + \left(a_1^* - a_2^*\right)^2 + \left(b_1^* - b_2^*\right)^2} \tag{1}$$

Among them, L_1^*, L_2^*, a_1^*, a_2^*, b_1^* and b_1^* separately represents the components of two different color in CIE1976 $L^*a^*b^*$ color space. Set the initial cluster centers, and then calculate the color difference of the pixel and the cluster centers. Iteratively Cluster the colors and adjust the cluster centers until color difference between the pixels and the clustering center comes to a minimal value until the final dominant color image was saved.

Step 3: Extract the chromaticity coordinates of each color according to the dominant color image. Count the percentage of each color in the dominant color image and show the histogram of the result.

2.2 Spots Feature Analyzing Module

Diameter can't be affected b i y the shape and direction of the pot and can effectively represent the size the each spot. Thus, in this paper diameter is used as a valid basis to describe the size of the spot in the background image. Spots Feature Analyzing Module includes the following main processing steps:

Step 1: Extract the spots with different colors in the background image and stored them in different layers. Convert the layers into binary images, the value of the pixels in the spot is 1, others 0.

Step 2: Use the closing operation of the mathematical morphology to process the binary image with a plate structure element of size 3×3. That is to form connected areas of the neighboring crushing spots. Then open the image with a plate structure element of size 3×3 to eliminate the noise and separate different spots.

Step 3: Label the spots in different color layer.

Step 4: Calculate the diameter of each spots sequentially and the count the probability of different size of the diameter. Draw the histogram of the distribution the diameter.

Step 5: Calculate the expectations of the diameter according to the histogram. If the number i size of the diameter in the image is represented by x_i. The probability of it is represented by p_i. Then the expectation of the diameter can be calculated by Eq. 2.

$$EX = \sum_i x_i \cdot p_i \tag{2}$$

If there are n kinds of color in the dominant color image and the expectation of the number j color spots in the dominant color image is represented by EX_j, the EX_{mean} represents the average of all the n kinds EX_j. EX_{mean} can be calculated by following Eq. 3.

$$EX_{mean} = \frac{\sum_{j=1}^{j=n} EX_j}{n} \tag{3}$$

2.3 Pattern Painting Generating Module

The function of the Pattern Painting Generating Module is to make the dominant color image into a camouflage pattern painting according to the color and spot features of the background image. The process of the Pattern Painting Generating Module includes three main steps:

Step 1: Read the dominant color image.
Step 2: Divide the dominant color image into small blocks. And the size of the blocks were decided by the size of the digital unit counted in the Spots Feature Analyzing Module.
Step 3: Fill the pixels in each blocks with the same dominant color. The pixel in the centre of the block was chosen to represent the pixels of the whole block. And fill the pixels in the block with the color of the pixel in the centre of the block. Save the final image and that is the camouflage pattern generated for fixed target.

3 Results and Analysis

The original background images were shown in Fig. 2. Background Image 1 to 3 are Forest Grassland and Desert Background Image. The pixel size of the image is 800 × 600. The dominant color images were extracted by K-means clustering algorithm and the RGB coordinates of the dominant colors (red, green, and blue components) were shown in Table 1. The probability statistics for each primary color in the background were shown in Table 2. The spot analysis process is shown in Fig. 3. The average size of the spots in the background image were 15.4076, 16.2101, 16.6855.

 (a) Background Image 1 (b) Background Image 2 (c) Background Image 3

Fig. 2. Background images

  The dominant color images were divided into blocks. And the pixels in each blocks were filled with the color of the pixel in the centre of the block. The dominant color images were turned into camouflage patterns for fixed target as shown in Fig. 4. The probability statistics for each primary color in the pattern paintings are shown in Table 3.

  The designed digital pattern painting used the dominant colors of the background images as shown in Table 1. By comparing Figs. 2 and 3 the conclusion that the

Table 1. RGB coordinates of the dominant colors

		Color 1	Color 2	Color 3	Color 4	Color 5
Background 1	R	31	148	174	72	211
	G	41	169	200	102	221
	B	26	97	149	55	172
Background 2	R	70	134	99	166	108
	G	106	174	129	203	156
	B	83	120	101	146	103
Background 3	R	115	181	204	151	224
	G	100	167	193	137	219
	B	73	136	162	108	197

Table 2. Probability for the colors in the dominant color images

	Color 1	Color 2	Color 3	Color 4	Color 5
Background 1	0.3528	0.1665	0.1369	0.2282	0.1155
Background 2	0.2054	0.2982	0.1734	0.1480	0.1750
Background 3	0.1478	0.3955	0.1525	0.2553	0.0490

(a) Spot Image   (b) Spot Labeling   (c) Spot Size Distribution

Fig. 3. Spot analysis of background image 1 (Color 1)

Table 3. Probability for the colors in the camouflage pattern

	Color 1	Color 2	Color 3	Color 4	Color 5
Camouflage pattern 1	0.3547	0.1623	0.1274	0.2406	0.1151
Camouflage pattern 2	0.2201	0.2930	0.1696	0.1544	0.1629
Camouflage pattern 3	0.1477	0.3964	0.1362	0.2608	0.0590

designed digital pattern painting coordinate with the background image can be made. The probabilities of Table 3 minus Table 2 are shown in Table 4. The error of the probabilities of the colors in the background dominant color images and the digital pattern painting is less than 2%. The maximum probability error was in the 1st pattern painting and the value is 0.0147. So the results illustrate that the probabilities of the colors in the background images and the coordinated pattern paintings are very close. The designed pattern paintings adapted to the background images in color features.

| (a) Pattern Painting 1 | (b) Pattern Painting 2 | (c) Pattern Painting 3 |

Fig. 4. Digital camouflge pattern

Table 4. Probability errors of the color

	Color 1	Color 2	Color 3	Color 4	Color 5
Pattern painting 1	0.0019	0.0042	0.0095	0.0124	0.0004
Pattern painting 2	0.0147	0.0052	0.0038	0.0064	0.0121
Pattern painting 3	0.0001	0.0009	0.0163	0.0055	0.0100

As is shown in Table 5, in digital camouflage pattern 1 to 3, the sizes of the digital block are 15, 16 and 17, they are close to the average sizes of the spots in the background images. The maximum error of the size was 0.4076 pixels in digital pattern painting 1. The value of the digital blocks in the pattern paining can be changes automatically with different background images. So the digital camouflage pattern painting adapted the spot features of the background images. In the design process of the digital camouflage pattern painting, the design constraints were all extracted from the background images. There was no human intervention. This digital camouflage pattern design algorithm was background adapted.

Table 5. The comparison of spots size

	Background 1	Background 2	Background 3
Average sizes of spots in original images	15.4076	16.2101	16.6855
Size of camouflage pattern unit	15	16	17

4   Conclusion

This paper presents a modified camouflage pattern generation algorithm for fixed target. This algorithm can effectively keep the color and spot features of the background images. The experimental result shows that the camouflage pattern generated by the presented algorithm fits the background in color and spots with good camouflage effect. The constraints of the algorithm (colors, probability distribution of the colors, size of the digital blocks) are extracted from the background images and can be automatically changed with the background images with no human intervention. So this algorithm is background adapted.

References

1. Zhang, J.C.: Pattern Painting Camouflage Technology, pp. 47–128. China Textile Press, Beijing (2002)
2. Hu, J.: Camouflage technology, pp. 15–17. National Defense Industry Press, Beijing (2012)
3. Yu, J., Yang, W.-X., Hu, Z.-Y., et al.: Research of digital camouflage generation algorithm. Opto-Electron. Eng. **37**(17), 110–114 (2010)
4. Zhou, B., Shen, J.-Y., Peng, Q.-K.: An Algorithm Based on Color Cluster Feature for Color Quantization, Mini-Micro Systems
5. Geng, G.H., Zhou, M.-Q.: Analyzing the quality of some common used algorithms of color quantization. Mini Micro Syst. **25**(11) (2004)
6. Liu, Z.-Y., Wang, Z.-R., Wang, J.-C., et al.: Design method of imitated pattern paiting based on main color clustering. Laser Infrared **39**(7), 793–796 (2009)
7. Zhang, Y., Wu, W.-J., Liu, Z.-M.: Design of bionic camouflage pattern. Comput. Eng. **35**(6), 35–38 (2009)
8. Yu, J., Wang, C., Hu, Z.-Y.: Design on digital disruptive pattern for fixed targets. Comput. Dig. Eng. **39**(4), 134–137 (2011)

Practical Bottom-up Golf Course Detection Using Multispectral Remote Sensing Imagery

Jingbo Chen[✉], Chengyi Wang, Dongxu He, Jiansheng Chen,
and Anzhi Yue

Institute of Remote Sensing and Digital Earth, Chinese Academy of Sciences,
Beijing 100101, China
chenjb@radi.ac.cn

Abstract. The rapid growth of golf course has constituted a nonnegligible threat to conservation of cropland and water resource in China. To monitor golf course at a large scale with low cost, a practical bottom-up golf course detection approach using multispectral remote sensing imagery is proposed. First of all, turfgrass, water-body and bunker are determined as the basic elements based on analyzing golf course land-use characteristics. Secondly, turfgrass and water-body are extracted using spectral indexes and these two basic elements are combined as region-of-interest under guidance of prior-knowledge. Afterwards, bunker is extracted by spectral mixture analysis restricted to region-of-interest. Finally, fuzzy C-means is adopted to recognize golf course using landscape metrics. A SPOT-5 HRG multispectral image of Beijing is used to validate the proposed method, and detection rate and false alarm rate are 86.67% and 38.10% respectively.

Keywords: Golf course · Remote sensing · Object detection
Landscape metrics

1 Introduction

Since the first golf course was opened in 1984, golf course has been undergoing rapid development in China, which has increased from 348 in 2009 to 521 in 2013 with growth rate of 49.71%. By contrast, sharp cropland decline and serious water shortage have drawn more and more attention from both the government and the public. Rapid expansion of golf course is regarded as a non negligible contributing factor leading to cropland and water resource-related issues for two reasons. On one hand, golf course is both land-consuming and water-consuming. On the other hand, most golf courses locate around developed cities where contradiction between people and environment is encountered persistently. In response to threats constituted by golf course, several regulations forbidding golf course construction have been released by the Government since 2004, and special investigations on golf course were carried out in 2009 and 2011 to control golf courses development.

Golf course is characterized by small overall number and large individual area, which make it appropriate to monitor golf course using remote sensing imagery. Medium-resolution multispectral imagery plays an important role in satellite remote

© Springer International Publishing AG 2017
Y. Zhao et al. (Eds.): ICIG 2017, Part II, LNCS 10667, pp. 552–559, 2017.
https://doi.org/10.1007/978-3-319-71589-6_48

sensing applications, the spatial resolution of which ranges from eight to 30 meters with visible and near-infrared spectral bands. Monitoring golf course using medium-resolution multispectral imagery is both efficient and economical. Besides, golf course is a typical kind of composite objects in contrast with simple objects, complex objects [1]. In several researches, golf course is treated as simple object and its detection problem is simplified to be turfgrass extraction. Dimock argued Landsat TM band 5, 4 and 3 could effectively enhance golf course visually, but automatic golf course extraction were unreliable [2]. Frankvich, Chen and Zhang detected golf course based on spectral and textural feature of turfgrass using Landsat TM and SPOT-5 imagery [3–5]. However, the low spectral separability between turfgrass and other well-growing vegetations makes these methods noneffective in discriminating golf course, cropland and grassland. To overcome the disadvantage, more recent researches turn to using or combining spatial feature in golf course detection. For example, Bhagavathy used spatial co-occurrence of turfgrass and rough which was termed as texture motif to recognize golf course in aerial image [6]. A hybrid evolutionary algorithm was used in Harvey's research to select features for golf course extraction in AVIRIS imagery and results proved regional spatial features made the biggest contribution [7]. Guo used Hyerpclique model to describe semantic feature of composite object and took golf course as an example in composite object detection [8]. In Yang's research on land-use classification using Bag-Of-Visual-Words, golf course was one of the 21 land-use objects of interest [9]. These methods regarded golf course as composite object and spatial relationship between components was taken into consideration, but the small Field-Of-View of aerial and hyperspectral imagery makes them unpractical on a large spatial scale.

In consideration of limitations of state-of-art methods, a practical bottom-up golf course detection approach is proposed in this paper. In terms of bottom-up manner, the approach is a flow composed of elements extraction and a subsequent area combination. In terms of practicality, the approach uses multispectral medium-resolution remote sensing imagery which can observe large area.

2 Study Area and Dataset

A geometrically and radiometrically corrected SPOT-5 HRG multispectral image of Beijing, China acquired on 17th, May, 2007 is used as experimental dataset. Four sub-images with size of 512×512 shown in Fig. 1 are selected to clearly show experimental results.

The number of golf course in Beijing increases at a high speed, and there are about 58 standard golf courses by 2013. Meanwhile, landscape characteristics of golf courses in Beijing vary a lot in terms of spatial composition and configuration. Sufficient number and various characteristics make Beijing an ideal experimental region for golf course detection.

As we can see that sub-image #1 and #4 lie in urban area where there exist park, while sub-image #2 and #3 lie in suburban area where there exist cropland. The experimental sub-images will demonstrate the capacity of proposed method in distinguishing golf course from other similar composite objects including park and cropland.

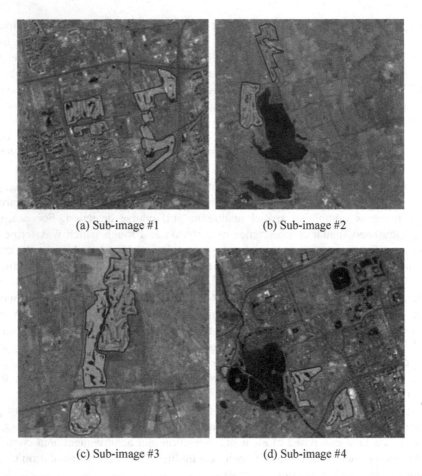

(a) Sub-image #1   (b) Sub-image #2

(c) Sub-image #3   (d) Sub-image #4

Fig. 1. Sub-images for golf course detection. Golf courses are delineated by green polygons through visual interpretation. (Color figure online)

3   Methodology

3.1   Basic Elements for Golf Detection

Basic elements should be determined in advance to detect a composite object in bottom-up manner. As for golf course detection using remote sensing, the basic elements should be determined according to two principles, i.e., they are significant components of golf course and they can be extracted easily from remote sensing data.

According to land-use characteristics [10], turfgrass, water-body and bunker are determined as the basic elements. The former two elements can be extracted easily because of distinguishing spectral response and overwhelming area percentage, i.e., 67% and 7% respectively. While bunker is a significant component for discriminating golf course with other similar composite object.

3.2   Region-of-Interest Extraction

A landscape mosaic must be given to restrict the outward spatial extent in landscape analysis. In golf course detection, the region-of-interest can be broadly defined as a localized region where turfgrass and water-body co-occur, which can be delineated using NDVI and MNDWI [11] respectively.

Morphological closing is used to merge neighboring turfgrass and water-body as a region-of-interest because it can connect adjacent objects, fill small holes and smooth boundary of region when keeping region area. Constraints of region minimum and maximum area as well as area proportion of turfgrass and water-body should be taken into consideration simultaneously. Specifically, region-of-interest area should range from 20 to 200 acreages, and area ratio of turfgrass to water-body should be larger than 1.

3.3   Bunker Extraction

Bunker usually appears as mixed pixels in medium-resolution images because of its small area and complex shape, and bunker cannot be well extracted by multispectral indexes as turfgrass and waterbody. In this paper, spectral mixture analysis (SMA) based on non-negative least squares is used for bunker extraction, which is considered to be a more suitable model for target detection applications [12].

An automated endmember selection method combining pixel purity index (PPI), categorical map and endmember spectral signature is designed to select pure pixels as endmember of basic elements. In each region-of-interest, endmember is selected by following steps:

1. Region-of-interest PPI is calculated and pixels with high value are extracted as spectral pure pixels.
2. Turfgrass endmember pixels are intersection of pure pixels and turfgrass area, and water-body endmember pixels are intersection of PPI and water-body area.
3. Bunker endmember pixels are intersection of pure pixels and pixels with high digital numbers in red band.

Thus, region-of-interest bunker abundance given by spectral unmixing is used to extract bunker.

3.4   Clustering Based on Landscape Metrics

Region-of-interest derived based on turfgrass and water-body may contain other similar composite objects such as parks (co-occurrence of grass and lake) and cropland (co-occurrence of dry and paddy cropland). Fortunately, spatial composition and spatial pattern quantified by landscape metrics make it possible to distinguish golf course from other similar composite objects. Spatial composition refers to what elements constitute a composite object and their area percentage, while spatial pattern refers to how elements distribute in a composite object. In this paper, seven patch-level and seven landscape-level metrics shown in Table 1 are chosen to analyze landscape characteristics of region-of-interest. The "scale" in Table 1 denotes the level at which landscape metrics are calculated. Class-level metrics refers to metrics characterizing a specific

Table 1. Metrics for landscape analysis.

Landscape metric	Scale
NP, Number of Patches	Class and landscape
PASD, Patch Area Standard Deviation	Class
LPI, Largest Patch Index	Class and landscape
PLAND, Percentage of LANDscape	Class
ED, Edge Density	Class
LSI, Landscape Shape Index	Class and landscape
SHAPEAM, Area Weighted Mean Patch Fractal Dimension	Class and landscape
ENNMN, Euclidian Mean Nearest Neighbor	Landscape
CONTAG, CONTAGion Index	Landscape
SHDI, SHannon's Diversity Index	Landscape

land-cover class of interest, i.e., turfgrass, water-body and bunker, existing in region-of-interest, while landscape-level metrics refers to metrics characterizing region-of-interest on the whole. More detailed description of these landscape metrics can be found in FragStats [13].

Following sequential forward searching (SFS) strategy in feature selection, J-M distance based filter is used to select optimal feature subset from the 14 metrics. Golf course is detected by two successive steps. Firstly, region-of-interest where there doesn't exist any patch of the three basic elements, i.e., turfgrass, water-body and bunker, are eliminated. Secondly, region-of-interest are grouped into two categories, i.e., golf course and other objects, using fuzzy C-means (FCM).

4   Experiment and Discussion

Thresholds for turfgrass and water-body extraction based on NDVI and MNDWI respectively are determined empirically. Experiments show that it's unnecessary to tune the two thresholds carefully. After golf course region-of-interest is derived by morphological closing of turfgrass and water-body images, SMA is used to unmix region-of-interest and pixels with bunker abundance higher than 0.3 are considered to be bunker. The region-of-interest land-cover thematic maps composed of turfgrass, water-body and bunker are shown in Fig. 2. There are 17, 9, 15 and 15 region-of-interest in sub-image #1, #2, #3 and #4 respectively.

J-M distance based filter gives an optimal feature subset, i.e., LSI_T, $SHAPEAM_T$, NP_W, LPI_B, ED_B, $SHAPEAM_L$ and $ENNMN_L$, where subscripts T, W, B and L denote metrics of turfgrass, water-body, bunker and landscape respectively. Each region-of-interest thus is quantified as a 7-dimension vector, based on which golf courses are recognized using FCM. Golf course detection results are shown in Fig. 3.

Visual interpretation of 4 sub-images shows there exist 15 golf courses in 56 region-of-interest, among which there are 13 true positive golf courses, 2 false negative golf courses, 33 true negative golf courses and 8 false positive golf courses. The overall detection rate is 86.67% and the overall false alarm rate is 38.10%.

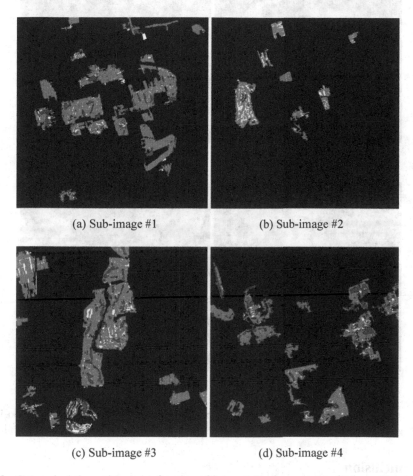

(a) Sub-image #1   (b) Sub-image #2

(c) Sub-image #3   (d) Sub-image #4

Fig. 2. Categorical thematic maps of region-of-interest. Turfgrass, water-body and bunker are shown by green, blue and white pixels respectively. (Color figure online)

False negative golf course in sub-image #1 is a golf course where bunker can be hardly recognized even by visual interpretation, and the other false negative golf course in sub-image #3 is a small part of an entire golf course. In both cases, false negative samples show non-typical golf course landscape characteristics. The main reason contributing to false alarm lies in confusion between water-body and other dark objects in urban area, e.g., building shadow, asphalt surface and dense vegetation. Experiments show false alarm rate may decrease sharply when water-body can be extract more accurately in urban area.

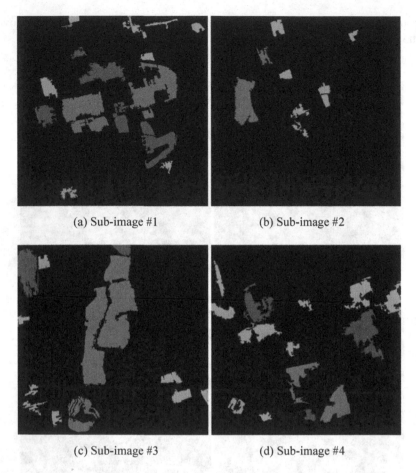

(a) Sub-image #1   (b) Sub-image #2

(c) Sub-image #3   (d) Sub-image #4

Fig. 3. Golf course detection results. Red, green, blue and yellow areas denote true positive, false negative, true negative and false positive golf courses respectively. (Color figure online)

5   Conclusion

A practical bottom-up golf course detection approach based on landscape metrics using multispectral remote sensing imagery is proposed in this paper. Experiments carried on SPOT-5 image achieve an acceptable golf course detection result with detection rate of 86.67% and false alarm rate of 38.10%. The bottom-up workflow enables detection of a specific composite object when its spatial composition and spatial pattern have been well understood. In other words, by presenting a case study of golf course, the proposed approach is proven to be promising for composite object detection which includes but is not limited to golf course.

Advantages of the proposed approach lie in two aspects. On one hand, the approach is essentially an unsupervised method because it doesn't need any training samples. Only three thresholds involved in extraction of turfgrass, water-body and bunker are indispensable. On the other hand, the proposed method is more practical than existing methods since it can work well on multispectral medium resolution imagery instead of aerial or hyperspectral imagery.

In the future, accuracy of basic elements extraction and its effect on golf course detection will be further explored. Meanwhile, the proposed approach will be compared or combined with deep learning models such as convolutional neural network.

Acknowledgement. This work was funded by National Nature Science Foundation of China with Grant No. 41501397, and partially funded by National Nature Science Foundation of China with Grant No. 41401376.

References

1. Xu, S., Fang, T., Li, D.R., Wang, S.W.: Object classification of aerial images with bag-of-visual words. IEEE Geosci. Remote Sens. Lett. 7(2), 366–370 (2010)
2. Dimock, W.J.: Spatial factors affecting white grub presence and abundance in golf course turf. Virginia Polytechnic Institute and State University, Blacksburg, VA (2004)
3. Frankovich, J.S.: Unsupervised classification of spectrally enhanced landsat TM data of Midland, MI. http://earthsensing.com/drs/stud_proj_f99/final.html. Accessed 9 May 2017
4. Chen, C.S., Chen, J.F., Zhang, X.L.: Extraction of golf course based on texture feature of SPOT5 image. In: Proceedings of 2011 International Conference on Electronics, Communications and Control (ICECC), pp. 254–257 (2011)
5. Zhang, J.F., Liu, Y., Cui, S.S., Wang, Z.Y., Zhao, Q.: Dynamic monitoring of golf course land in Beijing based on remote sensing technology. In: Proceedings of the Second International Conference on Remote Sensing, Environment and Transportation Engineering, pp. 1–4 (2012)
6. Bhagavathy, S., Manjunath, B.S.: Modeling and detection of geospatial objects using texture motifs. IEEE Trans. Geosci. Remote Sens. 44(12), 3706–3715 (2006)
7. Harvey, N.R., Perkins, S., Brumby, S.P., Theiler, J., Porter, R.B., Young, A.C., Varghese, A.K., Szymanski, J.J., Bloch, J.J.: Finding golf courses: the ultra high tech approach. In: Cagnoni, S. (ed.) EvoWorkshops 2000. LNCS, vol. 1803, pp. 54–64. Springer, Heidelberg (2000). https://doi.org/10.1007/3-540-45561-2_6
8. Guo, D., Xiong, H., Atluri, V., Adam, N.: Semantic feature selection for object discovery in high-resolution remote sensing imagery. In: Zhou, Z.-H., Li, H., Yang, Q. (eds.) PAKDD 2007. LNCS (LNAI), vol. 4426, pp. 71–83. Springer, Heidelberg (2007). https://doi.org/10.1007/978-3-540-71701-0_10
9. Yang, Y., Newsam, S.: Bag-of-visual-words and spatial extensions for land-use classification. In: Proceedings of the 18th SIGSPATIAL International Conference on Advances in Geographic Information Systems (GIS 2010), pp. 270–279. ACM (2010)
10. Lyman, G.T., Throssell, C.S., Johnson, M.E., Stacey, G.A., Brown, C.D.: Golf course profile describes turfgrass, landscape, and environmental stewardship features. Appl. Turfgrass Sci. 4, 1–25 (2007)
11. Xu, H.Q.: Modification of normalized difference water index (NDWI) to enhance open water features in remotely sensed imagery. Int. J. Remote Sens. 27, 3025–3033 (2006)
12. Chang, C.I., Heinz, D.C.: Constrained subpixel target detection for remotely sensed imagery. IEEE Trans. Geosci. Remote Sens. 38(3), 1144–1159 (2000)
13. McGarigal, K., Cushman, S.A., Ene, E.: FRAGSTATS v4: spatial pattern analysis program for categorical and continuous map, computer software program produced by the authors at the University of Massachusetts, Amherst. http://www.umass.edu/landeco/research/fragstats/fragstats.html. Accessed 9 May 2017

Efficient Decolorization via Perceptual Group Difference Enhancement

Hongchao Zhang[1] and Shiguang Liu[1,2(✉)]

[1] School of Computer Science and Technology, Tianjin University,
Tianjin 300350, People's Republic of China
lsg@tju.edu.cn
[2] Tianjin Key Laboratory of Cognitive Computing and Application,
Tianjin 300350, People's Republic of China

Abstract. This paper developed a new decolorization method by using perceptual group difference (PGD) enhancement. Based on the psychological studies, we regarded the perceptual group rather than the image pixels as the perception elements. Then, we respectively computed the relative group color difference and the global color to gray mapping. By combining and fusing them via perceptual group difference enhancement, our method can better preserve the contrast and details in the original image. Owing to the linear operations, our method is efficient. Various experiments and user studies validated our method.

Keywords: Decolorization · Perceptual group difference
Contrast preserving · Image editing

1 Introduction

Decolorization aims to convert color images to grayscale images while maintaining the visual features, e.g., the structures and contrasts in the original color images. Decolorization algorithms can be widely applied to color to gray applications such as grayscale printing in publishing due to economic reasons, making color blind people better 'see' visual features in color images.

Decolorization is generally regarded as a process of dimensional reduction which degrades a three-dimensional color space to the one-dimensional gray scale space, during which the loss of information will inevitably occur. The key of decolorization is to preserve people's perception of the original image as much as possible. Previous algorithms suffer from mistakenly transforming regions with different colors in the original color image into the same gray level in the gray scale image. It is therefore not trivial to specially cope with the grayscale contrast between different regions such that the magnitude of the grayscale contrast can reflect the magnitude of the color contrasts in the original color image. Most of the traditional color to gray algorithms perform decoloarization by converting RGB color space to Lab space in which the luminance

---

This work was partly supported by the Natural Science Foundation of China under grant Nos. 61672375 and 61170118.

Y. Zhao et al. (Eds.): ICIG 2017, Part II, LNCS 10667, pp. 560–569, 2017.
https://doi.org/10.1007/978-3-319-71589-6_49

information can be easily acquired, and then adopting the luminance information to group and transform the pixels into grayscales. Although this method is simple and easy to implement, it readily fails to preserve the image details, i.e., two regions with the same brightness but different colors would be transformed into the same grayscale. Additionally, the efficiency of decolorization is another essential factor of concern.

Based on the above observations and inspired by the recent successful color to gray algorithms [5, 9], we presented a novel, efficient decolorization method via perceptual group difference (PGD) enhancement. We formed the original color image into a few visual groups according to the color distributions of pixels. Then decolorization was performed for different groups separately so as to preserve the contrast between visual groups. A global color to gray mapping operator was adapted to obtain the overall grayscale information. Finally, the grayscale effects of each group were used to strengthen the global grayscale information so that the final transformed grayscale image can be distinguished accurately by the human eye and retain the important contrast magnitude. Our method has the following features:

- A new perceptually plausible decolorization framework was designed.
- Through PGD enhancement, our method can obtain better visual contrast effects and for different regions in the original color images.
- Our method is efficient and can preserve the image details as well.

2 Related Work

The direct decolorization method is color to gray using linear combination of R, G, and B channel information [1]. This method is efficient, but difficult to preserve the contrasts between regions with different colors. Song et al. [2] modified the rgb2gray() function in Matlab to avoid the failures in the regions with iso-luminance. Recently, decolorization is usually formulated as a mapping problem, which can be roughly classified into global mapping methods and local mapping methods.

Global mapping methods attempt to apply the same mapping to all the pixels in an image. Gooch et al. [3] proposed an algorithm called color2gray, in which the mapping is treated as an optimization of an objective function. This method is computationally expensive and suffers from image distort. Rasche et al. [4] introduced an algorithm, aiming to maintain the consistent luminance. Grundland and Dodgson [5] incorporated image sampling and dimensionality reduction and developed a new contrast enhancing color to grayscale conversion algorithm. Kuhn et al. [6] put forward a mass-spring model to enhance the color contrast. Kim et al. [7] proposed a nonlinear global gray mapping method, which can preserve the feature discriminability and reasonable color ordering.

Local mapping methods respect the local distribution of colors and perform the mapping for pixels locally. Bala and Eschbach [8] introduced a spatial approach for decolorization, in which the chrominace edges are retained locally by applying the high-frequency chrominance information into the luminance channel. Wu et al. [9] proposed an interactive two-scale color-to-gray method. This approach can effectively preserve the local information, but may cause distortion of the whole image so that the important features in the resulting grayscale image do not respect that from the original color image. Neumann et al. [10] described a gradient based decolorization method. This method is fast and suitable for handling high resolution images; however, it may fail for the regions with the same gradient in an image. Lu et al. [11] introduced a real time color to gray conversion method with contrast preservation. Smith et al. [12] developed a two-step decolorization, namely, first globally assigned gray values, and then locally enhanced the grayscale to reproduce the contrast. Zhu et al. [13] presented a new color to gray algorithm which can maintain the perceived appearance of color images. Decolorization was cast as visual cue preservation procedure [14], where the visual cue indicated the attentation [15], the chance of happening [16], etc.

3 Method

Our method mainly consists of four steps, namely, perceptual grouping, relative grayscale calculation, global mapping, and contrast enhancement.

3.1 Perceptual Grouping

According to the Gestalt theory, people tend to perceive elements similar color characteristics in an image as a whole. As a result, several segments of an image rather than each pixel are of concern. We would therefore cluster an image into several individual perceptual groups. For simplicity and efficiency, we adapted K-means algorithms. In our algorithm, a natural image is generally clustered into 3–6 groups. Thus it can avoid too scattered group distributions and can well distinguish viewers' perception. Experiments validated the above grouping strategy.

3.2 Group Processing

After obtaining the groups, we would decolorize them locally and globally. By specially handling the difference between the groups, the details and contrast in the original image can be pleasingly maintained in the decolorized grayscale image.

3.2.1 Average Group Color Calculation

For each group $S_t (t \in [1, K])$, we would compute its average color $c_t = (L_t, a_t, b_t)$ so as to express its color tone. We achieved this by averaging all the pixels' color in each group. Considering the difference between groups, the average color can well express the characteristic color tone of different groups.

3.2.2 Color Difference Evaluation and Group Decolorization

Since the color tone of each group can represent the overall color trends of the group, we adopted the average color differences to evaluate the color differences between groups. Further, we determined the gray value of different groups via their color differences with the goal to maximize the differences between groups as far as possible.

In the above sections, the image has been transformed into Lab color space, where the uniform change of the color in the space corresponds to the uniform change of human visual perception. Consequently, the relative perceptual difference between any two colors in the Lab space, can be expressed as calculating the Euclidean distance between two points in the 3D space. For an instance, the Euclidean distance between two points (L_1, a_1, b_1) and (L_2, a_2, b_2) in the space is

$$\Delta E_{(1, 2)} = \sqrt{(L_1 - L_2)^2 + (a_1 - a_2)^2 + (b_1 - b_2)^2}. \tag{1}$$

In this way, the color difference between any groups in the image can be computed; the more the color difference between two groups, the more the human perception difference for them. We thereby obtained a group difference matrix for the whole image,

$$\begin{pmatrix} 0 \, \Delta E_{(1,2)} \ldots \Delta E_{(1,k)} \\ \Delta E_{(2,1)} \, 0 \ldots \Delta E_{(2,k)} \\ \ldots \\ \Delta E_{(k,1)} \, \Delta E_{(k,2)} \ldots 0 \end{pmatrix}.$$

In the above matrix, we chose the element with the largest value as ΔE_{max}. Correspondingly, we set the greatest and the smallest gray value to the two groups with the largest color difference value; generally, the greatest gray value G_{max} was set to the group with larger average brightness, while the smallest gray value G_{min} was set to the one with relatively smaller average brightness. For other groups, we scale their gray values to their color difference as follows,

$$G_t = ((G_{max} - G_{min})/\Delta E_{max}) \times \Delta E_{(min, t)} \tag{2}$$

where t denotes the iteration of the groups.

Based on the above calculation, we can obtain the gray value for each group individually. Meanwhile, this strategy can best distinguish different group and thus maximize the differences among them. Moreover, it can dynamically allocate the gray value to other groups in a flexible manner. Figure 1 shows the calculation results of the average colors and the relative gray values for an image.

Fig. 1. The results of the average colors and the relative gray values for an image, (left) the original image, (middle) the result of the average color for different groups, and (right) the result of the relative gray values.

3.3   Global Gray Mapping

After the above group processing, we obtained the initial gray effects for the groups. However, the details in each group are completely lost; thus we need to recover the local details through the mapping between the original color image and the gray scale image. With the observation that the conventional dimension reduction method suffered from severe color information loss, we instead adapt a fast global mapping way to achieve the contrast enhancement [10]. In this procedure, we first randomly selected the points for calculating the color difference, then computed the color loss ratio during the transformation from the color image to the gray scale image, and finally recover the loss of the color information through evaluation of the chroma and the saturation. As demonstrated in Fig. 2, the mapping result of our method is better than traditional mapping method using only brightness information. Our method can preserve more visual details of the original image (see the marked area in Fig. 2).

Fig. 2. The results of the mapping between color and gray level, (left) is the original color image, (middle) is the mapping result considering only brightness information, and (right) shows the results generated by our global mapping method. (Color figure online)

Note that the global mapping is performed in YPQ color space, which is composed of a luminance channel Y and a pair of color independent color channels, namely, the yellow-blue channel P, and the red-green channel Q. Here we chose this color space due to its efficiency for evaluation of the chroma and the saturation by $H_i = \frac{1}{\pi}\tan^{-1}\left(\frac{Q_i}{P_i}\right)$ and $S_i = \sqrt{P_i^2 + Q_i^2}$.

By introducing the global mapping method in [10], the grayscale image can be regarded as an elegant linear mapping from the R, G, B, and the saturation valued of the original image to the grayscale image, which can be expressed as

$$T_i = r_i R_i + g_i G_i + b_i B_i + s_i S_i + t_i \tag{3}$$

where T_i is the gray value; R_i, G_i, B_i, and S_i are respectively the red component, green component, the blue component, and the saturation of the original image; t_i is a constant term.

This method can well maintain the details and contrast of the original image. On the other hand, it is fast owing to the low computation cost of the linear mapping operator.

3.4 Group Difference Enhancement

After we acquired the average gray value of each group and the global mapping gray value, we would combine them together to generate the final grayscale image. Our strategy is to enhance the group difference and then fuse the average gray value of each group with the global mapping gray value. In this section, we will detail on our group difference enhancement method.

3.4.1 Grouping Enhancement

The aforementioned group results can distinguish the difference between different groups as much as possible. However, the maximized difference result might not be directly integrated into the grayscale image generated using the global mapping, since it may destroy the edges and even can cause the distortion of the image contents. Therefore, we should handle the fusion coefficient and accommodate it to generate plausible results.

In the experiments, we observed that when dealing with an image with relatively smooth color gradient, we need to decrease the weighting coefficients so that the change of the gray values in the grayscale image also appears smooth, which can be more in line with the characteristics in the original image. On the other hand, for the image with relatively sharp color gradient, the weighting coefficients need to be increased so as to distinguish the grouping effects as much as possible; since the edges in these types of images tends to be sharp, the resulting image would not cause the image gray distortion.

3.4.2 Extrema Group Difference Enhancement

During the group difference enhancement, we first cope with the groups with the maximum and minimum gray values, which are called extrema group. Given the group with the maximum gray value, note its average gray value calculated in the above Section is G_s, the maximum global mapping gray value in this group is G_{max}, and the weighting coefficient is θ_{max}, the final enhancement result is written as

$$E_i = T_i + o_i|G_s - G_{max}|\theta_{max} \tag{4}$$

where E_i is the final enhanced result, T_i is the gray value obtained through the global mapping, and o_i is the coefficient sign which can be expressed

$$o_i = sign(G_s - G_{max}) \tag{5}$$

Here *sign* denotes the sign operation.

For the group with the minimum gray value, we enhancement it in the similar manner,

$$E_i = T_i + o_i|G_s - G_{min}|\theta_{min} \tag{6}$$

where $o_i = sign(G_s - G_{min})$.

After the above enhancement for the extrema group difference enhancement, the overall gray of the group with the maximum gray value generally would increase and conversely the overall gray of the group with the minimum gray value would decrease.

3.4.3 Difference Enhancement for Non-extrema Groups

For the enhancement of non-extrema groups, we would select the average gray value G_{mid} of each group and adopted it for gray contrast. The final enhancement can be expressed as

$$E_i = T_i + o_i |G_s - G_{mid}| \theta_{other} \tag{7}$$

where $o_i = sign(G_s - G_{mid})$. Figure 3 shows the final decolorization the group difference enhancement into account.

Fig. 3. The decolorization result contrast. (left) the original image, (middle) the result without the group difference enhancement, (right) the result with the group difference enhancement.

4 Experiments and Discussions

We have made some experiments based on the above algorithm. All the experiments were run on a common PC with 2.27 GHz dual-core Intel Core i5 processor, 4G RAM. The programs were written in Matlab.

Figure 4 demonstrates the comparison between the decolorization of our method and that generated using Adobe Photoshop. For the left flower image, although Photoshop can distinguish the red flower and green background, however their difference is relatively small, which may easily misled viewers that these two regions are similar. In contrast, our method can plausibly tell these two groups. Similarly for the right image, photoshop cannot deal with the grassland and the sky very well, but our method can generate pleasing gray difference for them.

We performed contrast with the state-of-the-art color to gray algorithms, including Gooch's method [3], Grundland's method [5], Simth's method [12], Kim's method [7], and Wu's method [9]. As shown in Fig. 5, our method can generate better decolorization results, especially with respect to the preservation of the contrast and details of the original color image. For example, in the second row, our method can distinguish the flower and leaves, and even maintain the details on the leaves; Although Wu's method can also well tell the difference between the flower and the leaves, the details on the leaves are lost. Both the perceptual grouping and the group difference enhancement help our method improve the decolorization quality. In all our experiments, we set $G_{max} = 255$ and $G_{min} = 0$. Figure 6 gives more decolorization results generated by our method.

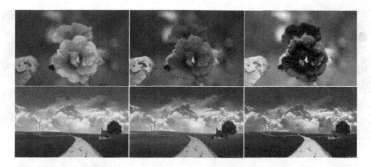

Fig. 4. Comparison between the result of our method and Adobe Photoshop. (Top line) the original color image, (middle line) the decolorization result of Adobe Photoshop, and (bottom line) the decolorization result of our method. (Color figure online)

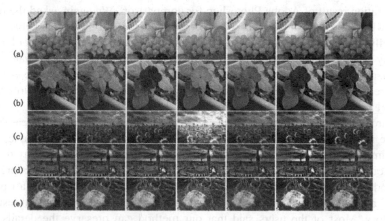

Fig. 5. Comparison with the state-of-the-art color to gray algorithms, from left to right: Gooch's method [3], Grundland's method [5], Simth's method [12], Kim's method [7], Wu's method [9], and our method

4.1 User Study

Inspired by the experiments in [9], we designed a group of user study experiments in order to further evaluate our decolorization method. We asked 23 users to participate our investigation. Among them, the numbers of the male and female are 13 and 10, respectively. Their ages are between 20 and 39. We also asked their professional background, e.g., if they are familiar with image processing or have the basic image knowledge.

In the first part of our user study experiment, we selected the original color image, the declorization image generated by our method, and the decolorization image produced by one of the state-of-the-art algorithms. Note that the state-of-the-art algorithm is selected randomly each time. We asked the users to select which one can better preserve the perceptual details of the original color image.

     (a)   (b)   (c)   (d)

Fig. 6. More decolourization results by our method

Next, in the second part, we also selected the original color image and the decolorization result generated by our method, but unlike the former part, we chose the decolorization result of Adobe Photoshop for comparison. We again asked the users to choose which one can better preserve the perceptual details of the original color image.

Finally, in the last part, we showed the original color image and the decolorization result by our method simultaneously to the user, and asked them to rate for the decolorization result. Here, we set score '5' to be the best and '1' to be the worst. Therefore, high scores mean that the decolorization result is satisfactory. Note that for each part we showed five groups of images to the users.

Figure 7 shows the statistical results of our user study experiments. It can be seen from the result that more users prefer our decolorization results. For example, for the second image in the first part, 19 users prefer our result and only 4 users say the result of previous work is better; for the fourth image in the second part, 18 users prefer our result and only 3 users say the result of Adode Photoshop is better. In the last part, we obtained a high average score of 4.41, which showed that our decolorization results are satisfactory. Most of the users said that our method can preserve the details of the original color image. A few users said that for some figure, it is hard to distinguish the decolorization result of our method and that produced by other methods.

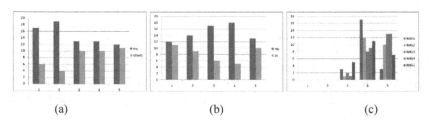

     (a)   (b)   (c)

Fig. 7. The statistical results of (a) the first part, (b) the second part, and (c) the last part of our user study experiment. Note that in (a) and (b) the horizontal axis is five groups of images while the horizontal axis in (c) represent the users' rate; the vertical axis in all the three figures denotes the number of the users.

5 Conclusions and Future Work

This paper proposed a novel, efficient decolorization method via PGD enhancement. This method is based on the human perception theory that perceptual groups rather than individual pixels are perceived by people. For each group, we calculated the average color value and adopted the average color value for the relative gray value evaluation. We then adapted global mapping to add the local details. Our method is efficient due to the low computational cost of the linear calculation. Moreover, our method can better preserve the details and contrast in the original color image.

In the future, we plan to develop an automatic, adaptive decolorization method so as to improve the efficiency and extend the applications of our method. Considering more characteristics of human visual perception might also further improve the decolorization results.

References

1. Wyszecki, G., Stileset, W.S.: Color Science, Concepts and Methods, Quantitative Data and Formulae. Wiley, New York (2000)
2. Song, Y., Bao, L., Xu, X., Yang, Q.: Decolorization: Is rgb2gray () out? In: Proceedings of ACM SIGGRAPH Asia Technical Briefs (2013)
3. Gooch, A., Olsen, S., Tumblin, J., Gooch, B.: Color2gray: salience-preserving color removal. ACM Trans. Graph. **24**(3), 634–639 (2005)
4. Rasche, K., Geist, R., Westall, J.: Re-coloring images for gamuts of lower dimension. Comput. Graph. Forum **24**(3), 423–432 (2005)
5. Grundland, M., Dodgson, N.: Decolorize: fast, contrast enhancing, color to grayscale conversion. Pattern Recogn. **40**(11), 2891–2897 (2007)
6. Kuhn, G.R., Oliveira, M.M., Fernandes, L.A.F.: An improved contrast enhancing approach for color to grayscale mappings. Vis. Comput. **24**(7), 505–514 (2008)
7. Kim, Y., Jang, C., Demouth, J., Lee, S.: Robust color-to-gray via nonlinear global mapping. ACM Trans. Graph. **28**(5), 1–4 (2009)
8. Bala, R., Eschbach, R.: Spatial color-to-grayscale transform preserving chrominance edge information. In: Proceedings of Color Imaging Conference, pp. 82–86 (2004)
9. Wu, J., Shen, X., Liu, L.: Interactive two-scale color-to-gray. Vis. Comput. **28**(6–8), 723–731 (2012)
10. Neumann, L., Cadik, M., Nemcsics, A.: An efficient perception based adaptive color to gray transformation. In: Proceedings of Computational Aesthetics, pp. 73–80 (2007)
11. Lu, C., Xu, L., Jia, J.: Real-time contrast preserving decolorization. In: Proceedings of SIGGRAPH Technical Briefs (2012)
12. Smith, K., Landes, P., Thollot, J., Myszkowsky, K.: Apparent greyscale: a simple and fast conversion to perceptually accurate images and video. Comput. Graph. Forum **27**(2), 193–200 (2008)
13. Zhu, W., Hu, R., Liu, L.: Grey conversion via perceived-contrast. Vis. Comput. **30**(3), 299–309 (2014)
14. Song, M., Tao, D., Chen, C., Li, X., Chen, C.: Color to gray: visual cue preservation. IEEE Trans. Pattern Anal. Mach. Intell. **32**(9), 1537–1552 (2010)
15. Yang, Y., Song, M., Bu, J., et al.: Color to gray: attention preservation. In: Proceedings of Pacific-Rim Symposium on Image and Video Technology (PSIVT), pp. 337–342 (2010)
16. Song, M., Tao, D., Bu, J., Chen, C., Yang, Y.: Color-to-gray based on chance of happening preservation. Neurocomputing **119**, 222–231 (2013)

A Spectral Unmixing Method Based on Co-Training

Qingyu Pang[1(✉)], Jing Yu[2(✉)], and Weidong Sun[1(✉)]

[1] State Key Laboratory of Intelligent Technology and Systems,
Tsinghua National Laboratory for Information Science and Technology,
Department of Electronic Engineering, Tsinghua University, Beijing 100084, China
pqy10@mails.tsinghua.edu.cn, wdsun@tsinghua.edu.cn
[2] College of Computer Science and Technology, Beijing University of Technology,
Beijing 100124, China
jing.yu@bjut.edu.cn

Abstract. With the gradual maturation of imaging spectroscopy, the demand for quantitative analysis of hyperspectral images grows with each passing day. Spectral unmixing has been considered as an efficient way to extract detailed information about land covers. In this paper, by introducing the co-training concept into the spectral unmixing method based on wavelet weighted similarity (WWS-SU), a spectral unmixing method based on co-training (CT-SU) is proposed. Compared with the WWS-SU method on synthetic hyperspectral image, the CT-SU method shows not only more practical but also more accurate in result.

Keywords: Hyperspectral remote sensing · Spectral unmixing
Co-training

1 Introduction

With the gradual maturation of imaging spectroscopy, hyperspectral remote sensing has received more and more attentions. Unlike the traditional imaging techniques, hyperspectral remote sensing can provide not only spatial information but also spectral information [21].

Due to the high altitude of the remote sensing platform and the low spatial resolution of the sensor, "mixed pixel", a combination of numerous individual components, usually exists in hyperspectral images. The measured spectra will be composite of various spectra, known as the "endmember", weighted by their corresponding fractions known as the "abundance" [15]. As the spectral unmixing can decompose mixed pixel into endmember and abundance, it has been considered as an efficient way to extract detailed information about the material properties [12].

This work was supported by the National Nature Science Foundation (No. 61171117) and the Capital Health Research and Development of Special (No. 2014-2-4025) of China.

Y. Zhao et al. (Eds.): ICIG 2017, Part II, LNCS 10667, pp. 570–579, 2017.
https://doi.org/10.1007/978-3-319-71589-6_50

The current spectral unmixing methods can be divided into two basic categories, the unsupervised method and the supervised method. The unsupervised unmixing method, which directly estimates the endmember and the abundance without using any priori knowledge, mainly contains these following methods [3,5,14]: geometric algorithms [16,19,22], statistical algorithms [11,17,18] and sparse regression-based algorithms [2,6].

The supervised unmixing methods mainly use spatial information [7,23] or the spectral library [10,13,20] as the priori knowledge. However the spectral library of the corresponding region does not always exist. Even if it exists, the spectra of the remote sensing image may differ with the spectra in the spectral library [1]. Facing this problem, a spectral unmixing method based on co-training is proposed in this paper. The remainder of this paper is as follows. Section 2 briefly describes the linear spectral mixture model and the spectral unmixing method based on wavelet weighted similarity. Section 3 details the spectral unmixing method based on co-training after introducing the co-training concept. Section 4 compares the CT-SU method with the WWS-SU method on synthetic hyperspectral image. Section 5 concludes this paper.

2 Spectral Mixture Model and Spectral Unmixing Method

The existing spectral mixture models can generally be divided into the linear spectral mixture model and the nonlinear spectral mixture model [15]. The linear spectral mixture model is widely used in spectral unmixing as it has a simple architecture and coincides with the actual situation in most cases. Therefore, the linear spectral mixture model will be first introduced in this section, followed by the wavelet weighted similarity and the spectral unmixing method based on wavelet weighted similarity.

2.1 Linear Spectral Mixture Model

The reflecting surface is generally portrayed as a chess board mixture, and the incident radiation interacts with only one component [15]. In this case, the fractions of the substances, namely, the abundance, have a linear relationship with reflected radiation, namely, the spectra of the mixed pixels. Mathematically, when M endmembers exist, the LMM is expressed as:

$$\mathbf{x} = \sum_{i=1}^{M} a_i \mathbf{s}_i + \mathbf{e} = \mathbf{Sa} + \mathbf{e} \tag{1}$$

where $\mathbf{x}$ denotes received pixel spectrum vector, $\mathbf{s}_i, i = 1, \ldots, M$ denotes the spectra vector of endmembers, $a_i, i = 1, \ldots, M$ denotes fractional abundance and $\mathbf{e}$ is additive observation noise vector. To be physically meaningful, there are two constraints on the abundance $\mathbf{a}$. The nonnegativity constraint requires all abundances to be nonnegative such that $a_i \geq 0, i = 1, \ldots, M$ and the full additivity constraint requires that $\sum_{i=1}^{M} a_i = 1$.

2.2   Wavelet Weighted Similarity

Generally different substances have different spectra, while the same substances have similar spectra. This type of similarity mainly embodies in the spectral absorption feature [21], hence the spectral absorption feature is essential to measure spectra similarity. However, current spectral similarity measurements, for instance the spectral angle mapper (SAM) and the correlation coefficient (COR), do not take into account the spectral absorption features. When $\mathbf{s}$ and $\mathbf{s}'$ are r band spectra vectors, the spectral angle mapper and correlation coefficient are defined as follows [21]:

$$\text{SAM}(\mathbf{s}, \mathbf{s}') = \arccos \frac{\mathbf{s}^T \mathbf{s}'}{\|\mathbf{s}\|_2 \|\mathbf{s}'\|_2} \tag{2}$$

$$\text{COR}(\mathbf{s}, \mathbf{s}') = \frac{(\mathbf{P}_r \mathbf{s})^T (\mathbf{P}_r \mathbf{s}')}{\|\mathbf{P}_r \mathbf{s}\|_2 \|\mathbf{P}_r \mathbf{s}'\|_2} \tag{3}$$

where $\mathbf{P}_r$ denotes a r dimensional projection matrix [9] defined as follow:

$$\mathbf{P}_r = 1 - \frac{1}{r} \mathbf{I}_r \mathbf{I}_r^T \tag{4}$$

In the paper [20], by computing the similarity of the wavelet coefficients between two spectra, the wavelet weighted similarity is defined as follow:

$$\text{WWS}(\mathbf{s}, \mathbf{s}') = \sum_{i=1}^{n} w_i \text{COR}(dx_i, dy_i) \tag{5}$$

In the formula, $\mathbf{s}$ and $\mathbf{s}'$ are spectra vectors, n denotes the scale of the wavelet transform, $dx_i, dy_i, i = 1, \ldots, n$ are the wavelet transform coefficients on i scale and $w_i, i = 1, \ldots, n$ are the given weight, which satisfy $\sum_{i=1}^{n} w_i = 1$.

2.3   Spectral Unmixing Method Based on Wavelet Weighted Similarity

In paper [20], based on measuring spectra similarity by wavelet weighted similarity between the endmember spectra and the spectra in spectral library, a regularization term is added to the optimization problem. The spectral unmixing method based on wavelet weighted similarity (WWS-SU) is described as follows:

minimize

$$f(\mathbf{S}, \mathbf{A}, \mathbf{OS}) = \frac{1}{2} \|\mathbf{X} - \mathbf{SA}\|_F^2 + \frac{\lambda}{2} \times trace(\mathbf{SP}_M \mathbf{S}^T)$$

$$+ \frac{\mu}{2} \sum_{i=1}^{M} \sum_{i'=1}^{M'} \delta(\mathbf{s}_i \sim \mathbf{os}_{i'}) \text{WWS}(\mathbf{s}_i, \mathbf{os}_{i'})$$

subject to $\mathbf{S} \geq 0, \mathbf{A} \geq 0, \mathbf{I}_M^T \mathbf{A} = \mathbf{I}_N^T$ $\tag{6}$

where λ and μ are Lagrange multipliers, $\mathbf{os}_{i'}, i = 1, \ldots, M'$ are spectra in spectral library, M' is the amount of spectra in spectral library, $\delta()$ is indicator function. If $\mathbf{s}_i$ and $\mathbf{os}_{i'}$ are matched, $\delta(\mathbf{s}_i \sim \mathbf{os}_{i'}) = 1$, otherwise $\delta(\mathbf{s}_i \sim \mathbf{os}_{i'}) = 0$.

3   Spectral Unmixing Method Based on Co-Training

By measuring spectra similarity with wavelet weighted similarity, the WWS-SU method is able to maintain the spectral absorption feature between the endmember spectra and the spectra in spectral library while reserving differences. However, the spectral library of the corresponding region does not always exist. Even if it exists, there still are differences between the spectra acquired from the remote sensing image and the spectra in the spectral library. Facing this problem, this paper proposes a spectral unmixing method based on co-training (CT-SU).

3.1   The Co-Training Model

The co-training model is proposed by Blum and Mitchell [4] in 1998. The instance space $X = X_1 \times X_2$ where X_1 and X_2 correspond to two different views and each view in itself is sufficient for classification, the algorithm is describe as follow:

Algorithm 1. Framework of the Co-Training

Require:
    The set of labeled training examples L
    The set of unlabeled samples U

Ensure:
1: Create a pool U' of examples by choosing u examples at random from L
2: **for** $i = 1$ to k **do**
3:    Use L to train a classifier h_1 that considers only the x_1 portion of x
4:    Use L to train a classifier h_2 that considers only the x_2 portion of x
5:    Allow h_1 to label p positive and n negative examples from U'
6:    Allow h_2 to label p positive and n negative examples from U'
7:    Randomly choose $2p + 2n$ examples from U to replenish U'
8: **end for**
9: **return** classifier h_1 and h_2

3.2   Spectral Unmixing Method Based on Co-Training

Although the spectral unmixing problem for two image might seem like the classification problem with two views, they are essentially different matters. Hence, the co-training model can not be directly applied to the spectral unmixing.

However, if we treat the endmembers from two images as two classifiers, and use the iterative gradient descent by Nesterov's algorithm to replace the iterative training of classification. Combining the concept of co-training algorithm and the WWS-SU method, this paper proposes the spectral unmixing method based on co-training, presented as follow:

Algorithm 2. Framework of the Spectral Unmixing Method Based on Co-Training

---

Require:
   The hyperspectral images X and X'
Ensure:
 1: Create two initial sets of endmembers S_0 and S_0' at random
 2: Calculate the corresponding abundances A_0 and A_0'
 3: **for** $k = 1$ to q **do**
 4:    Use S_k' as spectral library to guide the spectral unmixing of X
       Calculate S_{k+1} by Nesterov's algorithm

$$f(\mathbf{S_{k+1}}, \mathbf{A_k}, \mathbf{S_k'}) < f(\mathbf{S_k}, \mathbf{A_k}, \mathbf{S_k'})$$
$$= \frac{1}{2}\|\mathbf{X} - \mathbf{S_k A_k}\|_F^2 + \frac{\lambda}{2}trace(\mathbf{S_k P_M S_k}^T) \tag{7}$$
$$+ \frac{\mu}{2} \sum_{i=1}^{M} \sum_{i'=1}^{M'} \delta(\mathbf{s}_i \sim \mathbf{s}_{i'}') \text{WWS}(\mathbf{s}_i, \mathbf{s}_{i'}')$$

       Calculate A_{k+1}

$$f(\mathbf{S_{k+1}}, \mathbf{A_{k+1}}, \mathbf{S_k'}) < f(\mathbf{S_{k+1}}, \mathbf{A_k}, \mathbf{S_k'}) \tag{8}$$

 5:    Use S_{k+1} as spectral library to guide the spectral unmixing of X'
       Calculate S_{k+1}'

$$f(\mathbf{S_{k+1}'}, \mathbf{A_k'}, \mathbf{S_{k+1}}) < f(\mathbf{S_k'}, \mathbf{A_k'}, \mathbf{S_{k+1}}) \tag{9}$$

       Calculate A_{k+1}'

$$f(\mathbf{S_{k+1}'}, \mathbf{A_{k+1}'}, \mathbf{S_{k+1}}) < f(\mathbf{S_{k+1}'}, \mathbf{A_k'}, \mathbf{S_{k+1}}) \tag{10}$$

 6: **end for**
 7: **return** endmembers S and S'

---

4   Experiment and Analysis

4.1   Experiment Preparation

In this experiment, four spectra are randomly selected from the United States Geological Survey (USGS) digital spectral library [8], showed in Fig. 1, and namely they are clinoptilolite, glaucophane, axinite and grossular.

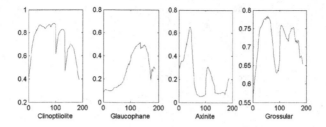

Fig. 1. Selected endmembers

Two hyperspectral image are synthesized by these spectra and the actual abundance images from other spectra unmixing result. The image we primarily focused and its corresponding abundance images are showed in Fig. 2.

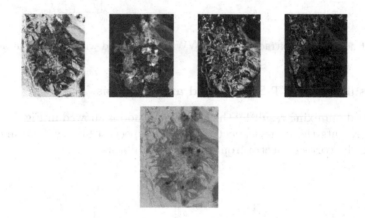

Fig. 2. Abundance images and synthesized hyperspectral image by color composition

4.2 Result of the WWS-SU Method

The spectral unmixing method based on wavelet weighted similarity (WWS-SU) requires a spectral library as priori knowledge to guide the unmixing procedure. Two different types of spectral library are tested in this experiment.

If the WWS-SU method uses the same spectral library as that used for synthetic hyperspectral image generation, it would get the best possible result. In this condition, the spectral unmixing result by the WWS-SU method is showed in Fig. 3. The line in red represents the correct spectra from the spectral library.

If the spectral library is fully uncorrelated with the hyperspectral image or does not exist at all, the WWS-SU method would degenerate into the unsupervised method. Mathematically, $\frac{\mu}{2} \sum_{i=1}^{M} \sum_{i'=1}^{M'} \delta(\mathbf{s}_i \sim \mathbf{os}_{i'}) \mathrm{WWS}(\mathbf{s}_i, \mathbf{os}_{i'}) = 0$. In this condition, the result is showed in Fig. 4. The line in red represents the correct spectra from the spectral library.

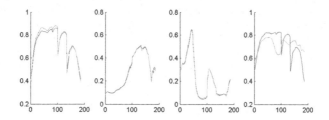

Fig. 3. Endmembers extracted by the WWS-SU method

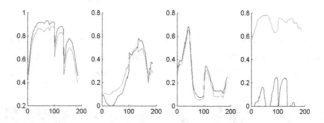

Fig. 4. Endmembers extracted by the WWS-SU method without spectral library

4.3   Result of the CT-SU Method and Analysis

The spectral unmixing result by the CT-SU method is showed in Fig. 5. The line in red represents the correct spectra from the spectral library. The line in red represents the correct spectra from the spectral library.

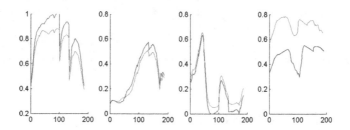

Fig. 5. Endmembers extracted by the CT-SU method

For the purpose of comparison, two measurements, COR and WWS, are adopted to evaluate the similarity between the true endmember and the extracted spectra. For COR and WWS, the larger the value is, the more similar the two spectra will be. The results of this experiment are showed in Table 1. The WWS-SU* means the WWS-SU method without the spectral library as priori knowledge.

For the endmember with large average abundance, namely clinoptilolite in this experiment, the content of this substance is plentiful in this region and the results show that WWS-SU and CT-SU perform equally well under both measure.

For the endmember with medium average abundance, the endmember extracted by WWS-SU* may have wrong spectral absorption feature as glaucophane in Fig. 4. COR does not correlate well with the differences of the spectral absorption feature, while WWS does.

For the endmember with small average abundance, namely grossular in this experiment, the content of this substance is scarce in this region and the WWS-SU and WWS-SU* may get completely wrong results (see in Figs. 3 and 4). With the help of the other hyperspectral image, CT-SU can still obtain the substantially correct result. This can indicate that CT-SU totally outperforms than WWS-SU. This also indicates WWS is much better than COR for measuring the similarity between spectra.

Table 1. Comparison of the similarity measured by COR and WWS extracted by WWS-SU and CT-SU, respectively

Average abundance		Clinoptilolite	Glaucophane	Axinite	Grossular
		0.48	0.23	0.23	0.07
COR	WWS-SU	0.997	0.999	0.999	0.366
	WWS-SU*	0.996	0.974	0.999	−0.074
	CT-SU	0.991	0.995	0.999	0.913
WWS	WWS-SU	0.991	0.995	0.999	0.255
	WWS-SU*	0.997	0.676	0.990	−0.685
	CT-SU	0.991	0.976	0.986	0.866

5   Conclusion

The co-training model is widely applied in semi-supervised learning. However due to the essential difference with the spectral unmixing problem, it cannot be directly used. By introducing the co-training concept into spectral unmixing, a spectral unmixing method base co-training (CT-SU) has been proposed in this paper. The CT-SU method considers two relevant hyperspectral images as different views in co-training algorithm instead of using the spectral library. Comparing with the spectral library, it is much easier to acquire another relevant hyperspectral image. Most times they are different part of the same image, or photographed by the same platform at different time. Hence the application of CT-SU is more extensive than WWS-SU or any other supervised method using the spectral library. After a comparison with WWS-SU on a synthetic hyperspectral image, CT-SU also shows promising results for all endmembers.

References

1. Asrar, G.: Theory and Applications of Optical Remote Sensing. Wiley, Hoboken (1989)
2. Bioucas-Dias, J.M., Figueiredo, M.A.: Alternating direction algorithms for constrained sparse regression: application to hyperspectral unmixing. In: 2010 2nd Workshop on Hyperspectral Image and Signal Processing: Evolution in Remote Sensing, pp. 1–4. IEEE (2010)
3. Bioucas-Dias, J.M., Plaza, A., Dobigeon, N., Parente, M., Du, Q., Gader, P., Chanussot, J.: Hyperspectral unmixing overview: geometrical, statistical, and sparse regression-based approaches. IEEE J. Sel. Top. Appl. Earth Obs. Remote Sens. **5**(2), 354–379 (2012)
4. Blum, A., Mitchell, T.: Combining labeled and unlabeled data with co-training. In: Proceedings of the Eleventh Annual Conference on Computational Learning Theory, pp. 92–100. ACM (1998)
5. Chang, C.: Hyperspectral Data Exploitation: Theory and Applications. Wiley, Hoboken (2007)
6. Charles, A.S., Olshausen, B.A., Rozell, C.J.: Learning sparse codes for hyperspectral imagery. IEEE J. Sel. Top. Sig. Process. **5**(5), 963–978 (2011)
7. Chen, X., Yu, J., Sun, W., et al.: Area-correlated spectral unmixing based on Bayesian nonnegative matrix factorization. Open J. Appl. Sci. **3**(1), 41 (2013)
8. Clark, R., Swayze, G., Wise, R., Livo, E., Hoefen, T., Kokaly, R., Sutley, S.: USGS Digital Spectral Library Splib06a. US Geological Survey, Denver (2007)
9. Dattorro, J.: Convex Optimization and Euclidean Distance Geometry. Meboo Publishing, Palo Alto (2005)
10. Dobigeon, N., Tourneret, J., Chang, C.: Semi-supervised linear spectral unmixing using a hierarchical Bayesian model for hyperspectral imagery. IEEE Trans. Sig. Process. **56**(7), 2684–2695 (2008)
11. Dobigeon, N., Moussaoui, S., Tourneret, J.Y., Carteret, C.: Bayesian separation of spectral sources under non-negativity and full additivity constraints. Sig. Process. **89**(12), 2657–2669 (2009)
12. Garini, Y., Young, I.T., McNamara, G.: Spectral imaging: principles and applications. Cytom. Part A **69**(8), 735–747 (2006)
13. Iordache, M.D., Plaza, A., Bioucas-Dias, J.: On the use of spectral libraries to perform sparse unmixing of hyperspectral data. In: 2010 2nd Workshop on Hyperspectral Image and Signal Processing: Evolution in Remote Sensing, pp. 1–4. IEEE (2010)
14. Keshava, N.: A survey of spectral unmixing algorithms. Linc. Lab. J. **14**, 55–78 (2003)
15. Keshava, N., Mustard, J.: Spectral unmixing. IEEE Trans. Sig. Process. **19**, 44–57 (2002)
16. Li, J., Bioucas-Dias, J.M.: Minimum volume simplex analysis: a fast algorithm to unmix hyperspectral data. In: 2008 IEEE International Geoscience and Remote Sensing Symposium, IGARSS 2008, vol. 3, pp. III–250 (2008)
17. Moussaoui, S., Carteret, C., Brie, D., Mohammad-Djafari, A.: Bayesian analysis of spectral mixture data using Markov chain Monte Carlo methods. Chemometr. Intell. Lab. Syst. **81**(2), 137–148 (2006)
18. Nascimento, J.M., Bioucas-Dias, J.M.: Hyperspectral unmixing algorithm via dependent component analysis. In: 2007 IEEE International Geoscience and Remote Sensing Symposium, pp. 4033–4036. IEEE (2007)

19. Nascimento, J.M., Dias, J.M.: Vertex component analysis: a fast algorithm to unmix hyperspectral data. IEEE Trans. Geosci. Remote Sens. **43**(4), 898–910 (2005)
20. Pang, Q., Yu, J., Sun, W.: A spectral unmixing method based on wavelet weighted similarity. In: 2015 IEEE International Conference on Image Processing (ICIP), pp. 1865–1869. IEEE (2015)
21. Tong, Q., Zhang, B., Zheng, L.: Hyperspectral Remote Sensing: the Principle, Technology and Application. Higher Education Press, Beijing (2006)
22. Winter, M.E.: N-FINDR: an algorithm for fast autonomous spectral end-member determination in hyperspectral data. In: SPIE's International Symposium on Optical Science, Engineering, and Instrumentation, pp. 266–275. International Society for Optics and Photonics (1999)
23. Zhang, B., Zhang, X., Liu, L., Zheng, L., Tong, Q., Zhang, B.: Spectral unmixing and image classification supported by spatial knowledge. In: Proceedings of SPIE, vol. 4897, pp. 279–283 (2002)

A Novel Algorithm of Image Fusion Based on Non-subsampled Shearlet-Contrast Transform

Dongpeng Wu[✉], Duyan Bi, Linyuan He, Shiping Ma, Zunlin Fan,
Wenshan Ding, Liyang Wu, Shiping Wang, and Kun Liu

Aeronautics and Astronautics Engineering College,
Air Force Engineering University, Baling Road, Xi'an 710038, China
Wdp_image@126.com

Abstract. To solve the shortcomings of results based on image fusion algorithm, such as lack of contrast and details, we proposed a novel algorithm of image fusion based on non-subsampled Shearlet-contrast transform (NSSCT). Firstly, we analyze the correlation and the diversity between different coefficients of non-subsampled Shearlet transform (NSST), build the high level coefficients which are the same orientation to NSSCT. Then, fuse the high level coefficients which can reserve details and contrast of image; fuse the low level coefficients based on the characters of it. Eventually, obtain the fused image by inverse NSSCT. To verify the advantage of the proposed algorithm, we compare with several popular algorithms such as DWT, saliency map, NSST and so on, both the subjective visual and objective performance conform the superiority of the proposed algorithm.

Keywords: Image fusion · Infrared and visible image
Non-subsampled Shearlet-contrast transform · Contrast

1 Introduction and Related Work

Infrared image identifies the thermal and hidden targets, it can unaffected by the external influences and occlusion, but it is poor contrast and details. In contrast, visible image can provide higher contrast and rich details, but its quality is easily affected by light intensity, occlusion and the impact of surroundings. Fuse the two type images can get a more informative image, it has been widely used in military reconnaissance, target recognition, society security and other fields [1].

Therefore, to fuse the different sensor images, there exits many algorithms which can be classified into two types: spatial domain and transform domain. The traditional algorithms fuse images based on spatial domain mainly, such as weighted average, principal component analysis [2] (PCA), gradient transform [3], contrast transform [4] and other algorithms. This kind of algorithms are simple and efficient. But the fused image is lack of image information and details, the edges of targets are not perfect.

To this end, scholars began to fuse images based on transform domain. The first transform domain algorithm is based on the wavelet transform domain [5], image can

© Springer International Publishing AG 2017
Y. Zhao et al. (Eds.): ICIG 2017, Part II, LNCS 10667, pp. 580–589, 2017.
https://doi.org/10.1007/978-3-319-71589-6_51

be decomposed into a low coefficient and a series of high level coefficients via wavelet transform. Those coefficients preserve the important information of the image, but high level coefficients express three directions only, so there are flaws in the details of performance. For the problem of wavelet transform, more transform domain fusion methods are proposed, such as Curvelet transform [6], contourlet transform [7] can decompose the image into more directions on different scales. Those methods perform well in processing the details, but the filter kernel is complex and hard to calculation. Guo and Labate proposed Shearlet transform [8, 9], this multi-scales geometric analysis is simple and effective, express the details and edges better.

Fusion methods based on the transform domain [10–12] enhance the quality of the details in fused image significantly, but their results are widespread lack of contrast information. Generally, the infrared image is larger than visible image in intensity, so most of those methods may lose a lot of information of visible image. Because those methods mainly use the coefficients directed without considering the connection between the coefficients, fused image contrast in not enough.

Summarizing the above problems, it is significant to proposed a novel transform. Hence, we try to proposed a novel transform named NSSCT to fuse infrared and visible images in this paper. Firstly, we introduce the framework of image fusion and build the NSSCT coefficients. Then, the fusion image achieved by the proposed rules in different coefficients. Finally, the experiment results prove that the performance of proposed fusion method.

2 Fusion Scheme and NSSCT

2.1 Framework for Image Fusion

In order to obtain a more informative fused image, the fused image should retain both hidden target information and contrast information. So we use NSSCT to decompose the infrared image and visible image, NSSCT is presented in the next section, obtain the coefficients which contain contrast information. Foinr the low coefficients, extract the saliency map to enhance the saliency target; for the high level coefficients fuse them to enhance the contrast of fused image. The schematic of proposed method is shown below (Fig. 1).

2.2 Non-subsampled Shearlet-Contrast Transform

NSST

Shearlet transform [8] is a multi-scales geometric analysis tool proposed by Guo and Labate. The direction filter kernel is simple, for the high level coefficients, there are more directions and is steerable.

For a two-dimensional affine system, it is constructed as:

$$\xi_{AB}(\psi) = \{\psi_{j,l,k}(x) = |\det A|^{j/2}\,\psi(B^l A^j x - k) : j, l \in Z, k \in Z^2\} \tag{1}$$

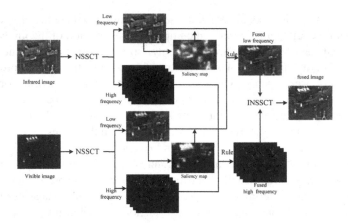

Fig. 1. Schematic diagram of the proposed method

where $\psi \in L^2(R^2)$, L is the integrable space, R is the set of real numbers, and Z is the set of integers. A and B are 2×2 reversible matrix, j is the decomposition level, l is the number of each decomposition direction, k is the transform parameter.

Suppose that $\xi_{AB}(\psi)$ satisfies the Parseval assumption (tight support condition) for any function $f \in L^2(R^2)$, as:

$$\sum_{j,l,k} |<f, \psi_{j,l,k}>|^2 = ||f||^2 \tag{2}$$

Then, the $\psi_{j,l,k}$ is the synthetic wavelet. Matrix A controls the scale and matrix B controls the direction. In general, $A = \begin{bmatrix} 4 & 0 \\ 0 & 2 \end{bmatrix}$ and $B = \begin{bmatrix} 1 & 1 \\ 0 & 1 \end{bmatrix}$ in the Shearlet transform.

NSST is based on the Shearlet transform using nonsubsampled scaling and direction filter processing. NSST is considered to be the optimal approximation of sparse representation for image. Hence, a lot of methods [13, 14] based on NSST are proposed, the results perform well in reserve image details and edges, but most of those methods use the coefficients directed, so the results is short of contrast.

NSSCT

Because of the lack of contrast in fusion results, we analyze the coefficients by NSST, and build a novel transform named NSSCT.

The image F is decomposed into a low coefficient I_L and a series of high level coefficients $[G_1, G_2 ... G_i ... G_n]$. For any adjacent high level coefficients, the coefficients direction of the scale $i + 1$ is double as more as the scale i. An example in shown in Fig. 2.

Figure 2 shows the results of the first scale high level coefficients G_1 and the second scale high level coefficients G_2 after decompose the image Lena. It is easily to know that the lower level coefficients can be the background of the higher level coefficients.

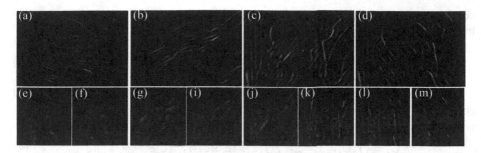

Fig. 2. The adjacent levels coefficients

It is obvious also that G_1^1 is correlate with G_2^1 and G_2^2, but uncorrelated with other coefficients inlevel 2. So we calculate the correlation [15] between G_1 and G_2. The Fig. 3 show the results.

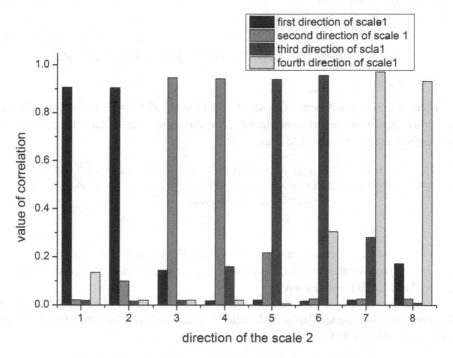

Fig. 3. The value of correlation between adjacent coefficients

It is apparently in Fig. 3 that lower level coefficients correlate with the two higher coefficients which are similar direction. In order to improve the contrast information of the fused images, it is necessary to make the relevant scales contain the contrast information of the images. To obtain the contrast information needs compare the adjacent scales. At that time, we need transform the coefficients to ensure the consistency and numbers between the adjacent scales. Hence, the coefficients of G_2 are transformed as:

$$G_2^{1*} = G_2^1 \odot G_2^2 \tag{3}$$

Before explain the operation $\odot$ we will analyze the process to calculate the hig level coefficients.

$$G_j^l = \left\langle f, \psi_{j,l,k}^{(d)} \right\rangle = 2^{\frac{3j}{2}} \int_{R^2} \hat{f}(\xi) \overline{V(2^{-2j}\xi) W_{j,l}^{(d)}(\xi)} e^{2\pi i \xi A_d^{-j} B_d^{-lk}} d\xi \tag{4}$$

For G_2^l, it is in the right frequency domain, so $d = 0$. The parameter $j = 2$ and $l = 1$. Hence, the direction of the coefficients is determined by l. The definition of V and W parameters in (7) is given in [9, 10]. We calculate the G_2^{1*} to explain the operation $\odot$.

$$\begin{aligned}
G_2^{1*} &= G_2^1 \odot G_2^2 \\
&= \left\langle f, \psi_{2,1}^{(0)} \right\rangle \odot \left\langle f, \psi_{2,2}^{(0)} \right\rangle \\
&= 2^3 \int_{R^2} \hat{f}(\xi) \overline{V(2^{-2}\xi)} e^{2\pi i \xi A_0^{-1}} (W_{2,1}^{(d)}(\xi) e^{B_0^{-l}} \odot W_{2,2}^{(d)}(\xi) e^{B_0^{-2}}) d\xi
\end{aligned} \tag{5}$$

There are two coefficients G_2^1 and G_2^2 which are the same scale but different directions. Hence, when calculate the G_2^{1*}, the direction filter W and the matrix B is most important. So we calculate it as:

$$W_{j,l}^{(d)}(\xi) e^{B_0^{-l}} \odot W_{j,l+1}^{(d)}(\xi) e^{B_0^{-l+1}} = \begin{cases} (\psi_2(2^j \frac{\xi_2}{\xi_1} - l/2) \times D_0(\xi) + \psi_2(2^j \frac{\xi_1}{\xi_2} - l/2 + 1) \times D_1(\xi)) e^{B_0^{-l}} & if, l = -2^{j-1} \\ (\psi_2(2^j \frac{\xi_2}{\xi_1} - l/2) \times D_0(\xi) + \psi_2(2^j \frac{\xi_1}{\xi_2} - l/2 - 1) \times D_1(\xi)) e^{B_0^{-l}} & if, l = 2^{j-1} - 1 \\ (\psi_2(2^j \frac{\xi_2}{\xi_1} - l/2)) e^{B_0^{-l}} \; otherwise \end{cases} \tag{6}$$

In (6), ψ_2 is the direction component of the Shearlet transform, $D_0(\xi)$ and $D_1(\xi)$ are the support frame of the Shearlet. Then, we can get the G_2^{1*}, the other coefficients can be calculated as above equations.

In order to preserve the contrast information, we contrast the coefficients which are different scales but are similarity in direction. So that the contrast information will be contained in the coefficients.

$$\begin{cases} G_i^k = \frac{G_{i+1}^{k*}}{G_i^k} - I & if, N > i \geq 1 \\ G_i^k = G_i^k & if, i = N \end{cases} (0 < k < 2^{i-1}) \tag{7}$$

3   Fusion Rules

3.1   Rule of High Level Coefficients

Based on the (4), (5) and (6), we have obtained the new coefficients. The new coefficients reflect the contrast and details information, to enhance the contrast and preserve the details, it is necessary to calculate the fusion coefficients in different region. Thus, $G_i^k(I_r)$ and $G_i^k(V_i)$, which are high level coefficients at level i and direction k of infrared and visible respectively, with approximation value can be considered to be redundant data. It means that they both are the details or regions with similar contrast, hence, it is applicative to obtain the fused coefficients by weighted summation. On the other hand, $G_i^k(I_r)$ and $G_i^k(V_i)$ with different characteristics which means that one of them are details or region with high contrast, the larger should be preserve. Thus, a threshold σ should be set. The specific calculate rule is shown as:

$$G_i^k(fus) = \begin{cases} \omega * G_i^k(I_r) + \omega * G_i^k(V_i) & |H(G_i^k(I_r)) - H(G_i^k(V_i))| < \sigma \\ G_i^k(I_r) & H(G_i^k(I_r)) - H(G_i^k(V_i)) > \sigma \\ G_i^k(V) & H(G_i^k(I_r)) - H(G_i^k(V_i)) < -\sigma \end{cases} \quad (8)$$

where $G_i^k(fus)$ denotes the fused coefficients. H(.) denotes the calculate of normalization. σ is the threshold to control different regions, in this paper, σ is set to 0.8. $\omega = 1 - \omega$, ω is a parameter to control fusion weights, the calculate of ω as:

$$\omega = \frac{H(G_i^k(I_r))}{H(G_i^k(I_r)) + H(G_i^k(V_i))} \quad (9)$$

After the fusion, we obtain the fused high level coefficients which preserve details and contrast, the fused image can avoid lacking of information.

3.2   Rule of Low Level Coefficients

The low level coefficients is the overview of source image, which contains the main information of the target and entropy of the image. To enhance the quality of the fused image, the fusion rule should based on the saliency [16] of the target.

Hence, we calculate the value of saliency for the image,

$$S_i = 1 - \exp\{-\frac{1}{M}\sum_{m=1}^{M}\frac{d_{inensity}(p_i, p_j^m)}{1 + \varepsilon \bullet d_{position}(p_i, p_j^m)}\} \quad (10)$$

In the (10), p_i and p_j denotes pixel patch which size is 3×3 centered on pixel i and j respectively. $d_{inensity}(p_i, p_j)$ denotes the intensity distance between the two pixel patches, and is calculated by the difference between the average value of the two pixel patches. $d_{position}(p_i, p_j)$ denotes the difference of Euler distances between two pixel patches. ε is a parameter to control the value saliency in pixel i, in this paper, ε is set to 0.6. (10) shows that intensity distance is positive correlation with the S_i, and Euler distance is negative correlation with the S_i. The value of S_i shows the saliency in the image, the more larger, the more salient. So the rule of low coefficient fusion need to compare the value of saliency.

$$L_i(fus) = \begin{cases} L_i(I_r) + \beta \bullet S_i(I_r) & H(S_i(I_r)) - H(S_i(V_i)) > \sigma_L \\ L_i(V_i) + \beta \bullet S_i(V_i) & H(S_i(I_r)) - H(S_i(V_i)) < -\sigma_L \\ \alpha(L_i(I_r) + \beta \bullet S_i(I_r)) + \alpha(L_i(V_i) + \beta \bullet S_i(V_i)) & otherwise \end{cases}$$

$$(11)$$

There are also necessary to build a threshold σ_L to distinguish different regions for different fusion rule, to make the target more salient, the σ_L need to be smaller than σ, σ_L is set to 0.5.

4   Experimental Results

4.1   Experiment Setting

To evaluate the performance of the proposed methods on image fusion, we select two sets of infrared images and visible image in this experiment and compare the performance between PCA [2], GT [3], CP [4], DWT [5] SAL (saliency) [17], NSCT [11] and NSST [12]. The number of levels in our method is 5.

4.2   Subjective Visual Test

Figure 4 shows the comparison on image with target. (a) and (b) are the source infrared and visible image, (c)–(j) are fused image by PCA, DWT, CP, GT, SAL, NSCT, NSST, and proposed methods, respectively. The targets in results are marked by blue rectangle and details of roof are marked by red rectangle. Target in proposed result is more saliency than PCA and NSST, compared with DWT, NSCT, SAL and GT results, the target are less bright, but those results are too bright to cover the contrast and details for the targets. It is also obvious that proposed result contain more details in the red rectangles. The results of PCA, DWT, SAL and NSCT brings the halo effects in the red rectangles. The CP results perform well in contrast of image, but is lack of some edges information, the result by the proposed methods perform better than it.

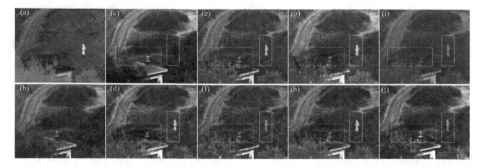

Fig. 4. The first set of experimental results (Color figure online)

Figure 5 shows the comparison on image with more details and different contrast between infrared and visible images. (a) and (b) are the source infrared and visible image, (c)–(j) are fused image by PCA, DWT, CP, GT, SAL, NSCT, NSST, and proposed methods, respectively.

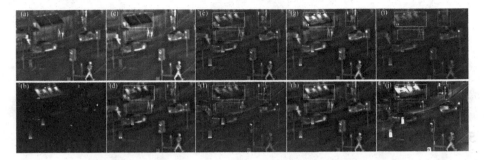

Fig. 5. The second set of experimental results (Color figure online)

The person targets in results are marked by green rectangle, the details of the seat within the store are marked by blue rectangle, and the texts in the roof are marked by red rectangle. The results by the proposed methods is superior to the other methods in the contrast. In the green rectangle, the results by the PCA, DWT, GT, SAL, NSCT are lack of contrast information, those results extract the most information form the infrared image, but the contrast information is mainly contained in visible image. The results by the NSST preserve the details well, but in the bule rectangle, it is fuzzy because of less contrast. CP methods perform well for the contrast of the image, but the details of the text in the roof are insufficient. So, the performance of the proposed methods is the best among those methods.

4.3 Quantitative Tests

To compare the performance on image fusion by above methods with quantitative measurement, the measure indexes of image quality (Q) [18], edge quality (Q_e) [19] and mutual information (MI) [20] are used in this paper (Table 1).

Table 1. Quantitative comparison for Fig. 4

Method	PCA	DWT	SAL	GT	CP	NSCT	NSST	Proposed
Q	4.114	4.521	4.905	4.528	5.669	4.535	4.564	**7.455**
Q_e	35.830	38.379	41.024	37.571	45.581	38.152	21.419	**59.891**
MI	1.436	1.322	1.987	1.381	0.939	1.631	1.571	**1.994**

It is obvious that proposed method achieves the largest value of Q and Q_e among other methods, which demonstrates that or method performs well in contrast and details of the fused image. The PCA result achieves larger value of MI for Fig. 5, because of the similar structure to visible, but loss the information of target from the infrared image (Table 2).

Table 2. Quantitative comparison for Fig. 5

Method	PCA	DWT	SAL	GT	CP	NSCT	NSST	Proposed
Q	5.748	6.085	5.943	6.033	6.340	6.018	5.427	**6.378**
Q_e	52.421	52.307	56.325	50.234	55.783	50.646	29.119	**57.230**
MI	**2.985**	1.048	1.285	1.045	1.037	1.145	1.099	1.414

5 Conclusion

Fused image has been widely used in many fields. But contrast loss and edge blurring limit its future development in industry application. To improve its quality, we construct a novel transform to decompose the image. For the high level coefficients, we fuse them to enhance the details and contrast; fuse the low level coefficients to enhance the salient of the target in source image. In addition, the experiment with subjective visual and quantitative tests show that the proposed methods can preserve details on the edges and enhance contrast of the image.

References

1. Ghassemian, H.: A review of remote sensing image fusion methods. Inf. Fusion **32**, 75–89 (2016)
2. Pan, Y., Zheng, Y.H., Sun, Q.S., Sun, H.J., Xia, D.S.: An image fusion framework based on principal component analysis and total variation model. J. Comput. Aided Design. Comput. Graph. **7**(23), 1200–1210 (2011)
3. Ma, J.Y., Chen, C., Li, C., Huang, J.: Infrared and visible image fusion via gradient transfer and total variation minimization. Inf. Fusion **31**, 100–109 (2016)
4. Xu, H., Wang, Y., Wu, Y.J., Qian, Y.S.: Infrared and multi-type images fusion algorithm based on contrast pyramid transform. Infrared Phys. Technol. **78**, 133–146 (2016)
5. Pajares, G., Manuel, J.: A wavelet-based image fusion tutorial. Pattern Recogn. **37**, 1855–1872 (2004)
6. Li, S.T., Yang, B.: Multifocus image fusion by combining curvelet and wavelet transform. Pattern Recogn. Lett. **29**, 1295–1301 (2008)
7. Do, M.N., Vetterli, M.: The contourlet transform: an efficient directional multiresolution image representation. IEEE Trans. Image Process. **14**(12), 2091–2106 (2005)
8. Guo, K.H., Labate, D.: Optimally sparse multidimensional representation using shearlets. SIAM J. Math. Anal. **39**, 298–318 (2007)
9. Labate, D., Lim, W.Q., Kutyniok, G., Weiss, G.: Sparse multidimensional representation using shearlets. In: The International Society for Optical Engineering SPIE, pp. 254–262, August 2005

10. Easley, G., Labate, D., Lim, W.Q.: Sparse directional image representations using the discrete shearlet transform. Appl. Comput. Harmon. Anal. **25**, 25–46 (2008)
11. Li, H.F., Qiu, H.M., Yu, Z.T., Zhang, Y.F.: Infrared and visible image fusion scheme based on NSCT and lowlevel visual features. Infrared Phys. Technol. **76**, 174–784 (2016)
12. Zhang, B.H., Lu, X.Q., Pei, H.Q., Zhao, Y.: A fusion algorithm for infrared and visible images based on saliency analysis and non-subsampled shearlet transform. Infrared Phys. Technol. **73**, 286–297 (2015)
13. Luo, X.Q., Zhang, Z.C., Wu, X.J.: A novel algorithm of remote sensing image fusion based on shift-invariant shearlet transform and regional selection. Int. J. Electron. Commun. **70**, 186–197 (2016)
14. Hou, B., Zhang, X.H.: SAR image despeckling based on nonsubsampled shearlet transform. IEEE J. Sel. Top. Appl. Earth Observ. Remote Sens. **5**(3), 809–823 (2012)
15. Zhang, C., Bai, L.F., Zhang, Y.: Method of fusing dual-spectrum low light level images based on grayscale spatial correlation. Acta Phys. Sin-ch Ed **6**(56), 3227–3233 (2007)
16. Itti, L., Koch, C., Niebur, E.: A model of saliencybased visual attention for rapid scene analysis. IEEE Trans. Pattern Anal. Mach. Intell. **20**(11), 1254–1259 (1998)
17. Bavirisetti, D.P., Dhuli, R.: Two-scale image fusion of visible and infrared images using saliency detection. Infrared Phys. Technol. **75**, 52–64 (2016)
18. Wang, Z., Bovik, A.C.: A universal image quality index. IEEE Signal Process. Lett. **9**(3), 81–84 (2002)
19. Piella, G., Heijmans, H.: A new quality metric for image fusion. In: IEEE ICIP, Barcelona, Spain (2003)
20. Qu, G.H., Zhang, D.L., Yan, P.F.: Information measure for performance of image fusion. Electron. Lett. **38**(7), 313–315 (2002)

Tricolor Pre-equalization Deblurring for Underwater Image Enhancement

Xiaofan Sun, Hao Liu[(⊠)], Xinsheng Zhang, and Kailian Deng

College of Information Science and Technology,
Donghua University, Shanghai 201620, China
`liuhao@dhu.edu.cn`

Abstract. To enhance the qualitative and quantitative performance of underwater images, this paper proposes a tricolor pre-equalization deblurring method. In the proposed methodology, the tricolor histogram equalization is firstly used to change the level of chroma, contrast and intensity of underwater images. Then, the tricolor background light can be robustly estimated by using the dark channel prior. Finally, the tricolor transmission map is estimated by optical properties of underwater imagery. As compared with other enhancement methods, the experimental results demonstrate that the proposed method can significantly improve visual quality of underwater imagery, and quantifiably enhance the objective quality of underwater images. Moreover, the proposed method obtains the moderate complexity performance.

Keywords: Underwater image · Enhancement · Histogram equalization
Blur removal

1 Introduction

With the resource exploration inside seas, lakes and rivers, underwater imagery has become an important research field. But, the problem with underwater scenario is the loss of colors and contrast in an image [1]. Underwater images often suffer from color distortion and low contrast because light is scattered and absorbed when traveling through water. An underwater image can be expressed as a linear superposition of a forward scattering component and a back scattering component. Such a forward scattering results in the blurring of image features whereas the back scattering obscures the details of the scene. Because each color differ in wavelength and energy level, every color absorbs at a different rate. The reason of most underwater images show green and/or blue in color is that the orange or red lights which has longer wavelengths are absorbed more quickly. Thus, underwater images usually perform predominantly in blue-green hue. As shown in Fig. 1, the forward scattering causes the blur degradation, and the back scattering causes the contrast degradation of underwater optical imaging. The underwater image is blurred from the actual characteristics, mainly caused by forward scattering of the light. While the back scattering actually tends to make the misty and foggy appearance of the distant object in the image and the scene has poor contrast. The capability to fully extract valuable information from underwater images for further processing such as aquatic robot inspection and marine mine detection is

© Springer International Publishing AG 2017
Y. Zhao et al. (Eds.): ICIG 2017, Part II, LNCS 10667, pp. 590–601, 2017.
https://doi.org/10.1007/978-3-319-71589-6_52

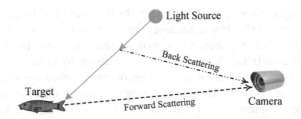

Fig. 1. The forward-scattering component and back-scattering component in underwater optical imaging (Color figure online).

deteriorated by the overall poor visibility. So, enhancing such underwater images is a valuable work. The recent reviews of underwater image enhancement can be found in [2, 3].

1.1 Related Works

The enhancement of underwater image is known to be an ill-posed problem. Some underwater image enhancement methods have been proposed mainly by (a) dehazing the image, (b) compensating non-uniform illumination, or (c) increasing the image contrast and correcting the color shift. Fattal [4] proposed a single image dehazing (SID) method for estimating the optical transmission in hazy scenes. Ground on this estimation, the scattered light is eliminated to increase scene visibility and recover blur-free scene contrasts. The SID method exploits the fact that the surface shading and transmission functions are locally statistically uncorrelated. Bianco et al. [5] presented a simple yet effective prior that utilizes the strong difference in attenuation among the three color channels in the water to estimate the depths of the underwater scene, which used a graph-cut method to refine the depth map of dark channel prior for obtaining the clear image. Chiang and Chen [6] improved underwater images by combining a dehazing method with wavelength compensation. He et al. [7] enhanced a dark channel prior (DCP) to remove blurry or foggy effects from the spoilt images. According to the amount of attenuation of each wavelength, reverse compensation is conducted to reduce the distortion from color cast. The defect of dark channel prior is to decrease the contrast and darken the resulting image in some situations. Ancuti et al. [8] enhanced the visual quality of underwater images and videos by using fusion principles. In the fusion-based method, various types of weight maps give us the enhancement of images with higher quality, but the image fusion can't be achieved simultaneously using this method. Galdran et al. [9] proposed a red channel method, where the lost contrast and color associated with short wavelength are recovered. The red-channel restoration method can be regarded as a simple extension of atmosphere dark channel prior, and the experiment results show that this method is good in the artificial lighting field, where the color correction and visibility can been improved.

Adaptive histogram equalization (AHE) is a typical technique which is used in image processing to enhance the contrast of images. AHE is different from ordinary histogram equalization. The adaptive method computes several histograms which respectively corresponds to a distinct section of an image, and utilizes them to redistribute the lightness values of the image. In this way, the local contrast can be improved. However, AHE has a tendency to overamplify the noise in relatively homogeneous regions of an image. A deviation of AHE called contrast limited adaptive histogram equalization (CLAHE) may avoid the tendency by limiting the amplification [10]. CLAHE is a generalization of adaptive histogram equalization where the contrast of an image are kept. The CLAHE model is originally developed for the enhancement of images with low contrast, and operates on the tiles of an image. Tiles are the small regions in the image which is divided according to a particular grid to exploit local spatial coherence in the scene. CLAHE enhances the contrast of each tile. To eliminate the induced artificial boundaries, the neighboring tiles are combined using bilinear interpolation. The contrast became limited to avoid amplifying any noise especially in homogeneous areas of an image. So, CLAHE limits the amplification by clipping the histogram at a user-defined value called clip limit. The probability-based (PB) method [11] is another image enhancement mechanism with simultaneous illumination and reflectance estimation, which is often used to enhance underwater images in related literatures.

Generally, the current deblurring methods unveil limited details and color of underwater images under several challenging scenes with the limited visible light, and they difficultly remove the effects of noise. For underwater image enhancement, the above methods possibly emphasize one aspect of either qualitative quality or quantitative quality, and ignore the comprehensive evaluation. In this work, the proposed method intends to address the above-mentioned problems.

1.2 Proposed Research

During underwater imagery, the scattering effect of light in the water causes the blur of the image. If the blurry image has a larger background area and low contrast, some deblurring methods possibly cause bad results as well as reduce the contrast of foreground. The existing methods have deserted the use of gamma correction and histogram stretching to reduce the noise problem which will be presented in the output image of the blur removal methods. In this work, we will propose a tricolor pre-equalization deblurring (TPD) method to remove foggy/hazy appearance in an underwater image. We firstly apply a histogram equalization technique with a color correction, and then optimize the deblurring mechanism by improving background light estimation and transmission map estimation, so as to obtain better visual results and to increase the objective quality and complexity performance.

1.3 Paper Organization

The rest of this paper is organized as follows. Section 2 introduces the proposed tricolor pre-equalization deblurring method. Section 3 evaluates and compares different enhancement methods' experimental results. Finally, Sect. 4 concludes this paper and discusses future works.

2 Tricolor Pre-equalization Deblurring

For underwater image enhancement, this section will review and summarize the tricolor pre-equalization deblurring (TPD) method by using the principle of contrast limited adaptive histogram equalization and dark channel prior. Figure 2 shows the module diagram of the proposed TPD method. First of all, underwater images are pre-processed by tricolor histogram equalization, and then enhanced through tricolor dark channel prior mechanism.

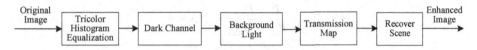

Fig. 2. Module diagram of the tricolor pre-equalization deblurring method.

Underwater lighting conditions are very complicated, and the color and contrast of underwater imagery undergoes a strong color-dependent attenuation. Following the previous research, a tricolor underwater imagery model can be represented as follows:

$$I^c(x) = J^c(x)t^c(x) + L^c[1 - t^c(x)], c \in \{r, g, b\} \tag{1}$$

where x is a pixel for each color-component image; $I^c(x)$ is the blur-mixed intensity of an observed image; $J^c(x)$ is the recovered scene; L^c is the background light that represents the contribution from the backscattering effect; $t^c(x) \in [0, 1]$ is the transmission map and it is used to describe the portion of the light which does not reach and scatter the camera. Again, $1 - t^c(x)$ represents the thickness of blur. Thus, $J^c(x)t^c(x)$ and $A^c[1 - t^c(x)]$ denote the forward scattered component and backscattered component in underwater optical imaging. The purpose of deblurring is to recover $J^c(x)$, L^c, and $t^c(x)$ from $I^c(x)$. $t^c(x)$ represents the percentage of residual energy when the foreground irradiance passes through the medium. Since $I^c(x)$ is the intensity of the actual image mixed with background light, $I^c(x)$ is usually brighter than $J^c(x)$, with a low value namely as the transmission map $t^c(x)$. So, the dark channel of $I^c(x)$ has a high value as compare with $J^c(x)$ and that is the distinction which helps to remove blur. To solve this kind of ill-posed problem, the proposed TPD method includes the following main steps.

2.1 Tricolor Histogram Equalization

Firstly, we take the physical spectral characteristics-based color correction. In this work, we improve the CLAHE method [10], where two different priors (local contrast and color) are combined. To remove the limitation of dark channel prior, we add a histogram equalization process before tricolor dark channel prior. In this process, the resulting image is divided into each channel and enhanced by adaptive histogram equalization. Then, the result is processed through a color correction technique which is the refined image. For color correction, the mean value and the mean square error are computed in RGB channels of original image. Then, the maximum and minimum of each channel is calculated by

$$
\begin{aligned}
I_{max}^c &= I_{mean}^c + \mu I_{var}^c \\
I_{min}^c &= I_{mean}^c - \mu I_{var}^c
\end{aligned}
\tag{2}
$$

where $c \in \{r, g, b\}$; I_{mean}^c and I_{var}^c are the mean value and the mean square error (MSE) in the RGB channel, respectively; μ is a parameter to control the image variation. Finally, the color-corrected image is obtained by

$$
I_{CR}^c = \frac{I^c - I_{min}^c}{I_{max}^c - I_{min}^c} \times 255 \times \alpha_c
\tag{3}
$$

where I_{CR}^c is single-color enhanced image, and I^c is single-color original image, and α_c is a weighting coefficient. The proposed TPD method is based on the statistics of histogram distribution of visually appealing natural-scene images. Intuitively, the histogram distributions of natural-scene images are wider and more consistent while the histogram distribution of each color channel of underwater image is shifted in a horizontal direction due to the effects of the absorption and scattering as well as the floating particles. The histogram of blue component concentrates on a brightest side, followed by the green component and then the red component. The histogram distributions of the contrast enhanced underwater image become wider and more consistent than those of the raw underwater image [12].

2.2 Calculating the Dark Channel

To robustly estimate the background light, we use a hierarchical searching technique, then remove the effects of suspended particles via the dark channel prior [7], and finally remove the disturbance of bright objects and determine the background light according to the properties of light travelling in the water. Dark channel prior is usually used to produce a natural blur-free image. However, we use this method to enhance underwater image. The presence of water particles and light scattering causes the blur in underwater images which can be removed by dark channel prior. The dark channel prior is used to remove blur from a single original image. It refers to the following observation on those images which don't blur: in most of the non-lightsource region, the intensity value of at least one color channel shows very low at some pixels. Namely, the minimum intensity in such a patch has a very low value. The main aim of the blur removal method is the estimation of $J^c(x)$, $t^c(x)$, L^c. The dark channel prior shows that the performance of most of the local regions which present in the background of the image, is consistent with the blur-free images. $J_{dark}(x)$ represents the dark channel at x. Formally, for an image, its underwater dark channel prior can be defined as:

$$
J_{dark}(x) = \min_{c \in \{r, g, b\}} \left(\min_{y \in \Omega(x)} J^c(y) \right)
\tag{4}
$$

In above equation, $J^c(y)$ is one of the RGB channels of an underwater image, and $\Omega(x)$ is a square region (local patch, 15×15 pixels) centered at x. If x doesn't belong to local regions, then $J_{dark}(x)$ is low and tends to be zero. Except for the lightsource patches, the intensity of $J_{dark}(x)$ is showing a low value and tending to zero when $J^c(y)$ is a blur-free image. And the above knowledge or statistical observation is called the dark channel prior.

2.3   Estimating the Background Light

In most of the previous methods, the background light L^c is estimated from the most blur-opaque pixel. For example, the pixel with highest intensity is used as the background light [4]. But in real images, the brightest pixel could on a white region. The dark channel of a blurry image approximates the blur denseness well. We can use the dark channel to improve the background light estimation. We first pick the top 0.1% brightest pixels in the dark channel. These pixels are most blur-opaque. Among these pixels, we select some pixels with highest intensity in the original image as the background light. Note that these pixels may not be brightest in the whole image. This method based on the dark channel prior is more robust and simple than the "brightest pixel" method. It is used to automatically evaluate the background lights for each image shown in this work. Based on the background light L^c, the transmission map is calculated by dividing the Eq. (1) by L^c. According to the dark channel prior, the dark channel of image without blur tends to zero [7], and He et al. provided the same transmission map for each color component:

$$t(x) = 1 - \omega \min_{c \in \{r,g,b\}} \left(\min_{y \in \Omega(x)} \frac{I^c(y)}{L^c} \right) \tag{5}$$

where the parameter $\omega(\omega = 0.9)$ keeps a small amount of blur in the image to perceive the depth of image. The above method didn't consider the difference of three color component. In our method, each color component has its transmission map $t^c(x)$ as follows:

$$t^c(x) = 1 - \frac{\beta_c \min_{c \in \{r,g,b\}} \left(\min_{y \in \Omega(x)} I^c(y) \right)}{L^c} \tag{6}$$

where $\beta_c(\beta_r = 1.0, \beta_g = 0.9, \beta_b = 0.95)$ is color-aware parameter. We adopt a guided image filtering method to refine the transmission map.

2.4   Refining the Transmission Map

Based on the observation that the dark and bright regions of underwater images become too dark or too bright after being enhanced by the proposed TPD method, a filtered transmission map is employed to adjust the results for better visual quality. After obtaining the transmission map block by block, we incorporate the guided filter to refine the transmission map, because the block-based transmission map usually yields blocking artifacts. By replacing soft matting [13], a guided filter [14] is applied to refine the transmission map, and to find the accurate transmission map.

2.5   Recovering the Scene Radiance

With the transmission map, the scene radiance can be recovered by the proposed TPD method according to Eq. (1). However, if the transmission $t^c(x)$ is close to zero, the direct attenuation term $J^c(x)t^c(x)$ will approximate to zero [15]. Noise will easily appear in the directly recovered scene $J^c(x)$. Based on this, we place restrictions on the transmission $t^c(x)$ to a lower bound t_0, therefore, a small certain amount of blur are preserved in very dense blurry regions. The goal of blur removal is to recover $J^c(x)$, L^c, and $t^c(x)$ from $I^c(x)$. Using the blur imaging equation and the dark channel prior together, the recovered scene can be represented by:

$$J^c(x) = \frac{I^c(x) - L^c}{\max(t^c(x), t_0)} + L^c, \ c \in \{r, g, b\} \tag{7}$$

where t_0 is a threshold value to avoid a low value of denominator, and t_0 is usually set to 0.1. Because the brightness of the scene is usually less bright than the background light, the image looks dim after blur removal. So, we increase the exposure of $J^c(x)$ for display. The dark channel prior is effective for a variety of hazy images, however, it may be invalid if the scene objects are inherently similar to the background light and no shadow is cast on them. The underwater images are similar with the blurry images as they are all degraded through the medium. Besides, they doesn't conform the failure condition [16]. Therefore, dark channel prior can be used to remove the blur in underwater images.

3   Experimental Results

To evaluate the proposed tricolor pre-equalization deblurring (TPD) method, extensive experiments are carried out. Without loss of generality, the underwater image enhancement methods include histogram equalization (HistEqu), single image dehazing (SID) [4], dark channel prior (DCP) [7], contrast limited adaptive histogram equalization (CLAHE) [10], Probability-based (PB) [11]. We used their Matlab codes to obtain different experimental results. To robustly compare the performance of different methods, we extracted the typical scenes which are also used by previous literatures, as shown in Fig. 3. For different underwater image enhancement methods, we present the comprehensive evaluation of qualitative quality, quantitative quality and runtime complexity.

Fig. 3. Typical underwater images: (a) *reef1*, 500 × 375; (b) *reef2*, 750 × 1000; (c) *reef3*, 1000 × 707; (d) *ocean2*, 550 × 412; (e) *Galdran_Im1*, 473 × 353; (f) *fish*, 512 × 384; (g) *Eustice4*, 690 × 560; (h) *Ancuti1*, 404 × 303, (i) *Ancuti2*, 1037 × 778; (j) *Ancuti3*, 512 × 384.

3.1 Qualitative Comparison

3.1.1 Typical Scenes

For different methods, Fig. 4 gives an example of qualitative quality comparisons. As can been observed, the appearance of some methods is either over-enhanced or under-enhanced. The HistEqu method introduces artifacts due to ignoring the spatially varying distance dependencies [17]. Although the contrast and details are increased by DCP and PB methods, the colors and visibility are poor because the attenuated energy is not compensated individually based on different wavelengths [18]. Our TPD method has successfully enhanced the contrast, relatively genuine color, and visibility of the original underwater images.

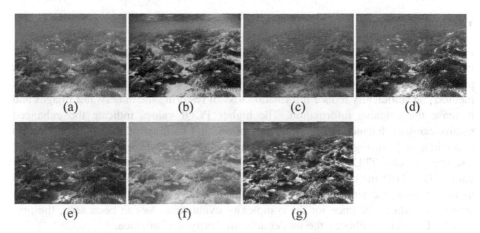

Fig. 4. Qualitative quality comparisons for the image *Galdran_Im1*: (a) Original underwater image; (b) HistEqu; (c) CLAHE; (d) SID; (e) DCP; (f) PB; (g) our TPD method.

3.1.2   Color Accuracy

Figure 5 shows the color-card example. Figure 5(a) shows the cards in bright sunlight with the spectral colors, and Fig. 5(b) shows the same cards at 60 ft in the Gulf of Mexico, and this photo is straight out of the camera with no filters or adjustments for white-balance, color, etc. As you can see, the spectral red is completely gone and difficult to distinguish from black. The orange now looks drab and almost an olive-green, and yellow holds fairly true, but green is now looking closer to yellow. Blue and indigo are OK, but contrasting with black, violet is similar to red. After enhancing the original photo by different methods, the result of our TPD method is more visible and has fewer color loss than the results of the compared methods.

Fig. 5. Color accuracy test. (a) The standard ColorChecker cards image; (b) The underwater ColorChecker cards image; (c) HistEqu; (d) CLAHE; (e) SID; (f) DCP; (g) PB; (h) our TPD method (Color figure online).

3.2   Quantitative Comparison

Following previous literatures, information Entropy and patch-based contrast quality index (PCQI) [19] are employed to evaluate the no-reference image quality of the proposed TPD method. The higher Entropy values indicate that the enhancement method can sufficiently reduce information loss of restoring the underwater images and increase the valuable information. The higher PCQI values indicate the enhanced results can well balance the chroma, saturation, and contrast of the enhanced underwater images [20]. Figure 6 gives the average values of the Entropy and PCQI for all test images. Our TPD method outperforms other methods in terms of the Entropy values. Our TPD method ranks first in terms of PCQI evaluation. Since all enhancement methods use similar basis instructions, their MATLAB implementations can provide a certain reference for the complexity evaluation. As can been seen, the proposed TPD method obtains the moderate complexity performance.

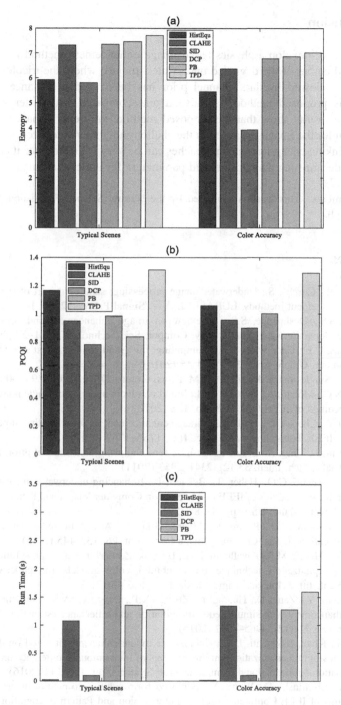

Fig. 6. Quantitative performance comparisons of different methods. (a) Entropy quality; (b) PCQI quality; (c) Runtime complexity.

4   Conclusion

In this work, we develop a physics-based image enhancement method for recovering visibility and colors of the degraded underwater images, where the tricolor histogram equalization followed by dark channel prior has been used to enhance underwater images. This proposed method is analyzed and compared with different methods. Experimental results show that the proposed method can better enhance underwater images, even for the images captured in the challenging underwater scenes. As a future work, we think that deep-learning approaches can be very valuable since it is difficult to empirically design such many priors and parameters for underwater image restoration.

Acknowledgments. This work is supported by the Natural Science Foundation of Shanghai (14ZR1400500).

References

1. Schettini, R., Corchs, S.: Underwater image processing: state of the art of restoration and image enhancement methods. EURASIP J. Adv. Signal Process. **2010**, 1–14 (2010)
2. Sankpal, S.S., Deshpande, S.S.: A review on image enhancement and color correction techniques for underwater images. Adv. Comput. Sci. Technol. **9**(1), 11–23 (2016)
3. Von Lukas, U.F.: Underwater visual computing: the grand challenge just around the corner. IEEE Comput. Graph. Appl. **36**(2), 10–15 (2016)
4. Fattal, R.: Single image dehazing. ACM Trans. Graph. **27**(3), 72:1–72:9 (2008)
5. Bianco, N.C., Mohan, A., Eustice, R.M.: Initial results in underwater single image dehazing. In: Proceedings of IEEE OCEANS, pp. 1–8 (2010)
6. Chiang, J.Y., Chen, Y.C.: Underwater image enhancement by wavelength compensation and dehazing. IEEE Trans. Image Process. **21**(4), 1756–1769 (2012)
7. He, K., Sun, J., Tang, X.: Single image haze removal using dark channel prior. IEEE Trans. Pattern Anal. Mach. Intell. **33**(12), 2341–2353 (2011)
8. Ancuti, C., Ancuti, C.O., Haber, T., Bekaert, P.: Enhancing underwater images and videos by fusion. In: Proceedings of IEEE Conference on Computer Vision and Pattern Recognition (CVPR), Rhode Island, USA, pp. 81–88 (2012)
9. Galdran, A., Pardo, D., Picón, A., Alvarez-Gila, A.: Automatic red-channel underwater image restoration. J. Vis. Commun. Image Represent. **26**, 132–145 (2015)
10. Yussof, W., Hitam, M.S., Awalludin, E.A., Bachok, Z.: Performing contrast limited adaptive histogram equalization technique on combined color models for underwater image enhancement. Int. J. Interact. Digit. Media **1**(1), 1–6 (2013)
11. Fu, X., Liao, Y., Zeng, D., Huang, Y., Zhang, X.P., Ding, X.: A probabilistic method for image enhancement with simultaneous illumination and reflectance estimation. IEEE Trans. Image Process. **24**(12), 4965–4977 (2015)
12. Mallik, S., Khan, S.S., Pati, U.C.: Underwater image enhancement based on dark channel prior and histogram equalization. In: Proceedings of International Conference on Innovations in Information Embedded and Communication Systems, pp. 139–144 (2016)
13. Levin, A., Lischinski, D., Weiss, Y.: A closed form solution to natural image matting. In: Proceedings of IEEE Conference on Computer Vision and Pattern Recognition (2006)
14. He, K., Sun, J., Tang, X.: Guided image filtering. IEEE Trans. Pattern Anal. Mach. Intell. **35**(6), 1397–1409 (2013)

15. Li, C.Y., Guo, J.C., Cong, R.M., Pang, Y.W., Wang, B.: Underwater image enhancement by dehazing with minimum information loss and histogram distribution prior. IEEE Trans. Image Process. **22**(12), 5664–5677 (2016)
16. Li, C.Y., Guo, J.C., Chen, S.J.: Underwater image restoration based on minimum information loss principle and optical properties of underwater imaging. In: Proceedings of IEEE International Conference on Image Processing, vol. 28(25), pp. 2381–8549 (2016)
17. Zhu, Y.F., Chang, L., Dai, J.L., Zheng, H.Y., Zheng, B.: Automatic object detection and segmentation from underwater images via saliency-based region merging. In: Proceedings of IEEE OCEANS, vol. 13(10), pp. 1–4 (2016)
18. Liu, Q.L., Zhang, H.Y., Lin, M.S., Wu, Y.D.: Research on image dehazing algorithms based on physical model. In: Proceedings of International Conference on Multimedia Technology, vol. 28(26), pp. 467–470 (2011)
19. Wang, S., Ma, K., Yeganeh, H., Wang, Z., Lin, W.: A patch-structure representation method for quality assessment of contrast changed images. IEEE Signal Process. Lett. **22**(12), 2387–2390 (2015)
20. Codevilla, F., Gaya, J.O., Duarte, N., Botelho, S.: Achieving turbidity robustness on underwater images local feature detection. In: Proceedings of British Machine Vision Conference (BMVC), pp. 1–13 (2012)

Link Functions and Training-Based in Reflectance Reconstruction from RGB Images

Lijun Zhang, Jun Jiang, Jingjing Zhang$^{(\boxtimes)}$, and Chen Wang

Hubei Key Laboratory of Advanced Control and Intelligent
Automation for Complex Systems, School of Automation,
China University of Geosciences, Wuhan 430074, China
zlj599@163.com, {junjiang,work.zhang,wangc}@cug.edu.cn

Abstract. Recovering the spectral reflectance is important for object analysis and visualization. Previous approaches use either specialized equipment or controlled illumination where the extra hardware and high cost prevent many practical applications. In this paper, we focuses on a training-based method to reconstruct the scene's spectral reflectance from RGB image. We use training images to model the mapping between camera-specific RGB values and scene-specific reflectance spectra. Our method is based on a radial basis function network that leverages RGB white-balancing to normalize the scene illumination and link function to transform the reflectance to recover the scene reflectance. Three link functions (logit, square root 1, square root 2) were evaluated in the training-based estimation of reflectance spectra of the RGB images in the 400–700 nm region. We estimate reflectance spectra from RGB camera responses in color patches's reflectance reconstruction and a normal scene reconstruction and show that a combination of link function and radial basis function network training-based decreases spectral errors when compared with without link function model.

Keywords: Link function · Training-based
Radial basis function network · RGB images
Reflectance reconstruction

1 Introduction

Over the past two decades, estimating spectral reflectance from objects surface has been widely used in object analysis and visualization [1] such as biometrics, medical diagnosis [2], color reproduction, art reproduction and cultural heritage [3]. Reflectance reconstruction for the 400–700 nm wavelength range from the responses of a digital camera has received considerable attention recently.

The traditional devices such as hyper- and multi-spectral imaging systems using existing spectral cameras (beyond trichromatic) can produce highly accurate information. While they can obtain highly accurate information, most of these methods require complex mechanical constructions and larger investments for imaging, which prevent many practical applications such as those in the outdoors compared to systems with consumer level RGB cameras [4].

© Springer International Publishing AG 2017
Y. Zhao et al. (Eds.): ICIG 2017, Part II, LNCS 10667, pp. 602–611, 2017.
https://doi.org/10.1007/978-3-319-71589-6_53

Using consumer cameras as relatively cheap measurement devices for estimating spectral color properties has become an interesting alternative to making pointwise high-precision spectral measurements compared with special equipment like photospectrometers [5]. The results obtained with consumer cameras cannot compete with the quality of the traditional devices, but they are very attractive since the equipment is relatively cheap and instant measurements are obtained for millions of measurement points. These advantages come, at the price of lower-quality, and it is thus of interest to improve the precision of the estimations [5].

Rang pointed out the prior approaches sensitive to input images captured under illuminations which were not present in the training data and proposed a novel training-based method to reconstruct a scene's spectral reflectance from a single RGB image in [6]. Which explore a new strategy to use training images to model the mapping between camera white-balancing RGB values and scene reflectance spectra. The method improved reconstruction performance compared with previous works, especially when the tested illumination is not included in the training data.

Heikkinen suggests that one way to increase the accuracy of reconstruction performance is via the inclusion of a priori knowledge in [1]. And Gijsenij make a non-linear transformation to reflectance in reflectance reconstruction and results demonstrate that non-linear transformation improved the accuracy of reconstruction in [7]. Inspired by these, we produce physically feasible estimations via combined with link functions and training-based approach. The general training-based approach using the method showed in [6], but we replace the reflectance with the specific reflectance via link function in the training stage and reconstruction stage. Our main focus is in the comparison of the performance of link functions when combined with the training-based approach. We evaluate the performance of three link functions (logit, square root 1, square root 2) reconstruction method in color patches reflectance reconstruction and a normal scene reconstruction, the experimental results demonstrate that the inclusion of link function improve the performance of the training-based reconstruction in terms of spectral error and shape.

2   Method

In this paper, we do not use RGB images taken directly from the camera. Instead, we synthesize RGB images from hyperspectral images using known camera's sensitivity functions. Synthesize RGB images in this way has two advantages compare with taken directly from the camera. Firstly, it removes the need to create a dataset of the images captured using the chosen camera for the same scenes as captured by the spectral camera. And the method can be used for any commercial camera so far as its sensitivity functions are known [6].

In this section, the details of link functions and training-based method were showed in Fig. 1. The method can be divided into two processes: the training stage and reconstruction stage.

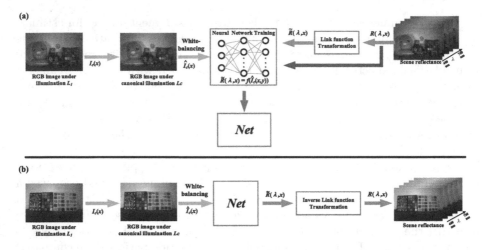

Fig. 1. The process of the training and reconstruction. (a) The training stage. (b) The reconstruction stage.

2.1   Training Stage

The method considers a mapping between RGB images under canonical illumination (using white-balancing) and their reflectance. The training process is shown in Fig. 1(a). The training process has four steps: synthesizing the RGB images, white-balancing the RGB images, link functions transform the reflectance, and computing the mapping.

Firstly, synthesized the RGB images corresponding to scenes and illuminations in spectral images can be formed by using the model as

$$I_c(x) = \int_\lambda P(\lambda)R(\lambda, x)C(\lambda)d\lambda \tag{1}$$

where $P(\lambda)$ is the spectrum of illumination, $R(\lambda, x)$ is the scene reflectance for the pixel intensity, $C(\lambda)$ is the camera spectral sensitivity.

After the RGB image $I_c(x)$ formed, we utilize transformation for the RGB image in a white balanced image $\widehat{I}_c(x)$ as follows:

$$\widehat{I}_c = diag(\frac{1}{t})I_c(x) = diag(\frac{1}{t_r}, \frac{1}{t_g}, \frac{1}{t_b})I_c(x) \tag{2}$$

where $\mathbf{t} = [\mathbf{t_r}, \mathbf{t_g}, \mathbf{t_b}]$ is the white balancing vector obtained by a chosen white balancing algorithm. For the white-balancing step, we used shades of grey (SoG) method [8] that was widely used for its simplicity, low computational requirement and proven efficacy over various datasets.

Next, the reflectance vectors $\mathbf{R}$ are replaced with transformed vectors $\widetilde{\mathbf{R}}$ via link functions. The link function made a non-linear transformation of reflectance vectors $\mathbf{R}$. Three link functions were evaluated in the experiments.

(1) The logit function

$$\tilde{\mathbf{R}} = \log \mathrm{it}(\mathbf{R}) = \log(\frac{\mathbf{R}}{1 - \mathbf{R}}) \tag{3}$$

where $log : [0, +\infty] \rightarrow R$ is the natural logarithm evaluated element-wise for $\mathbf{R} \in [\mathbf{0}, \mathbf{1}]^{\mathbf{n}}$.

(2) The square root 1

$$\tilde{\mathbf{R}} = \sqrt{\mathbf{R}} \tag{4}$$

(3) The square root 2

Tzeng and Berns proposed a new empirical space that gives a near-normal and reduced dimensionality for subtractive opaque processes in [7], the link function are given by Eq. 5, where $\mathbf{a}$ is an offset vector which is empirically derived.

$$\tilde{\mathbf{R}} = \mathbf{a} - \sqrt{\mathbf{R}} \tag{5}$$

Finally, the mapping f is learnt between the white balanced RGB images $\hat{I}_c(x)$ and their specific spectral reflectance $\tilde{R}$. We use scatter point interpolation based on a radial basis function (RBF) network for mapping. RBF network is a popular interpolation method in multidimensional space [6]. It is used to implement a mapping $f : R^3 \rightarrow R^P$ according to:

$$f(x) = \omega_0 + \sum_{i=1}^{M} \omega_i \emptyset(||x - c_i||) \tag{6}$$

where $x \in R^3$ is the RGB input value, $f(x) \in R^P$ is the spectral reflectance value in P-dimensional space, $\emptyset(.)$ is radial basis function, $||.||$ denotes the Euclidean distance, $\omega_i(0 \leq i \leq M)$ are the weights, $c_i \in R^3(1 \leq i \leq M)$ are the RBF centers, M is the number of center. The RBF centers c_i are chosen by the orthogonal least squares method. The weights ω_i are determined using linear least squares method.

To control the number of centers M for the RBF network model against overfitting, Nguyen had used repeated random sub-sampling validation to do cross-validation in [6], and found that the number of centers M which gave the best result for validation set was within 40–50, here the number of centers was set 50.

2.2   Reconstruction Stage

Once the training is performed, the mapping can be saved and used offline for spectral reflectance reconstruction. The reconstruction stage process is shown in Fig. 1(b).

To reconstruct spectral reflectance from a new RGB image, this image must be white-balanced to transform the image to the normalized illumination space $\hat{I}_c(x)$. The learned mapping f is used to map the white-balanced image to the specific spectral reflectance image as:

$$\tilde{R}(\lambda, x) = f(\hat{I}_c(x)) \tag{7}$$

Then the reconstructed reflectance $R(\lambda, x)$ can be get via inverse link function transformed $\tilde{R}(\lambda, x)$.

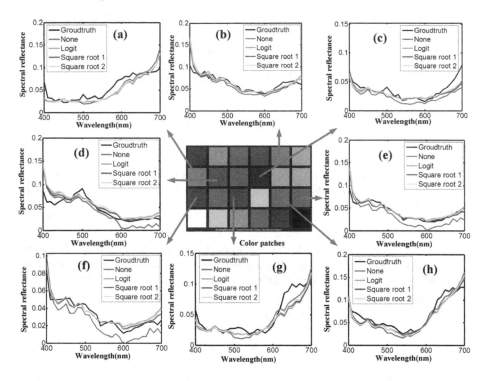

Fig. 2. This figure shows the reconstruction of eight color patches's reflectance using Canon 1D Mark III under indoor illumination using metal halid lamp of the 4300 K color temperature. The quantitative errors of eight patches are shown in Tables 1 and 2.

3   Experiments

3.1   Experiment Data

In this experiment, the hyperspectral images data from [6] and camera's sensitivity functions data from [9] has been used, the dataset contain spectral images and illumination spectra taken using Specim's PFD-CL-65-V10E (400 nm to 1000 nm) spectral camera. For light sources, natural sunlight and shade conditions were considered. Additionally, artificial wideband lights were also considered by using metal halide lamps with different color temperatures (2500 K, 3000 K, 3500 K, 4300 K, 6500 K) and a commercial off-the-shelf LED E400 light. For the natural light sources, outdoor images of natural objects (plants, human beings, etc.) as well as manmade objects has been taken. And a few images of buildings at very large focal length were also taken. The images corresponding to the other light sources have manmade objects as their scene content. For each spectral image, a total of 31 bands were used for imaging (400 nm to 700 nm at a spacing of about 10 nm).

There are a total of 64 spectral images, and 24 images with color charts taken as the test images for the reconstruction stage since explicit ground truth of their

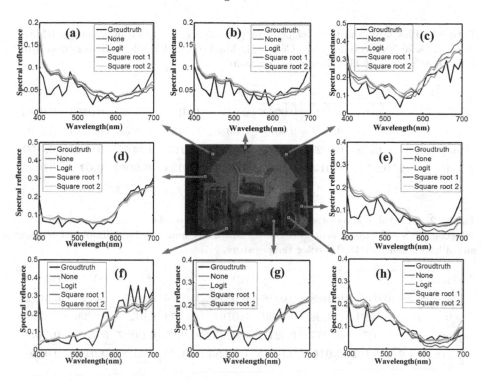

Fig. 3. This figure shows the reconstruction result of a normal scene using a Canon 1D Mark III under indoor illumination using metal halide lamp of 2500 K color temperature. The quantitative errors of the locations are shown in Tables 3 and 4.

spectral reflectance are available and thus the accuracy of reconstruction can be better assessed, the remaining 40 images are used for training.

3.2   Experiments

Since the pixel amount of 40 training images is very large and most of the training images are similar together, each training image was sub-sampled by using k-means clustering and totally collected around 16,000 spectral reflectance from all the images for the training stage. We used 24 images with color charts as the test images for the reconstruction stage, the ground truth of the spectral reflectance are obtained from the hyperspectral camera.

Four methods: without link function, logit link function, square root 1 link function, and square root 2 link function were compared. Firstly, the RGB test images for reconstruction are formed using the intrinsic image model in Eq. 1. The reflectance of 24 images (size of 1312 × 1924) were reconstructed.

In order to compare the performance of four reconstruction methods, the actual reconstruction results for eight color patches in the color chart were compared in Fig. 2 for Canon 1D Mark III. The quantitative results of these patches

Table 1. This table shows the eight color patches's reconstruction result (in RMSE) of colorchecker's reflectance using Canon 1D Mark III under indoor illumination using metal halide lamp of 4300 K color temperature.

Method	(a)	(b)	(c)	(d)	(e)	(f)	(g)	(h)
None	0.0165	0.0132	0.0092	0.019	0.0194	0.0139	0.0123	0.0144
Logit	0.0154	0.0131	0.0071	0.0086	0.0123	0.0058	0.0119	0.012
Square root 1	0.0148	0.0127	0.008	0.0099	**0.0121**	0.0051	0.0112	**0.0109**
Square root 2	**0.0145**	**0.0123**	**0.0064**	**0.0084**	0.0123	**0.0051**	**0.0112**	0.0125

Table 2. This table shows the eight color patches's reconstruction result (in PD) of colorchecker's reflectance using Canon 1D Mark III under indoor illumination using metal halide lamp of 4300 K color temperature.

Method	(a)	(b)	(c)	(d)	(e)	(f)	(g)	(h)
None	0.0316	0.0188	0.0276	0.0548	0.0516	0.0445	0.0228	0.0152
Logit	0.0289	0.0188	0.0169	0.0161	0.0279	0.0125	0.0226	0.0119
Square root 1	0.027	0.0177	0.0217	0.0205	**0.027**	**0.0097**	0.0199	**0.0099**
Square root 2	**0.0261**	**0.0167**	**0.0135**	**0.0154**	0.028	0.0098	**0.0199**	0.0126

Table 3. This table shows the reconstruction result (in RMSE) of a normal scene using a Canon 1D Mark III under indoor illumination using metal halide lamp of 2500 K color temperature.

Method	(a)	(b)	(c)	(d)	(e)	(f)	(g)	(h)
None	0.0213	0.02	0.0378	0.0264	0.0467	0.0658	0.0271	0.0371
Logit	**0.0194**	**0.018**	0.0368	0.0261	0.0367	0.0659	0.0271	**0.0255**
Square root 1	0.0195	0.0192	**0.0344**	0.0259	0.0373	0.0651	**0.0268**	0.0306
Square root 2	0.0198	0.0193	0.0349	**0.0258**	**0.0361**	**0.064**	0.0269	0.0285

Table 4. This table shows the reconstruction result (in PD) of a normal scene using a Canon 1D Mark III under indoor illumination using metal halide lamp of 2500 K color temperature.

Method	(a)	(b)	(c)	(d)	(e)	(f)	(g)	(h)
None	0.0728	0.0622	0.0226	0.0151	0.1253	0.0601	0.0276	0.058
Logit	**0.0622**	**0.056**	0.0215	0.015	0.0879	0.06	0.0277	**0.0326**
Square root 1	0.0631	0.0584	**0.0185**	0.0148	0.0899	0.0585	**0.027**	0.0442
Square root 2	0.0651	0.0592	0.0191	**0.0147**	**0.0866**	**0.0567**	0.0272	0.0406

for all methods are shown in Tables 1 and 2. Additionally, the reconstruction result of a normal scene were compared in Fig. 3, the RGB image is synthesized using a Canon 1D Mark III under indoor illumination (metal halide lamp with color temperature of 2500 K), and the quantitative results of the scene for all methods are shown in Tables 3 and 4.

3.3   Evaluation of Reconstruction Performance

To verify the quantitative performance for the spectral reflectance reconstruction in the experiments, we use root mean square error (RMSE) to measure the error,

$$RMSE(R, \widehat{R}) = \sqrt{\frac{\sum_x ||R(\lambda, x) - \widehat{R}(\lambda, x)||_2^2}{N}} \tag{8}$$

and Pearson Distance (PD) to measure the similarity,

$$PD(R, \widehat{R}) = 1 - \frac{1}{N} \sum_x \frac{|\sum_\lambda R(\lambda, x)\widehat{R}(\lambda, x)|}{\sqrt{\sum_\lambda [R(\lambda, x)]^2}\sqrt{\sum_\lambda [\widehat{R}(\lambda, x)]^2}} \tag{9}$$

The PD (1-PD is called as GFC [10]) is independent of the magnitude and therefore gives information about the shape of estimations. Where $R(\lambda, x)$ and $\widehat{R}(\lambda, x)$ are the actual and reconstructed spectral reflectance, N are the number of pixels in the image, and $||.||_2$ is $l^2 - norm$.

4   Results and Discussion

The numerical results for experiments in Tables 1, 2, 3 and 4, which can be summarized as follows:

A conclusion from these results is that model with link function improved the reconstruction performance in terms of RMSE and PD.

For the actual reconstruction results for eight color patches in the Tables 1 and 2, it can been seen that (when compared to the model without link function) three link function improve the reconstruction performance, and the square root 2 link function provides the best results in most cases which the RMSE metrics decrease 17.4%, 11.2%, 30.4%, 55.8%, 63.3% and 8.9% corresponding the patch a, b, c, d, f and g respectively. And the PD metrics decrease 17.4%, 11.2%, 30.4%, 71.9%, and 12.7% corresponding the patch a, b, c, d, and g corresponding the patch a, b, c, d, f and g respectively. Another result was the similarity (indicated by PD) of the reconstruction performance improved obviously.

For the reconstruction results of the normal scene in Tables 3 and 4, it can been seen that it can been seen that (when compared with the model without link function) three link function improve the reconstruction performance in terms of RMSE and PD, however, the performance of the different link functions is somewhat mixed.

The logit link function shows the best RMSE metrics results in location a, b, and h which decreases 8.9%, 10% and 31.3% respectively compared with the model without the link function, and similarly for PD metric in location a, b, and h which decreases 14.6%, 10%, and 43.8% respectively. The square root 2 link function provides the best RMSE metrics in location d, e, and f which decreases 2.3%, 22.7%, and 2.7% respectively compared with the model without the link function, and similarly for PD metric in location d, e, and f which decreases 2.6%, 30.9%, and 5.6% respectively. The square root 1 link function provides the best RMSE metrics result in location c, and g which decreases 9% and 1.1% respectively compared with the model without the link function, and similarly for PD metric in location c, and g which decreases 18.1% and 2% respectively. From the data, the PD improved obviousely.

The logit link function has been evaluated before in [5], also square root 2 link function has been used for reflectance estimation in [7] combined with principal component analysis. The link function combined with training-based has not been used for reflectance estimation before, but the link function has been proposed to be combined with kernel regression model in [1]. Nevertheless, it is possible to introduce the link function to the training-based approach for improve the reconstruction performance. In this paper, our main interest was in the evaluation of the models in Eq. 7 for the estimation with link functions.

5 Conclusion

In this paper, we proposed a new method to reconstruct spectral reflectance from RGB images, which combined with the link function and training-based approach. The training-based approach is based on a radial basis function network and using white-balancing as an intermediate step, the method is learning a mapping between the white balanced RGB images and their specific spectral reflectance which is a non-linear transformation to reflectance via link function. We compared with the performance of different link functions reconstruction method in the color patchess reflectance reconstruction and a normal scene reconstruction experiments.

Our results suggest that link functions improve the spectral accuracy for training-based spectral reconstruction from RGB images. The results show similar relative performance for different link functions and indicate that the spectral error (indicated by RMSE) and the spectral shape (indicated by PD) especially the spectral shape is estimated more accurately via link functions. Another, the model with square root 2 link function decreases several spectral errors significantly in most cases when compared to the model without link function.

Since the approach is combined with the link function and radial basis function network, the results of the training will seriously affect the reconstruction results, for the training stage, a limitation of the approach is the assumption that the scene is illuminated by an uniform illumination, for many scene in reality this is not the case. Moreover, although the training-based approach can handle well the reflectance which have smooth spectra, the approach like other approaches [6] still has poor results in case of spiky spectra. Spectral reconstruction under the narrow band illuminations will be interesting and challenging areas for future researching.

Acknowledgments. This research was supported partially by the National Natural Science Foundation of China (NSFC) (61604135).

References

1. Heikkinen, V., Mirhashemi, A., Alho, J.: Link functions and Matérn kernel in the estimation of reflectance spectra from RGB responses. J. Opt. Soc. Am. **30**, 2444–2454 (2013)
2. Heikkinen, V., Cámara, C., Hirvonen, T.: Spectral imaging using consumer-level devices and kernel-based regression. J. Opt. Soc. Am. A: **33**, 1095–1110 (2016)
3. Zhao, Y., Berns, R.S.: Image-based spectral reflectance reconstruction using the matrix R method. Color Res. Appl. **32**(5), 343–351 (2010)
4. Jiang, J., Gu, J.: Recovering spectral reflectance under commonly available lighting conditions. In: IEEE Computer Vision and Pattern Recognition Workshops, pp. 1–8 (2012)
5. Heikkinen, V., Lenz, R., Jetsu, T., Parkkinen, J., Hauta-Kasari, M.: Evaluation and unification of some methods for estimating reflectance spectra from RGB images. J. Opt. Soc. Am. **25**(10), 2444–2458 (2008)
6. Nguyen, R.M.H., Prasad, D.K., Brown, M.S.: Training-based spectral reconstruction from a single RGB image. In: Fleet, D., Pajdla, T., Schiele, B., Tuytelaars, T. (eds.) ECCV 2014. LNCS, vol. 8695, pp. 186–201. Springer, Cham (2014). https://doi.org/10.1007/978-3-319-10584-0_13
7. Imai, F., Berns, R.S., Tzeng, D.: A comparative analysis of spectral reflectance estimation in various spaces using a trichromatic camera system. J. Imaging Sci. Technol. **44**, 280–287 (2000)
8. Finlayson, G.D., Trezzi, E.: Shades of gray and colour constancy. In: Color and Imaging Conference, pp. 37–41 (2004)
9. Jiang, J., Liu, D., Gu, J., Susstrunk, S.: What is the space of spectral sensitivity functions for digital color cameras? In: IEEE Workshop on Applications of Computer Vision, pp. 168–179 (2013)
10. Valero, E.M., Hu, Y., Hernández-Andrés, J., et al.: Comparative performance analysis of spectral estimation algorithms and computational optimization of a multispectral imaging system for print inspection. Color Res. Appl. **39**(1), 16–27 (2012)

Multi-modal Image Registration Based on Modified-SURF and Consensus Inliers Recovery

Yanjia Chen, Xiuwei Zhang$^{(\boxtimes)}$, Fei Li, and Yanning Zhang

Northwestern Polytechnical University, 127 West Youyi Road,
Xi'an 710072, Shaanxi, People's Republic of China
xwzhang@nwpu.edu.cn

Abstract. Multi-modal image registration has been received significant research attention in past decades. In this paper, we proposed a solution for rigid multi-modal image registration, which focus on handling gradient reversal and region reversal problems happened in multimodal images. We also consider the common property of multi-modal images in geometric structure for feature matching. Besides the improvements in features extraction and matching step, we use a correspondences recovery step to obtain more matches, thus improving the robustness and accuracy of registration. Experiments show that the proposed method is effective.

1 Introduction

Image registration is a fundamental task in computer vision. It is an application of feature detection, feature description, feature matching, image transformation and interpolation. Each step is a classic problem and there exist many solutions to it. Recently, multi-sensor technology achieves huge progress benefit from physics researches. Traditional single-modal image registration enlarges the view of visible modality, while multi-modal image registration makes the view much deeper and expose essential characteristic of targets.

Solutions to single-modal image registration have been proposed in literatures, most of them utilize the common properties in intensity and describe local features with gradient information. Thus, the intensity-based registration methods cannot be used in multi-modal image registration, and these gradient feature-based methods cannot handle multi-modal image registration as the intensities and gradient usually show inconsistency in multi-modal images, which is as point A illustrated in Fig. 1. To solve this problem, some modified variation of classic feature descriptors have been proposed. Chen and Tian proposed a Symmetric Scale Invariant Feature Transform (symmetric-SIFT) descriptor [3], which is symmetric to contrast, thus suitable to multi-modal images. Hossian [6] improve symmetric-SIFT in the process of descriptor merging. Dong Zhao proposed a variance of the SURF [2] named Multimodal-SURF (MM-SURF)

© Springer International Publishing AG 2017
Y. Zhao et al. (Eds.): ICIG 2017, Part II, LNCS 10667, pp. 612–622, 2017.
https://doi.org/10.1007/978-3-319-71589-6_54

[12], inherits the advantages of the SURF and is able to generate a large number of keypoints. It is superior to symmetric-SIFT and CS-LBP [5], which is a modified version of the well-known local binary pattern (LBP) [9]. However, the adaptive ability of MM-SURF is obtained by changing the way of dominant orientation assignment, and limiting the gradient direction in $[0, \pi)$. This kind of revise decreases the distinguishability of descriptors. Thus resulting in a consequence of more but wrong matches, which cannot been removed by Random sample consensus (RANSAC) [4].

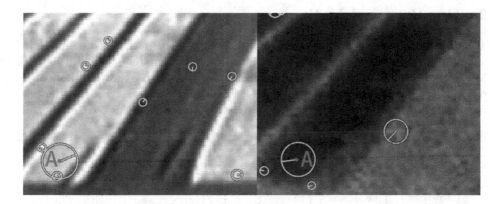

Fig. 1. Gradient reversal in multi-modal images

Another problem of multi-modal image registration is that existing feature-based methods cannot retain adequate accurate correspondences between different modal images. Lack of correspondences or inaccurate correspondences will result in bad transformation and errors. It is usually because of strict matching and outlier remove algorithms. Aguilar [1] proposed a simple and highly robust point-matching method named Graph Transformation Matching (GTM), it finds a consensus nearest-neighbor graph emerging from candidate matches and eliminates dubious matches to obtain the consensus graph. GTM shows superior to RANSAC for high outlier rates. However, it cannot handle some contradictory circumstances, for instance, two falsely matches points have the same neighbors. Then Izadi [7] proposed a weighted graph transformation matching (WGTM) method to overcome the limitations with a more strict matching rules. They are all end with a few matches, and the result is vulnerable even there only one pair of wrong match points. Zhao [13] proposed a dual-graph-based matching method, it generates Delaunay graphs for outlier removal, and recover inliers located in the corresponding graph of Voronoi cells, the inliers recovery make the result to be more robust and stable.

In this paper, we aim to solve the problems above mentioned in multi-modal image registration. First, we propose the modified-SURF (M-SURF) to describe keypoints, and match them refer to the ratio of nearest neighbor and second-closest neighbor. The raw matches set contains many outliers, then we eliminate them through a graph-based method. The graph-based outlier remove method uses geometry consistency between different modal images, which is believed to be survived in a wide range of geometric and photometric transformation. Second, in order to bring back inliers eliminated former and delete persistent outliers, we create a correspondences recovery step in a reverse way of RANSAC.

The rest of the paper is organized as follows. Section 2 explains the proposed method. Section 3 analyzes the performances of the proposed method in some realworld datasets. Section 4 states conclusions and outlines future work.

2   Our Proposed Method

The overall diagram of the proposed method is shown in Fig. 2. It is obvious that our method includes three step. Firstly is to find a raw matches set utilizes the M-SURF. Secondly, a graph-based matching step is used to remove outliers and retain correct matches as many as possible. Finally, a consensus correspondences recovery step is applied. The results of each step are all matches set.

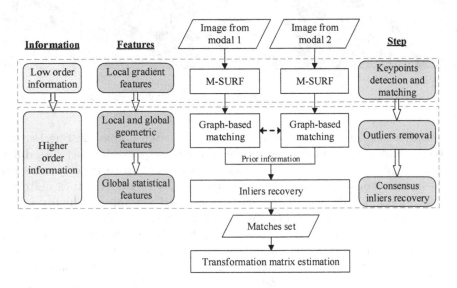

Fig. 2. The overall diagram of the proposed method

2.1   Modified-SURF

Review of SURF: The SURF is much fast than the SIFT and also can ensure the repeatability, distinctiveness and robustness. The SURF is a three stage procedure: (1) keypoints detection; (2) local feature description; (3) keypoints matching. In keypoints detection, the integral image is employed to reduce computation time, Gaussian scale-space and Hessian matrix is employed for keypoints location. In feature description, the dominant orientation of a keypoint is the orientation of summed haar wavelet responses within a circular neighborhood of radius 6 scale around it. The SURF descriptor for a keypoint is generated in a 20 scale square region centered the keypoint and oriented along its dominant orientation, then the 20 scale square region which is divided into $4*4$ subregions, each subregion contains $5*5$ sample points. For each subregion, the SURF calculate its haar wavelet responses and weighted with a Gaussian distribution, then obtain a 4 length's vector $(\sum d_x, \sum d_y, \sum |d_x|, \sum |d_y|)$. d_x and d_y are the haar wavelet responses in horizontal direction and vertical direction, $\sum |d_x|$ and $\sum |d_y|$ are their absolute values. Finally, the SURF descriptor is composed of all feature vectors of 16 subregions. After obtain the SURF descriptor, it is usually employ distance ratio between the closest neighbor and second-closest neighbor.

M-SURF: In the SURF, the dominant orientation assignment is based on the horizontal and vertical haar wavelet responses within radius 6 scale around the keypoint. However, haar wavelet responses are related to gradient, which is unstable in multi-modal images. Thus, the SURF cannot obtain desirable results in multi-modal image registration. Inspired by the gradient reversal phenomenon, we modified the dominant orientation assignment in the SURF and limited it in $[0, \pi)$. For the dominant orientation θ calculated in SURF, the modified orientation θ_m defined below.

$$\theta_m = \begin{cases} \theta, & \theta \in [0°, 180°] \\ \theta - 180°, & \theta \in (180°, 360°) \end{cases} \tag{1}$$

Except for the revise in dominant orientation, we then limited the direction of haar wavelet responses to the interval $[0, \pi)$ according to equation below.

$$(d_x, d_y) = sgn(d_y)(dx, dy) \tag{2}$$

where

$$sgn(x) = \begin{cases} 1, & x \geq 0 \\ -1, & x < 0 \end{cases} \tag{3}$$

The modification of dominant orientation assignment and haar wavelet responses' direction are a kind of relaxation, it handle the problem of gradient reversal in multi-modal images but also decreases the distinctiveness of descriptor for wrong matches. Therefore, we employ a graph-based matching algorithm to remove these outliers.

2.2   Outliers Removal

After applying the M-SURF, we obtain two sets of corresponding keypoints $P = \{p_i\}$ and $P' = \{p_i'\}$ where p_i matches p_i'. Outliers removal is to delete wrong matches in these two sets using certain rules and remain correct matches as accuracy as possible. Recently, graph has been utilized for establishing a higher level geometrical or spatial relationship between feature points. No matter what transformation relationship is between the two images, the spatial relationship between feature points can be maintained.

Many graph-based matching algorithms have been proposed recently. They used adjacency matrix to describe the spatial relationship between feature points and their adjacent feature points. The weighted graph transformation matching (WGTM) algorithm is inspired by GTM algorithm to remove outliers using K-nearest-neighbor (K-NN) graph. It takes the angular distance as a criterion to judge the outliers (false matches).

WGTM starts with creating median K-NN directed graph G for each image, a directed edge $e(i,j)$ exists when p_j is one of the closest neighbors of p_i and also $\|p_i - p_j\| \leq \eta$, and all directed edges formed a edge set E. η is defined by:

$$\eta = \underset{(l,m) \in P \times P}{median} \|p_l - p_m\| \tag{4}$$

A adjacency matrix A is defined by:

$$A(i,j) = \begin{cases} 1 & e(i,j) \in E \\ 0 & otherwise \end{cases} \tag{5}$$

In addition, points without any neighbors are removed as we cannot identify their spatial relationship with other feature points.

Next, a weight matrix W is generated for each point p_i using graph G_p. For another point p_m and their correspondences p_i' and p_m', the weight value is defined by:

$$W(i,m) = \left| \arccos \left(\frac{(p_m - p_i)((p_m' - p_i')Rot(\theta(k_{min}, i)))}{\|p_m - p_i\| \|p_m' - p_i'\|} \right) \right| \tag{6}$$

where

$$Rot(\theta(k_{min}, i)) = \begin{bmatrix} cos(\theta(k_{min}, i)) & sin(\theta(k_{min}, i)) \\ -sin(\theta(k_{min}, i)) & cos(\theta(k_{min}, i)) \end{bmatrix} \tag{7}$$

Here k_{min} represents the optimal rotation angle between each pair of matches. The optimal rotation angle is defines as the angle that minimizes the sum of angular distances between p_i and p_m'. For more information about WGTM, please refer to [7], its performances proved superior to that of GTM and RANSAC. However, there are still problems when applied it to multi-modal image registration.

WGTM uses angular distance as the criterion to find outliers, it is invariant to scale, rotation and sensitive to noise. However, its sensitivity shows more obvious in multi-modal images as the attributes in heterologous modals are quite different, these differences are easy to be identified as noise and removed finally.

2.3   Consensus Inliers Recovery

After outliers removal, the least square method is usually used in literatures to estimate transformation matrix. However, due to the strict rules of graph-based outliers removal and massive noise, there are few correspondences remained after WGTM. It will make the registration result inaccurate if the remained keypoints are not extracted accurate enough or there still exist one pair of false match points. It is found that some true matches are eliminated in outliers removal because of the strict rule of WGTM. Thus, we focus on how to recover these true matches.

Random sample consensus (RANSAC) is an iterative method to estimate parameters of a mathematical model from a set of observed data that contains outliers, when outliers are to be accorded no influence on the values of estimates. It is usually used to fine correspondences. However, RANSAC is not suitable for multi-modal image registration as there exist too many false matches and it would fail to find a satisfied consensus set. In this case, inspired by RANSAC, we design a consensus inlier recovery method, which use inliers identified by WGTM as prior. Its steps are as follows.

(1) Assume that the correspondences sets are P_i and P_i^*, which are remained after WGTM. We estimate the transformation relationship H_0 between them using the method of least squares.
(2) Use H_0 to check all keypoints with a threshold ε. For a keypoint v_k and its corresponding keypoint v_k^*, the transformed point of v_k is $v_{k2} = H_0 \cdot v_k$, if $\|v_k^* - v_{k2}\| \leq \varepsilon$, then the keypoint is viewed as the consensus inliers, and its corresponding point are also inliers and recovered.
(3) Update the correspondences set P_i and P_i^* with recovered inliers. if there has no point recovered or the sum error reach the top value, stop iteration, otherwise, re-computing the transformation matrix H_0 and back to step (2) and continue the iteration.

3   Experiments

We applied the proposed method to three datasets: (1) The dataset released by Shen [11], which is composed of different exposures images, flash and noflash images, RGB images and Depth images, RGB images and NIR images; (2) The dataset released by Palmero [10], which is composed of RGB images, Depth images and infrared images; (3) Our own dataset, which contains visible/infrared image pairs and visible/hyperspectral (band 66) image pairs. Figure 3 shows some typical examples of datasets. The development environment of experiments is Intel Core i5-4570 CPU @3.20 GHz, 32 GB RAM. The operating system is 64 bit Windows 10. The development platform is Visual Studio 2013 with OpenCV 2.4.9 and Matlab 2016b.

3.1   Evaluation Measures

The accuracy of a registration technique is highly depended on the match sets. The more correct matches, the better registration result. Therefore, we evaluate our results in two ways. One is the final correct matches, another is the target registration error (TRE) [8]. They are defined as follows.

The final correct matches means the number of final correct matches, they are used to estimate the transformation matrix. As long as enough correct

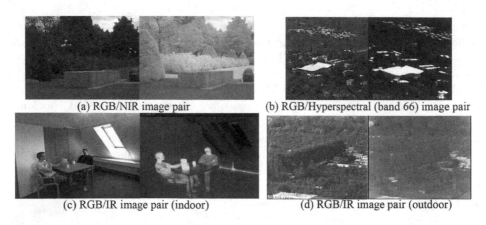

(a) RGB/NIR image pair   (b) RGB/Hyperspectral (band 66) image pair

(c) RGB/IR image pair (indoor)   (d) RGB/IR image pair (outdoor)

Fig. 3. Example image pairs of datasets

matches are retained, the final correspondences and transformation matrix can be obtained by RANSAC algorithm. The final correct matches is obtained in this way. Due to the transformation matrix is estimated by the method of least square, the more true matches, the little influence of false match and inaccurate feature point extraction, and the better result.

For the TRE, assume that the transformation relationship is $T_1 = \begin{bmatrix} R_1 & t_1 \\ 0 & 1 \end{bmatrix}$ and the ground truth is $T_2 = \begin{bmatrix} R_2 & t_2 \\ 0 & 1 \end{bmatrix}$, where R_1, R_2 are 2×2 rotation matrices and t_1, t_2 are translation vectors. For a point $p = (x, y)^T$ in the reference image, thus

$$p_1 = T_1(p) = R_1 p + t_1 \tag{8}$$

$$p_2 = T_2(p) = R_2 p + t_2 \tag{9}$$

On eliminating p, it follows that,

$$p_2 = R_2 R_1^{-1} p_1 + t_2 - R_2 R^{-1} t_1 \tag{10}$$

The TRE Δp is, thus

$$\Delta p = p_2 - p_1 = (R_2 R_1^{-1} - I) p_1 + t_2 - R_2 R^{-1} t_1 \tag{11}$$

The TRE is a measurement of image registration in a way of reprojection. The value of TRE means the distance between reference image and transformed image in pixel level.

3.2   Matching Comparisons

The matching comparisons is conducted between initial matches identified by M-SURF, matches before recovery and matches after recovery. Figures 4, 5, 6

Fig. 4. Matching comparison between RGB/NIR image pair

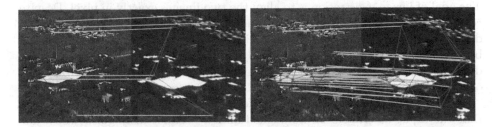

Fig. 5. Matching comparison between RGB/Hyperspectral (band 66) image pair

Fig. 6. Matching comparison between RGB/IR image pair (indoor)

Fig. 7. Matching comparison between RGB/IR image pair (outdoor)

and 7 show the experimental results. The k in WGTM used to create K-NN graph is set to be 5 in our experiments.

From the comparisons, it is obvious that the consensus inliers recovery is worked effectively. In RGB/NIR image pair, although the initial matches obtained by M-SURF and WGTM is enough, we still recovered more matches. Because the NIR image is similar with RGB image in gradient and texture, M-SURF is enough to describe the correspondences. However, in RGB/Hyperspectral (band 66) image pair and RGB/IR image pairs, the initial matches are just exactly enough to estimate the transformation. Any one of false match or inaccurate feature point extraction can result in a failure registration. For example, there are only three matches in the initial matches of Fig. 6, but the points around the window in the upright of the image are not match. The consensus inliers recovery step not only recover more matches, but also eliminated the false match.

3.3   The TRE Comparisons

The goal of image registration is to align the two images exactly in pixel. Despite comparing the matching results, we evaluate the proposed method with the TRE described before in the final fusion of images. The ground truth is obtained by selecting more than twenty matches per image manually, these points are distributed evenly. To compute the average TRE, we randomly choose 70% pixels of each image as sample points.

We divide the results into two part for considering the TRE results. One is that the input images (set1) are aligned and we cannot distinguish which one is better from the fusion image ($TRE < 5$), Table 1 shows the TRE results of these images. Another one is that the input images (set2) are hard to be aligned or traditional method cannot perform well ($TRE > 5$), Table 2 shows the TRE results of these images.

Table 1. The TRE comparison of set1

Image	1	2	3	4	5	6	7
Before recovery	17.1075	8.5796	49.7602	24.3963	17.521	6.3292	7.7719
After recovery	0.8769	5.1742	2.0491	0.5429	2.0013	1.5387	2.9594
Image	8	9	10	11	12	13	
Before recovery	11.5286	12.6282	17.1823	10.5873	8.12535	12.535	
After recovery	2.241	5.3173	2.5131	2.8637	5.4977	4.7348	

Table 2. The TRE comparison of set2

Image	1	2	3	4	5	6	7
Before recovery	5.6674	2.11	3.6151	4.748	3.2283	5.1124	2.0531
After recovery	2.1828	1.8065	1.9424	2.776	1.9247	2.9118	1.8819
Image	8	9	10	11	12	13	
Before recovery	4.9546	4.4336	1.8301	1.3644	3.4728	4.9187	
After recovery	3.1551	0.8652	1.7125	0.8249	4.4033	1.5867	

From the comparisons of the TRE, we can conclude that the proposed method is effective and robust to multimodal image registration. M-SURF and WGTM filter most outliers, the inliers recovery find matches with more accurate feature points. Moreover, the consensus inliers recovery step also can eliminate the stubborn outliers that graph-based outliers removal cannot identify. Therefore, From the comparisons of the TRE, for those images (set1) that traditional method cannot align, the proposed method performs well. For those images (set2) that traditional method can align with ordinary results, the proposed method performs better.

4 Conclusions

In this paper, we proposed a novel multimodal image registration method. It is based a modified SURF to extract feature points and create the poor correspondences. By introducing the spatial relationship of matching points, a graph-based outliers removal method (WGTM) is applied then to eliminate false matches. By considering too few inliers were reserved and some stubborn outliers still existed in the residual matches set, the results of the previous two steps are viewed as a prior to recover the consensus inliers. The matching and registration results in the experiments have indicated the effectiveness and robustness of the proposed method. Image registration is a foundation work of image processing, our future work will include incorporating multimodal information to improve the performances in other computer vision tasks.

Acknowledgements. This work is supported by the National Natural Science Foundation of China (Nos. 61231016, 61303123, 61273265), the Natural Science Foundation of Shaanxi Province (No. 2015JQ6256), the Fundamental Research Funds for the Central Universities (No. 3102015JSJ0008), the NPU Foundation for Fundamental Research (No. JCT20130108).

References

1. Aguilar, W., Frauel, Y., Escolano, F., Martinez-Perez, M.E., Espinosa-Romero, A., Lozano, M.A.: A robust graph transformation matching for non-rigid registration. Image Vis. Comput. **27**(7), 897–910 (2009)
2. Bay, H., Ess, A., Tuytelaars, T., Van Gool, L.: Speeded-up robust features. Comput. Vis. Image Underst. **110**(3), 404–417 (2008)
3. Chen, J., Tian, J.: Real-time multi-modal rigid registration based on a novel symmetric-SIFT descriptor. Prog. Nat. Sci.: Mater. Int. **19**(5), 643–651 (2009)
4. Fischler, M.A., Bolles, R.C.: Random sample consensus: a paradigm for model fitting with applications to image analysis and automated cartography. ACM (1981)
5. Heikkilä, M., Pietikäinen, M., Schmid, C.: Description of interest regions with local binary patterns. Pattern Recogn. **42**(3), 425–436 (2009)
6. Hossain, M.T., Lv, G., Teng, S.W., Lu, G., Lackmann, M.: Improved symmetric-sift for multi-modal image registration. In: International Conference on Digital Image Computing Techniques and Applications, pp. 197–202 (2011)
7. Izadi, M., Saeedi, P.: Robust weighted graph transformation matching for rigid and nonrigid image registration. IEEE Trans. Image Process. **21**(10), 4369–4382 (2012)

8. Maurer, C., Maciunas, R.J., Fitzpatrick, J.M.: Registration of head CT images to physical space using a weighted combination of points and surfaces [image-guided surgery]. IEEE Trans. Med. Imaging **17**(5), 753–761 (1998)
9. Ojala, T., Pietikäinen, M., Mäenpää, T.: Multiresolution gray-scale and rotation invariant texture classification with local binary patterns. In: European Conference on Computer Vision, pp. 404–420 (2000)
10. Palmero, C., Claps, A., Bahnsen, C., MØgelmose, A., Moeslund, T.B., Escalera, S.: Multi-modal rgbcdepthcthermal human body segmentation. Int. J. Comput. Vis. **118**(2), 217–239 (2016)
11. Shen, X., Xu, L., Zhang, Q., Jia, J.: Multi-modal and multi-spectral registration for natural images. In: European Conference on Computer Vision, pp. 309–324 (2014)
12. Zhao, D., Yang, Y., Ji, Z., Hu, X.: Rapid multimodality registration based on MM-SURF. Neurocomputing **131**(131), 87–97 (2014)
13. Zhao, M., An, B., Wu, Y., Chen, B., Sun, S.: A robust delaunay triangulation matching for multispectral/multidate remote sensing image registration. IEEE Geosci. Remote Sens. Lett. **12**(4), 711–715 (2014)

Author Index

Printed in the United States
By Bookmasters